RECCHIONI - MAMMUCARI

ORPHANS

VOLUME FOUR
WINNERS AND LOSERS

ORPHANS series created by Roberto Recchioni and Emiliano Mammucari

Original lettering by Marina Sanfelice
Original logo created by Paolo Campana
Original book design by Officine Bolzoni with Cosimo Torsoli

English translation by Elena Cecchini and Valeria Gobbato
Localization, layout, and editing by Mike Kennedy

MAGNETIC™   **LION**™ **FORGE**

ISBN: 978-1-942367-86-4
Library of Congress Control Number: 2019908901

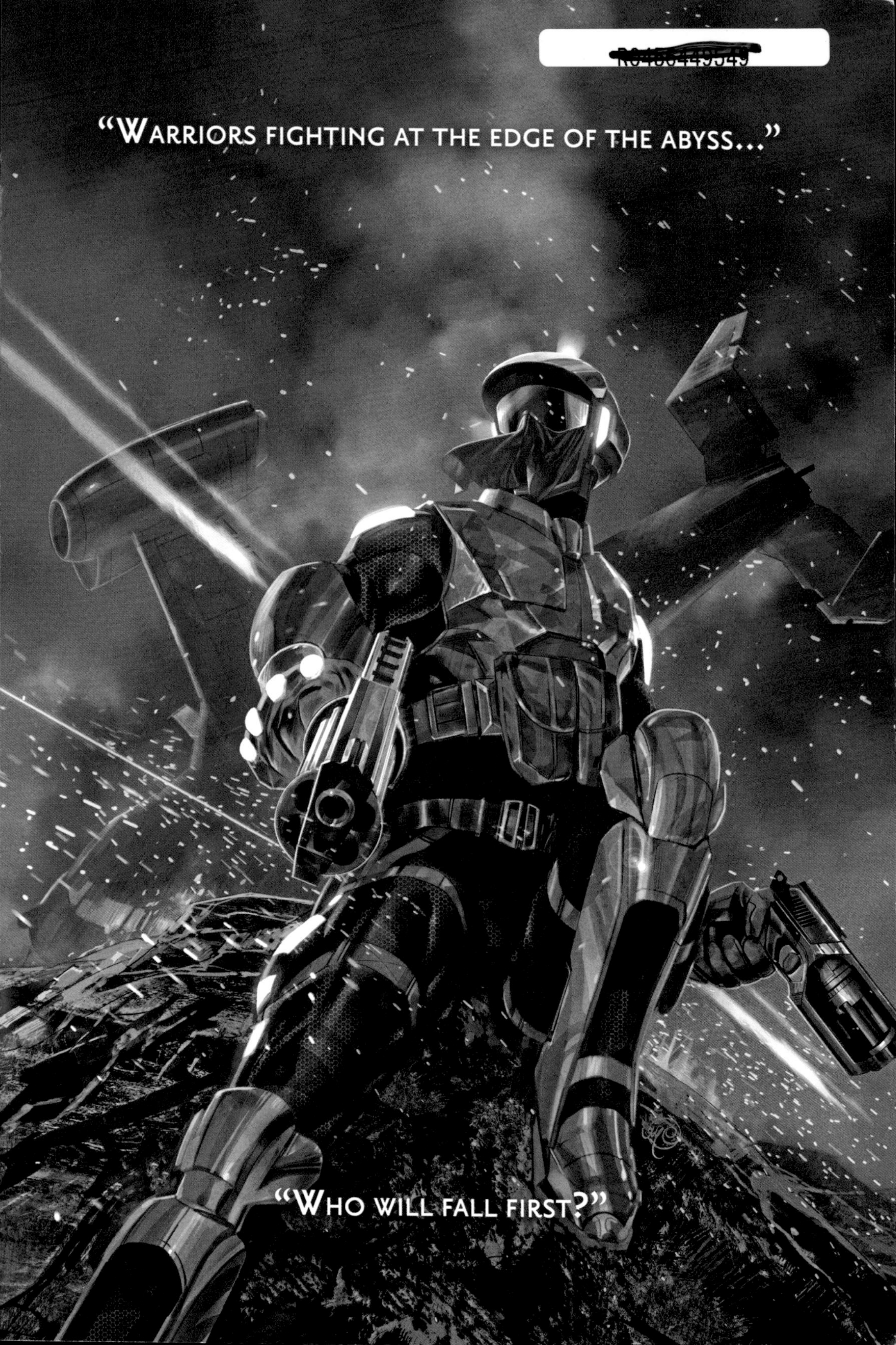
"WARRIORS FIGHTING AT THE EDGE OF THE ABYSS..."
"WHO WILL FALL FIRST?"

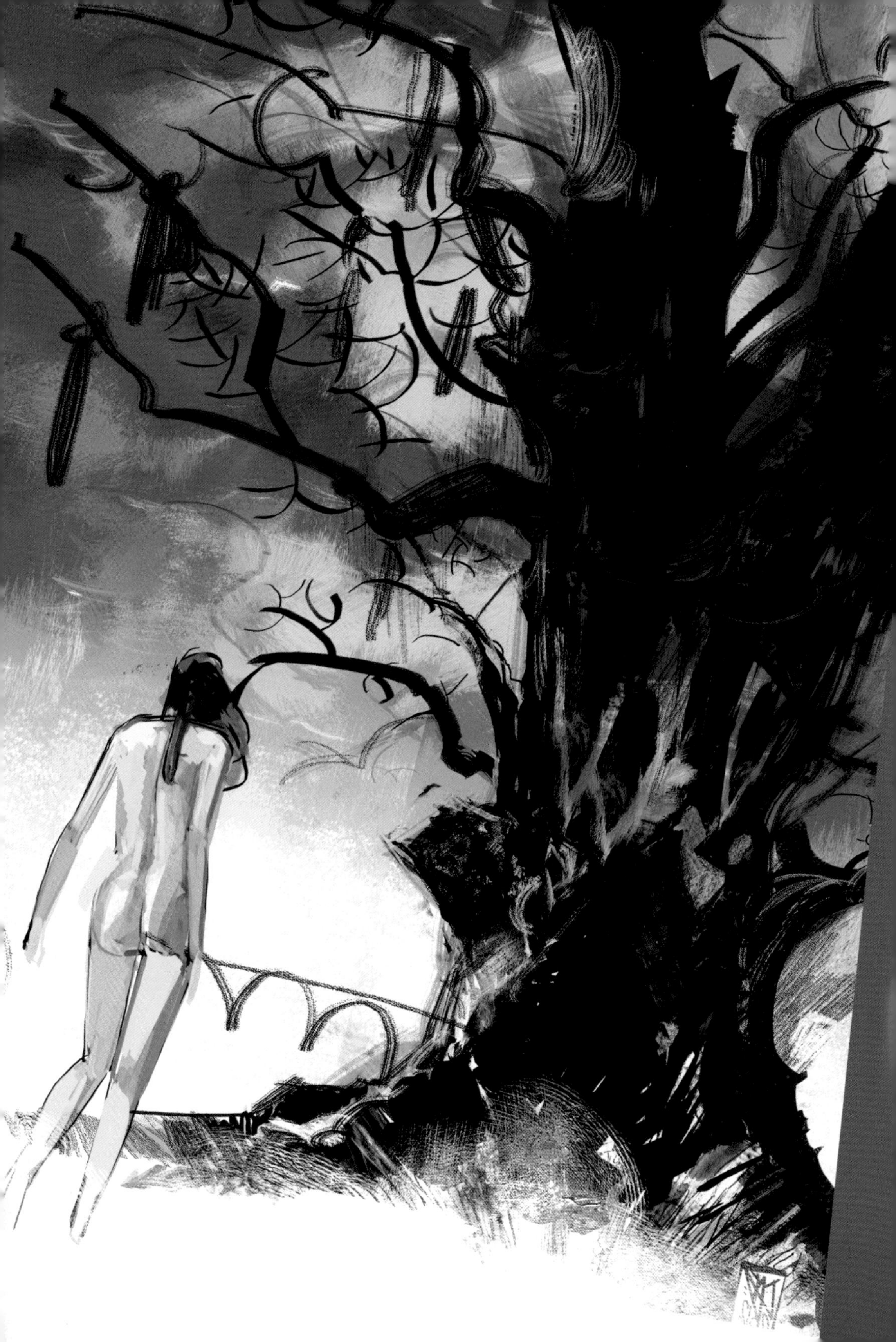

START

This volume collects the last of the first twelve chapters, originally released over a twelve month period -- nearly 1200 pages of action and drama carefully planned and plotted from the start like a carefully crafted television series. In fact, these twelve chapters are even referred to as "season one" -- yes, there is much more to the tale introduced in these pages, this is just the tip of the iceberg!

Roberto Recchioni and Emiliano Mammucari envisioned not only a collection of deep and engaging character arcs, but in the process created an entirely new universe of military conspiracies, political intrigue, and moral conundrums set against a wholly unique version of the apocalyptic dystopia. These twelve chapters are merely the seeds from which a forest of bold ideas and masterful sci-fi storytelling has grown.

So buckle up, this ride is coming to a close, and you might be surprised where things end up...

PREVIOUS PAGE: ILLUSTRATION BY GIGI CAVENAGO

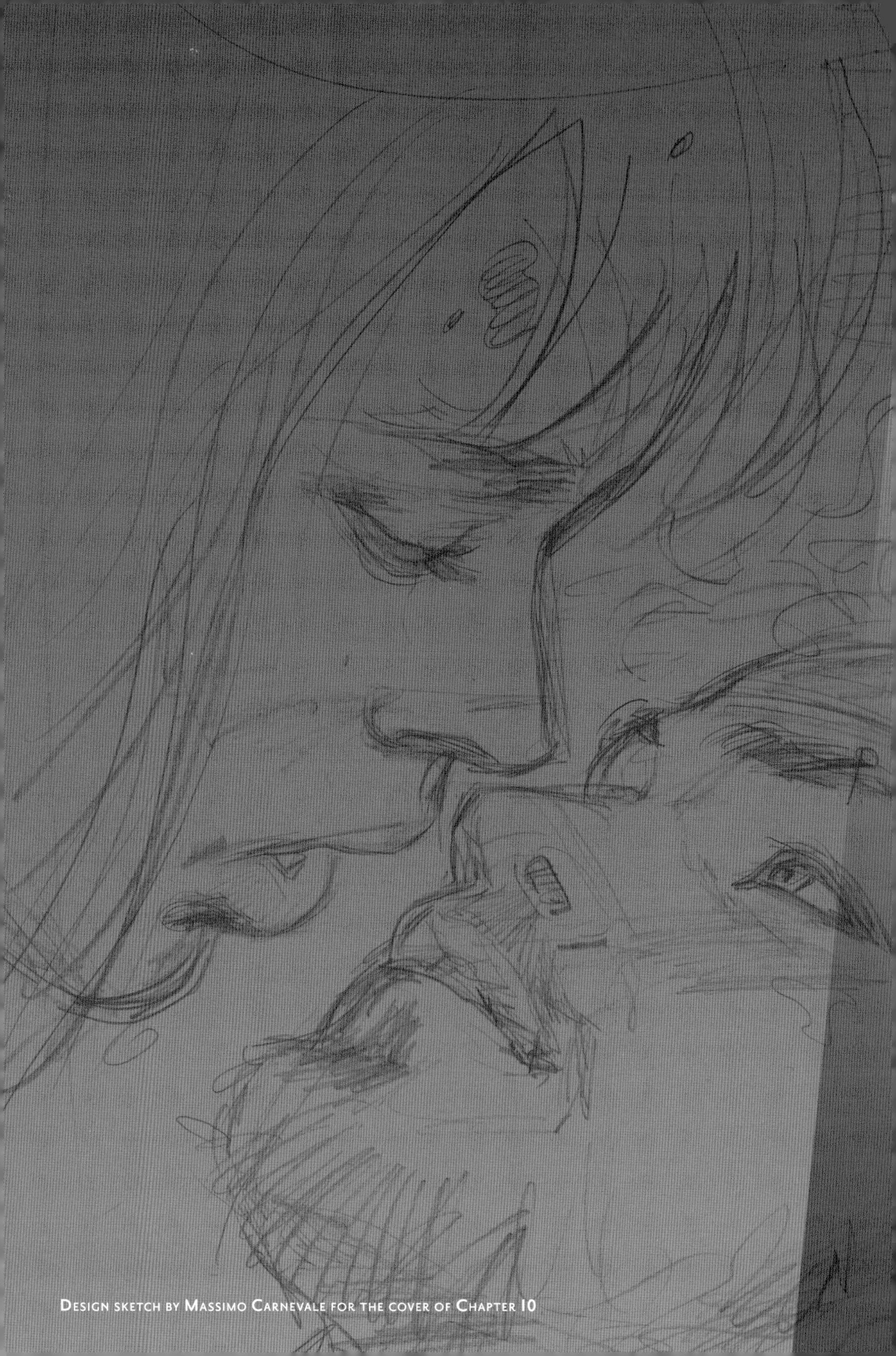

Design sketch by Massimo Carnevale for the cover of Chapter 10

HEARTS IN THE ABYSS

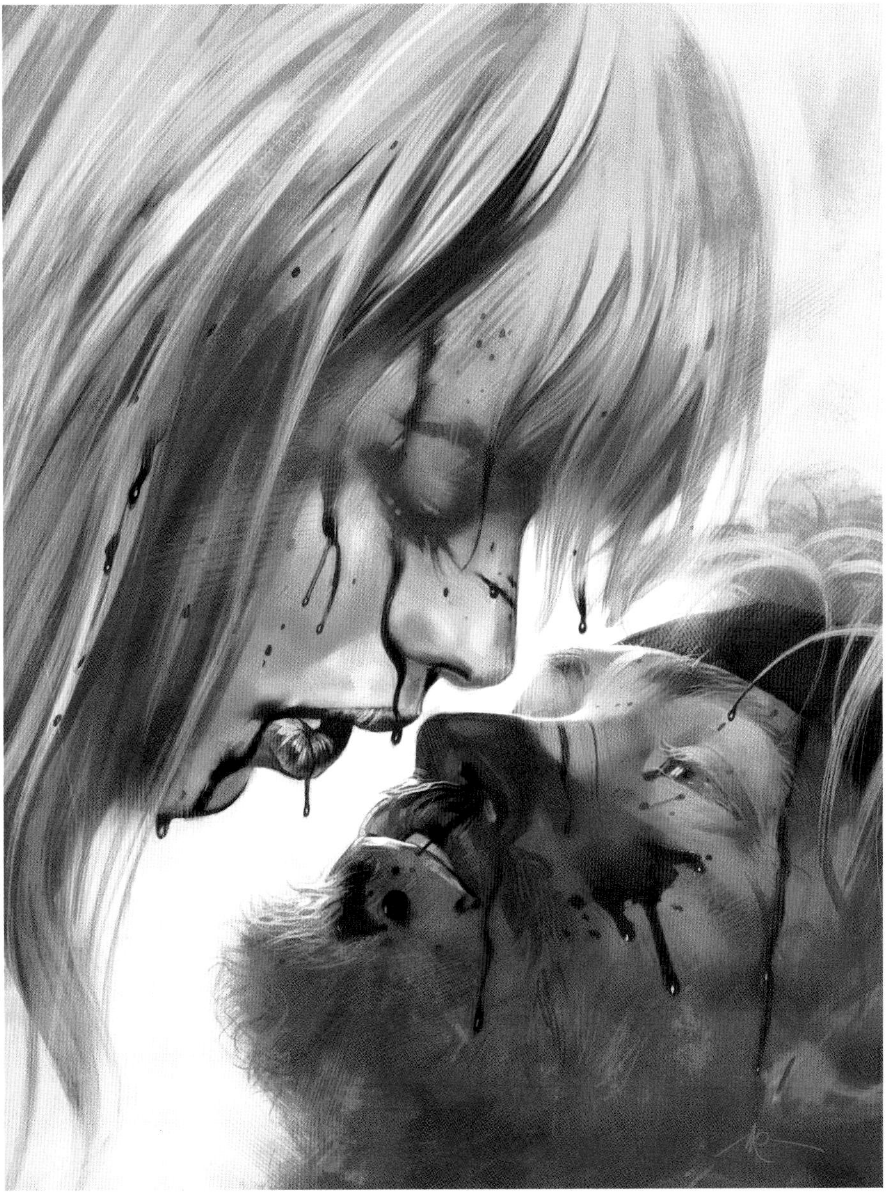

ORPHANS: CHAPTER 10

story: ROBERTO RECCHIONI
art: MATTEO CREMONA
colors: ANNALISA LEONI
cover: MASSIMO CARNEVALE

CHAPTER 10

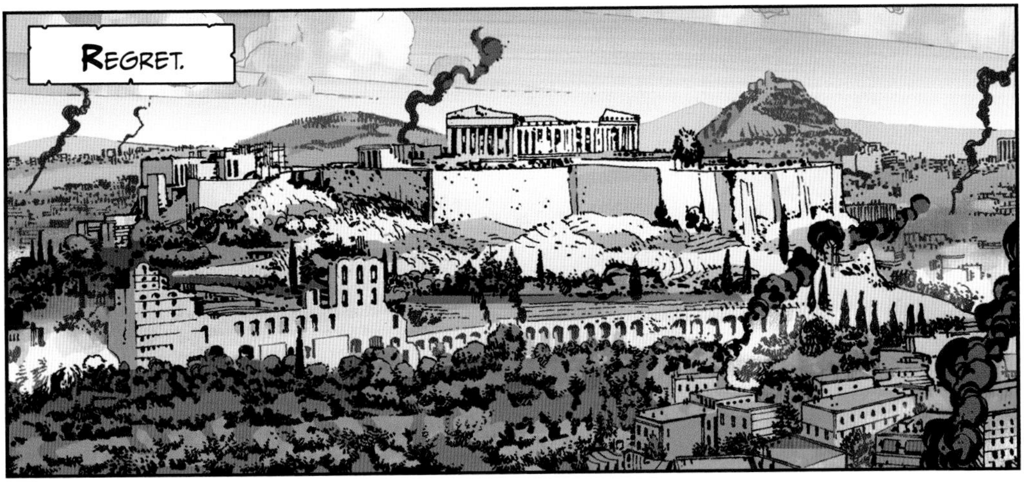
REGRET.

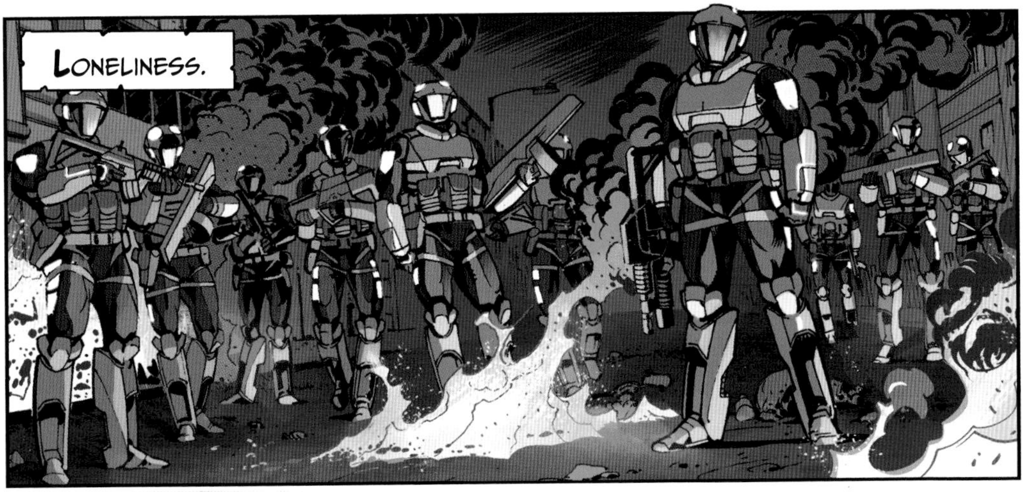
LONELINESS.

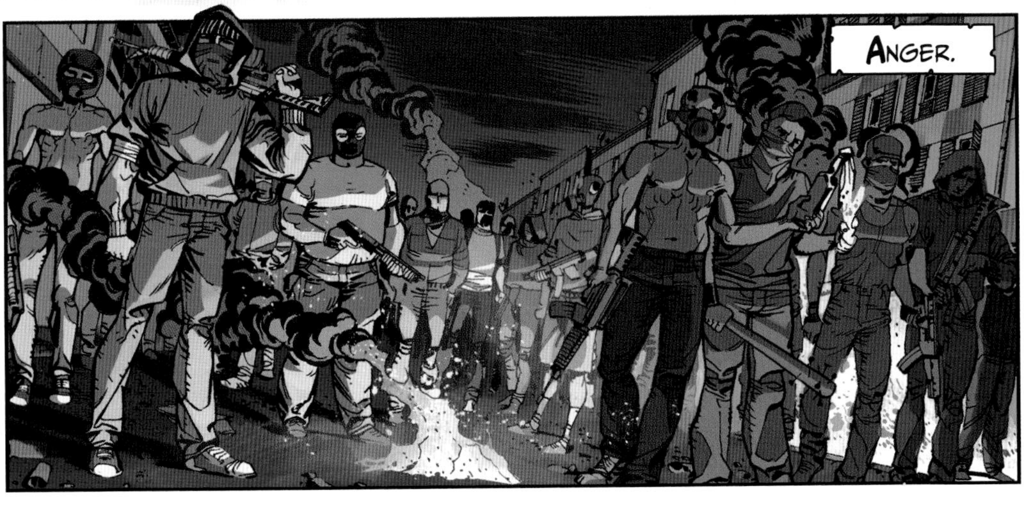
ANGER.

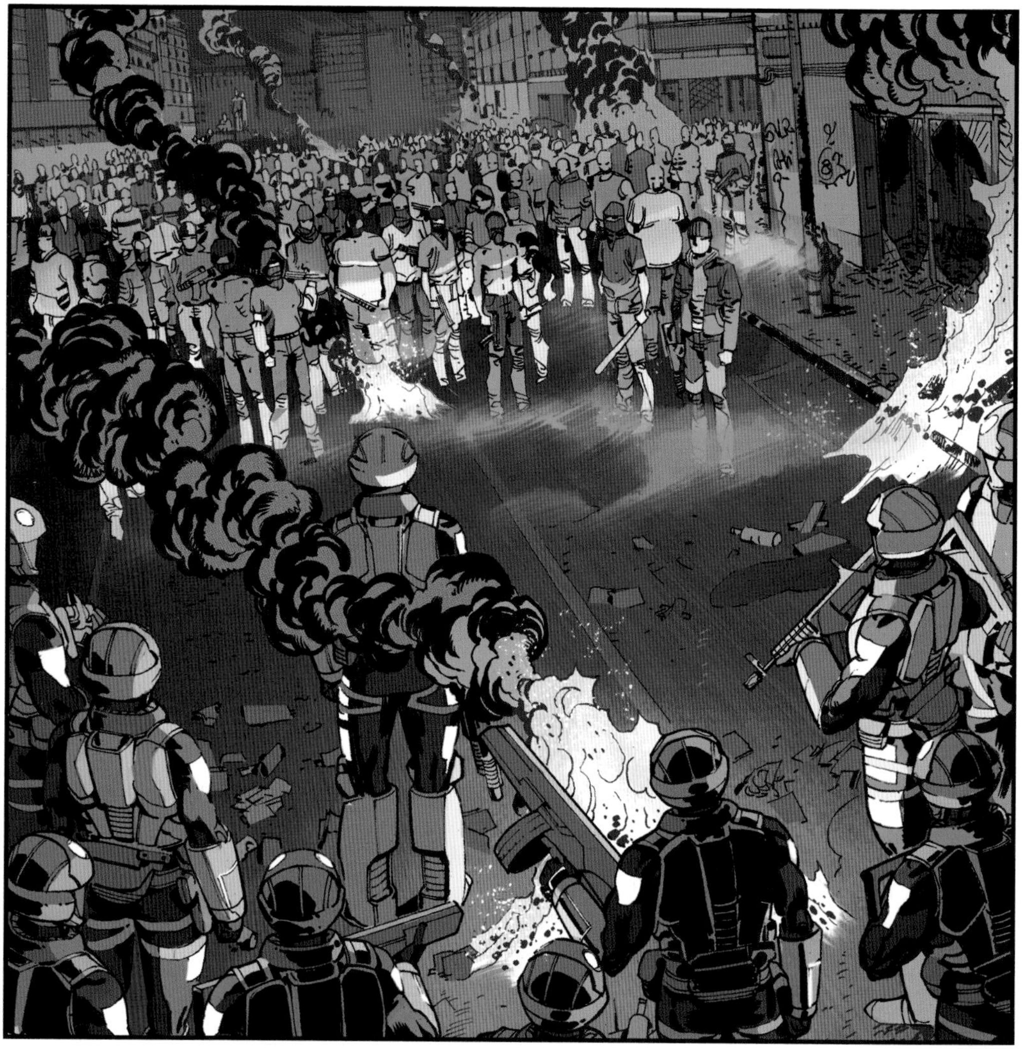

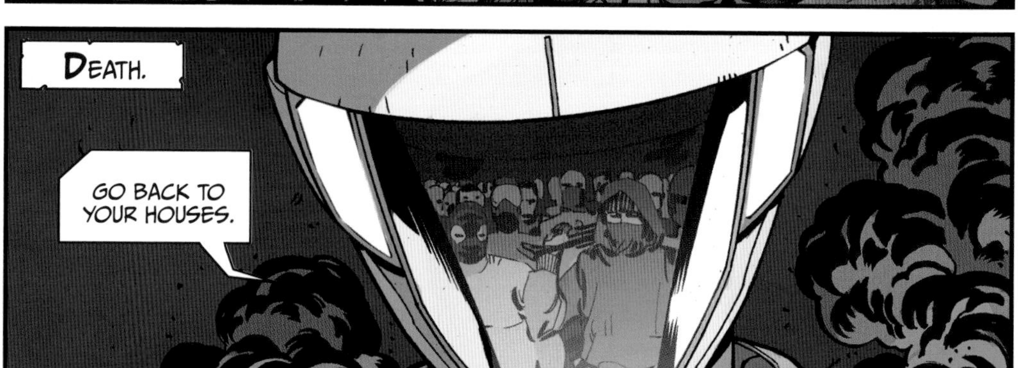
DEATH.
GO BACK TO YOUR HOUSES.

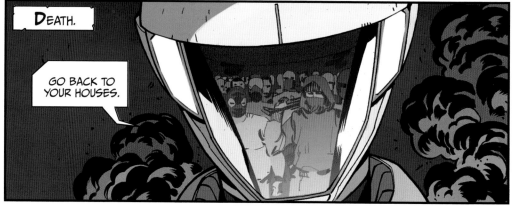

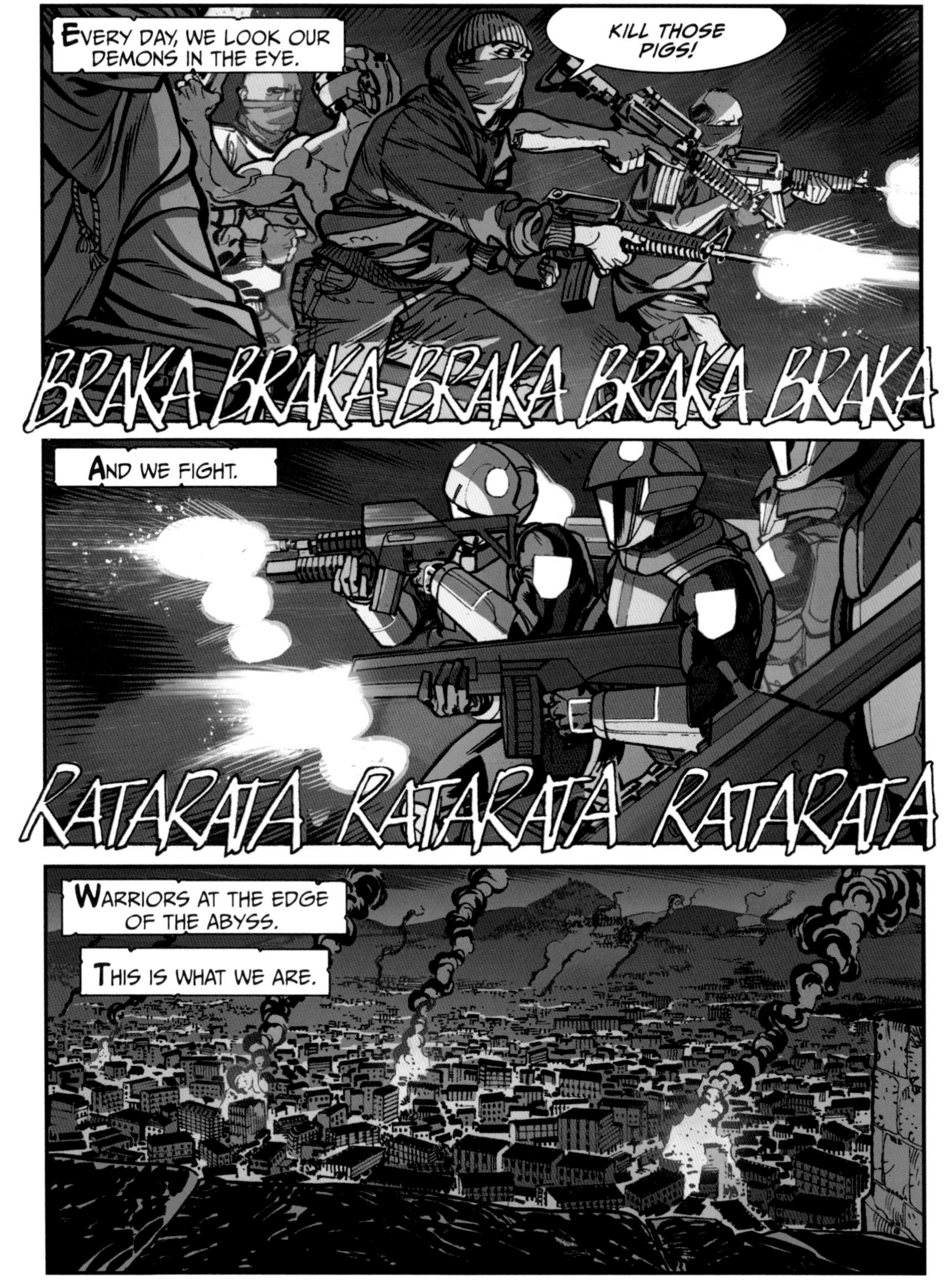
EVERY DAY, WE LOOK OUR DEMONS IN THE EYE.
KILL THOSE PIGS!
BRAKA BRAKA BRAKA BRAKA BRAKA
AND WE FIGHT.
RATARATA RATARATA RATARATA
WARRIORS AT THE EDGE OF THE ABYSS.
THIS IS WHAT WE ARE.

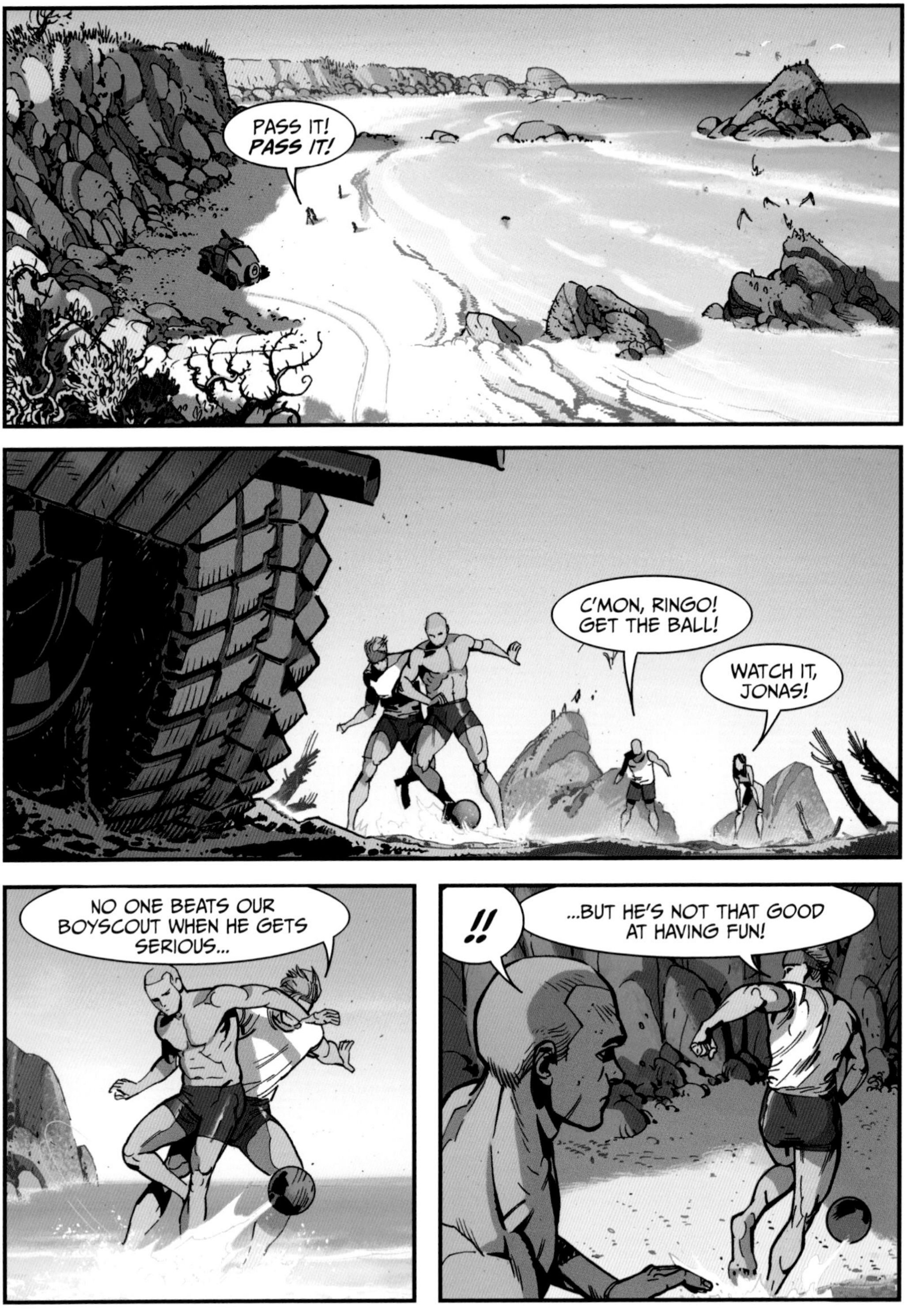
PASS IT! PASS IT!
C'MON, RINGO! GET THE BALL!
WATCH IT, JONAS!
NO ONE BEATS OUR BOYSCOUT WHEN HE GETS SERIOUS...
!!
...BUT HE'S NOT THAT GOOD AT HAVING FUN!

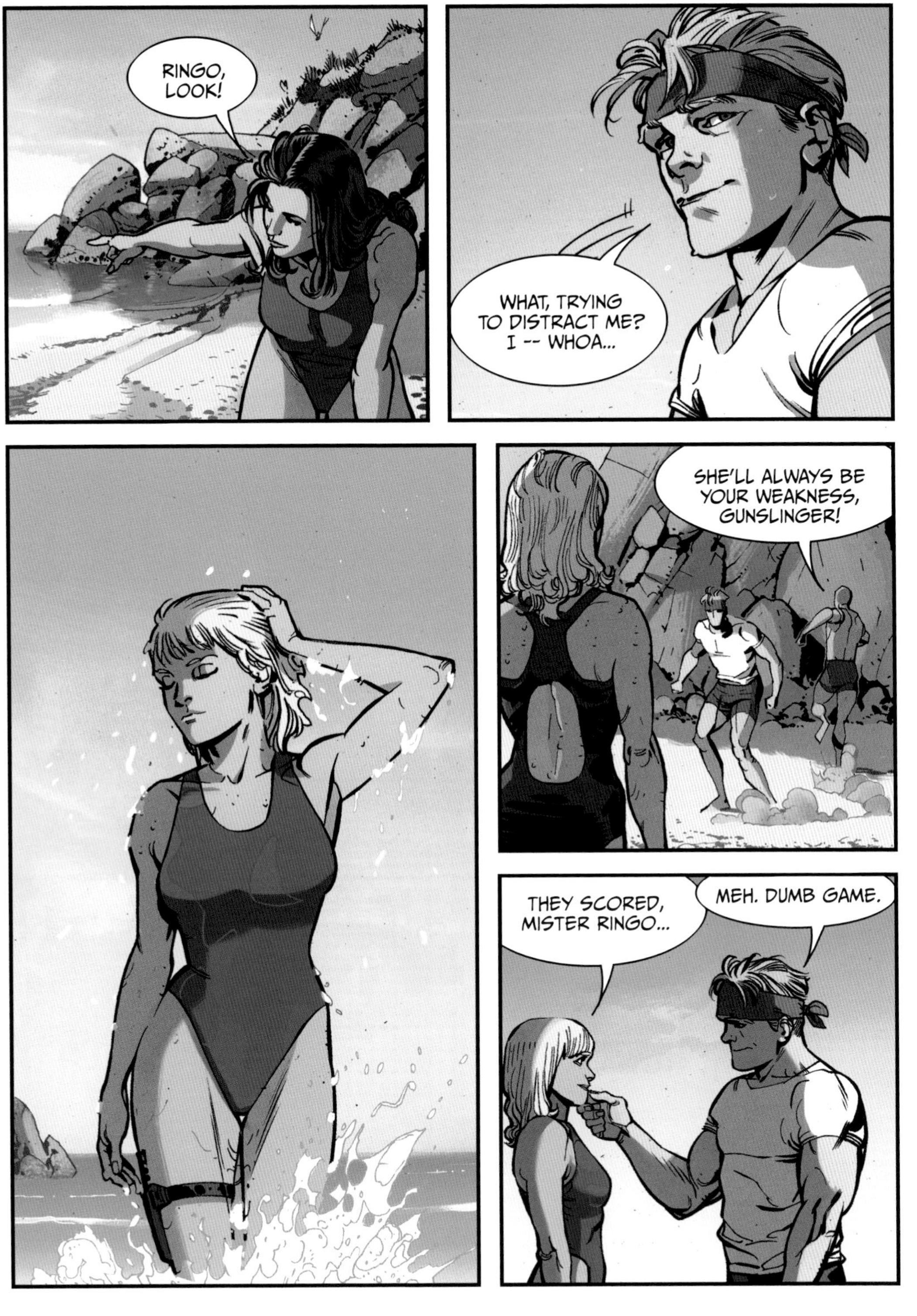
RINGO, LOOK!
WHAT, TRYING TO DISTRACT ME? I -- WHOA...
SHE'LL ALWAYS BE YOUR WEAKNESS, GUNSLINGER!
THEY SCORED, MISTER RINGO...
MEH. DUMB GAME.

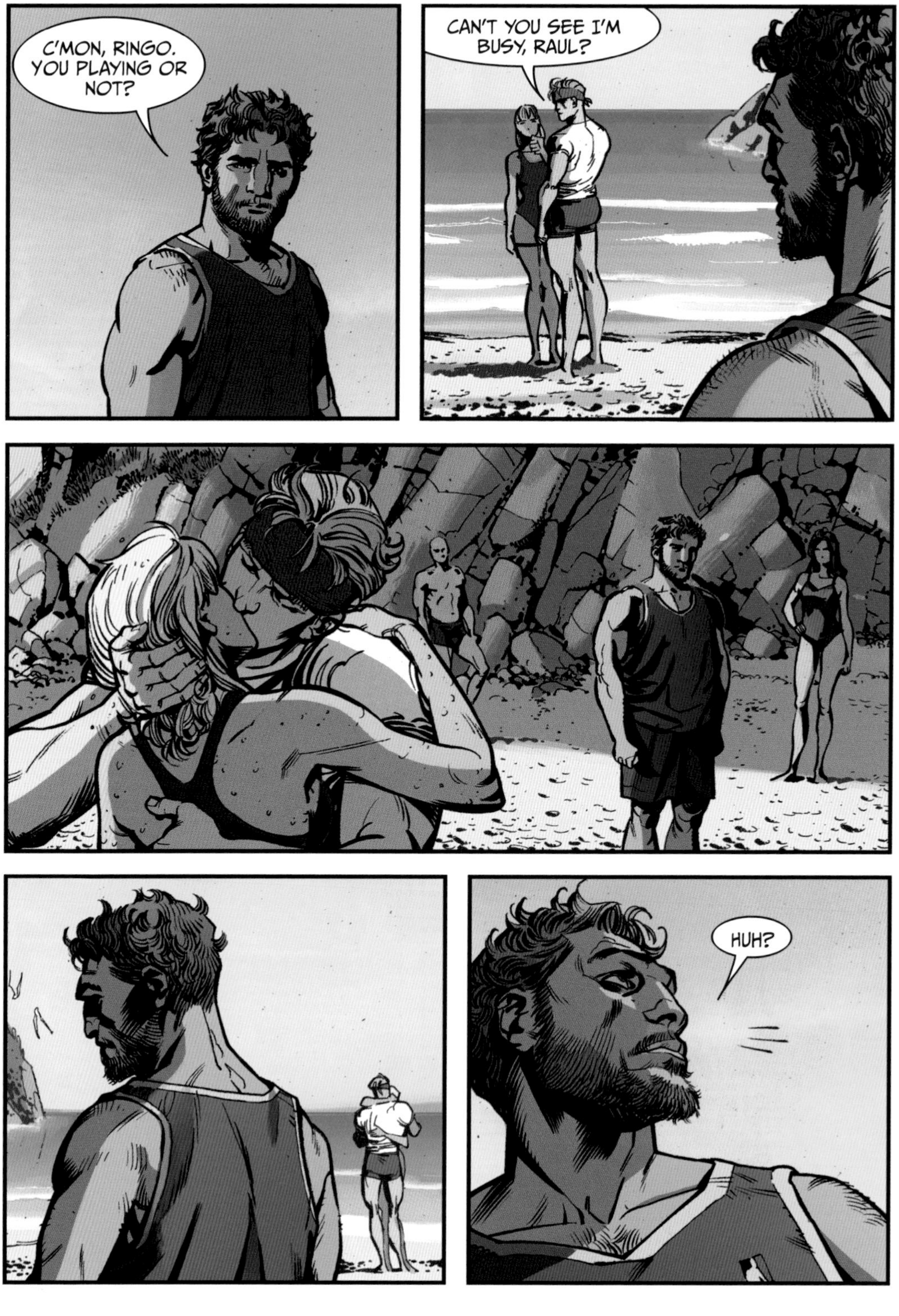
C'MON, RINGO. YOU PLAYING OR NOT?
CAN'T YOU SEE I'M BUSY, RAUL?
HUH?

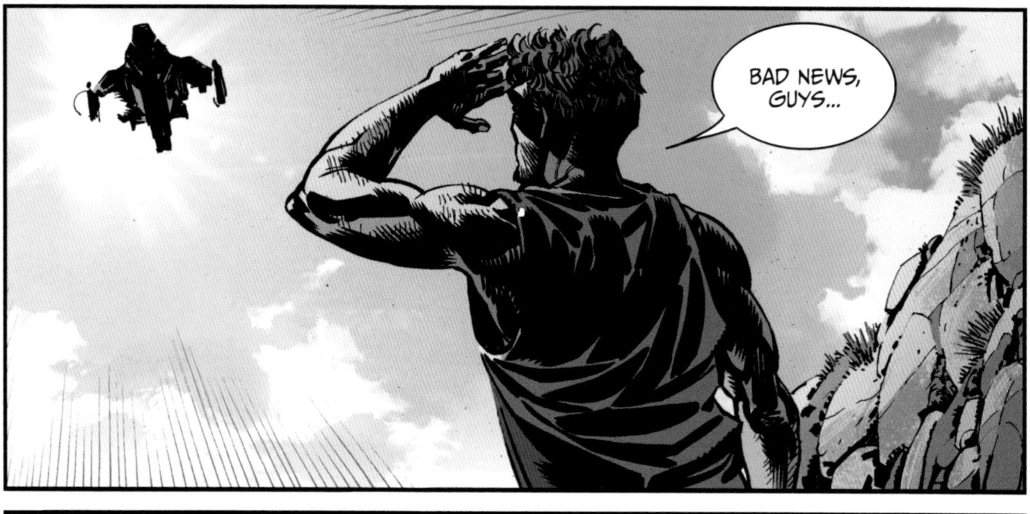
BAD NEWS,
GUYS...

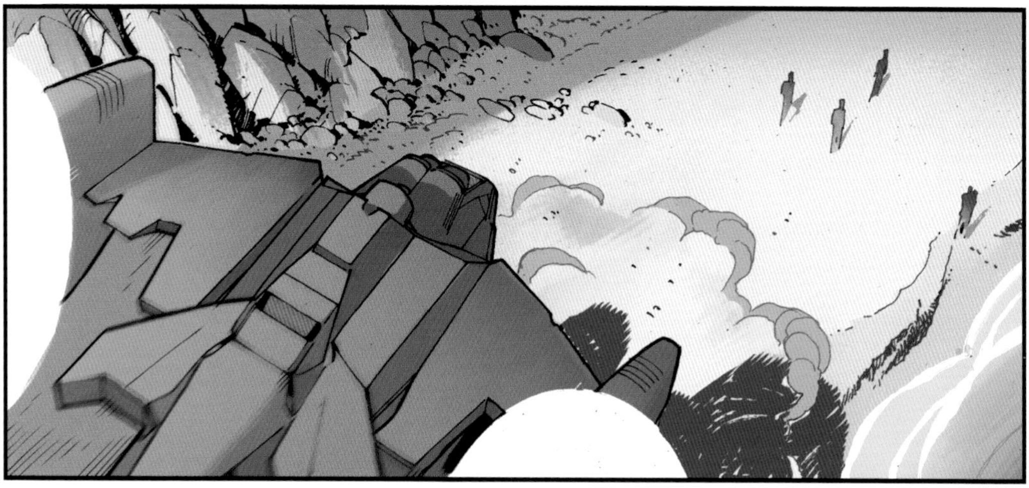

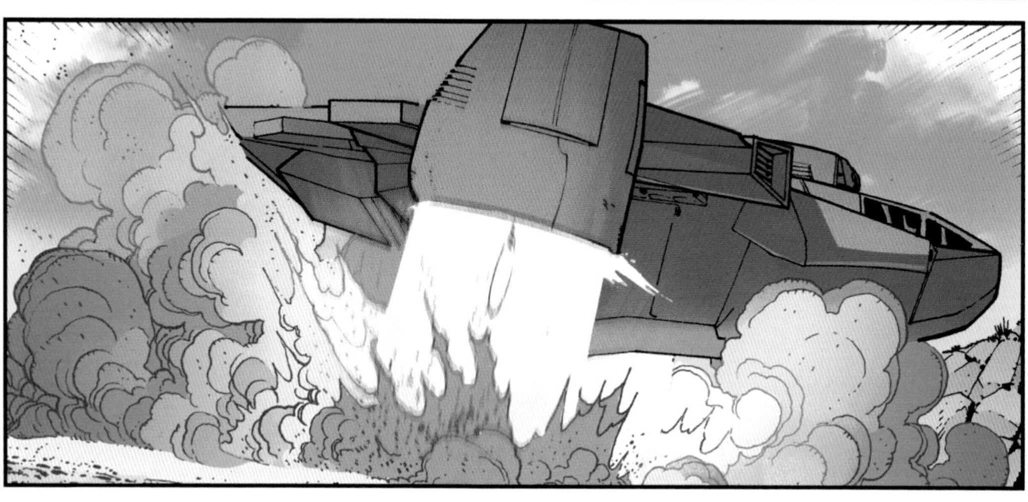

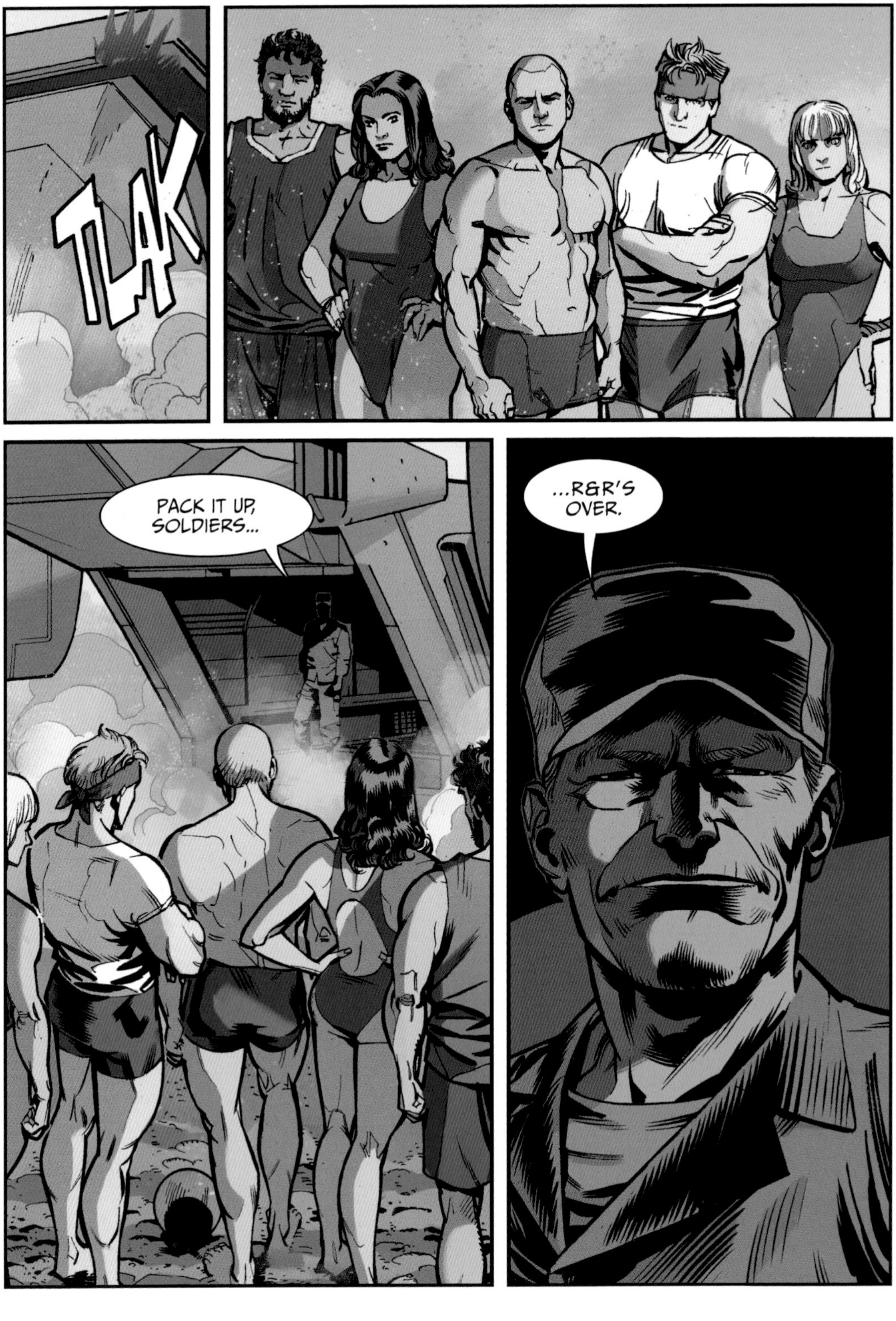
TLAK
PACK IT UP, SOLDIERS...
...R&R'S OVER.

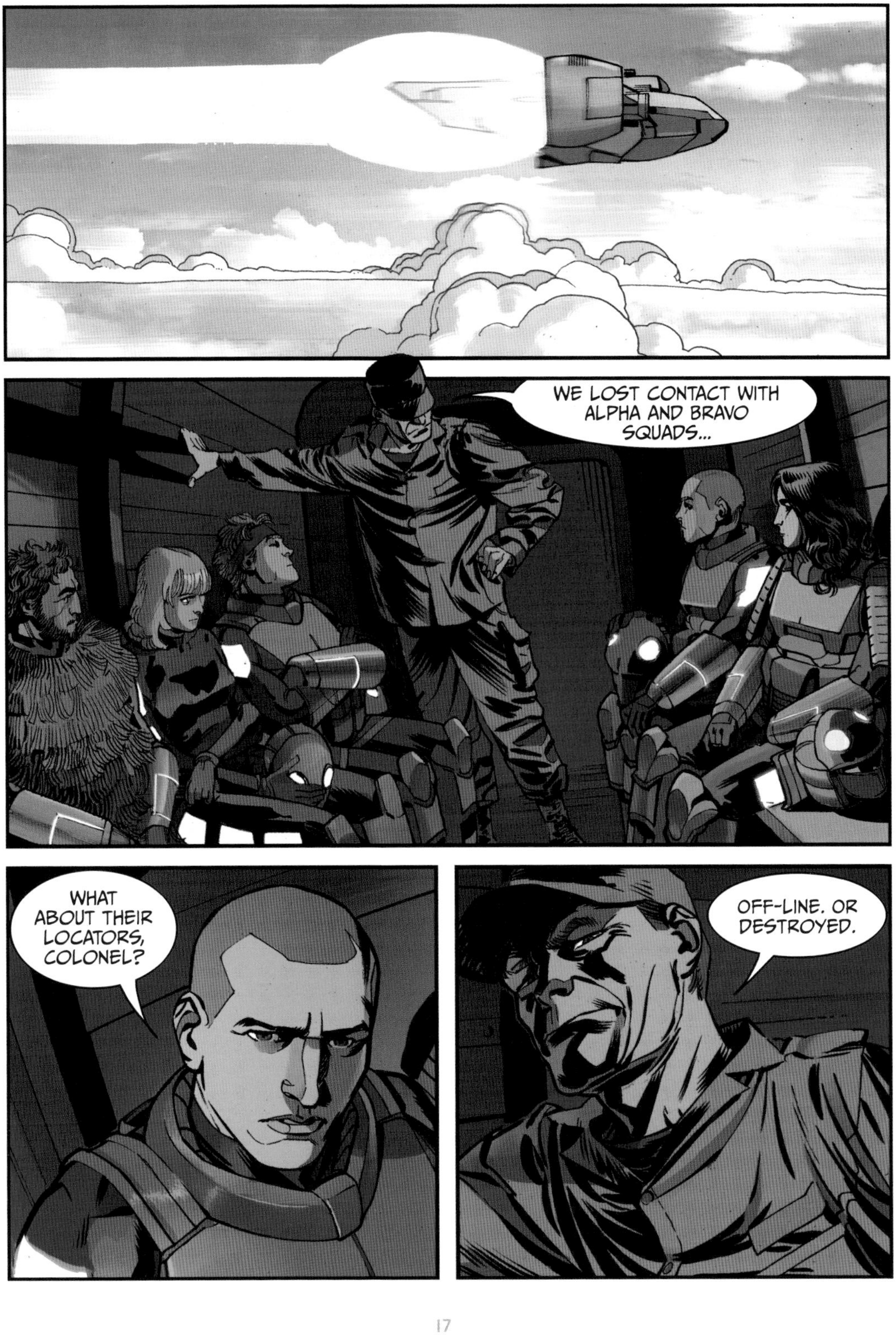
WE LOST CONTACT WITH ALPHA AND BRAVO SQUADS...
WHAT ABOUT THEIR LOCATORS, COLONEL?
OFF-LINE. OR DESTROYED.

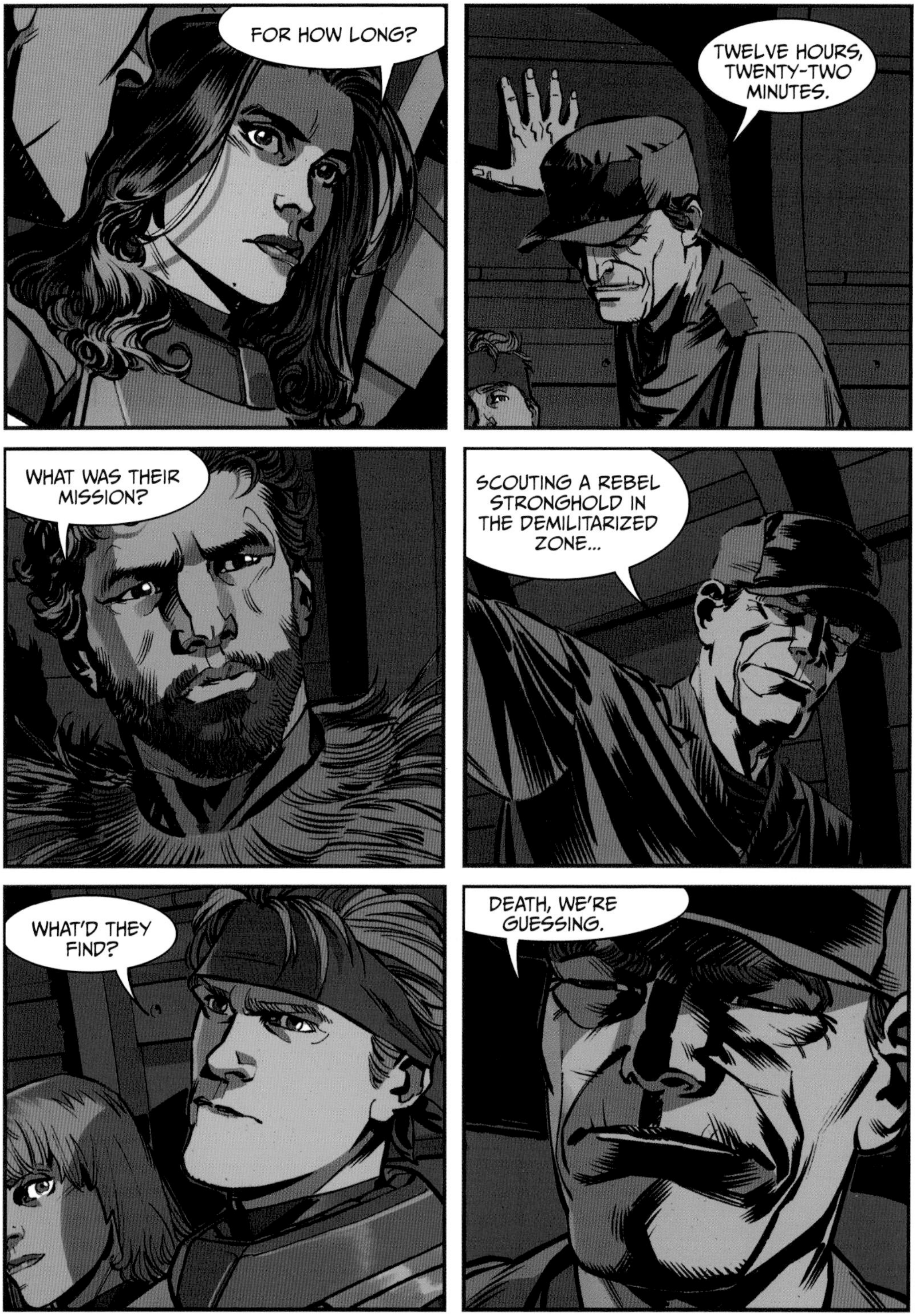
FOR HOW LONG?
TWELVE HOURS, TWENTY-TWO MINUTES.
WHAT WAS THEIR MISSION?
SCOUTING A REBEL STRONGHOLD IN THE DEMILITARIZED ZONE...
WHAT'D THEY FIND?
DEATH, WE'RE GUESSING.

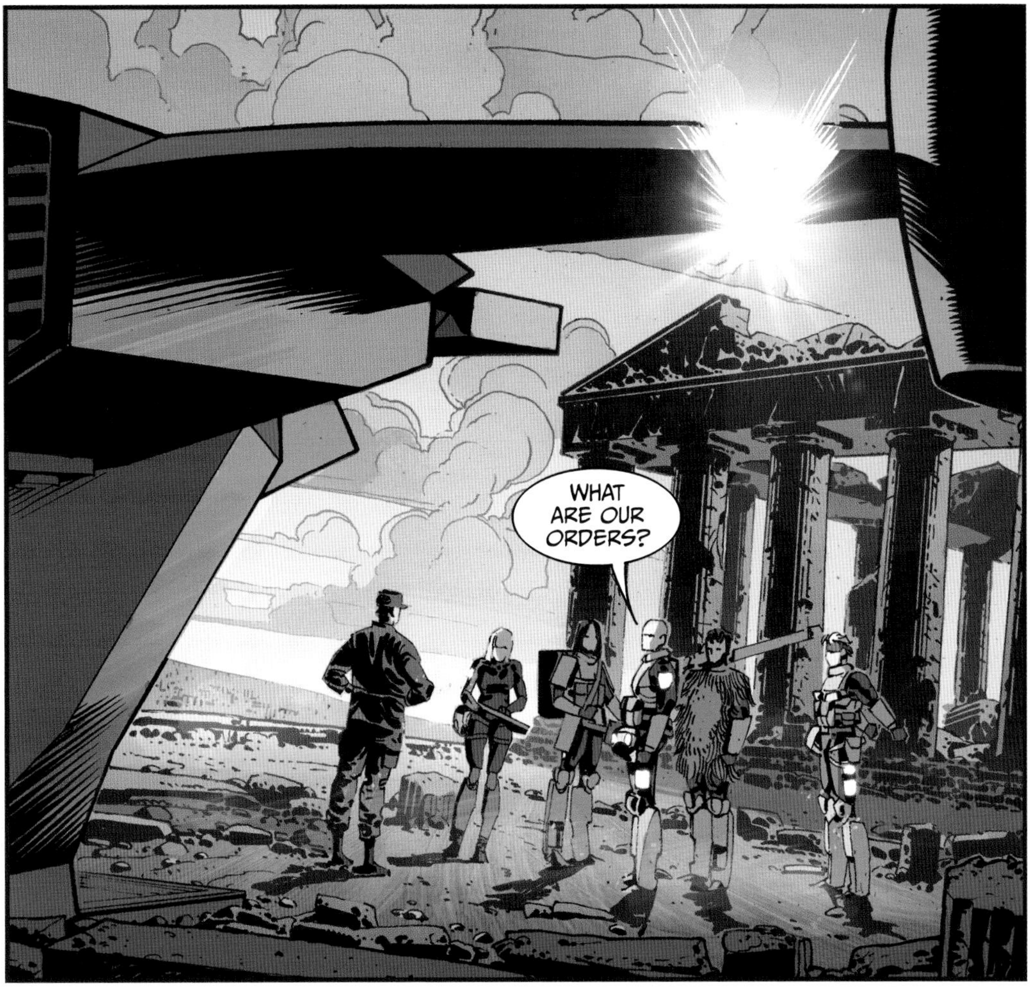
WHAT ARE OUR ORDERS?

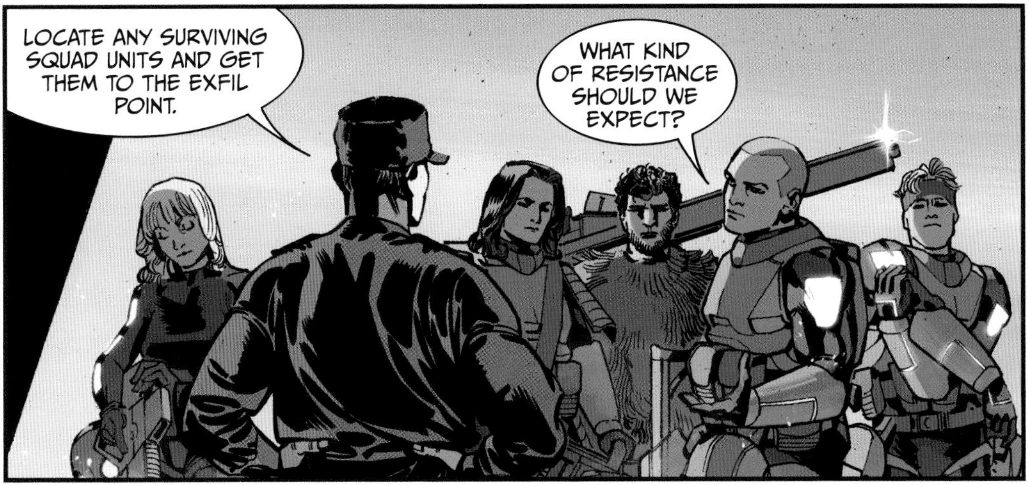
LOCATE ANY SURVIVING SQUAD UNITS AND GET THEM TO THE EXFIL POINT.
WHAT KIND OF RESISTANCE SHOULD WE EXPECT?

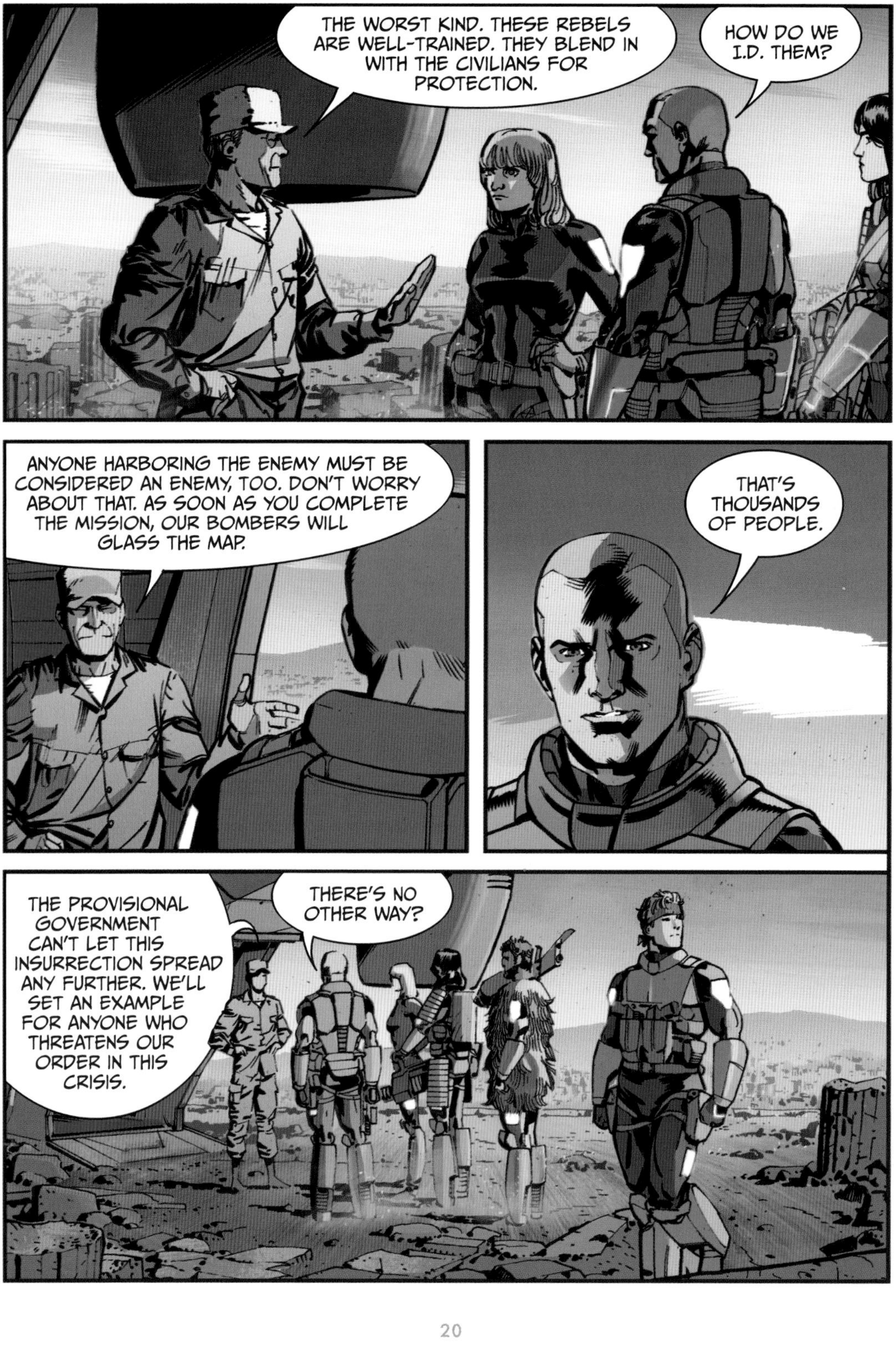
THE WORST KIND. THESE REBELS ARE WELL-TRAINED. THEY BLEND IN WITH THE CIVILIANS FOR PROTECTION.
HOW DO WE I.D. THEM?
ANYONE HARBORING THE ENEMY MUST BE CONSIDERED AN ENEMY, TOO. DON'T WORRY ABOUT THAT. AS SOON AS YOU COMPLETE THE MISSION, OUR BOMBERS WILL GLASS THE MAP.
THAT'S THOUSANDS OF PEOPLE.
THE PROVISIONAL GOVERNMENT CAN'T LET THIS INSURRECTION SPREAD ANY FURTHER. WE'LL SET AN EXAMPLE FOR ANYONE WHO THREATENS OUR ORDER IN THIS CRISIS.
THERE'S NO OTHER WAY?

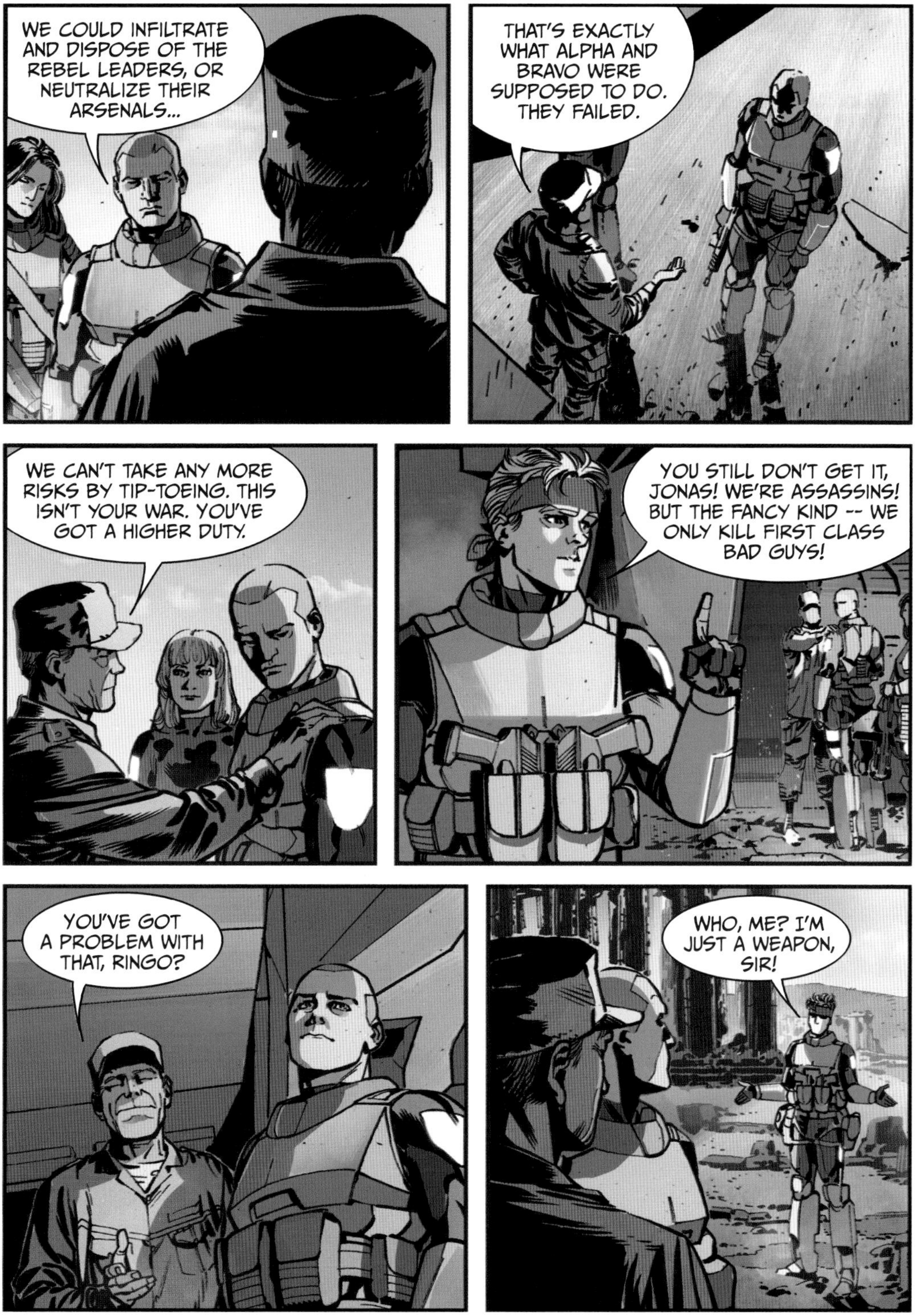
WE COULD INFILTRATE AND DISPOSE OF THE REBEL LEADERS, OR NEUTRALIZE THEIR ARSENALS...
THAT'S EXACTLY WHAT ALPHA AND BRAVO WERE SUPPOSED TO DO. THEY FAILED.
WE CAN'T TAKE ANY MORE RISKS BY TIP-TOEING. THIS ISN'T YOUR WAR. YOU'VE GOT A HIGHER DUTY.
YOU STILL DON'T GET IT, JONAS! WE'RE ASSASSINS! BUT THE FANCY KIND -- WE ONLY KILL FIRST CLASS BAD GUYS!
YOU'VE GOT A PROBLEM WITH THAT, RINGO?
WHO, ME? I'M JUST A WEAPON, SIR!

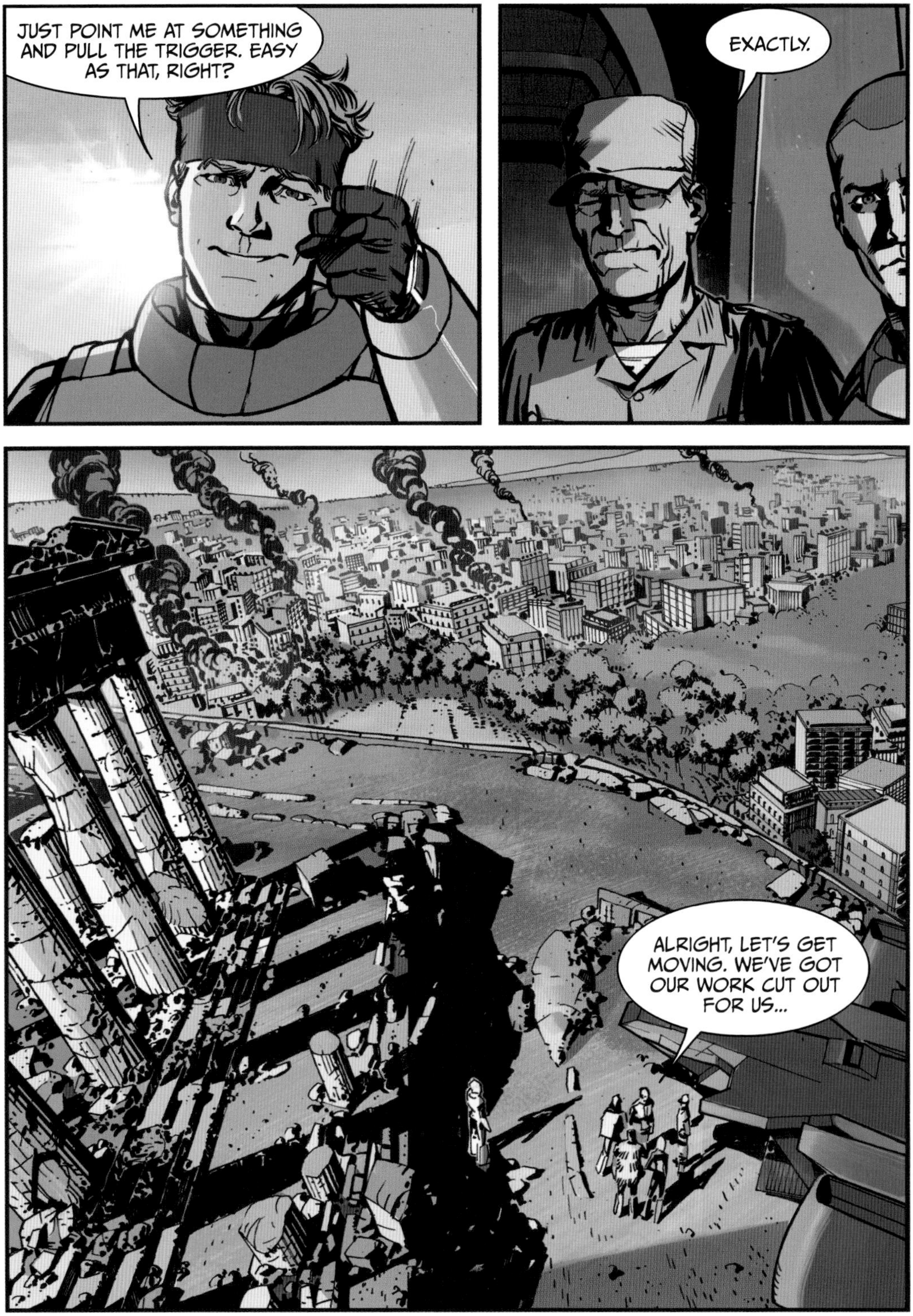
JUST POINT ME AT SOMETHING AND PULL THE TRIGGER. EASY AS THAT, RIGHT?
EXACTLY.
ALRIGHT, LET'S GET MOVING. WE'VE GOT OUR WORK CUT OUT FOR US...

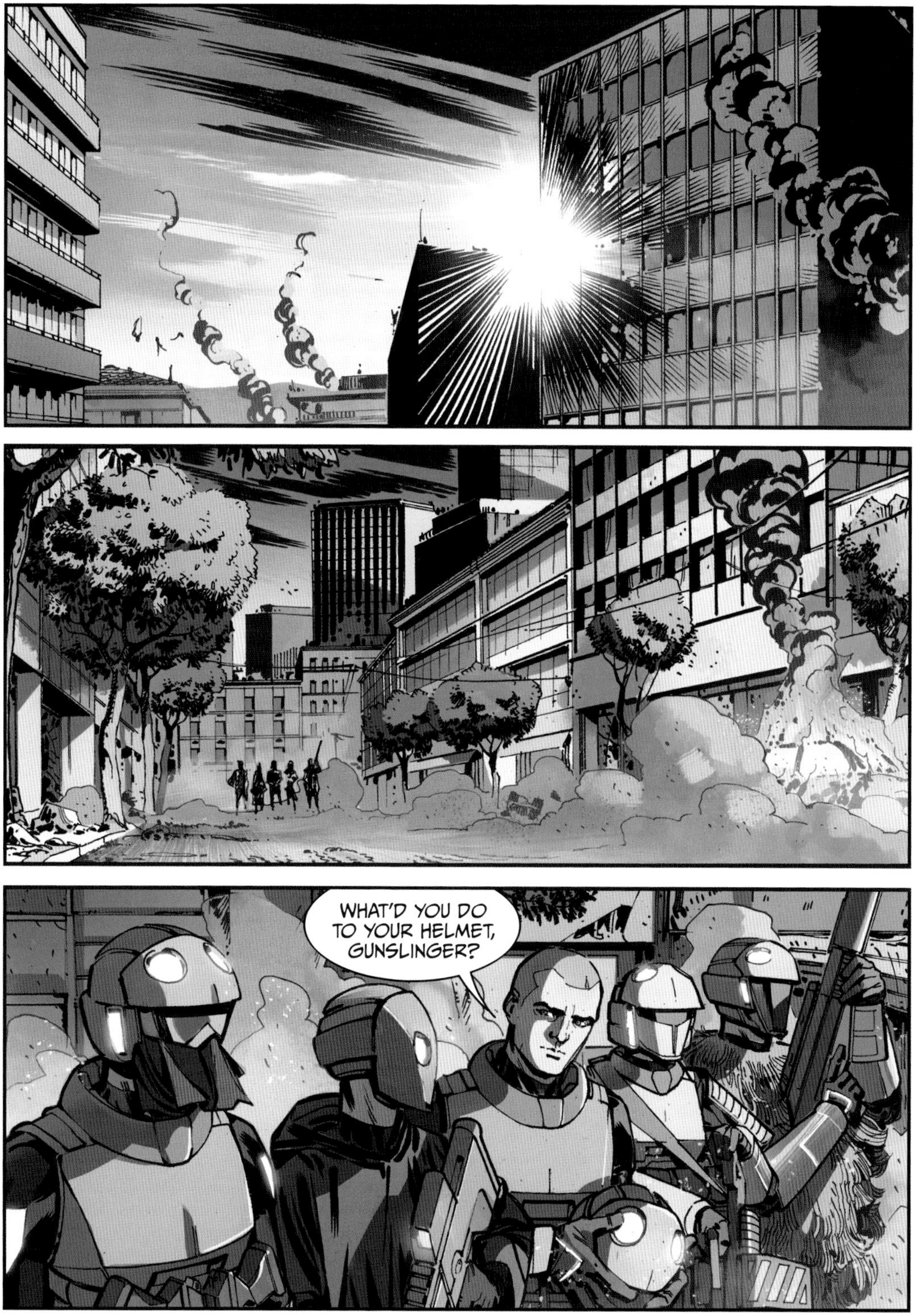
WHAT'D YOU DO TO YOUR HELMET, GUNSLINGER?

I GAVE IT A PERSONAL TOUCH. LIKE IT?

NO. IT'S STUPID. AND TAMPERING WITH GEAR IS AGAINST CODE.

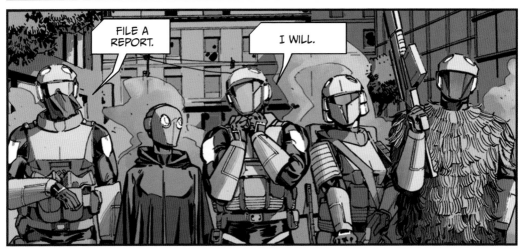

FILE A REPORT.

I WILL.

CUT IT OUT, GUYS.

BRAT'S RIGHT -- TIME TO GET TO WORK!

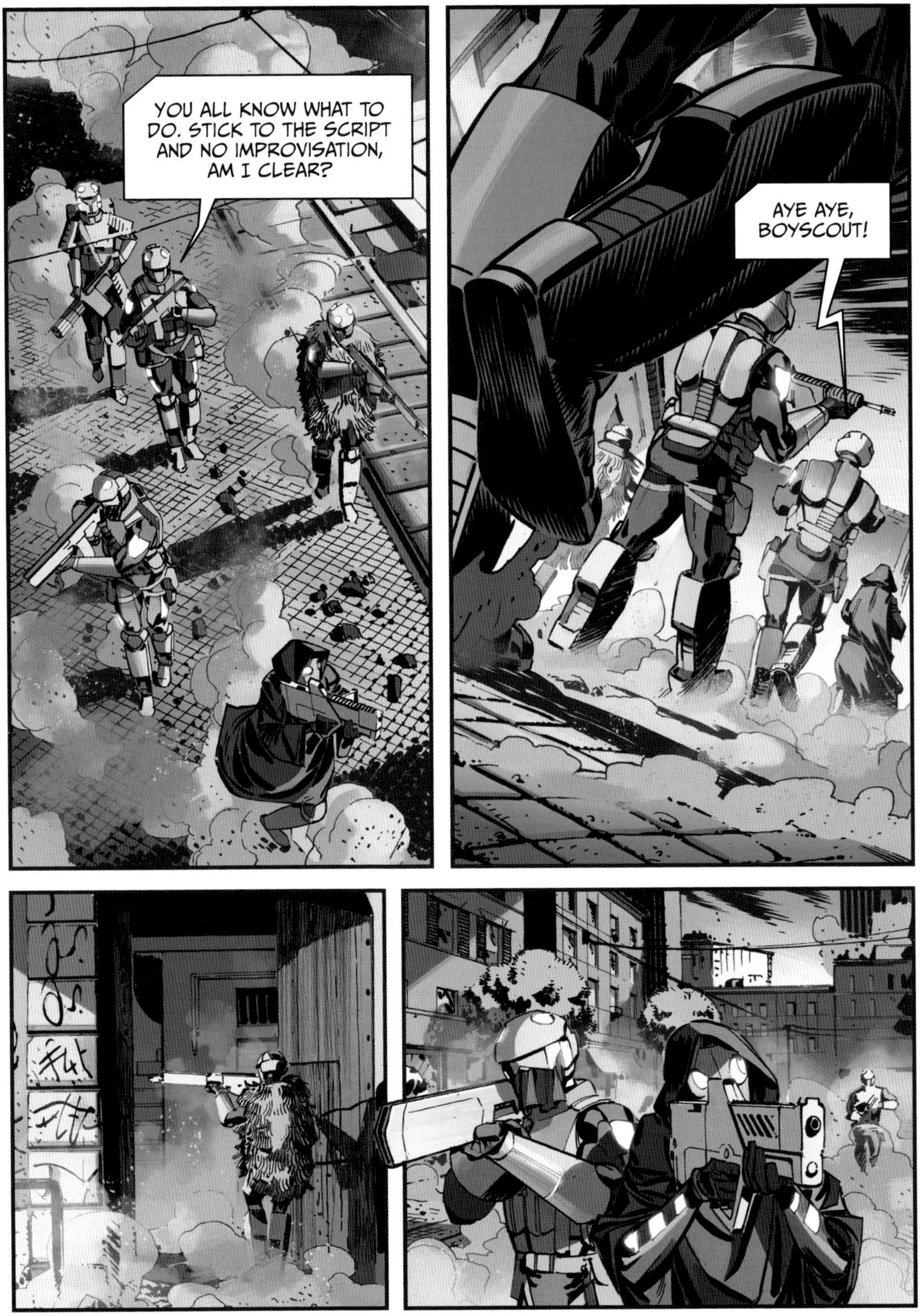
YOU ALL KNOW WHAT TO DO. STICK TO THE SCRIPT AND NO IMPROVISATION, AM I CLEAR?
AYE AYE, BOYSCOUT!

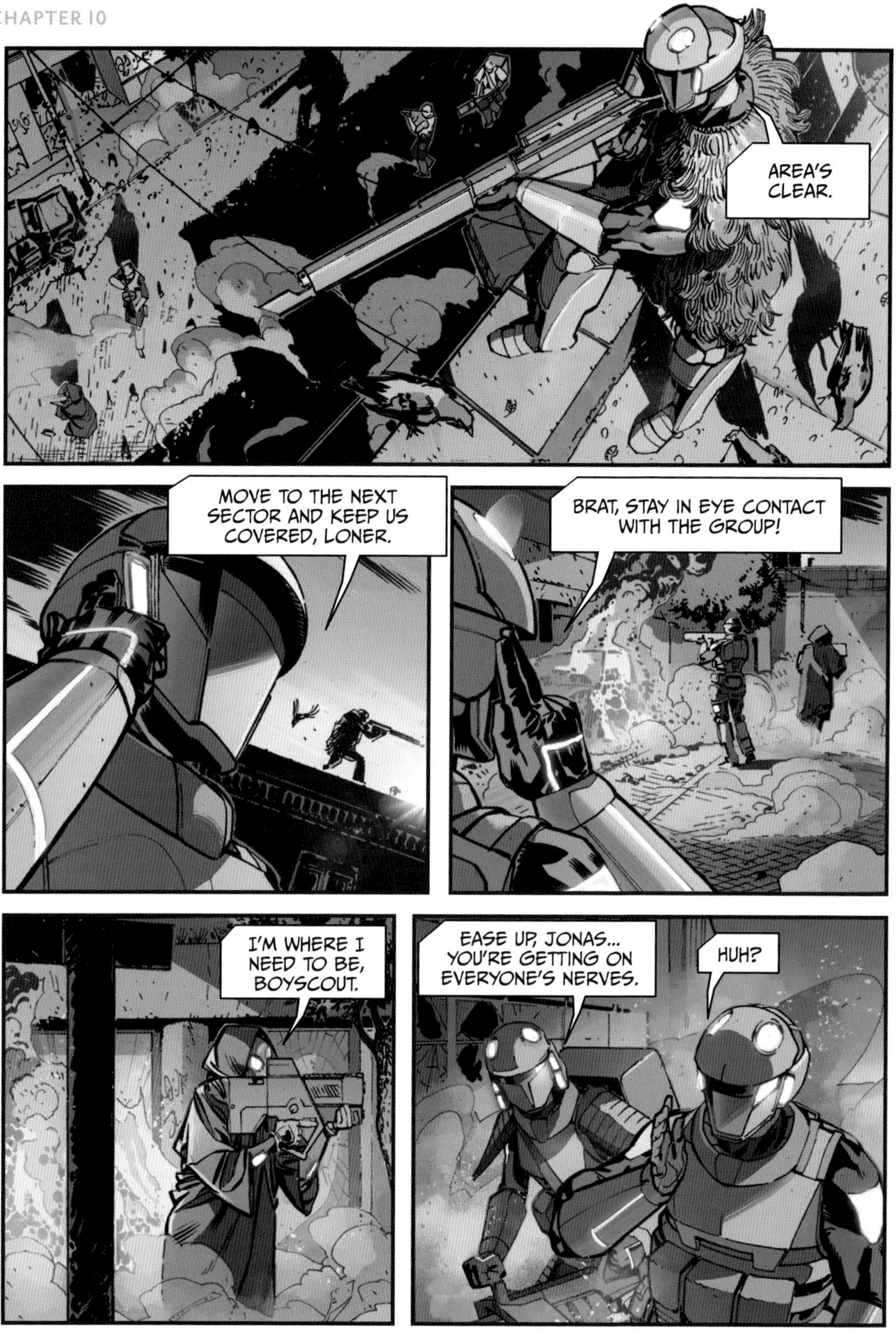
AREA'S CLEAR.
MOVE TO THE NEXT SECTOR AND KEEP US COVERED, LONER.
BRAT, STAY IN EYE CONTACT WITH THE GROUP!
I'M WHERE I NEED TO BE, BOYSCOUT.
EASE UP, JONAS... YOU'RE GETTING ON EVERYONE'S NERVES.
HUH?

WE KNOW OUR JOB. YOU DON'T HAVE TO TREAT US LIKE CHILDREN.

THEN YOU'D KNOW THAT WE USE CODE NAMES ON THE BATTLEFIELD, ANGEL. THIS ISN'T A TRAINING DRILL!

YOU'RE RIGHT. THIS IS REALITY, AND REALITY SUCKS... BOYSCOUT.

TRUST THE TRAINING. TRUST US.

AND TRUST YOURSELF.

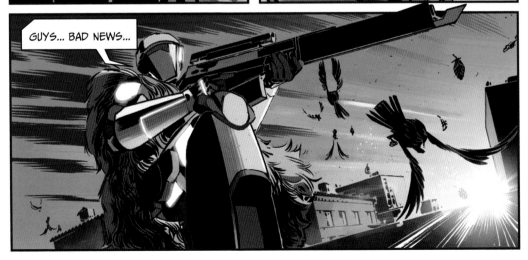

GUYS... BAD NEWS...

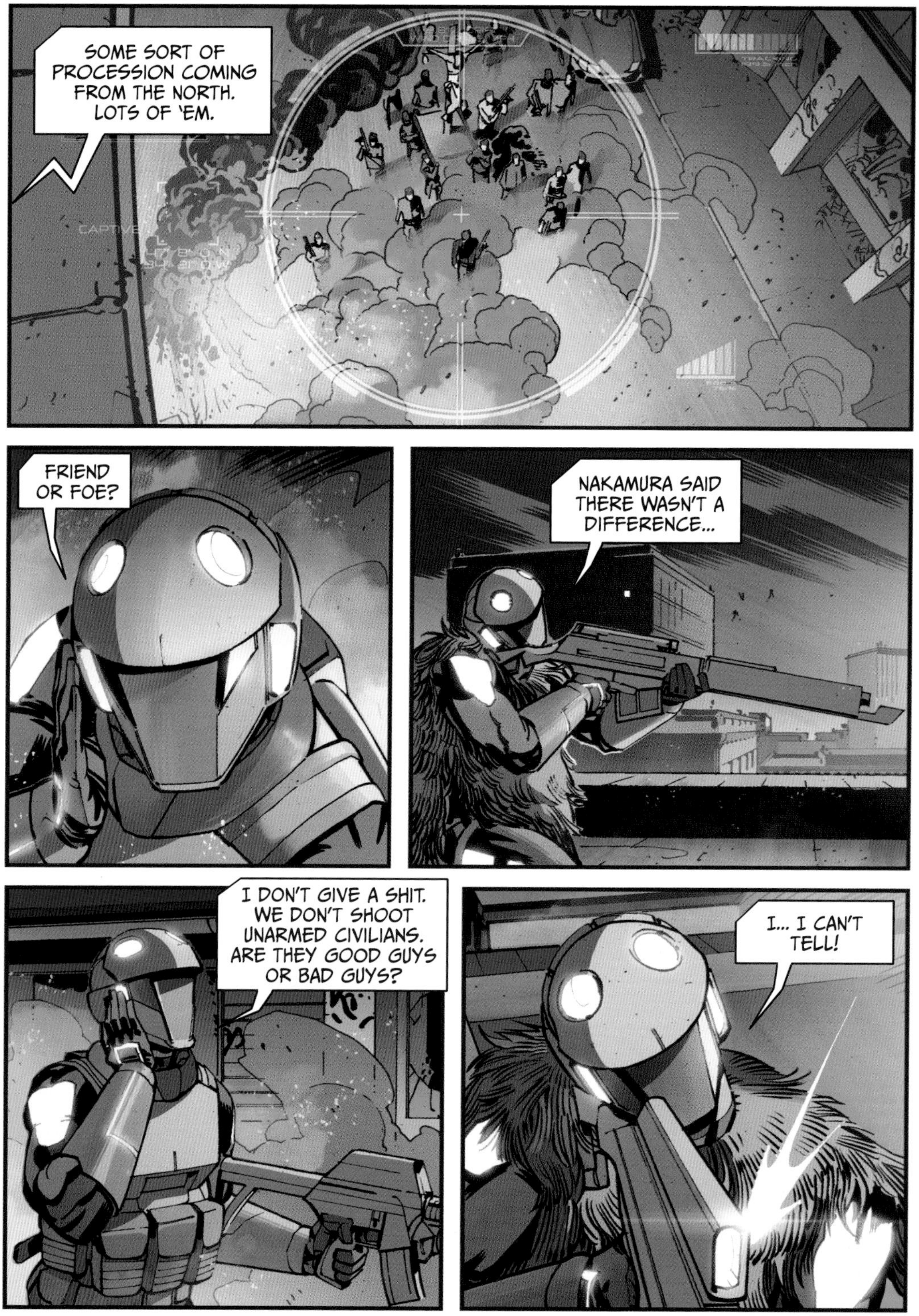
SOME SORT OF PROCESSION COMING FROM THE NORTH. LOTS OF 'EM.
FRIEND OR FOE?
NAKAMURA SAID THERE WASN'T A DIFFERENCE...
I DON'T GIVE A SHIT. WE DON'T SHOOT UNARMED CIVILIANS. ARE THEY GOOD GUYS OR BAD GUYS?
I... I CAN'T TELL!

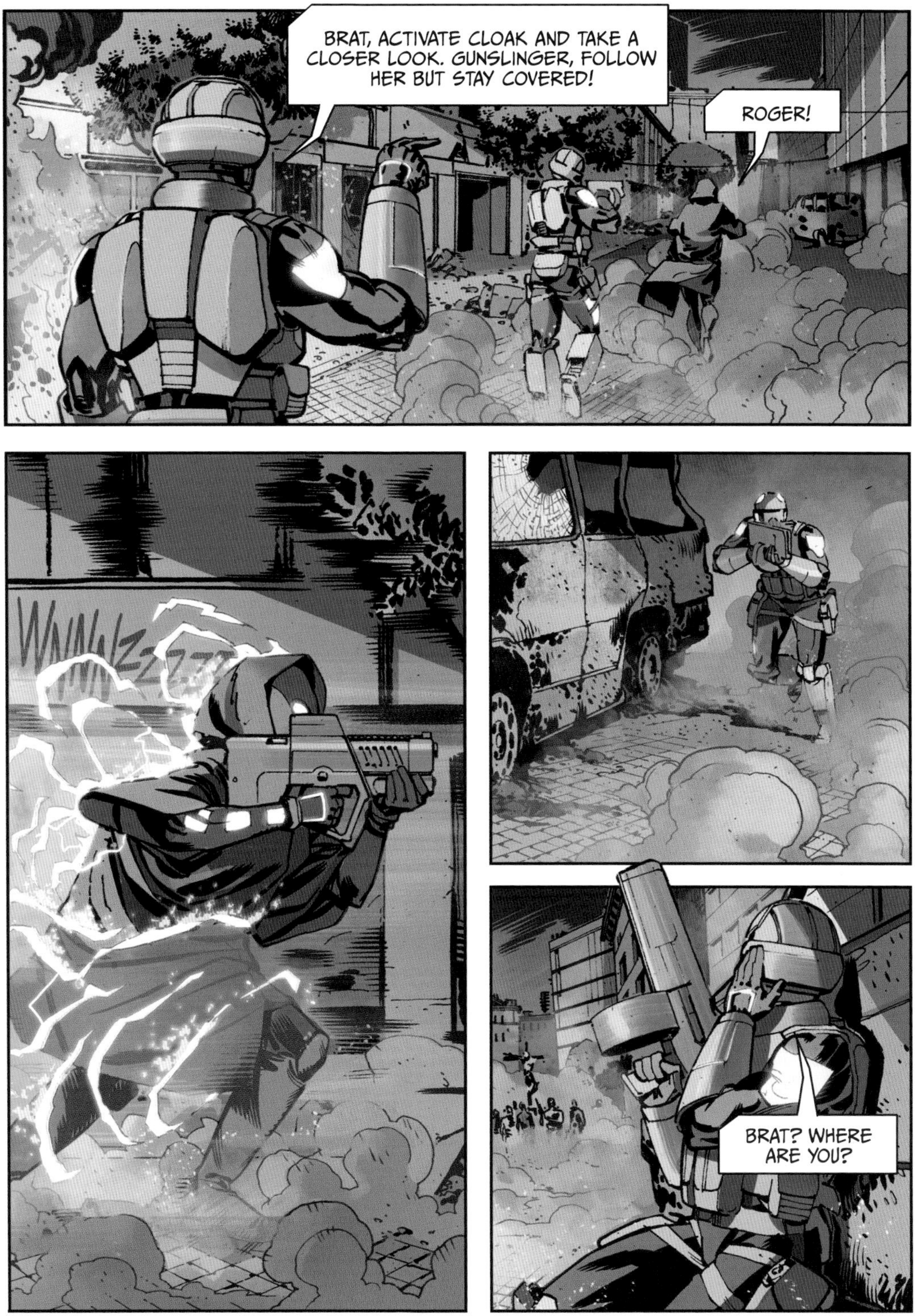
BRAT, ACTIVATE CLOAK AND TAKE A CLOSER LOOK. GUNSLINGER, FOLLOW HER BUT STAY COVERED!
ROGER!
WNNNZZZZ
BRAT? WHERE ARE YOU?

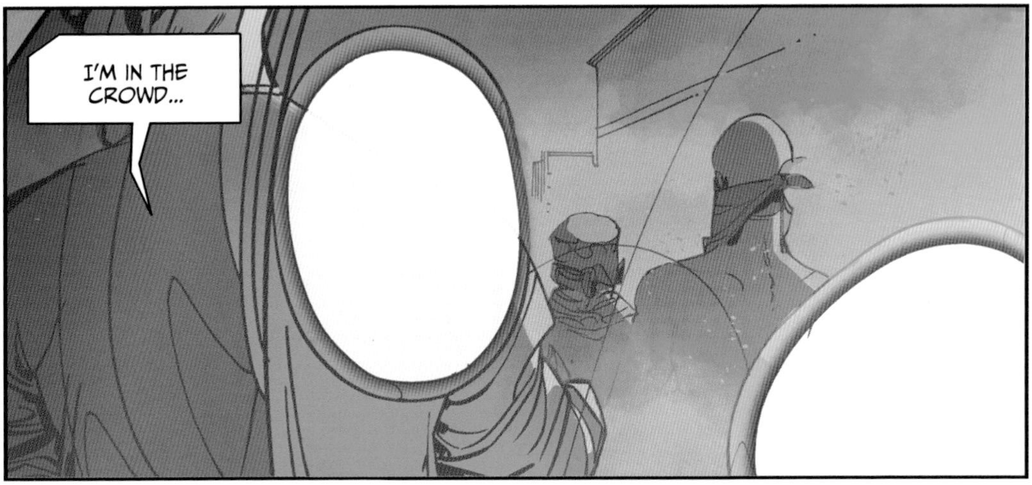
I'M IN THE CROWD...

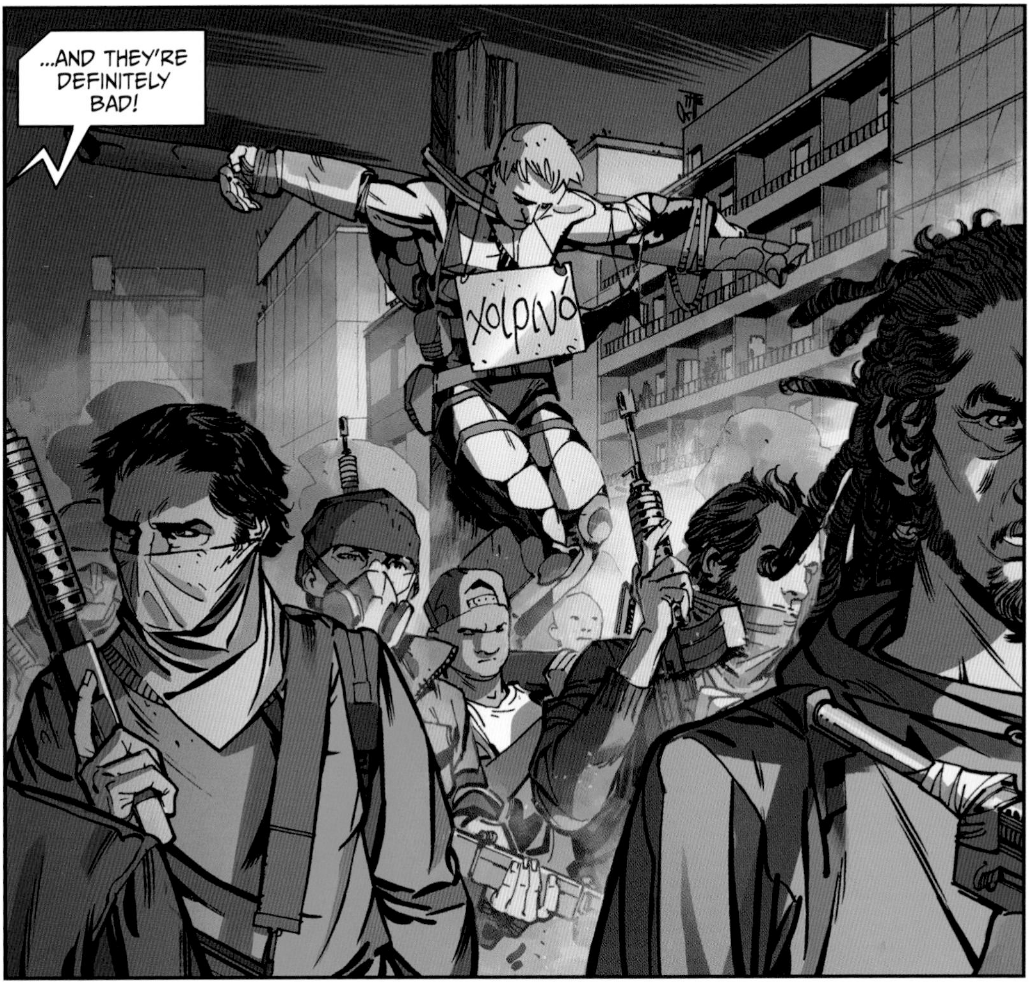
...AND THEY'RE DEFINITELY BAD!

DO NOT ENGAGE, BRAT. I REPEAT, *DO NOT ENGAGE!*

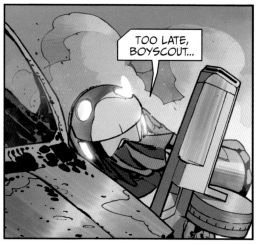

TOO LATE, BOYSCOUT...

...SHE THREW THE FIRST PITCH!

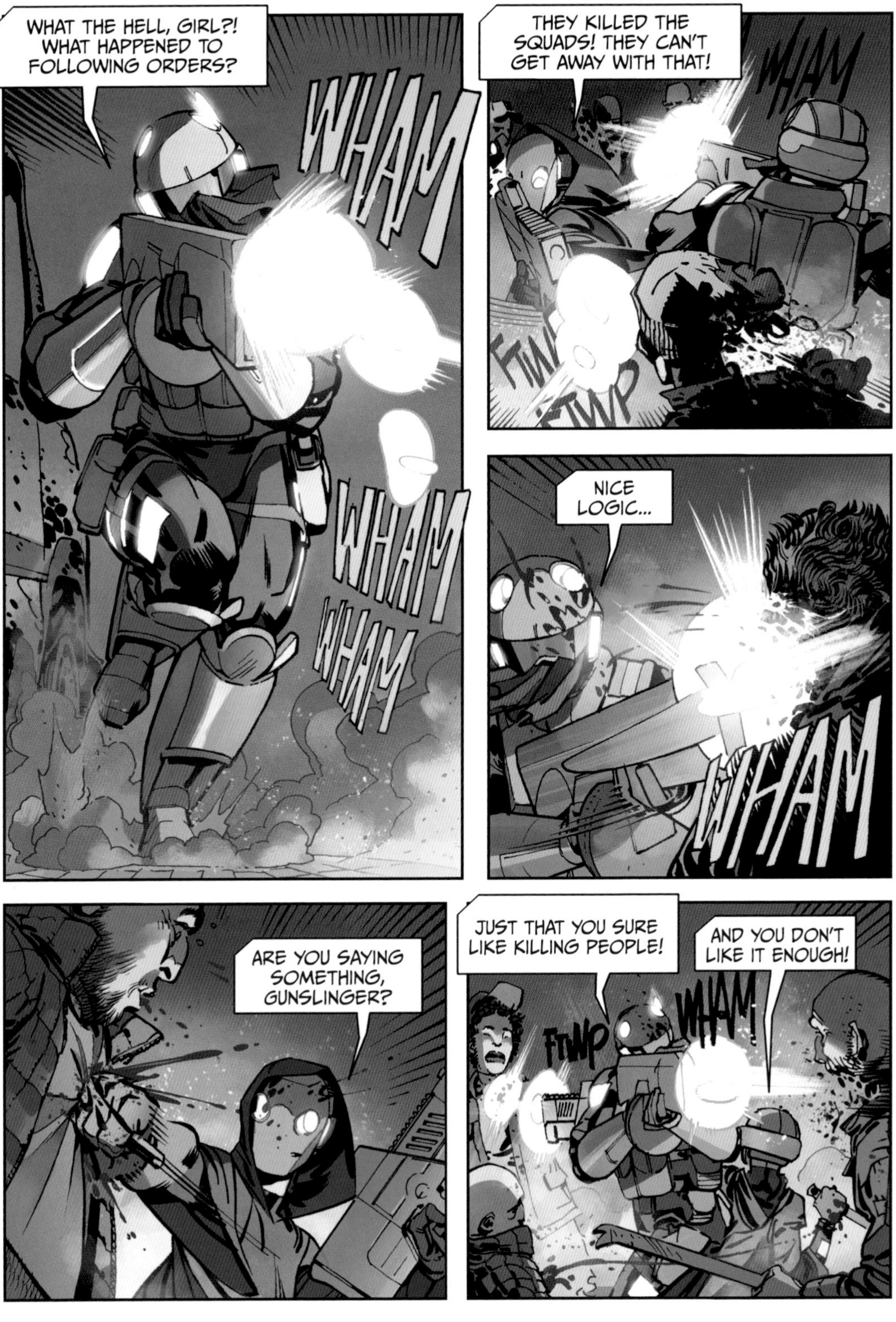
WHAT THE HELL, GIRL?! WHAT HAPPENED TO FOLLOWING ORDERS?
WHAM
WHAM
WHAM
THEY KILLED THE SQUADS! THEY CAN'T GET AWAY WITH THAT!
WHAM
FTWP
NICE LOGIC...
WHAM
ARE YOU SAYING SOMETHING, GUNSLINGER?
JUST THAT YOU SURE LIKE KILLING PEOPLE!
FTWP
WHAM
AND YOU DON'T LIKE IT ENOUGH!

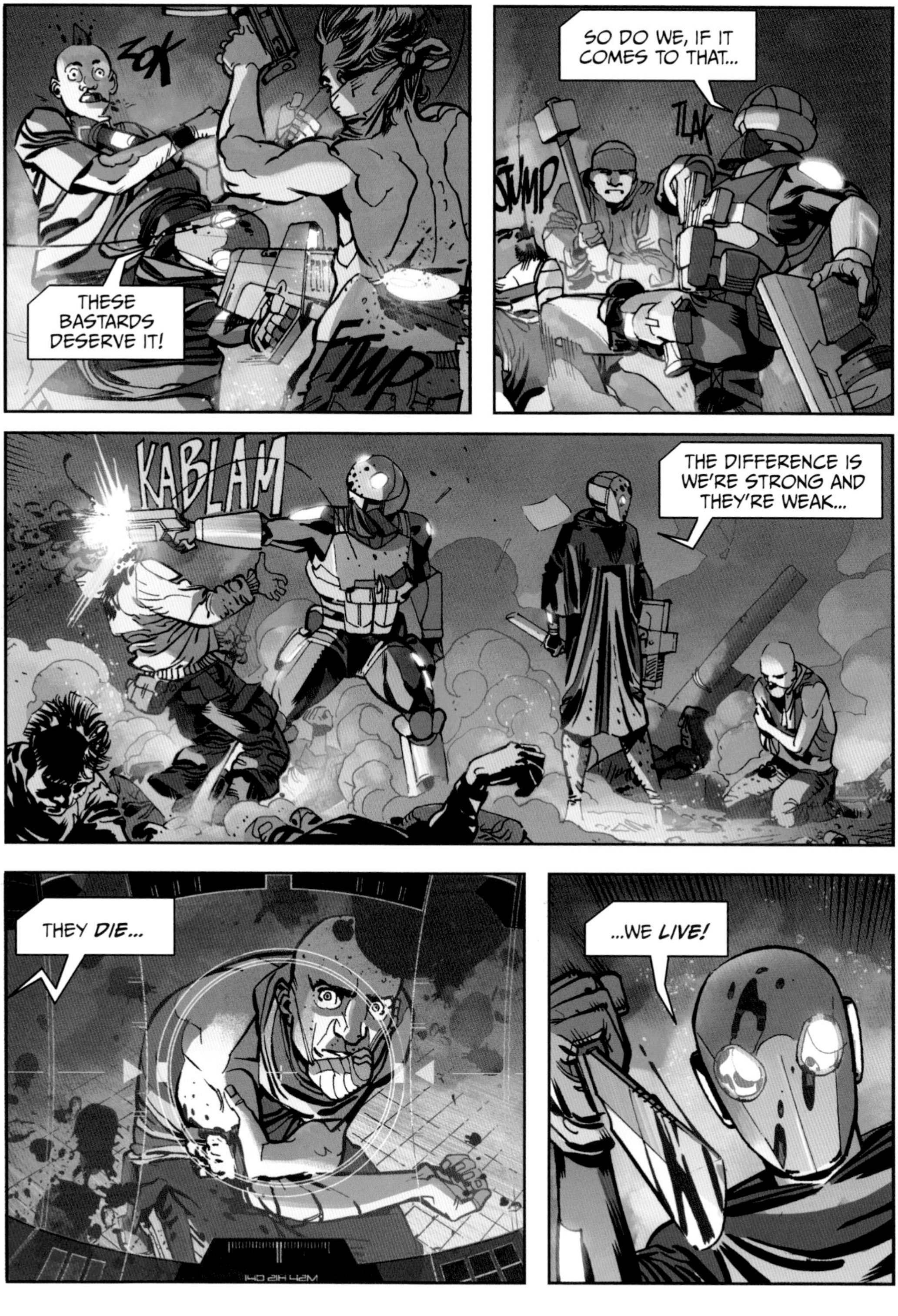
THESE BASTARDS DESERVE IT!
SO DO WE, IF IT COMES TO THAT...
TLAK
KABLAM
THE DIFFERENCE IS WE'RE STRONG AND THEY'RE WEAK...
THEY *DIE*...
...WE *LIVE!*

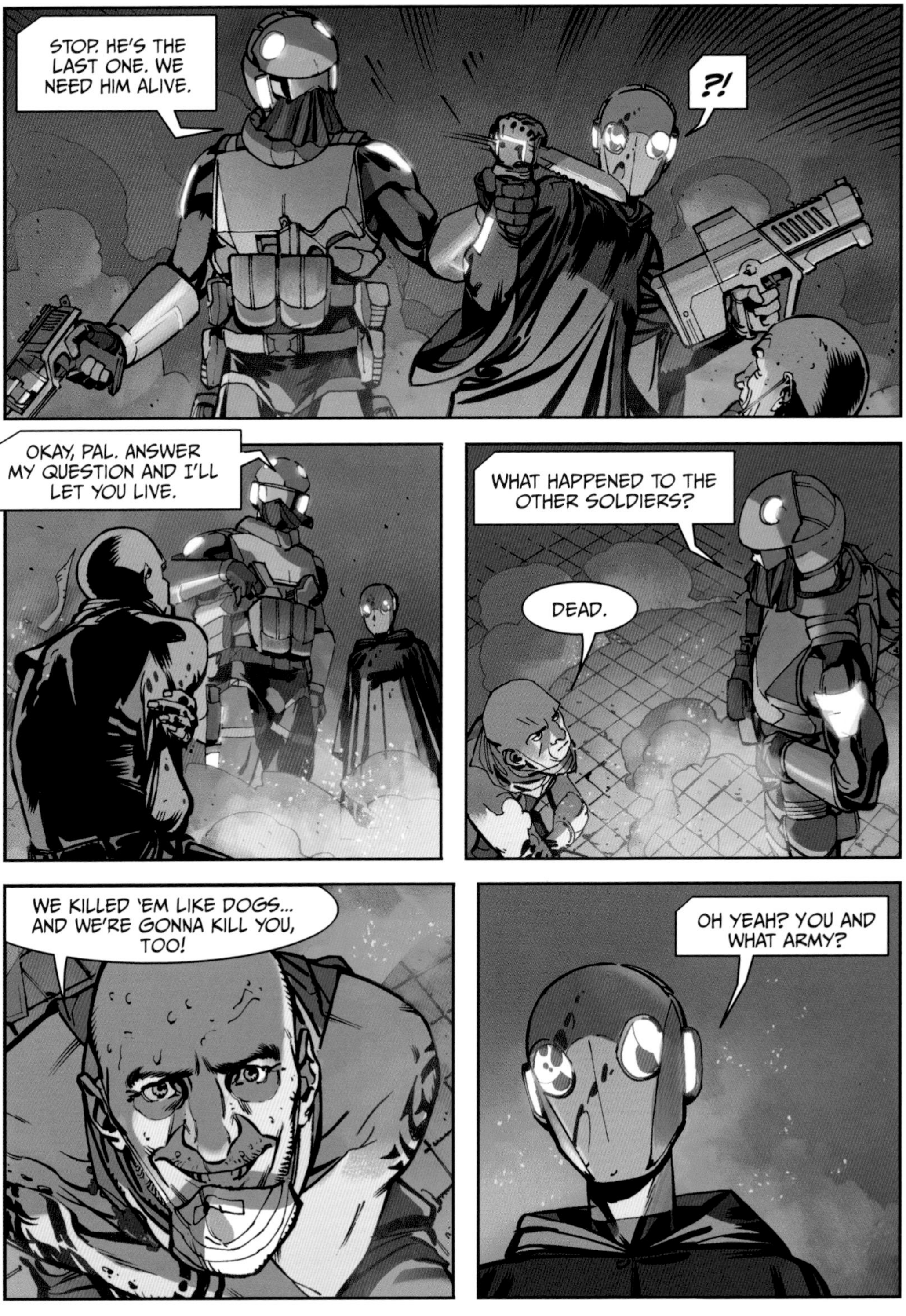
STOP. HE'S THE LAST ONE. WE NEED HIM ALIVE.
?!
OKAY, PAL. ANSWER MY QUESTION AND I'LL LET YOU LIVE.
WHAT HAPPENED TO THE OTHER SOLDIERS?
DEAD.
WE KILLED 'EM LIKE DOGS... AND WE'RE GONNA KILL YOU, TOO!
OH YEAH? YOU AND WHAT ARMY?

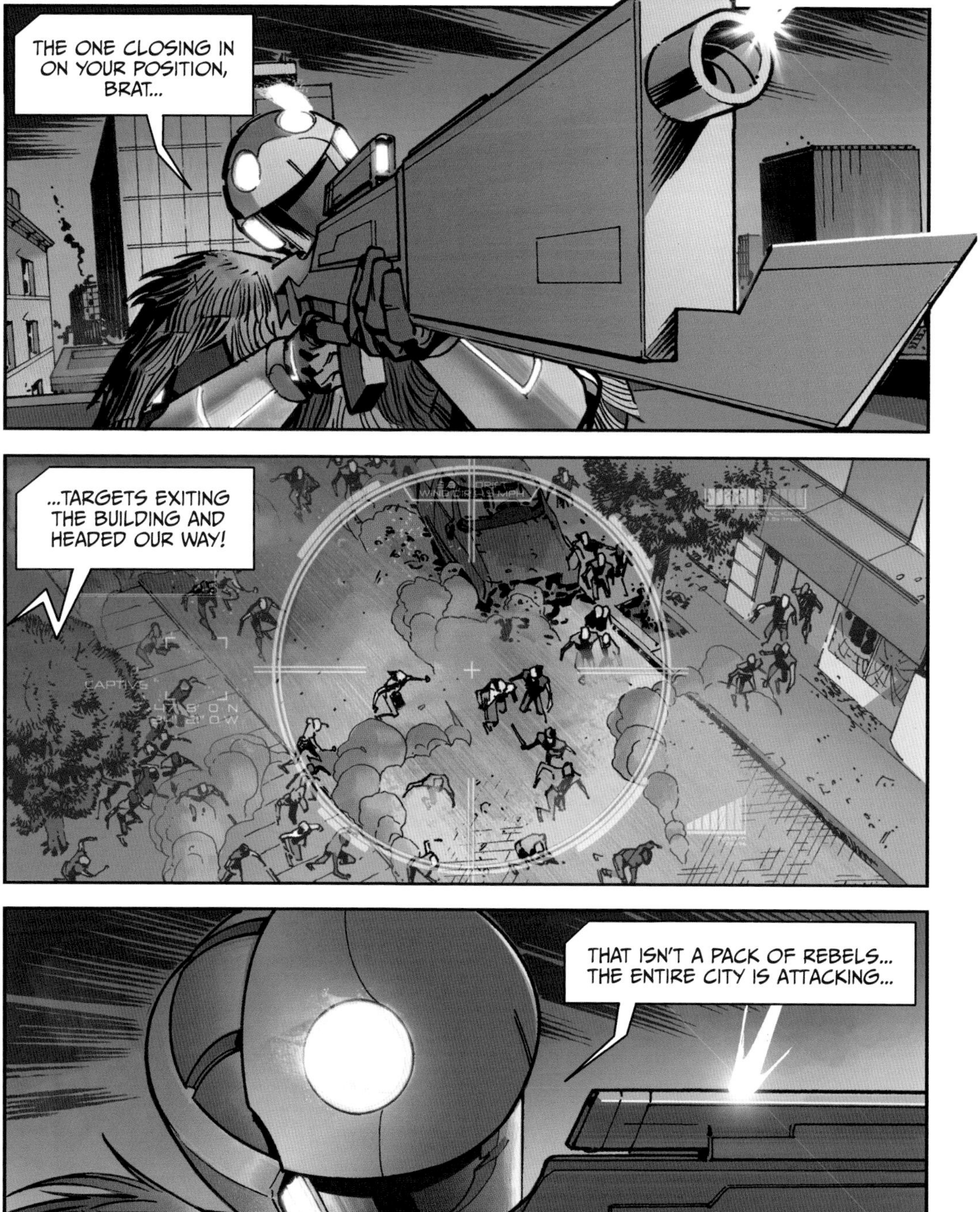
THE ONE CLOSING IN ON YOUR POSITION, BRAT...
...TARGETS EXITING THE BUILDING AND HEADED OUR WAY!
THAT ISN'T A PACK OF REBELS... THE ENTIRE CITY IS ATTACKING...

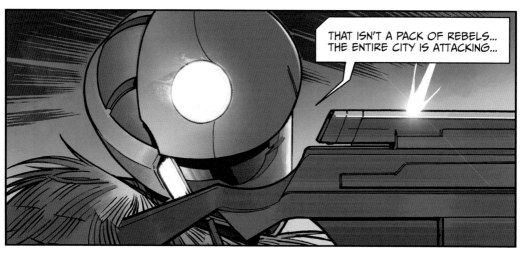

GUNSLINGER, BRAT, FALL BACK. THIS POSITION IS COMPROMISED. WE GOT WHAT WE NEEDED, WE'RE DONE HERE.

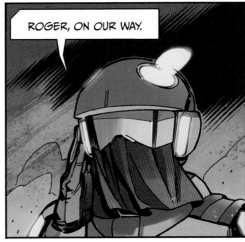

ROGER, ON OUR WAY.

DON'T NEED YOU...!

NO!

HNGH!

Zak!

DAMN IT, SAM! I GAVE HIM MY WORD!

AND YOU KEPT IT.

I KILLED HIM, NOT *YOU*.

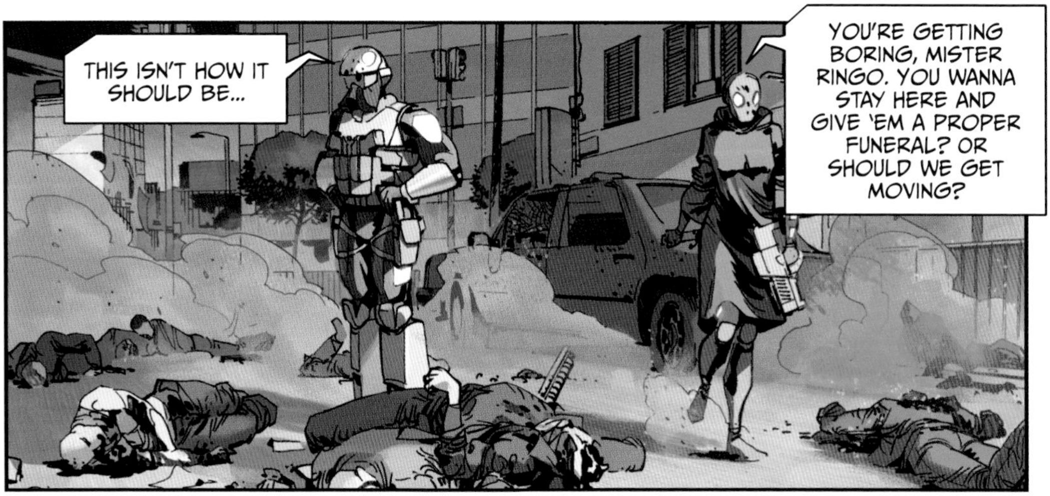
THIS ISN'T HOW IT SHOULD BE...
YOU'RE GETTING BORING, MISTER RINGO. YOU WANNA STAY HERE AND GIVE 'EM A PROPER FUNERAL? OR SHOULD WE GET MOVING?

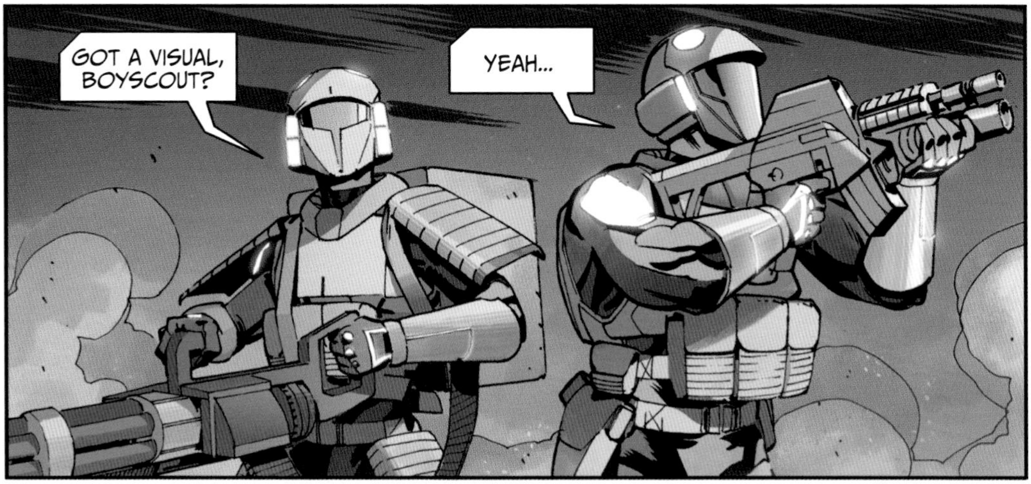
GOT A VISUAL, BOYSCOUT?
YEAH...

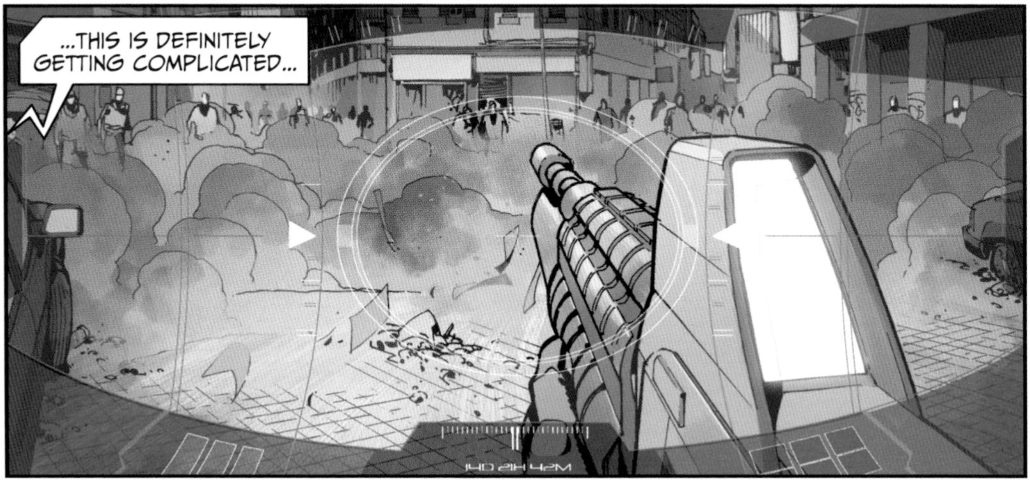
...THIS IS DEFINITELY GETTING COMPLICATED...

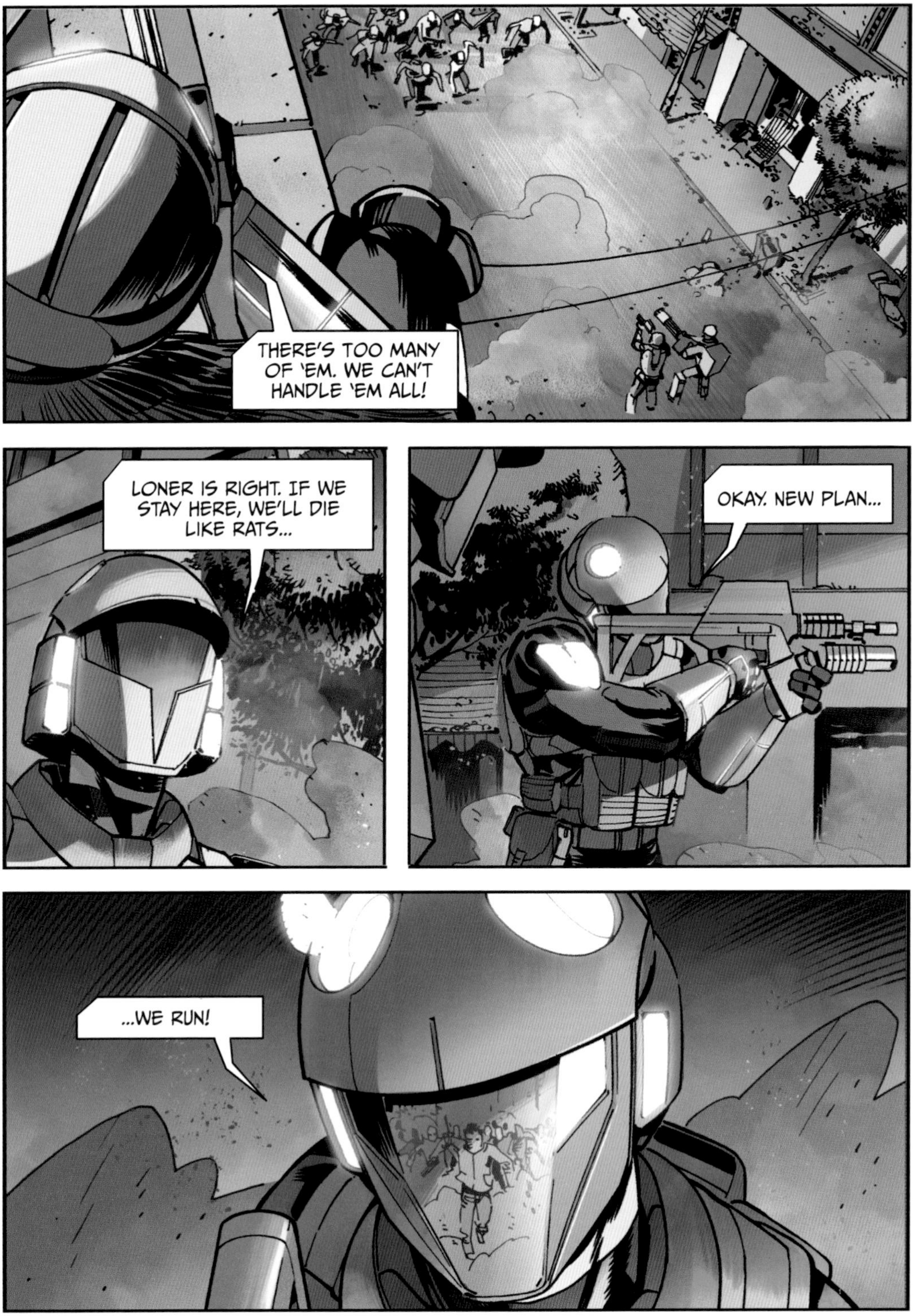
THERE'S TOO MANY OF 'EM. WE CAN'T HANDLE 'EM ALL!
LONER IS RIGHT. IF WE STAY HERE, WE'LL DIE LIKE RATS...
OKAY. NEW PLAN...
...WE RUN!

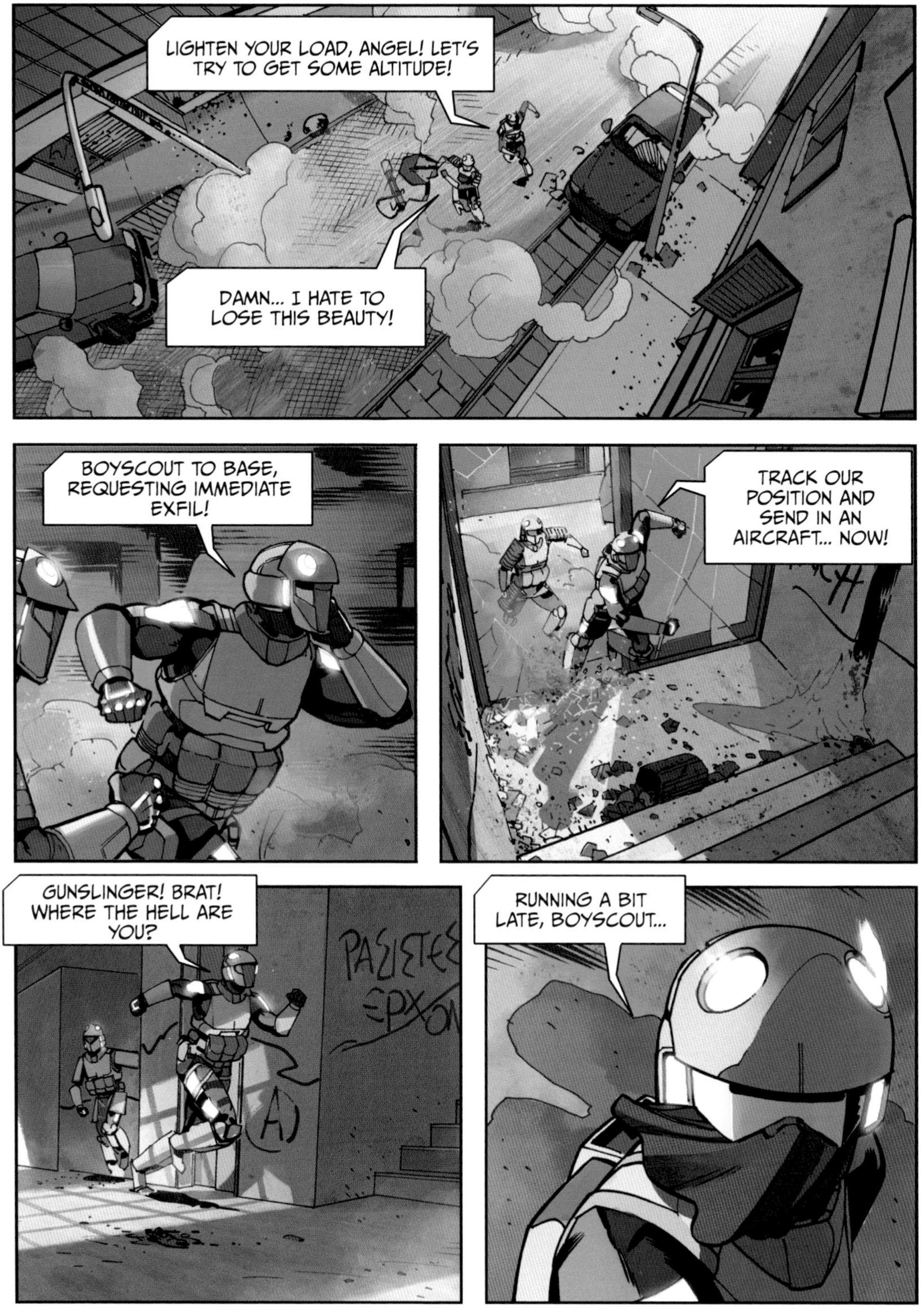
LIGHTEN YOUR LOAD, ANGEL! LET'S TRY TO GET SOME ALTITUDE!
DAMN... I HATE TO LOSE THIS BEAUTY!
BOYSCOUT TO BASE, REQUESTING IMMEDIATE EXFIL!
TRACK OUR POSITION AND SEND IN AN AIRCRAFT... NOW!
GUNSLINGER! BRAT! WHERE THE HELL ARE YOU?
RUNNING A BIT LATE, BOYSCOUT...

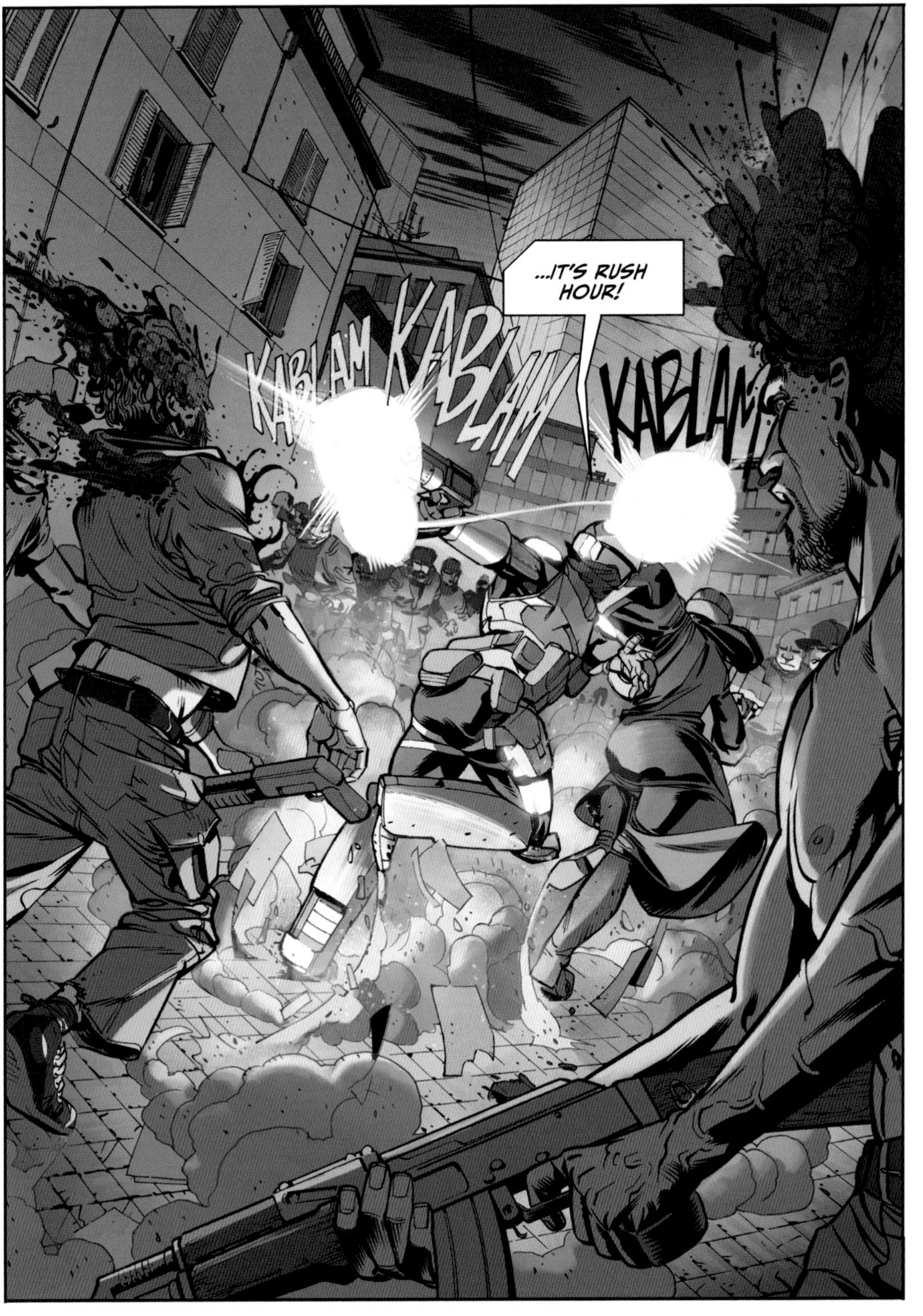
KABLAM KABLAM
...IT'S RUSH HOUR!
KABLAM

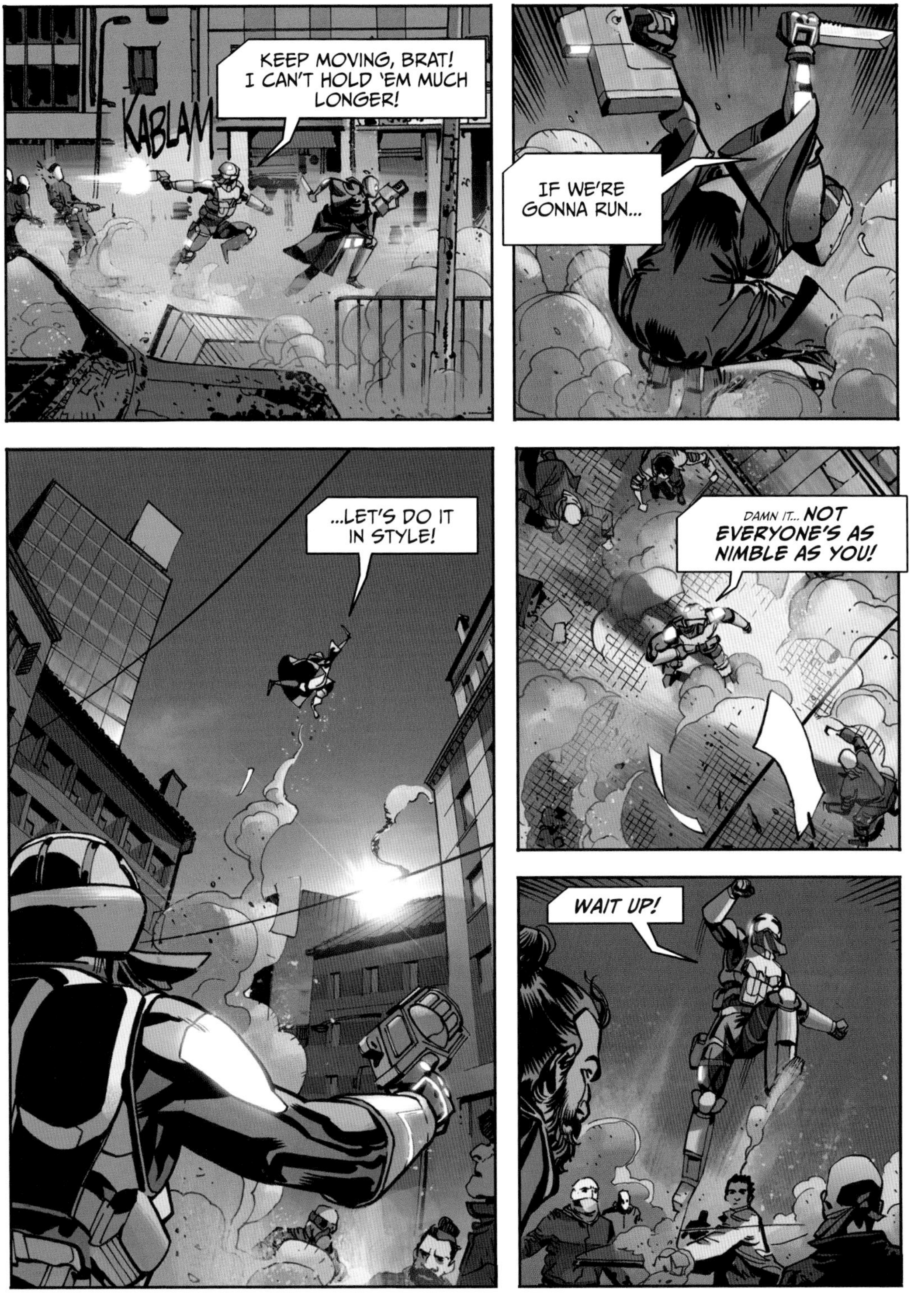
KEEP MOVING, BRAT! I CAN'T HOLD 'EM MUCH LONGER!
KABLAM
IF WE'RE GONNA RUN...
...LET'S DO IT IN STYLE!
DAMN IT... NOT EVERYONE'S AS NIMBLE AS YOU!
WAIT UP!

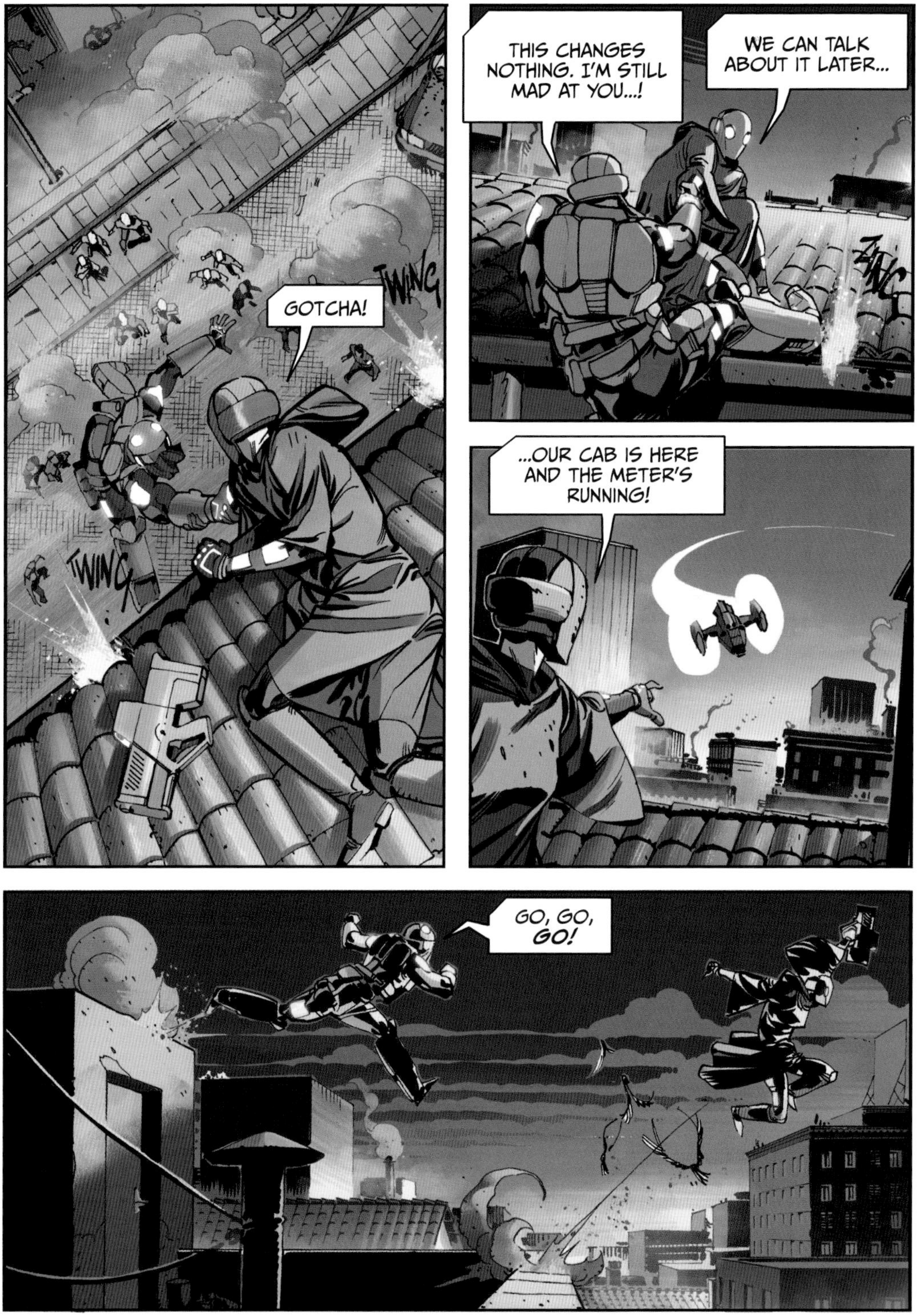
TWING
GOTCHA!
TWING
THIS CHANGES NOTHING. I'M STILL MAD AT YOU...!
WE CAN TALK ABOUT IT LATER...
ZWING
...OUR CAB IS HERE AND THE METER'S RUNNING!
GO, GO, **GO!**

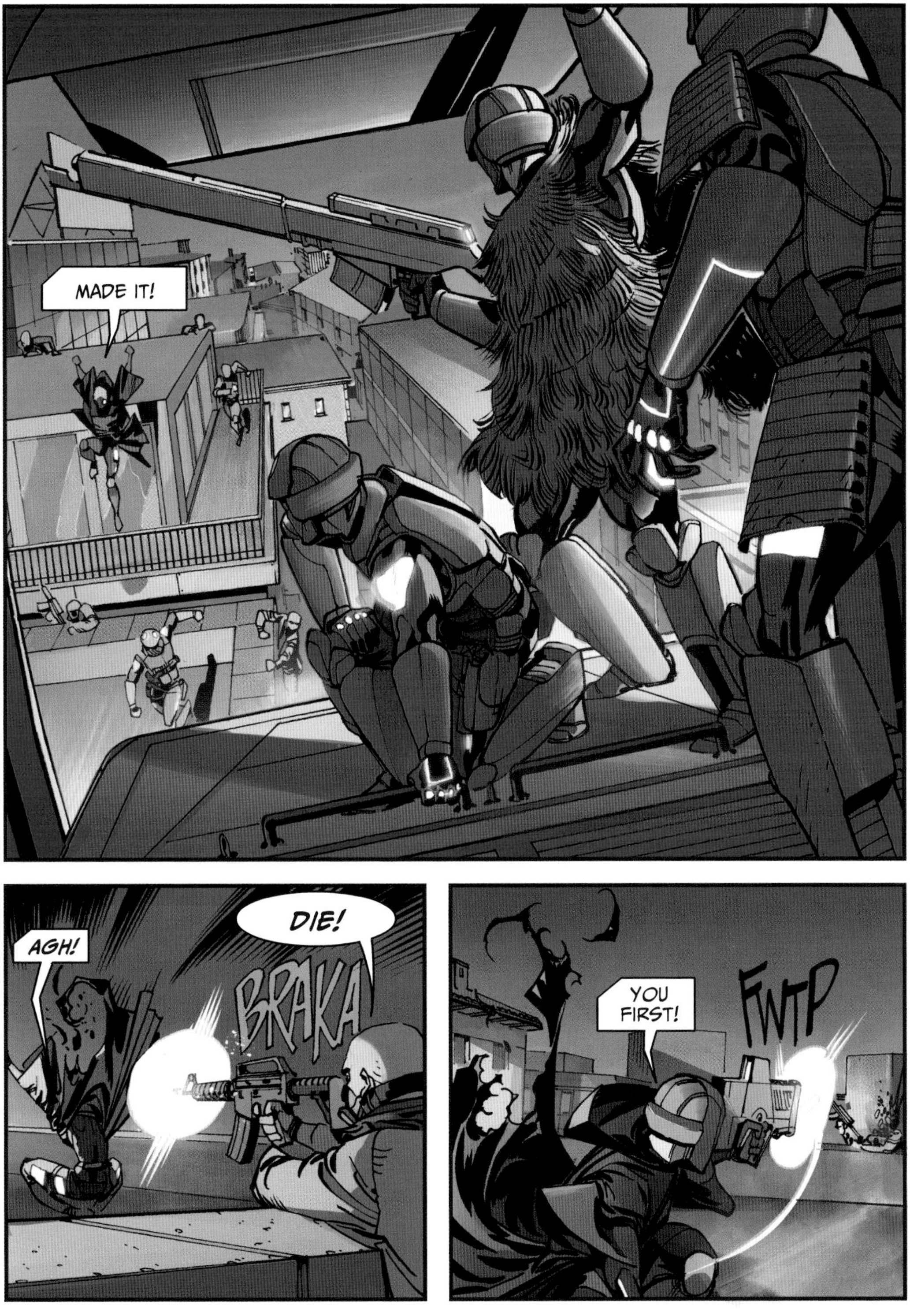
MADE IT!
AGH!
DIE!
BRAKA
YOU FIRST!
FWTP

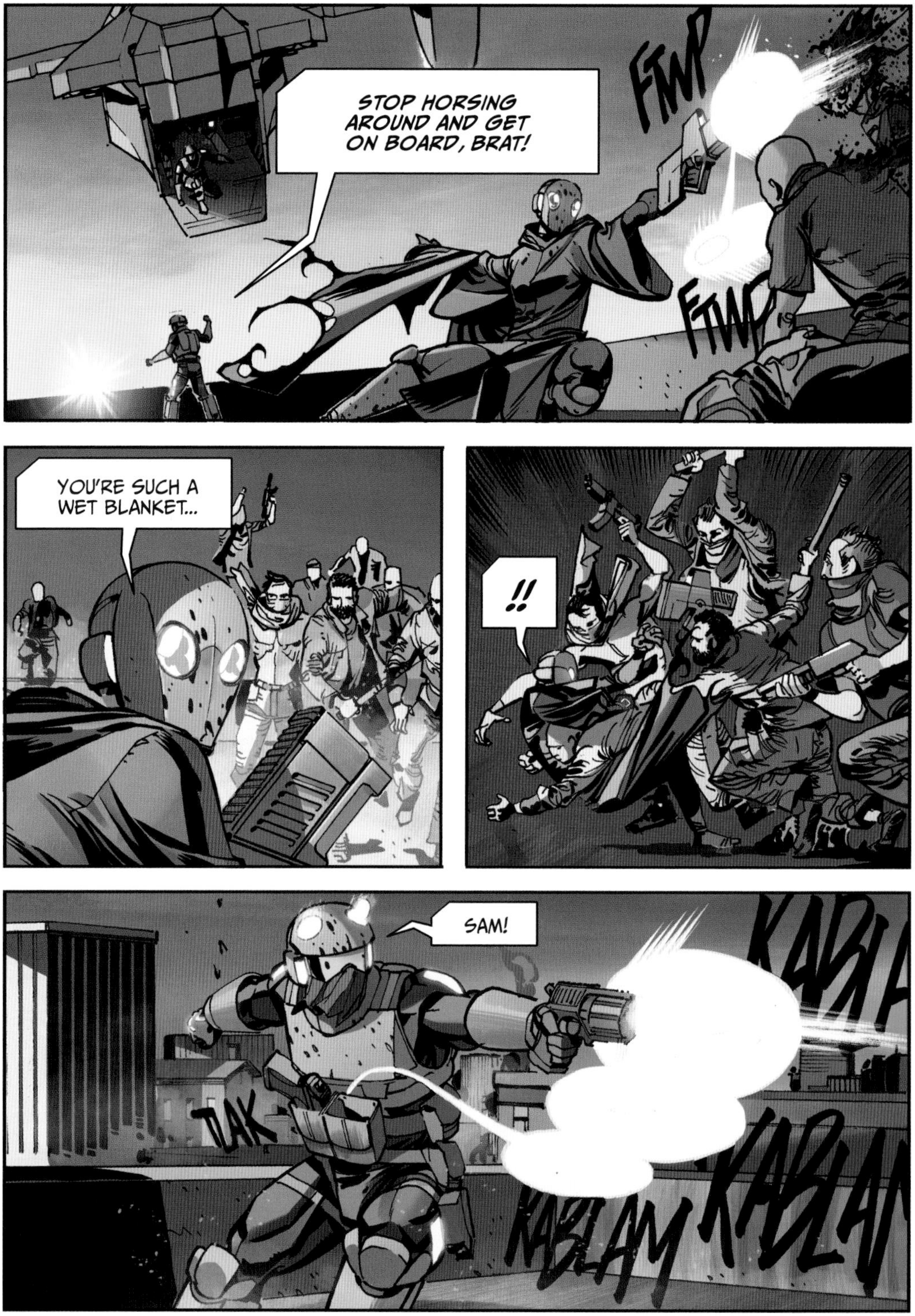
STOP HORSING AROUND AND GET ON BOARD, BRAT!
FTWP
FTWP
YOU'RE SUCH A WET BLANKET...
!!
SAM!
KABLAM

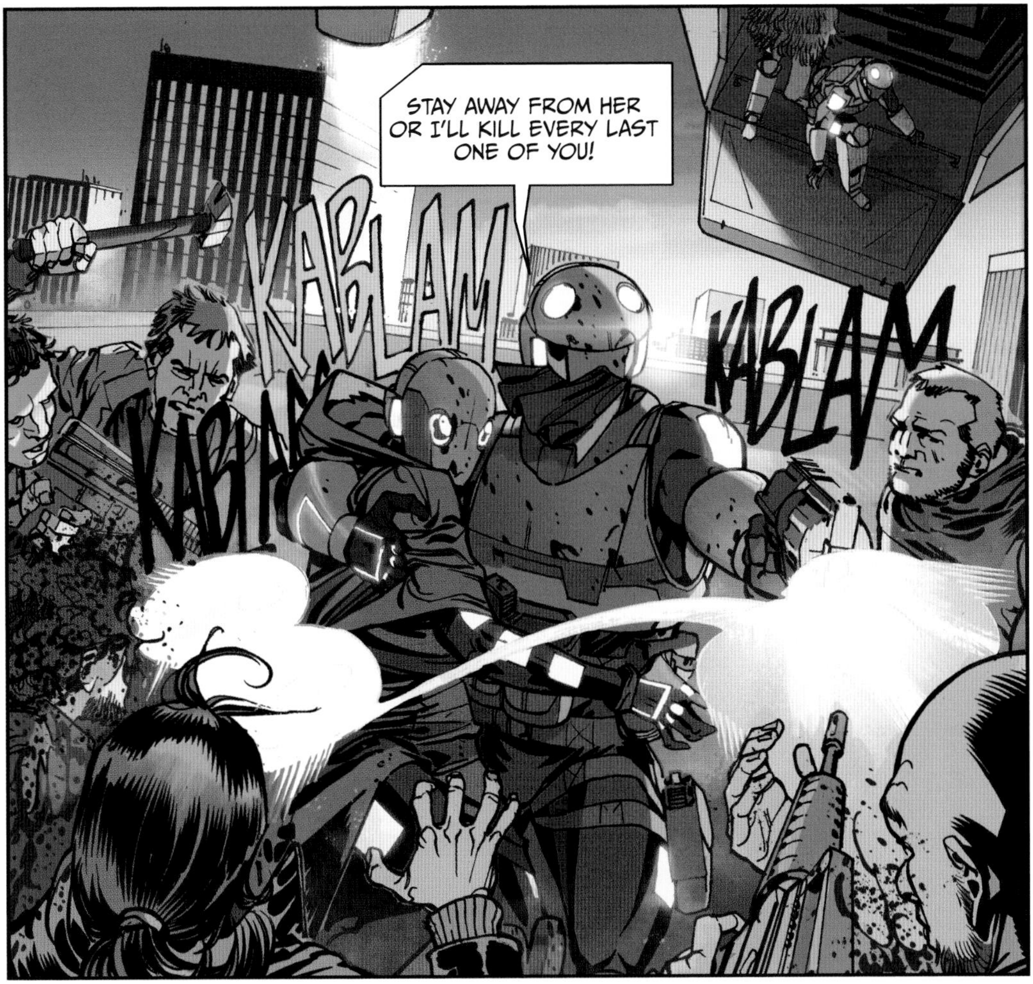
STAY AWAY FROM HER OR I'LL KILL EVERY LAST ONE OF YOU!
KABLAM
KABLAM
KABLAM

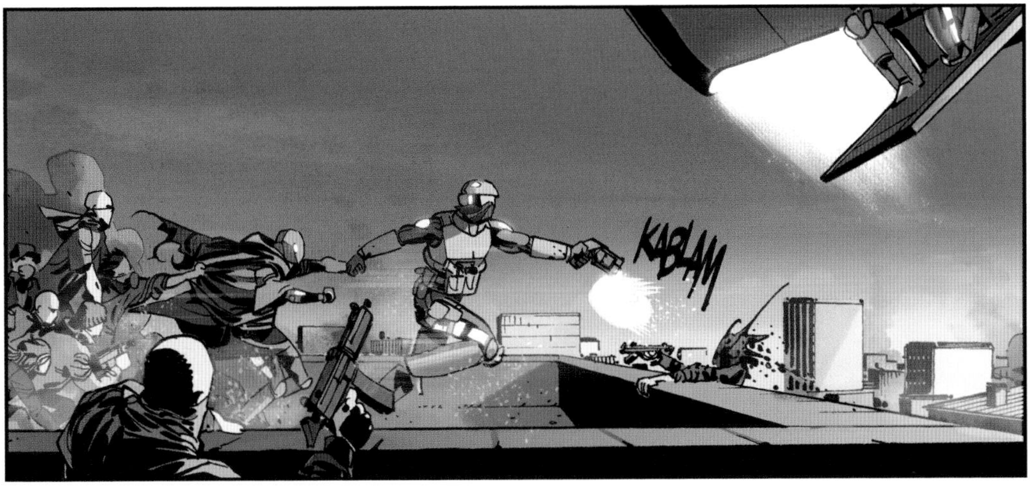
KABLAM

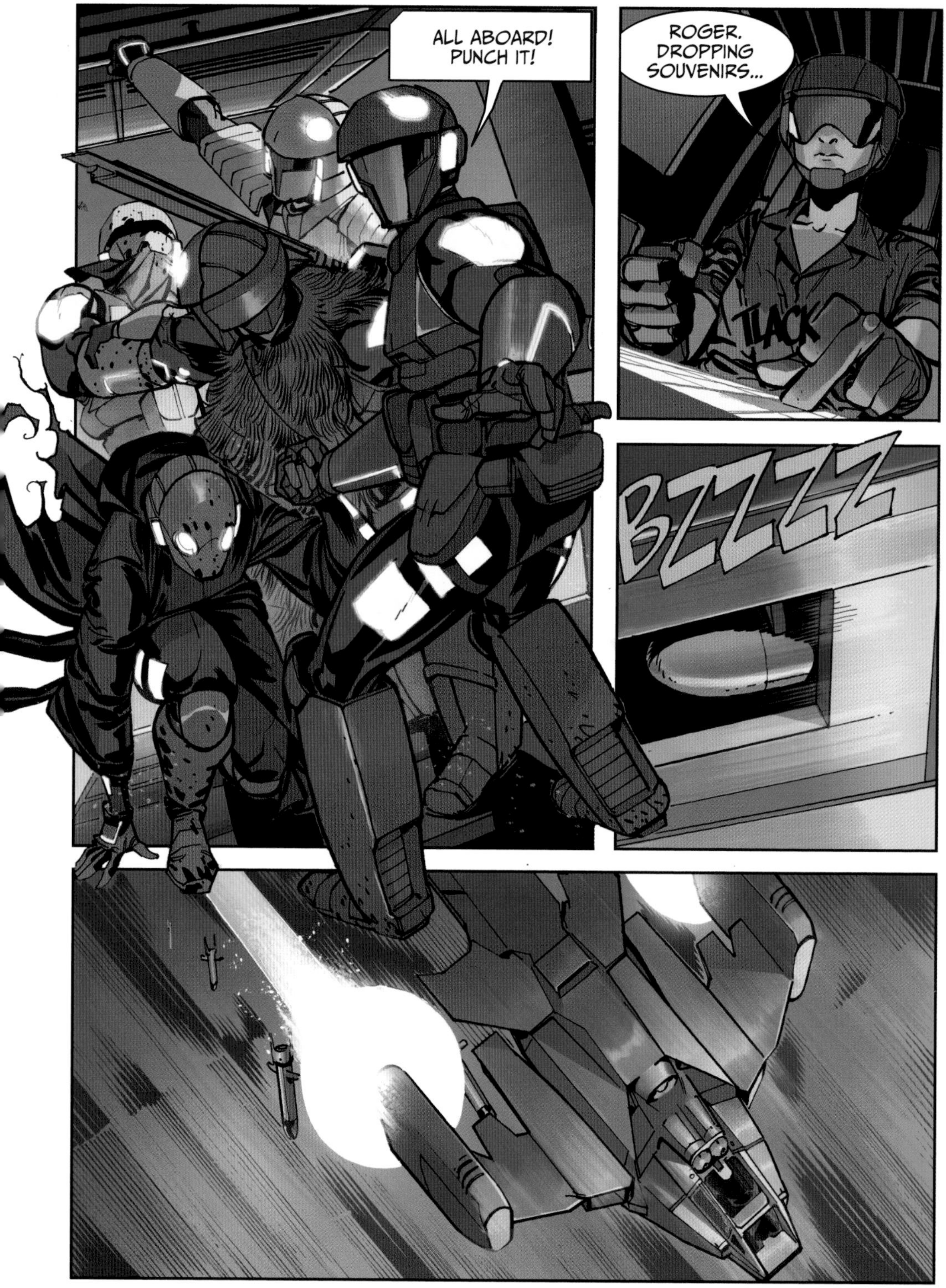
ALL ABOARD! PUNCH IT!
ROGER. DROPPING SOUVENIRS...
TLACK
BZZZZ

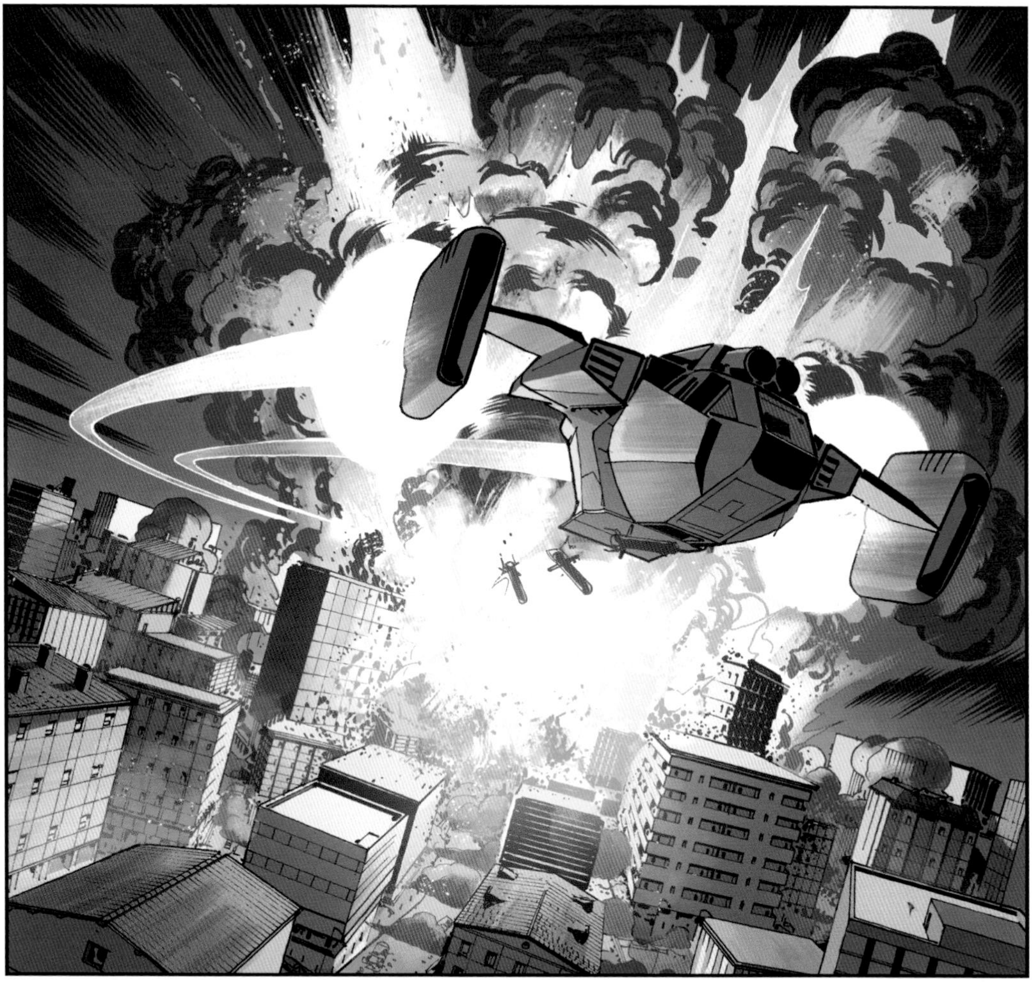

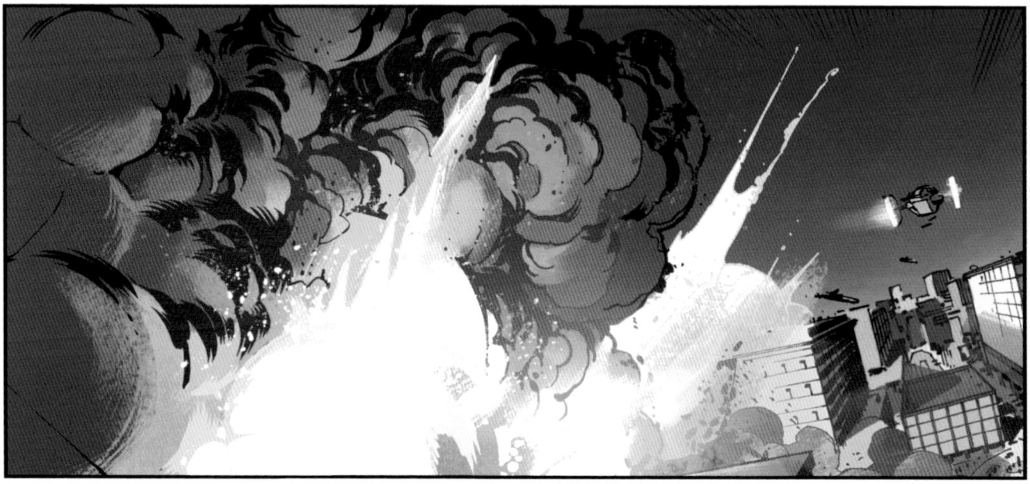

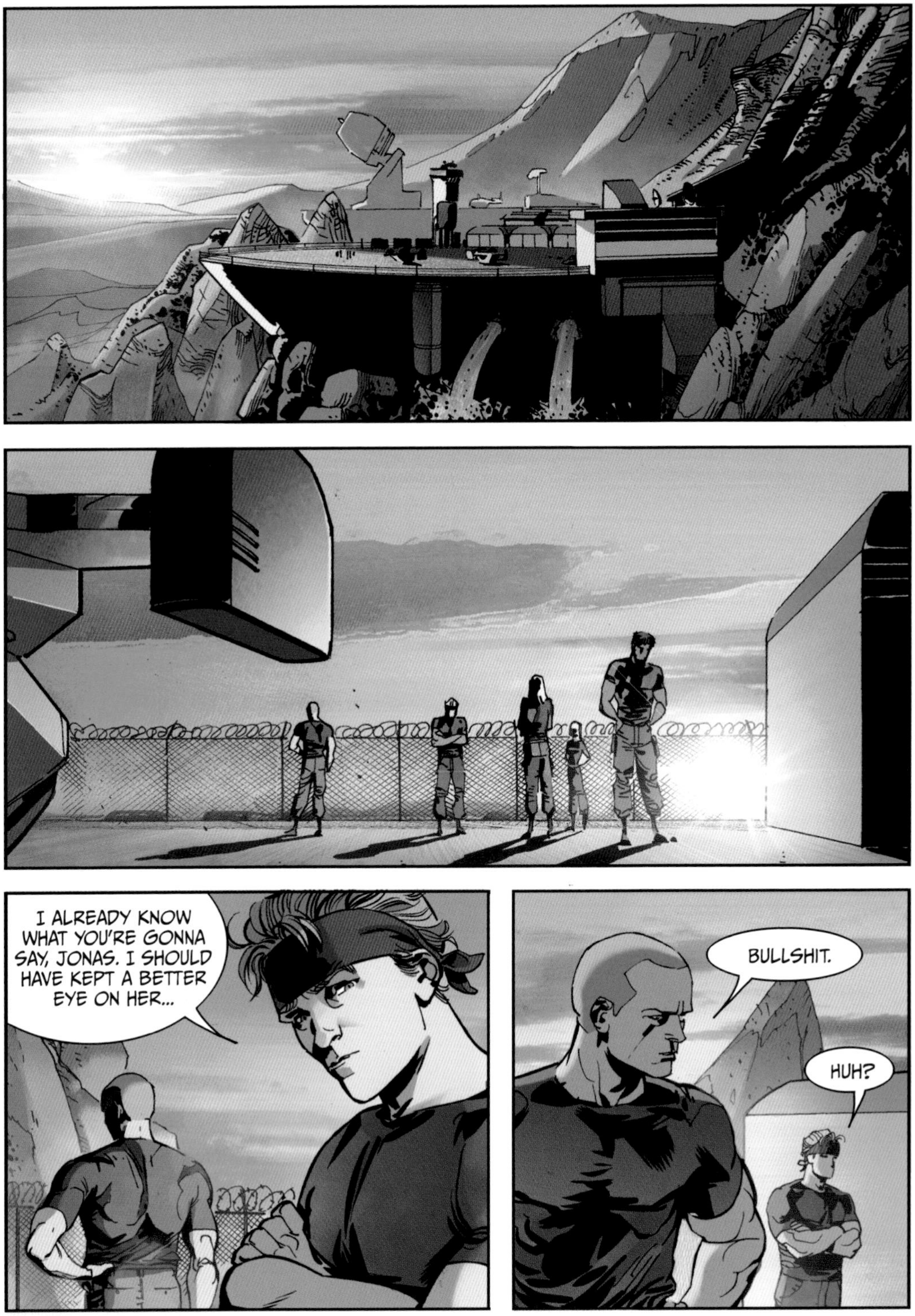
I ALREADY KNOW WHAT YOU'RE GONNA SAY, JONAS. I SHOULD HAVE KEPT A BETTER EYE ON HER...
BULLSHIT.
HUH?

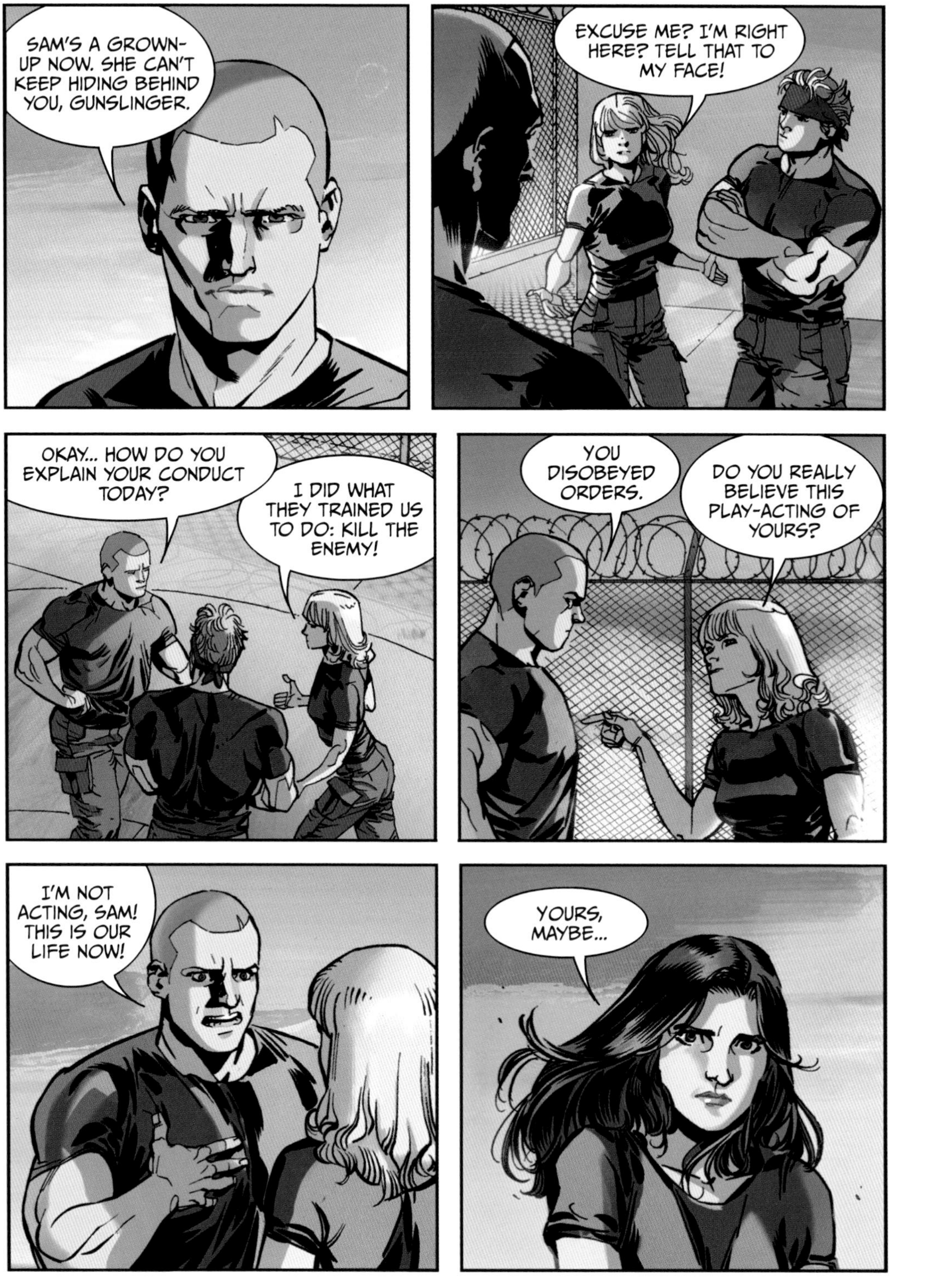
SAM'S A GROWN-UP NOW. SHE CAN'T KEEP HIDING BEHIND YOU, GUNSLINGER.
EXCUSE ME? I'M RIGHT HERE? TELL THAT TO MY FACE!
OKAY... HOW DO YOU EXPLAIN YOUR CONDUCT TODAY?
I DID WHAT THEY TRAINED US TO DO: KILL THE ENEMY!
YOU DISOBEYED ORDERS.
DO YOU REALLY BELIEVE THIS PLAY-ACTING OF YOURS?
I'M NOT ACTING, SAM! THIS IS OUR LIFE NOW!
YOURS, MAYBE...

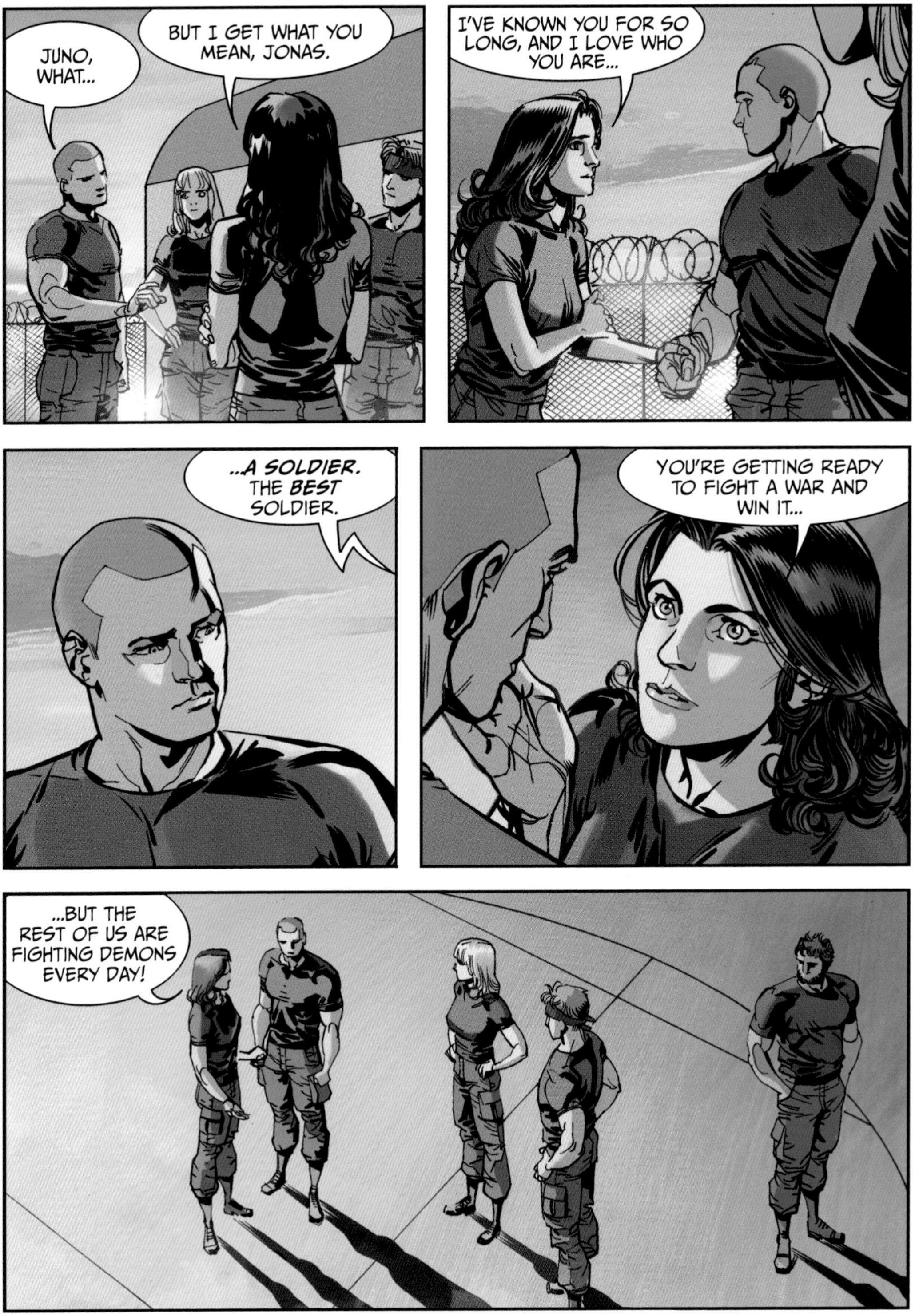
JUNO, WHAT...
BUT I GET WHAT YOU MEAN, JONAS.
I'VE KNOWN YOU FOR SO LONG, AND I LOVE WHO YOU ARE...
...A SOLDIER. THE BEST SOLDIER.
YOU'RE GETTING READY TO FIGHT A WAR AND WIN IT...
...BUT THE REST OF US ARE FIGHTING DEMONS EVERY DAY!

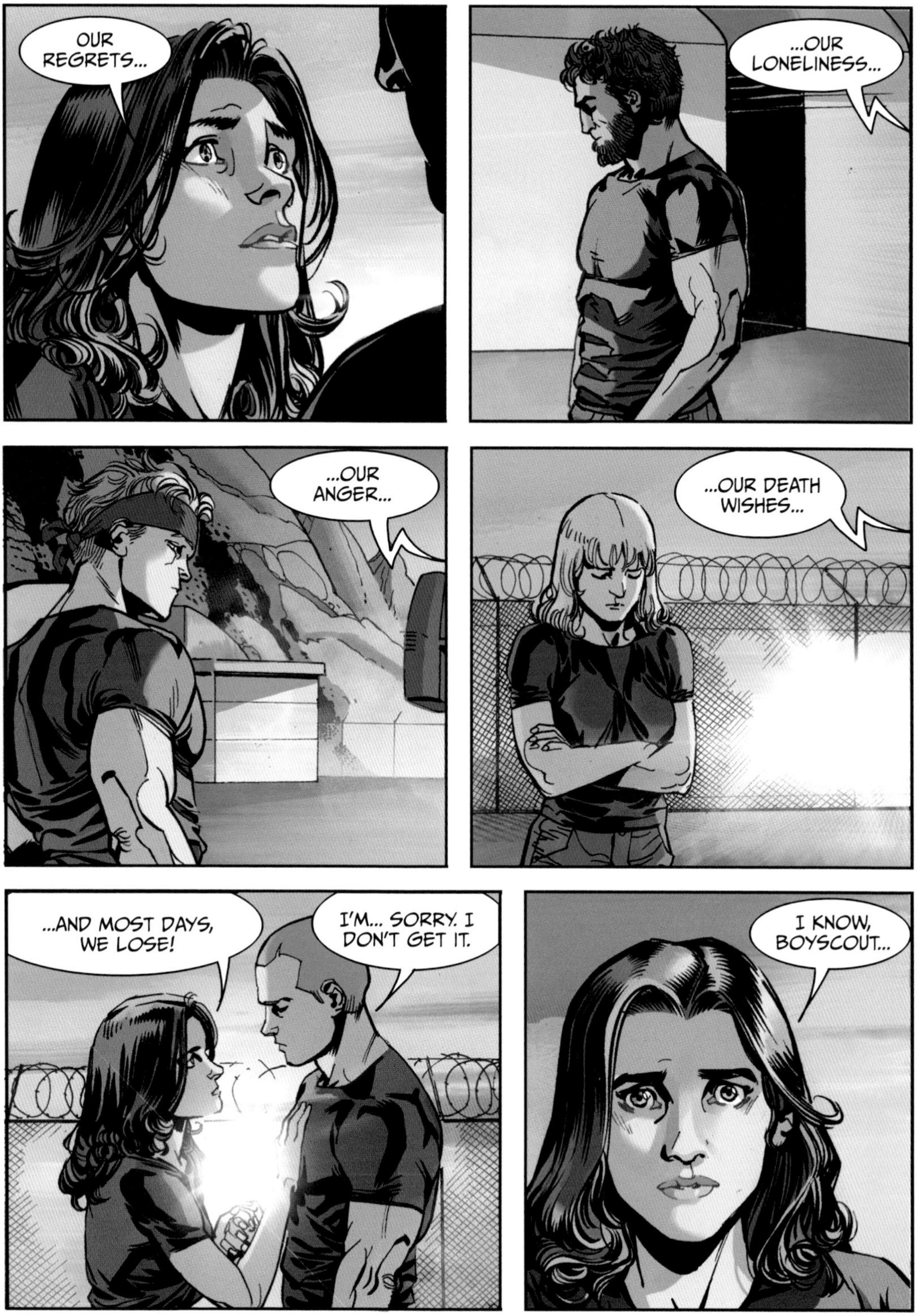
OUR REGRETS...
...OUR LONELINESS...
...OUR ANGER...
...OUR DEATH WISHES...
...AND MOST DAYS, WE LOSE!
I'M... SORRY. I DON'T GET IT.
I KNOW, BOYSCOUT...

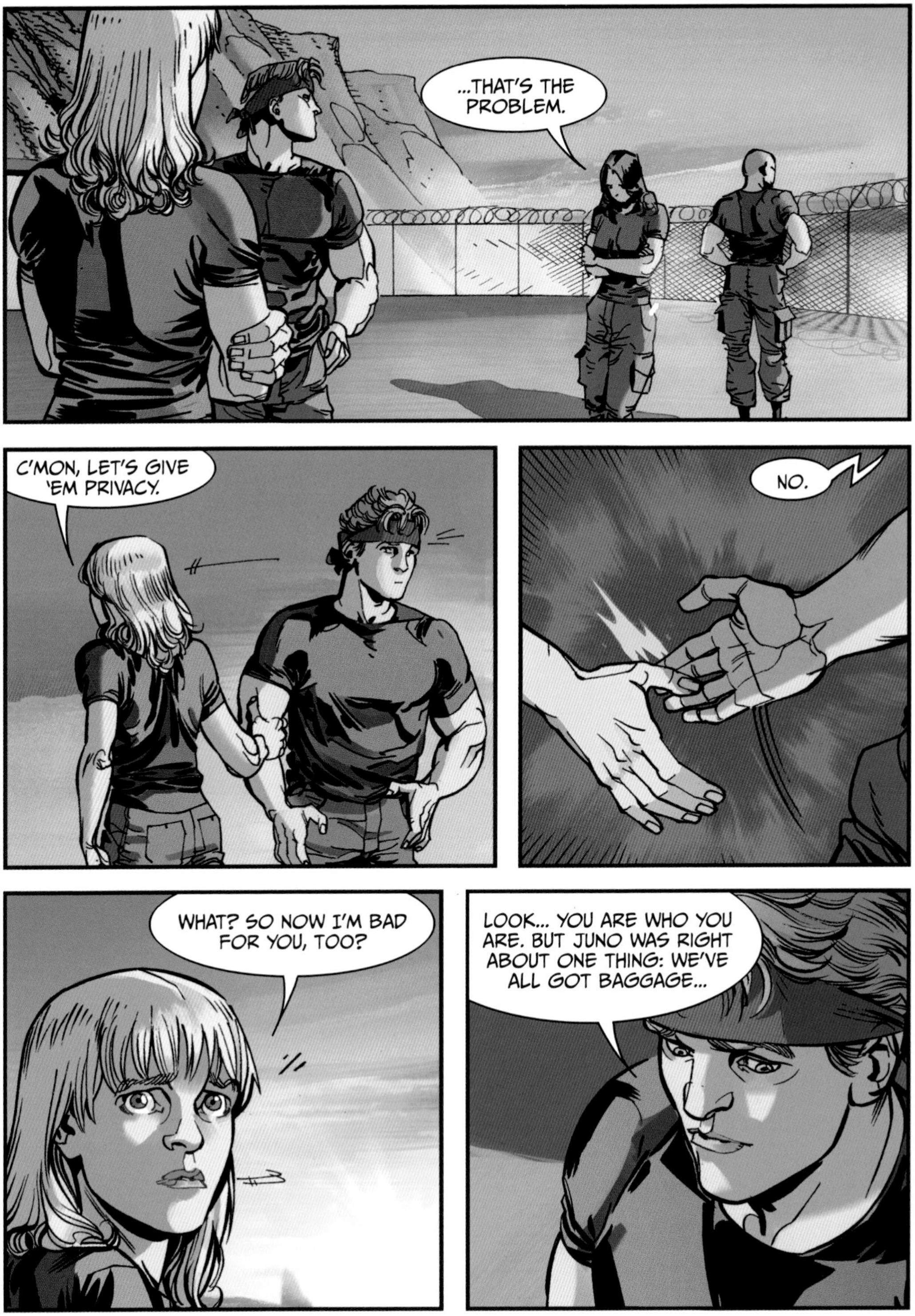
...THAT'S THE PROBLEM.
C'MON, LET'S GIVE 'EM PRIVACY.
NO.
WHAT? SO NOW I'M BAD FOR YOU, TOO?
LOOK... YOU ARE WHO YOU ARE. BUT JUNO WAS RIGHT ABOUT ONE THING: WE'VE ALL GOT BAGGAGE...

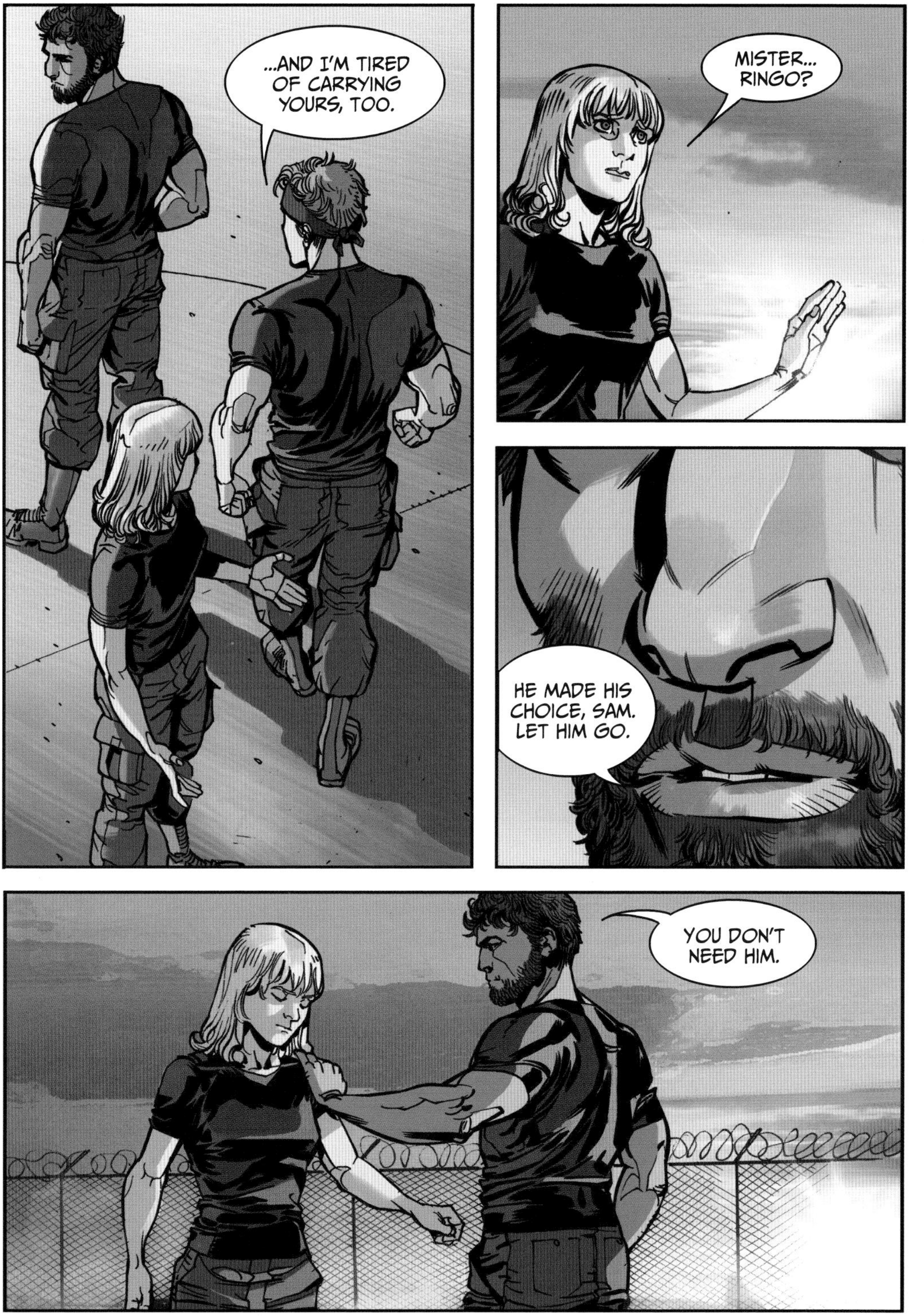
...AND I'M TIRED OF CARRYING YOURS, TOO.
MISTER... RINGO?
HE MADE HIS CHOICE, SAM. LET HIM GO.
YOU DON'T NEED HIM.

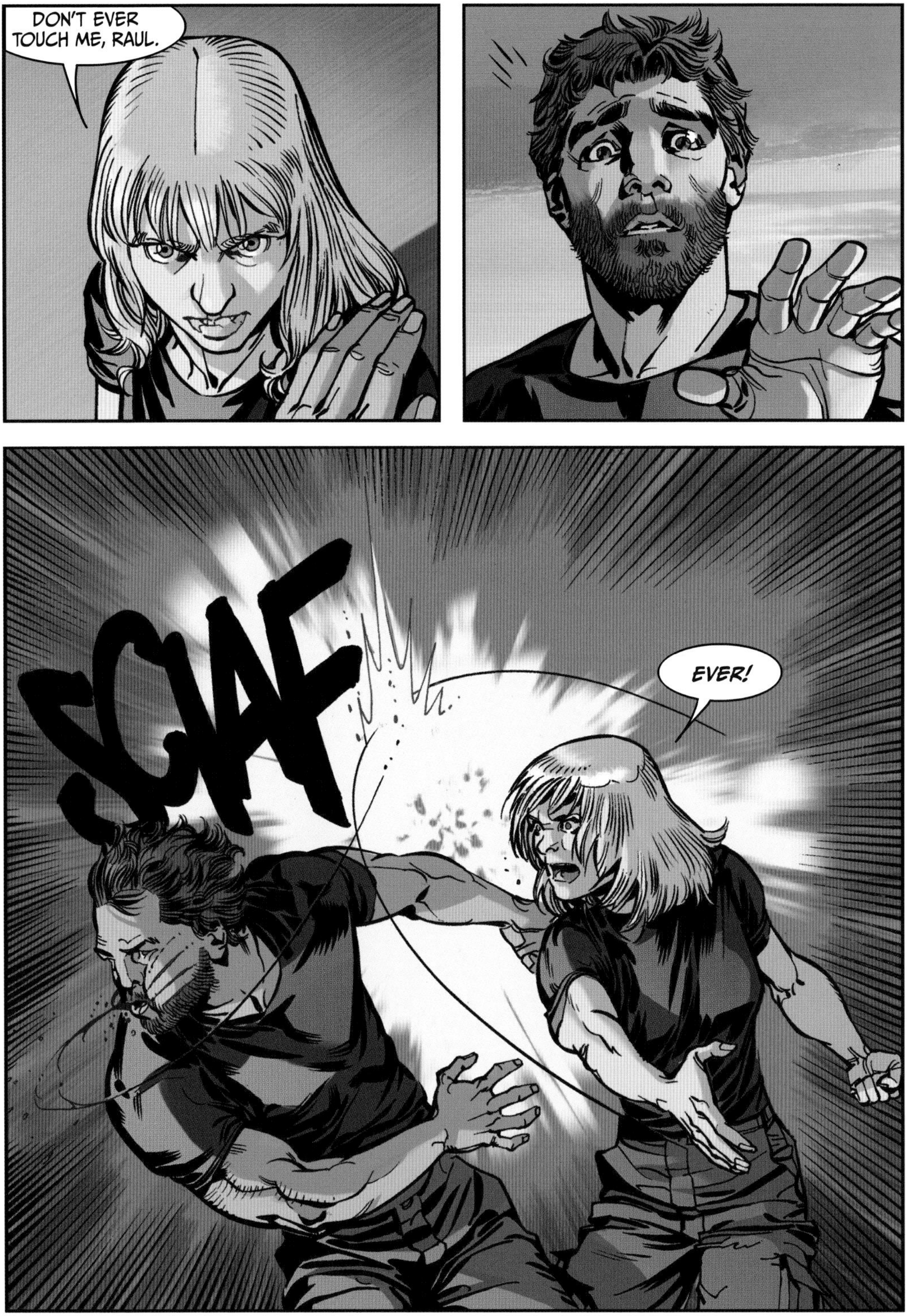
DON'T EVER TOUCH ME, RAUL.
SCIAF
EVER!

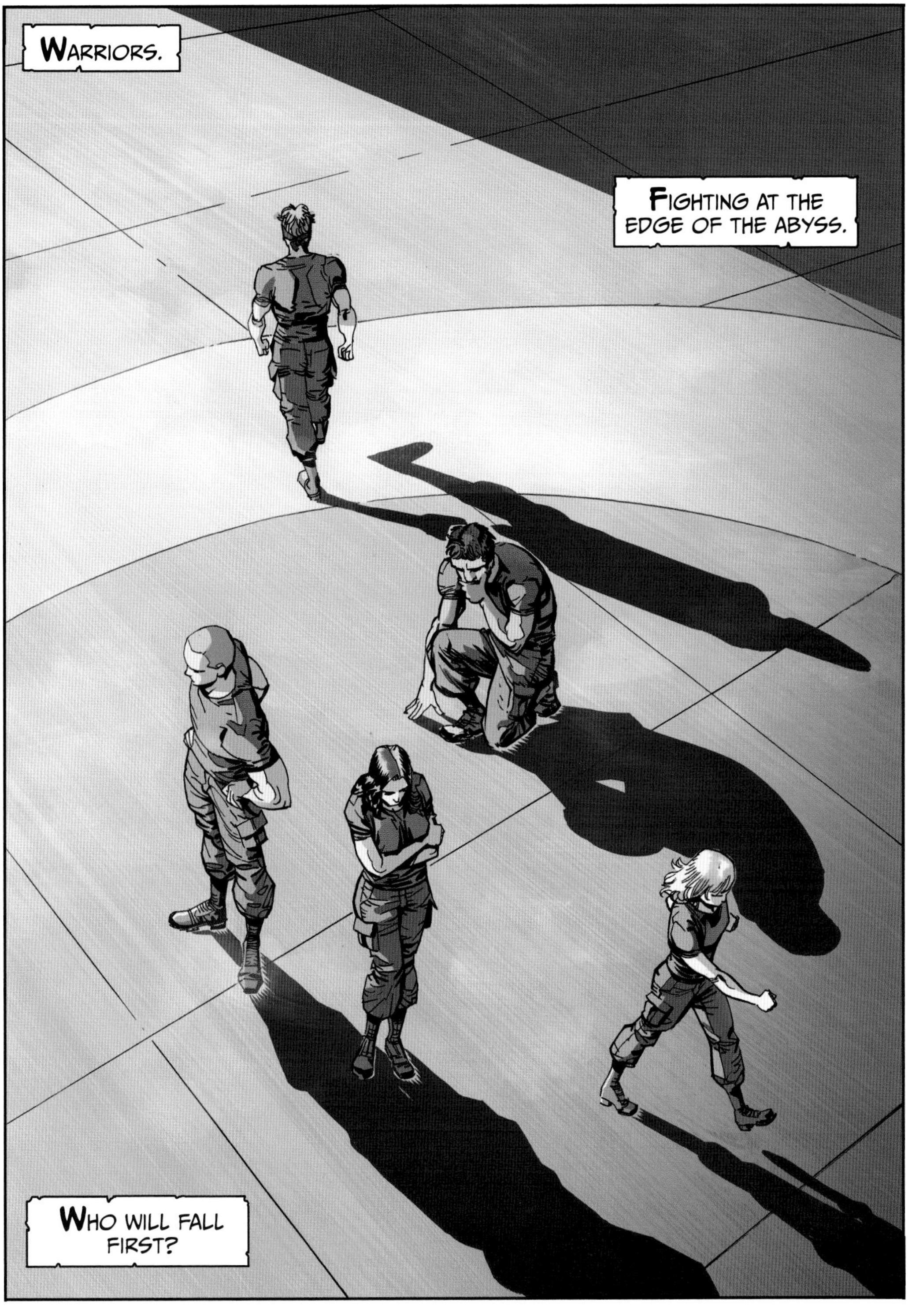
WARRIORS.
FIGHTING AT THE EDGE OF THE ABYSS.
WHO WILL FALL FIRST?

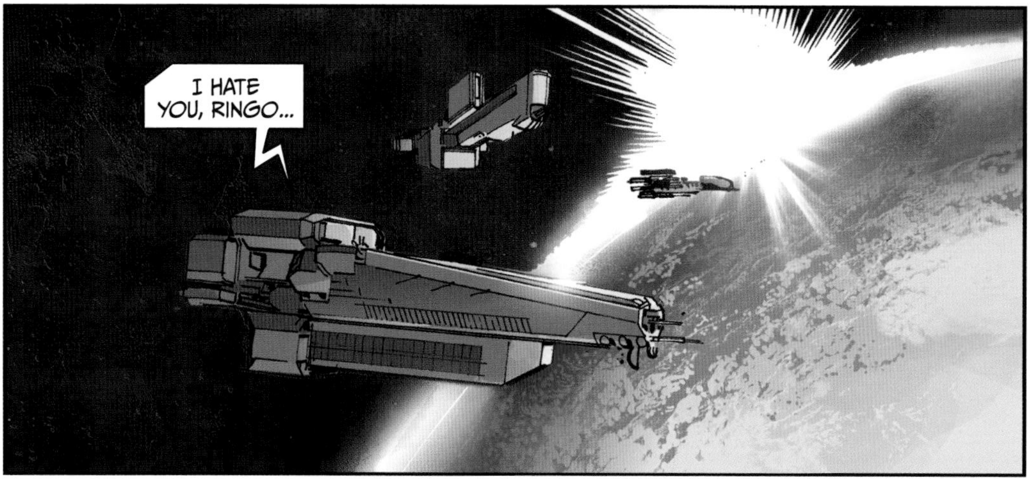
I HATE YOU, RINGO...

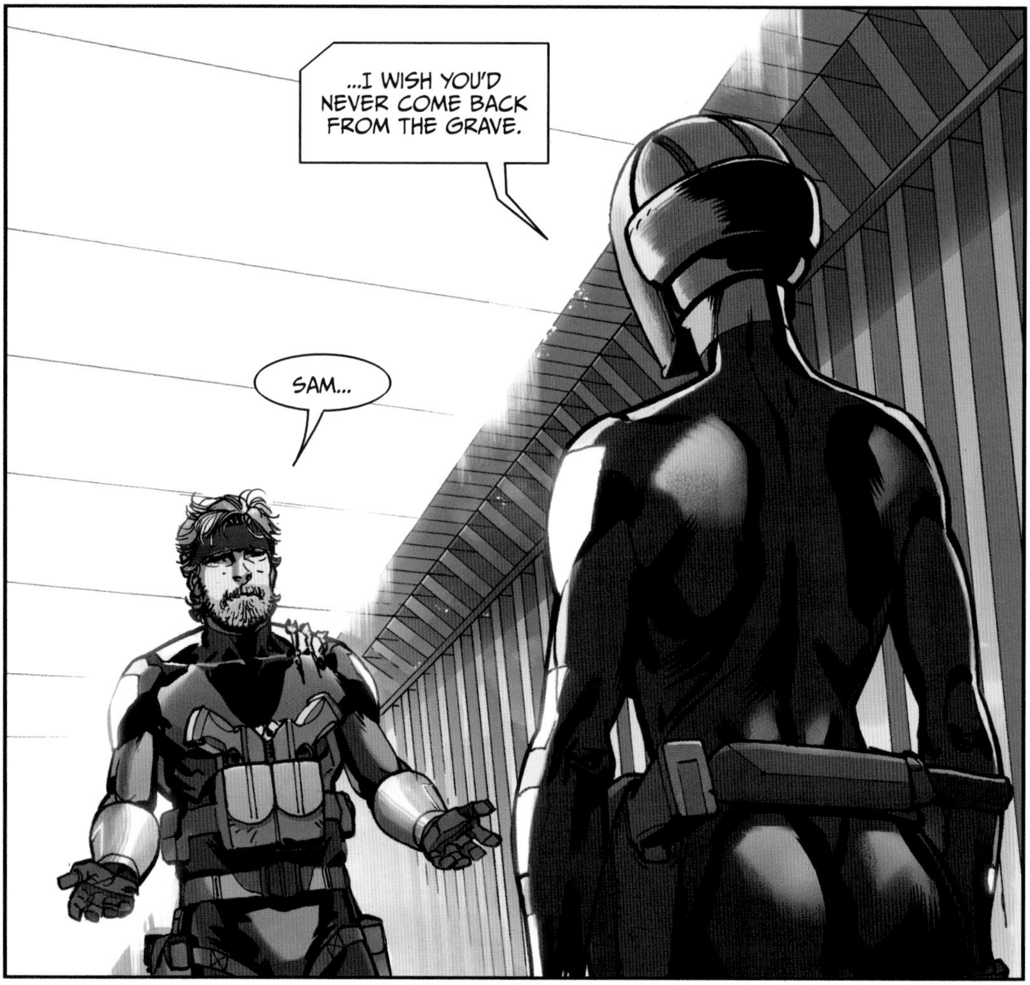
...I WISH YOU'D NEVER COME BACK FROM THE GRAVE.
SAM...

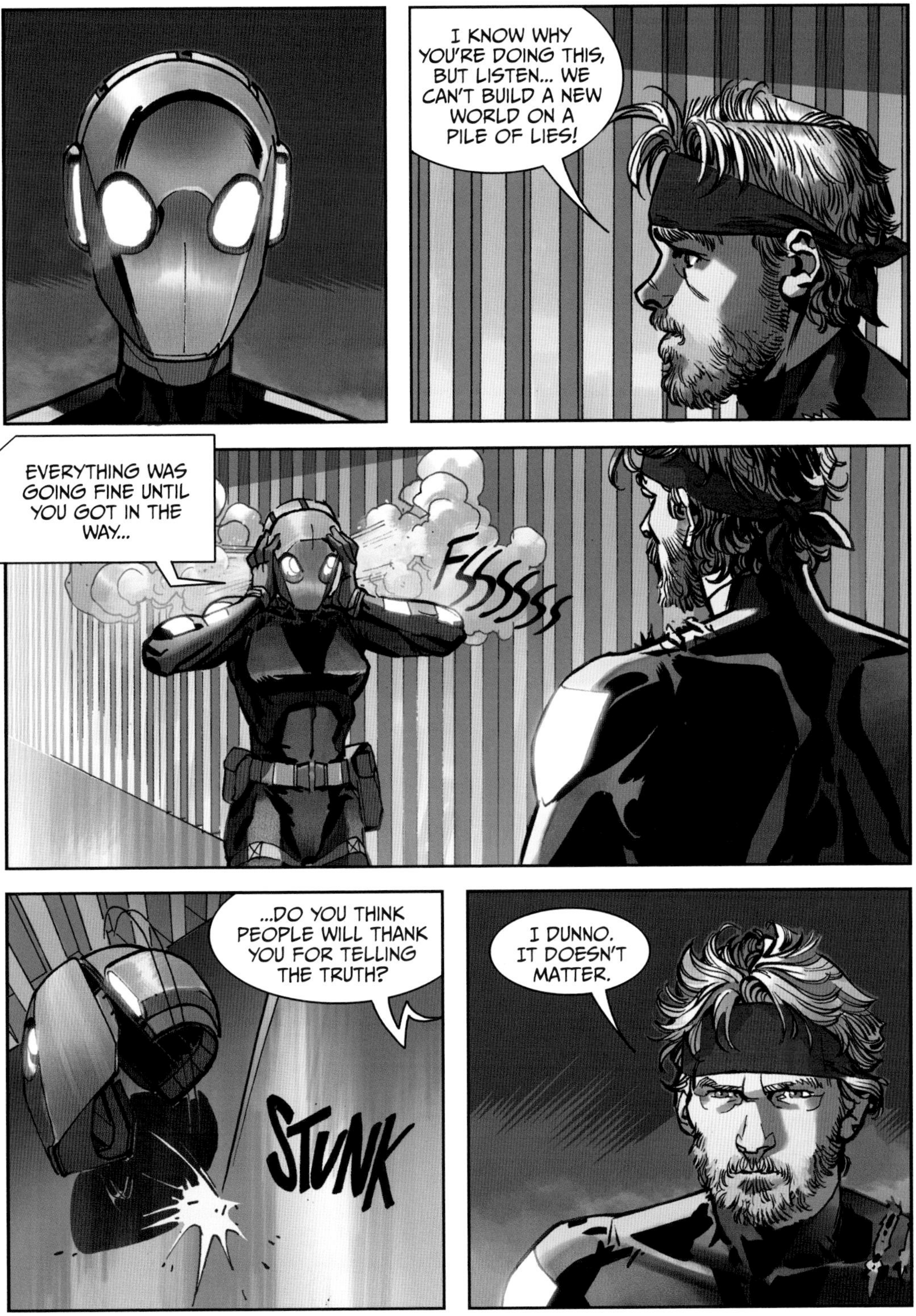
I KNOW WHY YOU'RE DOING THIS, BUT LISTEN... WE CAN'T BUILD A NEW WORLD ON A PILE OF LIES!
EVERYTHING WAS GOING FINE UNTIL YOU GOT IN THE WAY...
FSSSSS
...DO YOU THINK PEOPLE WILL THANK YOU FOR TELLING THE TRUTH?
STUNK
I DUNNO. IT DOESN'T MATTER.

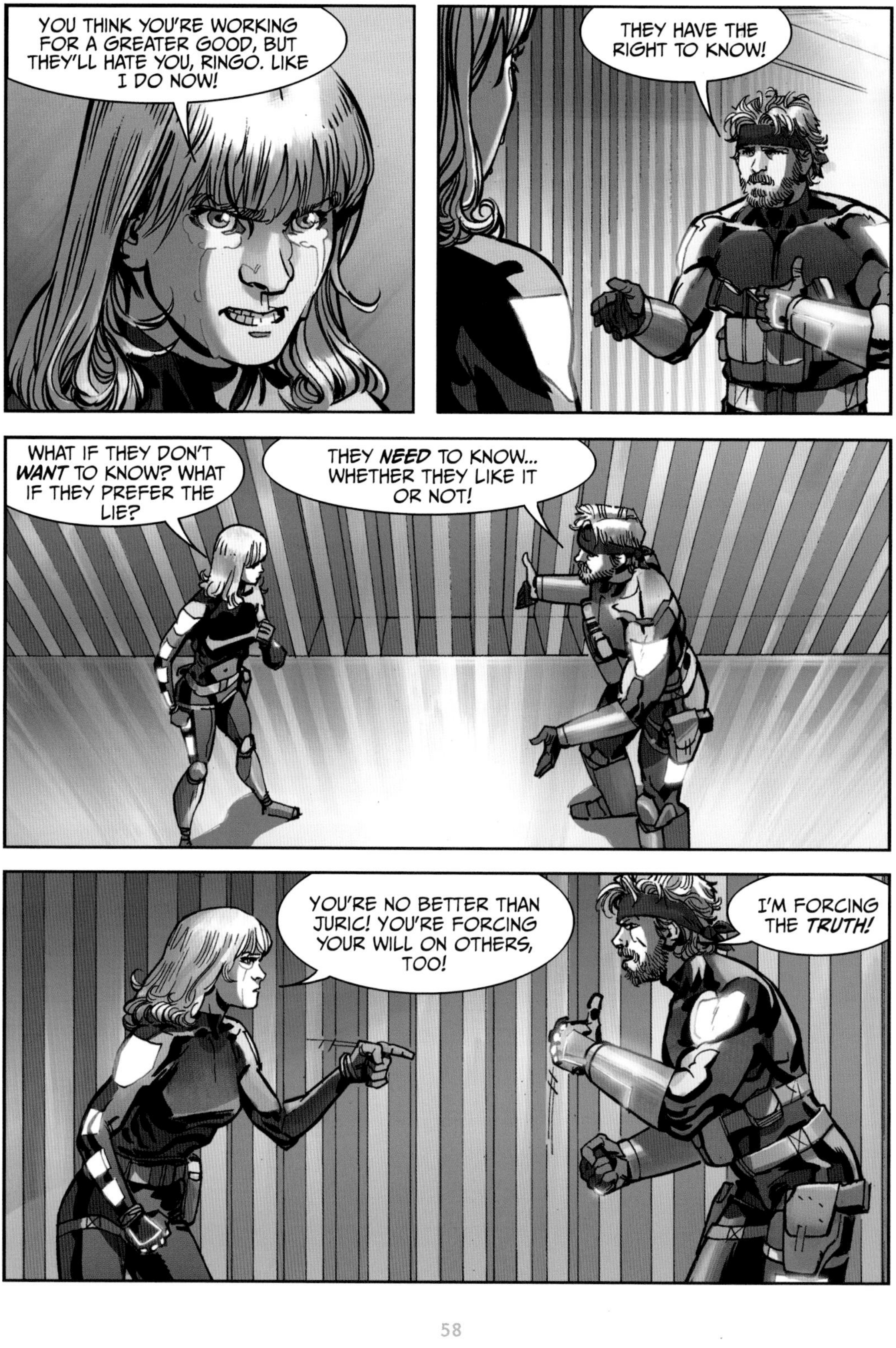
YOU THINK YOU'RE WORKING FOR A GREATER GOOD, BUT THEY'LL HATE YOU, RINGO. LIKE I DO NOW!
THEY HAVE THE RIGHT TO KNOW!
WHAT IF THEY DON'T *WANT* TO KNOW? WHAT IF THEY PREFER THE LIE?
THEY *NEED* TO KNOW... WHETHER THEY LIKE IT OR NOT!
YOU'RE NO BETTER THAN JURIC! YOU'RE FORCING YOUR WILL ON OTHERS, TOO!
I'M FORCING THE *TRUTH!*

TRUTH? TRUTH DOESN'T EXIST. ONLY WHAT YOU CHOOSE TO BELIEVE...

YOU KNOW I GOTTA KILL YOU. NOTHING PERSONAL.

OH, IT'S VERY PERSONAL...

...I KILLED YOUR BOYFRIEND.

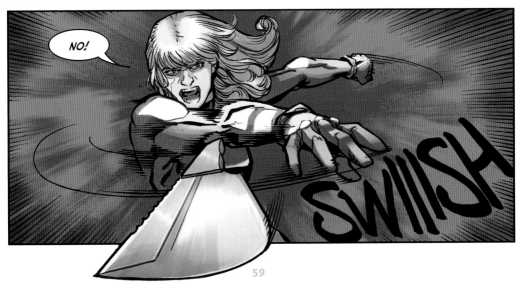

NO!

SWIIISH

59

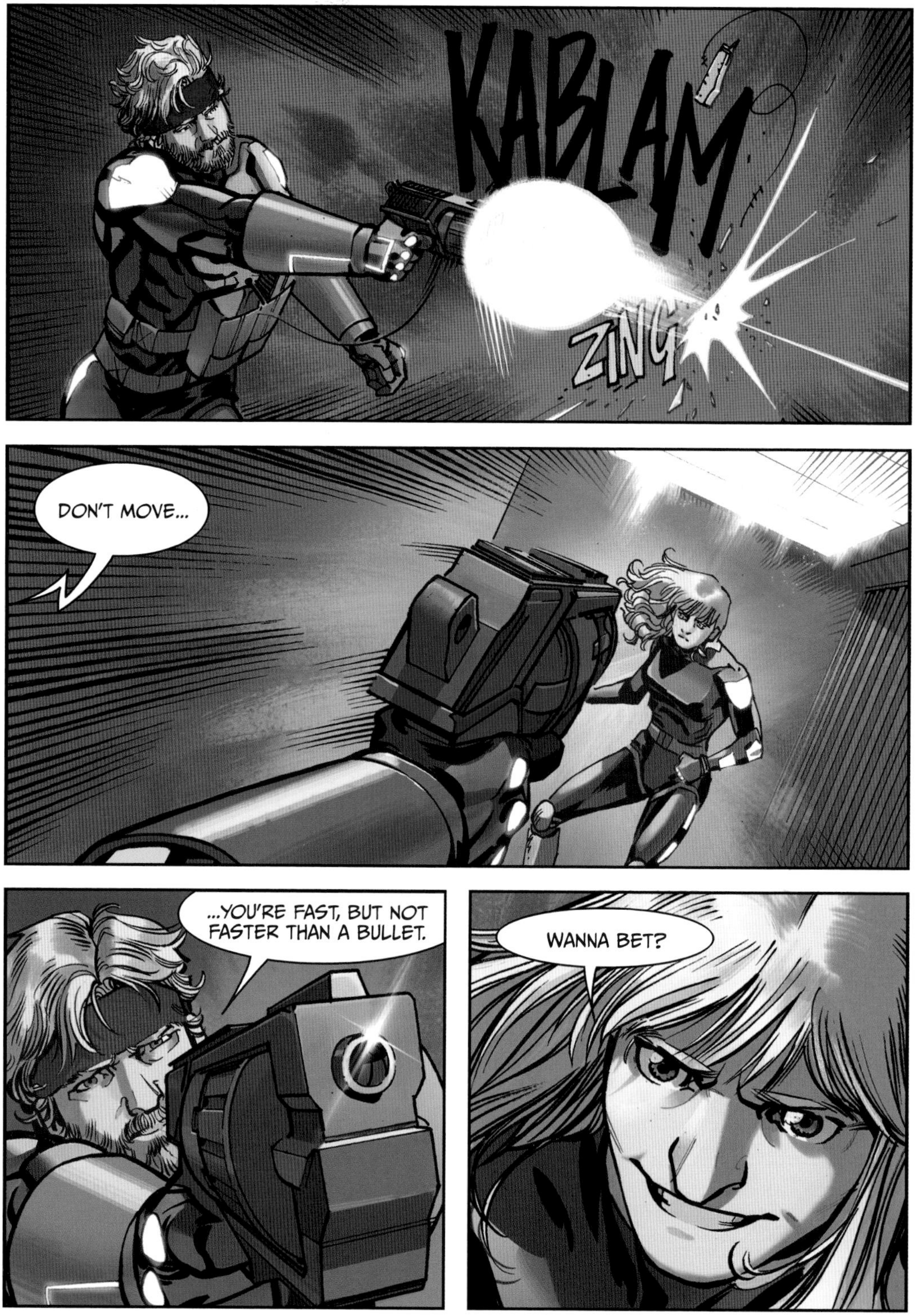
KABLAM
ZING
DON'T MOVE...
...YOU'RE FAST, BUT NOT FASTER THAN A BULLET.
WANNA BET?

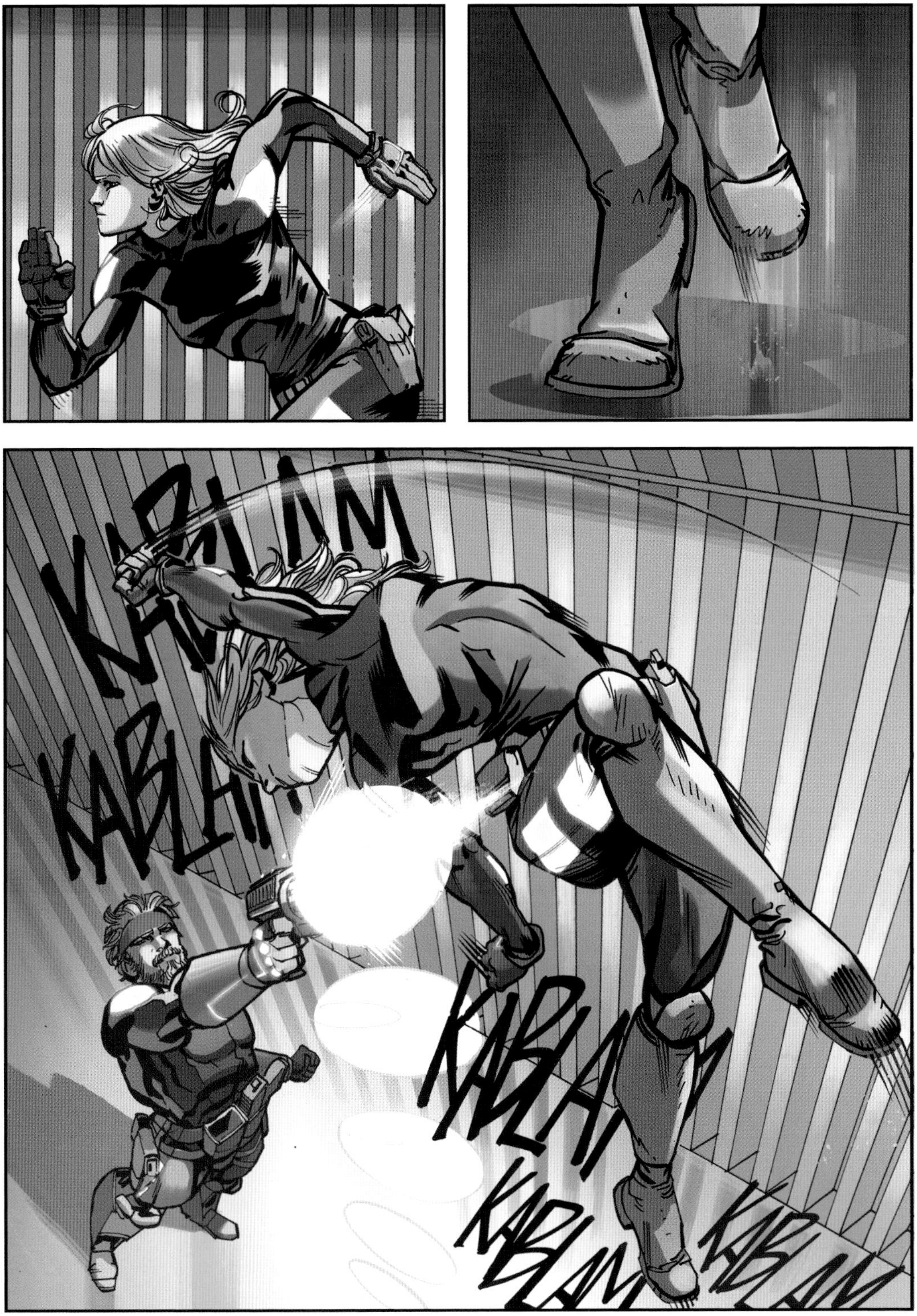
KABLAM
KABLAM
KABLAM
KABLAM
KABLAM

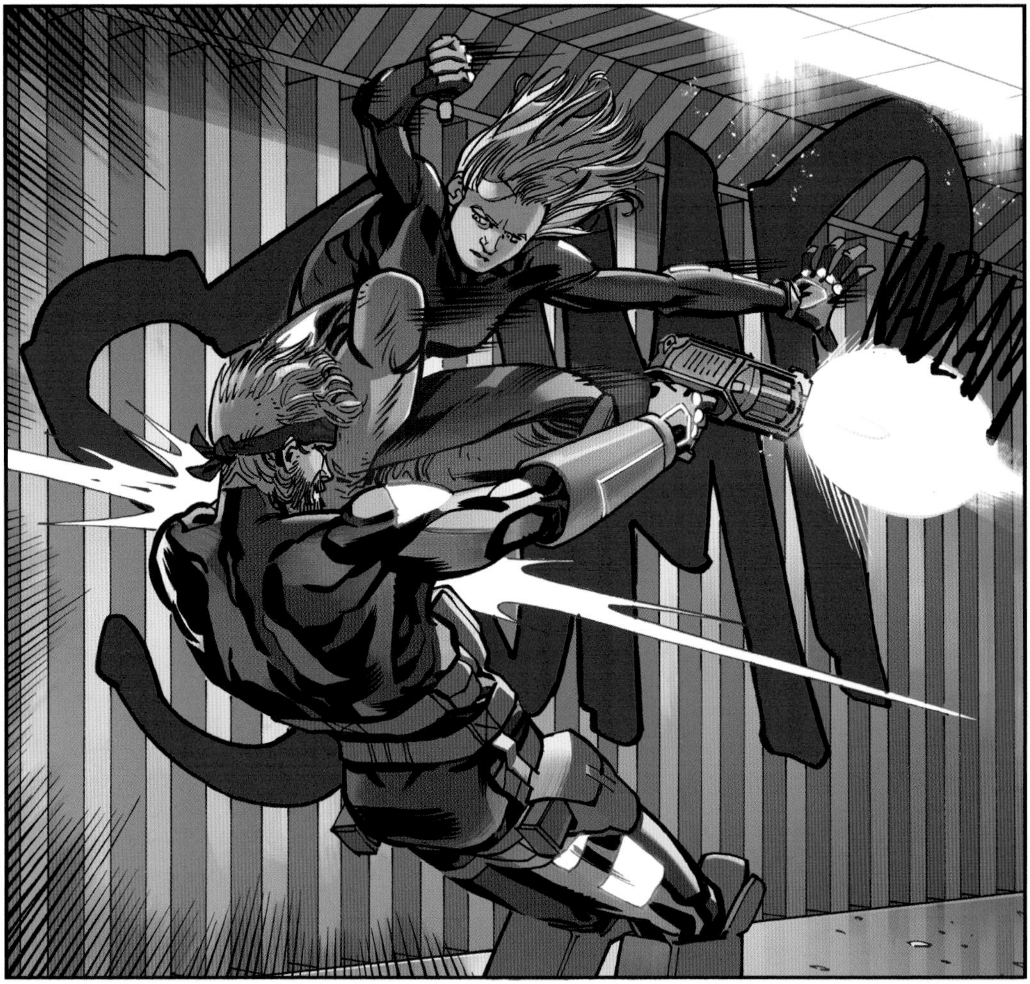

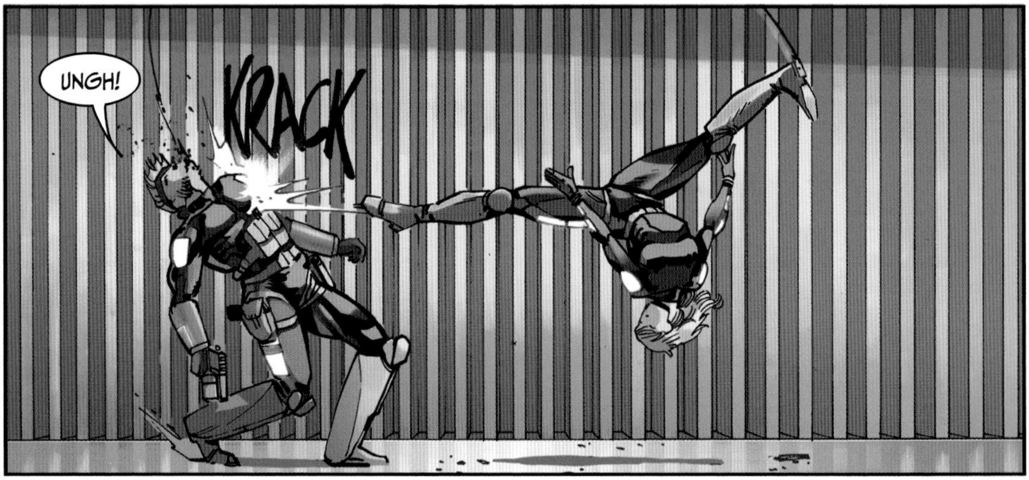
UNGH!
KRACK

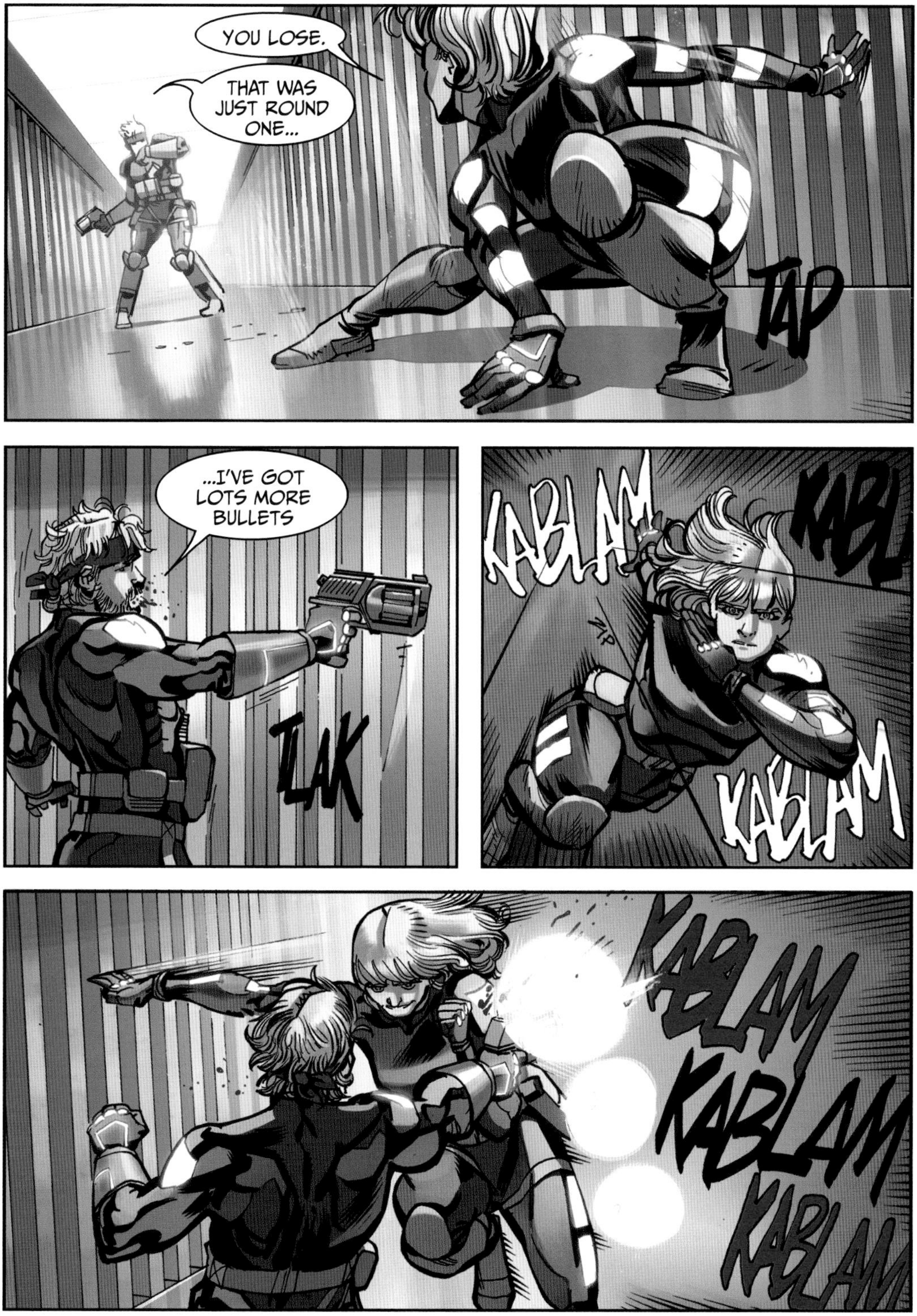
YOU LOSE.
THAT WAS JUST ROUND ONE...
TAP
...I'VE GOT LOTS MORE BULLETS
TLAK
KABLAM
KABL
ZIP
KABLAM
KABLAM
KABLAM
KABLAM

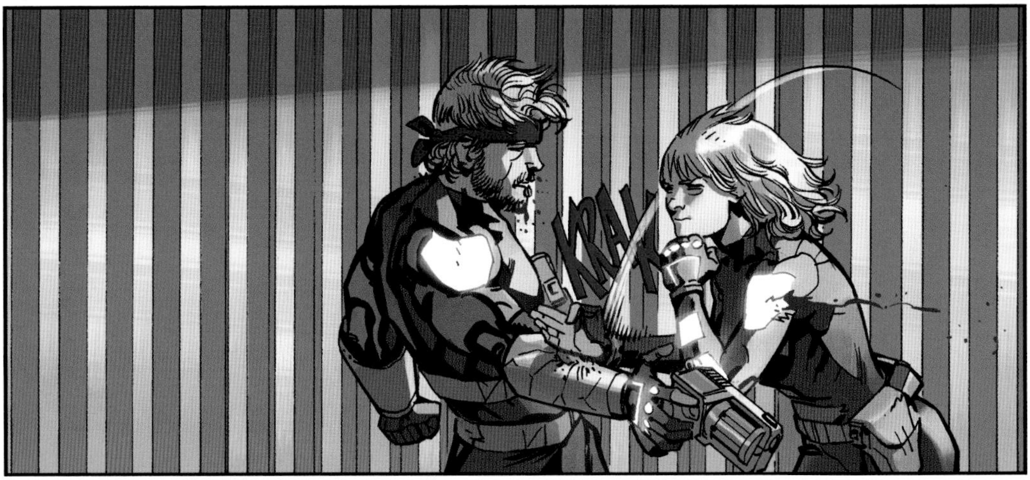
KRAK

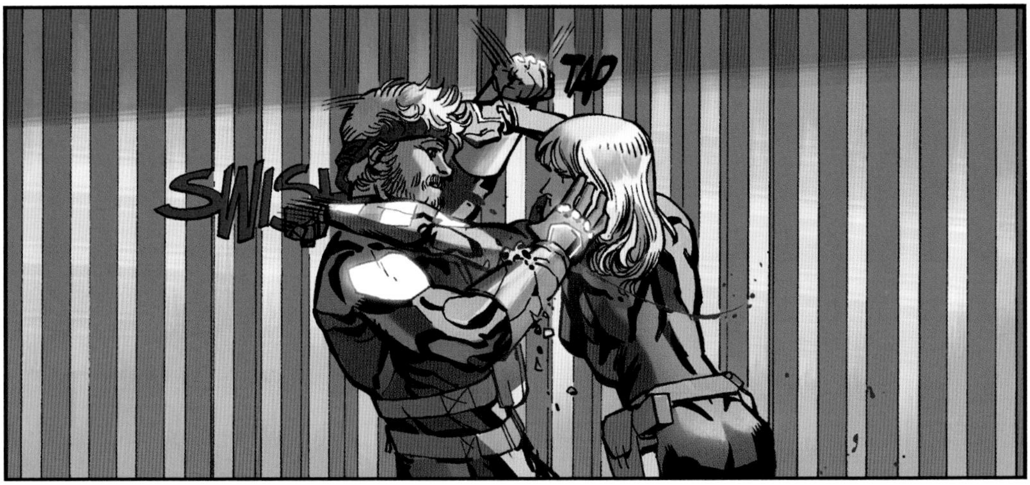
TAP
SWIS

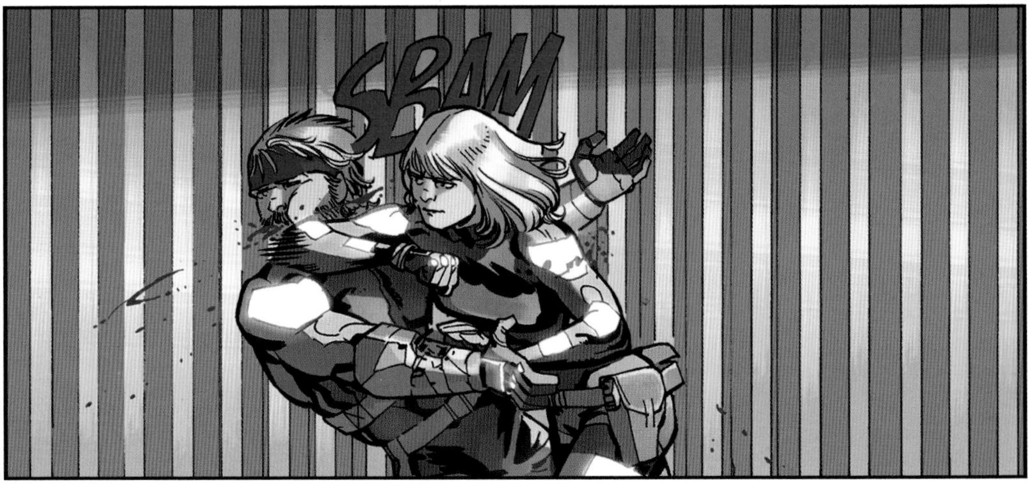
SBAM

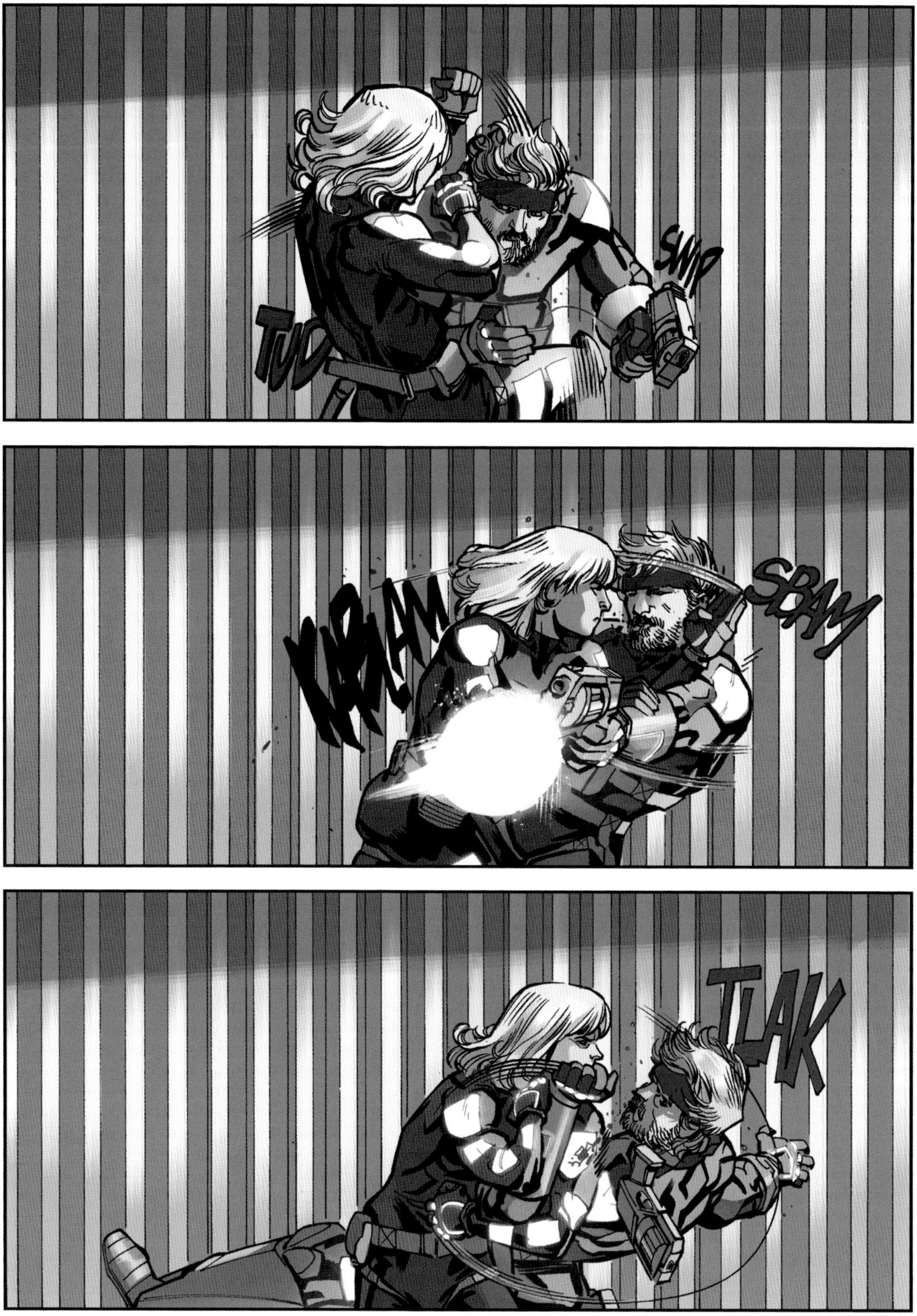
TUD
SWIP
KABLAM
SBAM
TLAK

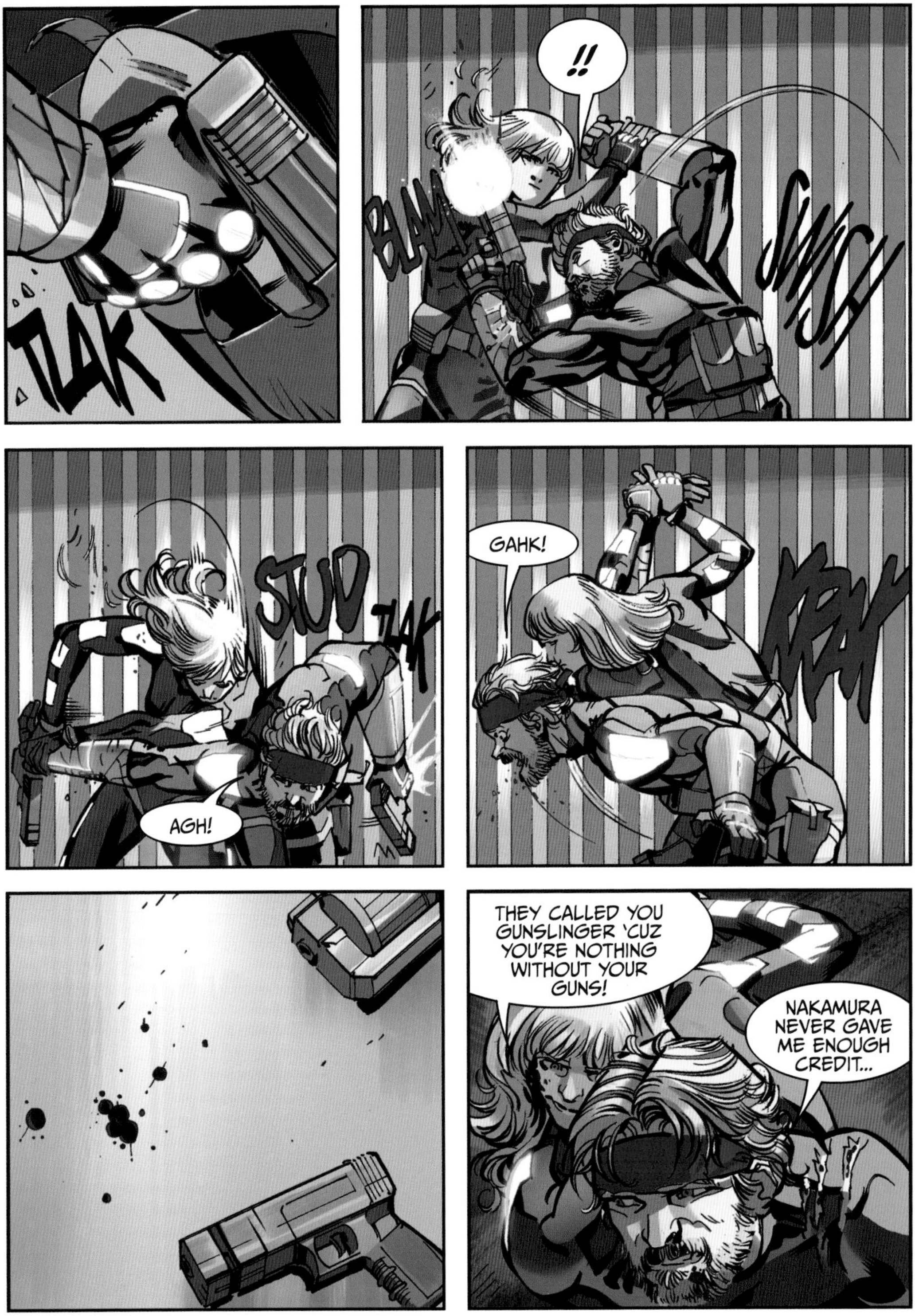
TZAK
BLAM
!!
STUD
TZAK
AGH!
GAHK!
THEY CALLED YOU GUNSLINGER 'CUZ YOU'RE NOTHING WITHOUT YOUR GUNS!
NAKAMURA NEVER GAVE ME ENOUGH CREDIT...

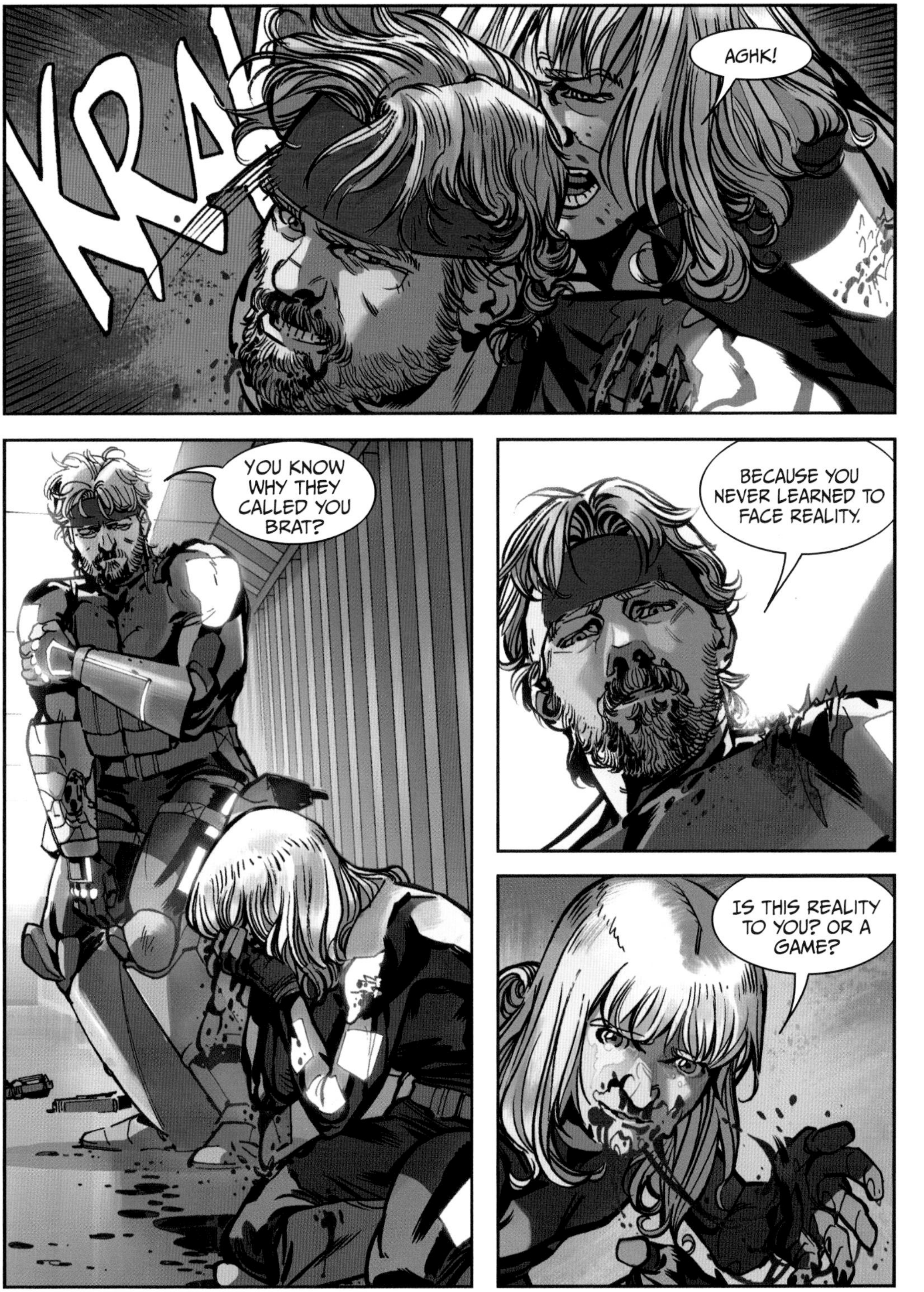
KRA
AGHK!
YOU KNOW WHY THEY CALLED YOU BRAT?
BECAUSE YOU NEVER LEARNED TO FACE REALITY.
IS THIS REALITY TO YOU? OR A GAME?

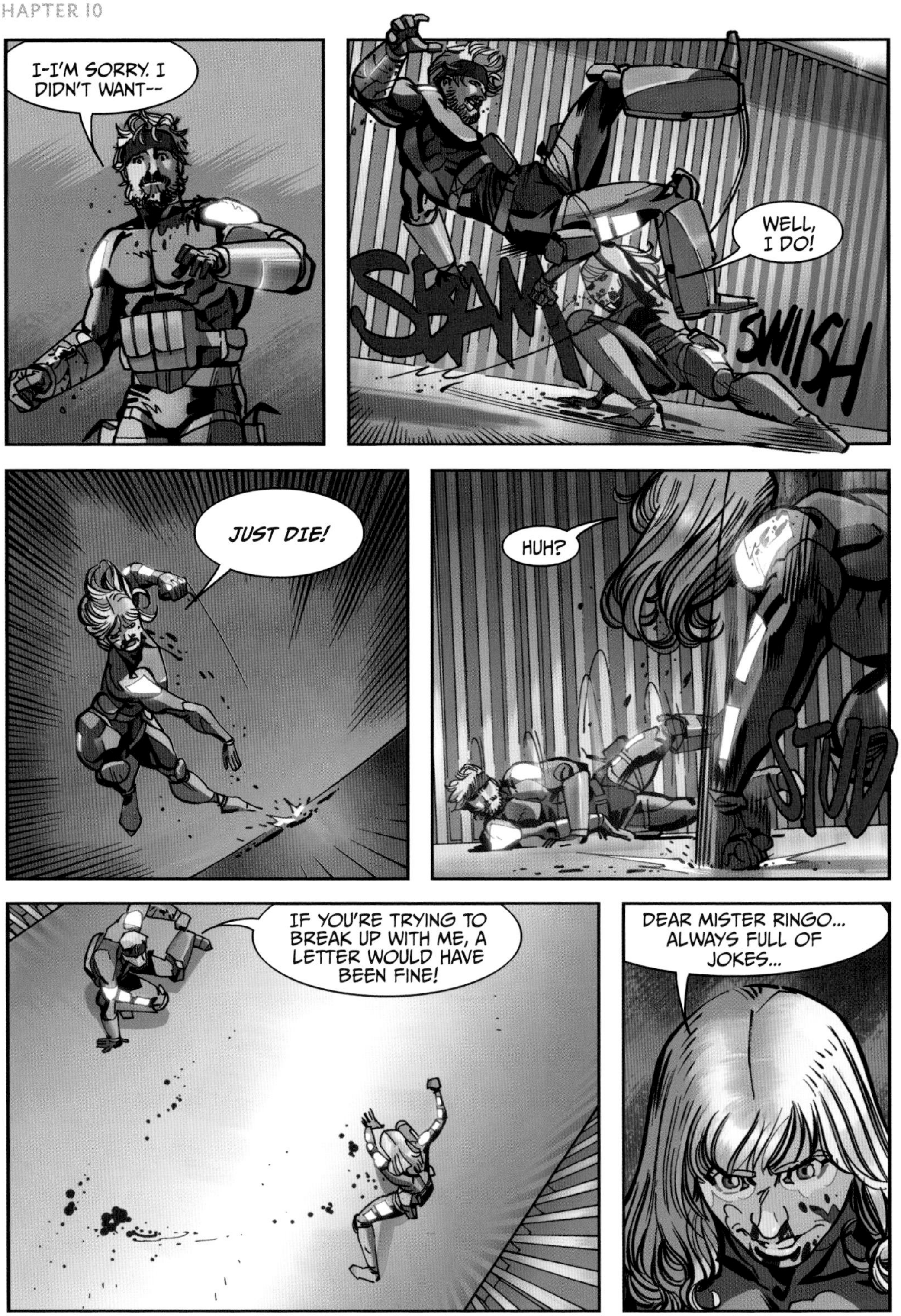
I-I'M SORRY. I DIDN'T WANT--
WELL, I DO!
SLAM
SWISH
JUST DIE!
HUH?
STUD
IF YOU'RE TRYING TO BREAK UP WITH ME, A LETTER WOULD HAVE BEEN FINE!
DEAR MISTER RINGO... ALWAYS FULL OF JOKES...

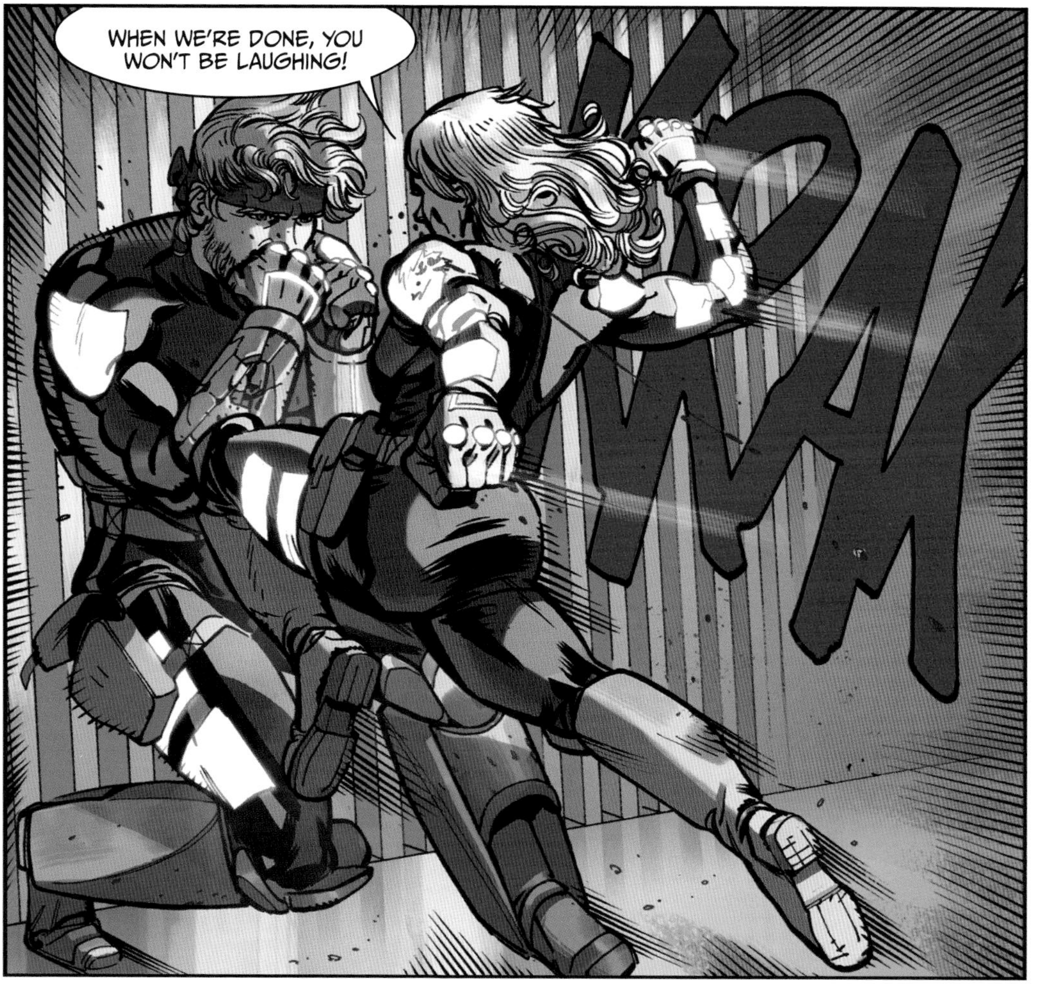
WHEN WE'RE DONE, YOU WON'T BE LAUGHING!
WAM

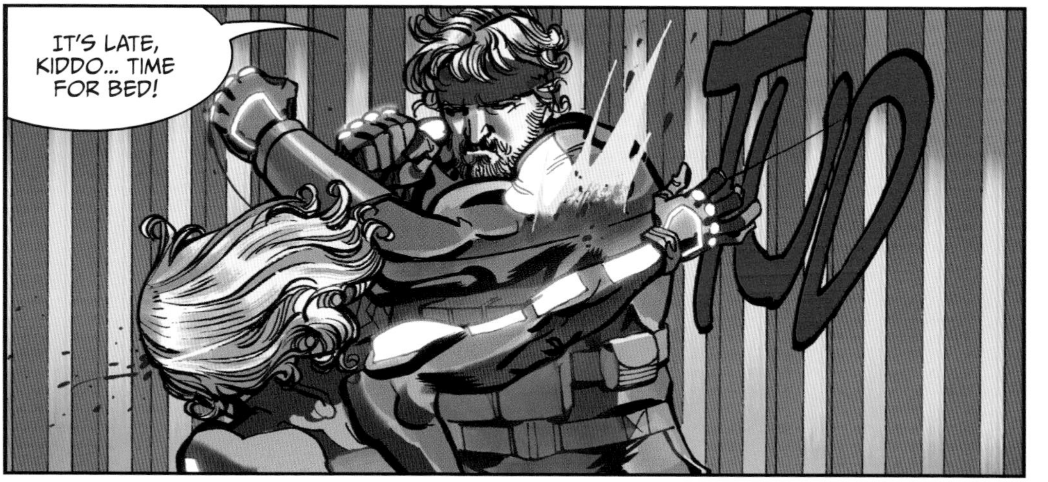
IT'S LATE, KIDDO... TIME FOR BED!
TUD

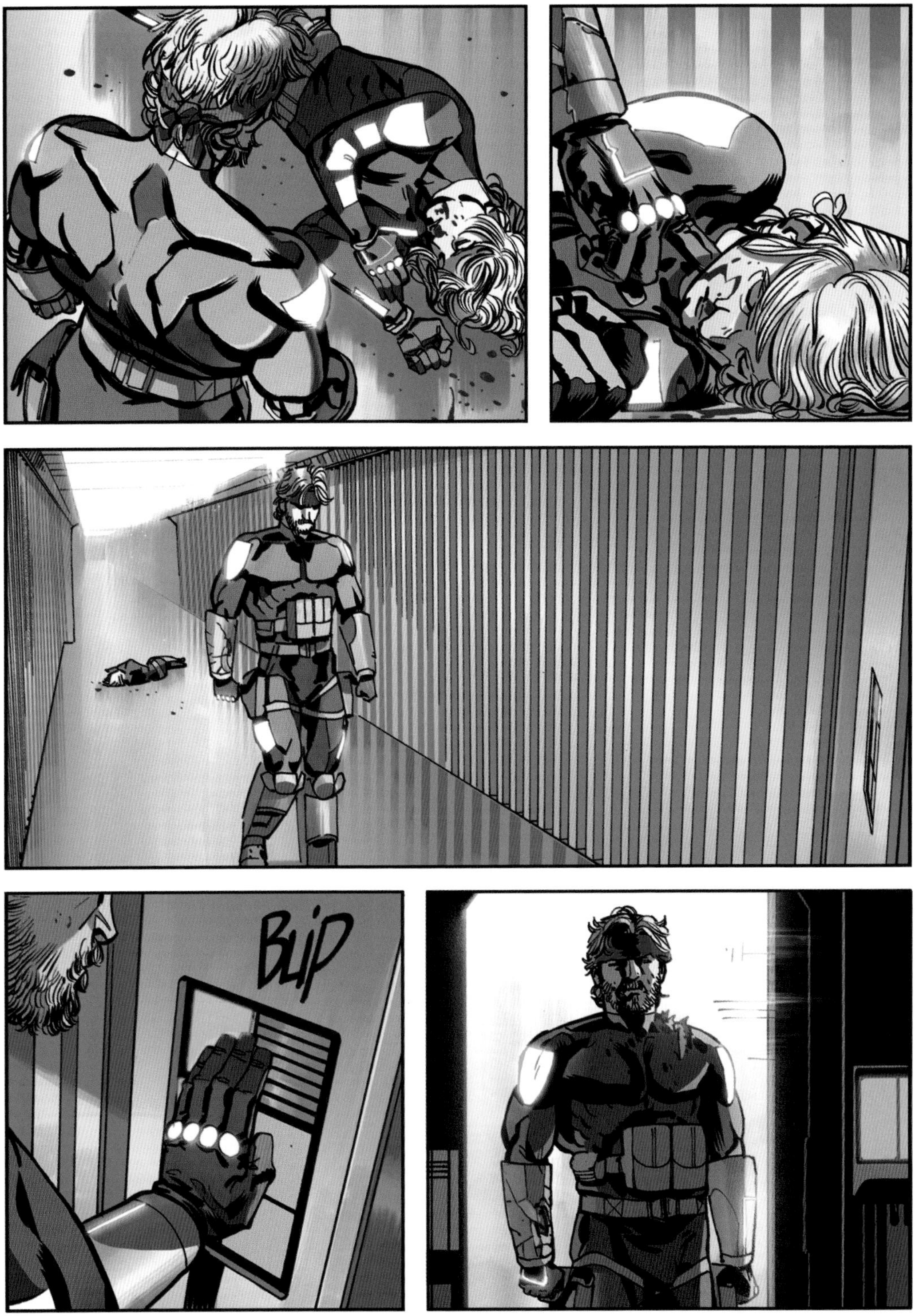
BLIP

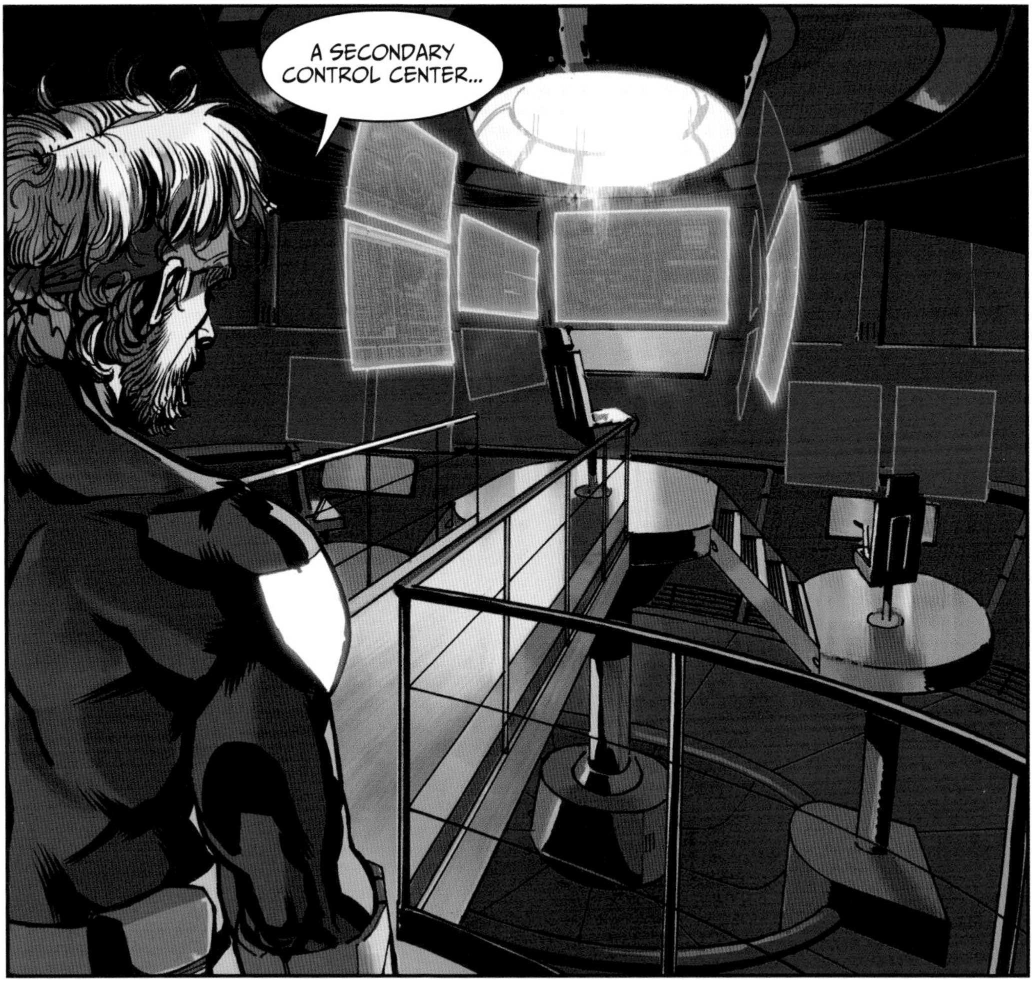
A SECONDARY CONTROL CENTER...

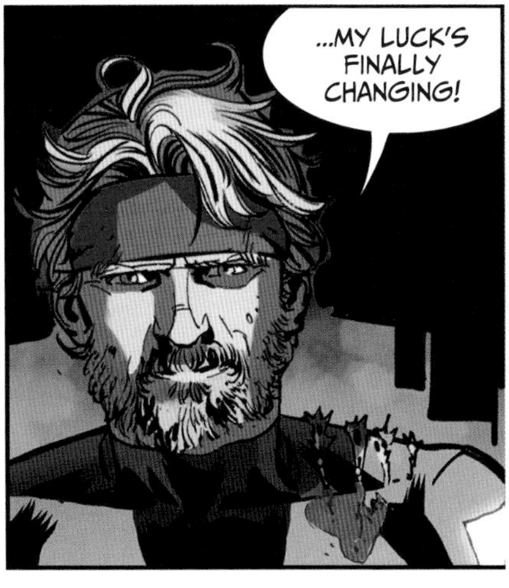
...MY LUCK'S FINALLY CHANGING!

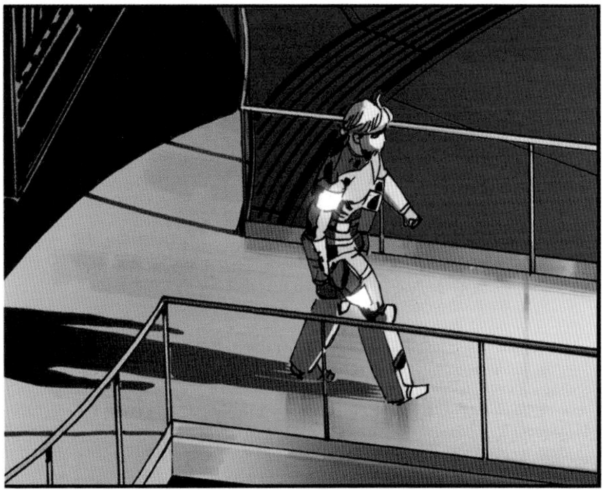

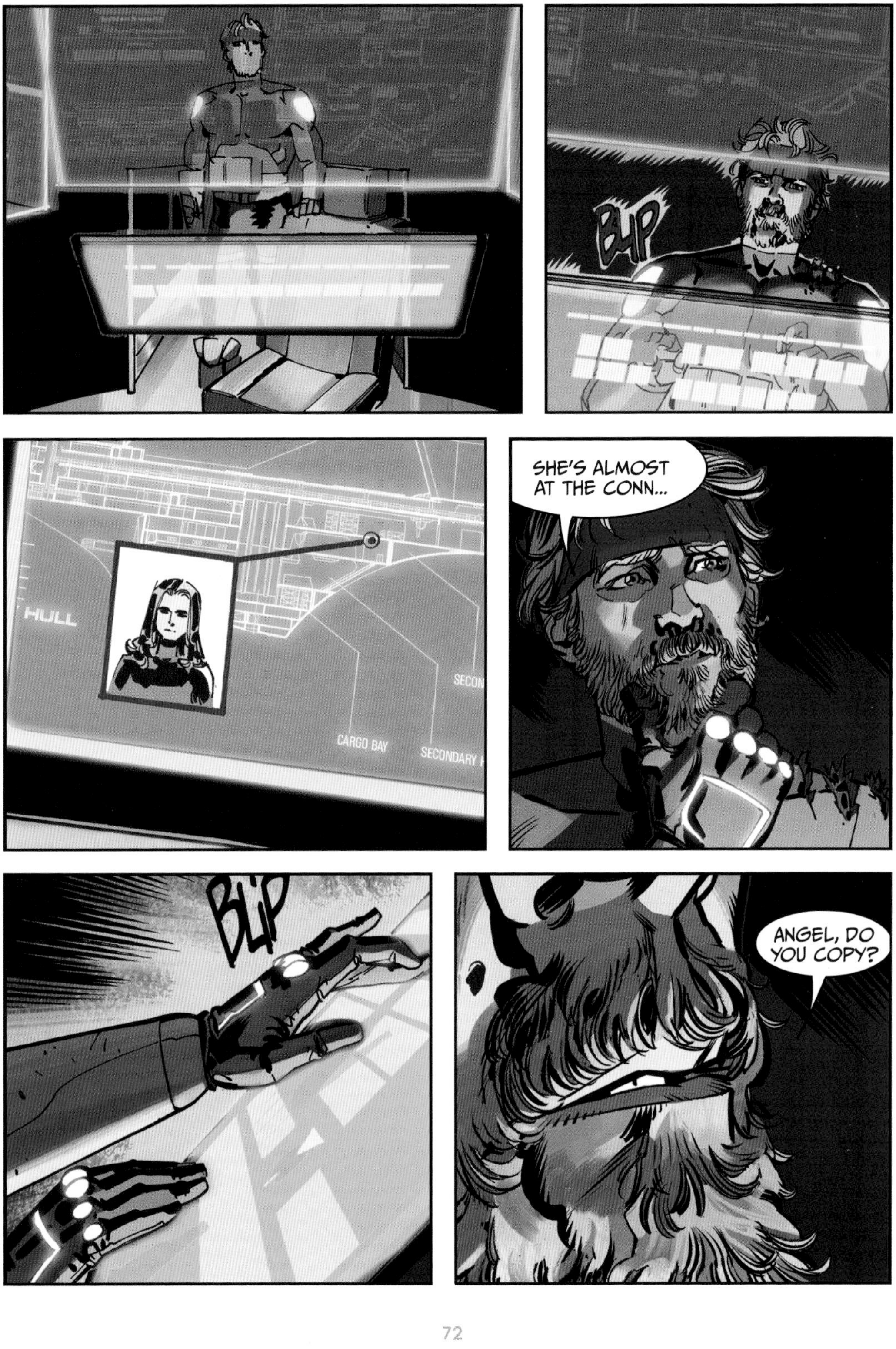
BLIP
HULL
CARGO BAY
SHE'S ALMOST AT THE CONN...
BLIP
ANGEL, DO YOU COPY?

ANGEL? CAN YOU HEAR ME?

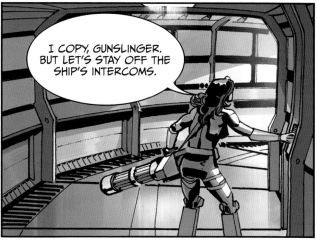

I COPY, GUNSLINGER. BUT LET'S STAY OFF THE SHIP'S INTERCOMS.

SNEAKING AROUND IS POINTLESS. THEY HAVE US ON THEIR SENSORS. JONAS IS ABOUT TO MEET YOU ON THE BRIDGE...

...AND HE'S GOT A SQUAD WITH HIM.

GOOD THING MOST OF THE FIGHTING FORCE IS ON THE OTHER SHIP OR WE'D BE FACING A WHOLE ARMY BY NOW...

IT WON'T BE EASY EITHER WAY. YOU'D BETTER HURRY UP AND GET OVER HERE...

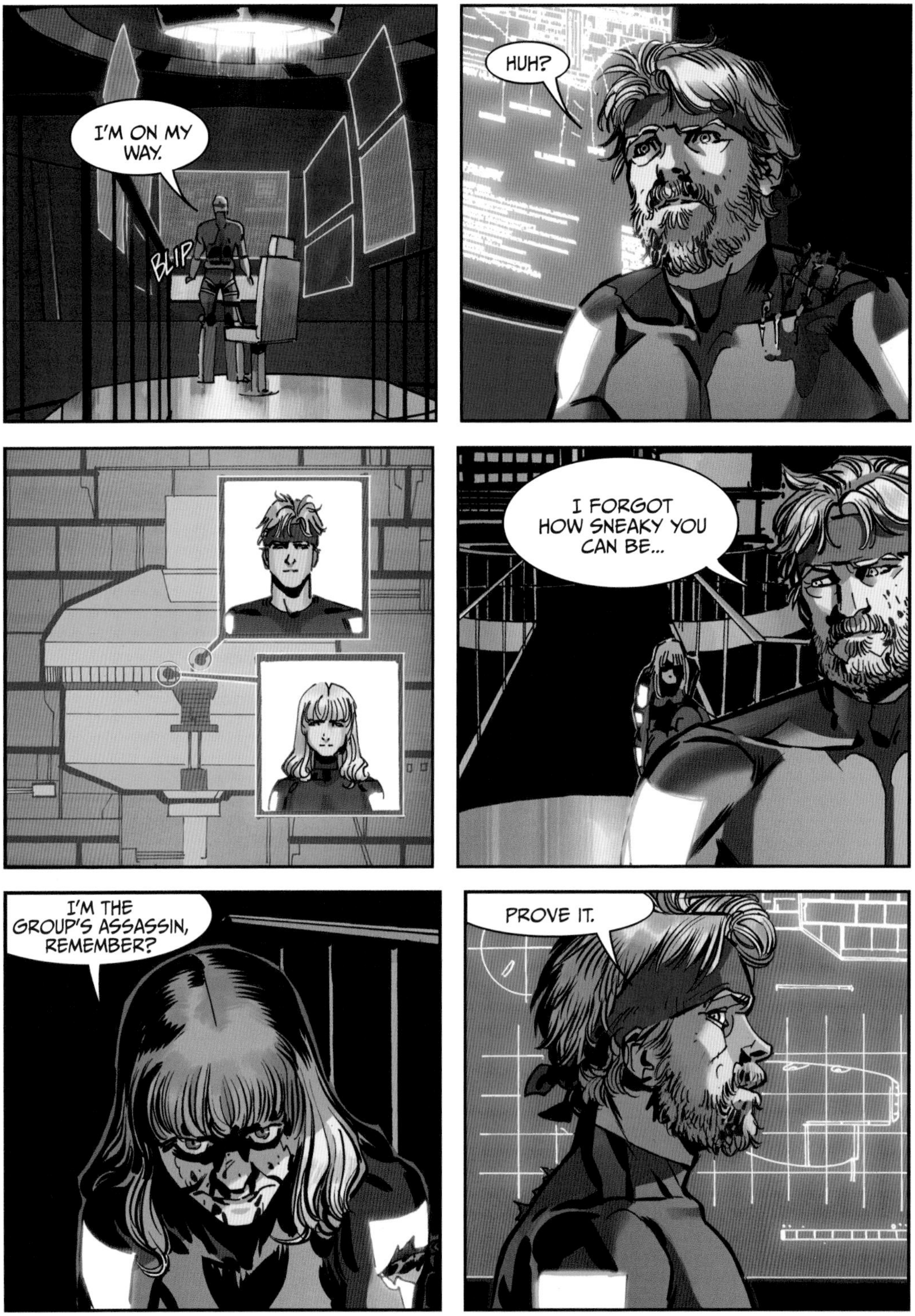
I'M ON MY WAY.
BLIP
HUH?
I FORGOT HOW SNEAKY YOU CAN BE...
I'M THE GROUP'S ASSASSIN, REMEMBER?
PROVE IT.

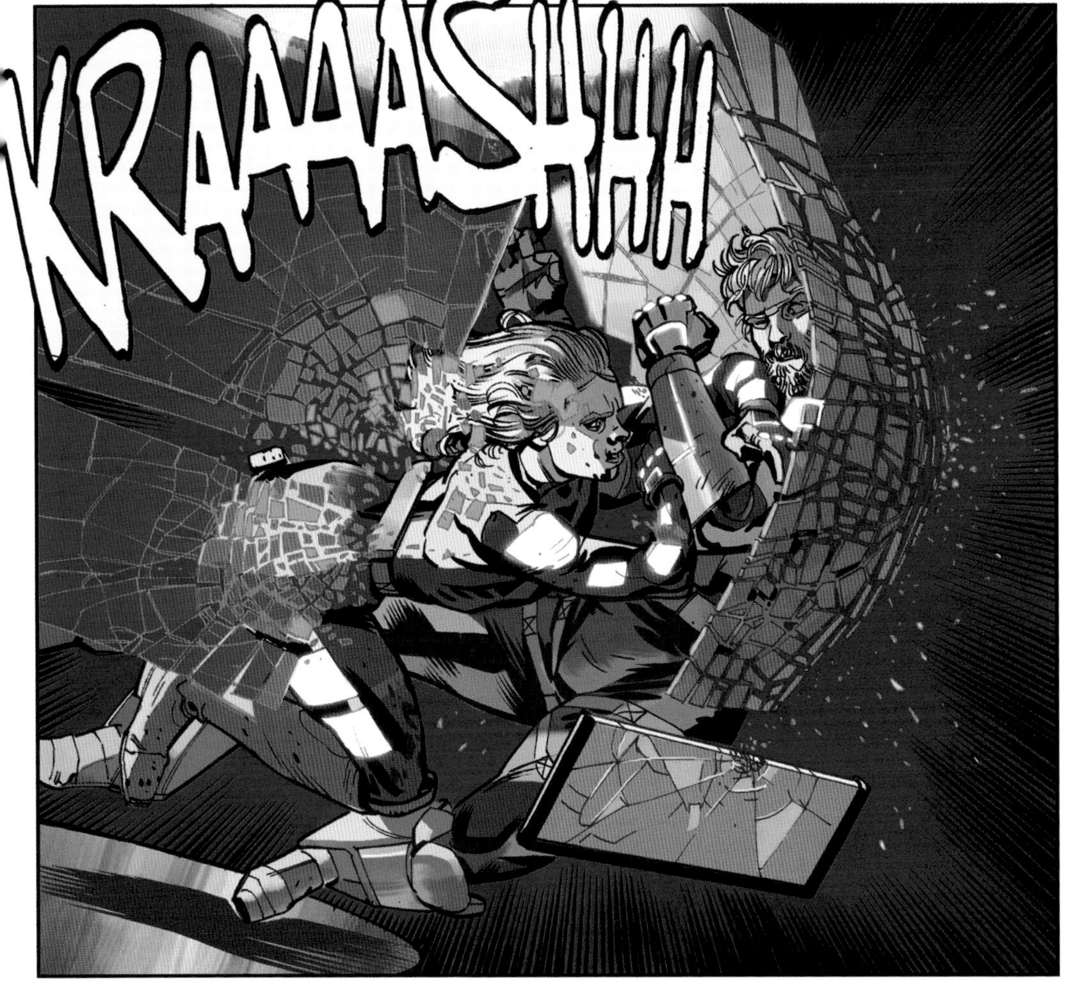
KRAAASHHH

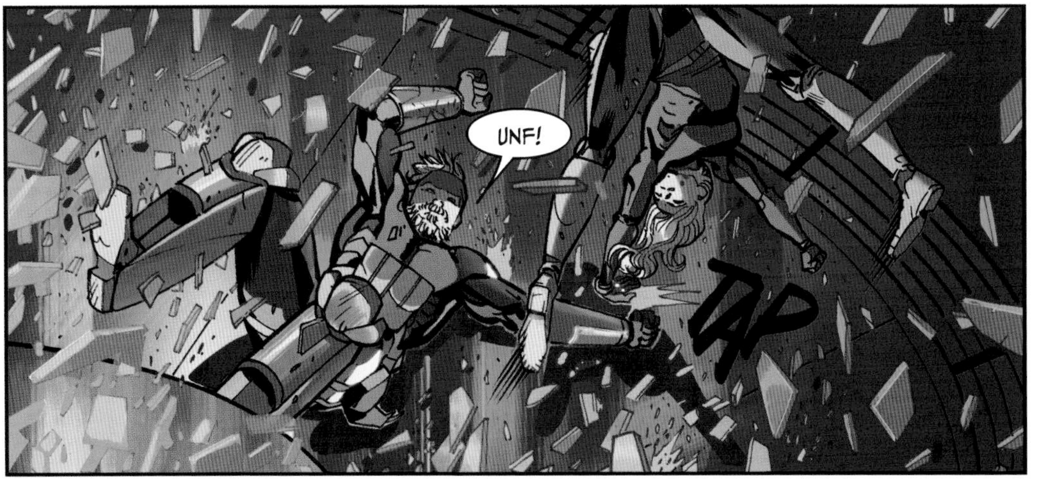
UNF!
TAP

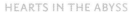

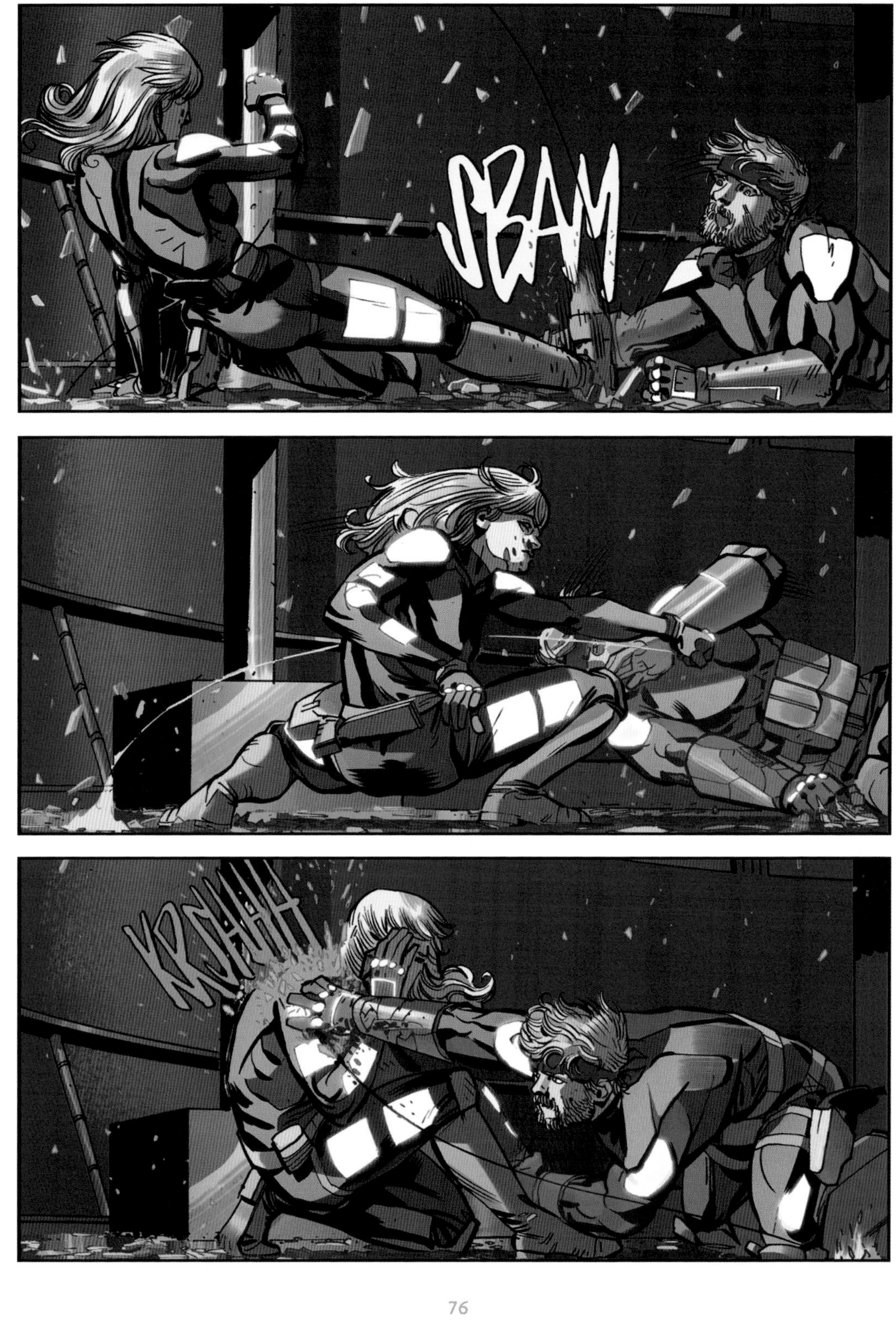
SBAM
KRSHHH

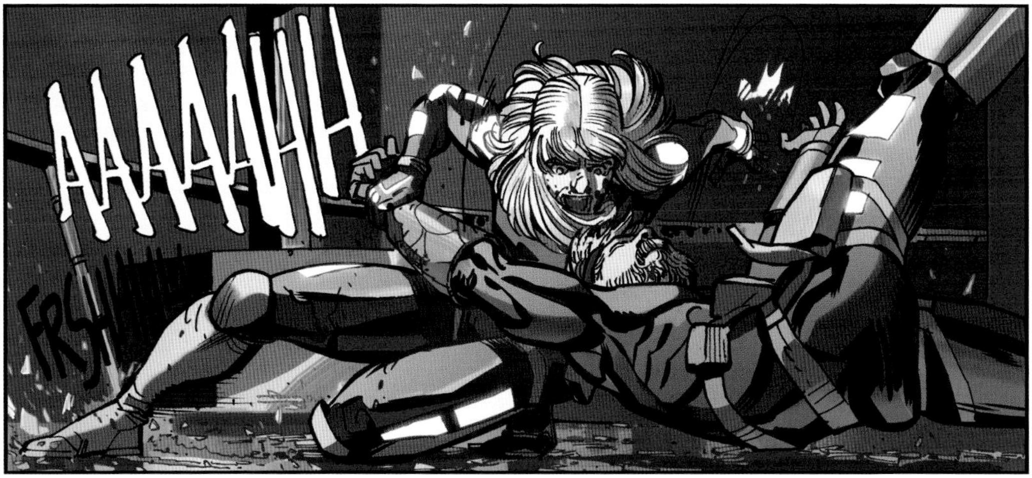
AAAAAHH
FRSH

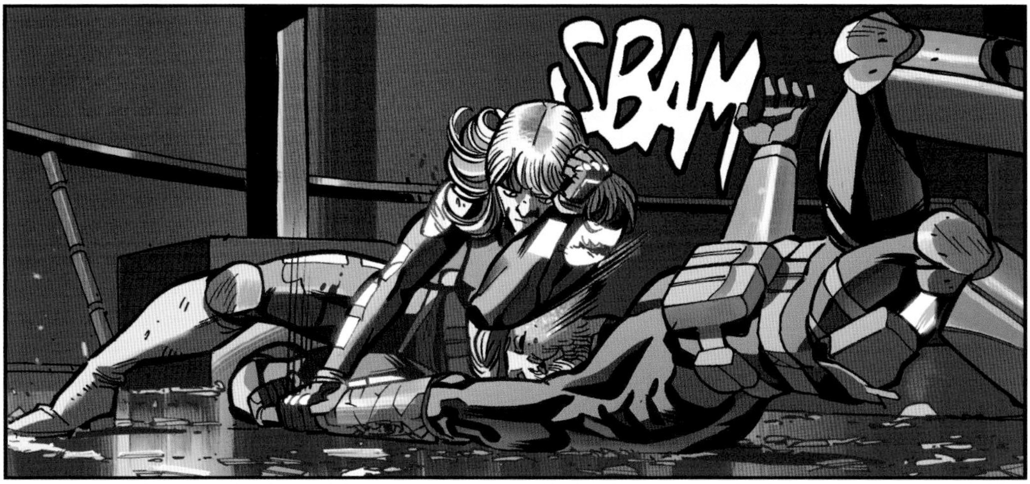
SBAM

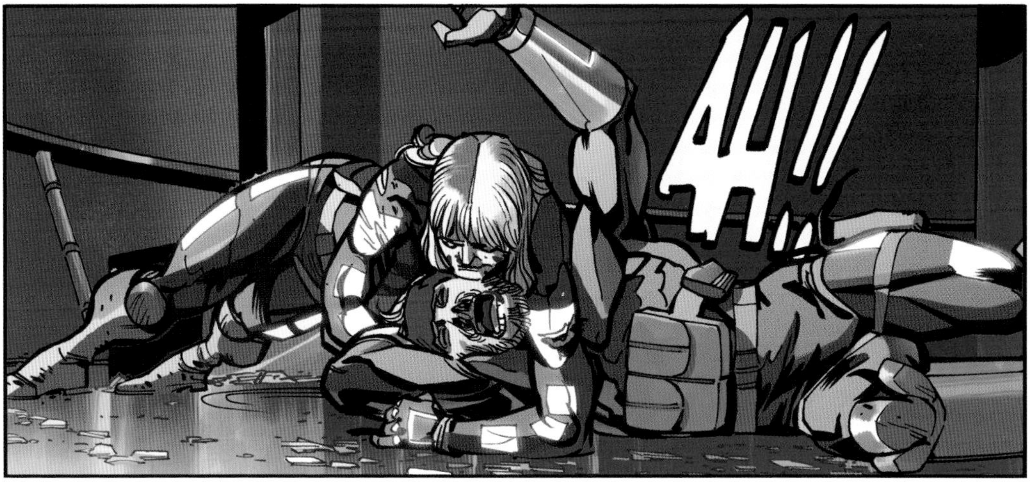
AH!!

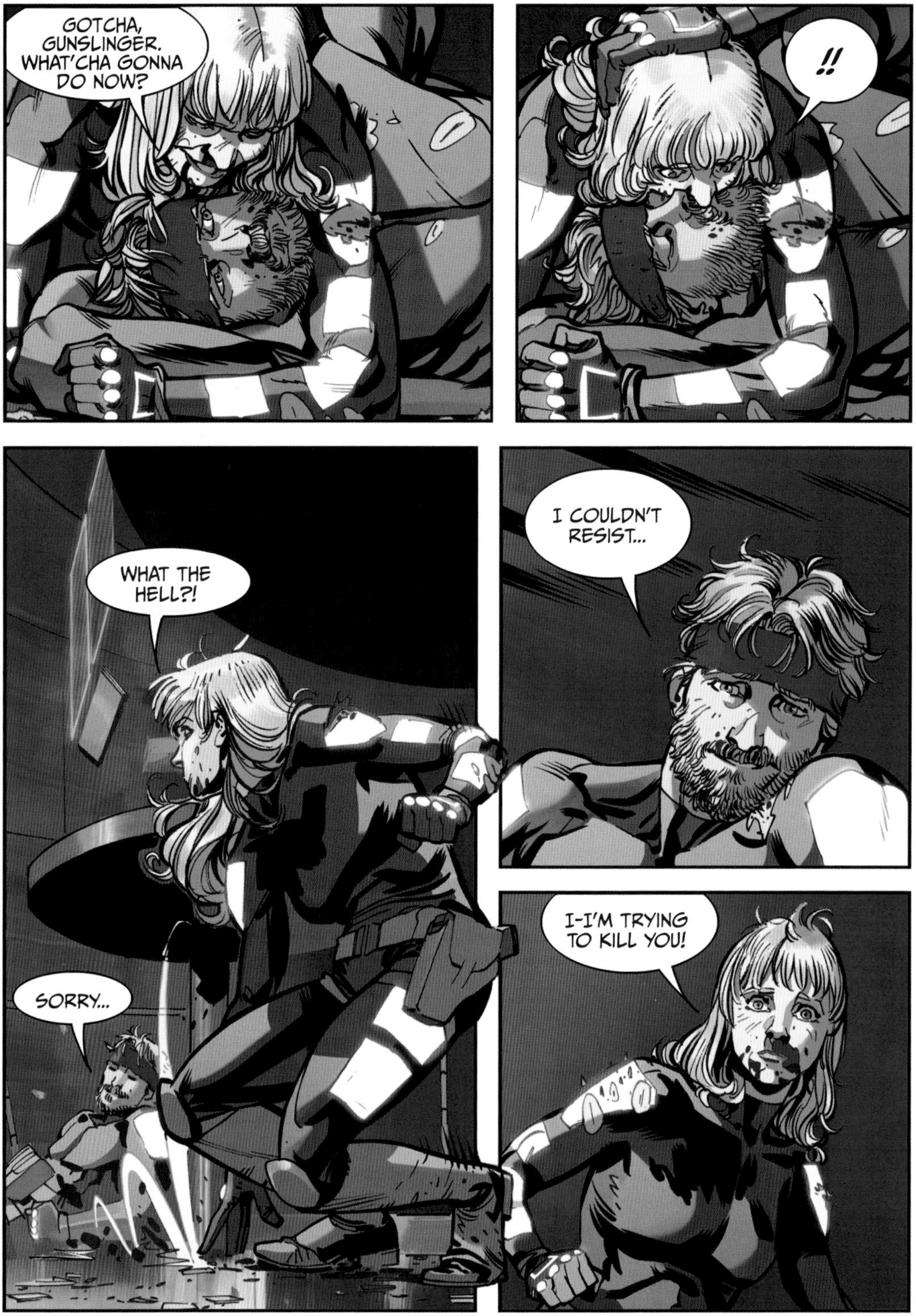
GOTCHA, GUNSLINGER. WHAT'CHA GONNA DO NOW?
!!
WHAT THE HELL?!
SORRY...
I COULDN'T RESIST...
I-I'M TRYING TO KILL YOU!

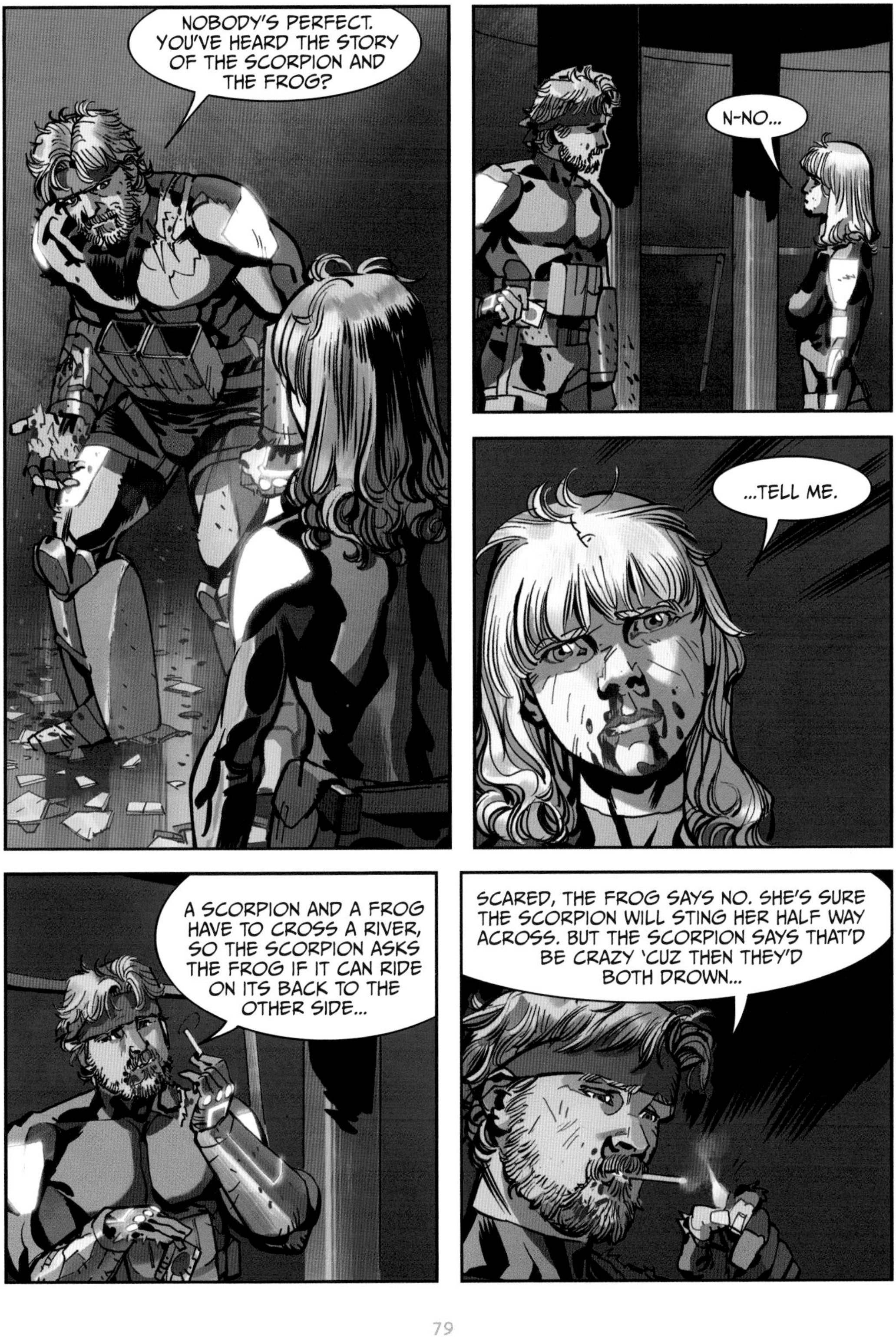
NOBODY'S PERFECT. YOU'VE HEARD THE STORY OF THE SCORPION AND THE FROG?
N-NO...
...TELL ME.
A SCORPION AND A FROG HAVE TO CROSS A RIVER, SO THE SCORPION ASKS THE FROG IF IT CAN RIDE ON ITS BACK TO THE OTHER SIDE...
SCARED, THE FROG SAYS NO. SHE'S SURE THE SCORPION WILL STING HER HALF WAY ACROSS. BUT THE SCORPION SAYS THAT'D BE CRAZY 'CUZ THEN THEY'D BOTH DROWN...

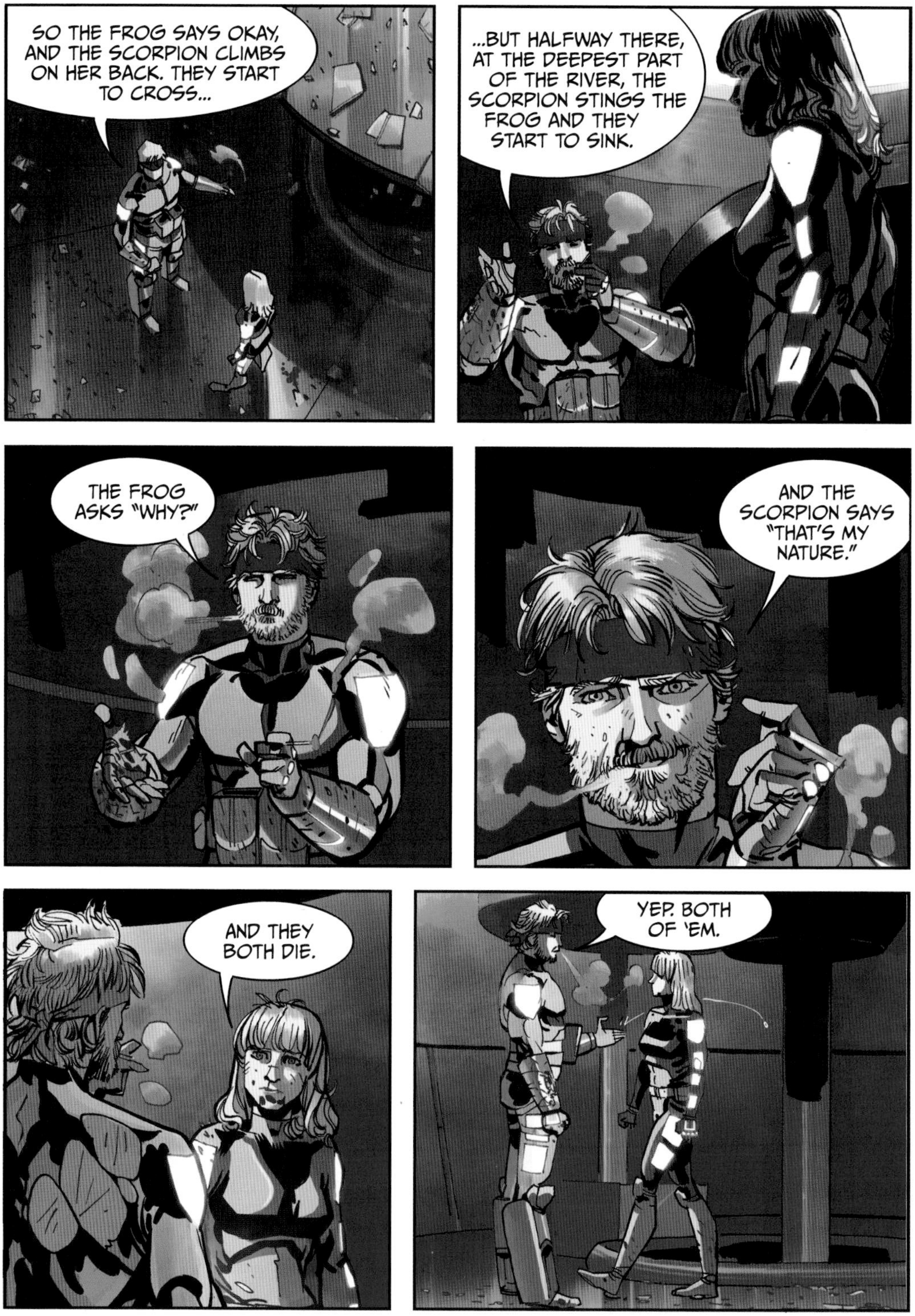
SO THE FROG SAYS OKAY, AND THE SCORPION CLIMBS ON HER BACK. THEY START TO CROSS...
...BUT HALFWAY THERE, AT THE DEEPEST PART OF THE RIVER, THE SCORPION STINGS THE FROG AND THEY START TO SINK.
THE FROG ASKS "WHY?"
AND THE SCORPION SAYS "THAT'S MY NATURE."
AND THEY BOTH DIE.
YEP. BOTH OF 'EM.

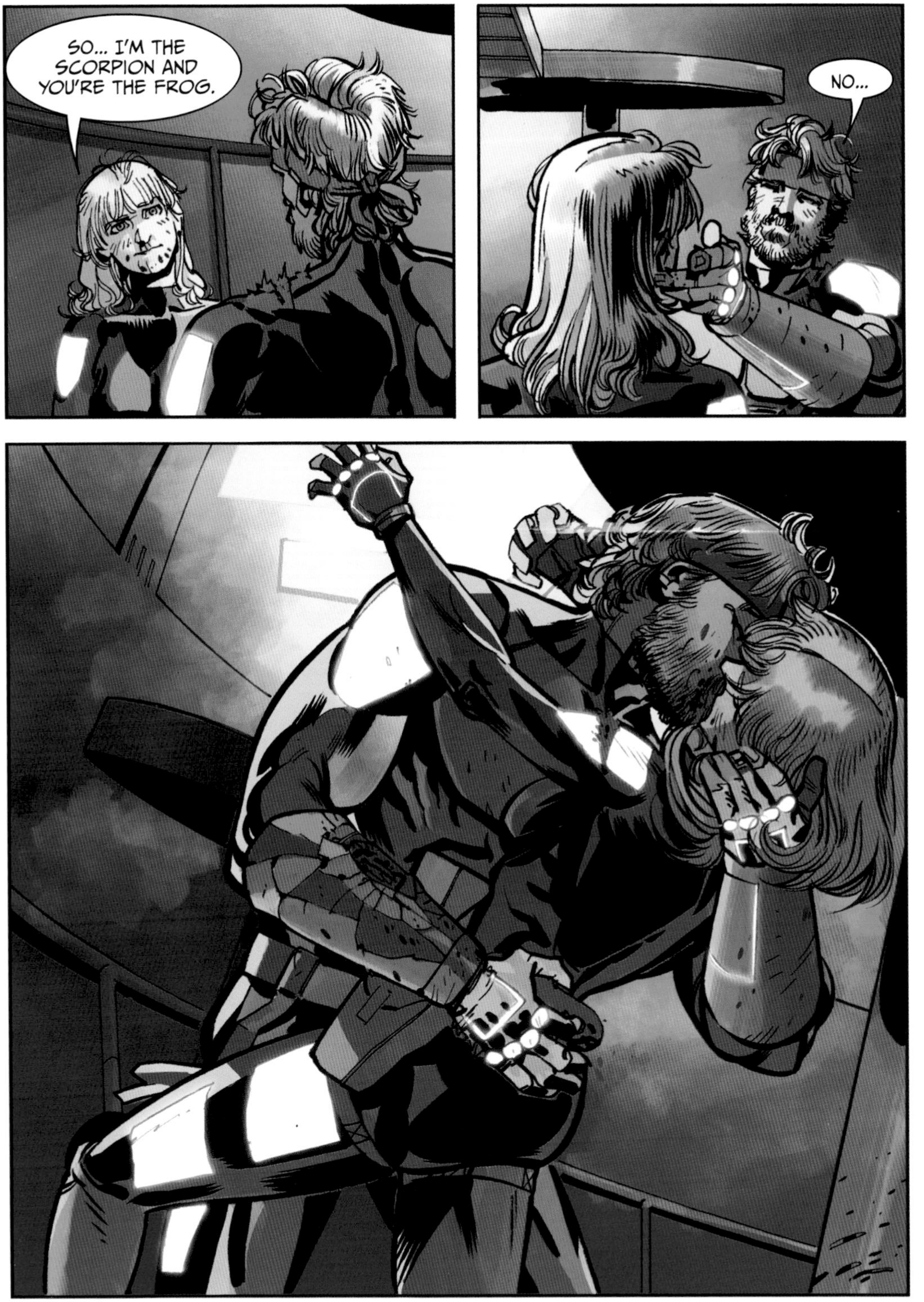
SO... I'M THE SCORPION AND YOU'RE THE FROG.
NO...

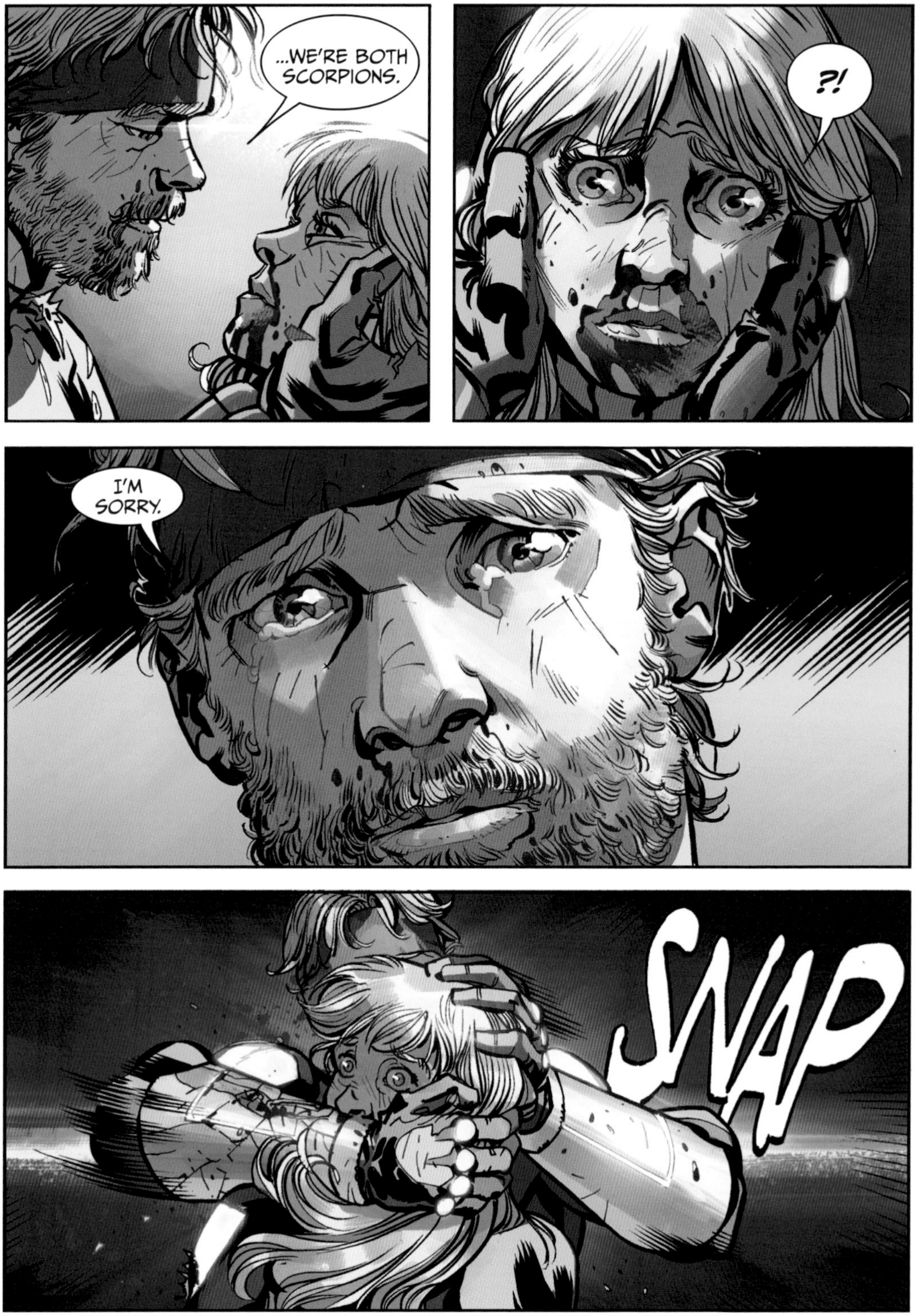
...WE'RE BOTH SCORPIONS.
?!
I'M SORRY.
SNAP

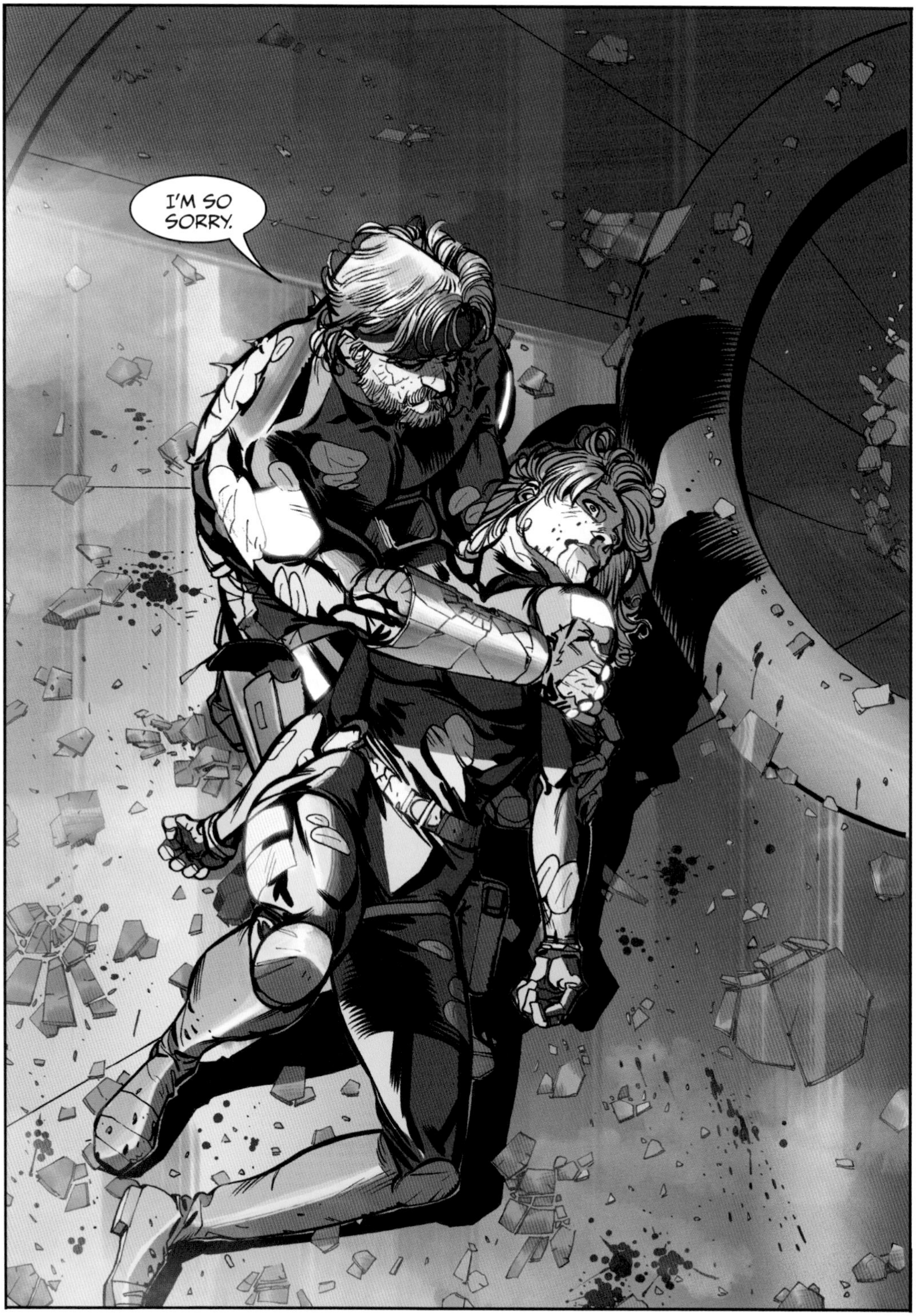
I'M SO SORRY.

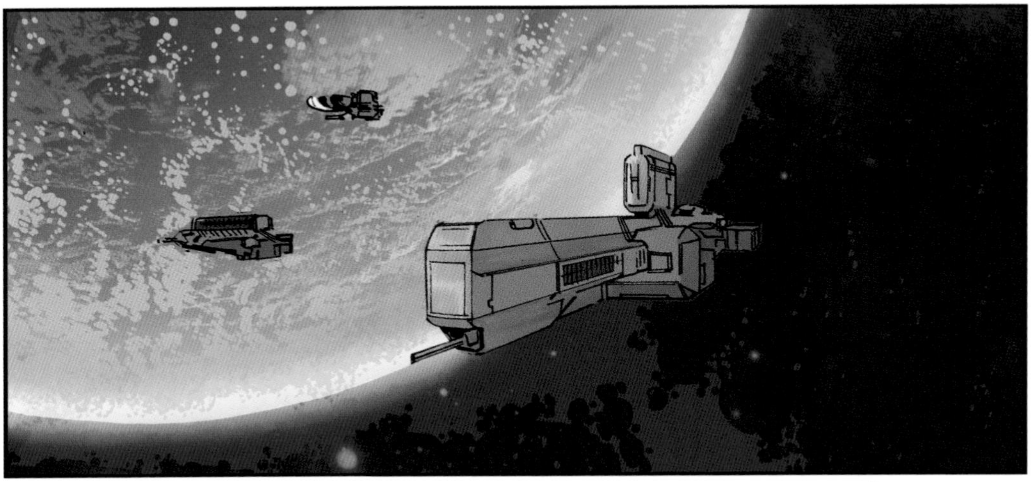

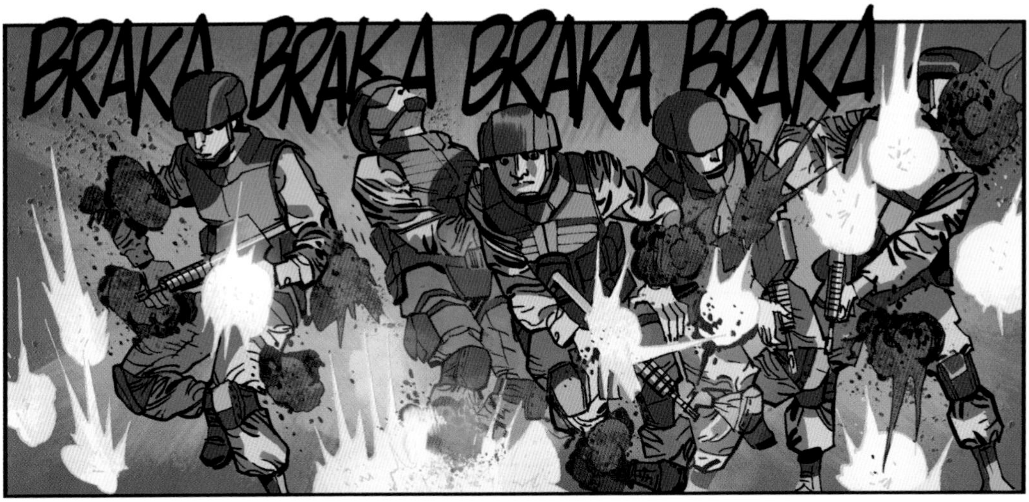
BRAKA BRAKA BRAKA BRAKA

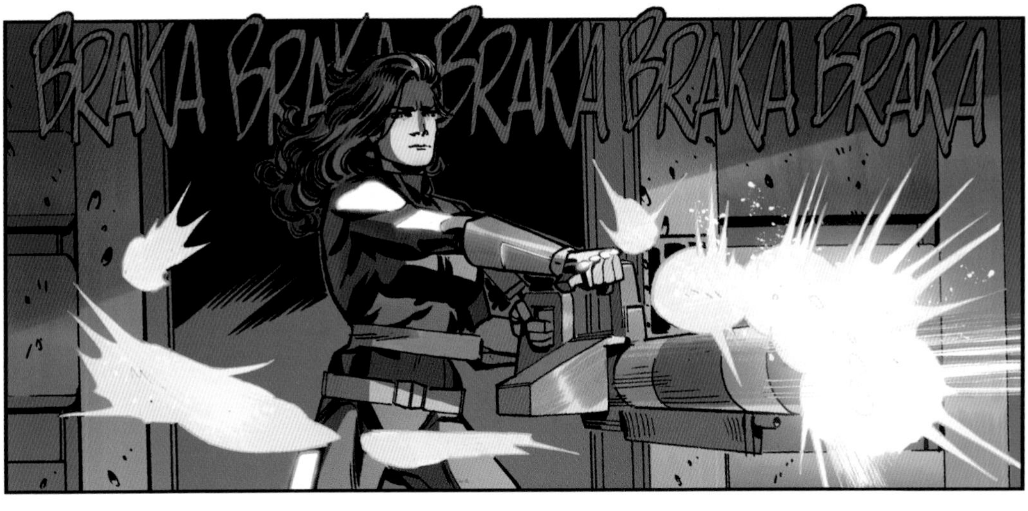
BRAKA BRAKA BRAKA BRAKA BRAKA

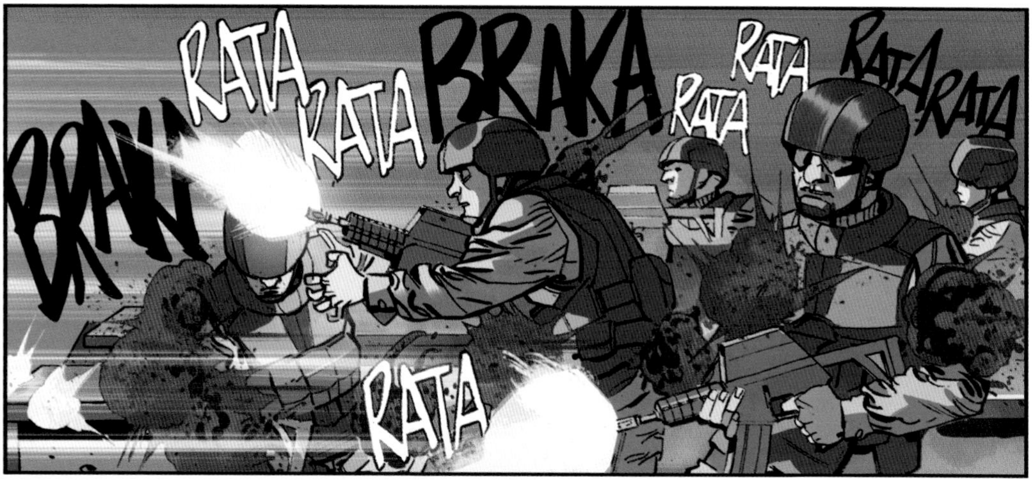
BRAKA
RATA
RATA
BRAKA
RATA
RATA
RATARATA
RATA

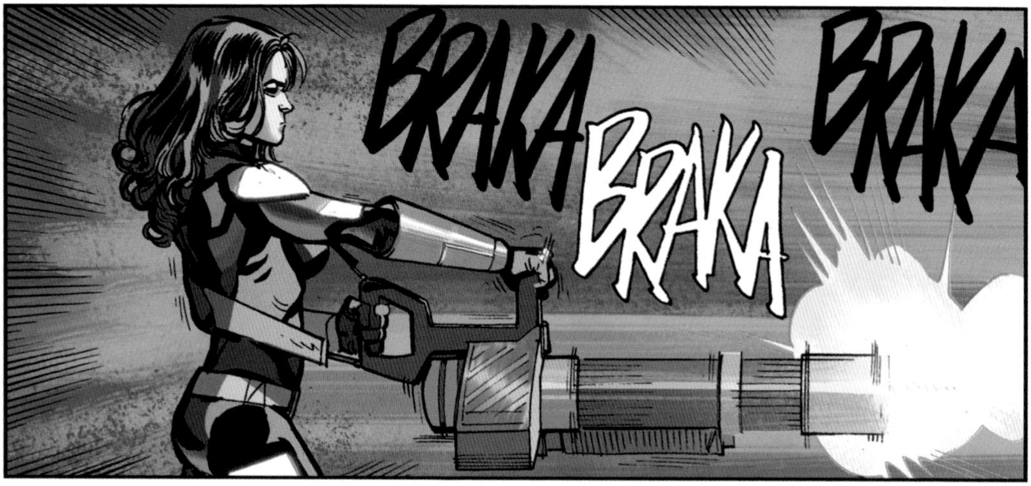
BRAKA
BRAKA
BRAKA

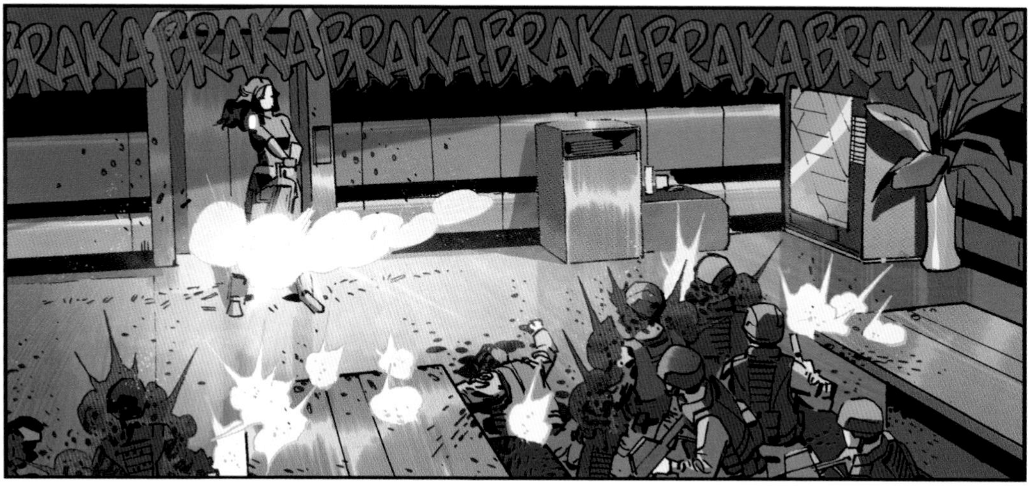
BRAKABRAKABRAKABRAKABRAKABRAKABR

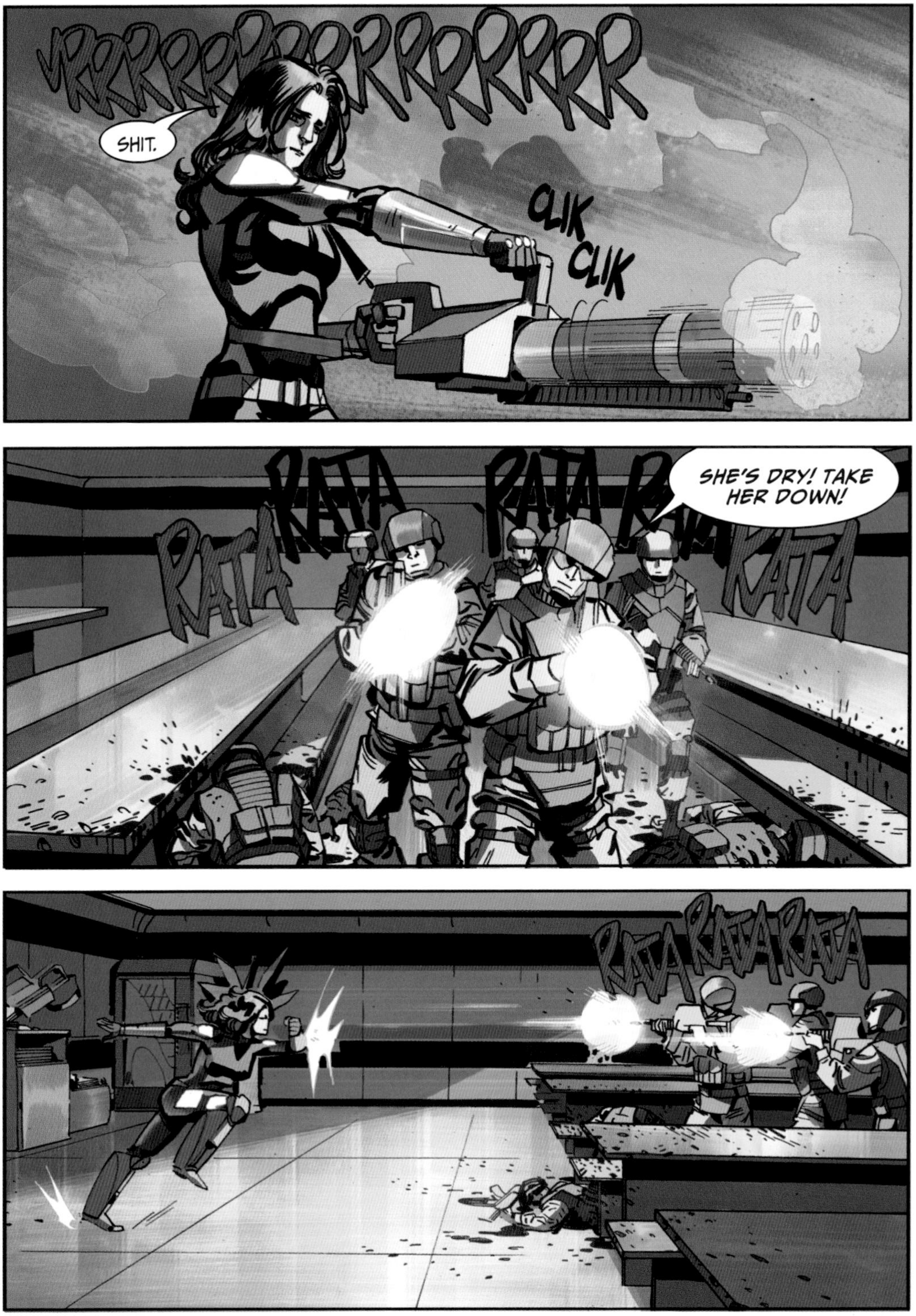
VRRRRRRRRRRRRRRR
SHIT.
CLIK
CLIK
RATA
RATA
RATA
SHE'S DRY! TAKE HER DOWN!
RATA
RATA RATA RATA

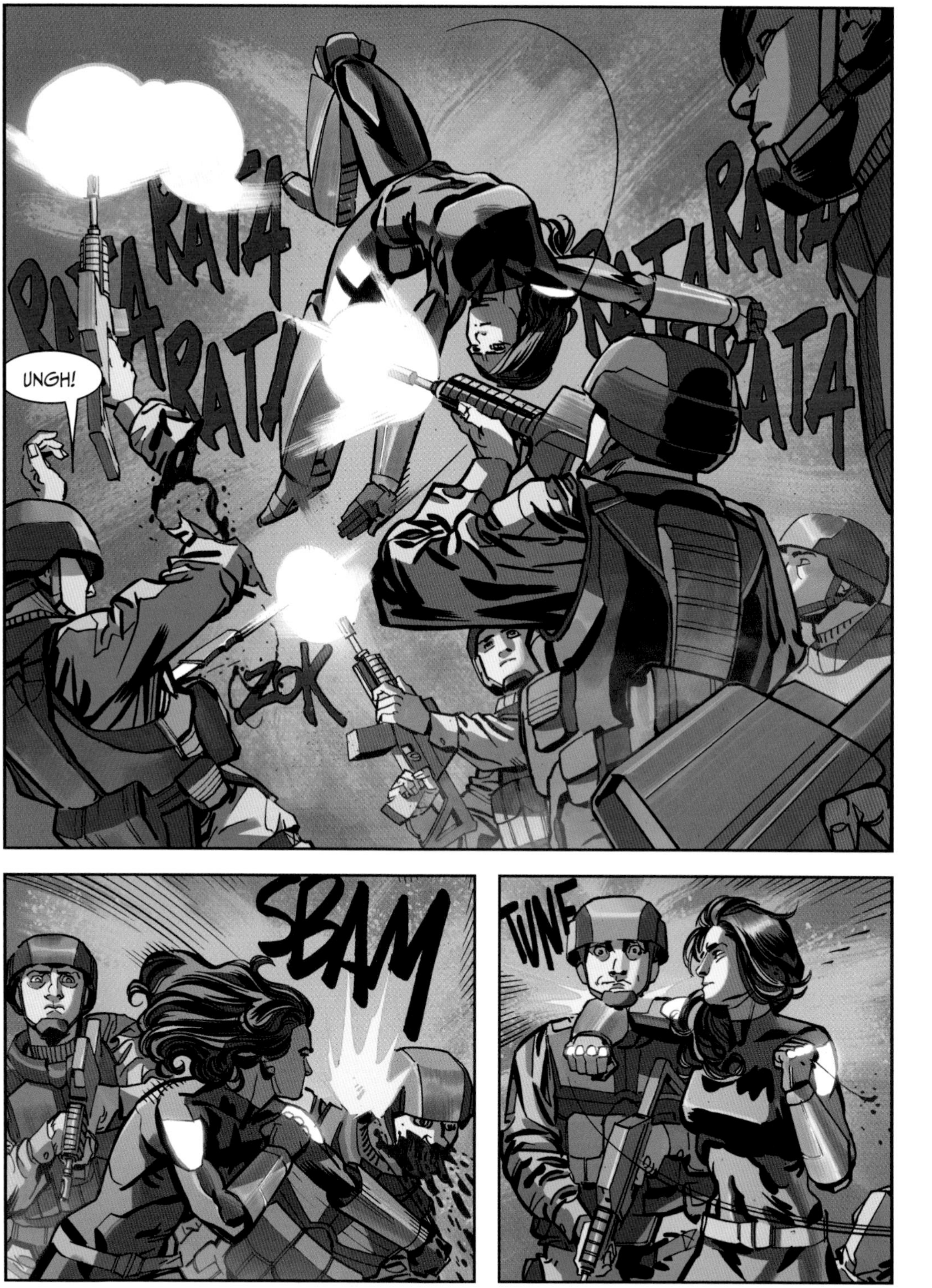
RATATA RATATA
RATATA
UNGH!
RATATA
RATATA
ZOK
SBAM
TUNF

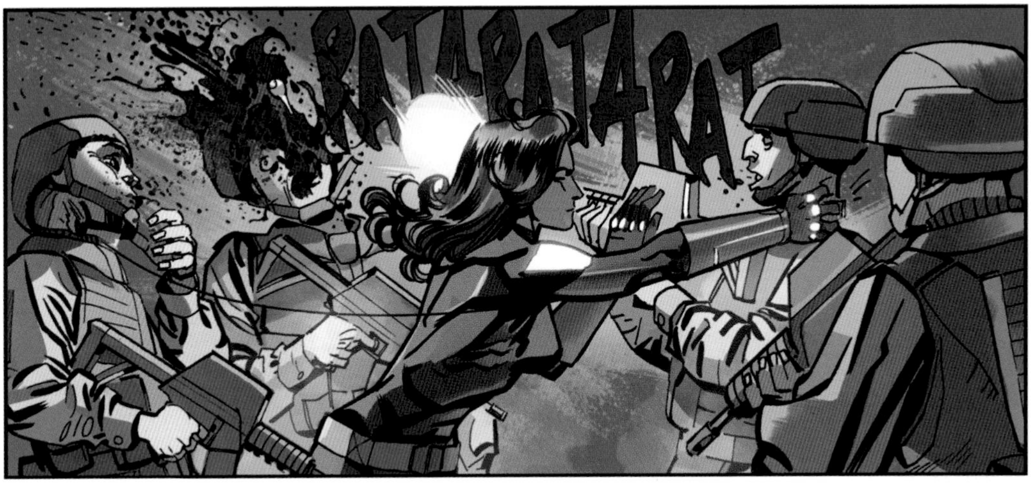
RATARATATARAT

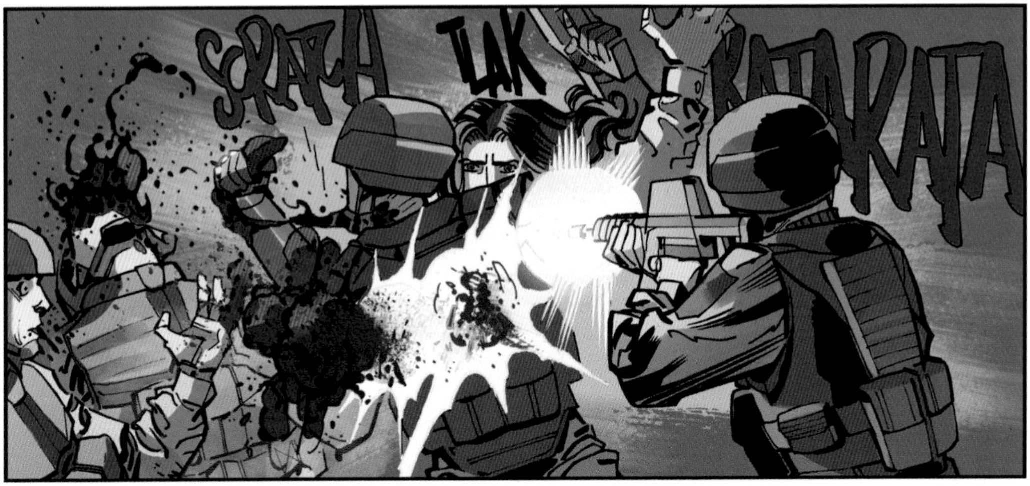
TLAK
RATARATA

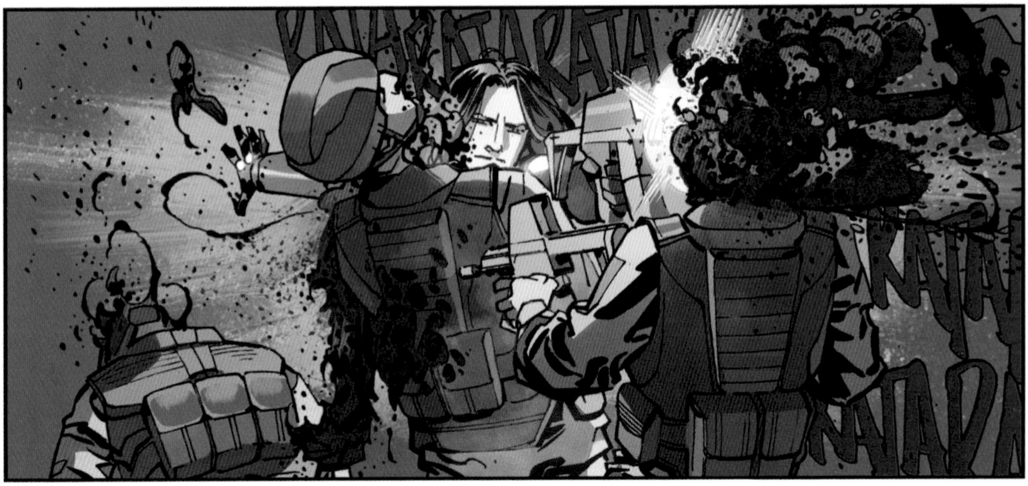

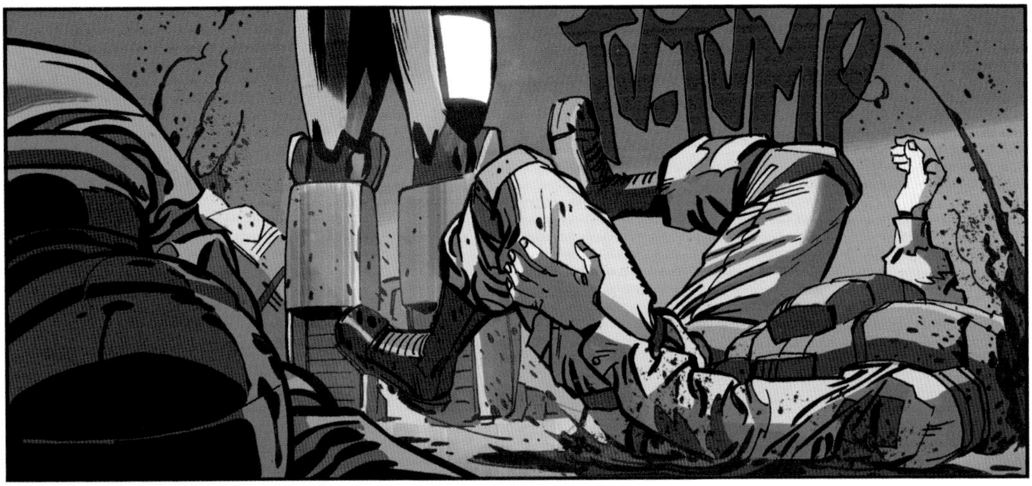
TV.TUMP

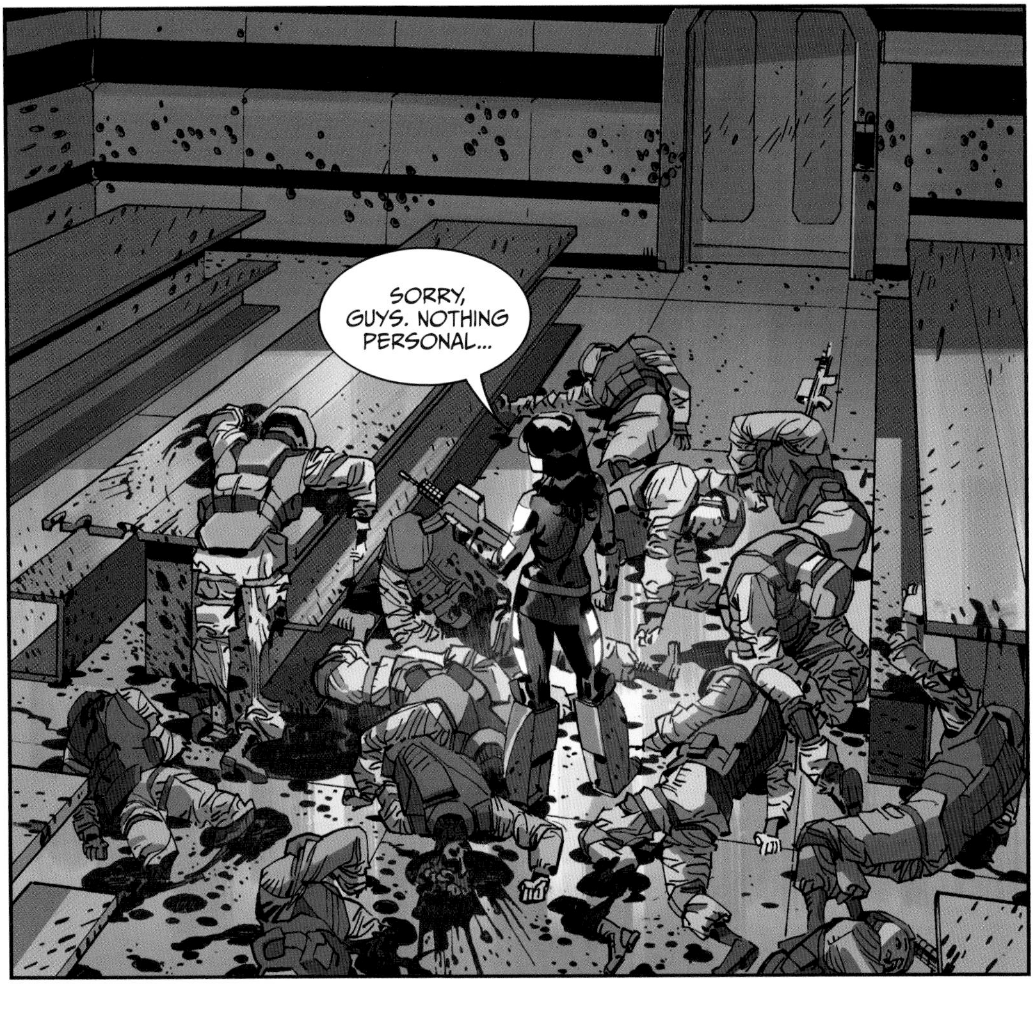
SORRY, GUYS. NOTHING PERSONAL...

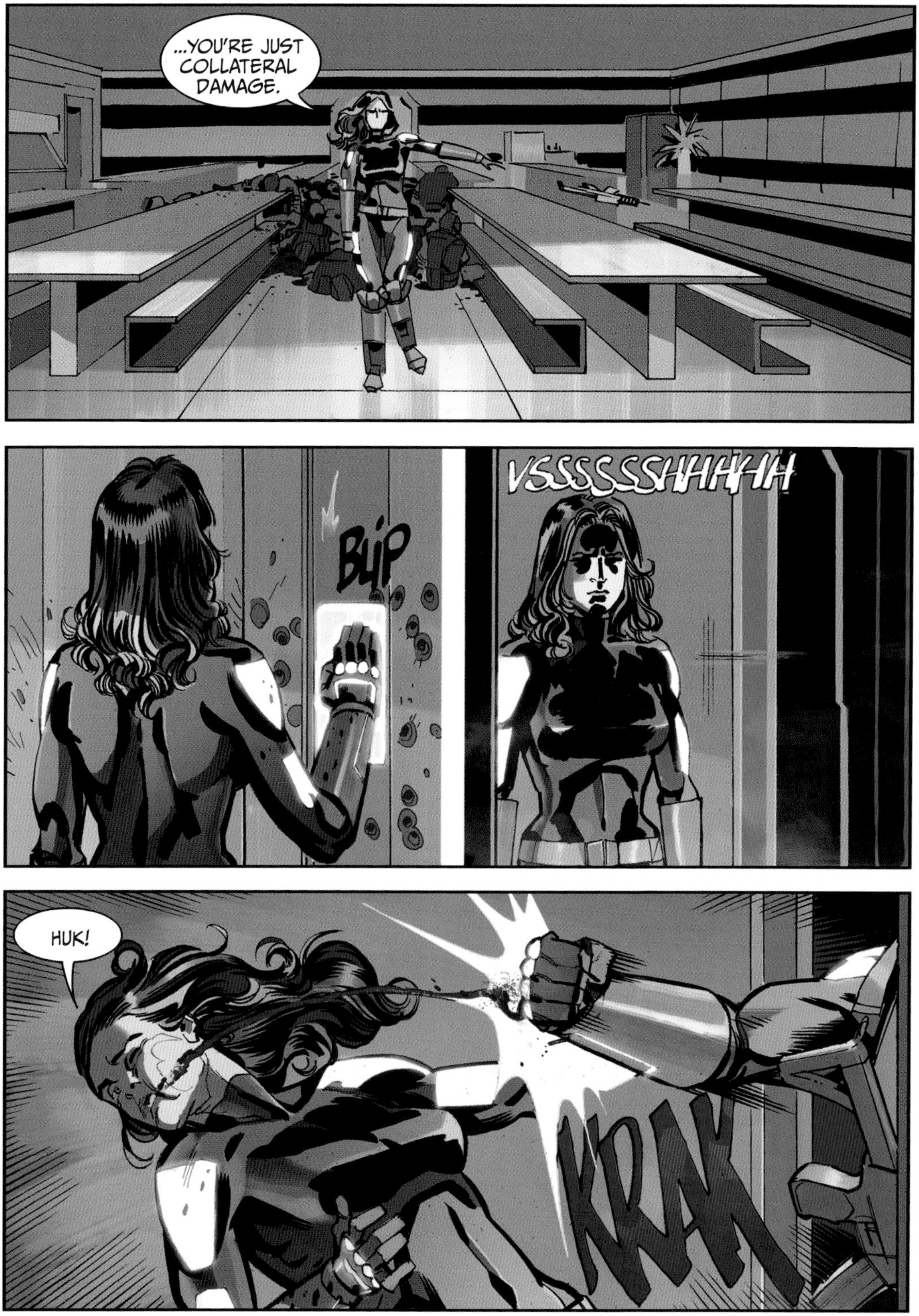
...YOU'RE JUST COLLATERAL DAMAGE.
BLIP
VSSSSSSHHHHH
HUK!
KRAK

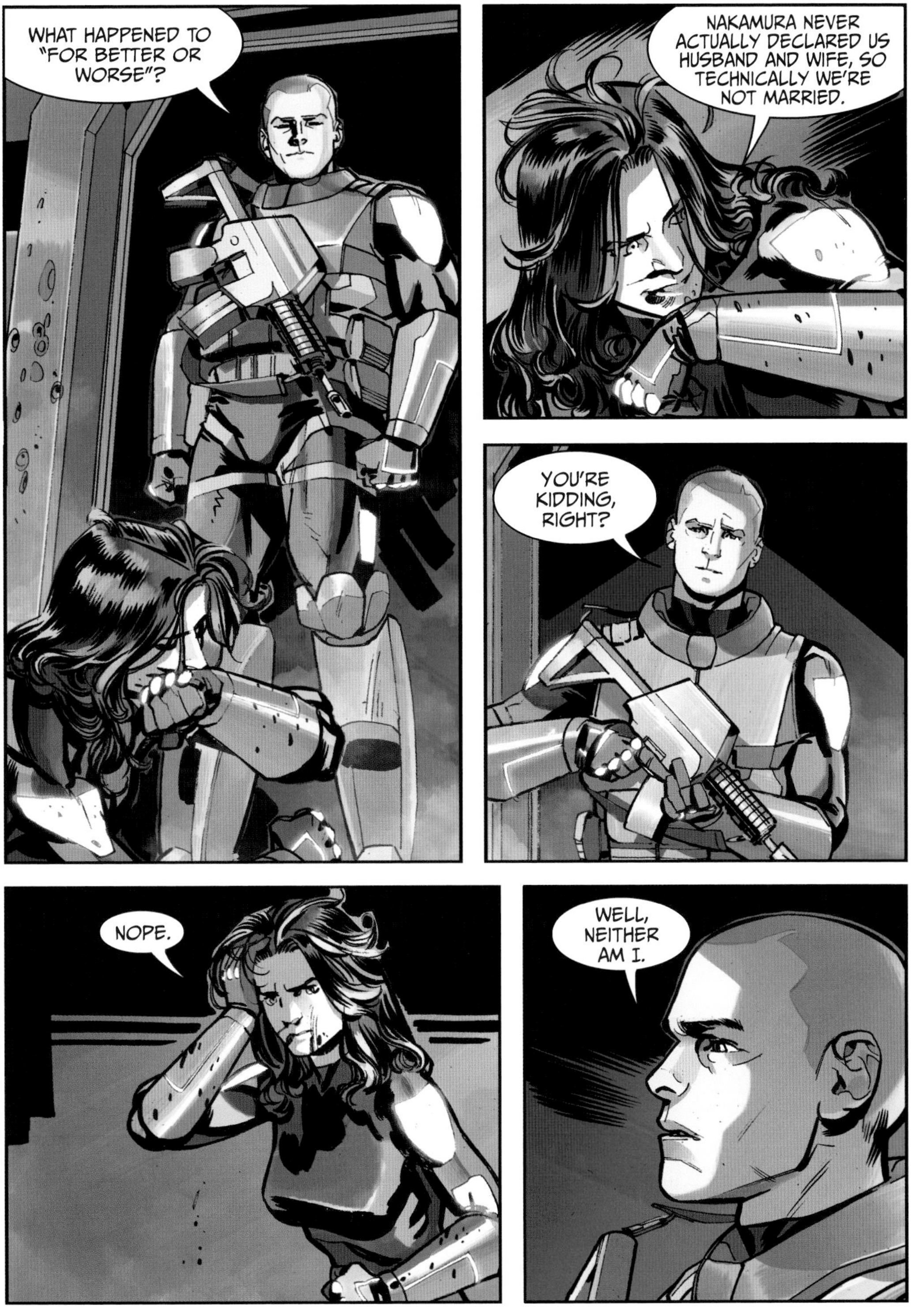
WHAT HAPPENED TO "FOR BETTER OR WORSE"?
NAKAMURA NEVER ACTUALLY DECLARED US HUSBAND AND WIFE, SO TECHNICALLY WE'RE NOT MARRIED.
YOU'RE KIDDING, RIGHT?
NOPE.
WELL, NEITHER AM I.

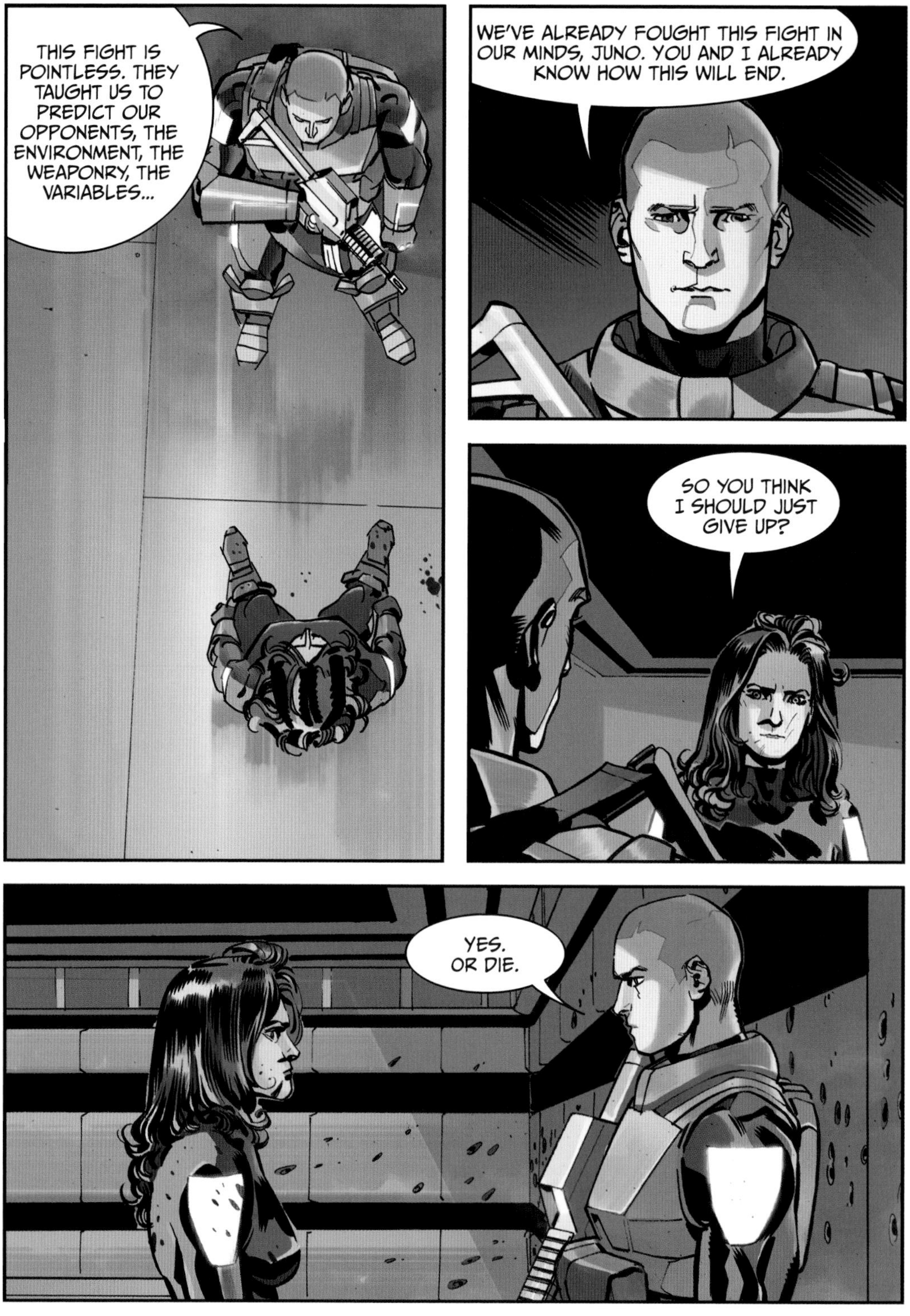
THIS FIGHT IS POINTLESS. THEY TAUGHT US TO PREDICT OUR OPPONENTS, THE ENVIRONMENT, THE WEAPONRY, THE VARIABLES...
WE'VE ALREADY FOUGHT THIS FIGHT IN OUR MINDS, JUNO. YOU AND I ALREADY KNOW HOW THIS WILL END.
SO YOU THINK I SHOULD JUST GIVE UP?
YES. OR DIE.

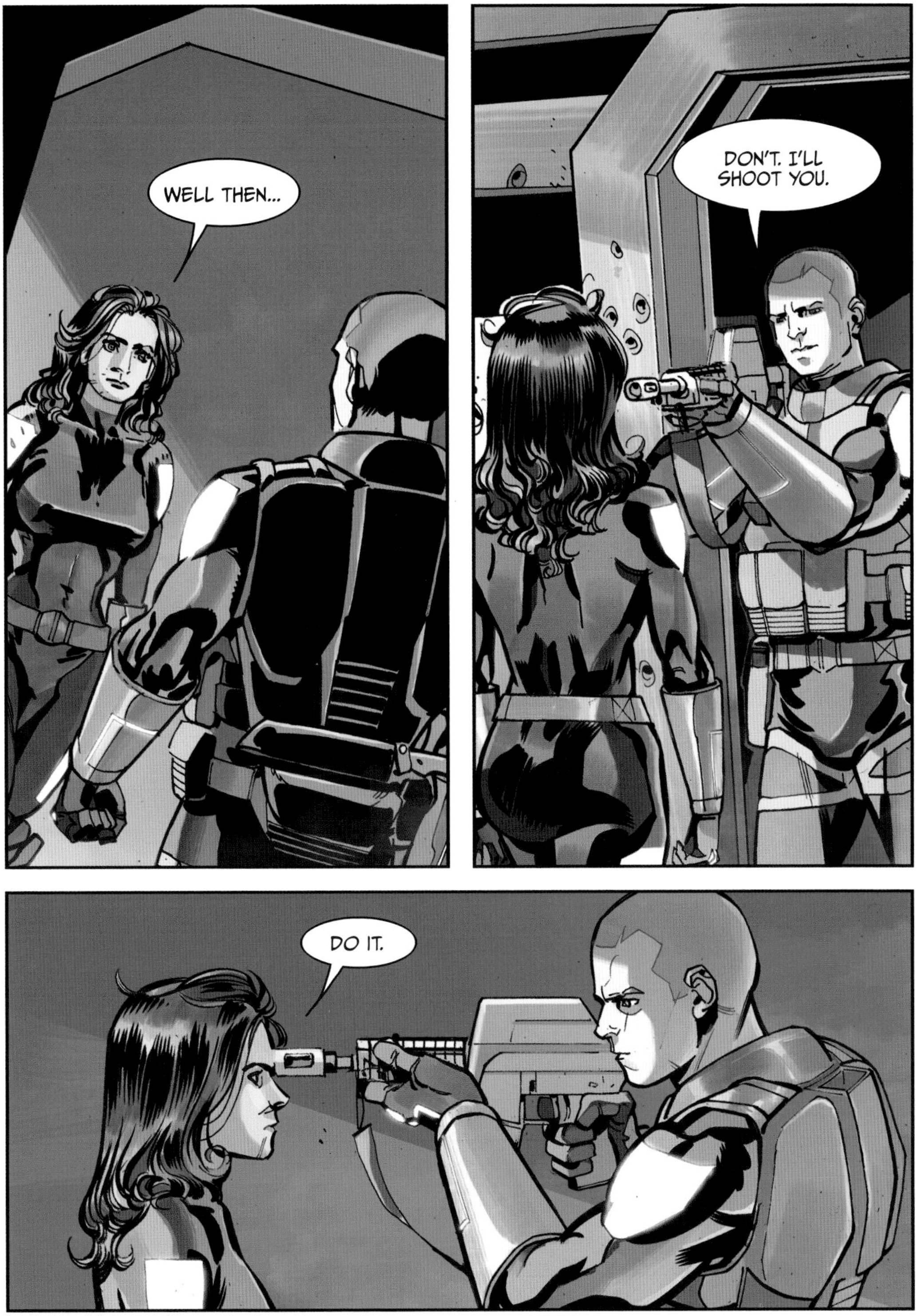
WELL THEN...
DON'T. I'LL SHOOT YOU.
DO IT.

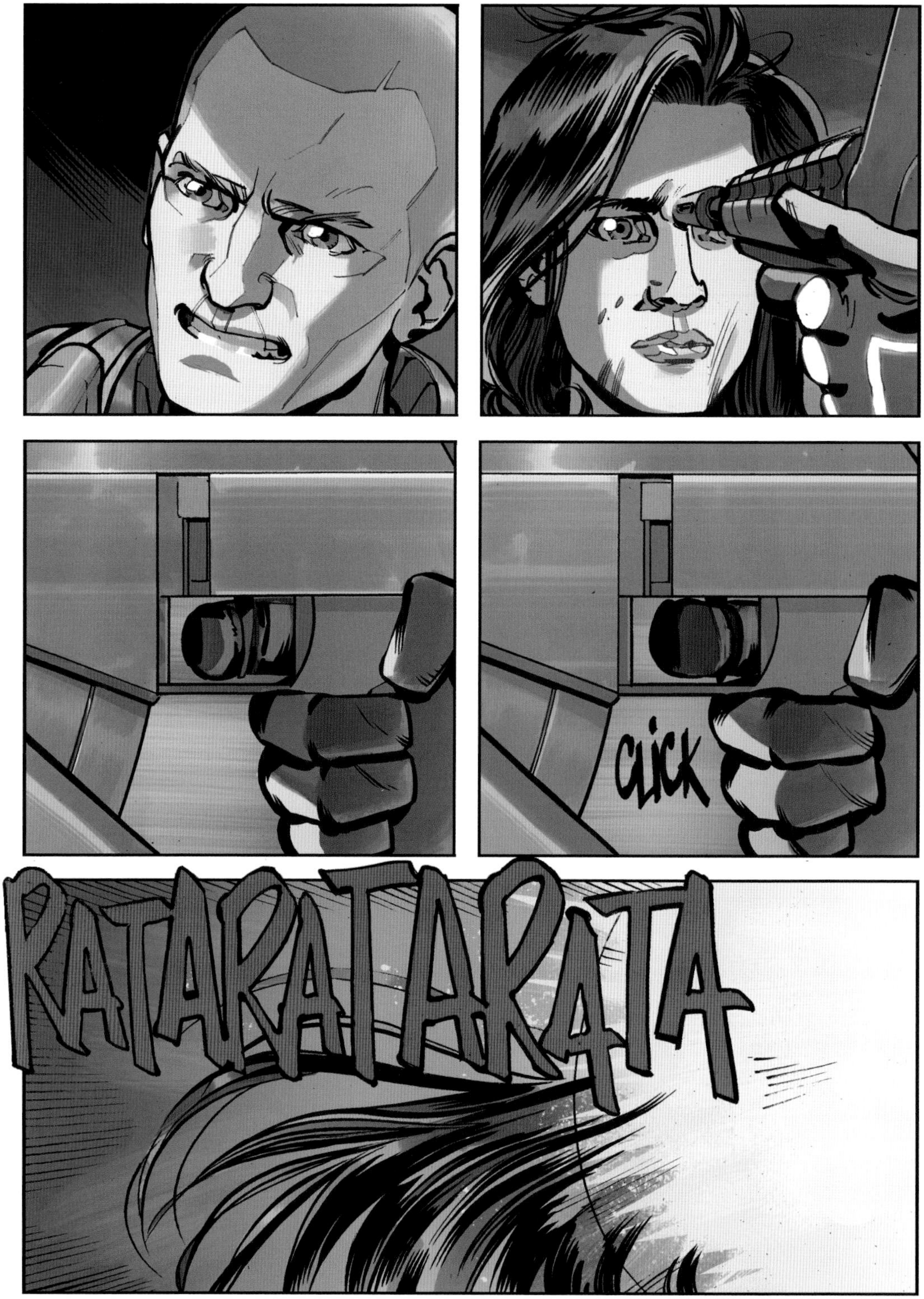
CLICK
RATATARATATARATA

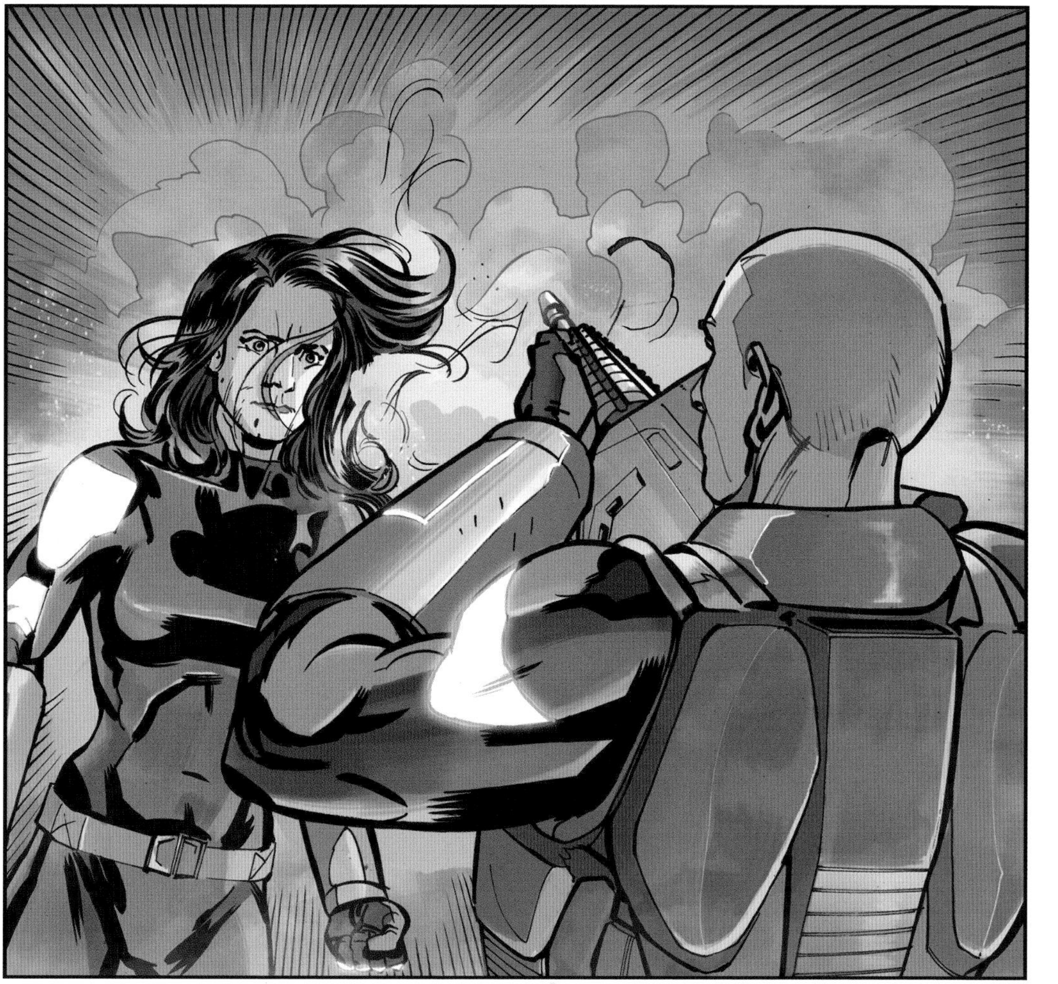

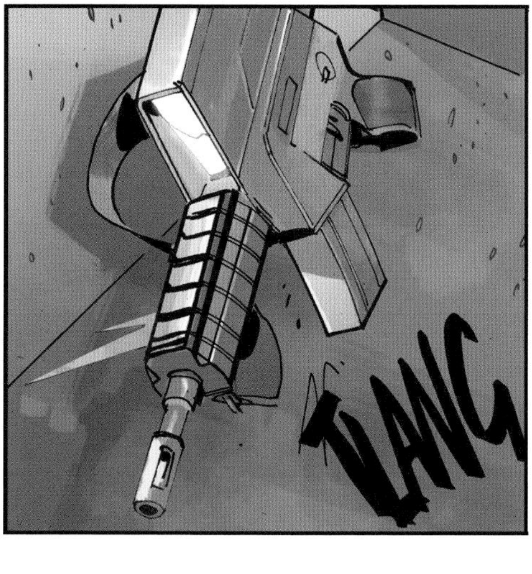
TANG

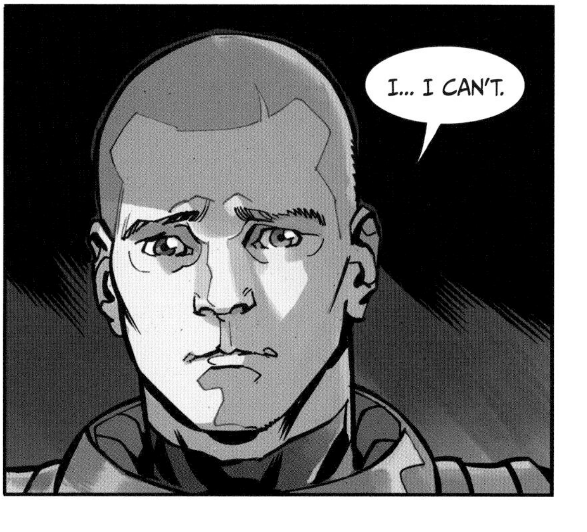
I... I CAN'T.

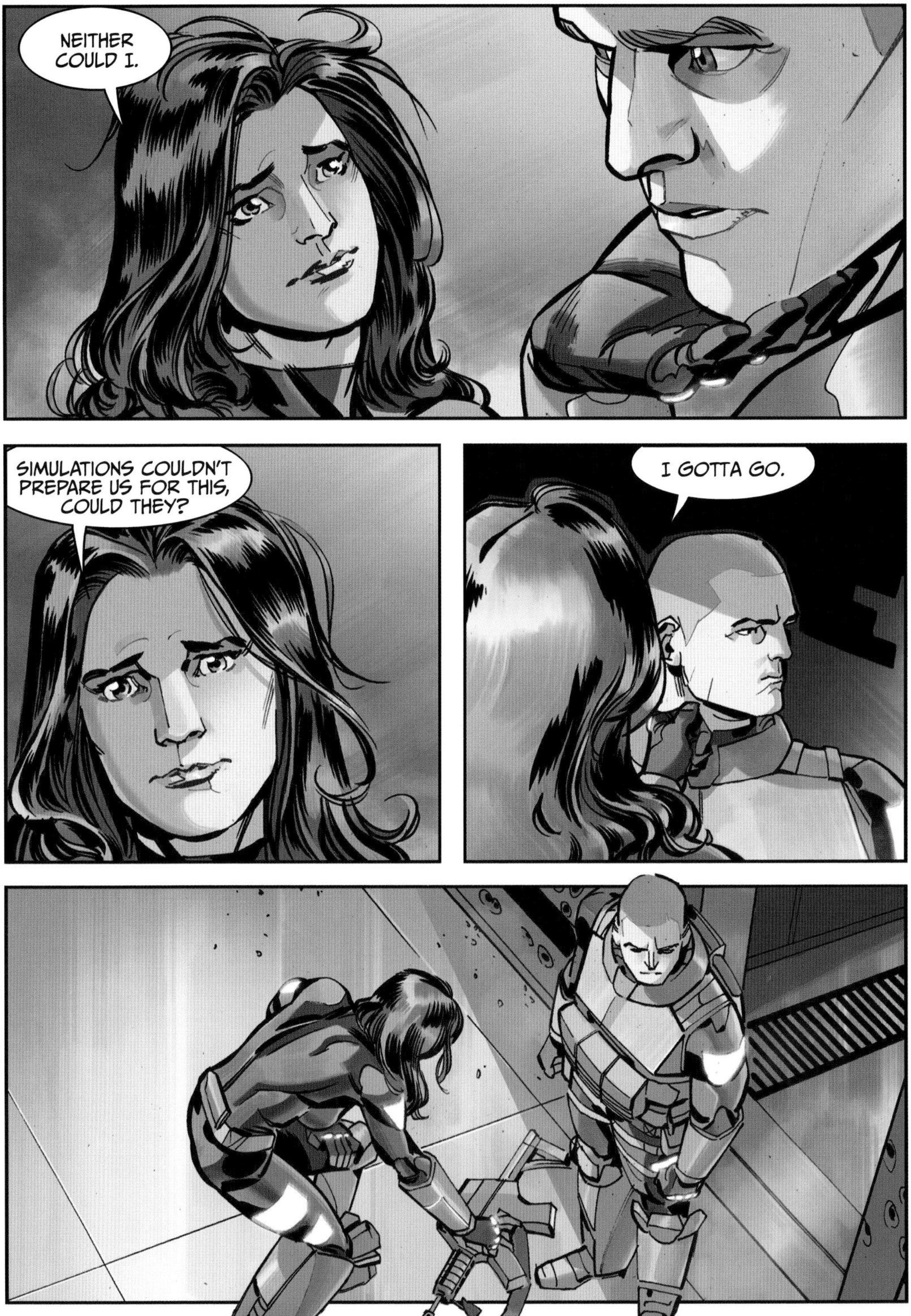
NEITHER COULD I.
SIMULATIONS COULDN'T PREPARE US FOR THIS, COULD THEY?
I GOTTA GO.

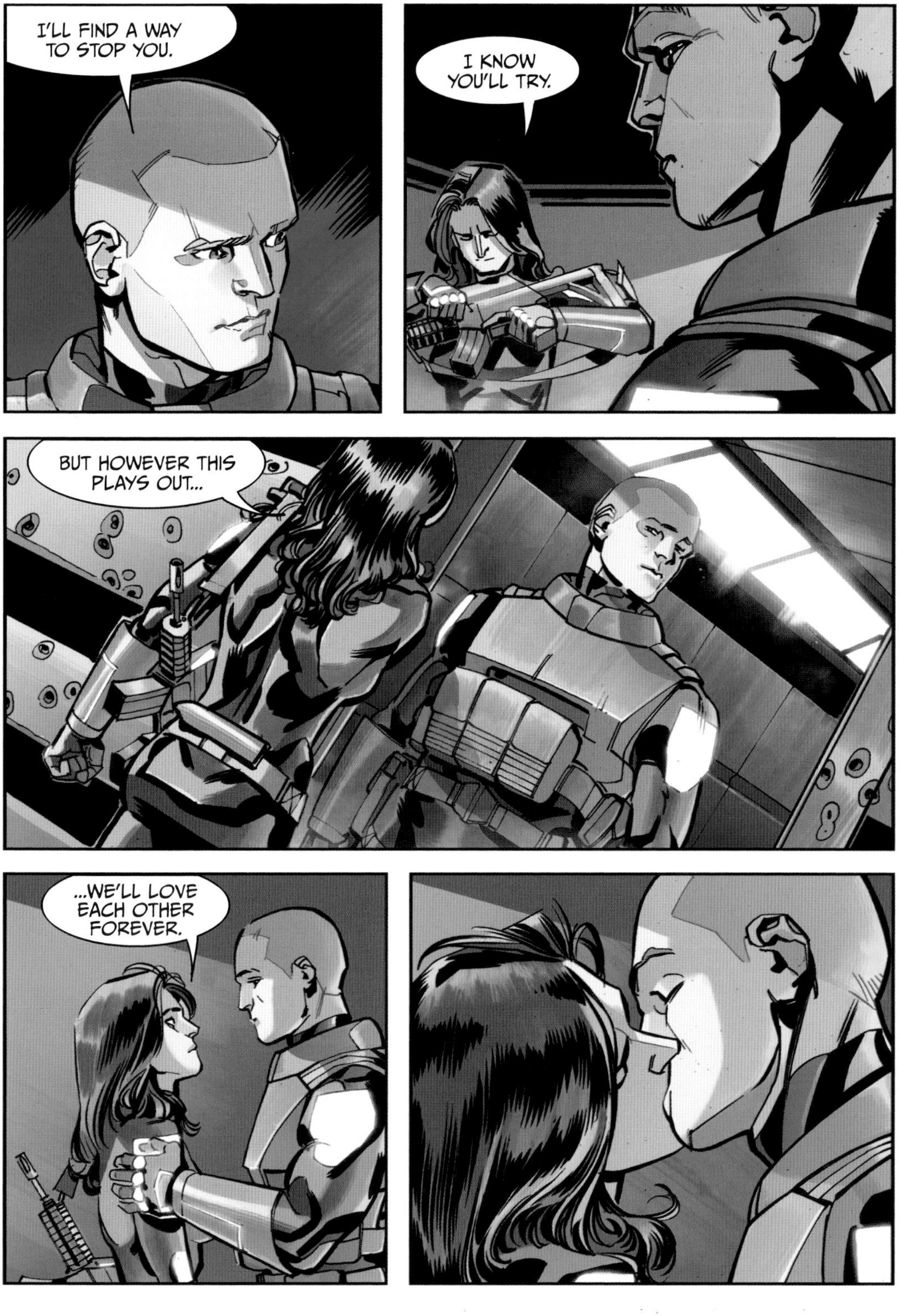
I'LL FIND A WAY TO STOP YOU.
I KNOW YOU'LL TRY.
BUT HOWEVER THIS PLAYS OUT...
...WE'LL LOVE EACH OTHER FOREVER.

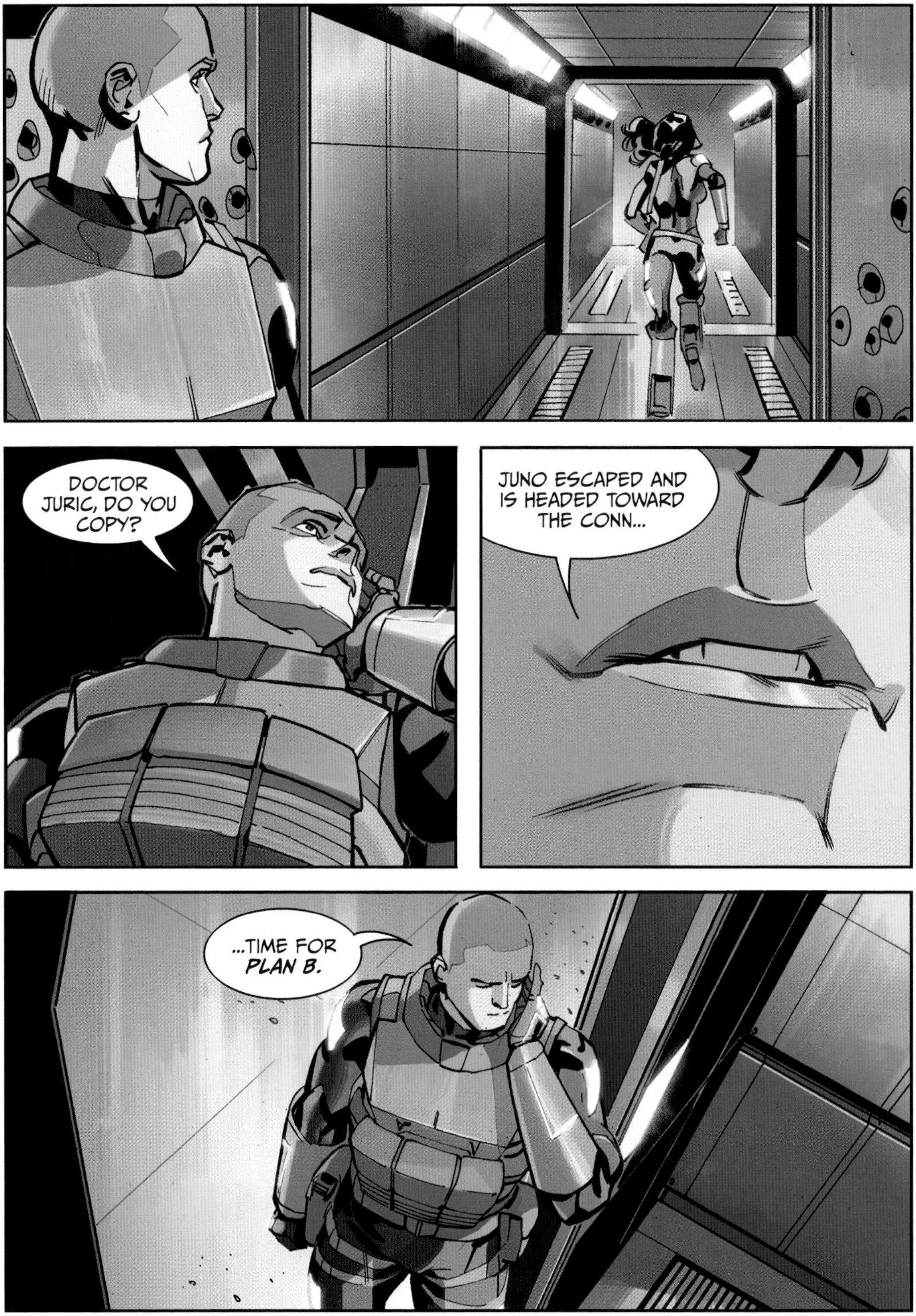
DOCTOR JURIC, DO YOU COPY?
JUNO ESCAPED AND IS HEADED TOWARD THE CONN...
...TIME FOR *PLAN B.*

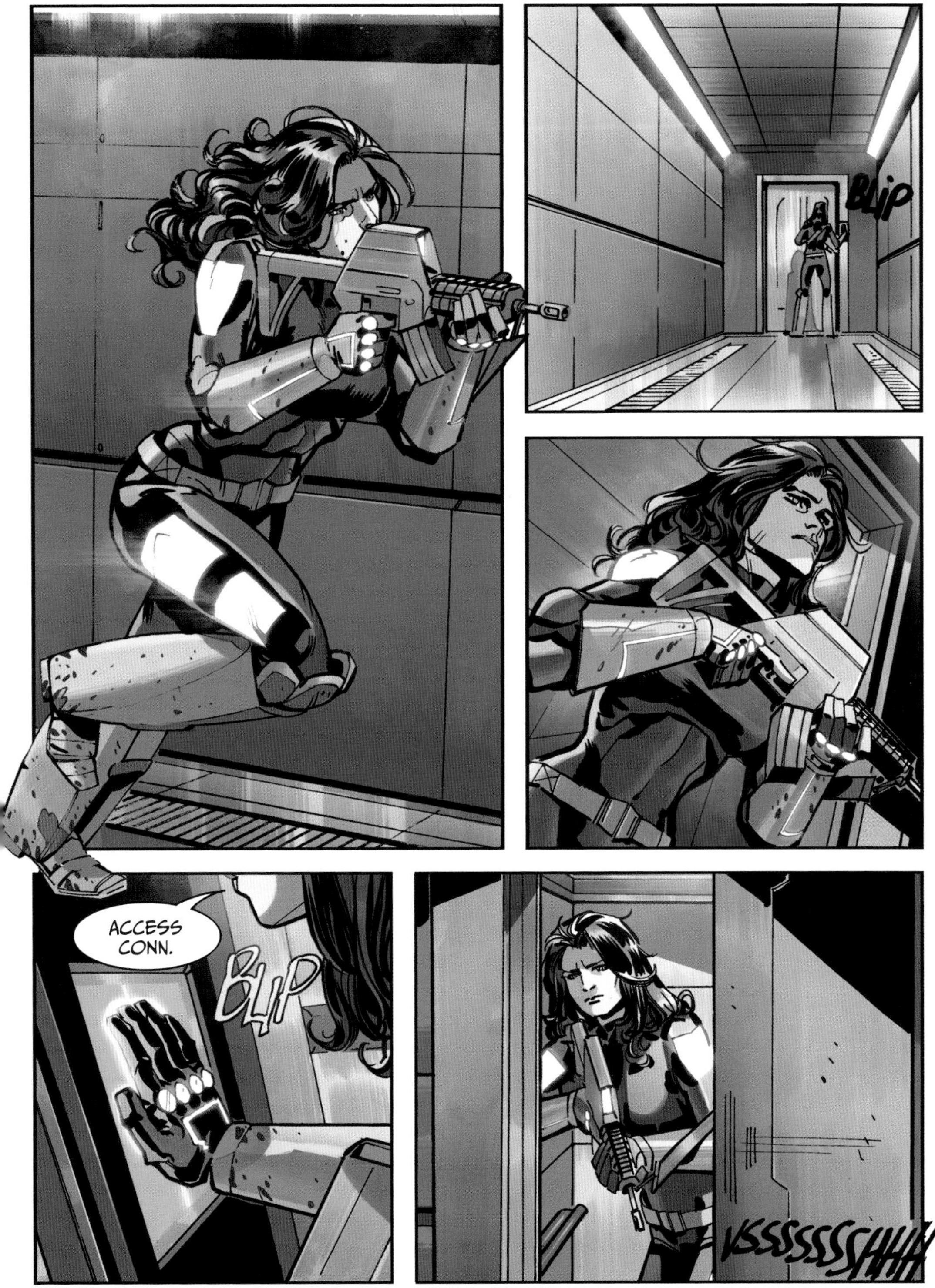
BLIP
ACCESS CONN.
BLIP
VSSSSSSSSHHH

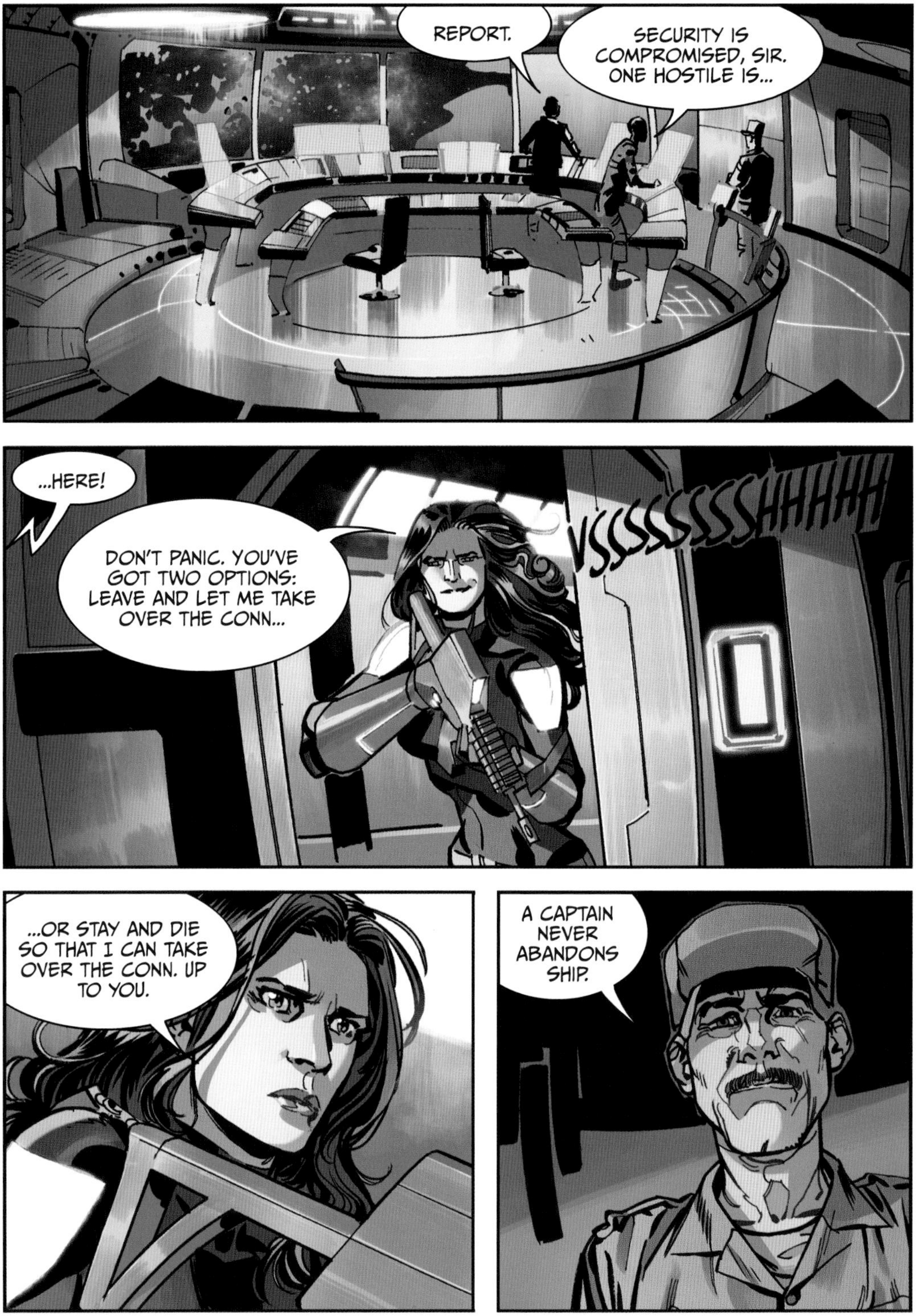
REPORT.
SECURITY IS COMPROMISED, SIR. ONE HOSTILE IS...
...HERE!
DON'T PANIC. YOU'VE GOT TWO OPTIONS: LEAVE AND LET ME TAKE OVER THE CONN...
VSSSSSSSSHHHHH
...OR STAY AND DIE SO THAT I CAN TAKE OVER THE CONN. UP TO YOU.
A CAPTAIN NEVER ABANDONS SHIP.

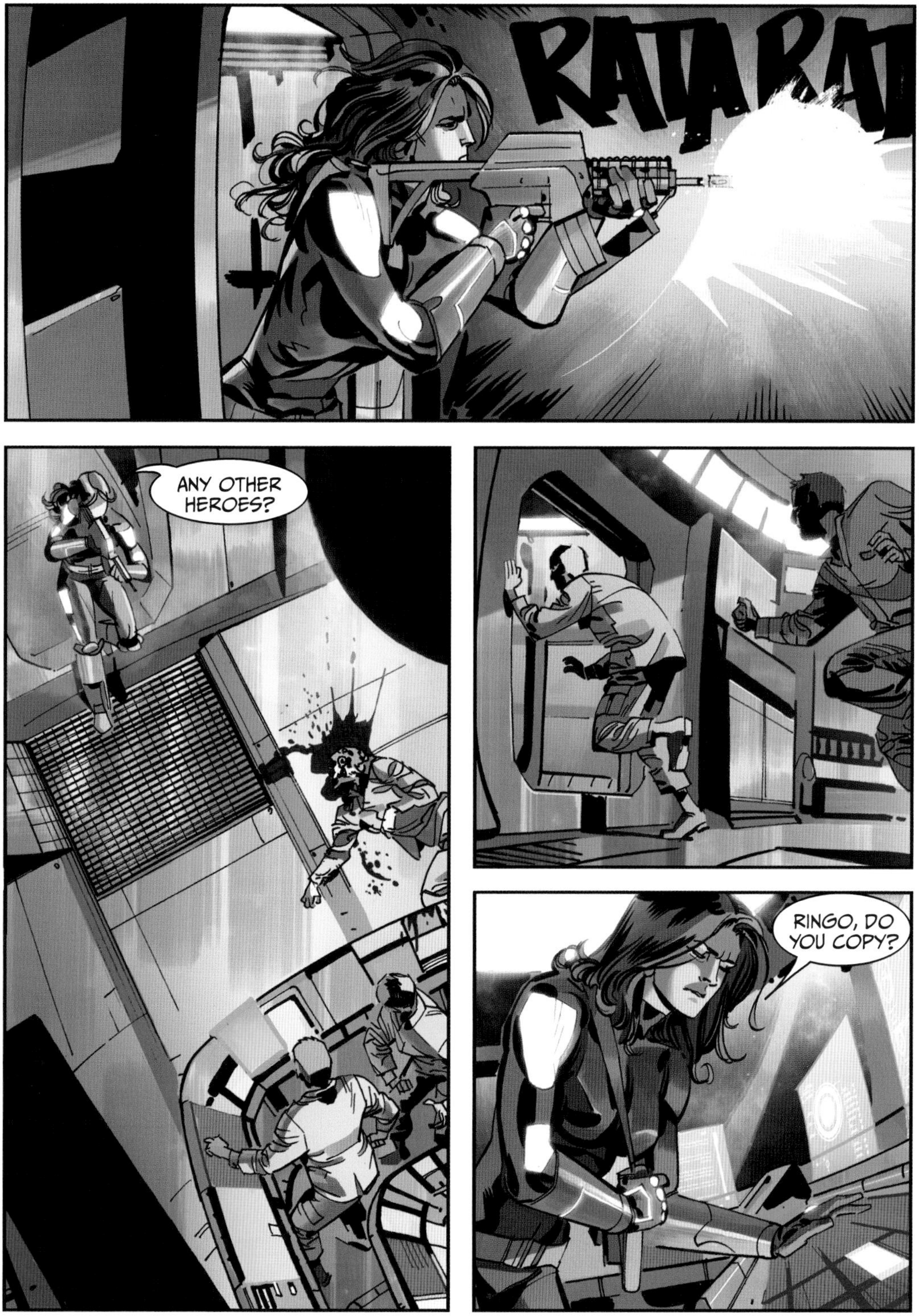
RATARAT
ANY OTHER HEROES?
RINGO, DO YOU COPY?

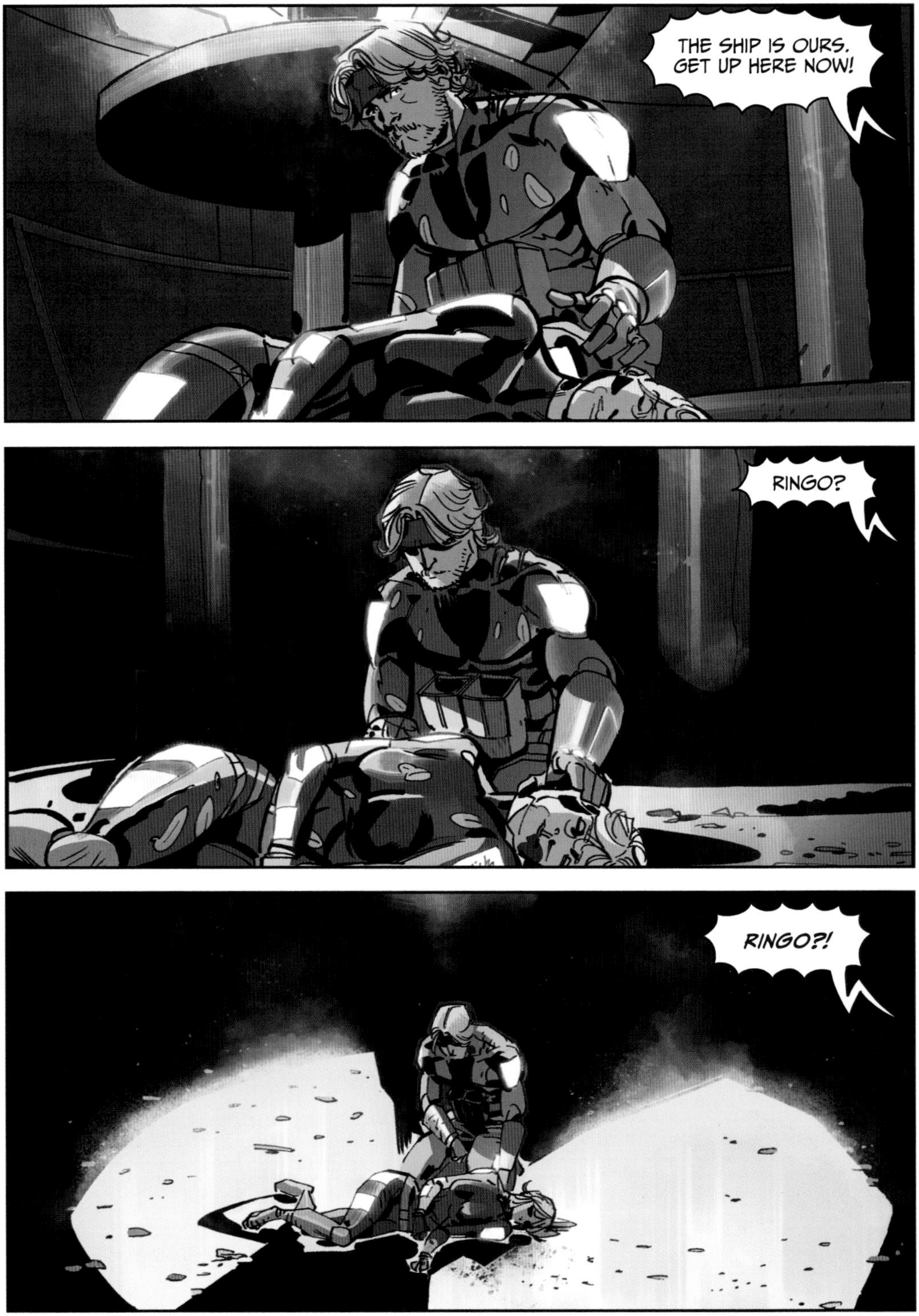
THE SHIP IS OURS. GET UP HERE NOW!
RINGO?
RINGO?!

MATTEO CREMONA   **ARTIST**

When and where were you born? Where do you live now?
I was born in Como, Italy, on March 20, 1981, and I currently live in Milan.

What sort of artistic education did you have?
I attended the Technical Institute for textile design in Como. Then, after five years of tablecloths and ties, I enrolled at the Comics School in Milan, where I studied for two years.

Tell us about your previous works, before *Orphans*.
I was part of the art team for *John Doe*, published by Eura Editoriale, for which I drew three issues. After that, I worked with Roberto Recchioni on *Eddie Murphy: 911*, a four-volume mini-series published by Panini Comics.

When did you start working on *Orphans*, and when did you finish drawing this chapter?
I started at the beginning of 2013 and finished in April 2014.

What tools did you use?
I did everything on paper, with pencil and ink. For the inking part, I used a brush almost exclusively.

What was the most difficult scene, and which one did you have to redraw more times?
In terms of difficulty, the toughest pages were the first twenty, not due to actual complexity of the drawings, but mainly because of the trouble I had getting used to the style and the characters; I hope I managed to figure these issues out and solve them as best as I could while drawing this chapter.

If you could go back in time, what would you change about this chapter?
The whole mid-sequence with the "static" dialogue among the five orphans gathered on the landing strip at Ridgeback Camp. I'd work on the characters' movements some more, their acting and expressions.

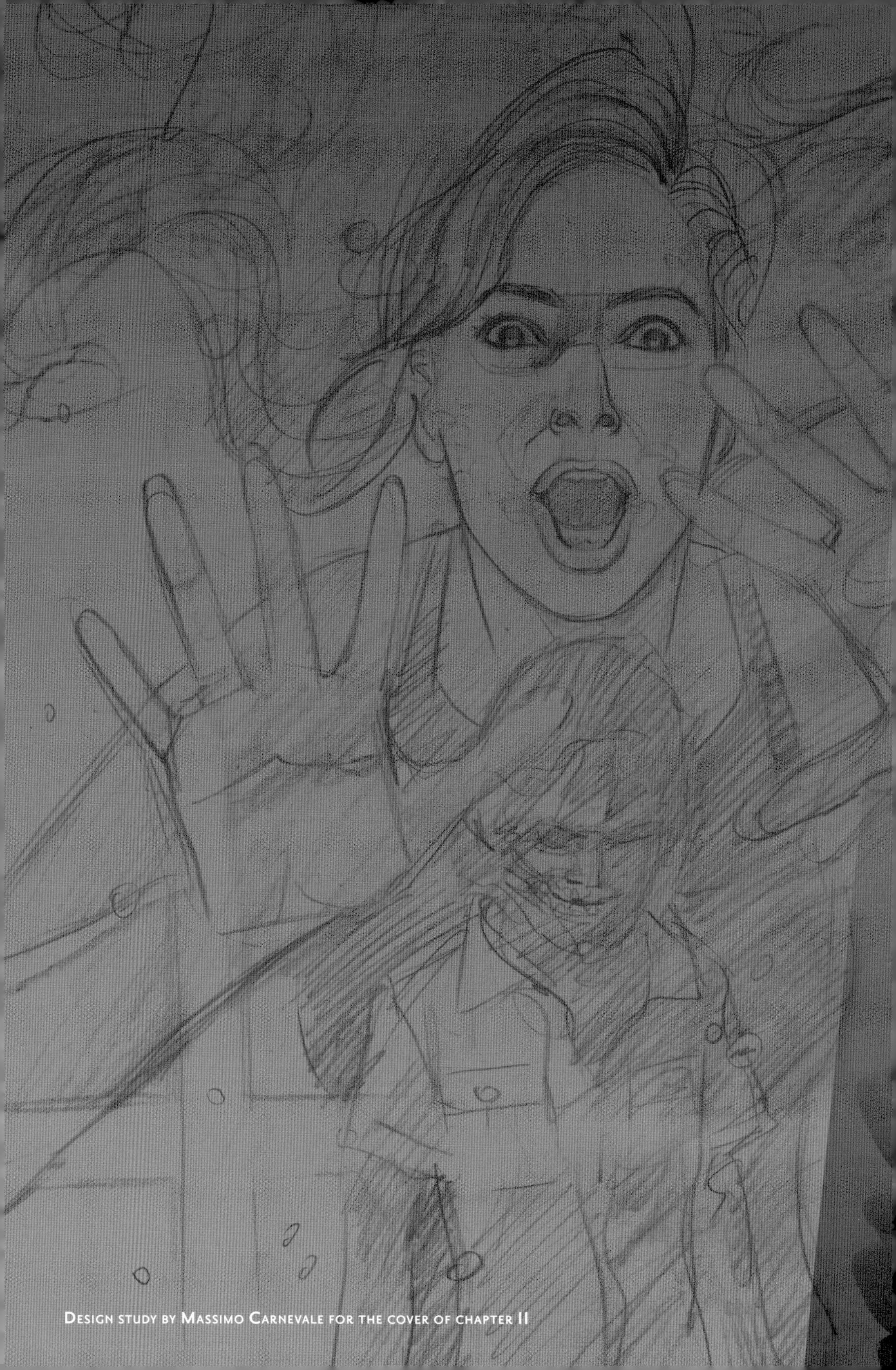

Design study by Massimo Carnevale for the cover of chapter II

WE ALL FALL DOWN

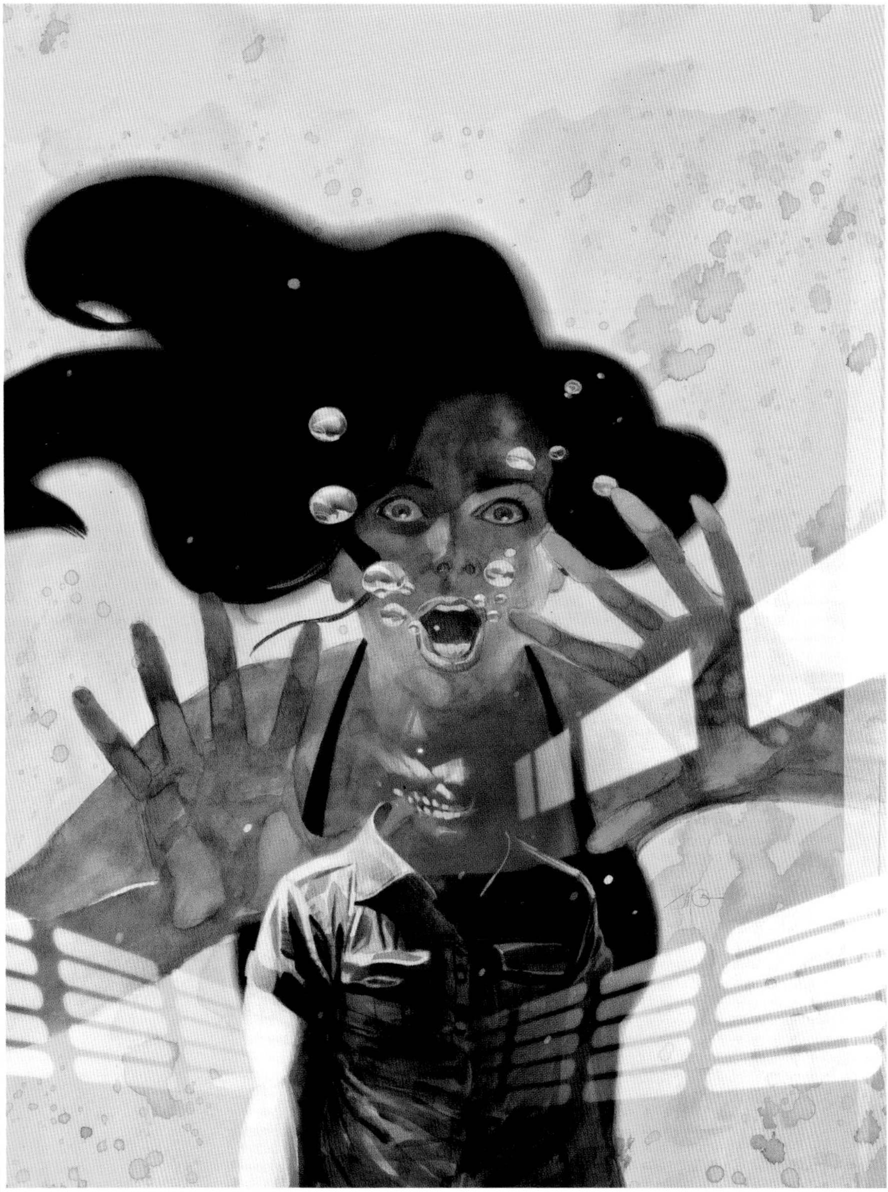

ORPHANS: CHAPTER 11

story: ROBERTO RECCHIONI
art: WERTHER DELL'EDERA and GIGI CAVENAGO
colors: GIOVANNA NIRO, ALESSIA PASTORELLO and GIGI CAVENAGO
cover: MASSIMO CARNEVALE

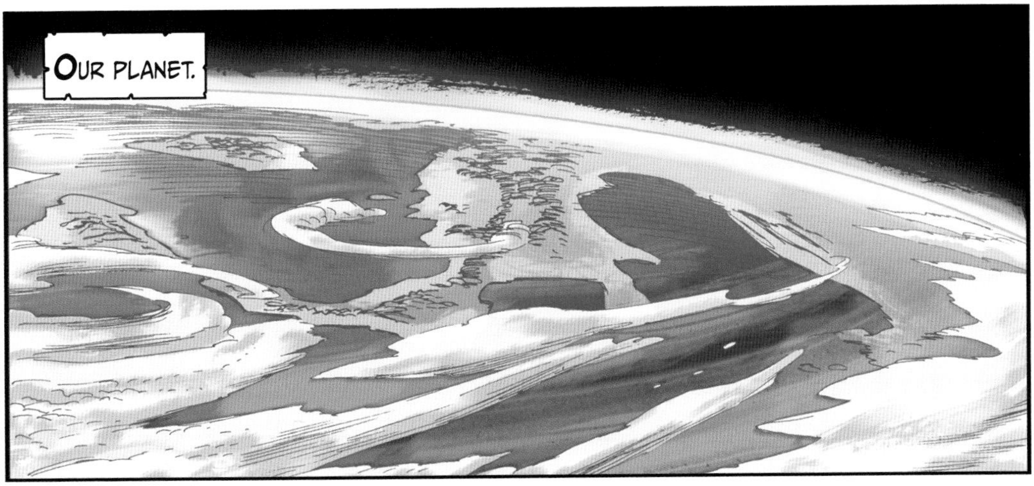
OUR PLANET.

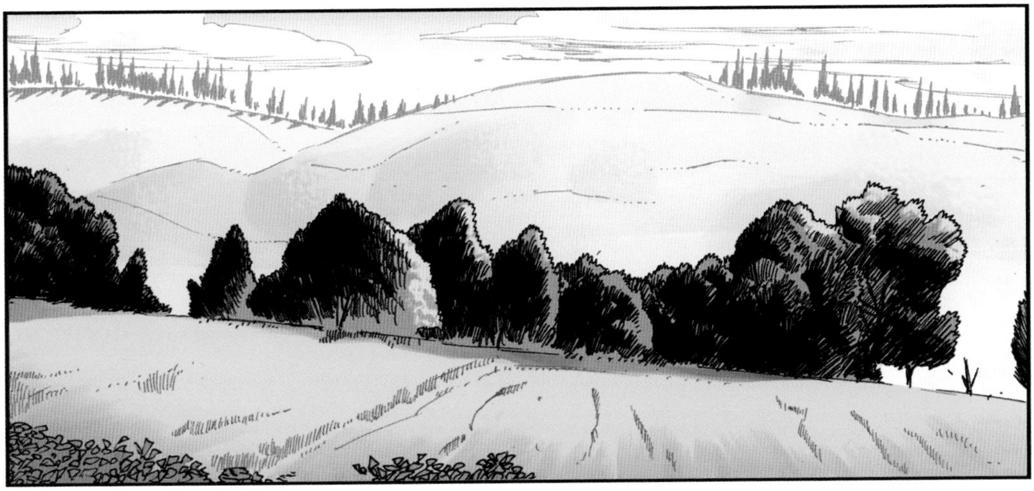

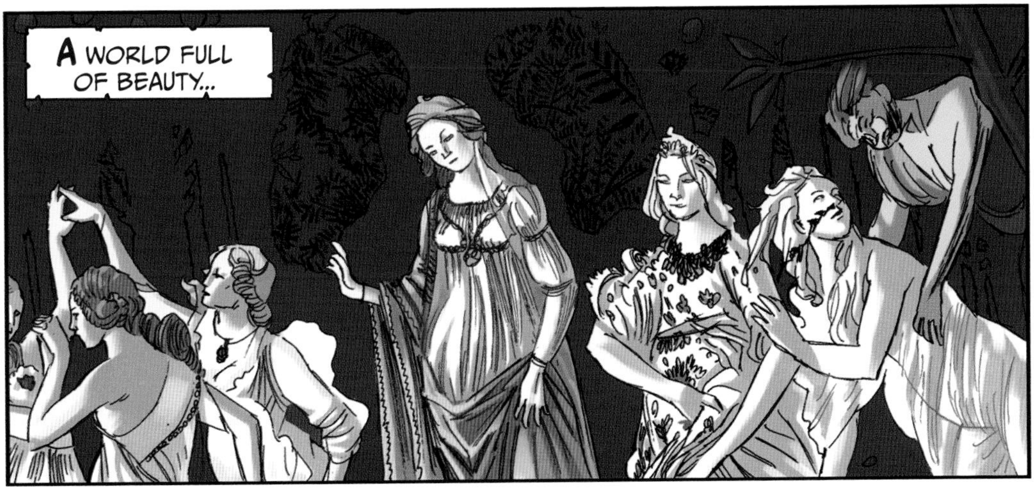
A WORLD FULL
OF BEAUTY...

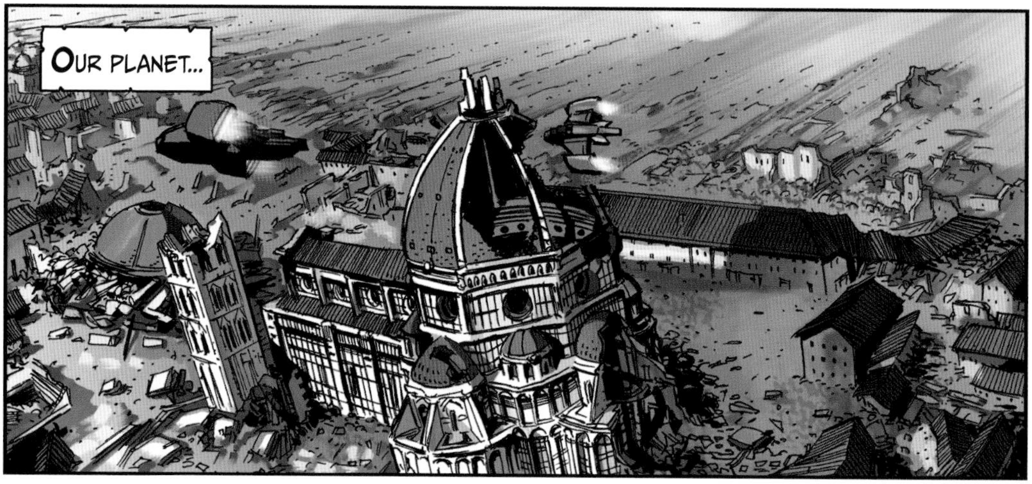
OUR PLANET...

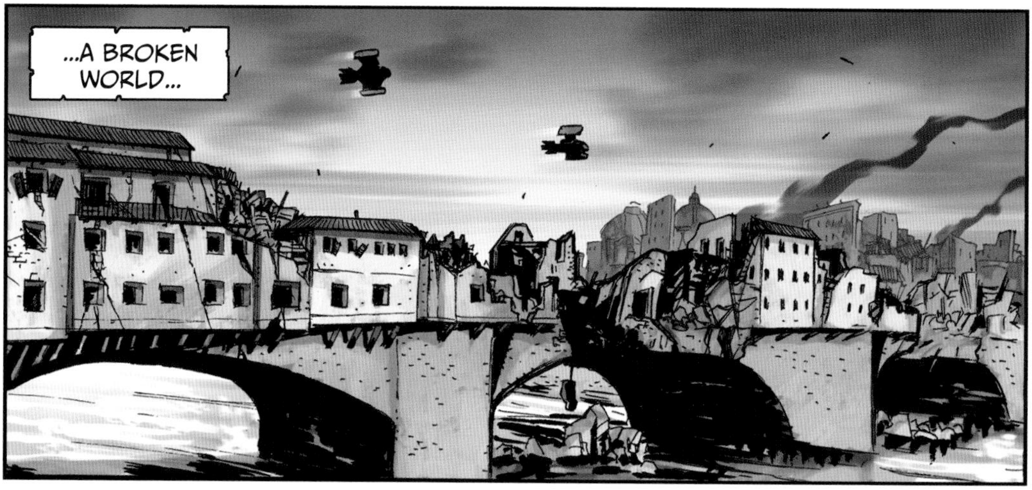
...A BROKEN WORLD...

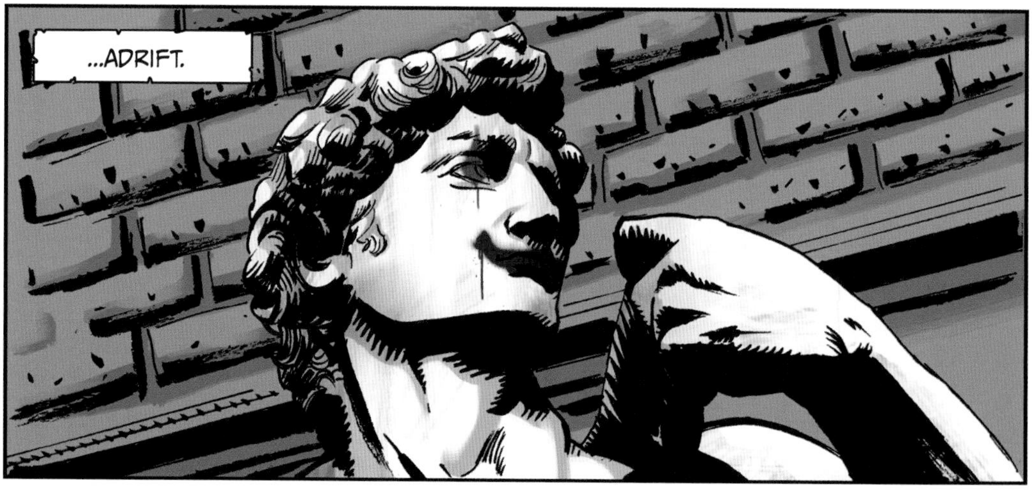
...ADRIFT.

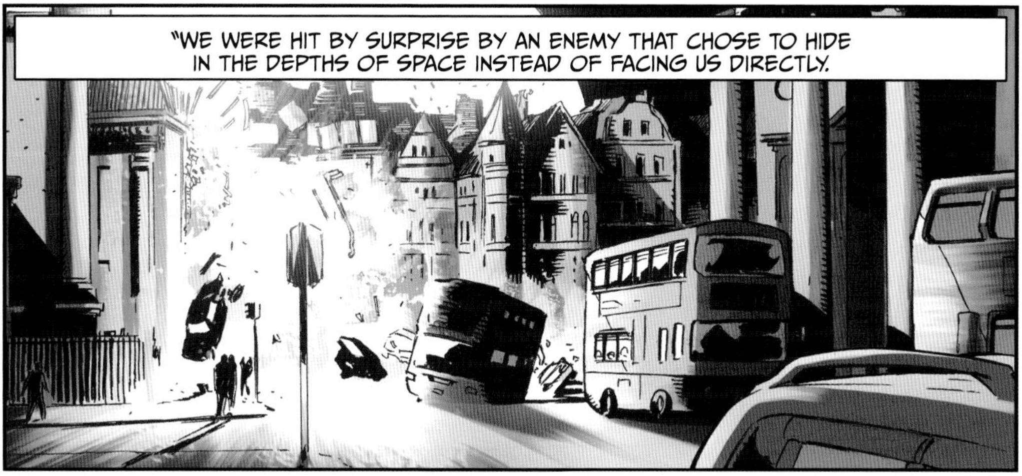
"WE WERE HIT BY SURPRISE BY AN ENEMY THAT CHOSE TO HIDE IN THE DEPTHS OF SPACE INSTEAD OF FACING US DIRECTLY.

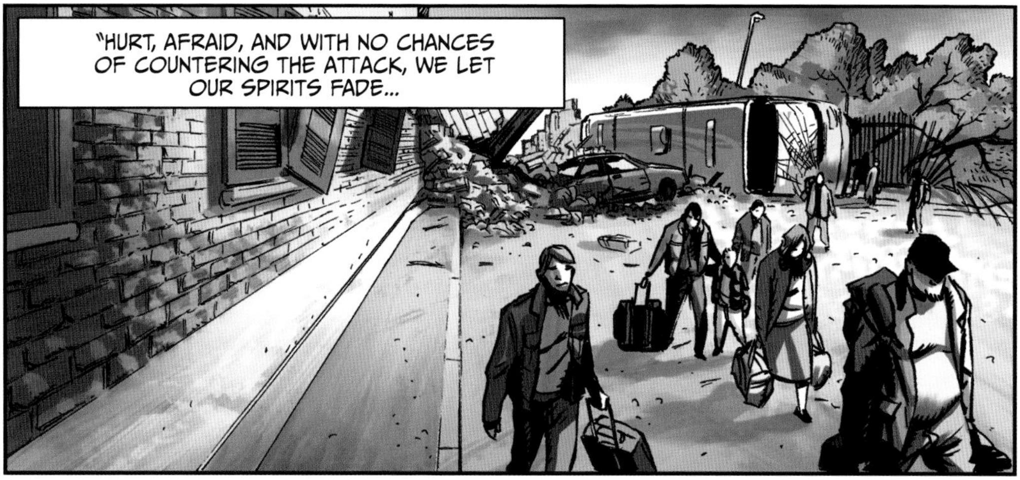
"HURT, AFRAID, AND WITH NO CHANCES OF COUNTERING THE ATTACK, WE LET OUR SPIRITS FADE...

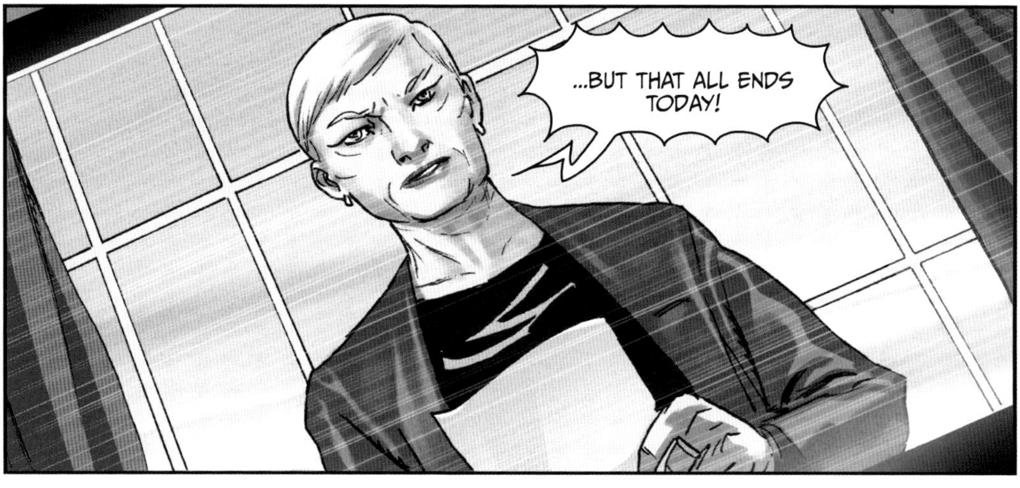
...BUT THAT ALL ENDS TODAY!

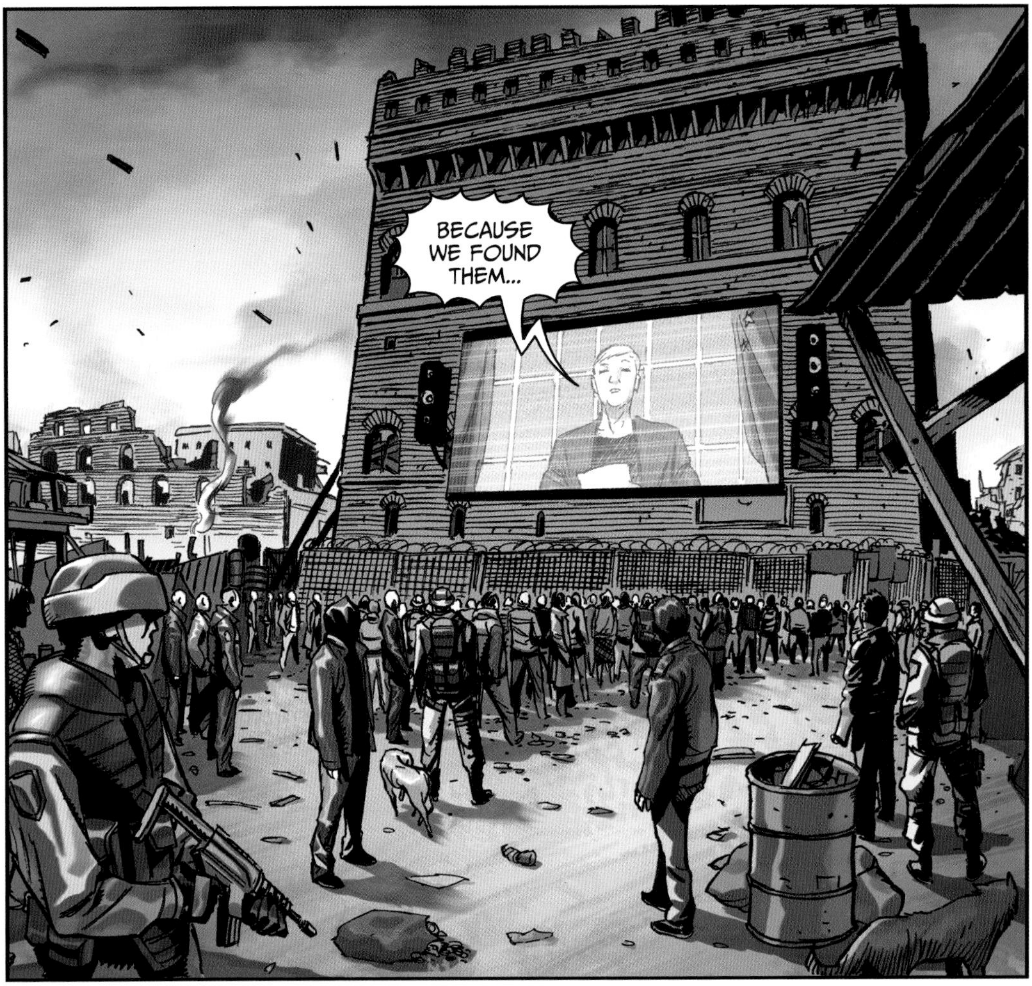
BECAUSE WE FOUND THEM...

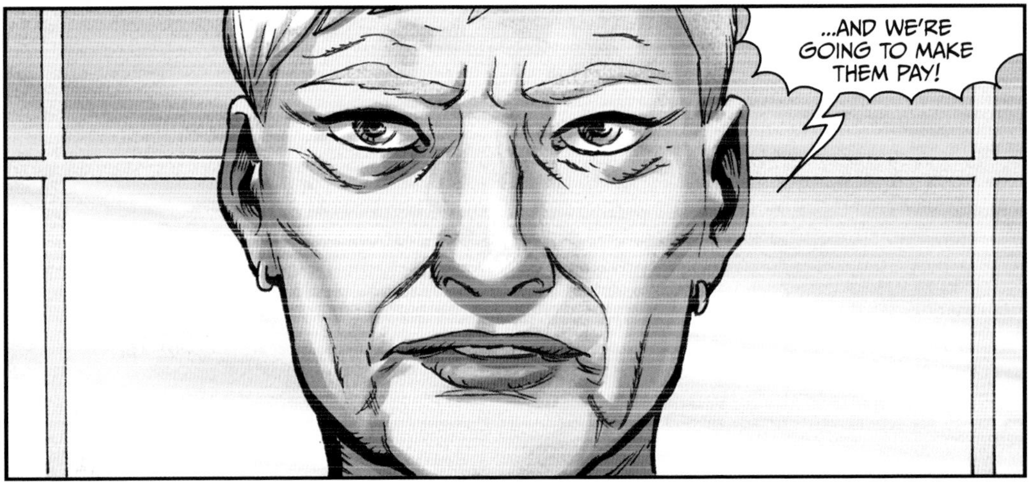
...AND WE'RE GOING TO MAKE THEM PAY!

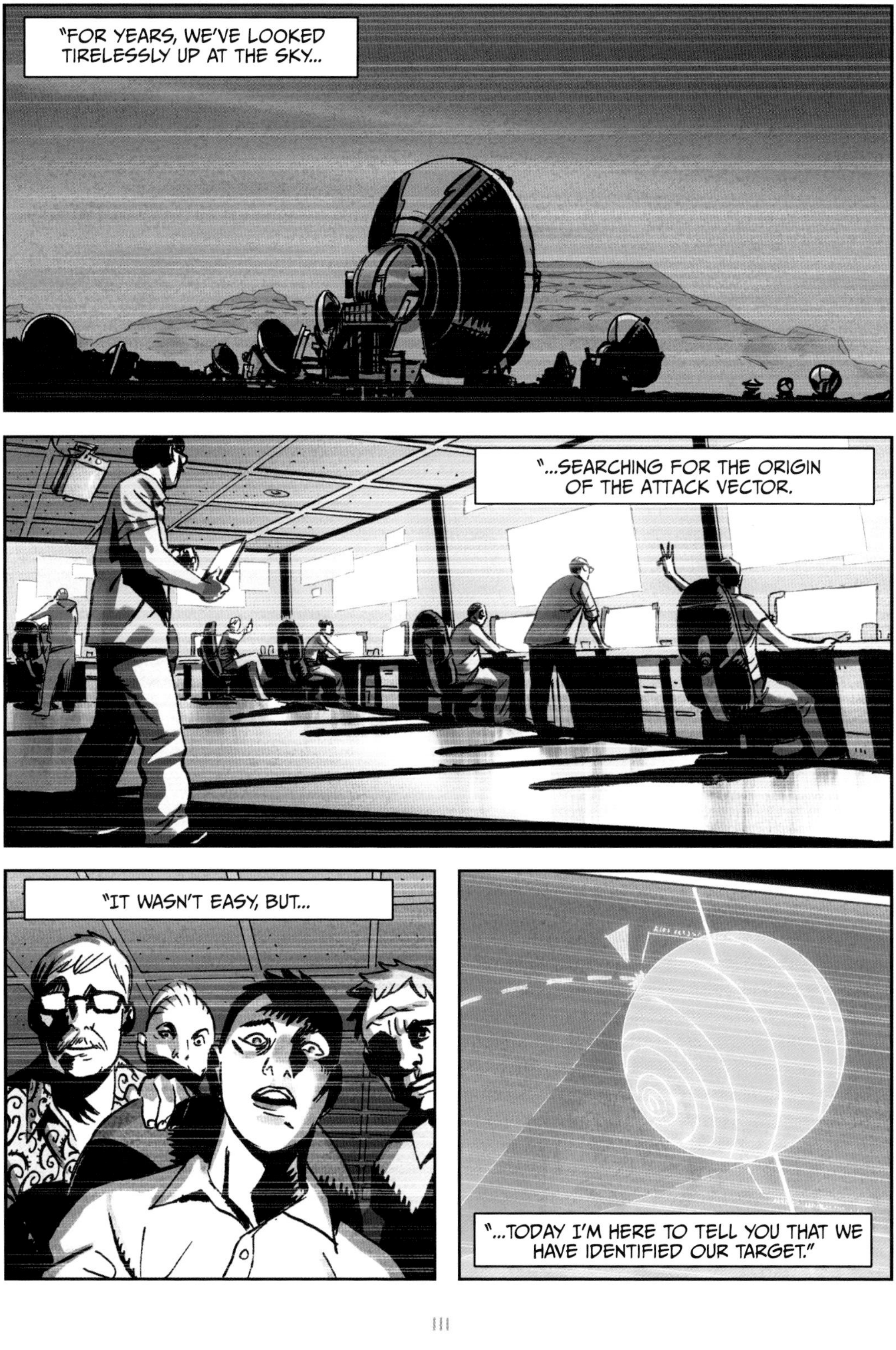
"FOR YEARS, WE'VE LOOKED TIRELESSLY UP AT THE SKY...
"...SEARCHING FOR THE ORIGIN OF THE ATTACK VECTOR.
"IT WASN'T EASY, BUT...
"...TODAY I'M HERE TO TELL YOU THAT WE HAVE IDENTIFIED OUR TARGET."

THE ENEMY PLANET IS FAR AWAY, UNIMAGINABLY FAR. BUT THAT WON'T STOP US!

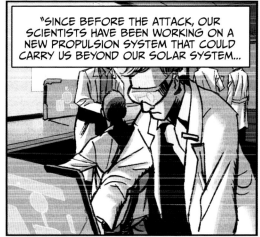

"SINCE BEFORE THE ATTACK, OUR SCIENTISTS HAVE BEEN WORKING ON A NEW PROPULSION SYSTEM THAT COULD CARRY US BEYOND OUR SOLAR SYSTEM...

"THEY CALL IT THE *EPR ACCELERATOR.*

"THREE BATTLESHIPS ARE BEING COMPLETED AS I NOW SPEAK TO YOU..."

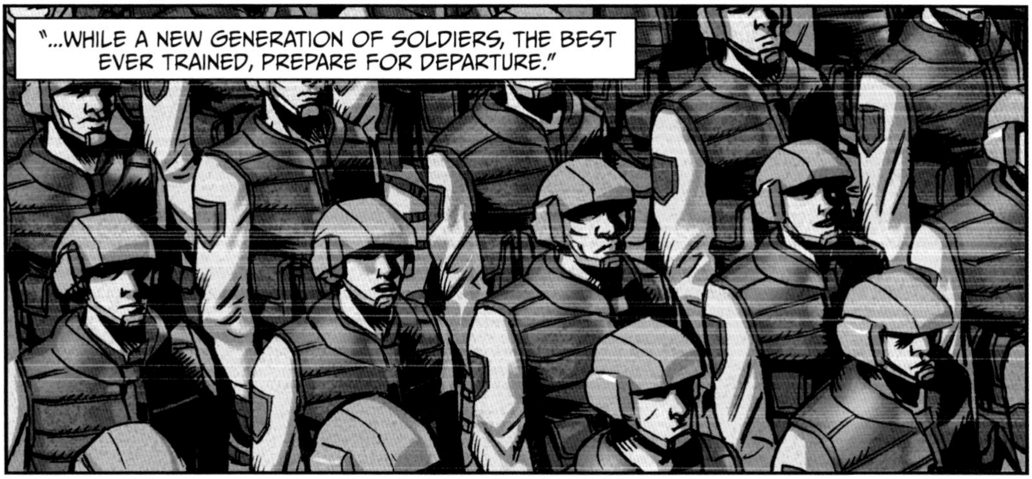
"...WHILE A NEW GENERATION OF SOLDIERS, THE BEST EVER TRAINED, PREPARE FOR DEPARTURE."

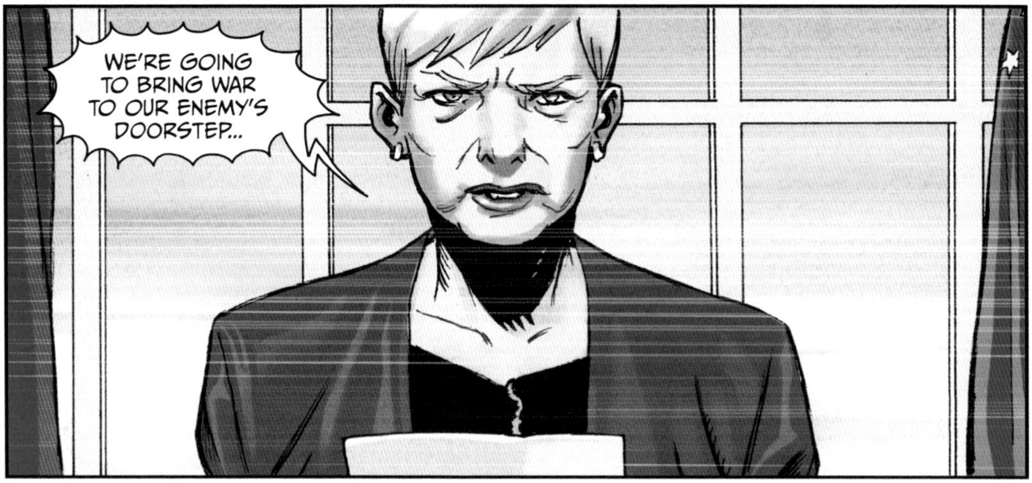
WE'RE GOING TO BRING WAR TO OUR ENEMY'S DOORSTEP...

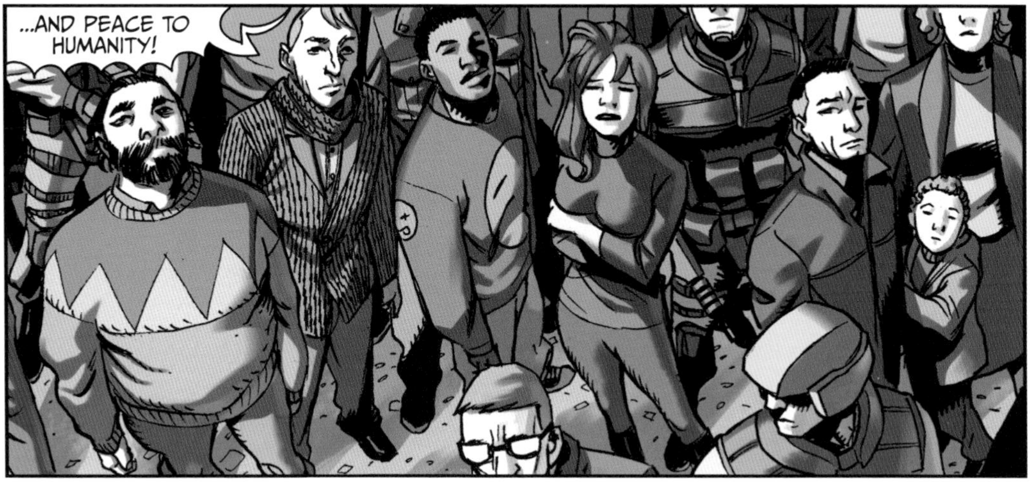
...AND PEACE TO HUMANITY!

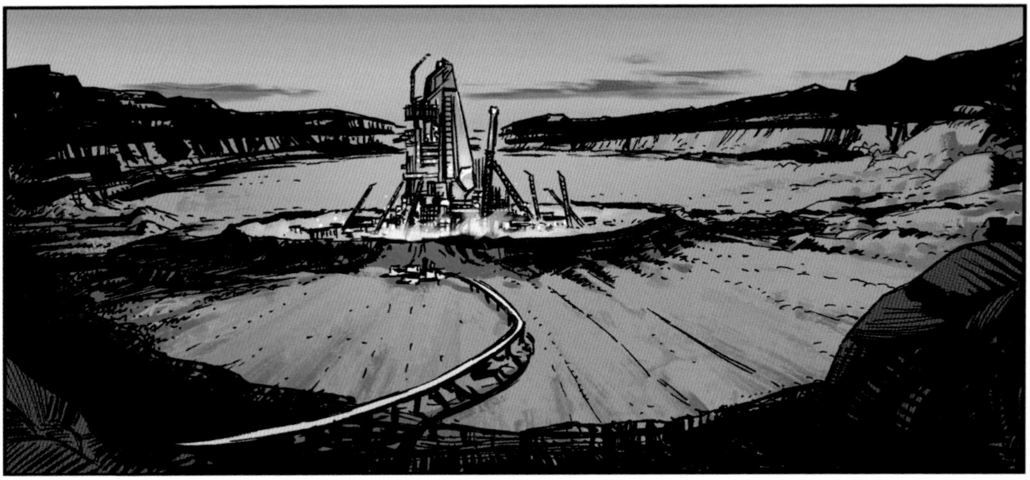

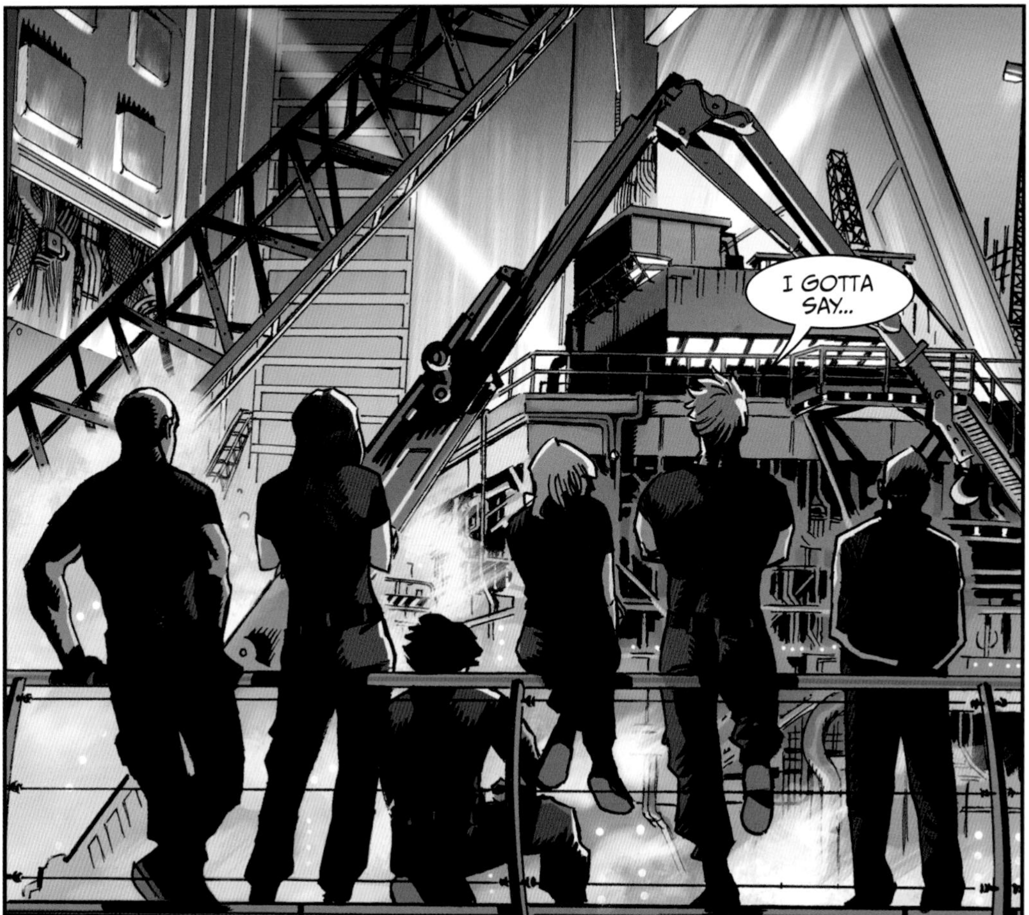
I GOTTA SAY...

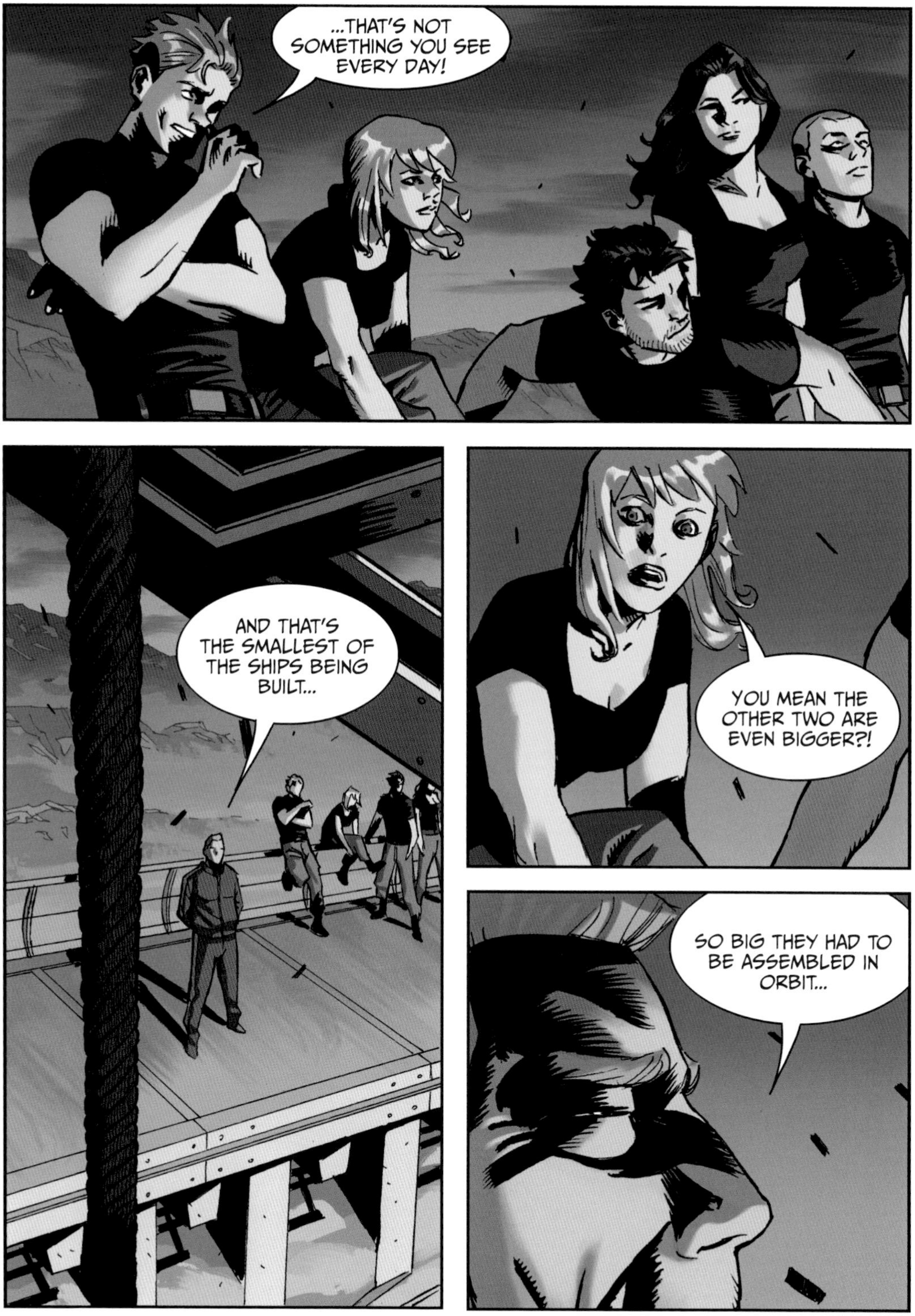
...THAT'S NOT SOMETHING YOU SEE EVERY DAY!
AND THAT'S THE SMALLEST OF THE SHIPS BEING BUILT...
YOU MEAN THE OTHER TWO ARE EVEN BIGGER?!
SO BIG THEY HAD TO BE ASSEMBLED IN ORBIT...

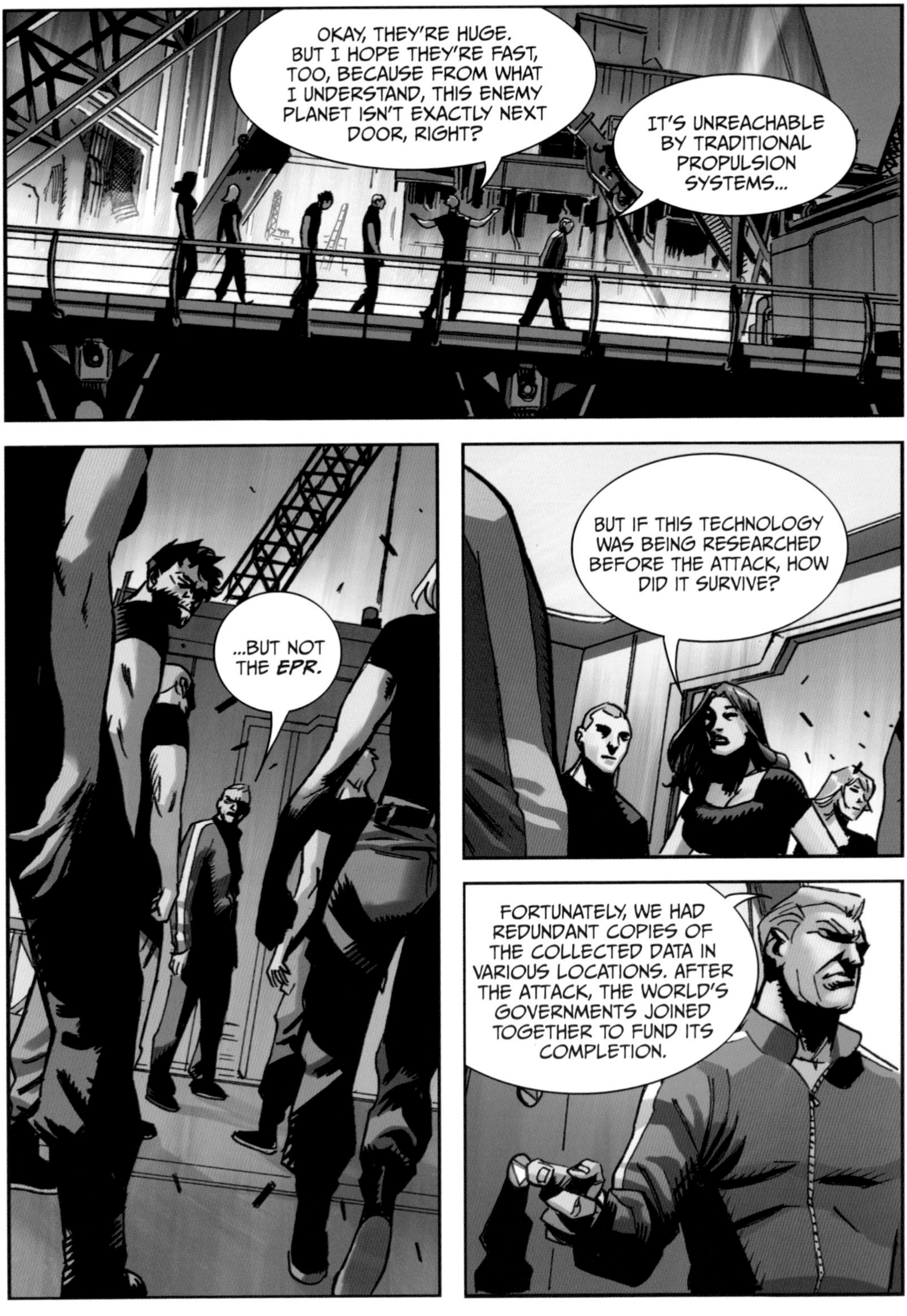
OKAY, THEY'RE HUGE. BUT I HOPE THEY'RE FAST, TOO, BECAUSE FROM WHAT I UNDERSTAND, THIS ENEMY PLANET ISN'T EXACTLY NEXT DOOR, RIGHT?
IT'S UNREACHABLE BY TRADITIONAL PROPULSION SYSTEMS...
...BUT NOT THE *EPR.*
BUT IF THIS TECHNOLOGY WAS BEING RESEARCHED BEFORE THE ATTACK, HOW DID IT SURVIVE?
FORTUNATELY, WE HAD REDUNDANT COPIES OF THE COLLECTED DATA IN VARIOUS LOCATIONS. AFTER THE ATTACK, THE WORLD'S GOVERNMENTS JOINED TOGETHER TO FUND ITS COMPLETION.

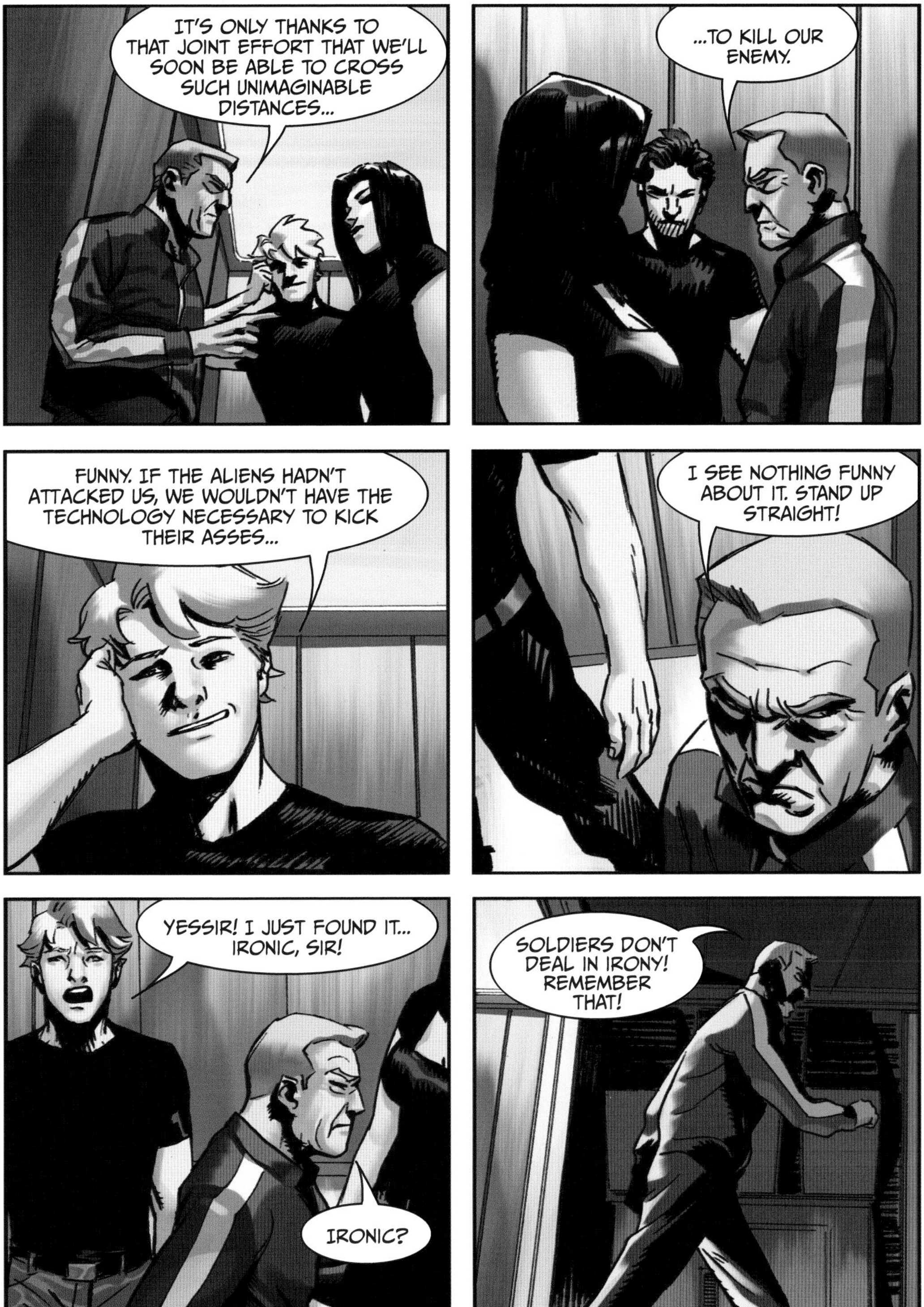
IT'S ONLY THANKS TO THAT JOINT EFFORT THAT WE'LL SOON BE ABLE TO CROSS SUCH UNIMAGINABLE DISTANCES...
...TO KILL OUR ENEMY.
FUNNY. IF THE ALIENS HADN'T ATTACKED US, WE WOULDN'T HAVE THE TECHNOLOGY NECESSARY TO KICK THEIR ASSES...
I SEE NOTHING FUNNY ABOUT IT. STAND UP STRAIGHT!
YESSIR! I JUST FOUND IT... IRONIC, SIR!
IRONIC?
SOLDIERS DON'T DEAL IN IRONY! REMEMBER THAT!

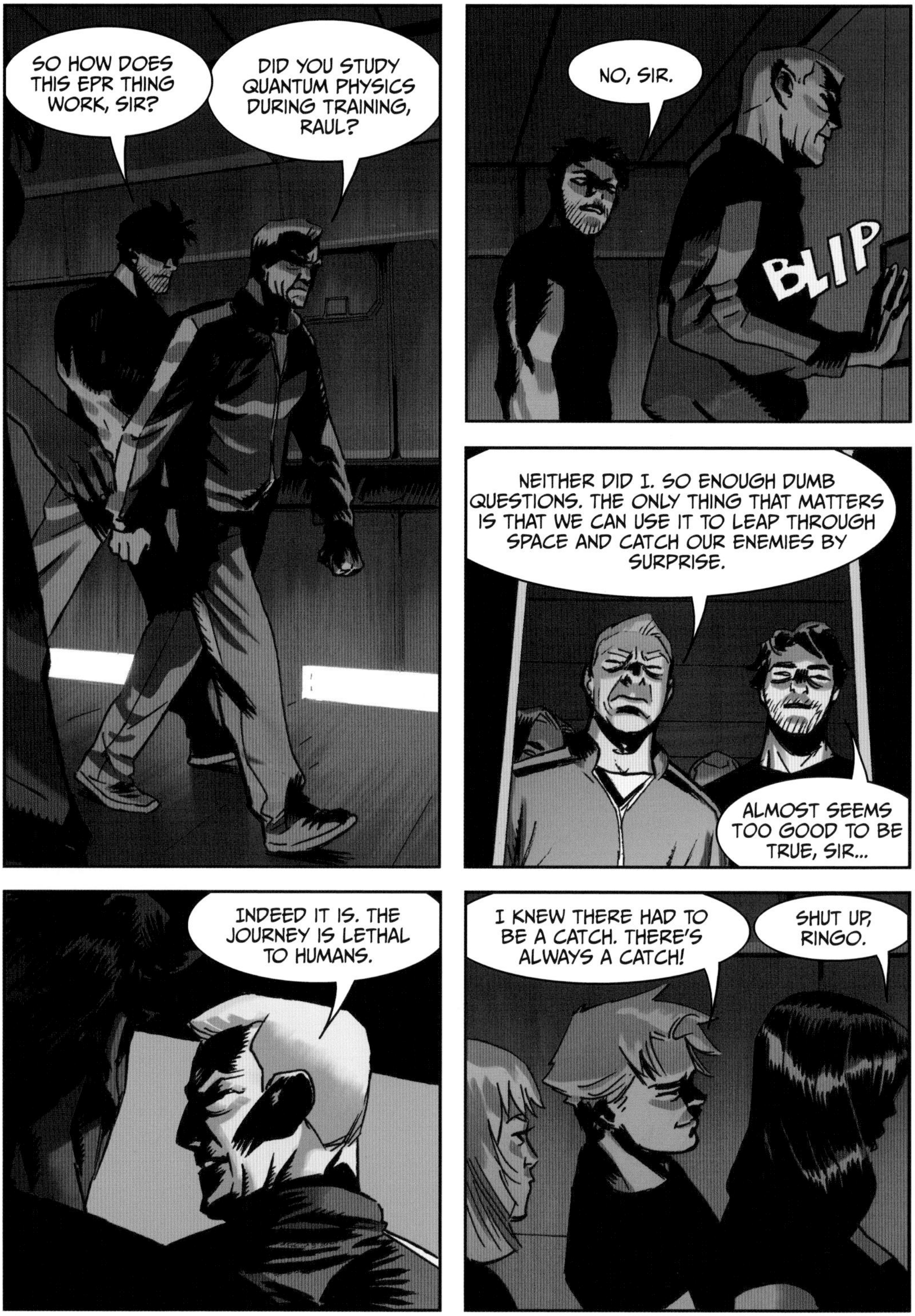
SO HOW DOES THIS EPR THING WORK, SIR?
DID YOU STUDY QUANTUM PHYSICS DURING TRAINING, RAUL?
NO, SIR.
BLIP
NEITHER DID I. SO ENOUGH DUMB QUESTIONS. THE ONLY THING THAT MATTERS IS THAT WE CAN USE IT TO LEAP THROUGH SPACE AND CATCH OUR ENEMIES BY SURPRISE.
ALMOST SEEMS TOO GOOD TO BE TRUE, SIR...
INDEED IT IS. THE JOURNEY IS LETHAL TO HUMANS.
I KNEW THERE HAD TO BE A CATCH. THERE'S ALWAYS A CATCH!
SHUT UP, RINGO.

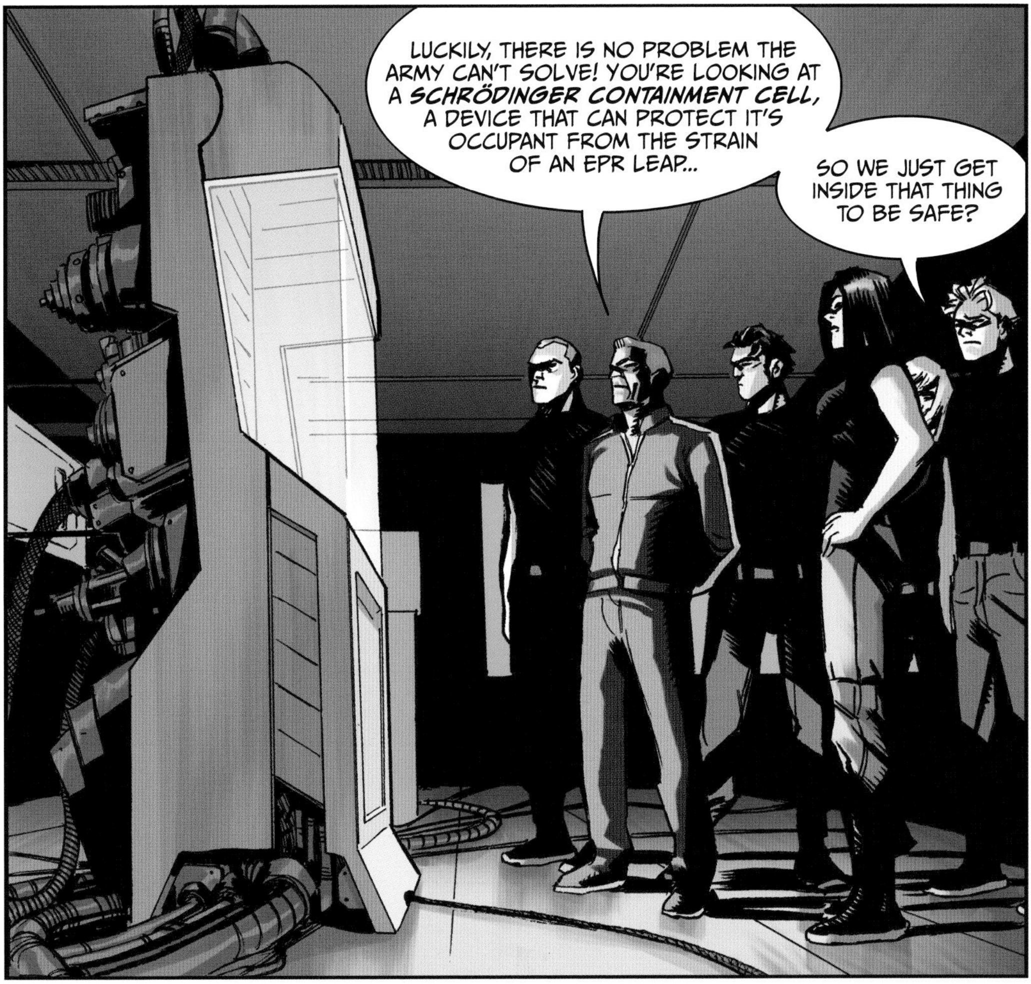
LUCKILY, THERE IS NO PROBLEM THE ARMY CAN'T SOLVE! YOU'RE LOOKING AT A **SCHRÖDINGER CONTAINMENT CELL,** A DEVICE THAT CAN PROTECT IT'S OCCUPANT FROM THE STRAIN OF AN EPR LEAP...
SO WE JUST GET INSIDE THAT THING TO BE SAFE?

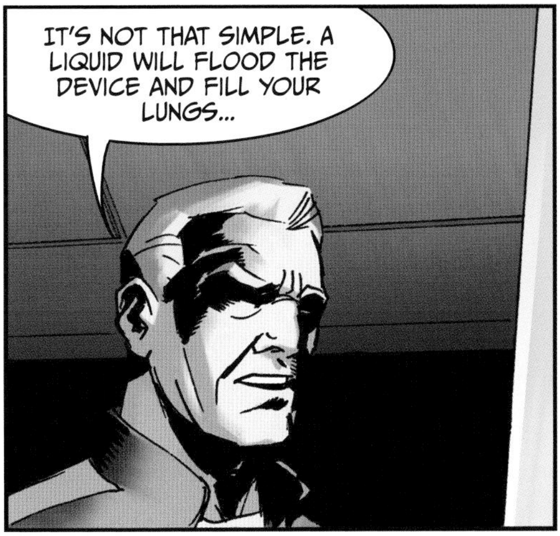
IT'S NOT THAT SIMPLE. A LIQUID WILL FLOOD THE DEVICE AND FILL YOUR LUNGS...

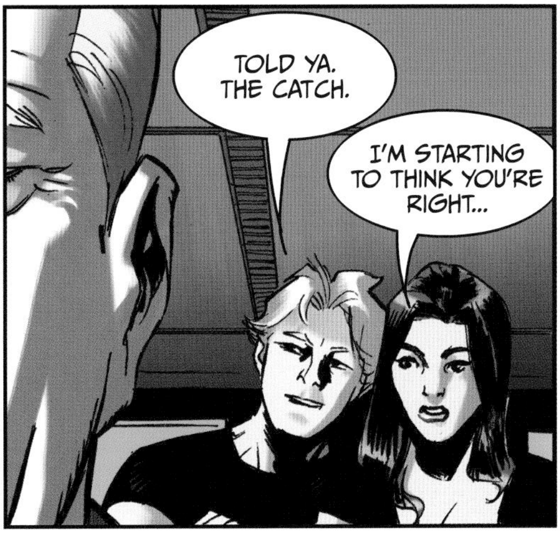
TOLD YA. THE CATCH.
I'M STARTING TO THINK YOU'RE RIGHT...

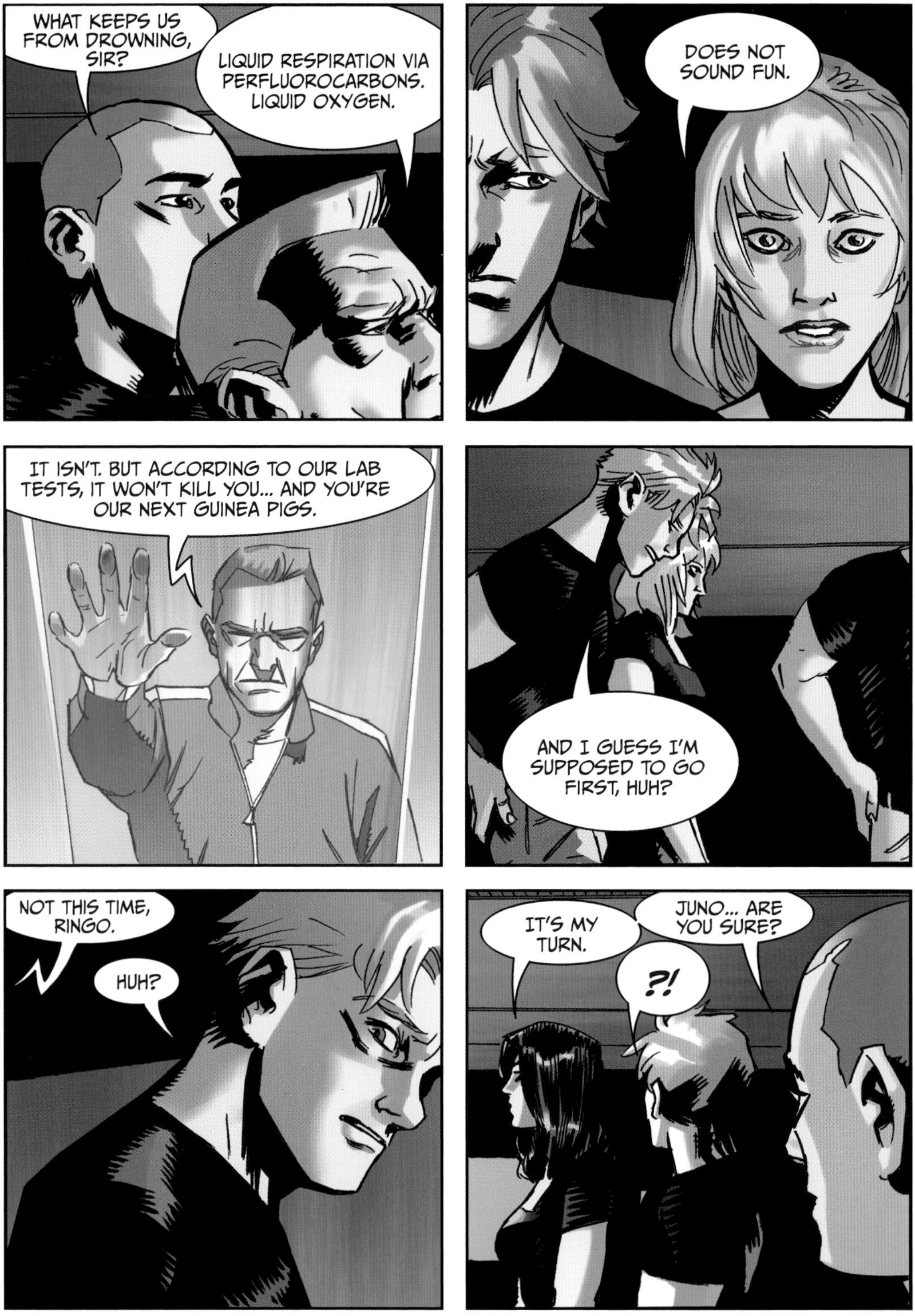
WHAT KEEPS US FROM DROWNING, SIR?
LIQUID RESPIRATION VIA PERFLUOROCARBONS. LIQUID OXYGEN.
DOES NOT SOUND FUN.
IT ISN'T. BUT ACCORDING TO OUR LAB TESTS, IT WON'T KILL YOU... AND YOU'RE OUR NEXT GUINEA PIGS.
AND I GUESS I'M SUPPOSED TO GO FIRST, HUH?
NOT THIS TIME, RINGO.
HUH?
IT'S MY TURN.
JUNO... ARE YOU SURE?
?!

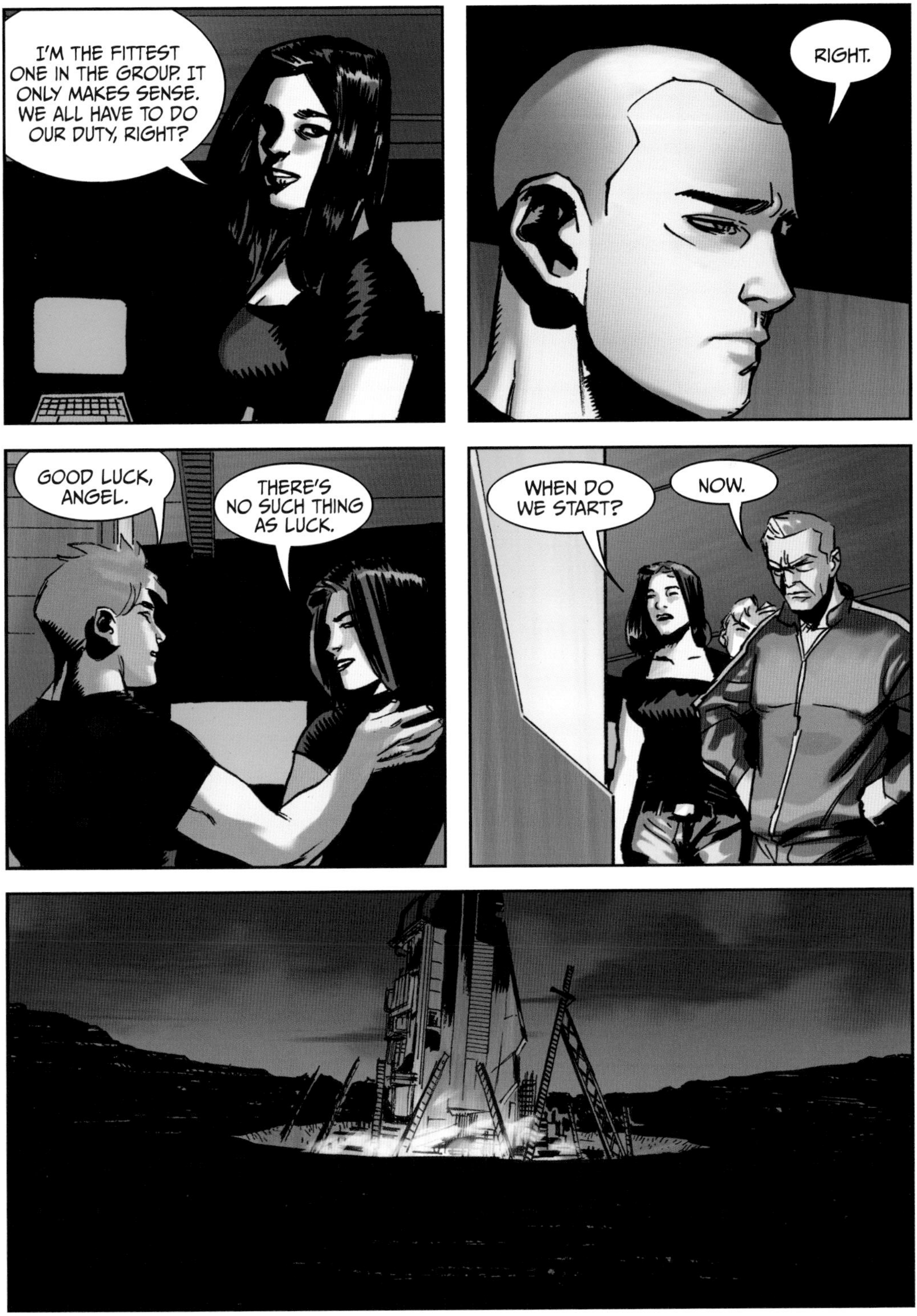
I'M THE FITTEST ONE IN THE GROUP. IT ONLY MAKES SENSE. WE ALL HAVE TO DO OUR DUTY, RIGHT?
RIGHT.
GOOD LUCK, ANGEL.
THERE'S NO SUCH THING AS LUCK.
WHEN DO WE START?
NOW.

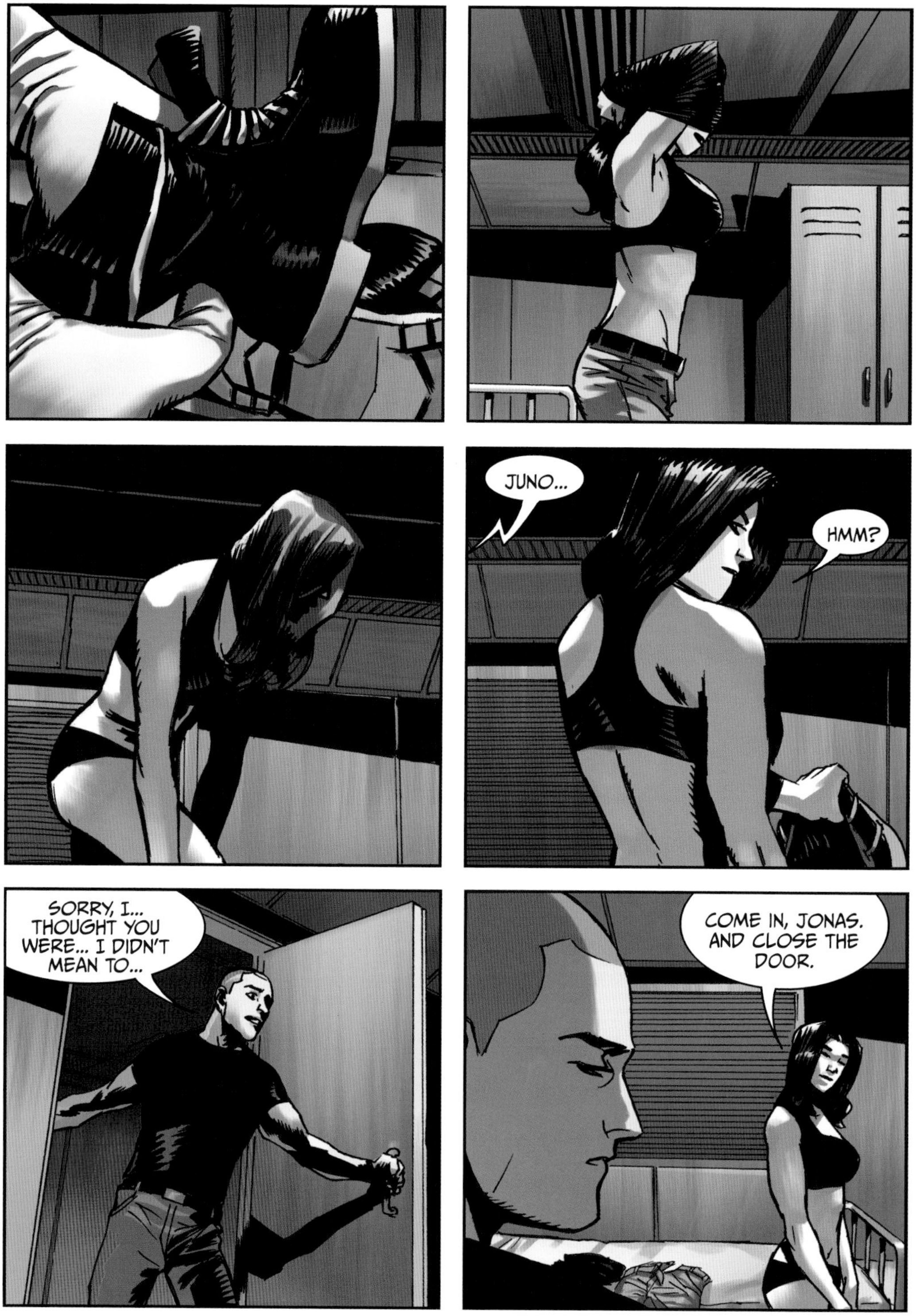
JUNO...
HMM?
SORRY, I... THOUGHT YOU WERE... I DIDN'T MEAN TO...
COME IN, JONAS. AND CLOSE THE DOOR.

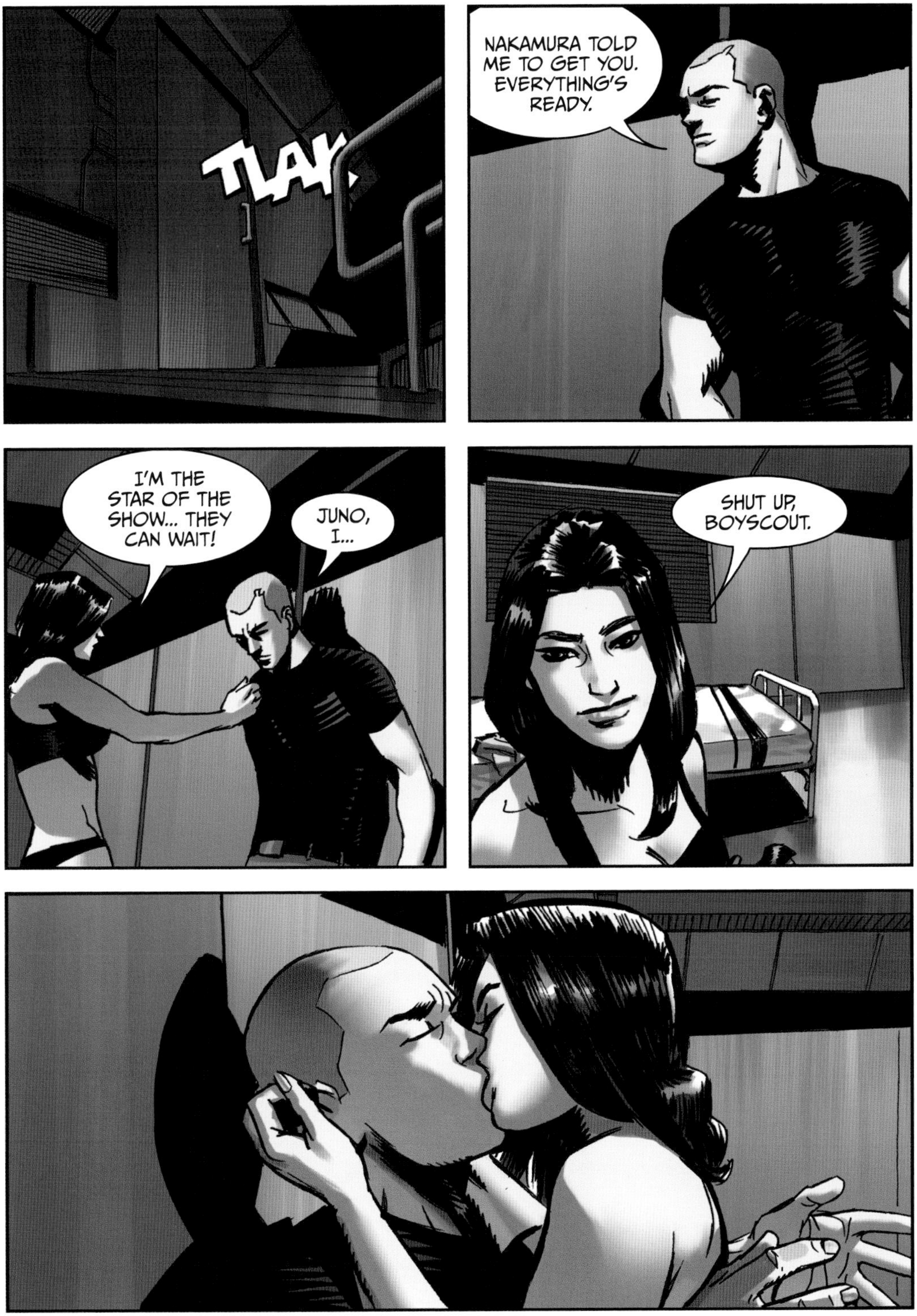
TLAK
NAKAMURA TOLD ME TO GET YOU. EVERYTHING'S READY.
I'M THE STAR OF THE SHOW... THEY CAN WAIT!
JUNO, I...
SHUT UP, BOYSCOUT.

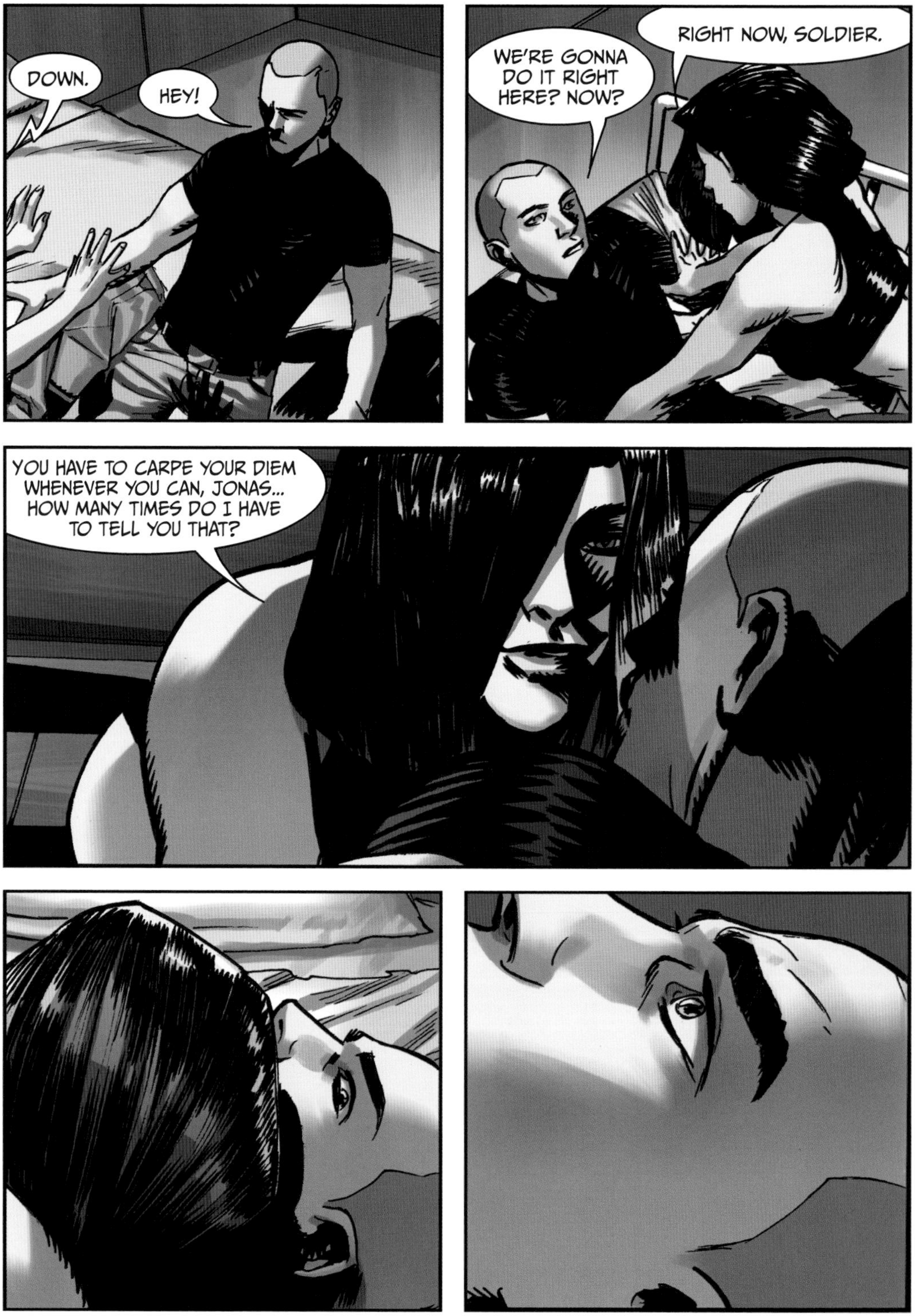
DOWN.
HEY!
WE'RE GONNA DO IT RIGHT HERE? NOW?
RIGHT NOW, SOLDIER.
YOU HAVE TO CARPE YOUR DIEM WHENEVER YOU CAN, JONAS... HOW MANY TIMES DO I HAVE TO TELL YOU THAT?

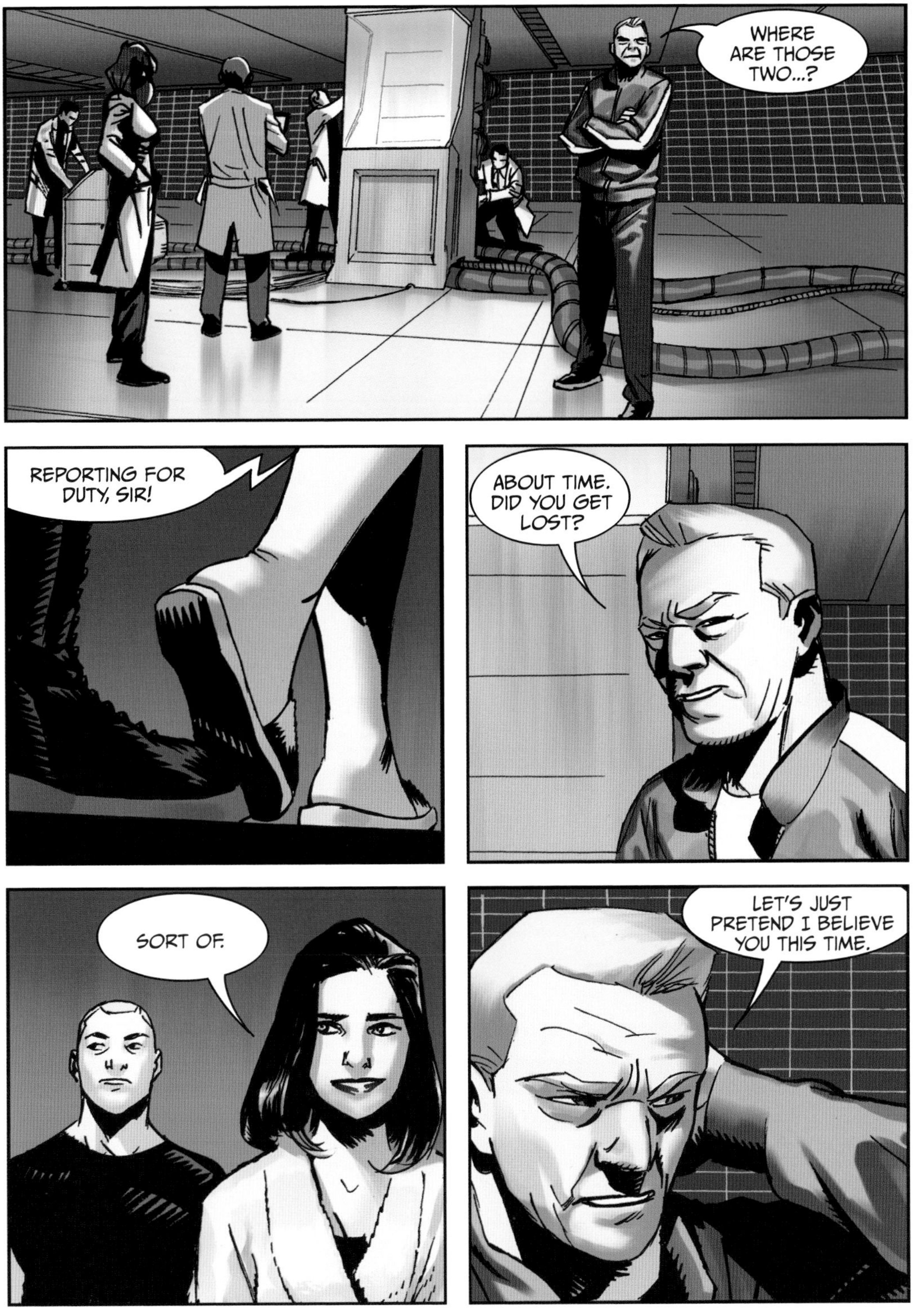
WHERE ARE THOSE TWO...?
REPORTING FOR DUTY, SIR!
ABOUT TIME. DID YOU GET LOST?
SORT OF.
LET'S JUST PRETEND I BELIEVE YOU THIS TIME.

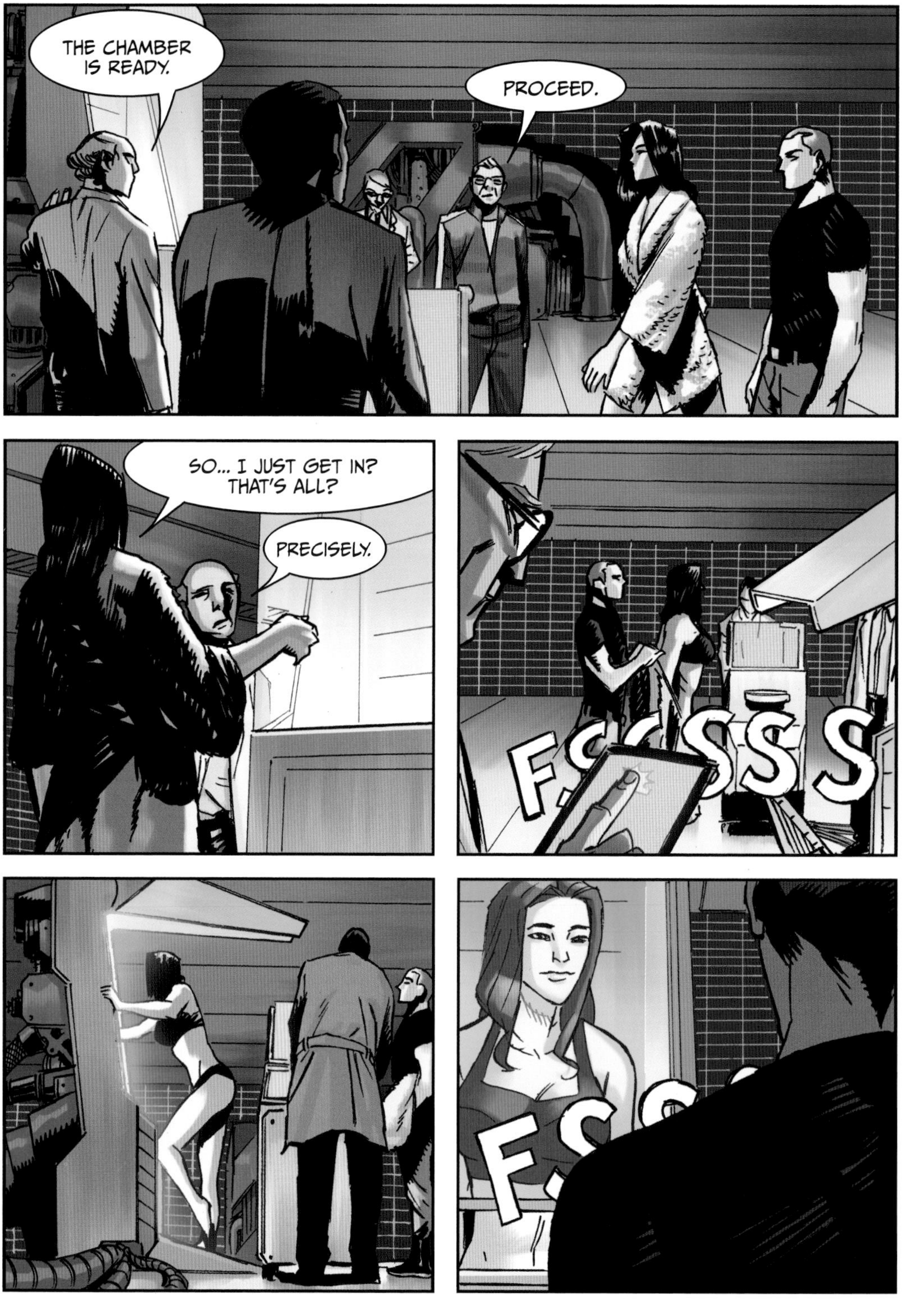
THE CHAMBER IS READY.
PROCEED.
SO... I JUST GET IN? THAT'S ALL?
PRECISELY.
FSSSSS

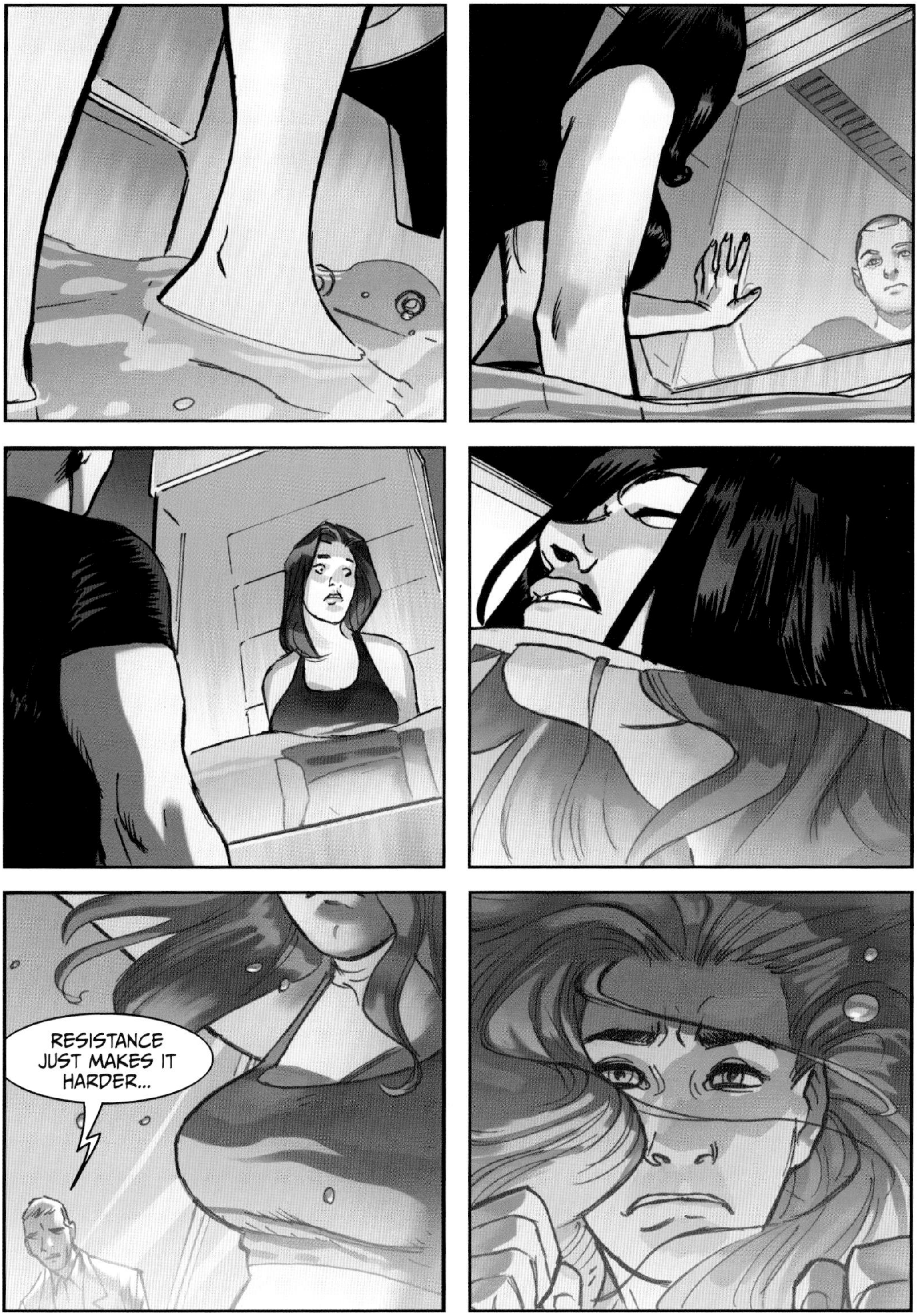
RESISTANCE JUST MAKES IT HARDER...

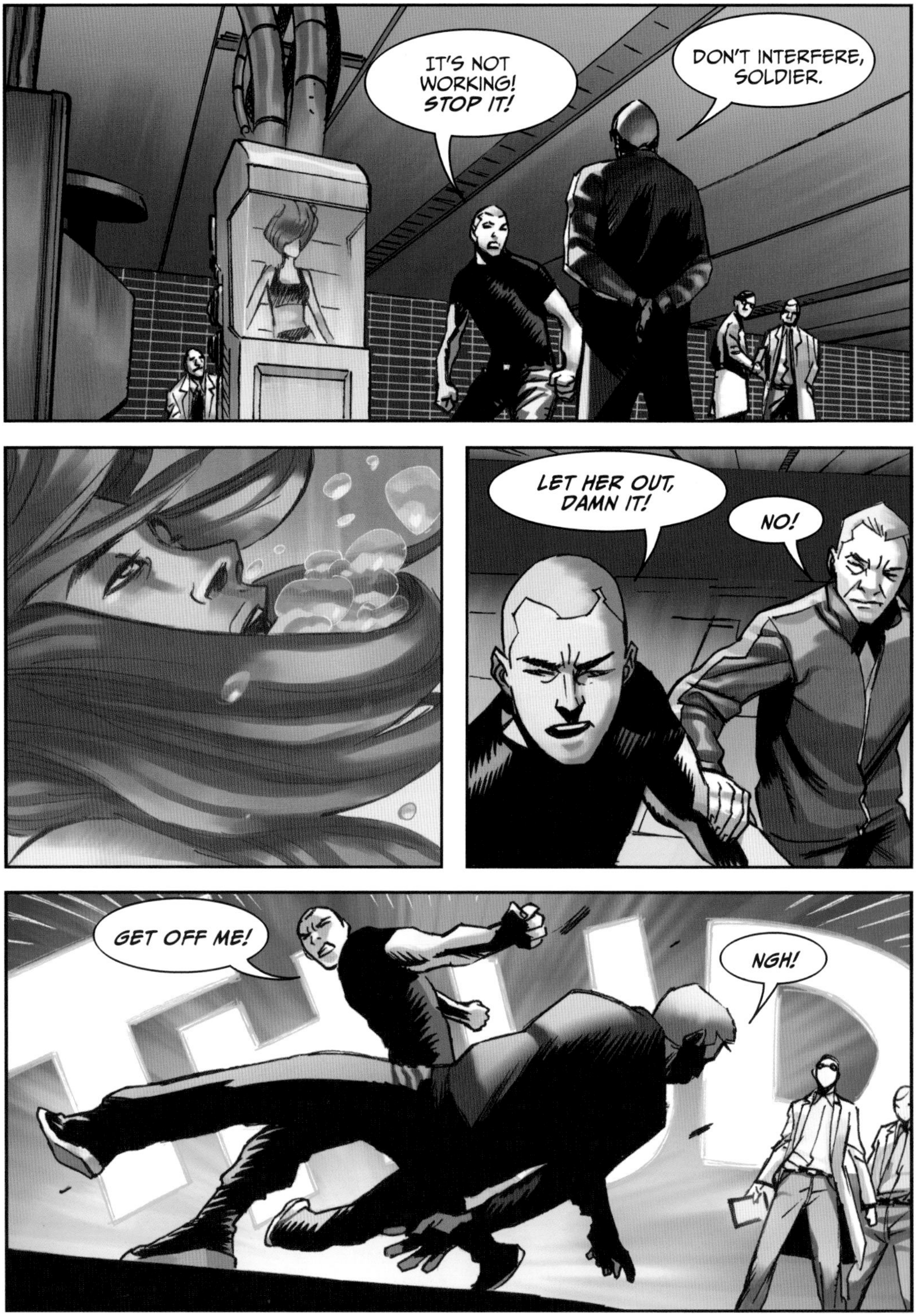
IT'S NOT WORKING! STOP IT!
DON'T INTERFERE, SOLDIER.
LET HER OUT, DAMN IT!
NO!
GET OFF ME!
NGH!

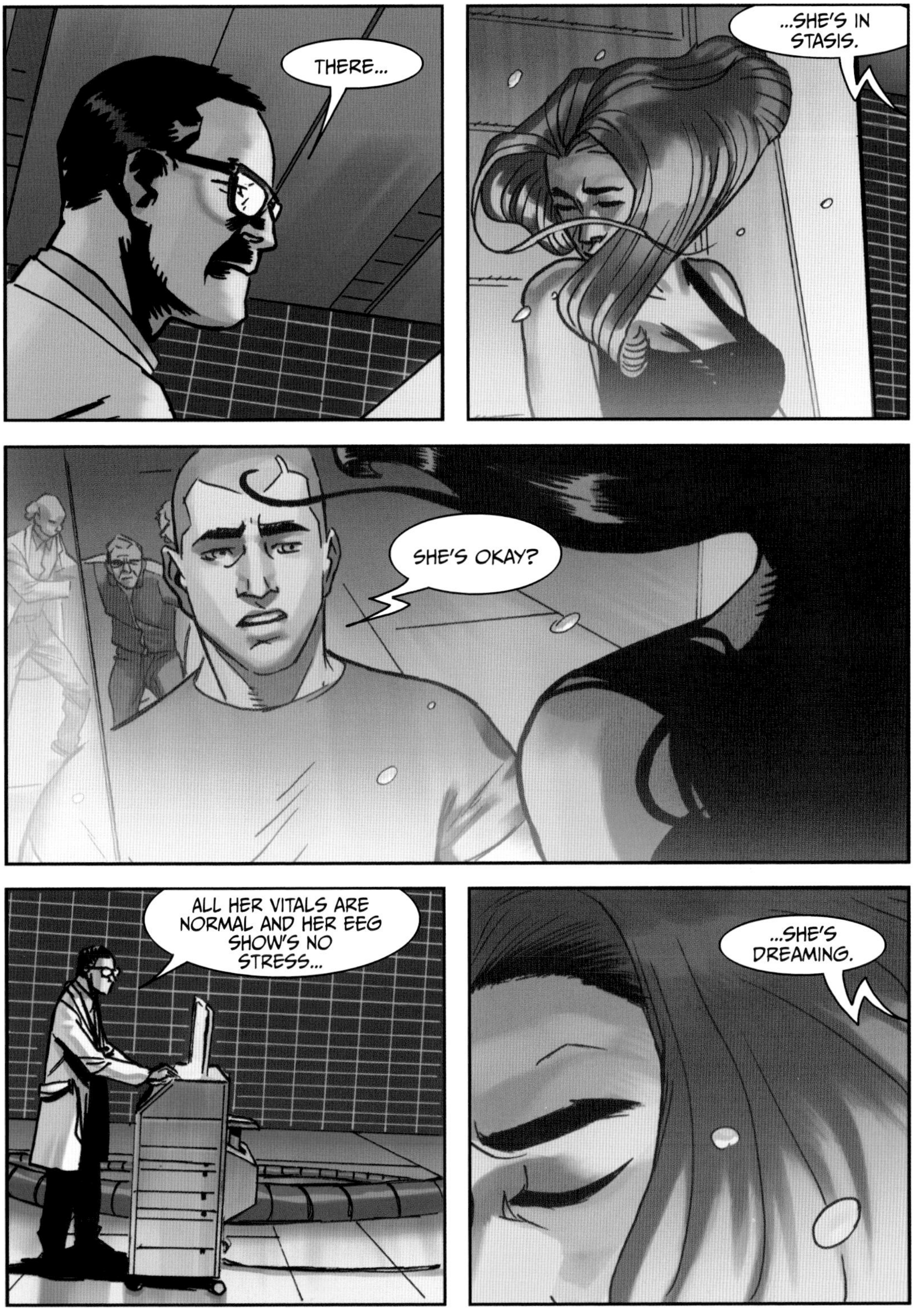
THERE...
...SHE'S IN STASIS.
SHE'S OKAY?
ALL HER VITALS ARE NORMAL AND HER EEG SHOW'S NO STRESS...
...SHE'S DREAMING.

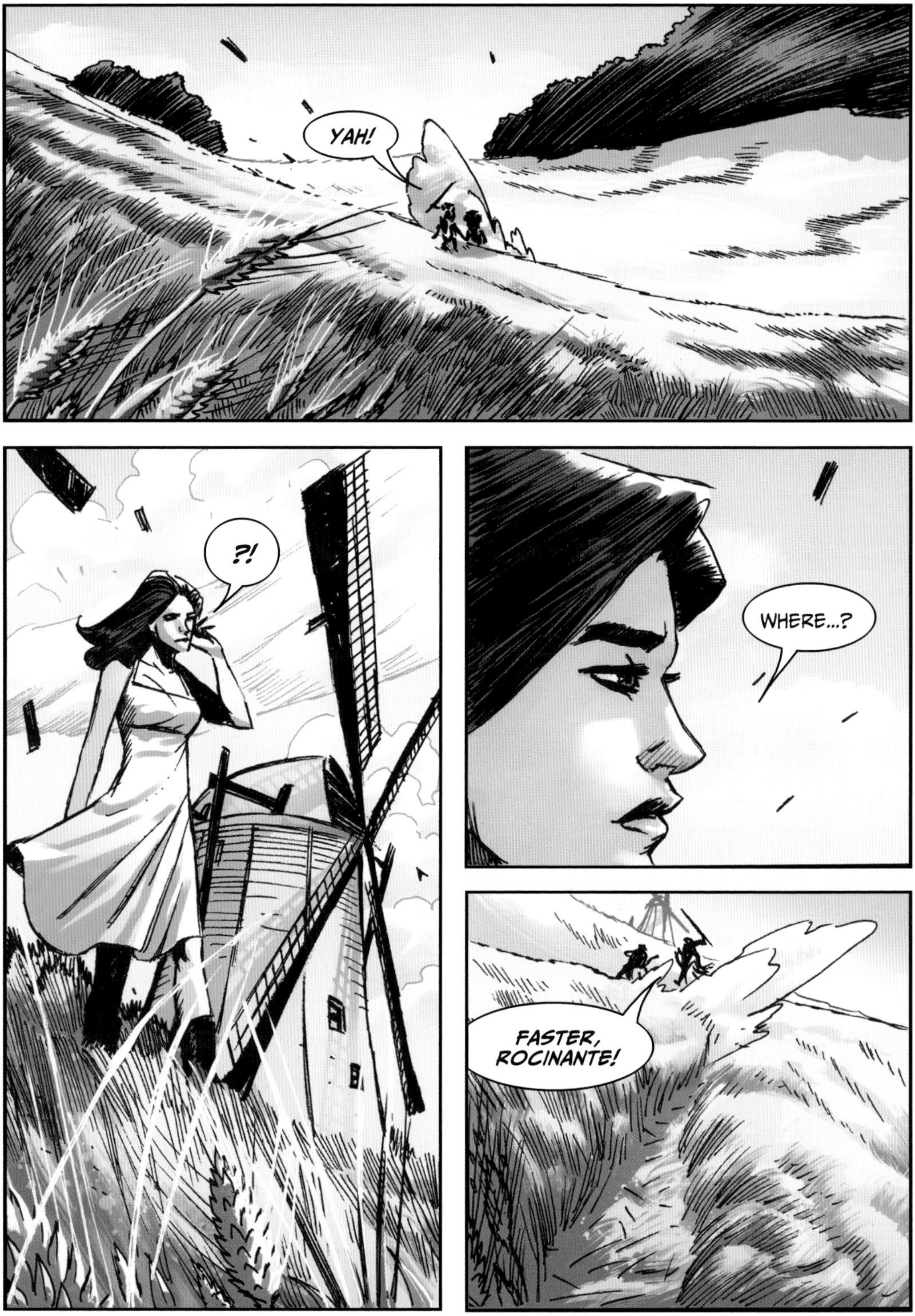
YAH!
?!
WHERE...?
FASTER, ROCINANTE!

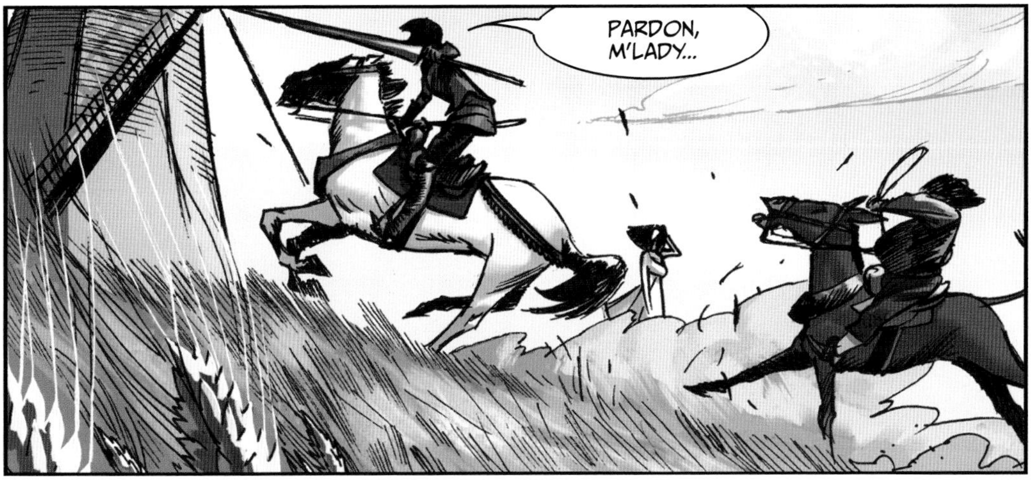
PARDON, M'LADY...

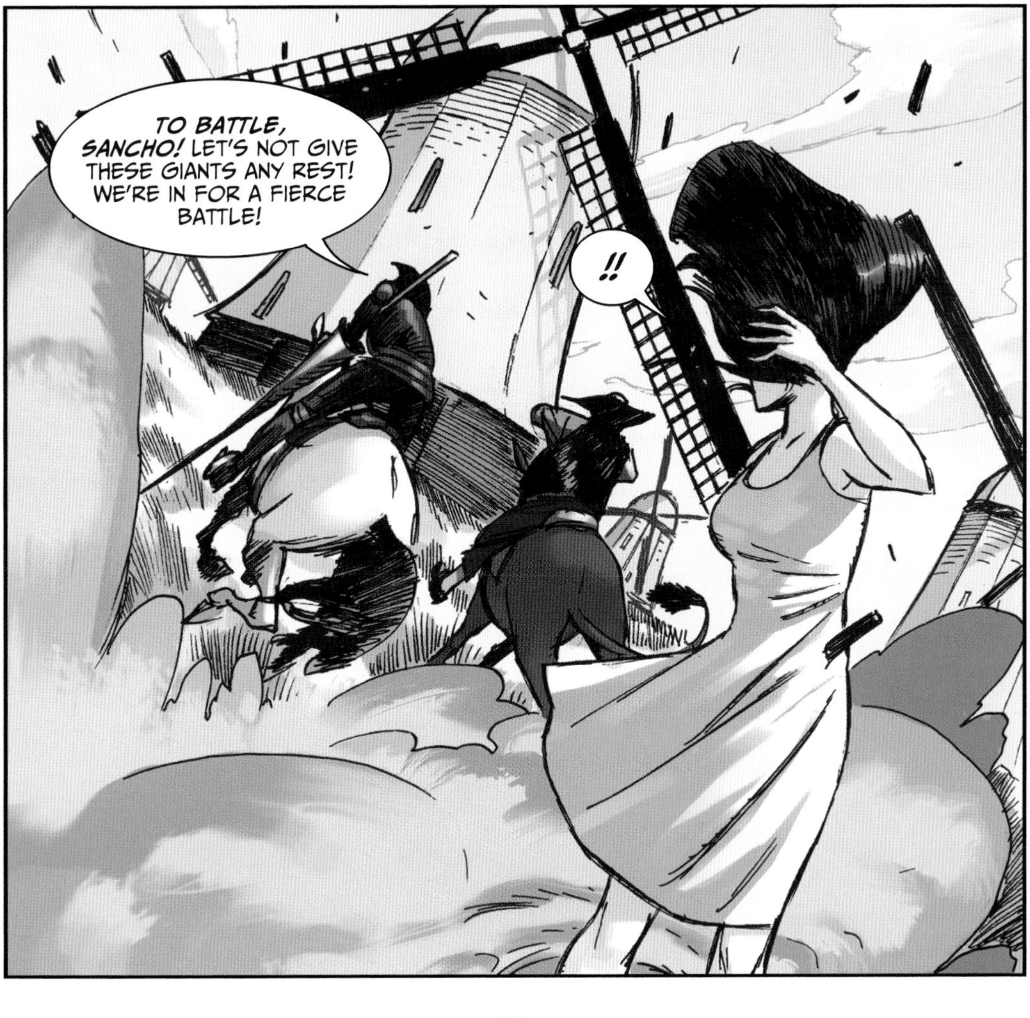
TO BATTLE, SANCHO! LET'S NOT GIVE THESE GIANTS ANY REST! WE'RE IN FOR A FIERCE BATTLE!
!!

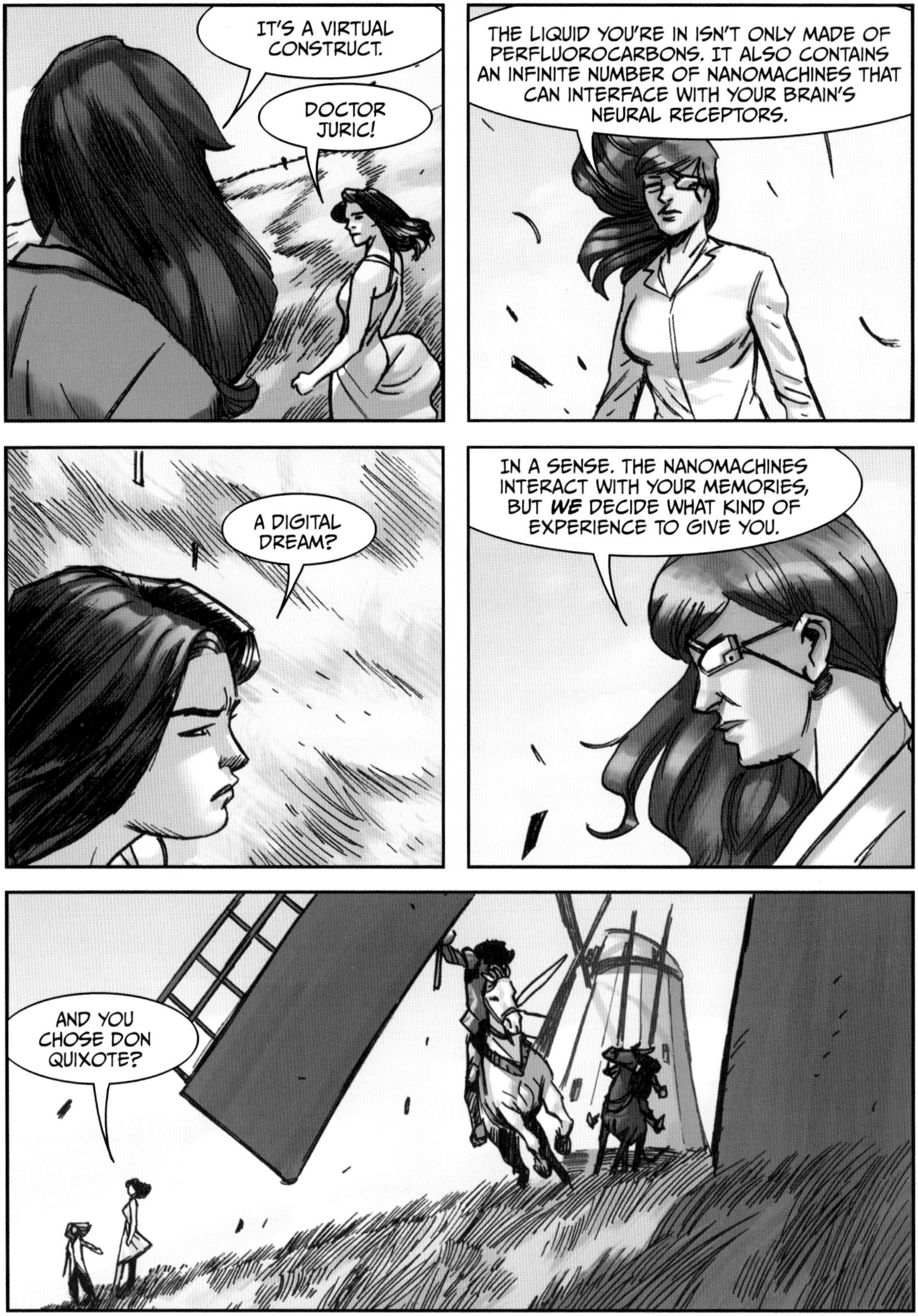
IT'S A VIRTUAL CONSTRUCT.
DOCTOR JURIC!
THE LIQUID YOU'RE IN ISN'T ONLY MADE OF PERFLUOROCARBONS. IT ALSO CONTAINS AN INFINITE NUMBER OF NANOMACHINES THAT CAN INTERFACE WITH YOUR BRAIN'S NEURAL RECEPTORS.
A DIGITAL DREAM?
IN A SENSE. THE NANOMACHINES INTERACT WITH YOUR MEMORIES, BUT *WE* DECIDE WHAT KIND OF EXPERIENCE TO GIVE YOU.
AND YOU CHOSE DON QUIXOTE?

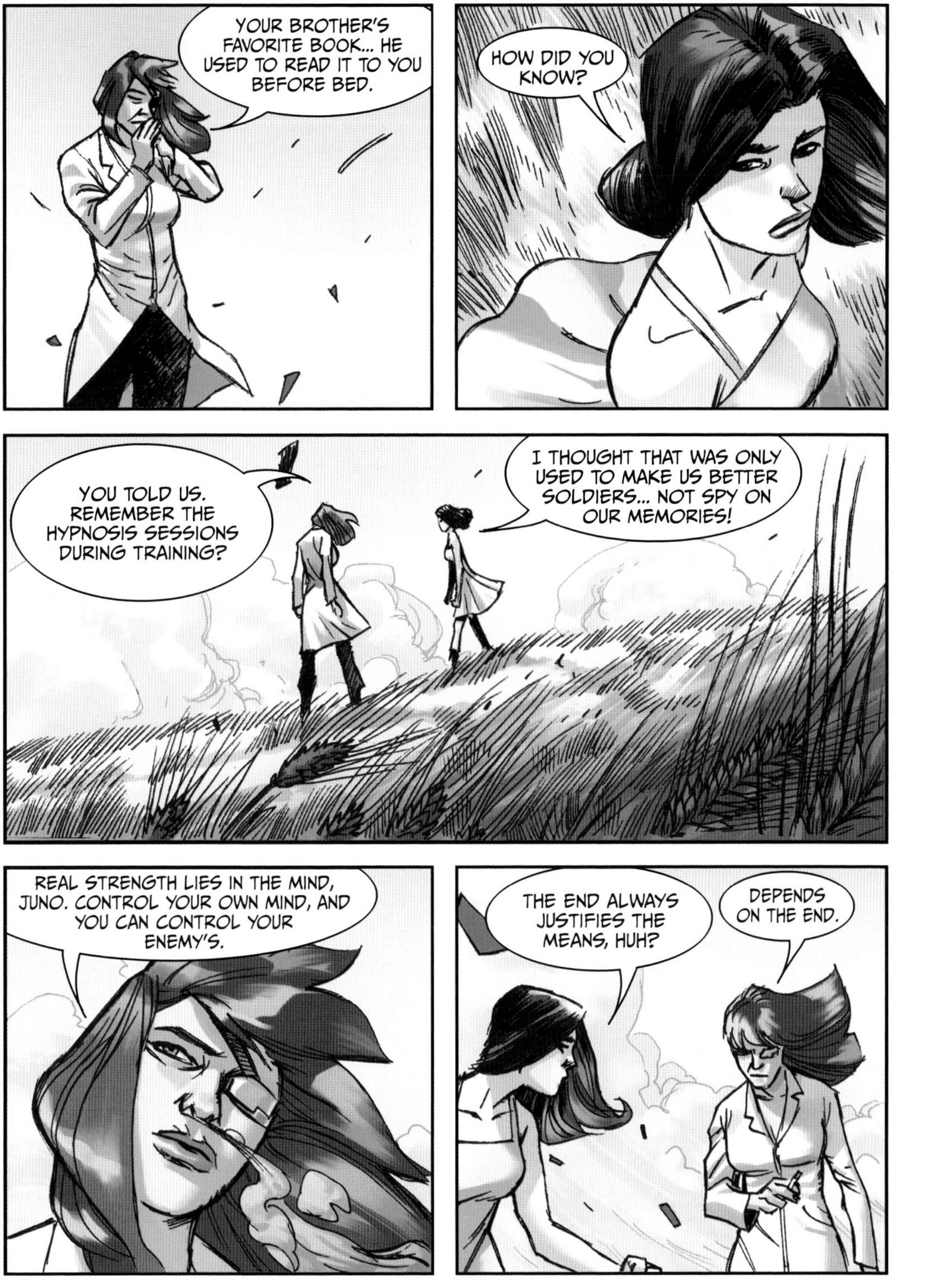
YOUR BROTHER'S FAVORITE BOOK... HE USED TO READ IT TO YOU BEFORE BED.
HOW DID YOU KNOW?
YOU TOLD US. REMEMBER THE HYPNOSIS SESSIONS DURING TRAINING?
I THOUGHT THAT WAS ONLY USED TO MAKE US BETTER SOLDIERS... NOT SPY ON OUR MEMORIES!
REAL STRENGTH LIES IN THE MIND, JUNO. CONTROL YOUR OWN MIND, AND YOU CAN CONTROL YOUR ENEMY'S.
THE END ALWAYS JUSTIFIES THE MEANS, HUH?
DEPENDS ON THE END.

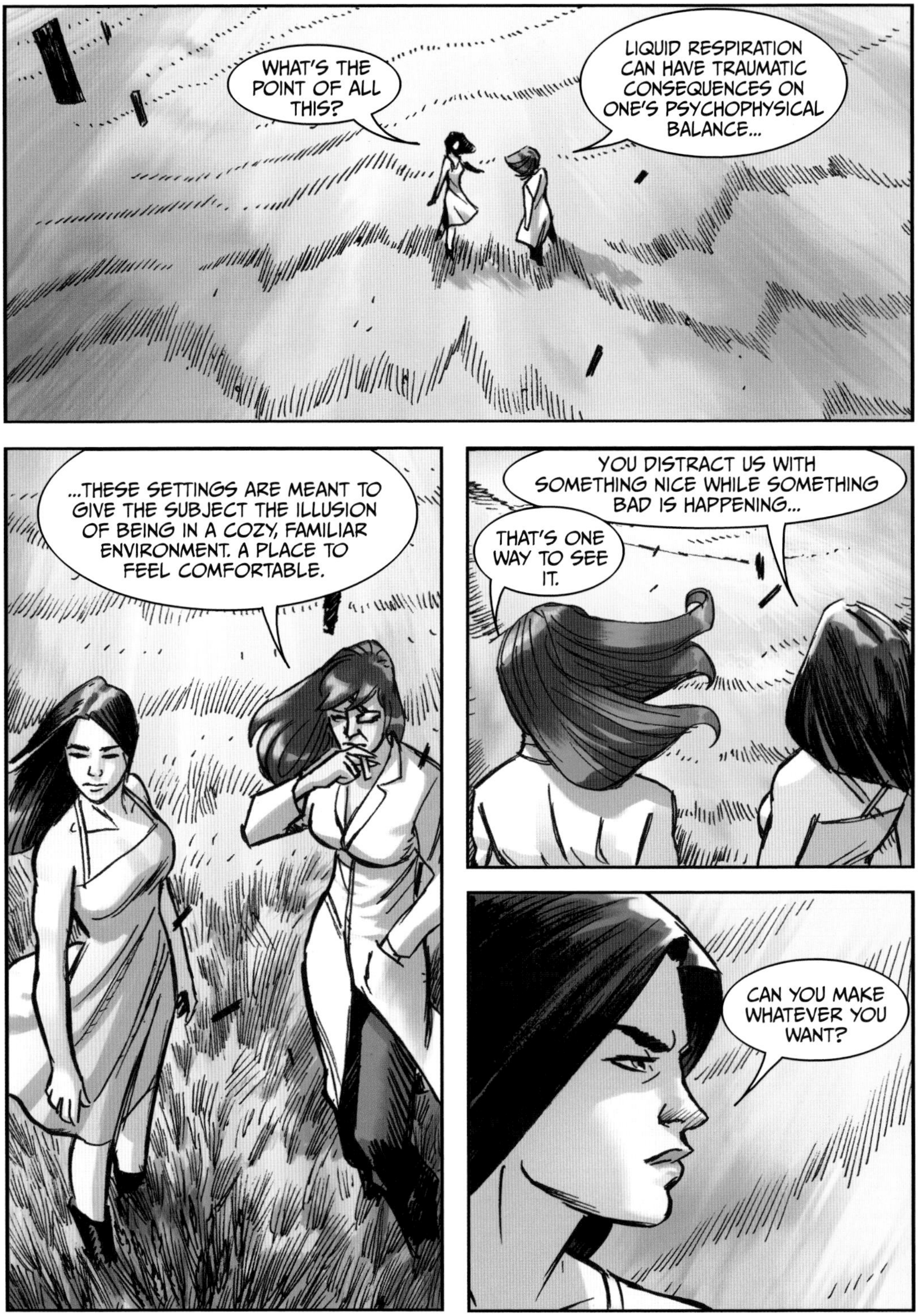
WHAT'S THE POINT OF ALL THIS?
LIQUID RESPIRATION CAN HAVE TRAUMATIC CONSEQUENCES ON ONE'S PSYCHOPHYSICAL BALANCE...
...THESE SETTINGS ARE MEANT TO GIVE THE SUBJECT THE ILLUSION OF BEING IN A COZY, FAMILIAR ENVIRONMENT. A PLACE TO FEEL COMFORTABLE.
YOU DISTRACT US WITH SOMETHING NICE WHILE SOMETHING BAD IS HAPPENING...
THAT'S ONE WAY TO SEE IT.
CAN YOU MAKE WHATEVER YOU WANT?

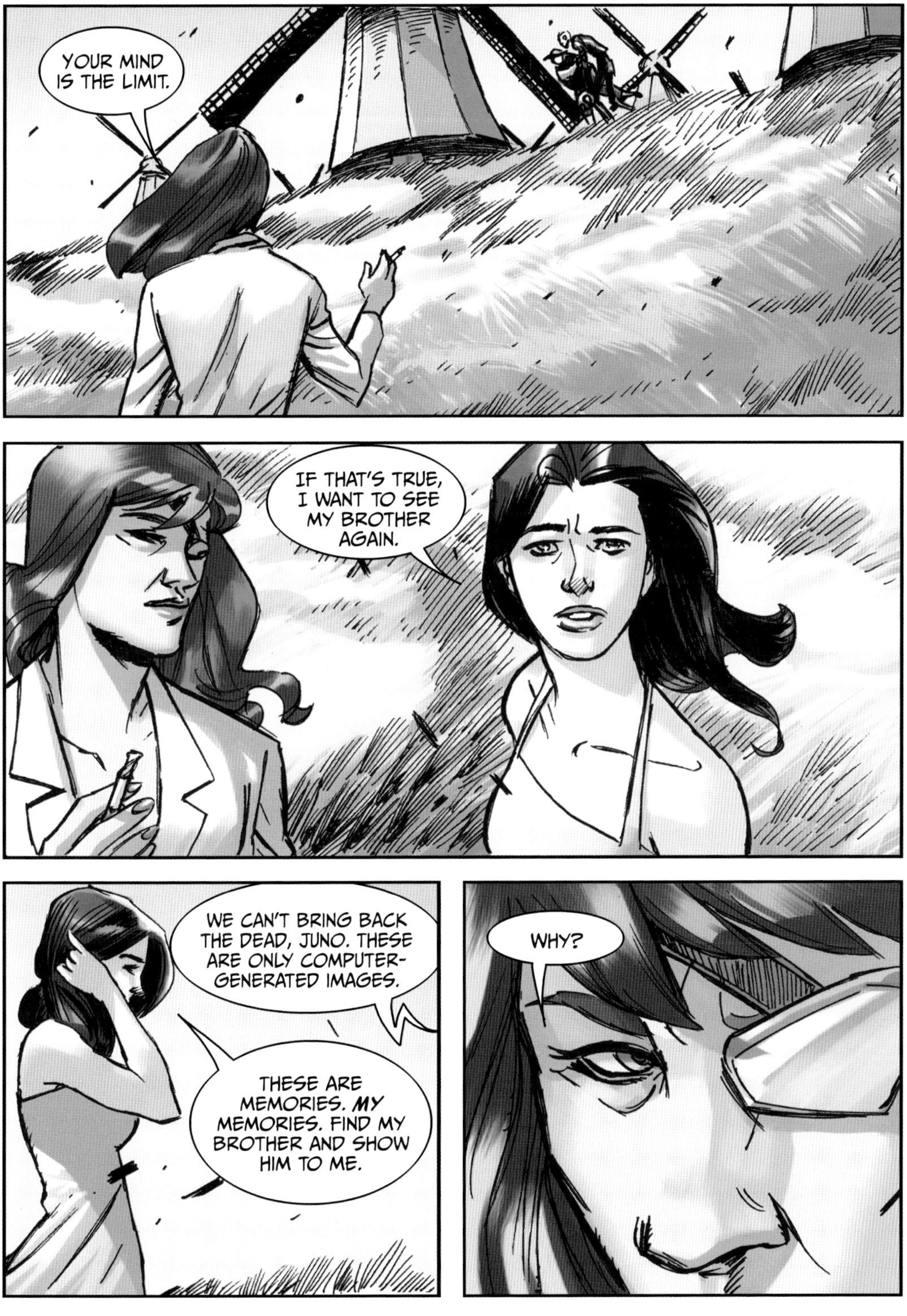
YOUR MIND IS THE LIMIT.
IF THAT'S TRUE, I WANT TO SEE MY BROTHER AGAIN.
WE CAN'T BRING BACK THE DEAD, JUNO. THESE ARE ONLY COMPUTER-GENERATED IMAGES.
THESE ARE MEMORIES. *MY* MEMORIES. FIND MY BROTHER AND SHOW HIM TO ME.
WHY?

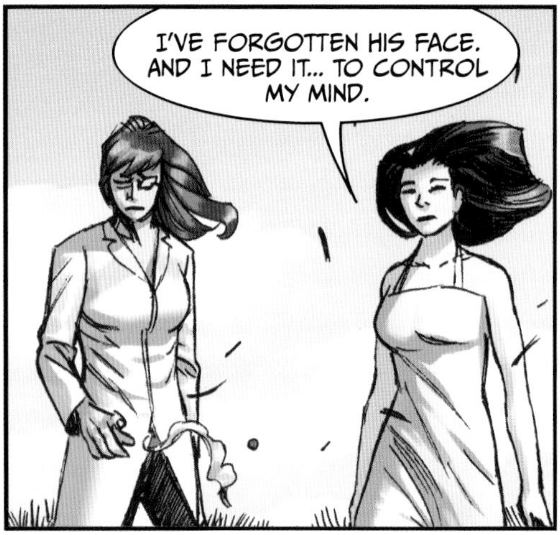
I'VE FORGOTTEN HIS FACE. AND I NEED IT... TO CONTROL MY MIND.

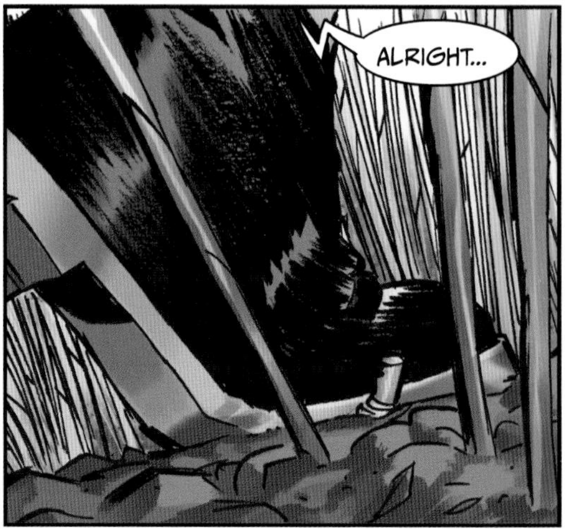
ALRIGHT...

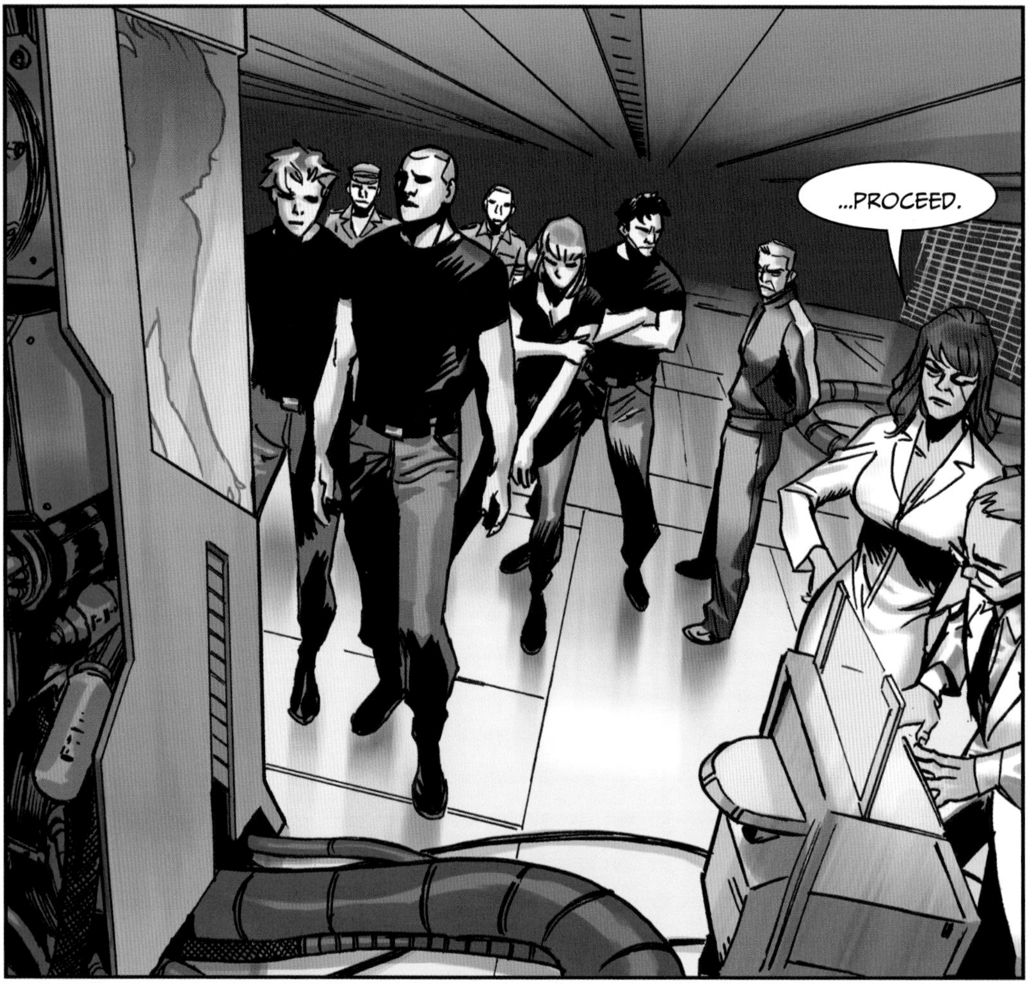
...PROCEED.

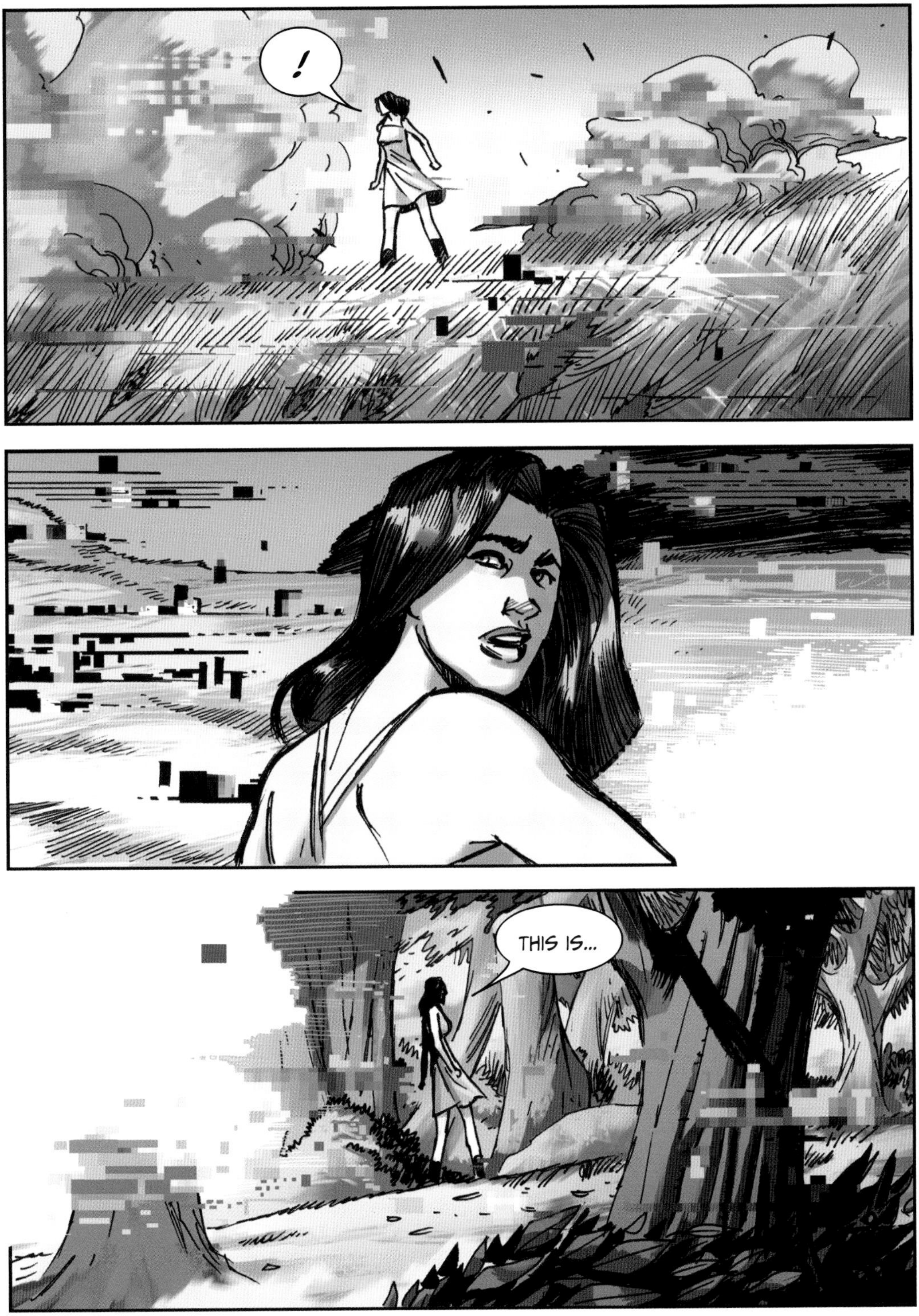
!
THIS IS...

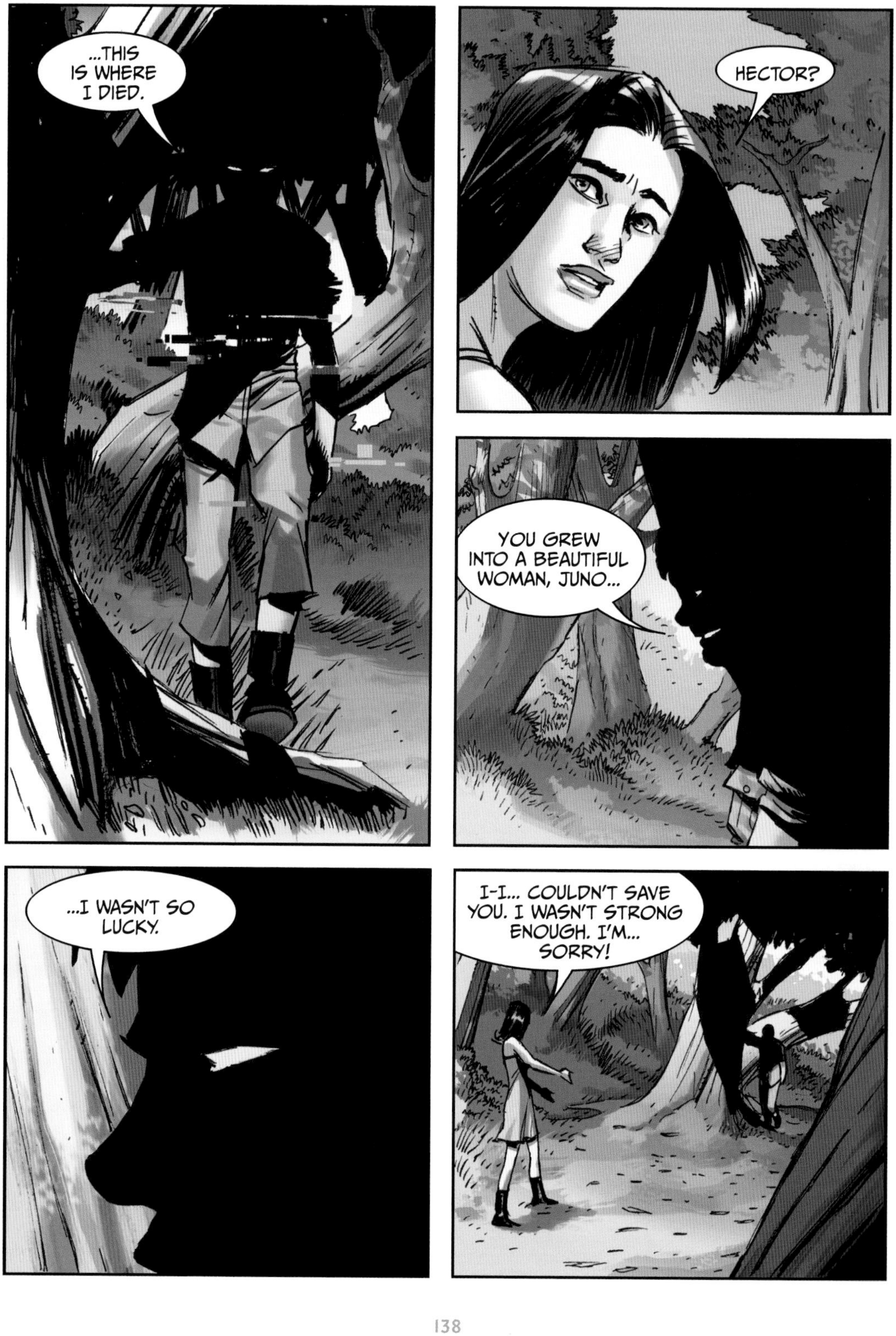
...THIS IS WHERE I DIED.
HECTOR?
YOU GREW INTO A BEAUTIFUL WOMAN, JUNO...
...I WASN'T SO LUCKY.
I-I... COULDN'T SAVE YOU. I WASN'T STRONG ENOUGH. I'M... SORRY!

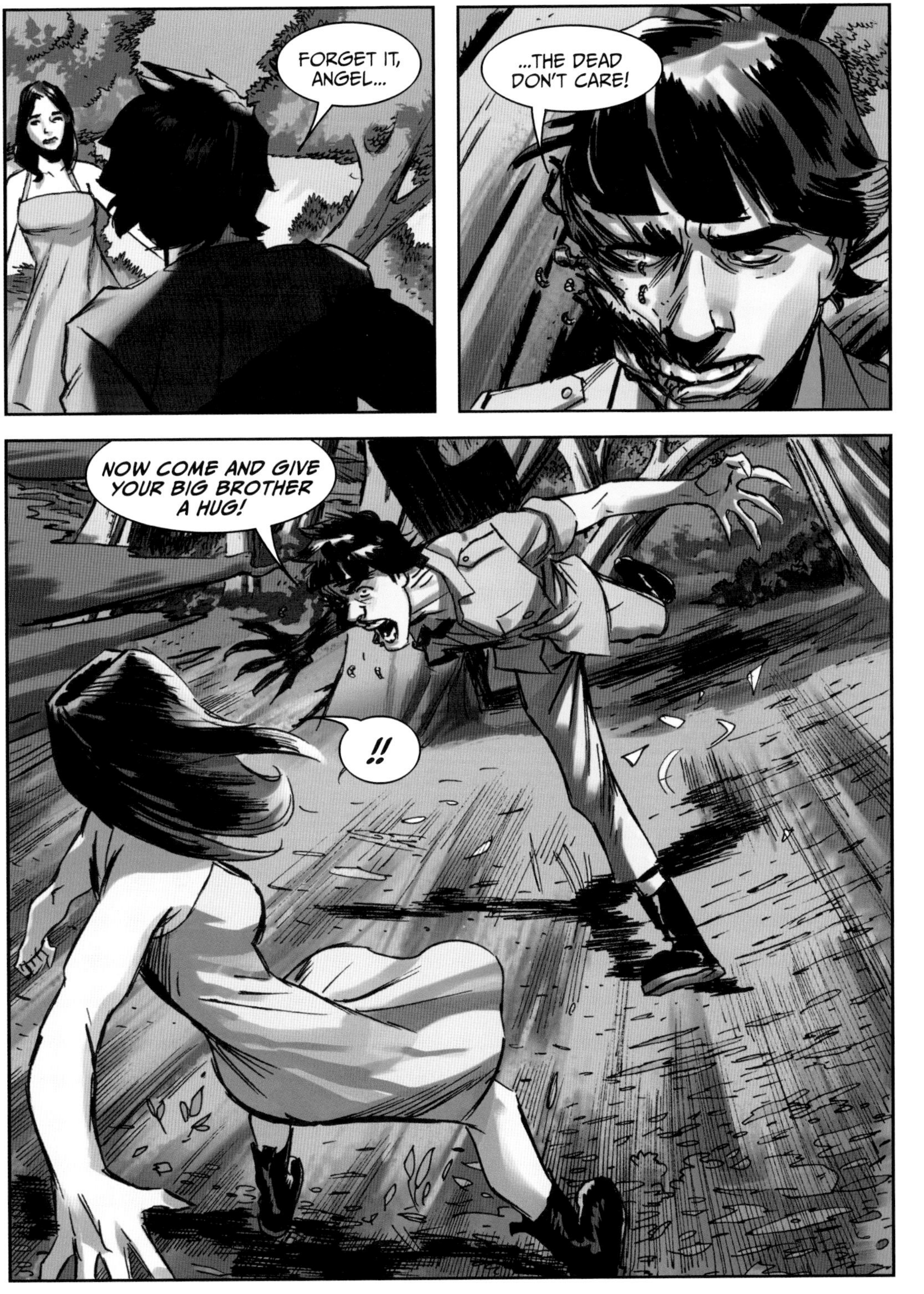
FORGET IT, ANGEL...
...THE DEAD DON'T CARE!
NOW COME AND GIVE YOUR BIG BROTHER A HUG!
!!

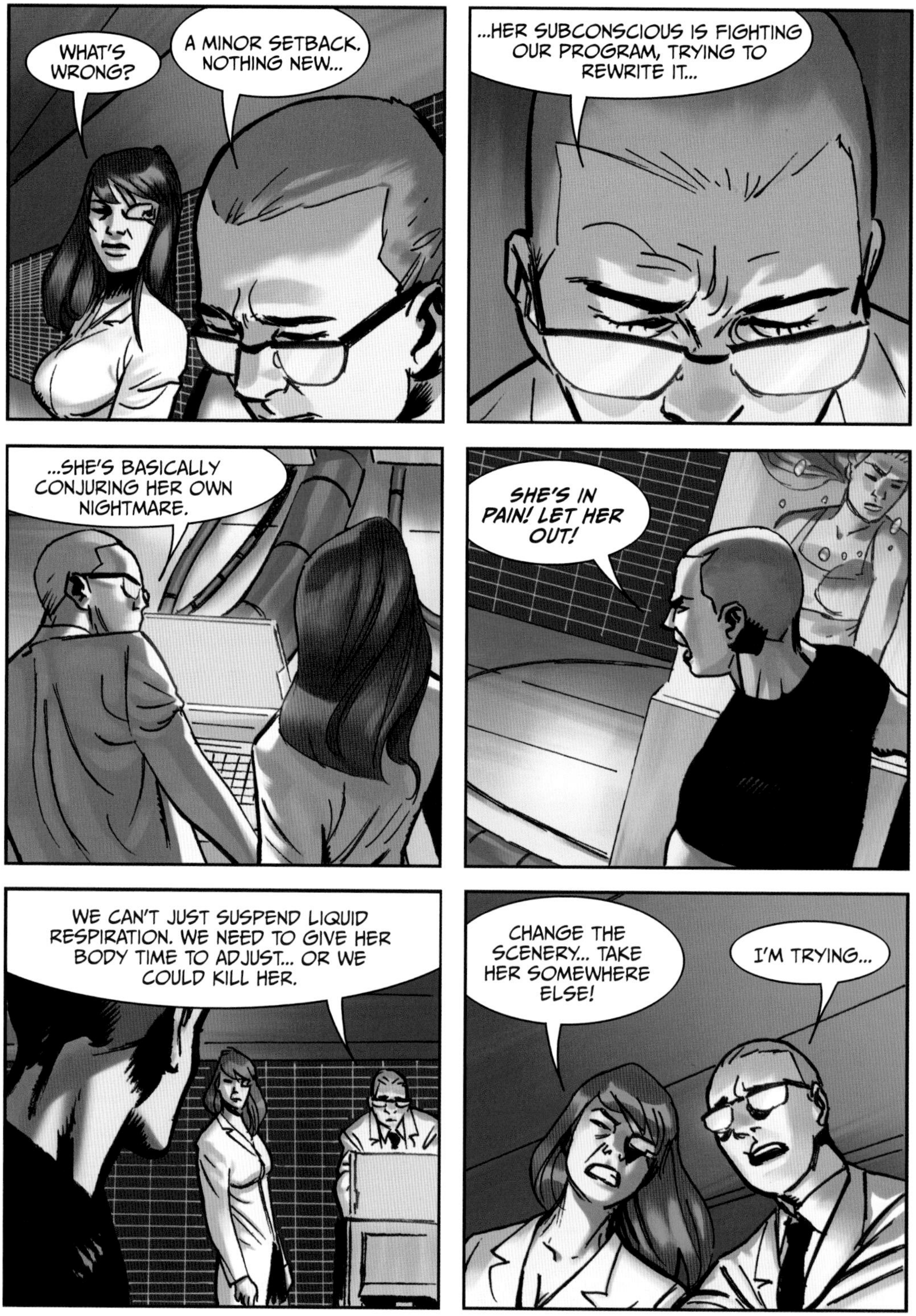
WHAT'S WRONG?
A MINOR SETBACK. NOTHING NEW...
...HER SUBCONSCIOUS IS FIGHTING OUR PROGRAM, TRYING TO REWRITE IT...
...SHE'S BASICALLY CONJURING HER OWN NIGHTMARE.
SHE'S IN PAIN! LET HER OUT!
WE CAN'T JUST SUSPEND LIQUID RESPIRATION. WE NEED TO GIVE HER BODY TIME TO ADJUST... OR WE COULD KILL HER.
CHANGE THE SCENERY... TAKE HER SOMEWHERE ELSE!
I'M TRYING...

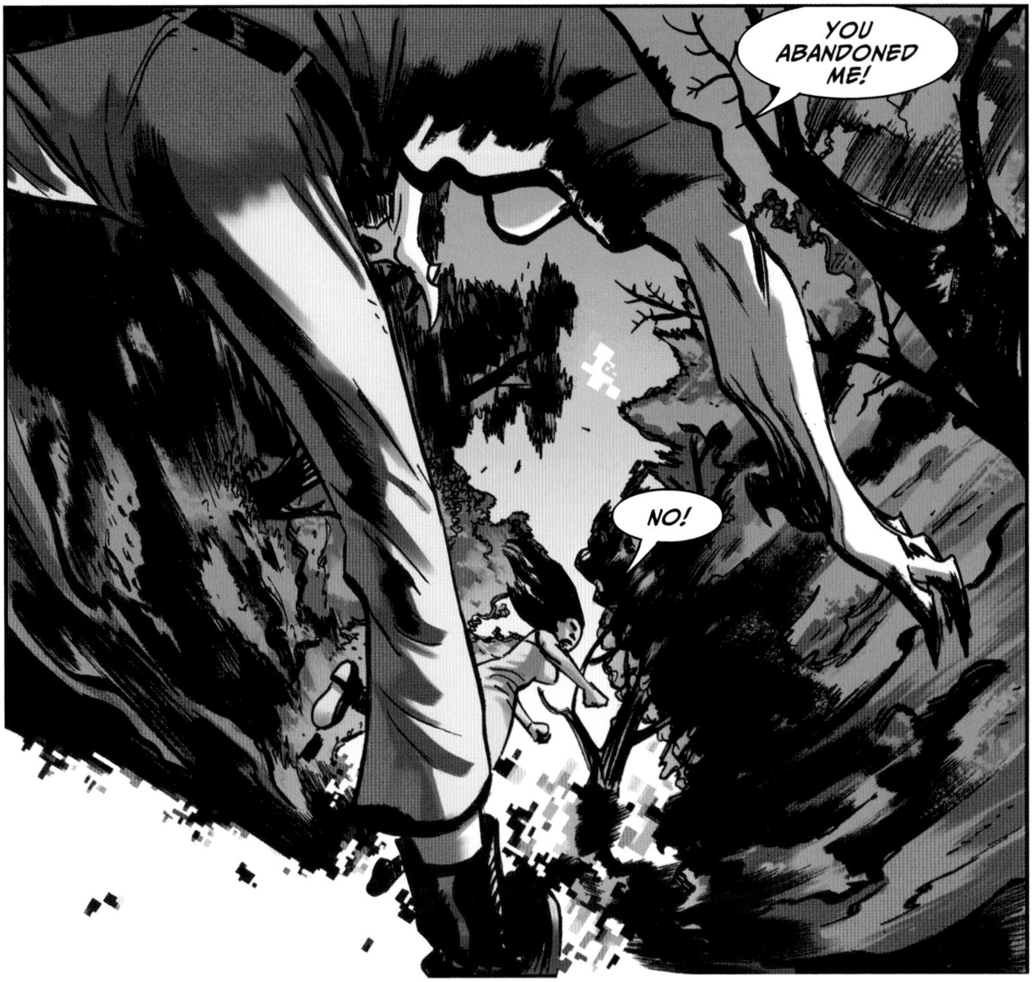
YOU ABANDONED ME!
NO!

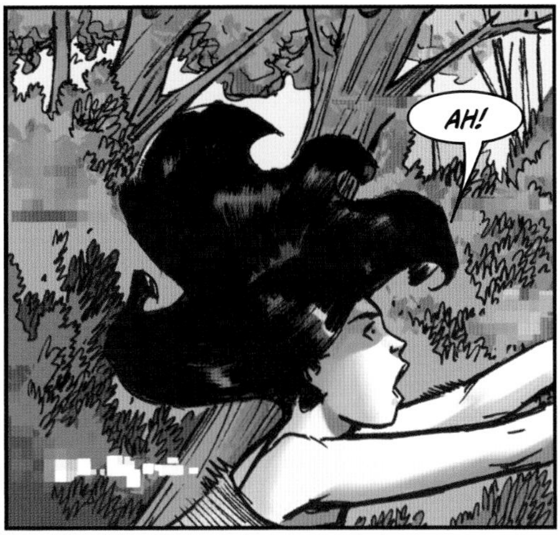
AH!

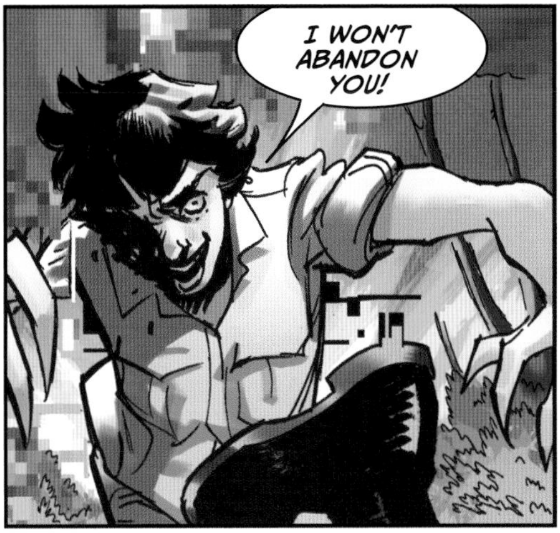
I WON'T ABANDON YOU!

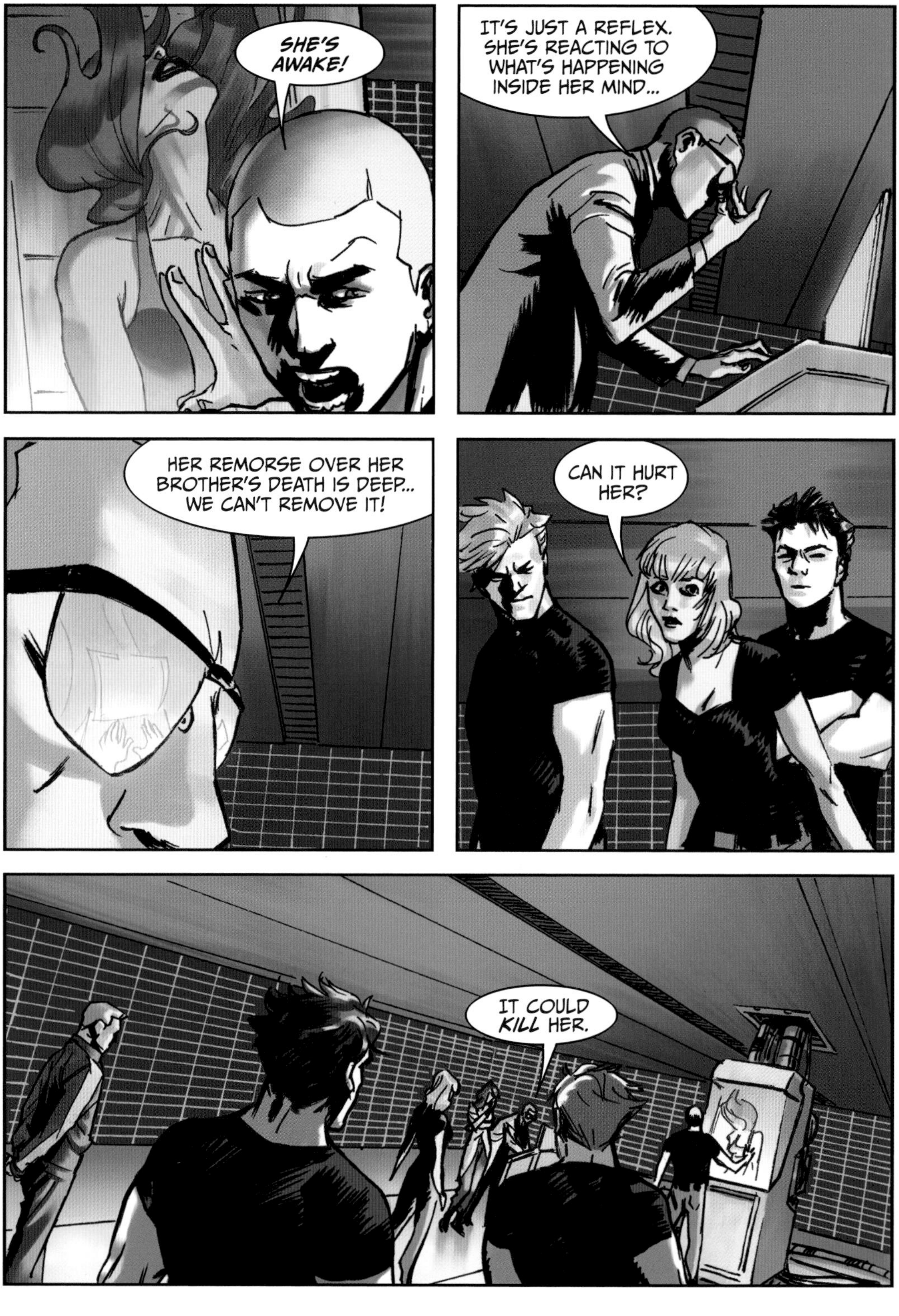
SHE'S AWAKE!
IT'S JUST A REFLEX. SHE'S REACTING TO WHAT'S HAPPENING INSIDE HER MIND...
HER REMORSE OVER HER BROTHER'S DEATH IS DEEP... WE CAN'T REMOVE IT!
CAN IT HURT HER?
IT COULD *KILL* HER.

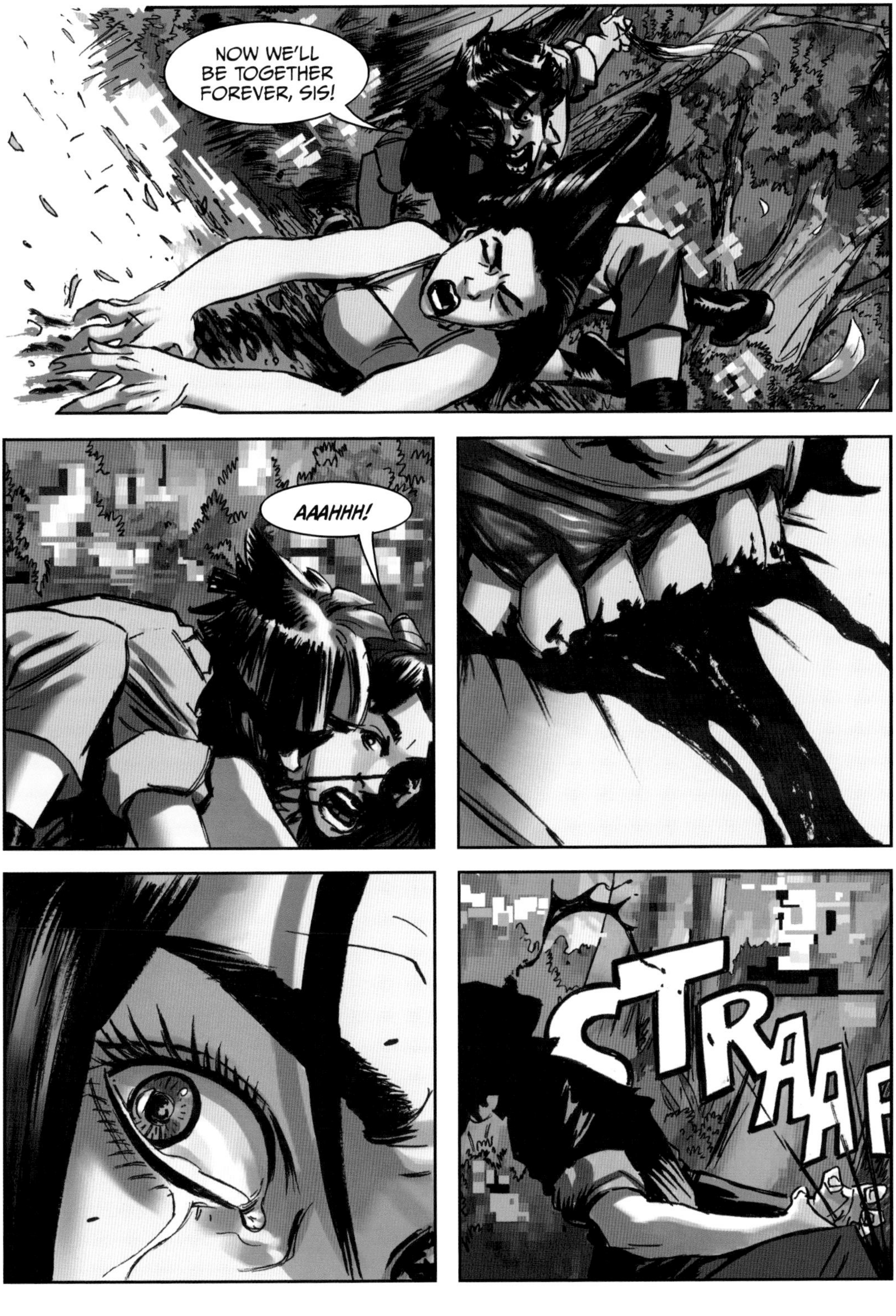
NOW WE'LL BE TOGETHER FOREVER, SIS!
AAAHHH!
STRAAF

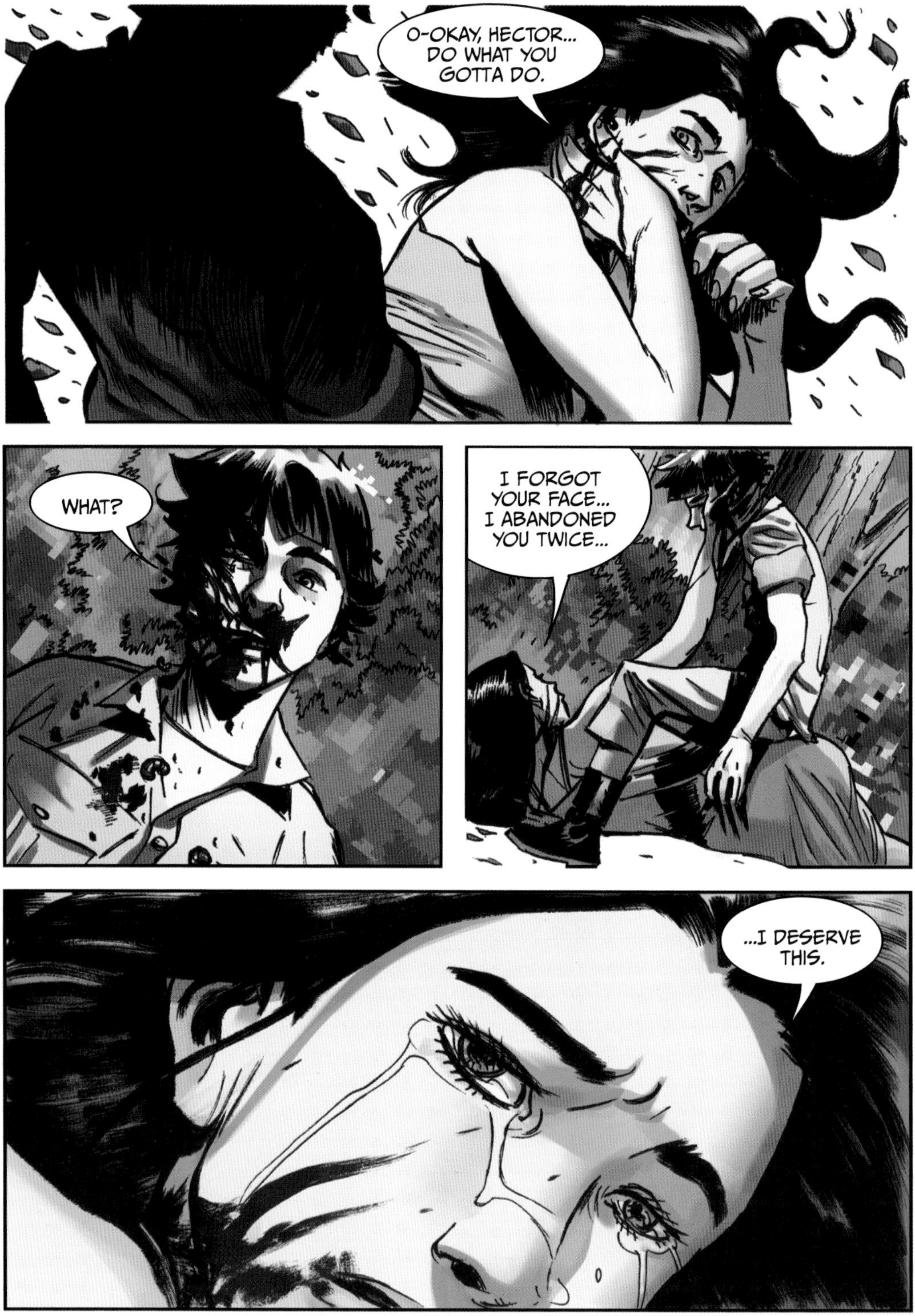
O-OKAY, HECTOR... DO WHAT YOU GOTTA DO.
WHAT?
I FORGOT YOUR FACE... I ABANDONED YOU TWICE...
...I DESERVE THIS.

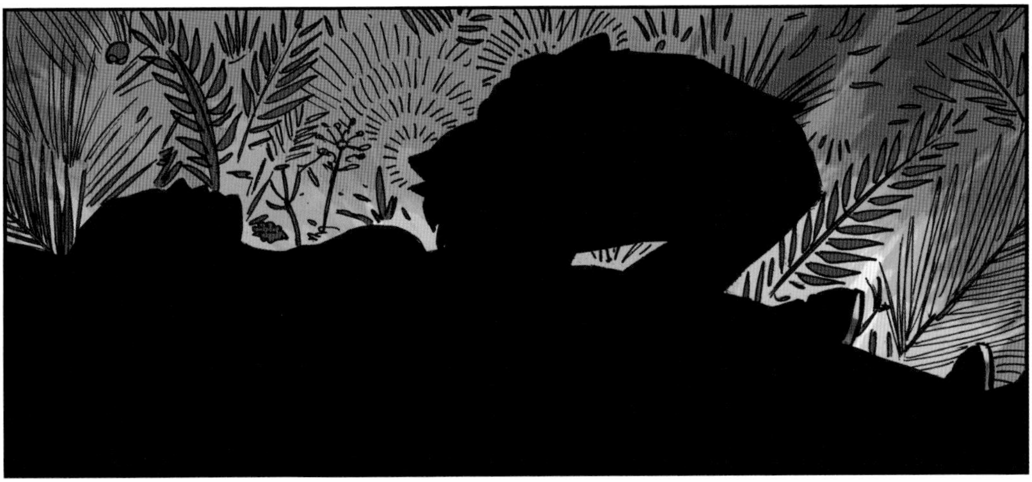

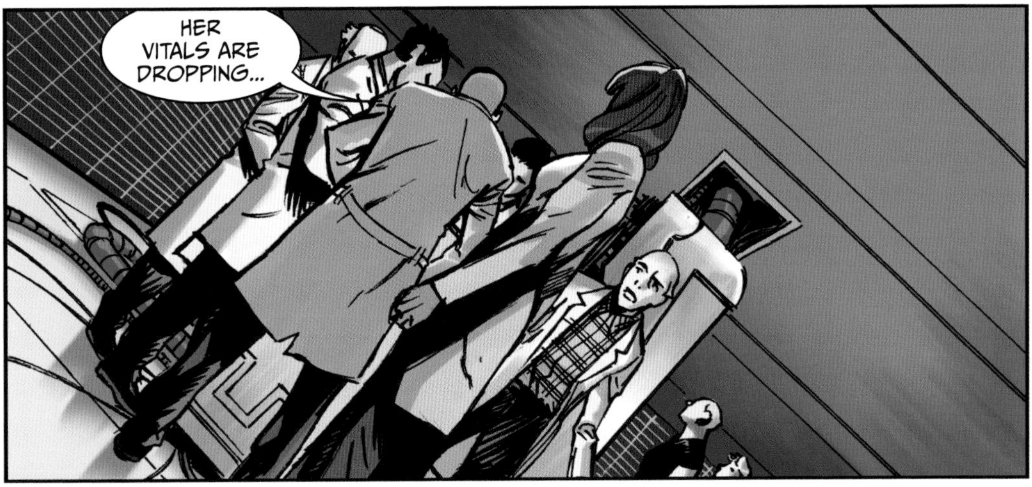
HER VITALS ARE DROPPING...

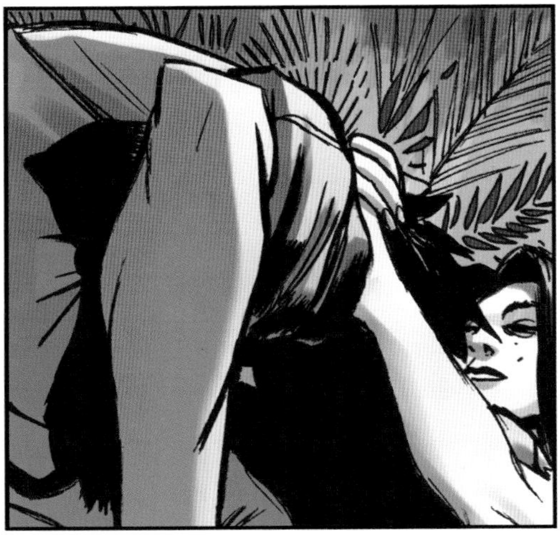

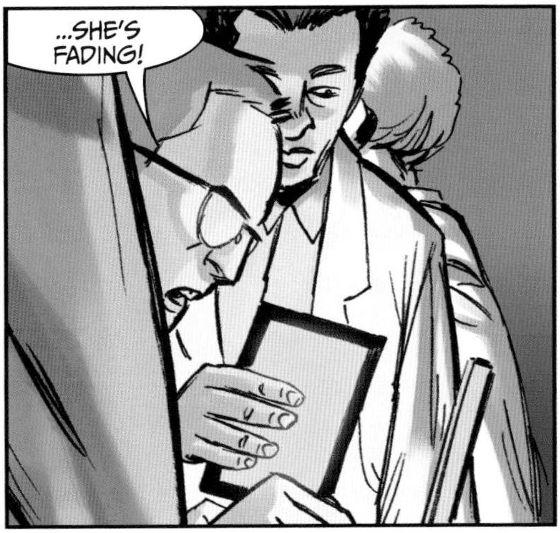
...SHE'S FADING!

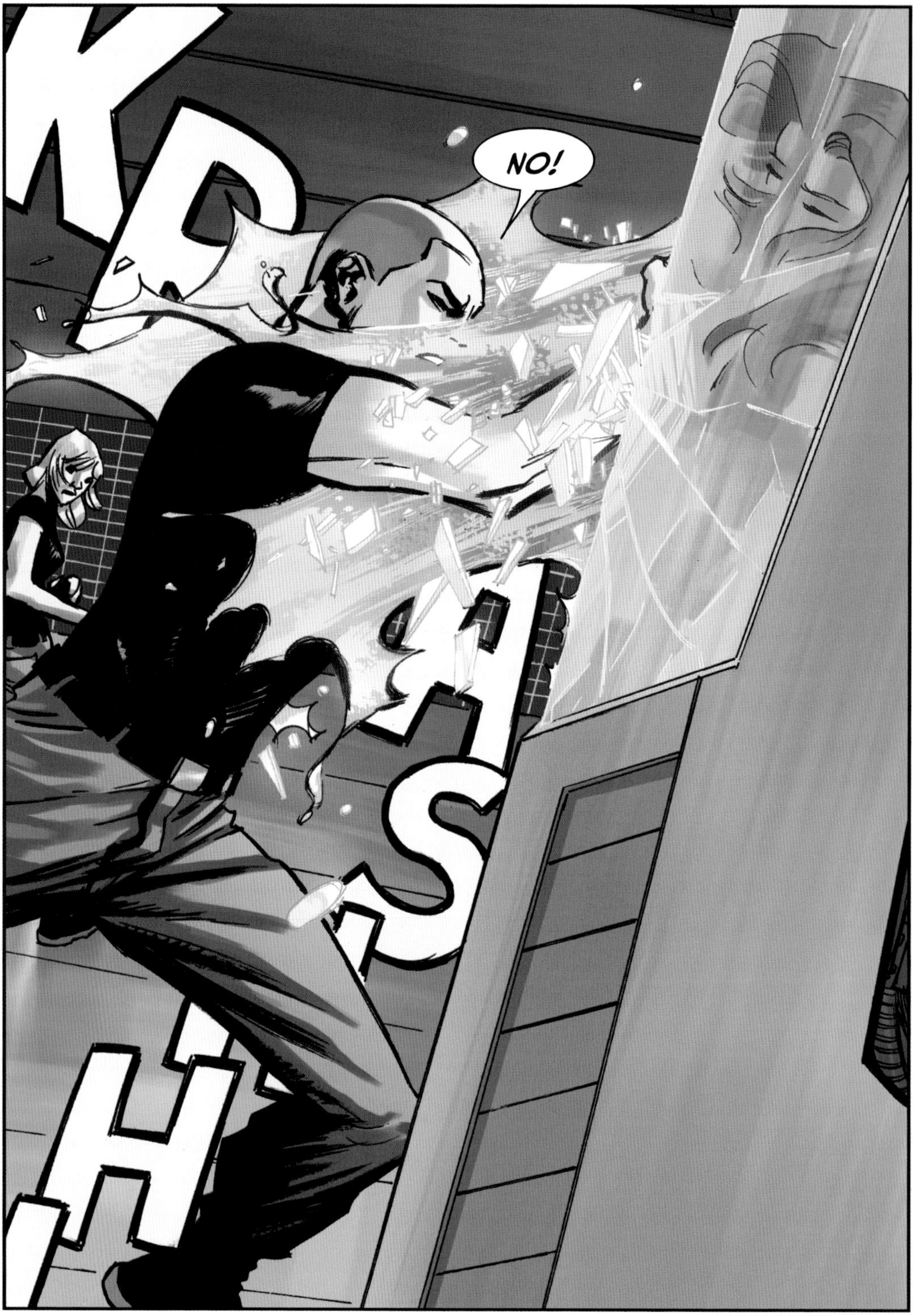
NO!

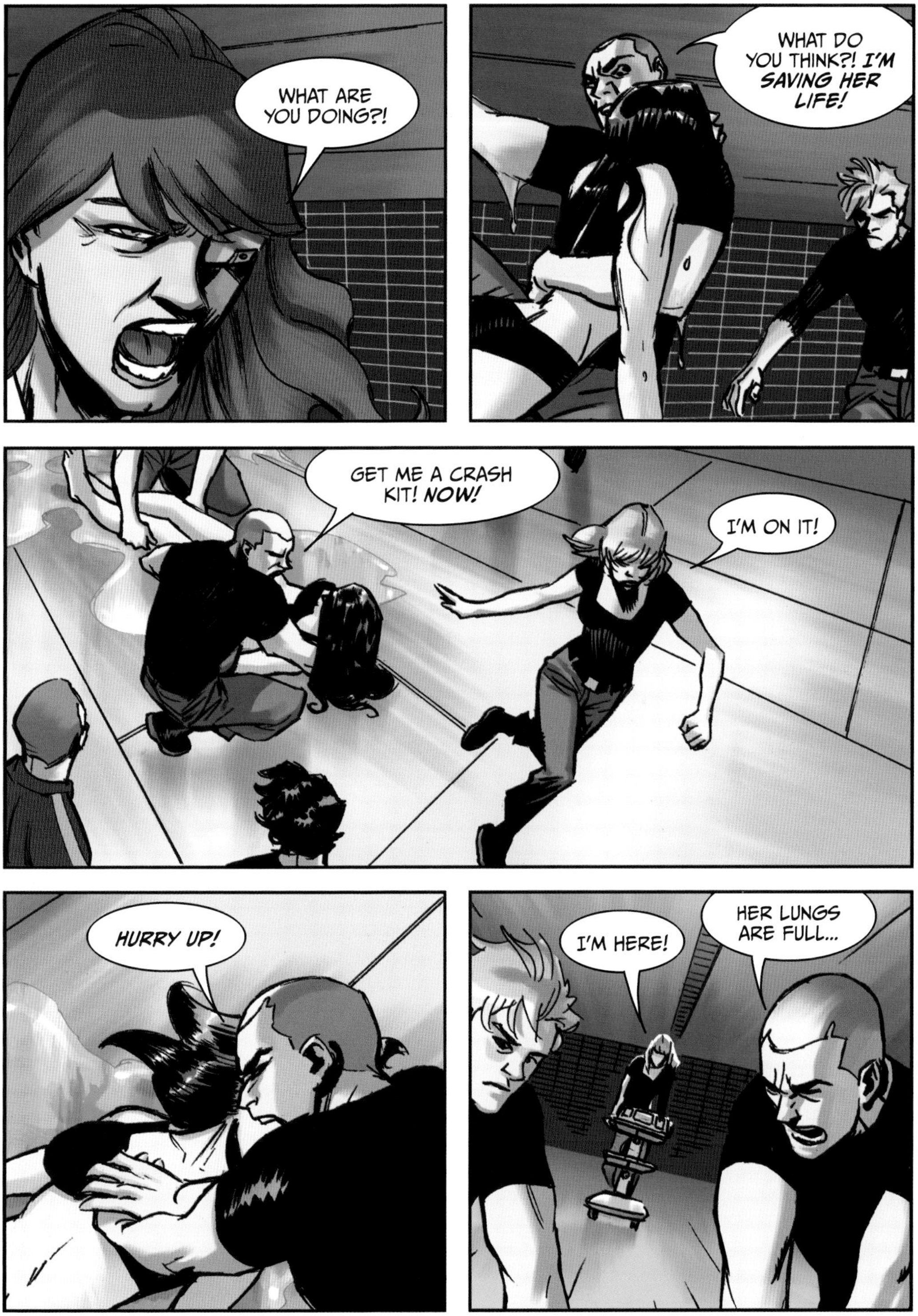
WHAT ARE YOU DOING?!
WHAT DO YOU THINK?! *I'M SAVING HER LIFE!*
GET ME A CRASH KIT! *NOW!*
I'M ON IT!
HURRY UP!
I'M HERE!
HER LUNGS ARE FULL...

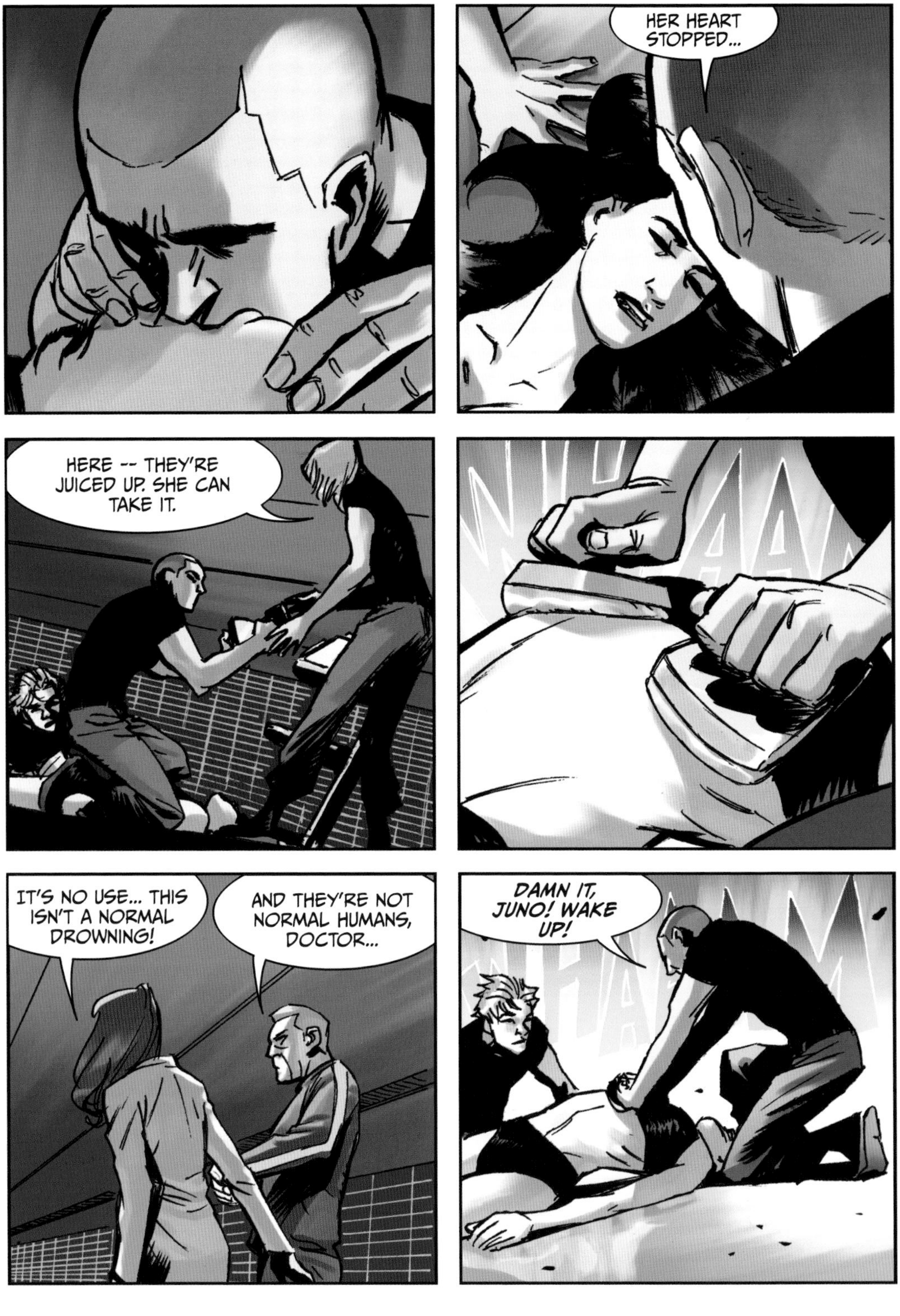
HER HEART STOPPED...
HERE -- THEY'RE JUICED UP. SHE CAN TAKE IT.
IT'S NO USE... THIS ISN'T A NORMAL DROWNING!
AND THEY'RE NOT NORMAL HUMANS, DOCTOR...
DAMN IT, JUNO! WAKE UP!

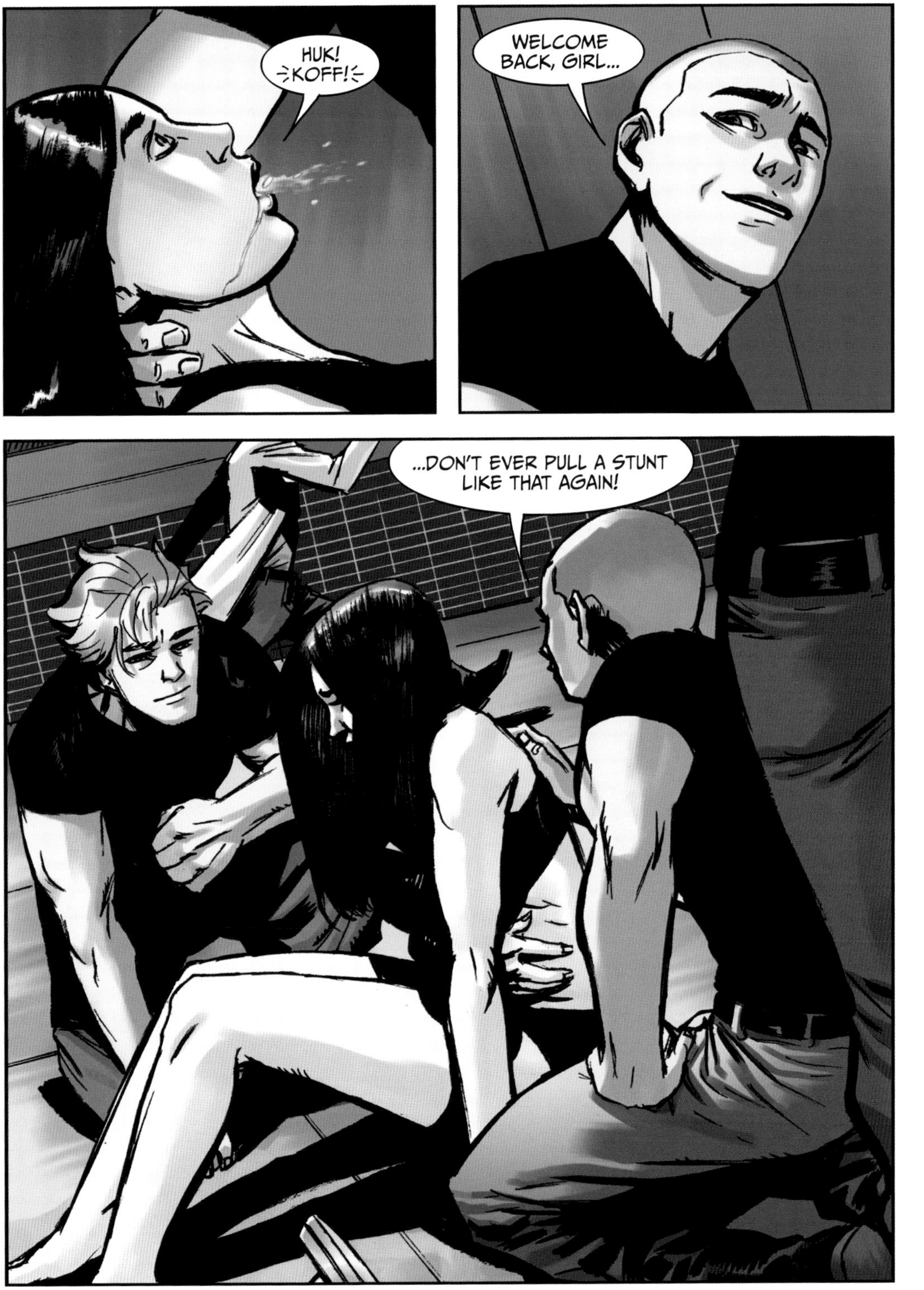
HUK!
-KOFF!-
WELCOME BACK, GIRL...
...DON'T EVER PULL A STUNT LIKE THAT AGAIN!

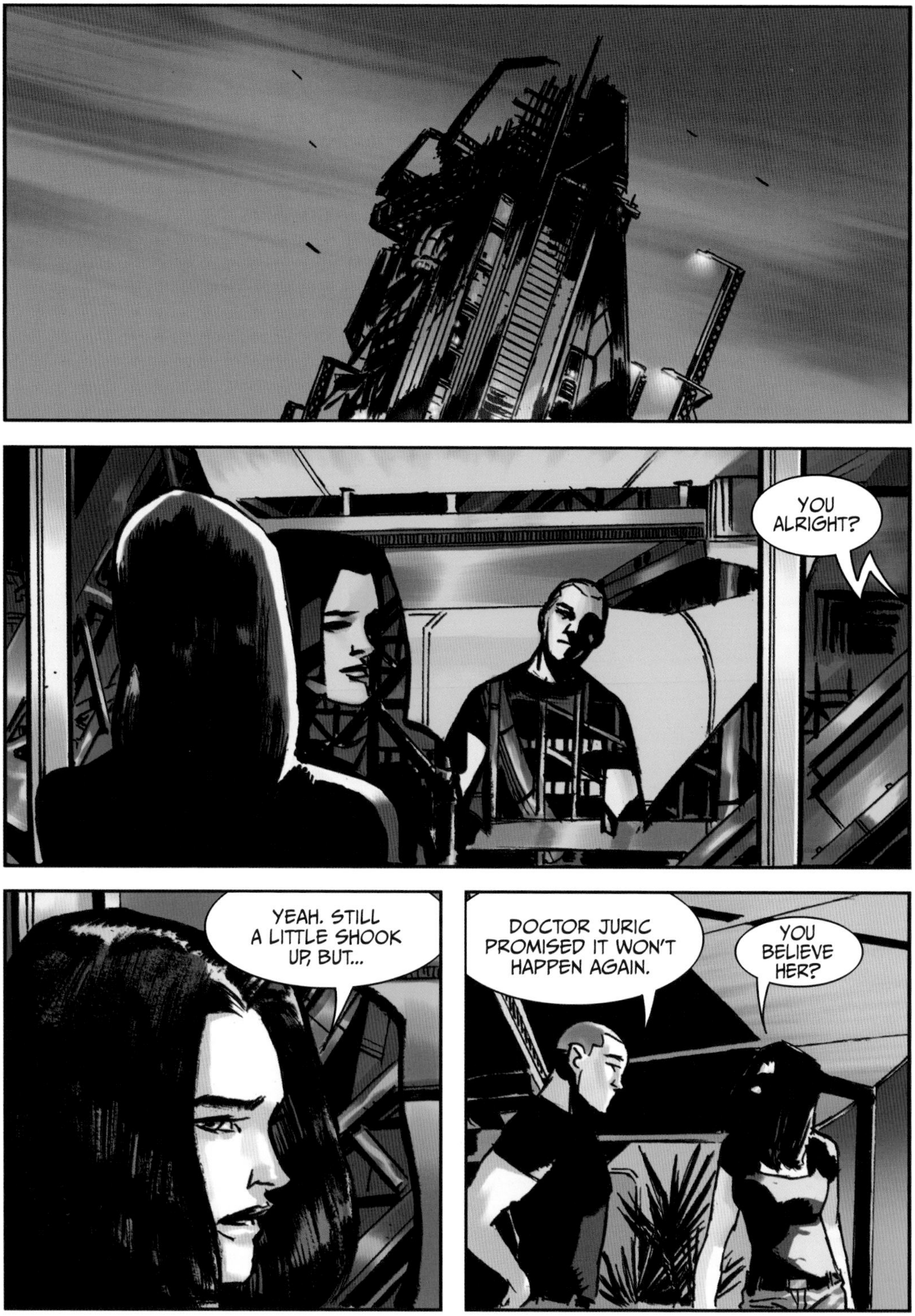
YOU ALRIGHT?
YEAH. STILL A LITTLE SHOOK UP, BUT...
DOCTOR JURIC PROMISED IT WON'T HAPPEN AGAIN.
YOU BELIEVE HER?

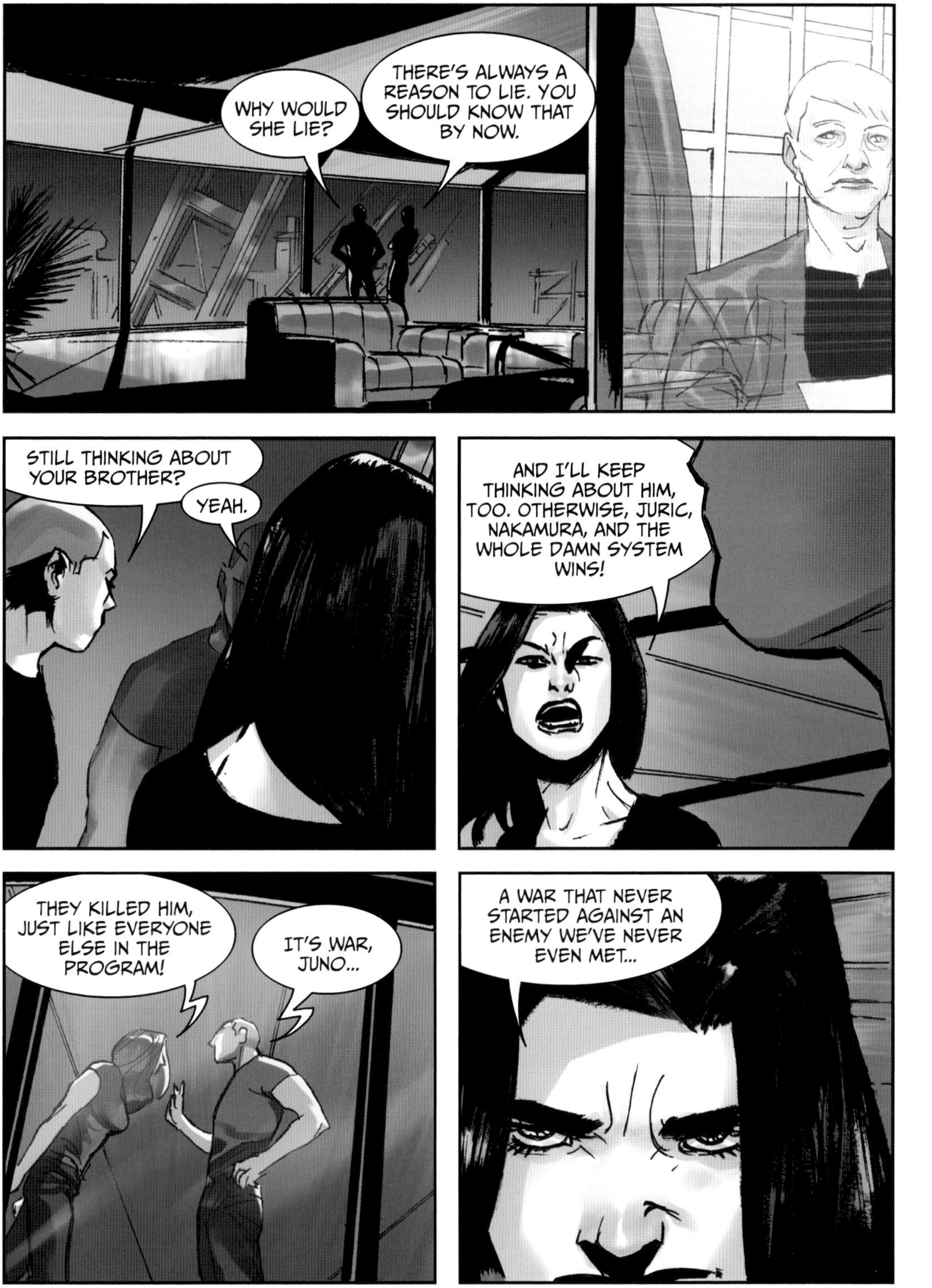
WHY WOULD SHE LIE?
THERE'S ALWAYS A REASON TO LIE. YOU SHOULD KNOW THAT BY NOW.
STILL THINKING ABOUT YOUR BROTHER?
YEAH.
AND I'LL KEEP THINKING ABOUT HIM, TOO. OTHERWISE, JURIC, NAKAMURA, AND THE WHOLE DAMN SYSTEM WINS!
THEY KILLED HIM, JUST LIKE EVERYONE ELSE IN THE PROGRAM!
IT'S WAR, JUNO...
A WAR THAT NEVER STARTED AGAINST AN ENEMY WE'VE NEVER EVEN MET...

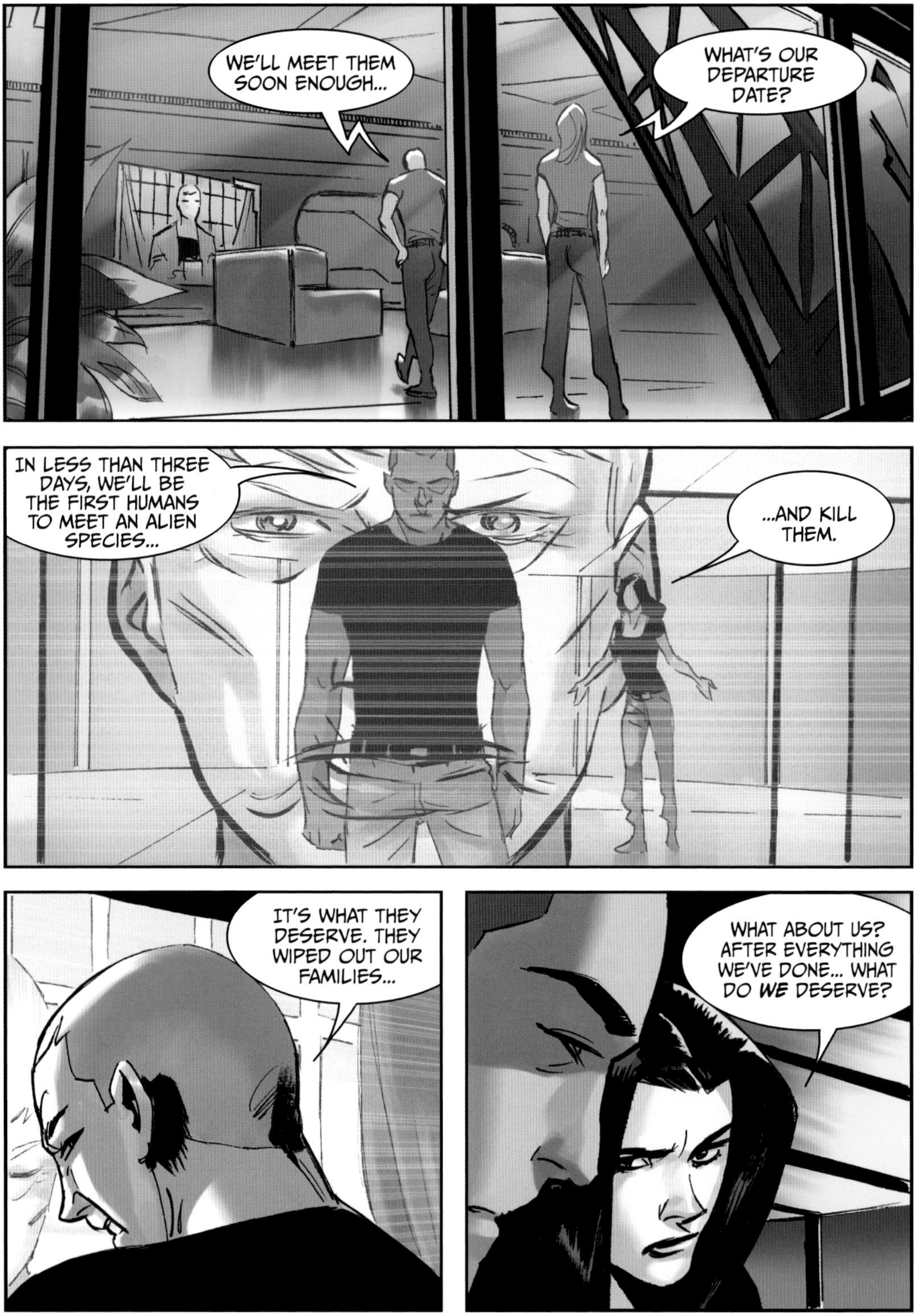
WE'LL MEET THEM SOON ENOUGH...
WHAT'S OUR DEPARTURE DATE?
IN LESS THAN THREE DAYS, WE'LL BE THE FIRST HUMANS TO MEET AN ALIEN SPECIES...
...AND KILL THEM.
IT'S WHAT THEY DESERVE. THEY WIPED OUT OUR FAMILIES...
WHAT ABOUT US? AFTER EVERYTHING WE'VE DONE... WHAT DO **WE** DESERVE?

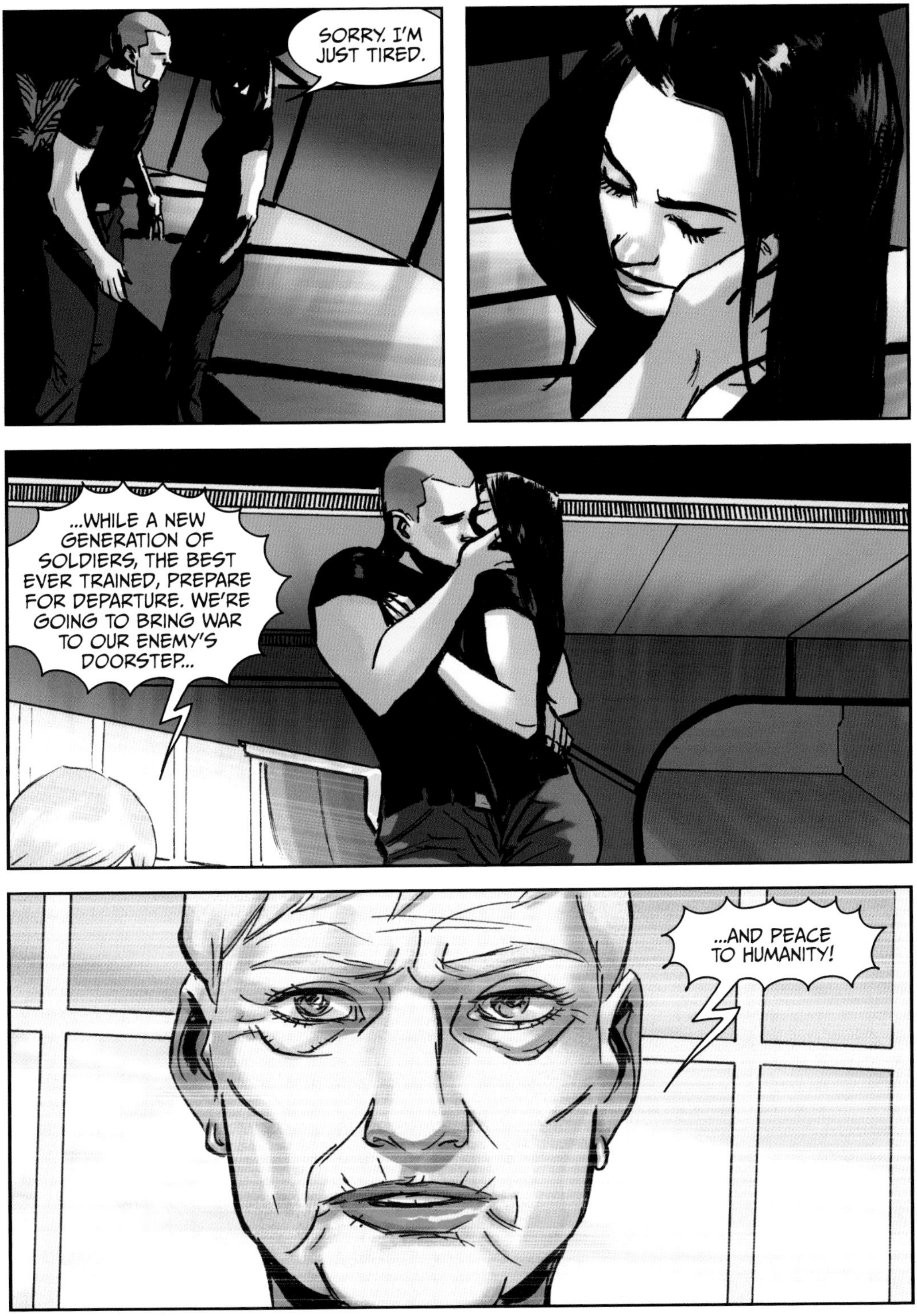
SORRY. I'M JUST TIRED.
...WHILE A NEW GENERATION OF SOLDIERS, THE BEST EVER TRAINED, PREPARE FOR DEPARTURE. WE'RE GOING TO BRING WAR TO OUR ENEMY'S DOORSTEP...
...AND PEACE TO HUMANITY!

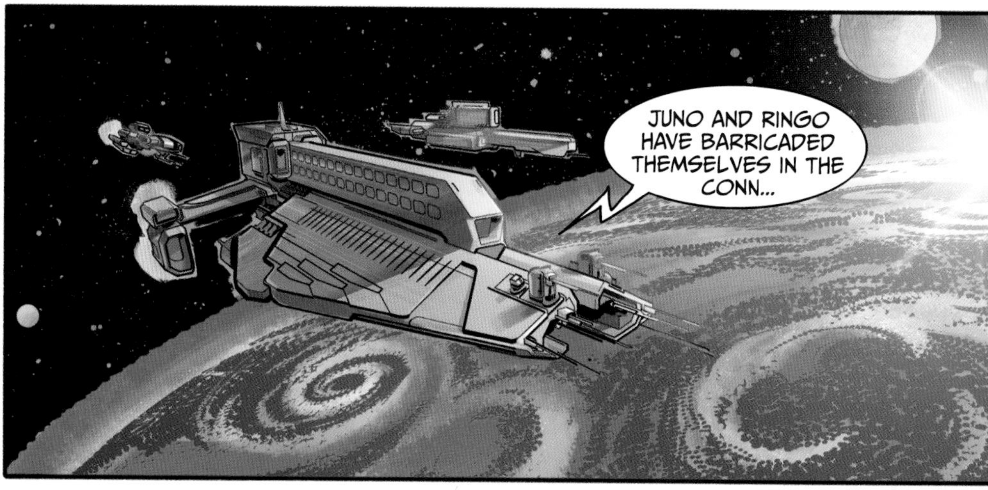
JUNO AND RINGO HAVE BARRICADED THEMSELVES IN THE CONN...

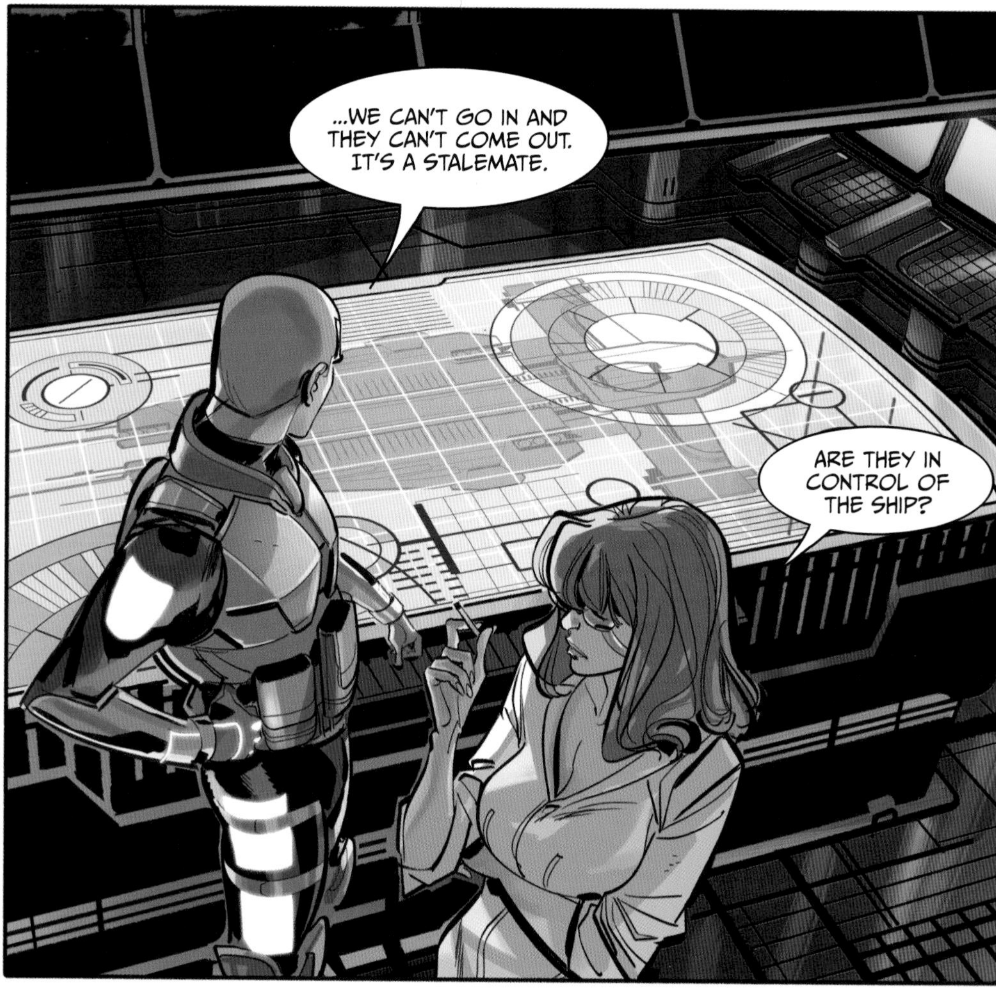
...WE CAN'T GO IN AND THEY CAN'T COME OUT. IT'S A STALEMATE.
ARE THEY IN CONTROL OF THE SHIP?

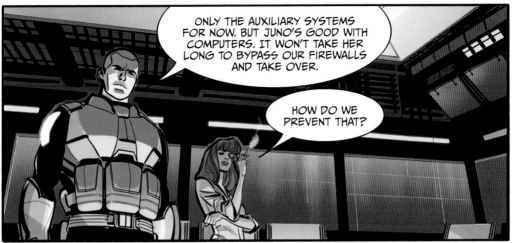

ONLY THE AUXILIARY SYSTEMS FOR NOW. BUT JUNO'S GOOD WITH COMPUTERS. IT WON'T TAKE HER LONG TO BYPASS OUR FIREWALLS AND TAKE OVER.

HOW DO WE PREVENT THAT?

I'VE ORDERED FULL EVACUATION. AS SOON AS IT'S CLEAR, THE OTHER SHIPS WILL OPEN FIRE ON THIS ONE AND DESTROY IT. ITS OUR ONLY CHOICE.

WHY WAIT?

IF THE LIVES OF THE HUNDREDS OF SOLDIERS ON BOARD AREN'T ENOUGH FOR YOU, DOCTOR... I'D REMIND YOU WE'D BOTH DIE IF THEY WERE TO ATTACK NOW, TOO.

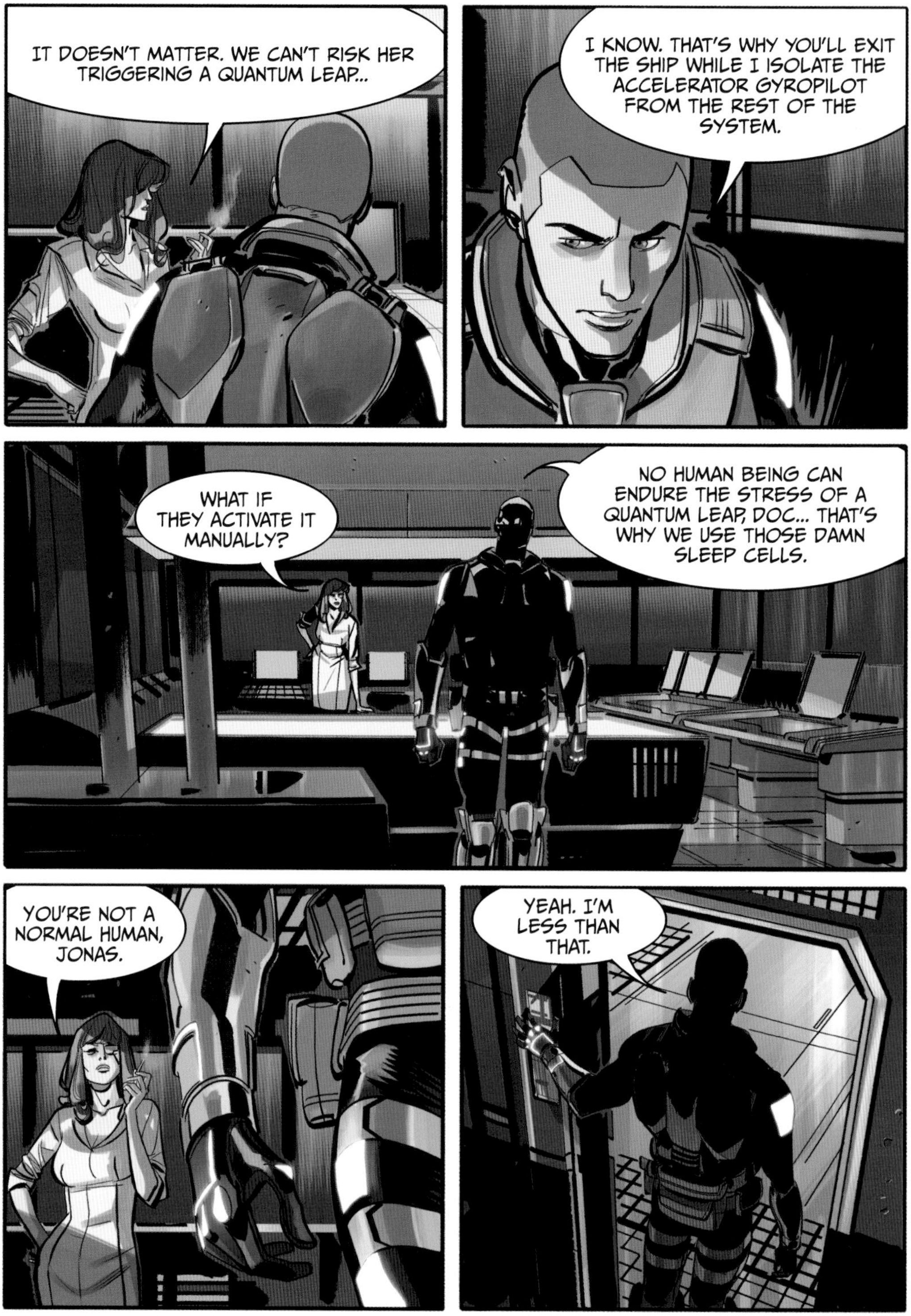
IT DOESN'T MATTER. WE CAN'T RISK HER TRIGGERING A QUANTUM LEAP...
I KNOW. THAT'S WHY YOU'LL EXIT THE SHIP WHILE I ISOLATE THE ACCELERATOR GYROPILOT FROM THE REST OF THE SYSTEM.
WHAT IF THEY ACTIVATE IT MANUALLY?
NO HUMAN BEING CAN ENDURE THE STRESS OF A QUANTUM LEAP, DOC... THAT'S WHY WE USE THOSE DAMN SLEEP CELLS.
YOU'RE NOT A NORMAL HUMAN, JONAS.
YEAH. I'M LESS THAN THAT.

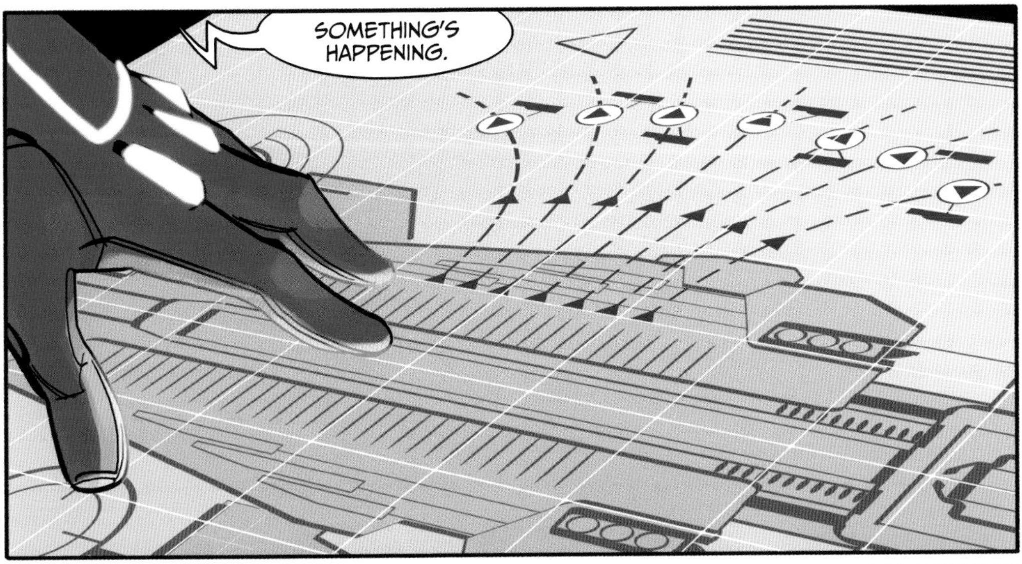
SOMETHING'S HAPPENING.

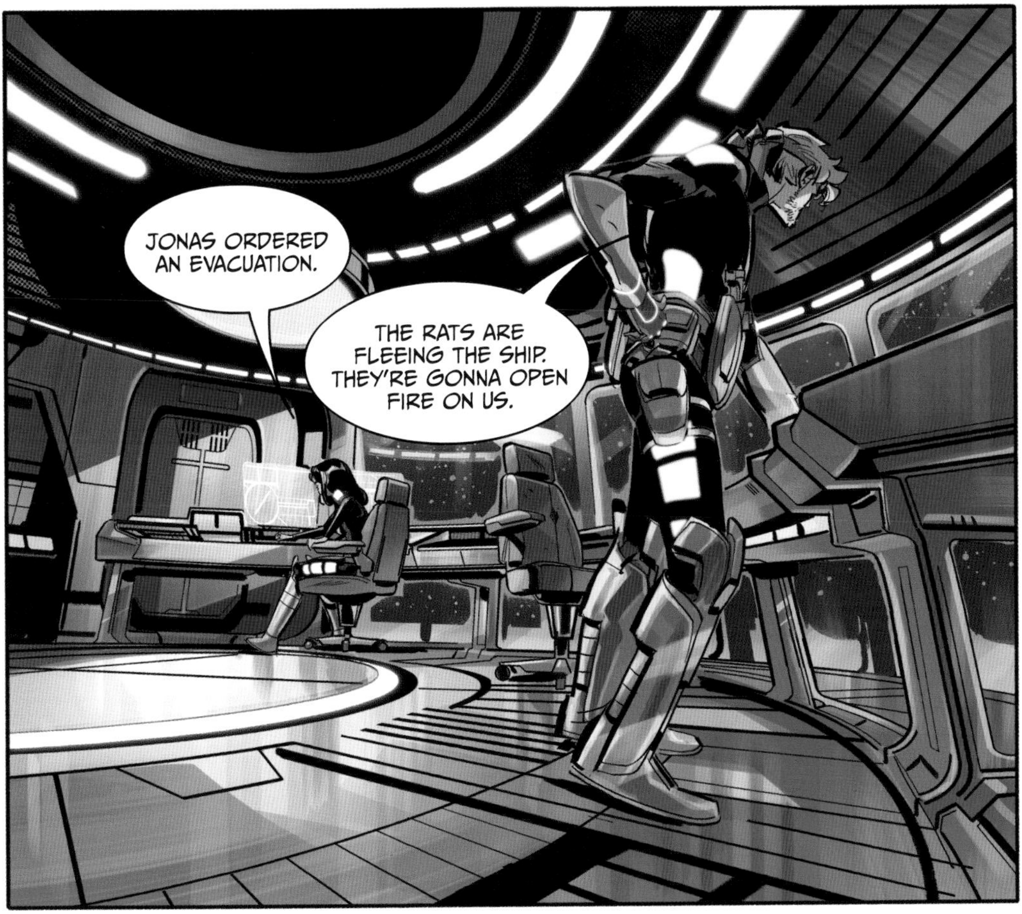
JONAS ORDERED AN EVACUATION.
THE RATS ARE FLEEING THE SHIP. THEY'RE GONNA OPEN FIRE ON US.

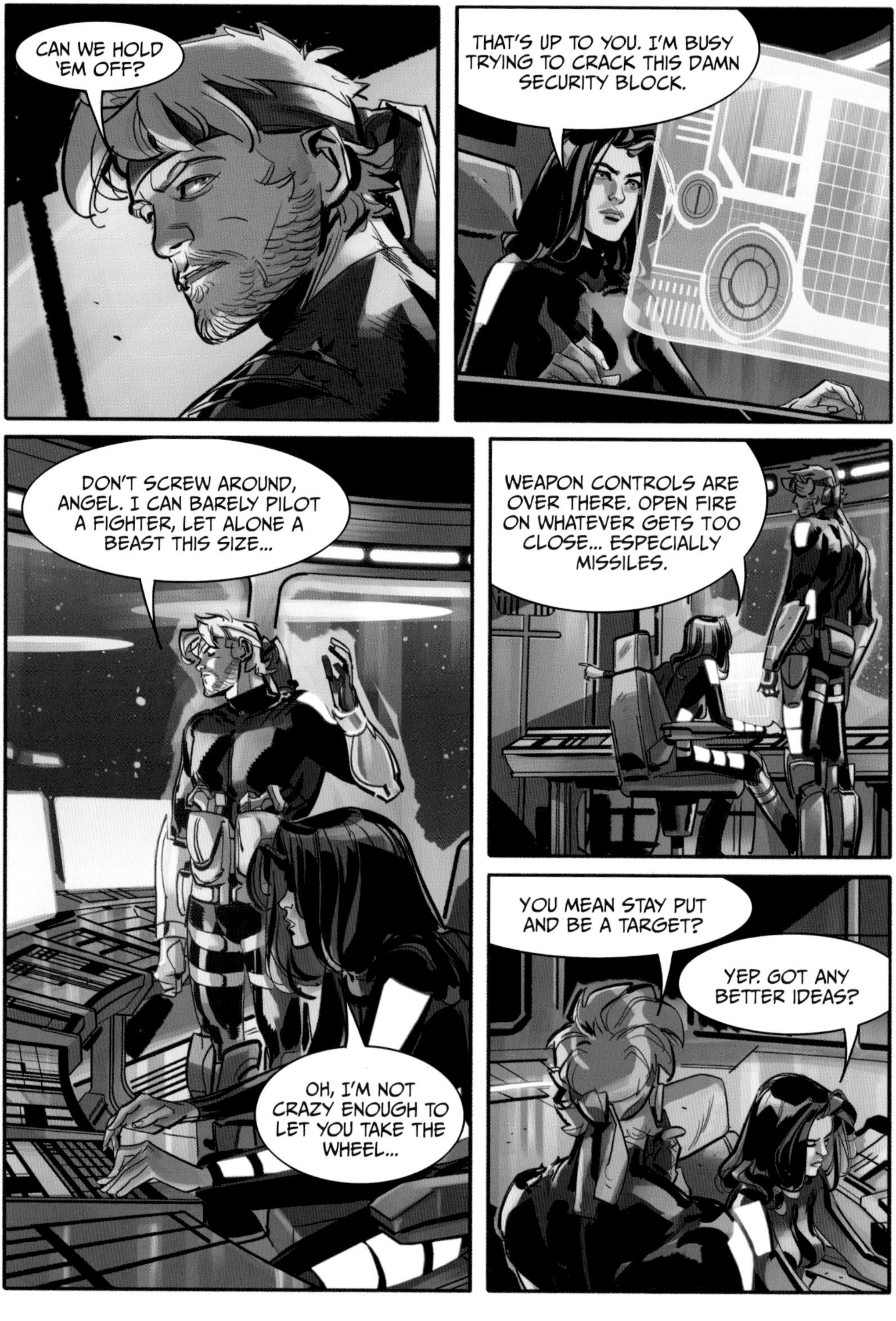
CAN WE HOLD 'EM OFF?
THAT'S UP TO YOU. I'M BUSY TRYING TO CRACK THIS DAMN SECURITY BLOCK.
DON'T SCREW AROUND, ANGEL. I CAN BARELY PILOT A FIGHTER, LET ALONE A BEAST THIS SIZE...
OH, I'M NOT CRAZY ENOUGH TO LET YOU TAKE THE WHEEL...
WEAPON CONTROLS ARE OVER THERE. OPEN FIRE ON WHATEVER GETS TOO CLOSE... ESPECIALLY MISSILES.
YOU MEAN STAY PUT AND BE A TARGET?
YEP. GOT ANY BETTER IDEAS?

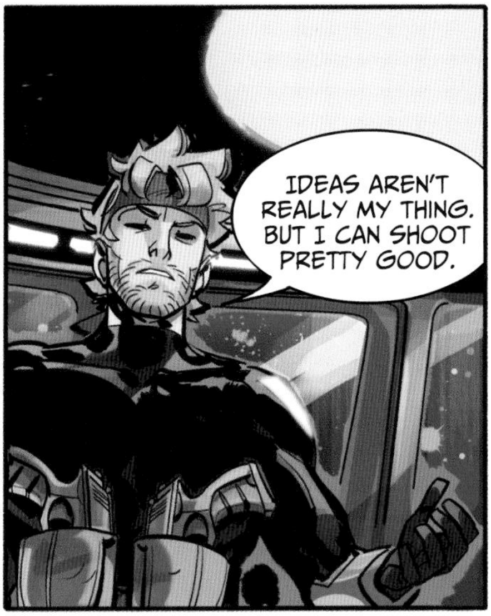
IDEAS AREN'T REALLY MY THING. BUT I CAN SHOOT PRETTY GOOD.

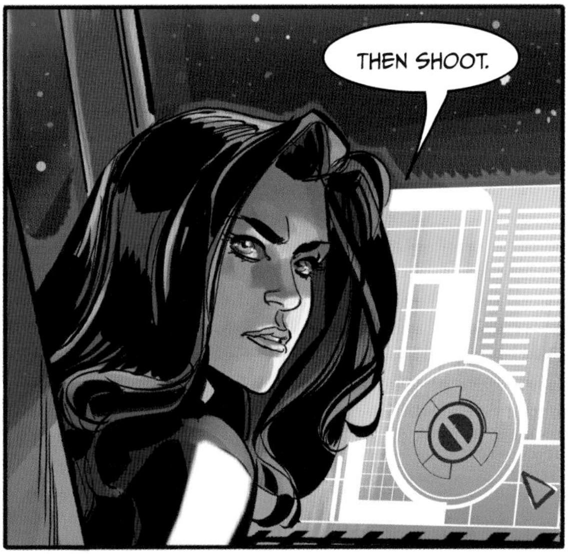
THEN SHOOT.

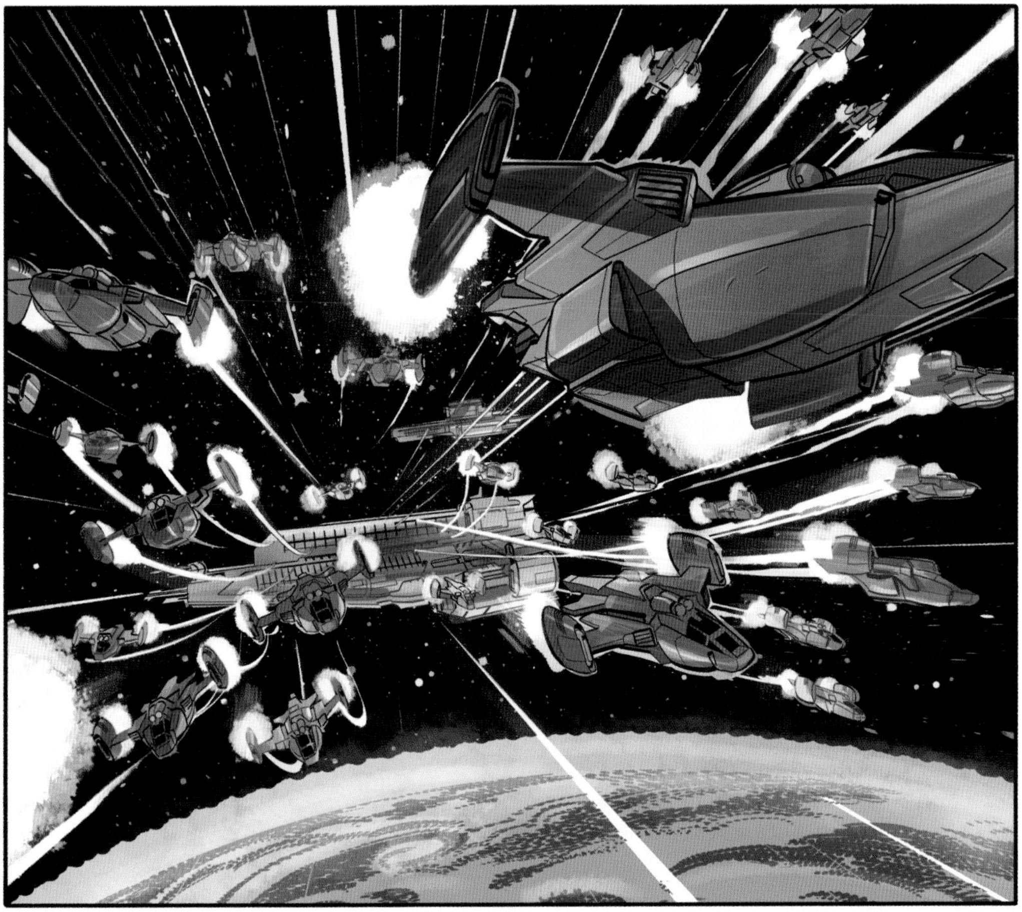

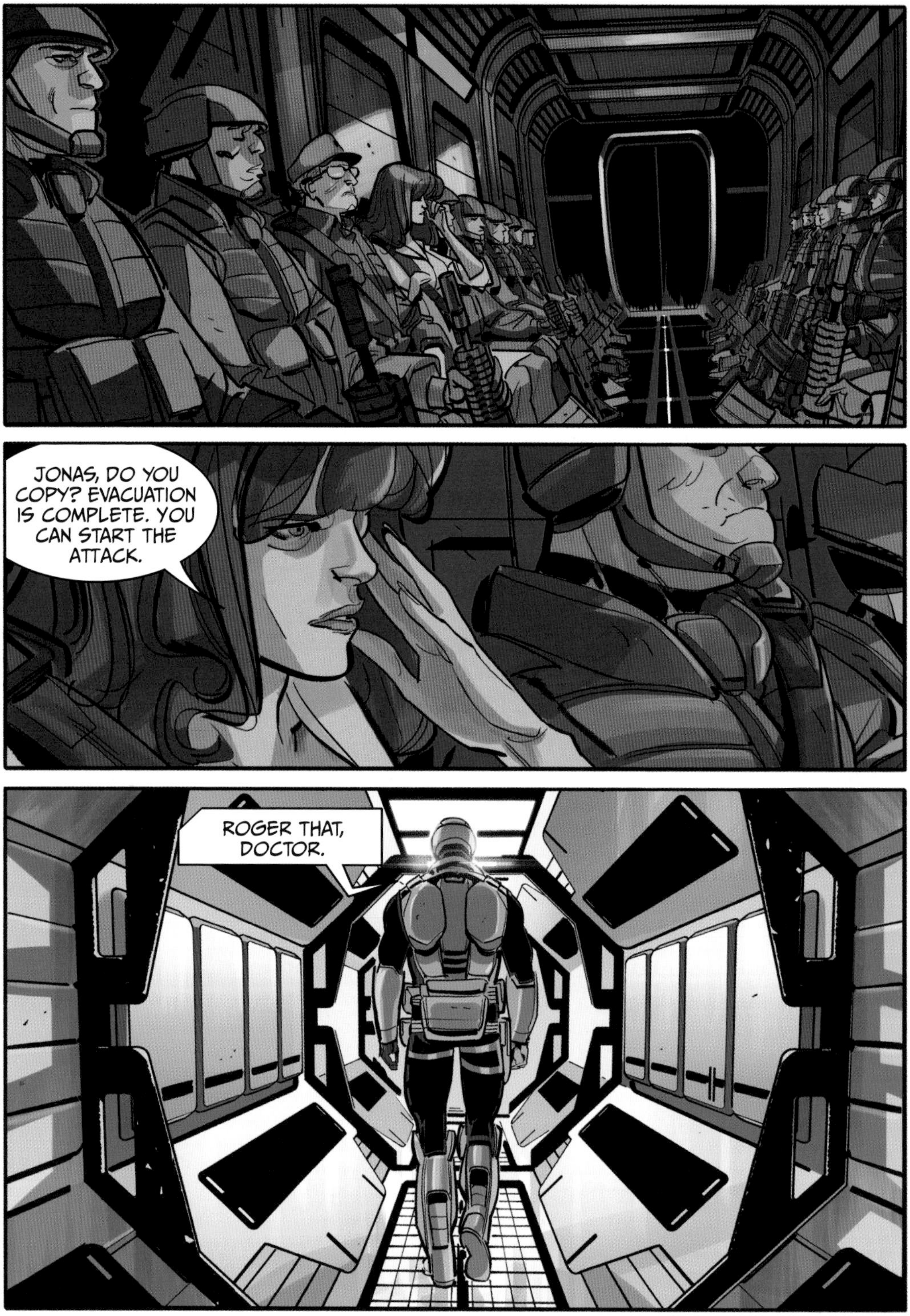
JONAS, DO YOU COPY? EVACUATION IS COMPLETE. YOU CAN START THE ATTACK.
ROGER THAT, DOCTOR.

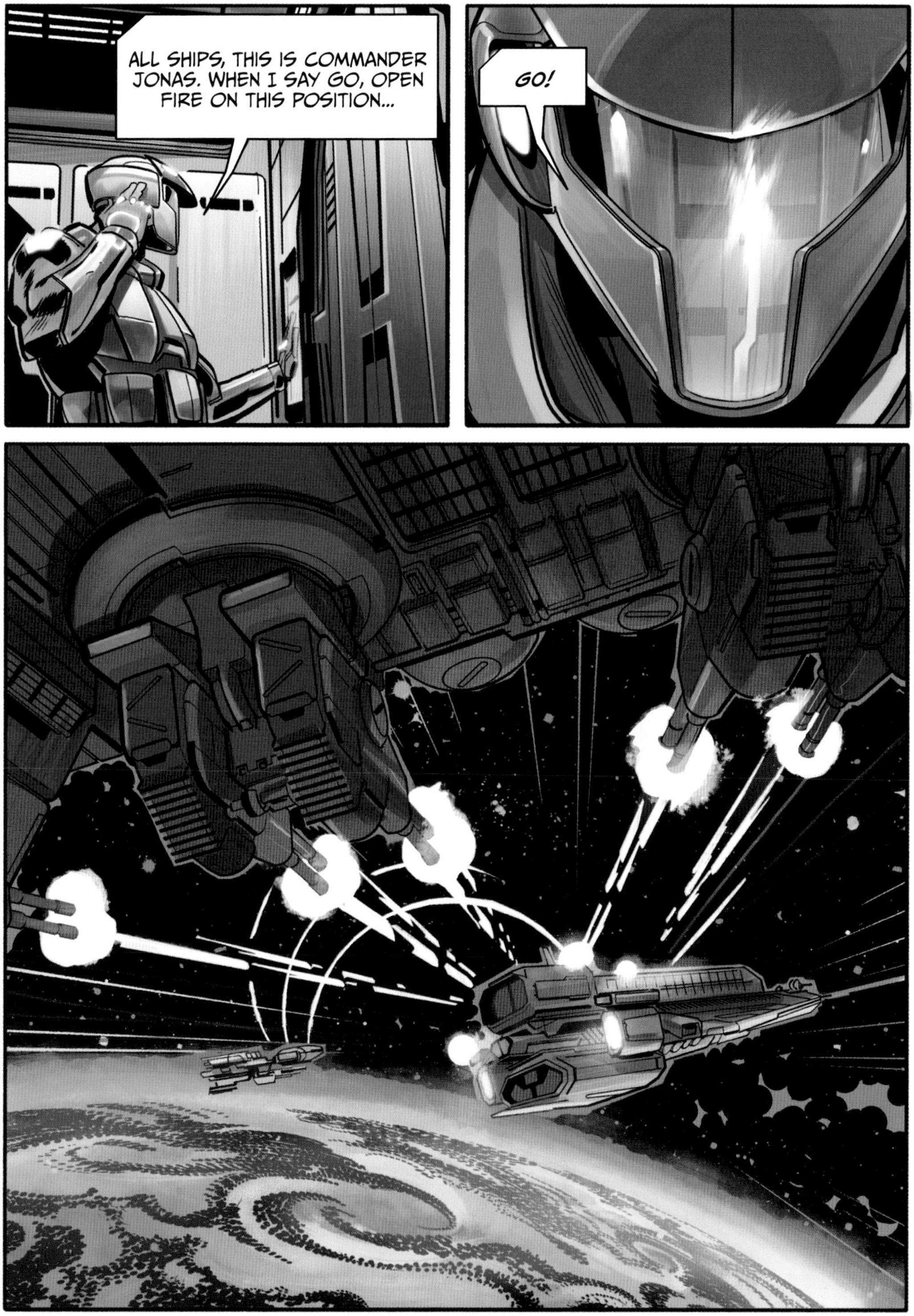
ALL SHIPS, THIS IS COMMANDER JONAS. WHEN I SAY GO, OPEN FIRE ON THIS POSITION...
GO!

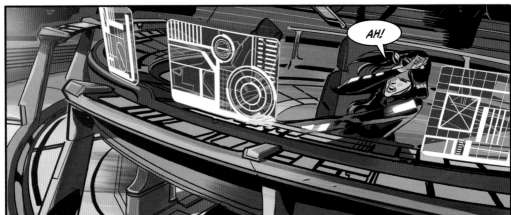

CHAPTER II

AH!

THE CURTAIN'S UP, RINGO! THAT'S YOUR CUE!

ALMOST THERE...

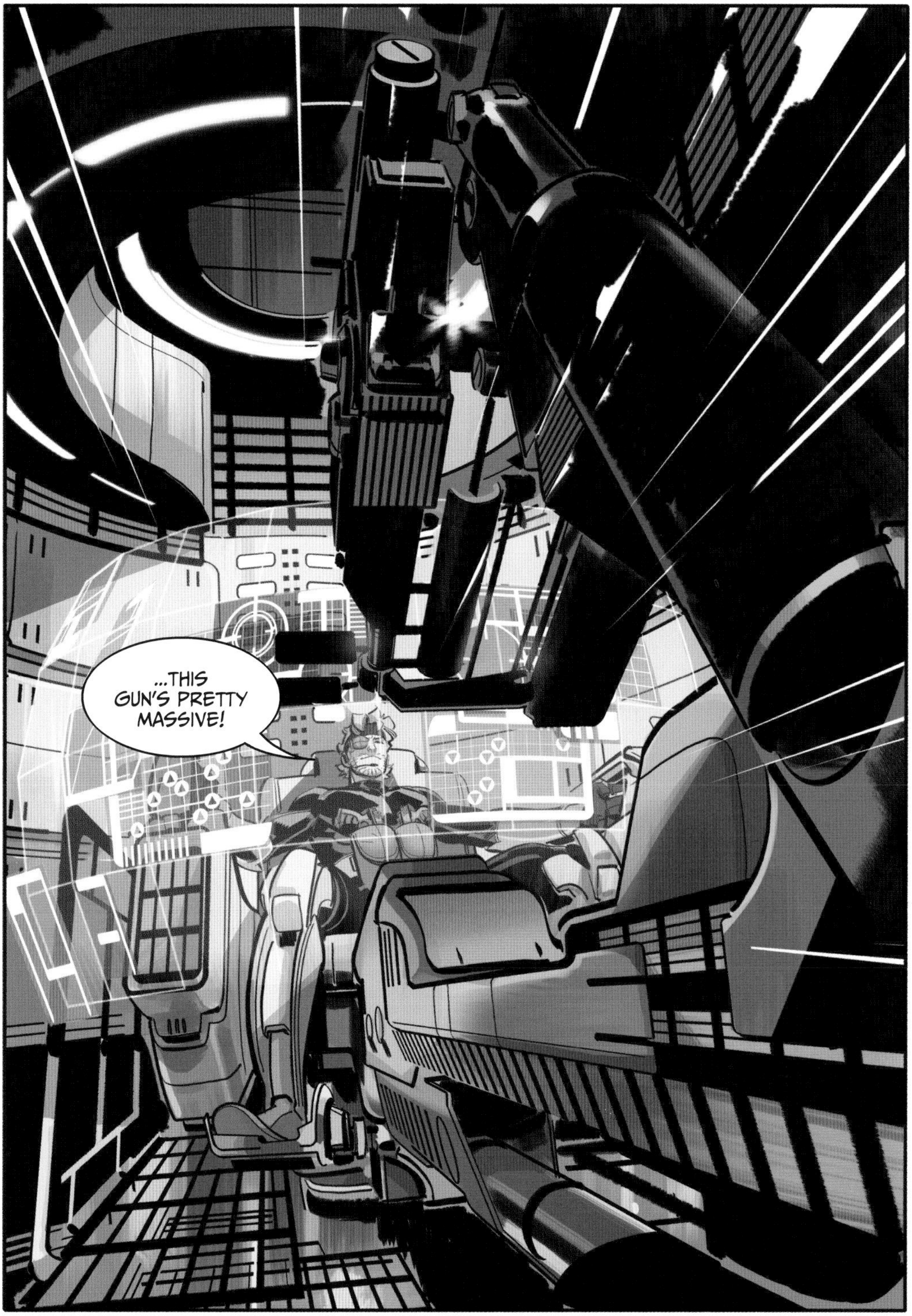
...THIS GUN'S PRETTY MASSIVE!

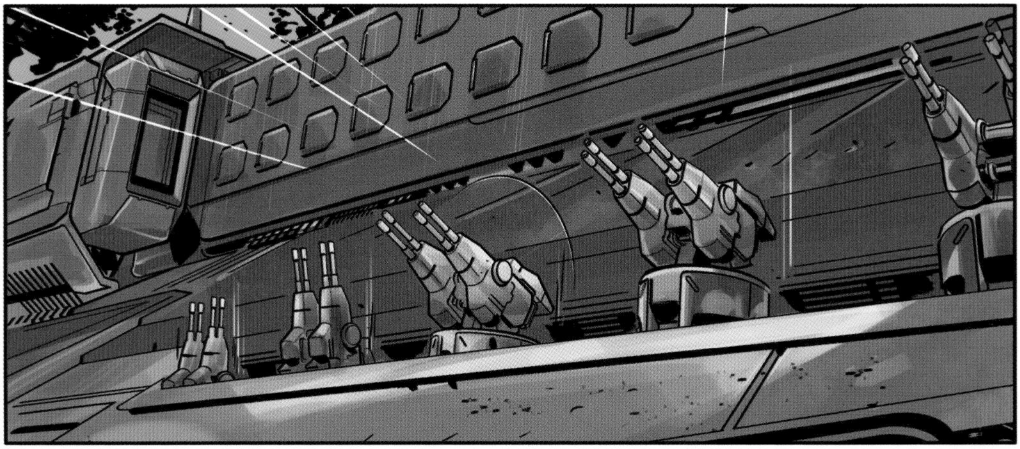

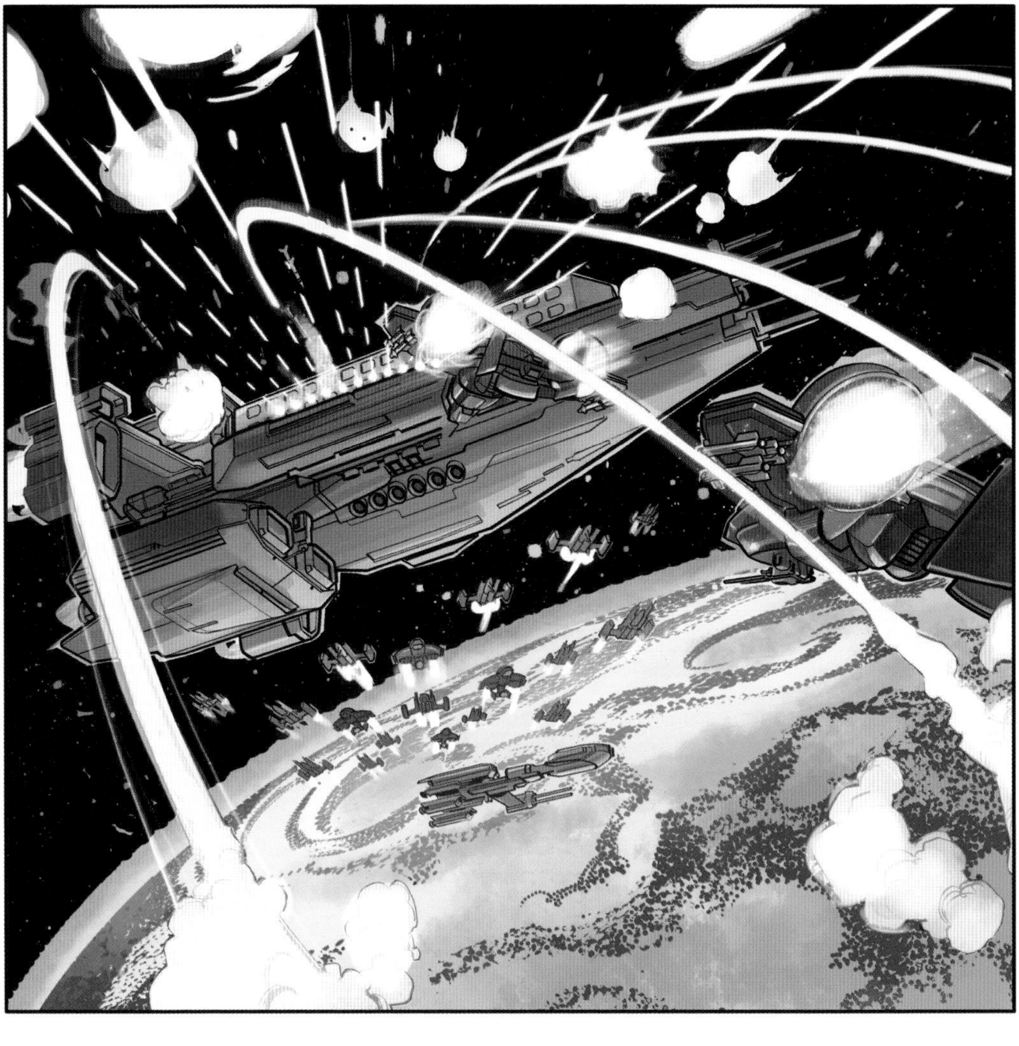

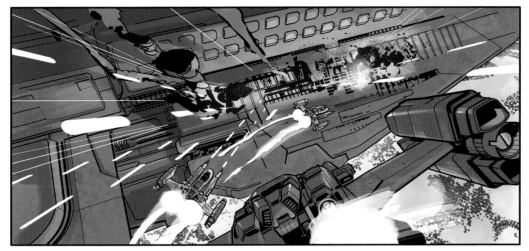

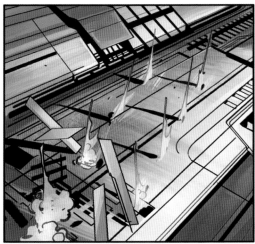

DAMN IT, RINGO! DEAL WITH THOSE FIGHTERS! THEY'RE BUTCHERING US!

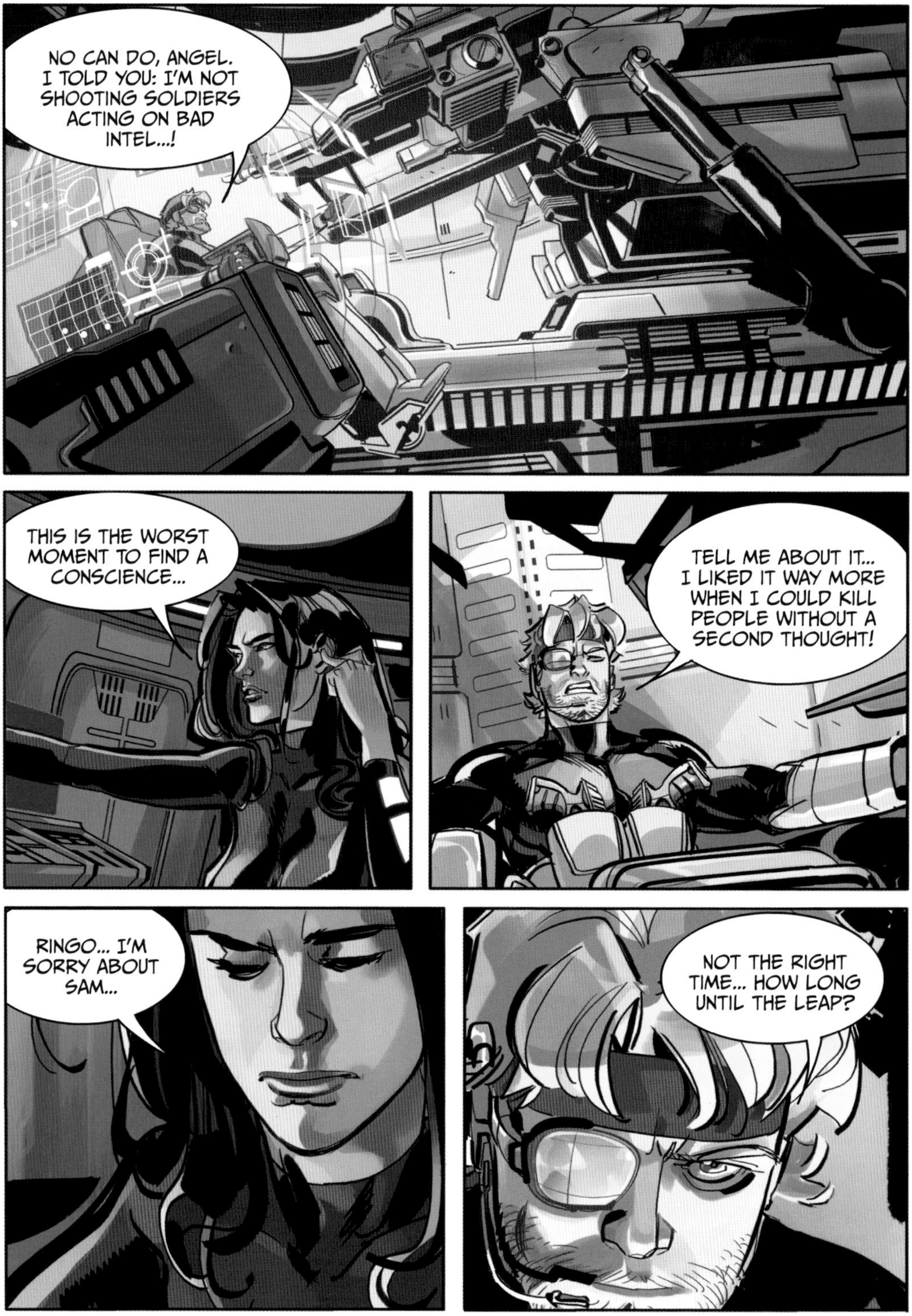
NO CAN DO, ANGEL. I TOLD YOU: I'M NOT SHOOTING SOLDIERS ACTING ON BAD INTEL...!
THIS IS THE WORST MOMENT TO FIND A CONSCIENCE...
TELL ME ABOUT IT... I LIKED IT WAY MORE WHEN I COULD KILL PEOPLE WITHOUT A SECOND THOUGHT!
RINGO... I'M SORRY ABOUT SAM...
NOT THE RIGHT TIME... HOW LONG UNTIL THE LEAP?

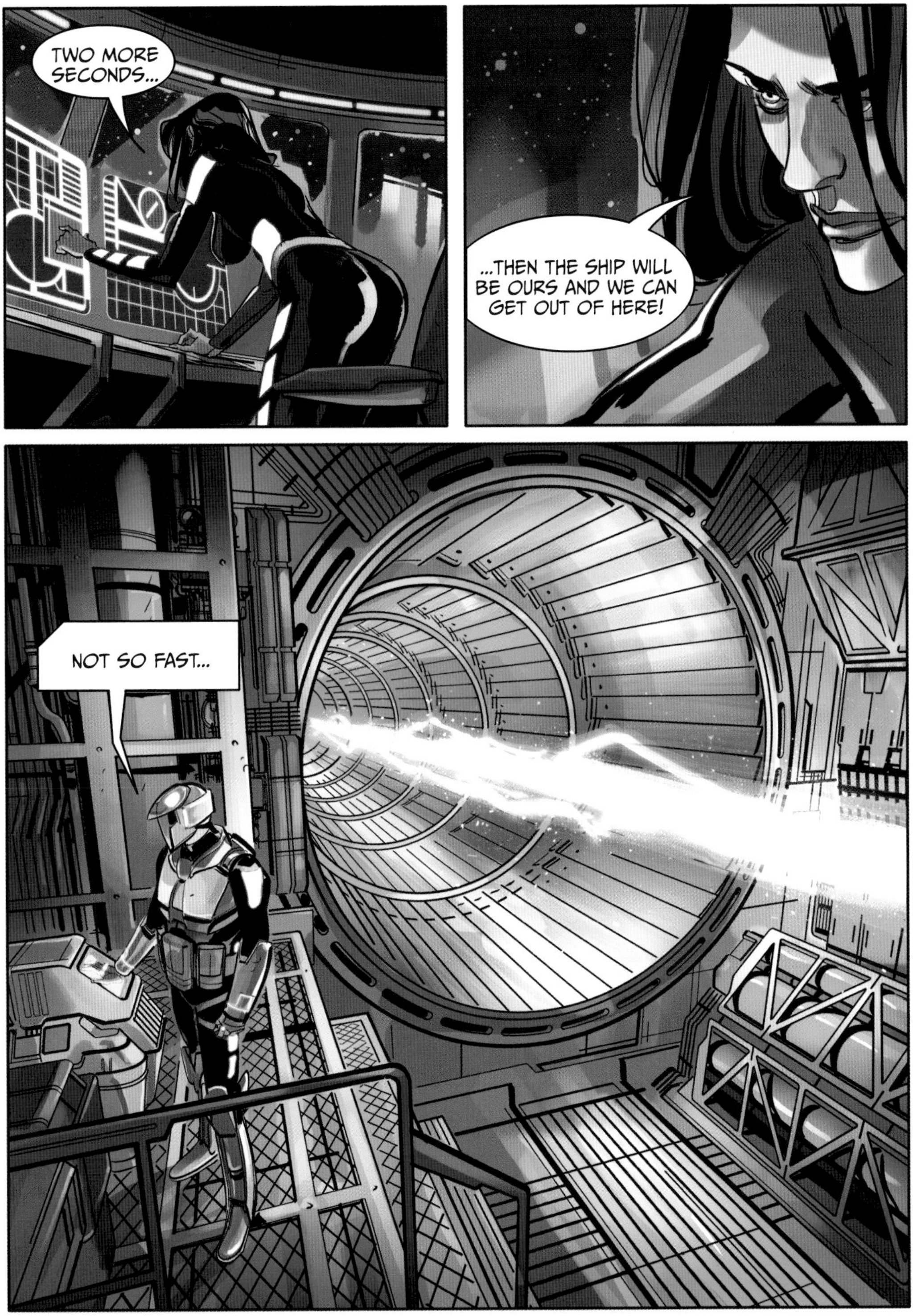
TWO MORE SECONDS...
...THEN THE SHIP WILL BE OURS AND WE CAN GET OUT OF HERE!
NOT SO FAST...

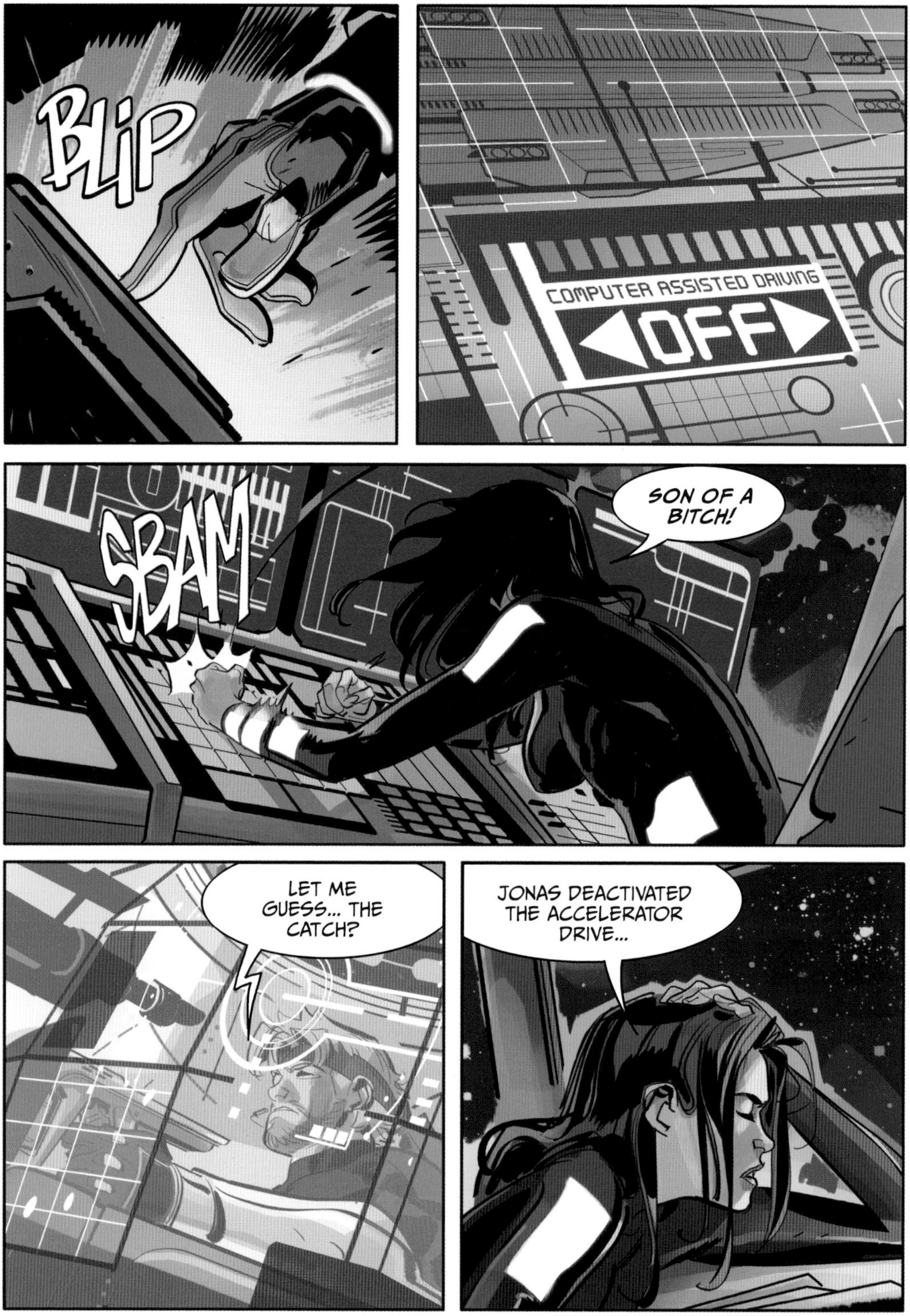
BLIP
COMPUTER ASSISTED DRIVING
OFF
SBAM
SON OF A BITCH!
LET ME GUESS... THE CATCH?
JONAS DEACTIVATED THE ACCELERATOR DRIVE...

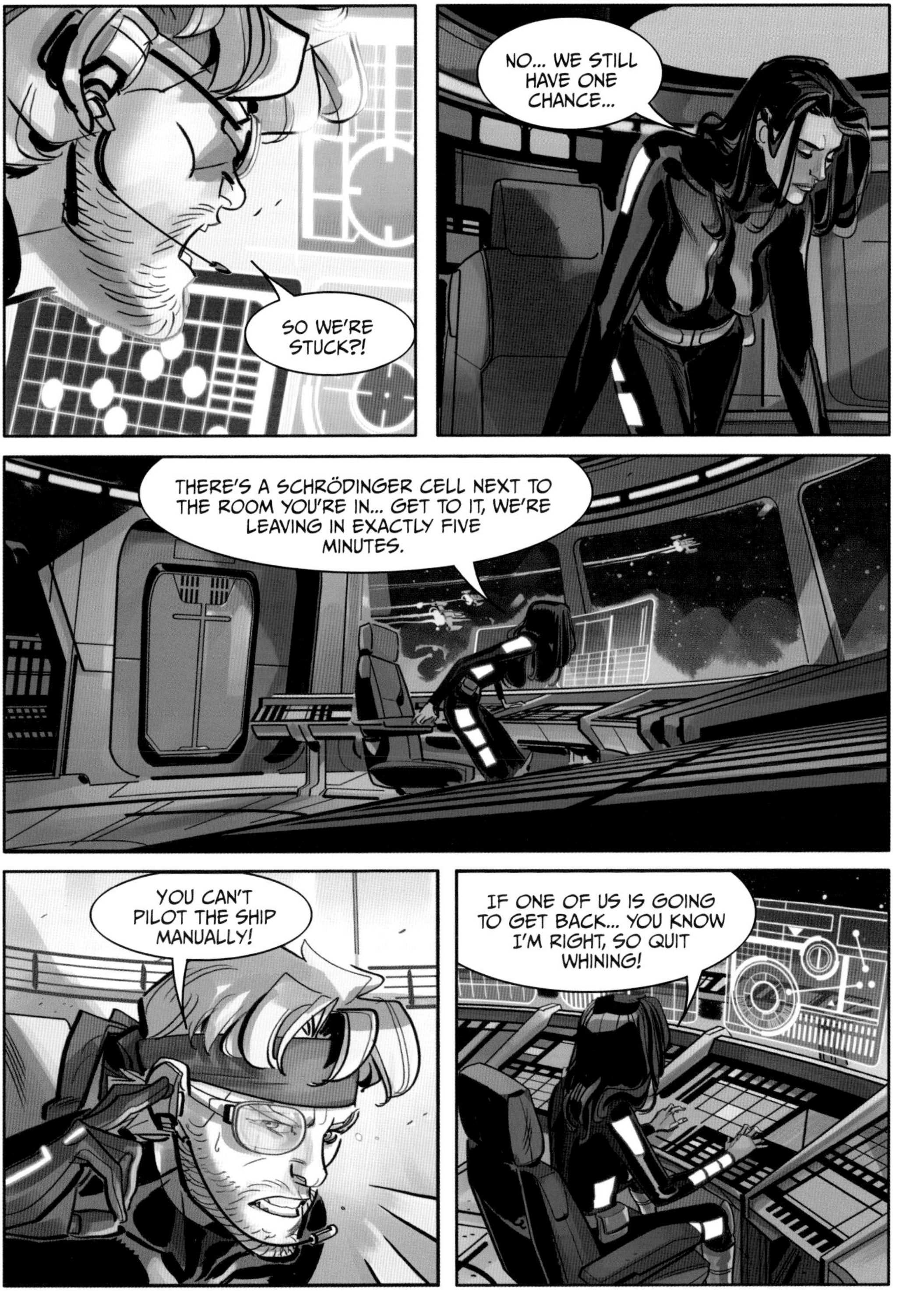
SO WE'RE STUCK?!
NO... WE STILL HAVE ONE CHANCE...
THERE'S A SCHRÖDINGER CELL NEXT TO THE ROOM YOU'RE IN... GET TO IT, WE'RE LEAVING IN EXACTLY FIVE MINUTES.
YOU CAN'T PILOT THE SHIP MANUALLY!
IF ONE OF US IS GOING TO GET BACK... YOU KNOW I'M RIGHT, SO QUIT WHINING!

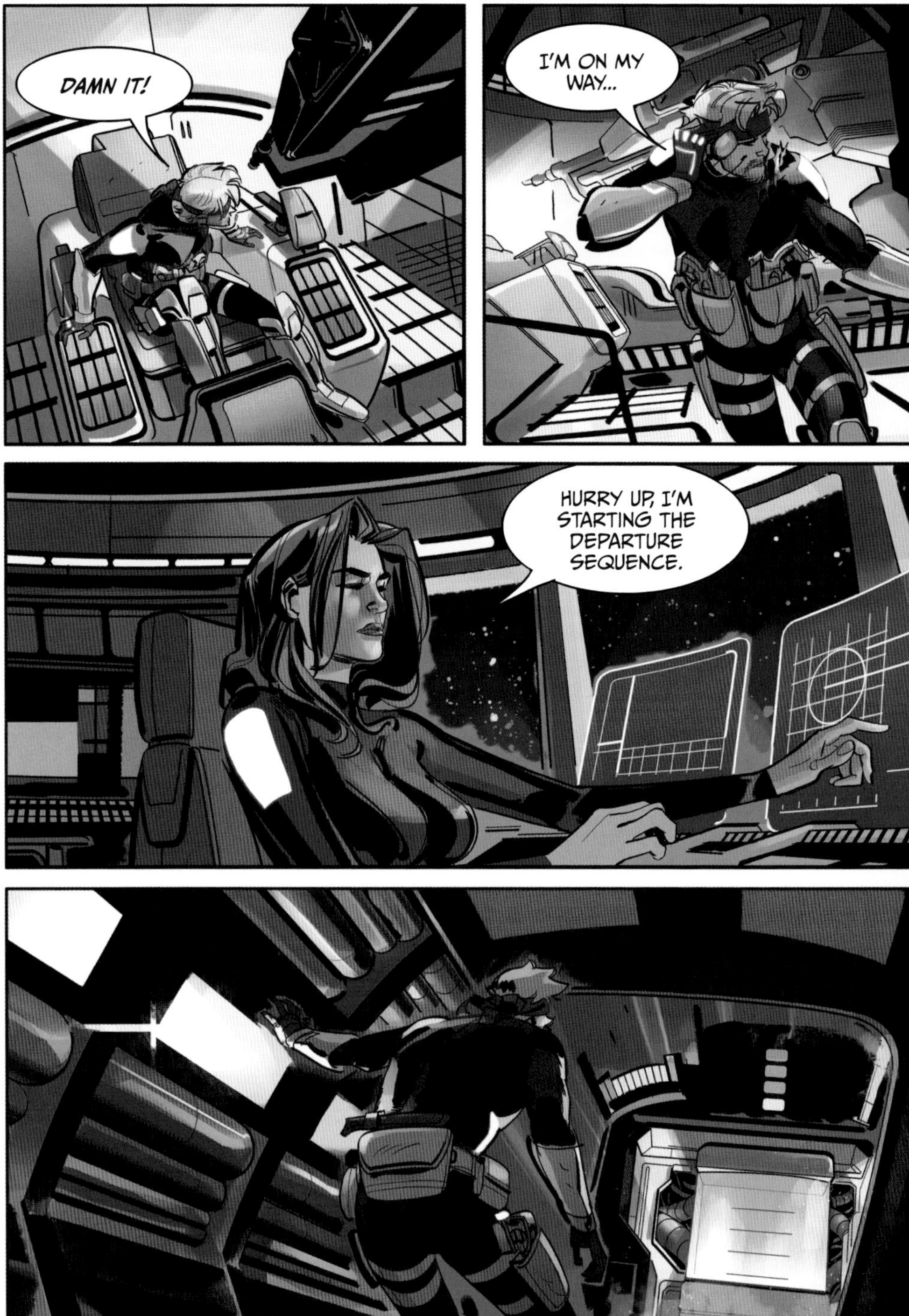
DAMN IT!
I'M ON MY WAY...
HURRY UP, I'M STARTING THE DEPARTURE SEQUENCE.

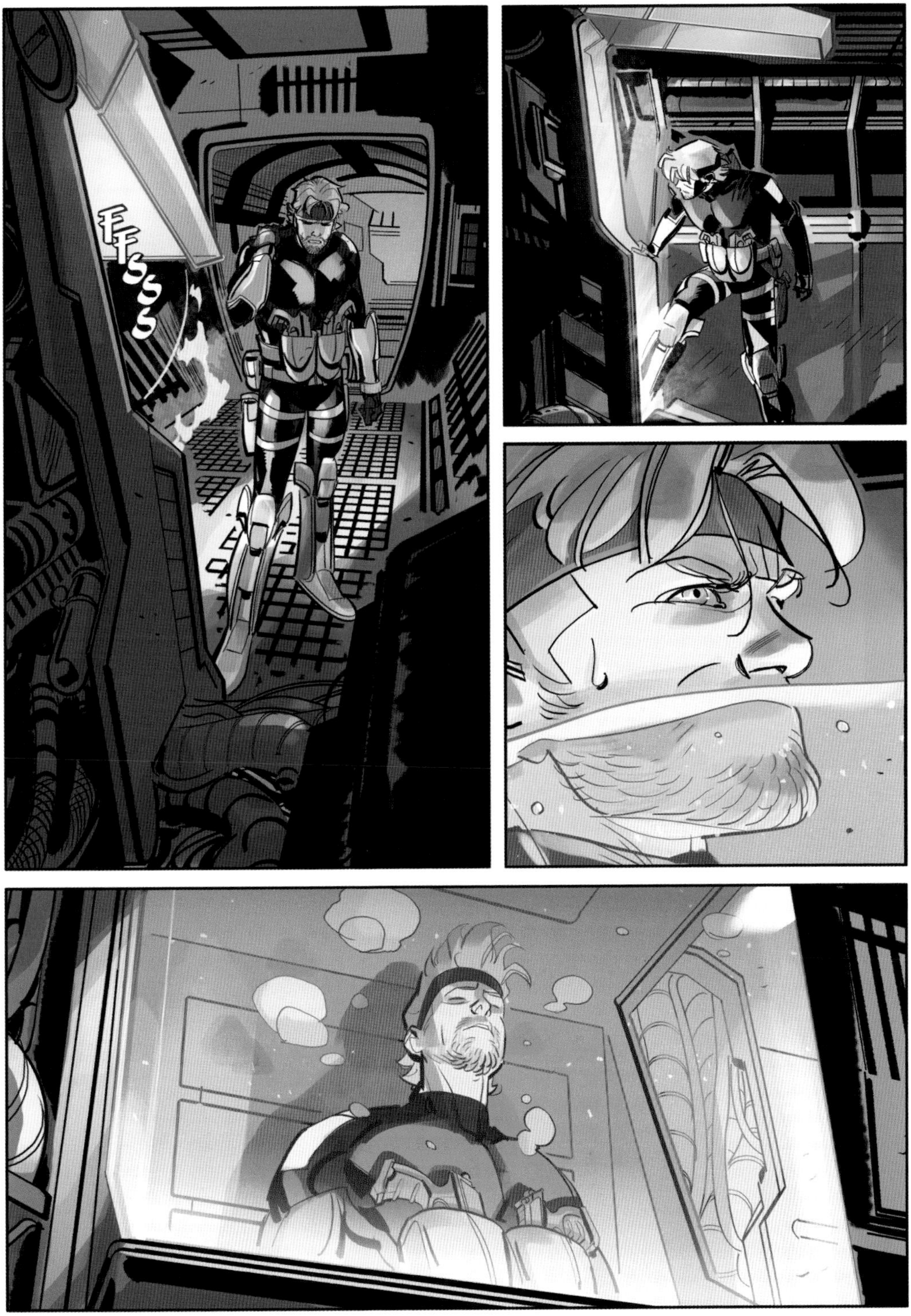
FFSSS

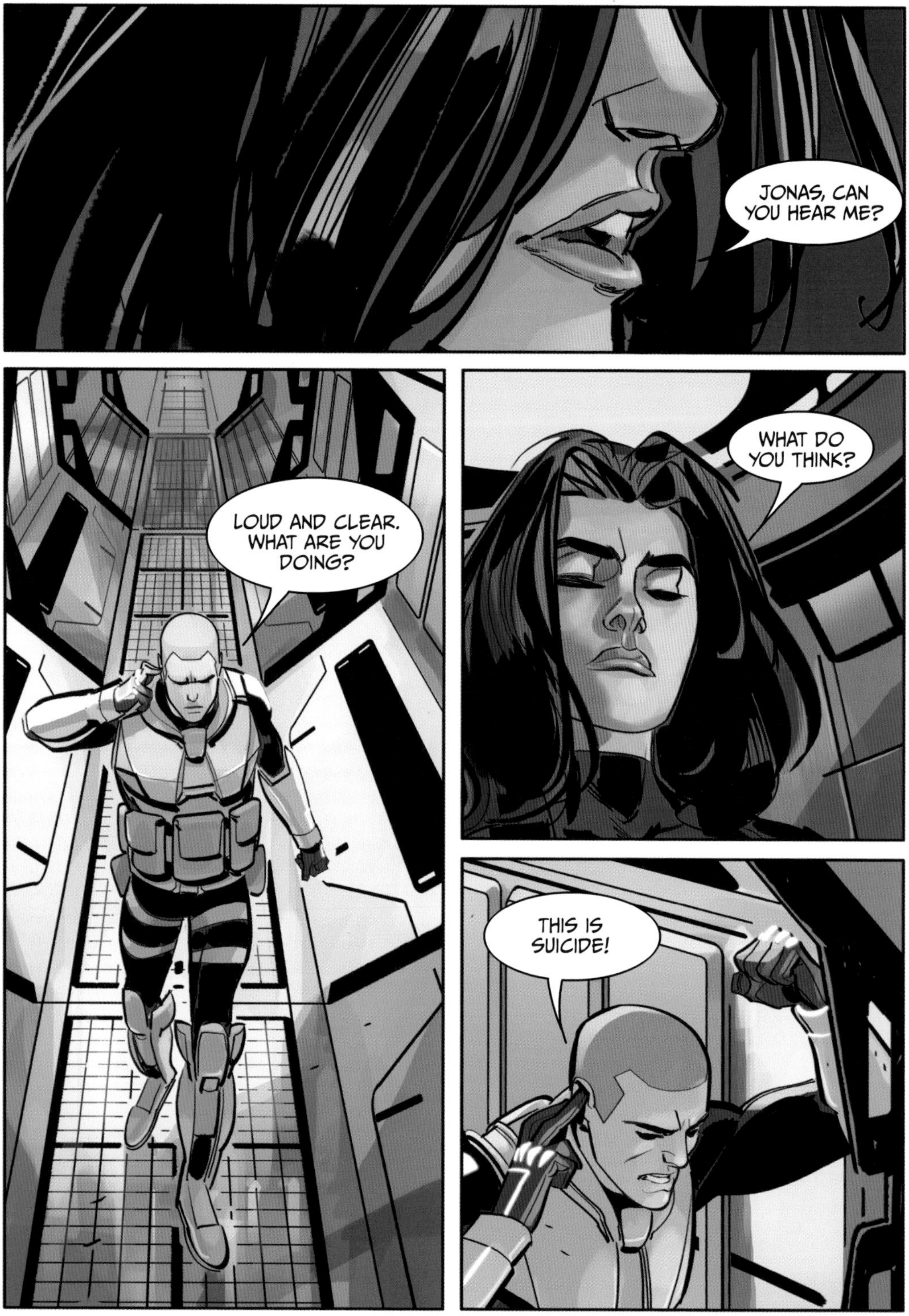
JONAS, CAN YOU HEAR ME?
LOUD AND CLEAR. WHAT ARE YOU DOING?
WHAT DO YOU THINK?
THIS IS SUICIDE!

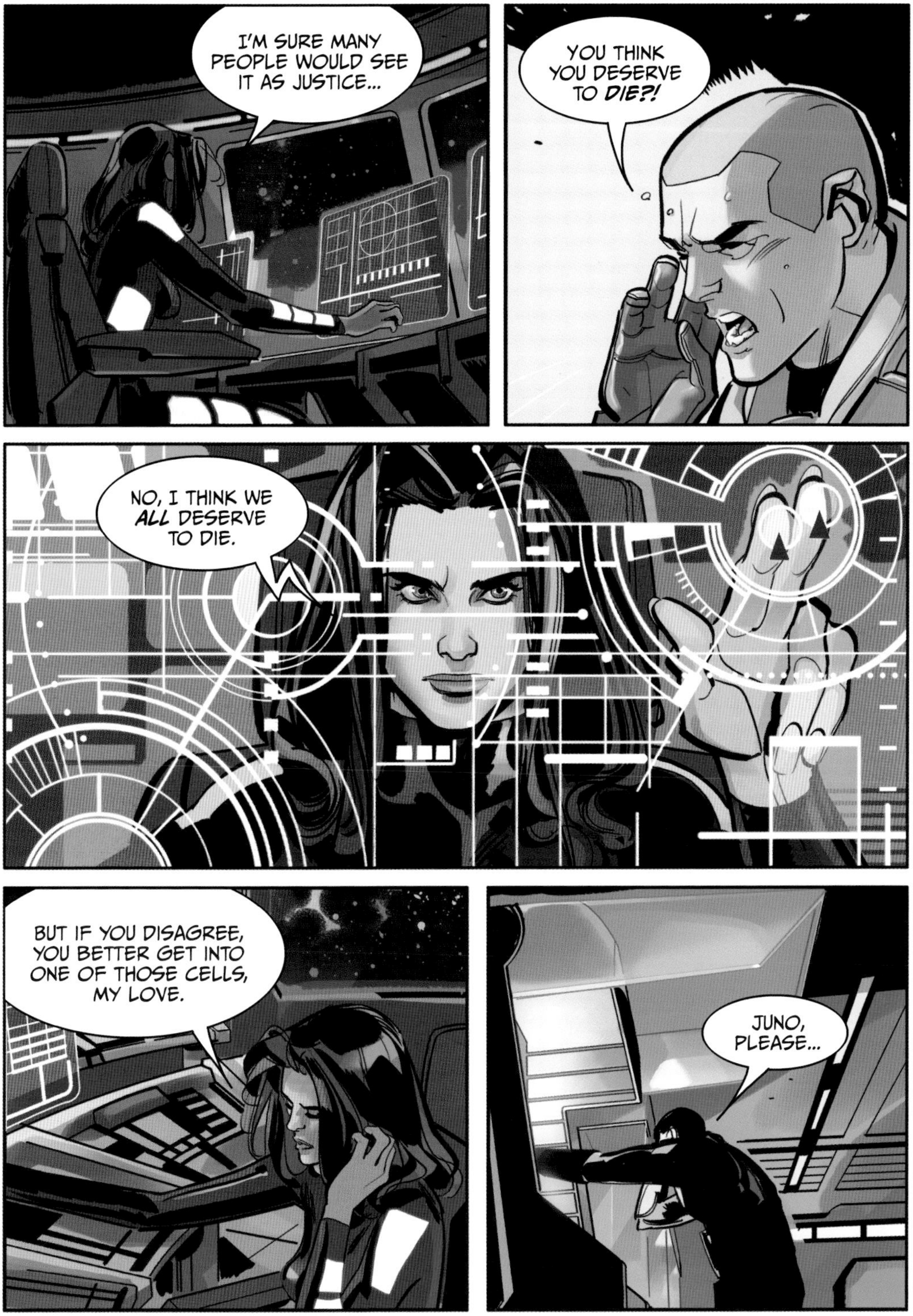
I'M SURE MANY PEOPLE WOULD SEE IT AS JUSTICE...
YOU THINK YOU DESERVE TO DIE?!
NO, I THINK WE ALL DESERVE TO DIE.
BUT IF YOU DISAGREE, YOU BETTER GET INTO ONE OF THOSE CELLS, MY LOVE.
JUNO, PLEASE...

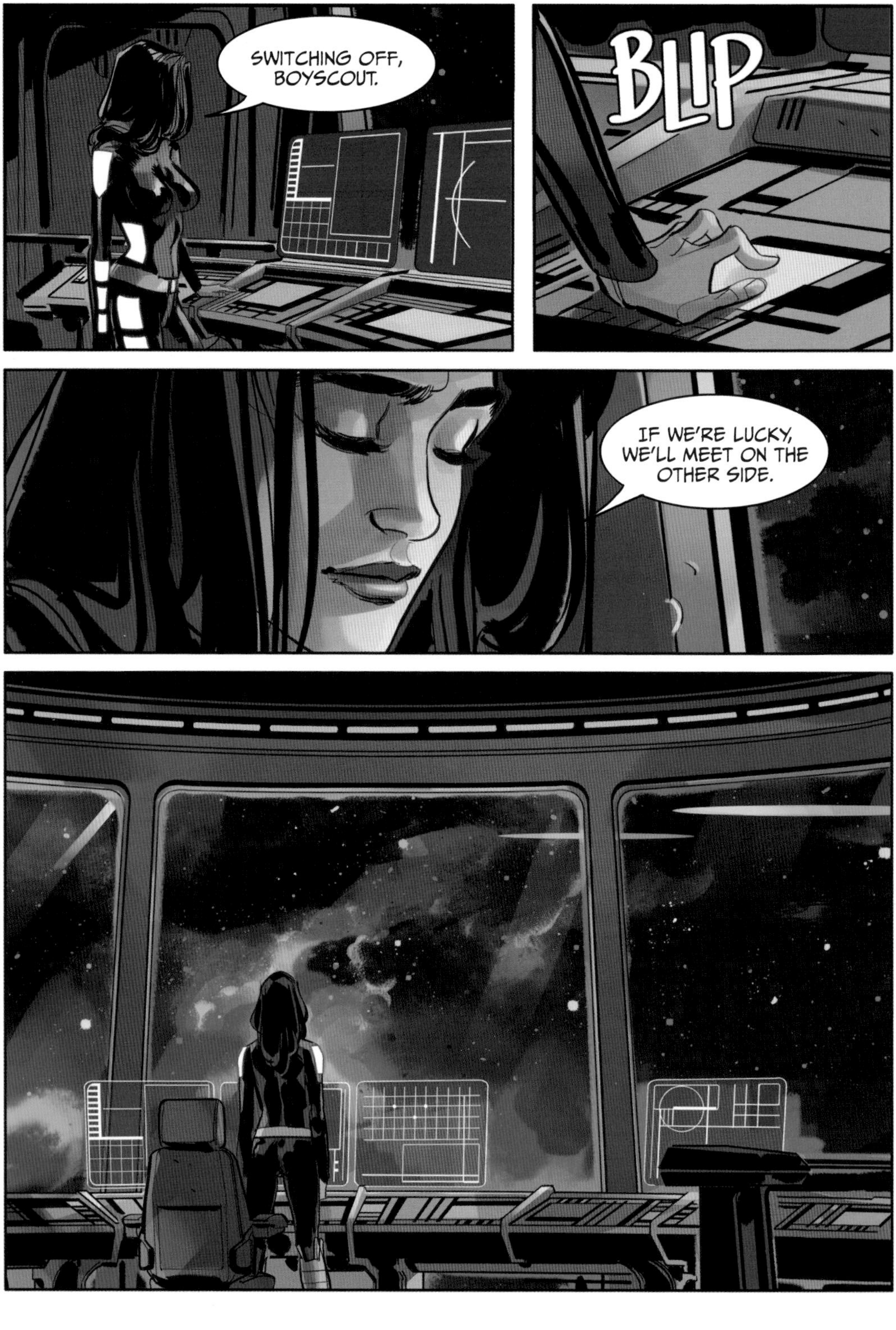
SWITCHING OFF, BOYSCOUT.
BLIP
IF WE'RE LUCKY, WE'LL MEET ON THE OTHER SIDE.

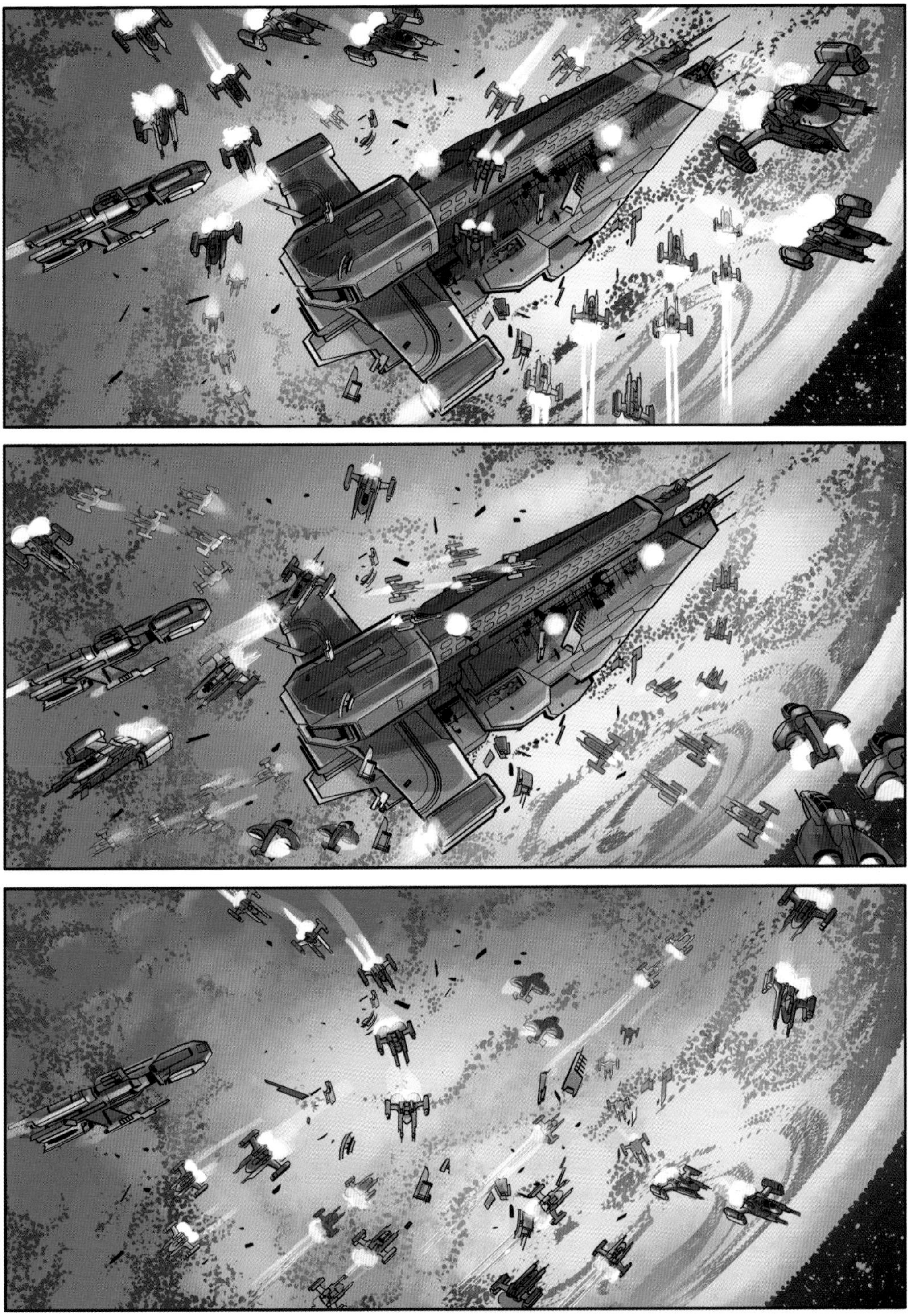

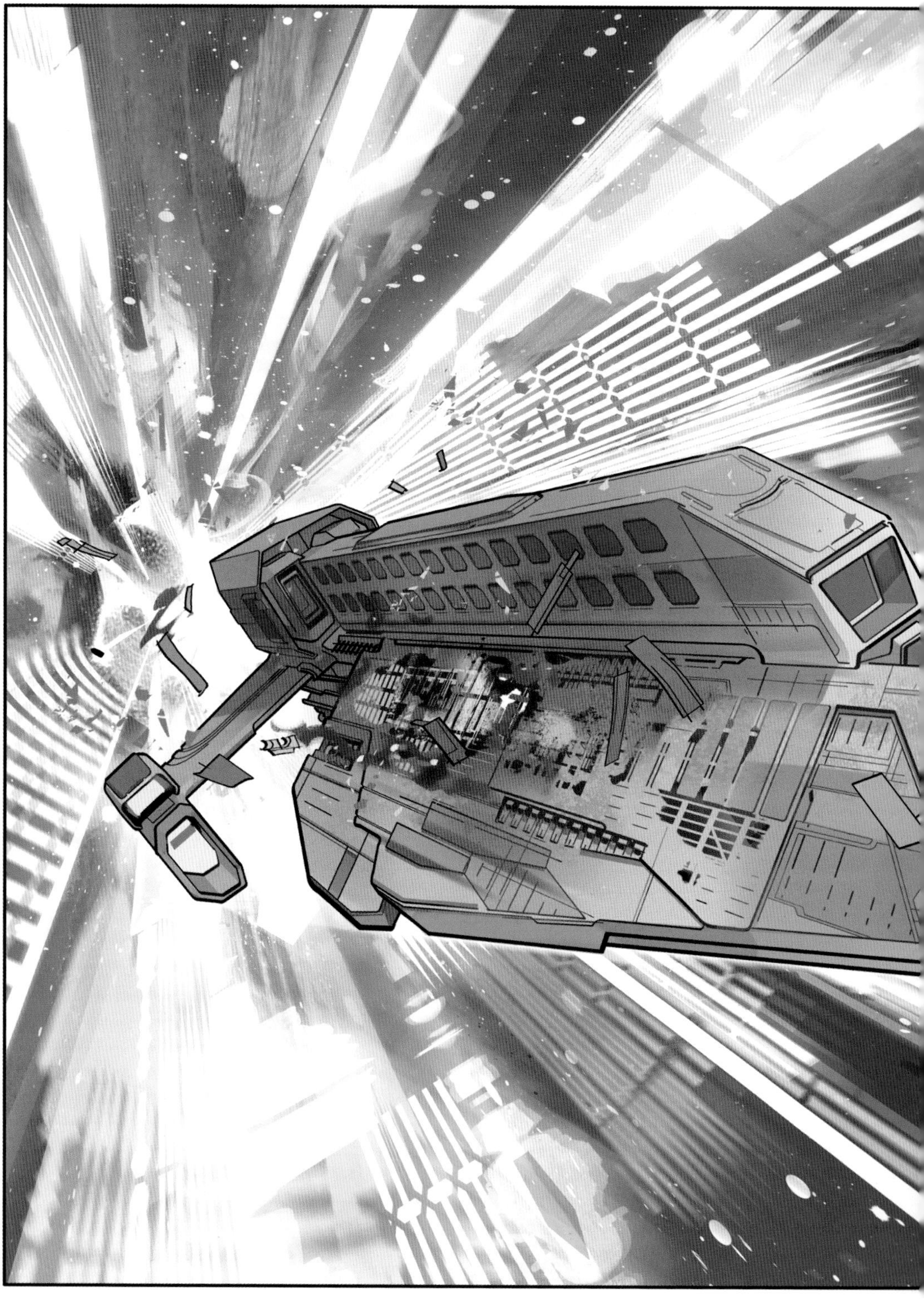

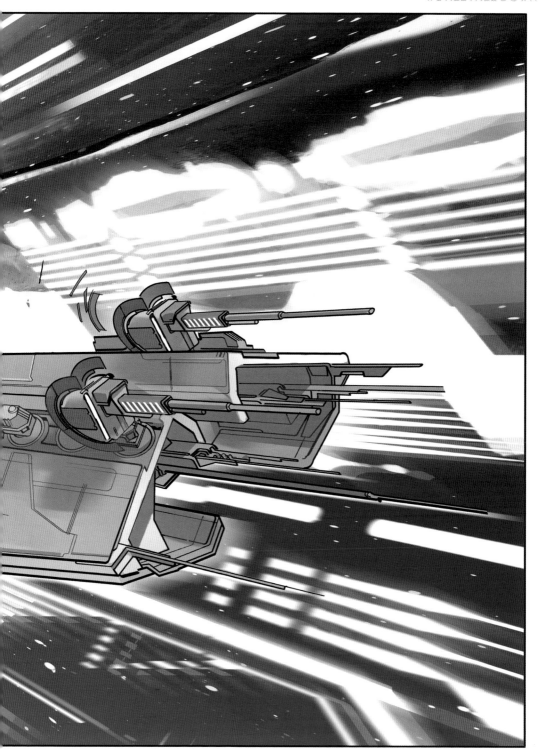

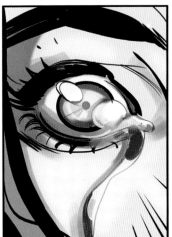

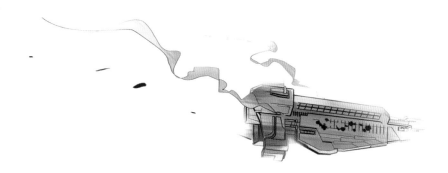

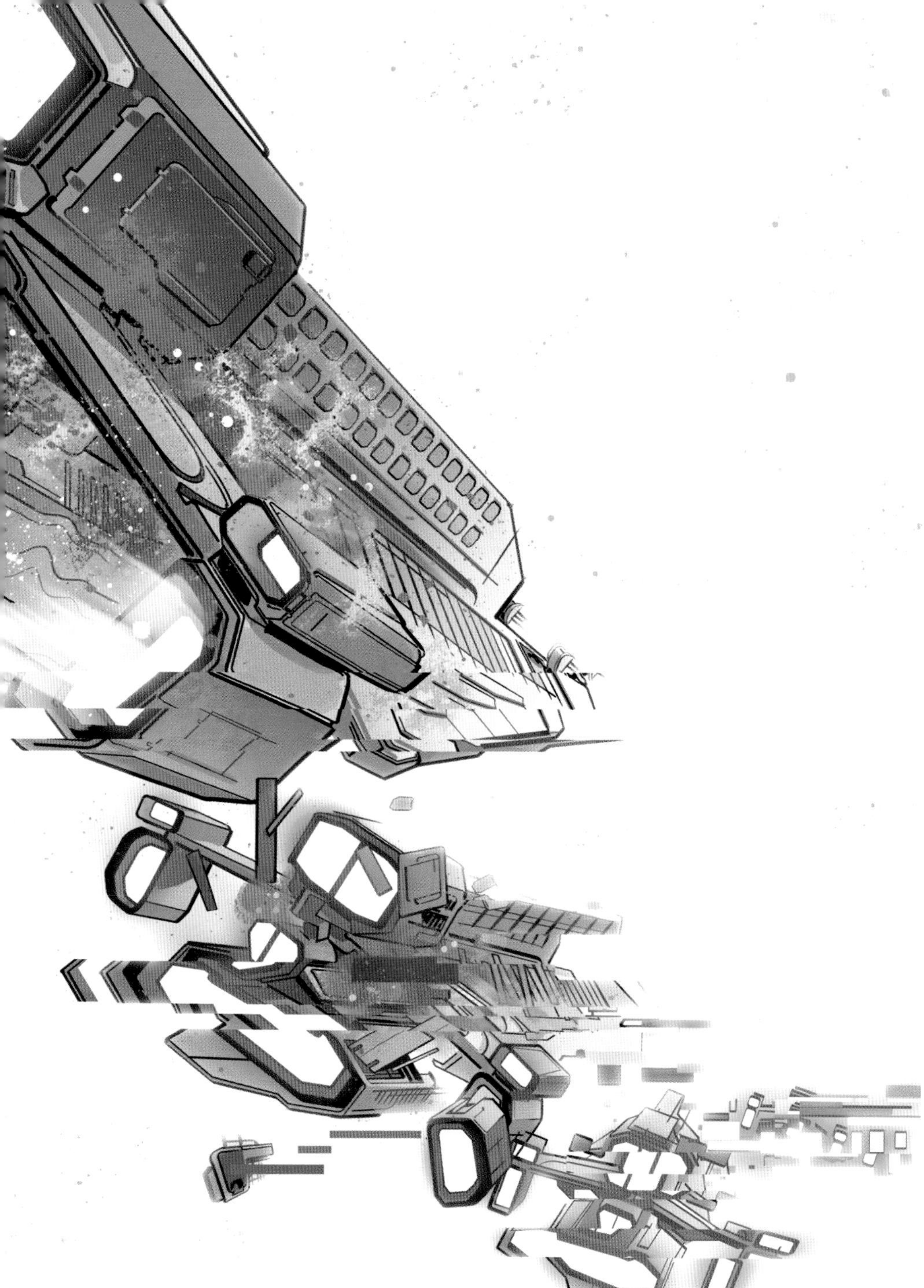

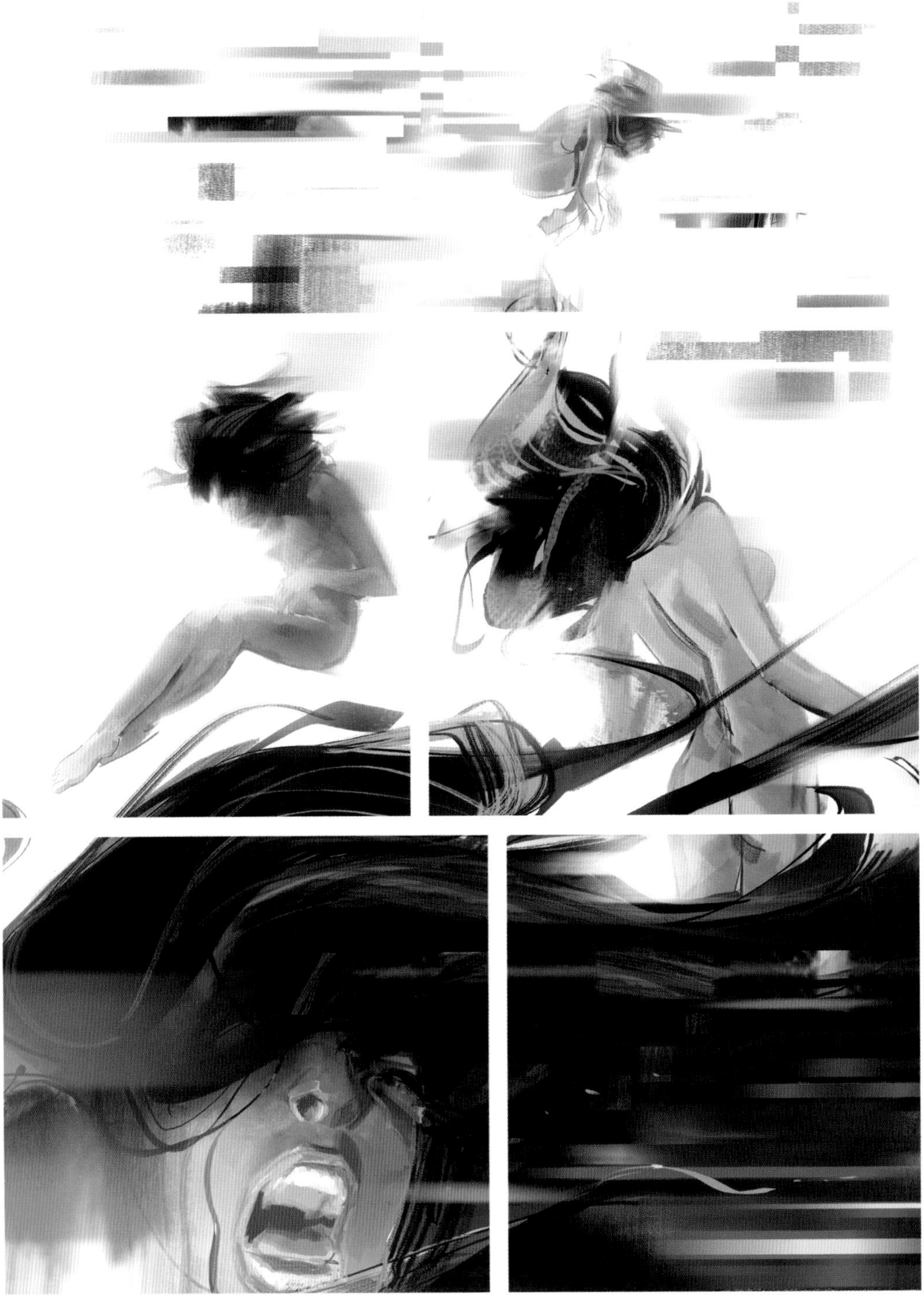

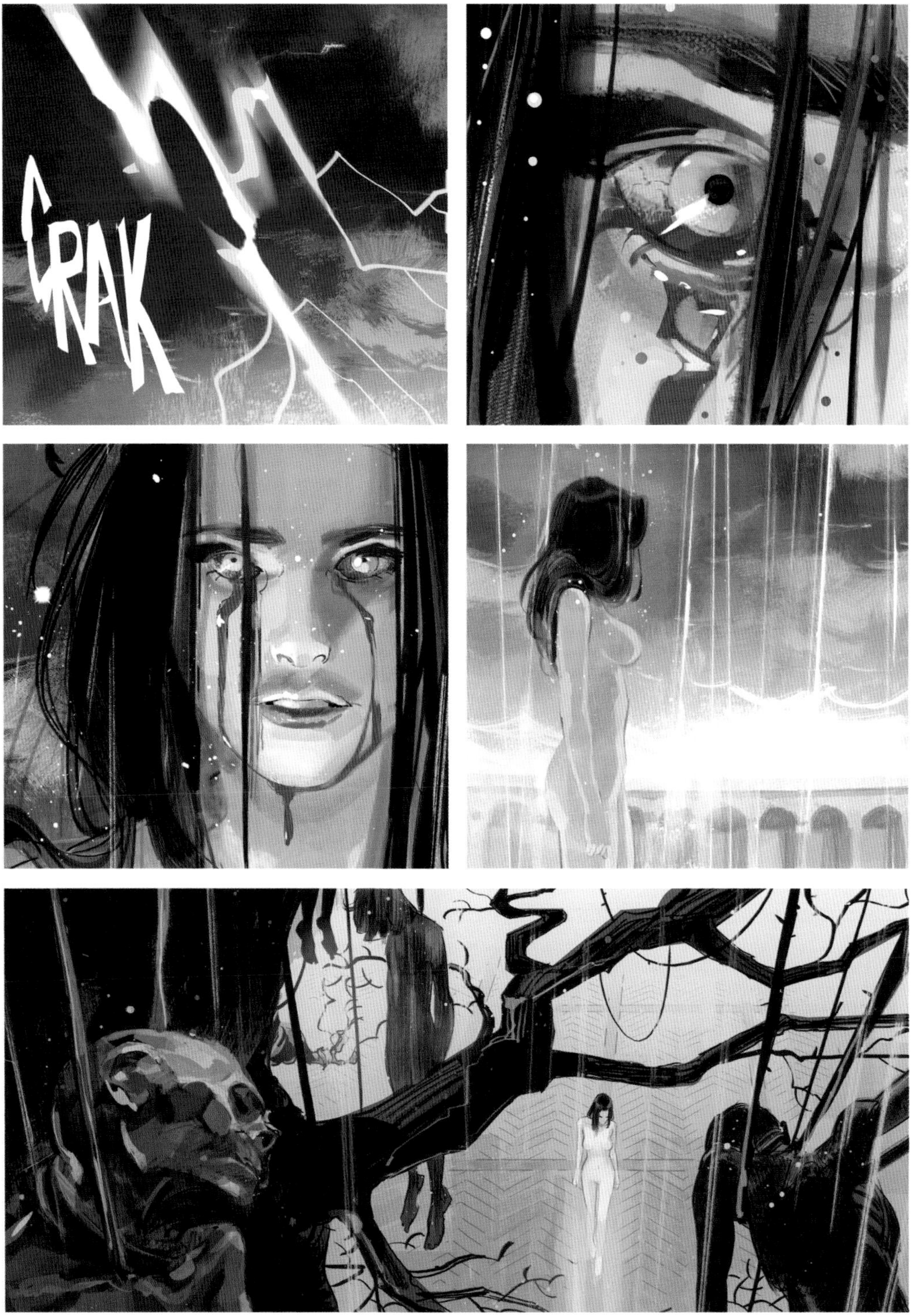
CRAK

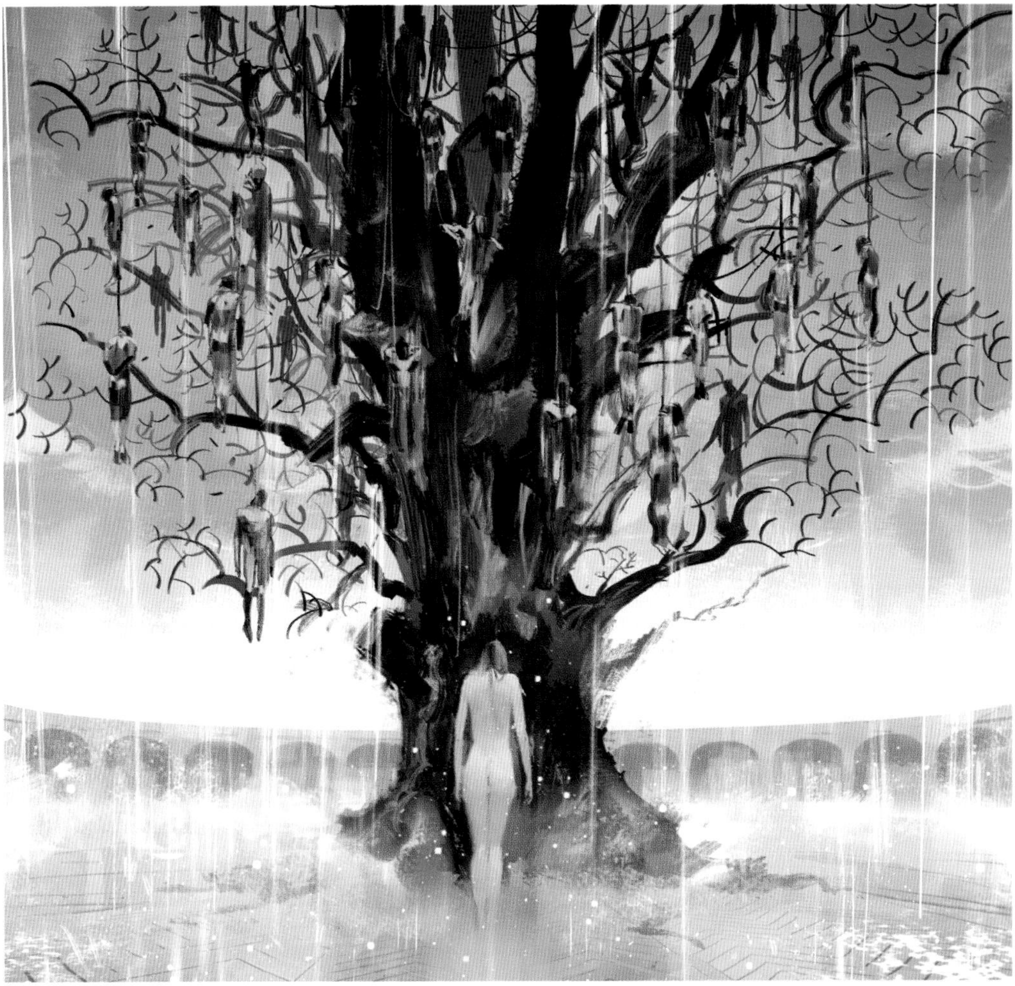

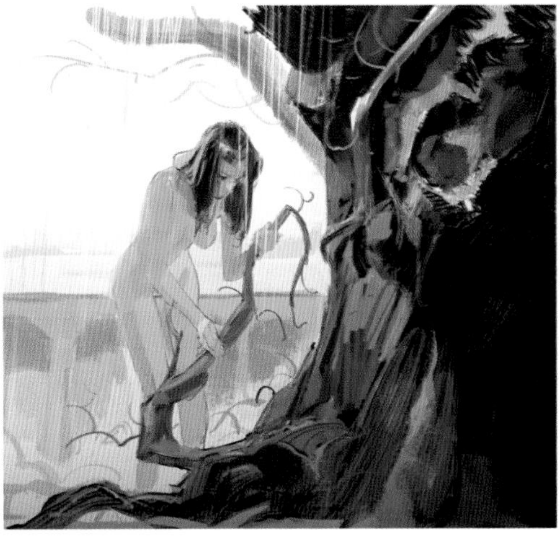

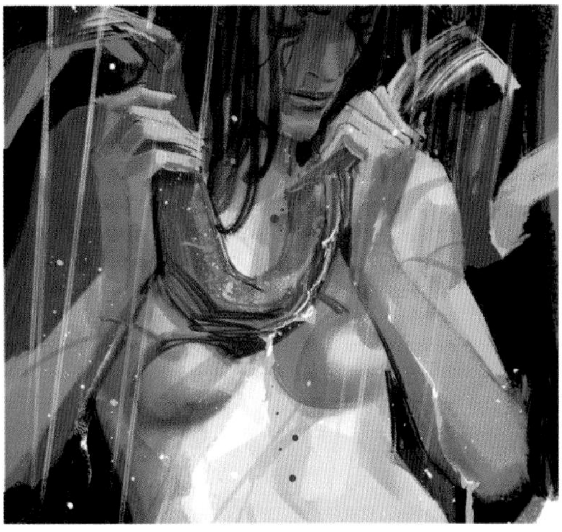

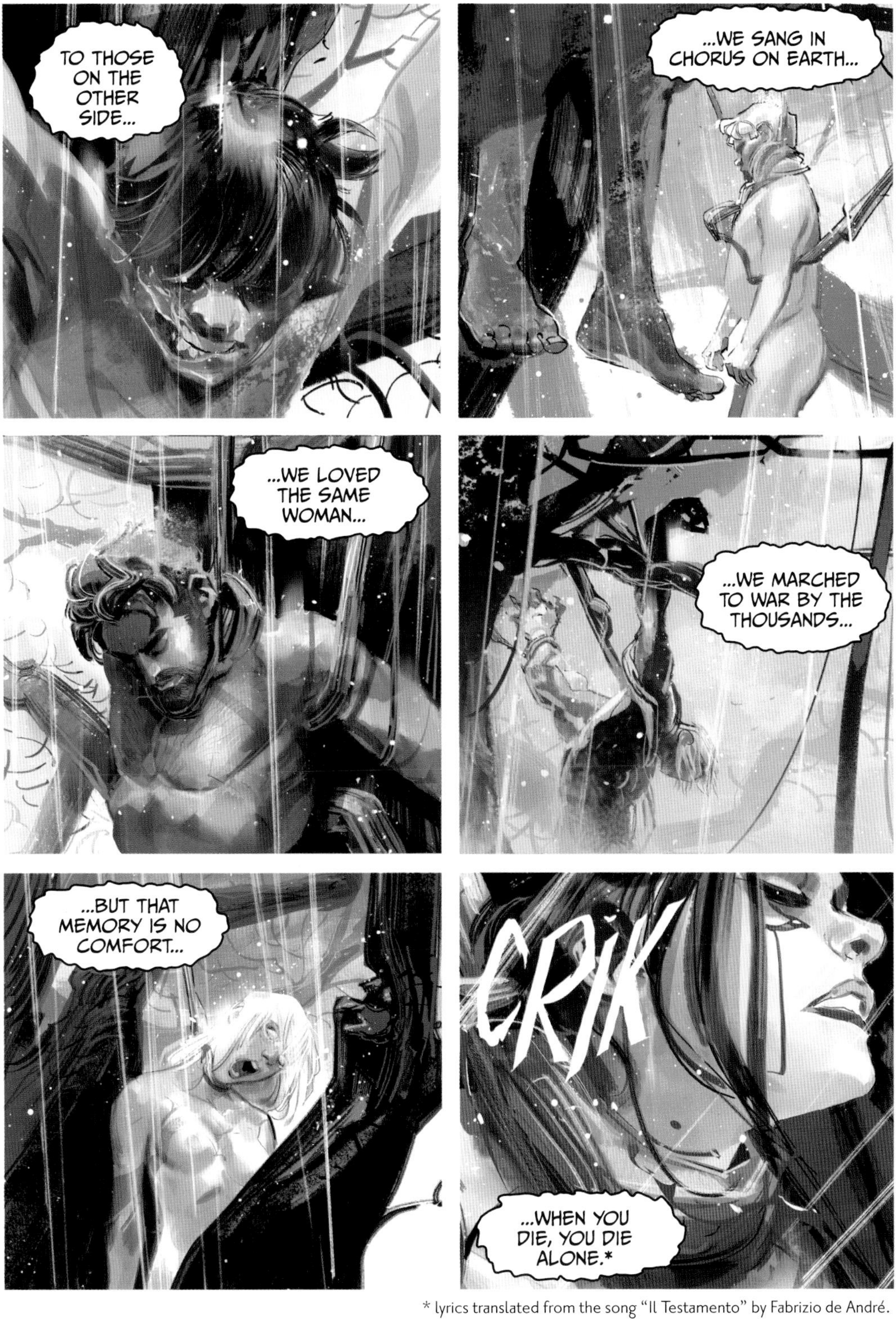
TO THOSE ON THE OTHER SIDE...
...WE SANG IN CHORUS ON EARTH...
...WE LOVED THE SAME WOMAN...
...WE MARCHED TO WAR BY THE THOUSANDS...
...BUT THAT MEMORY IS NO COMFORT...
CRIK
...WHEN YOU DIE, YOU DIE ALONE.*

* lyrics translated from the song "Il Testamento" by Fabrizio de André.

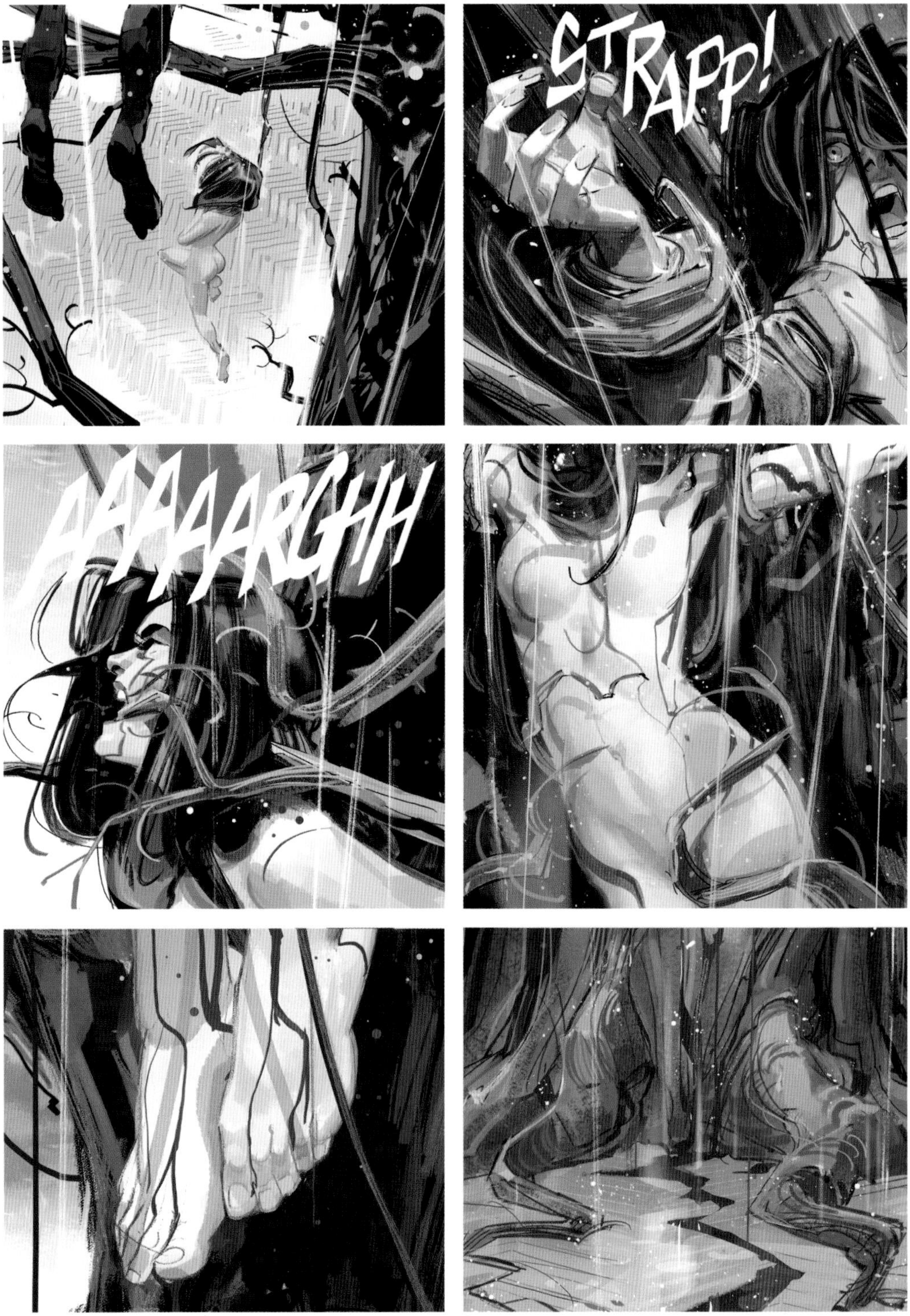
STRAPP!
AAAARGHH

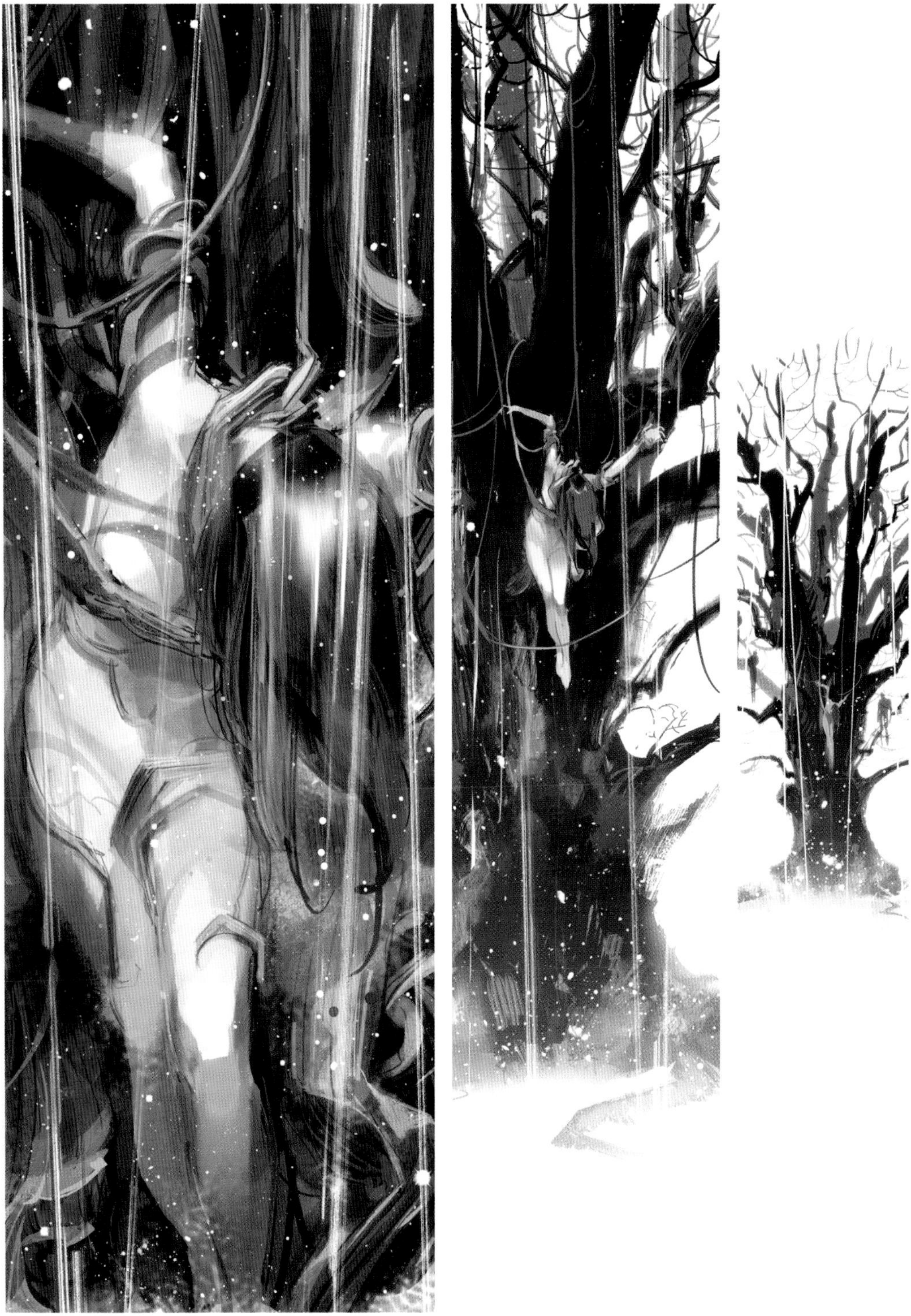

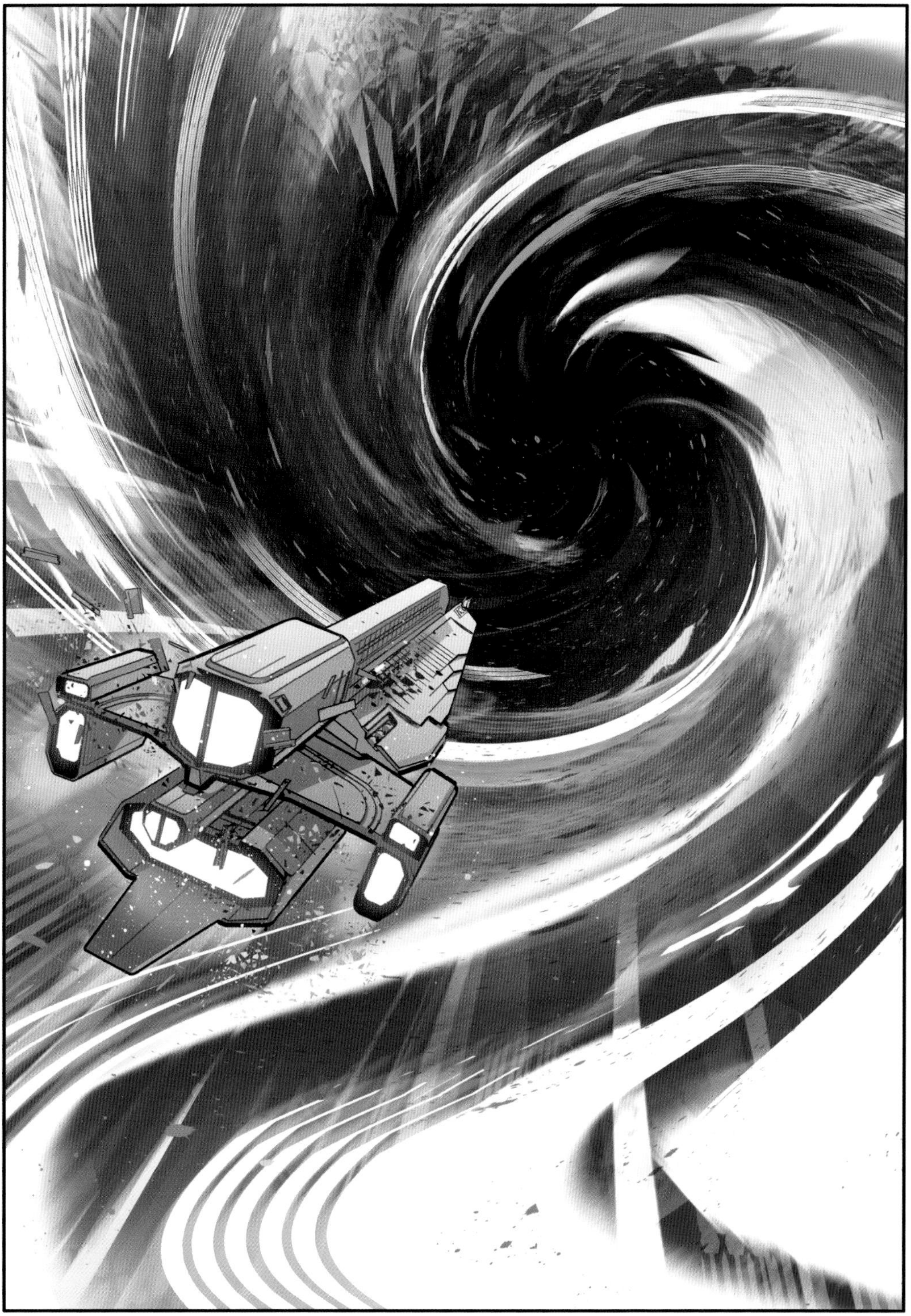

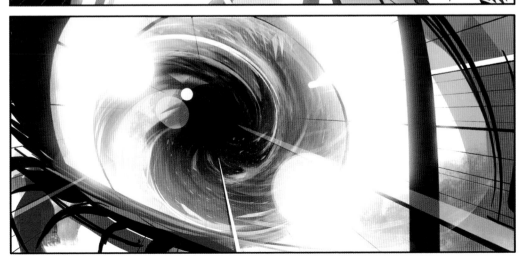

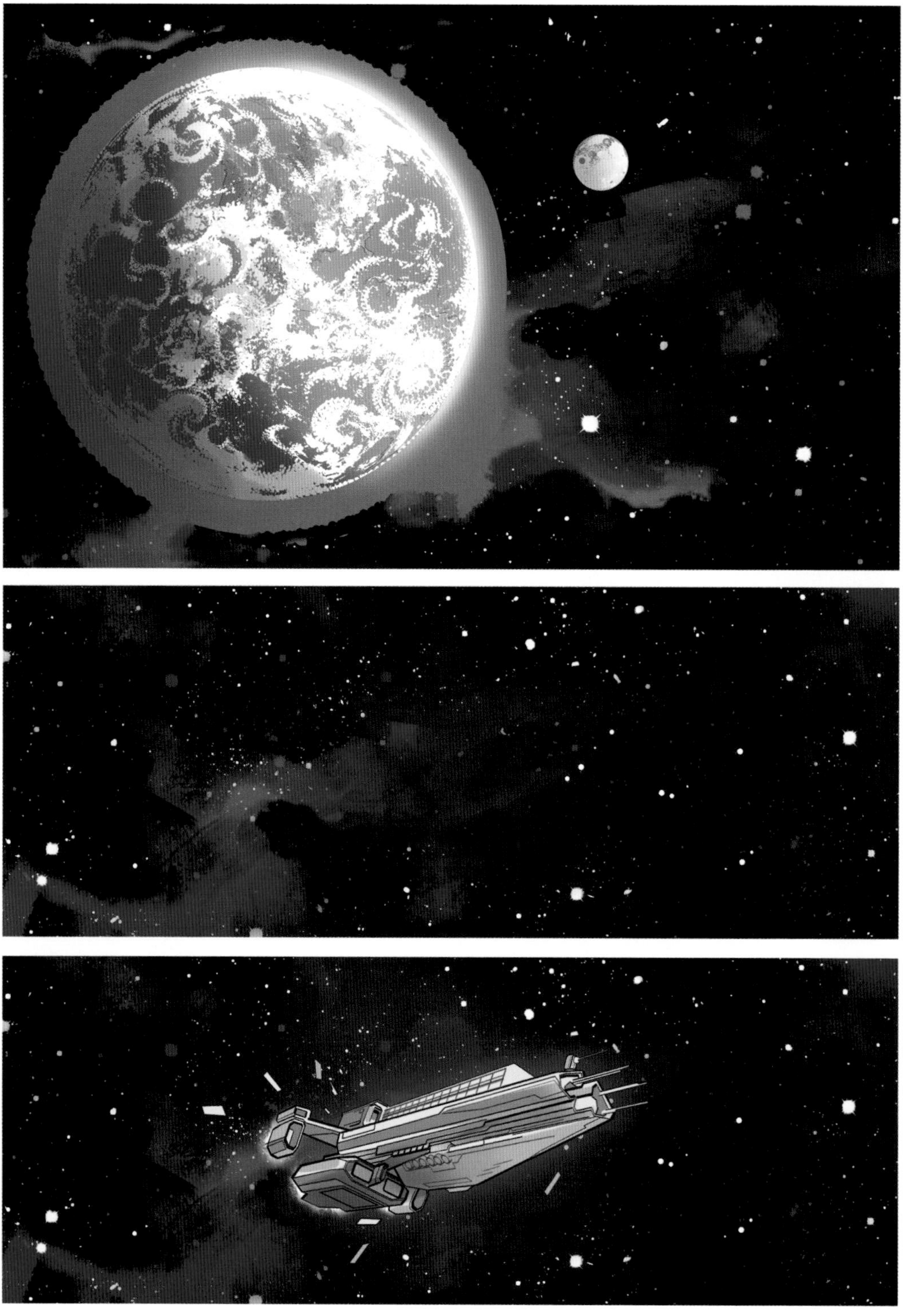

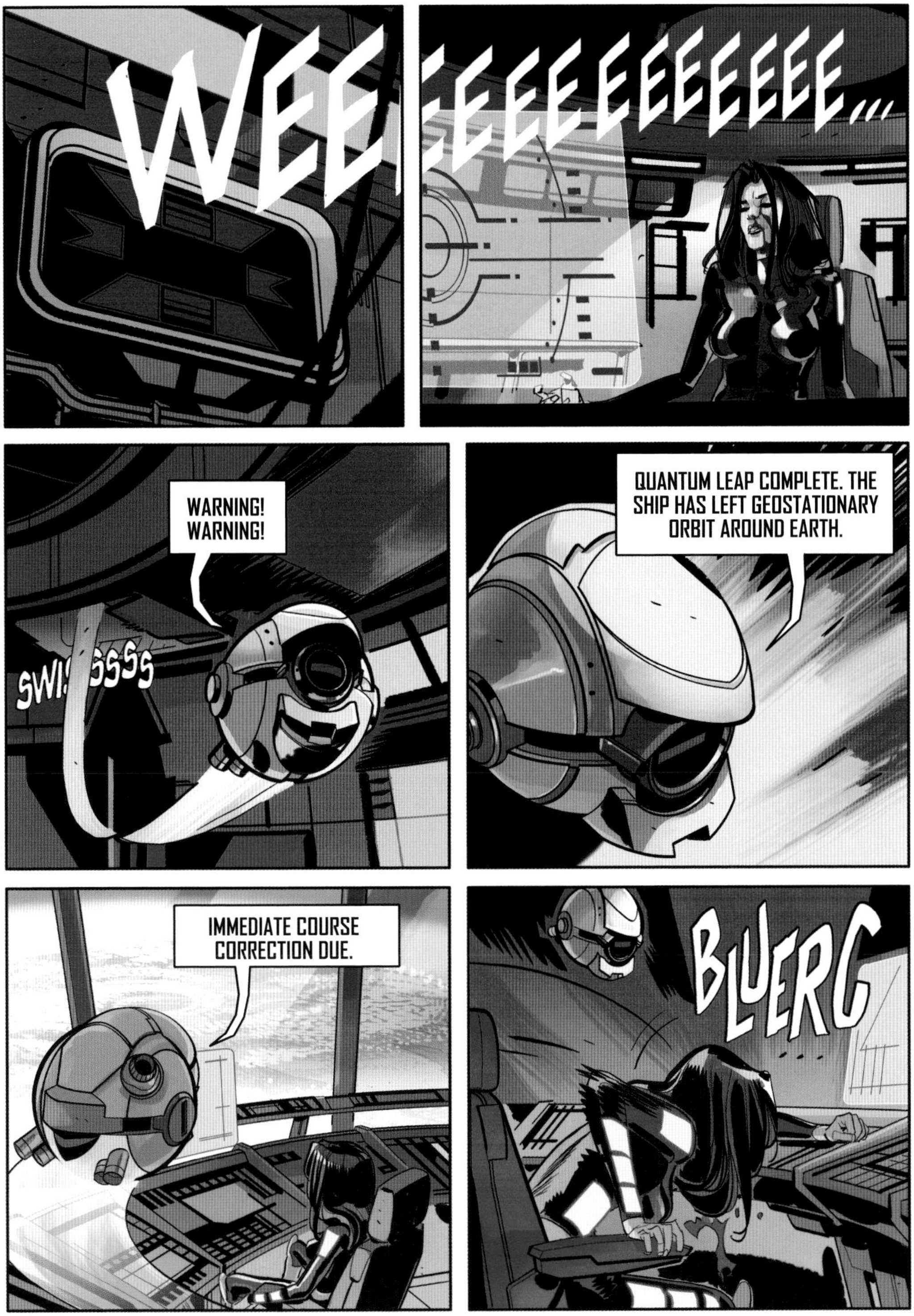
WEEEEEEEEEEE...
WARNING! WARNING!
SWISSSSS
QUANTUM LEAP COMPLETE. THE SHIP HAS LEFT GEOSTATIONARY ORBIT AROUND EARTH.
IMMEDIATE COURSE CORRECTION DUE.
BLUERG

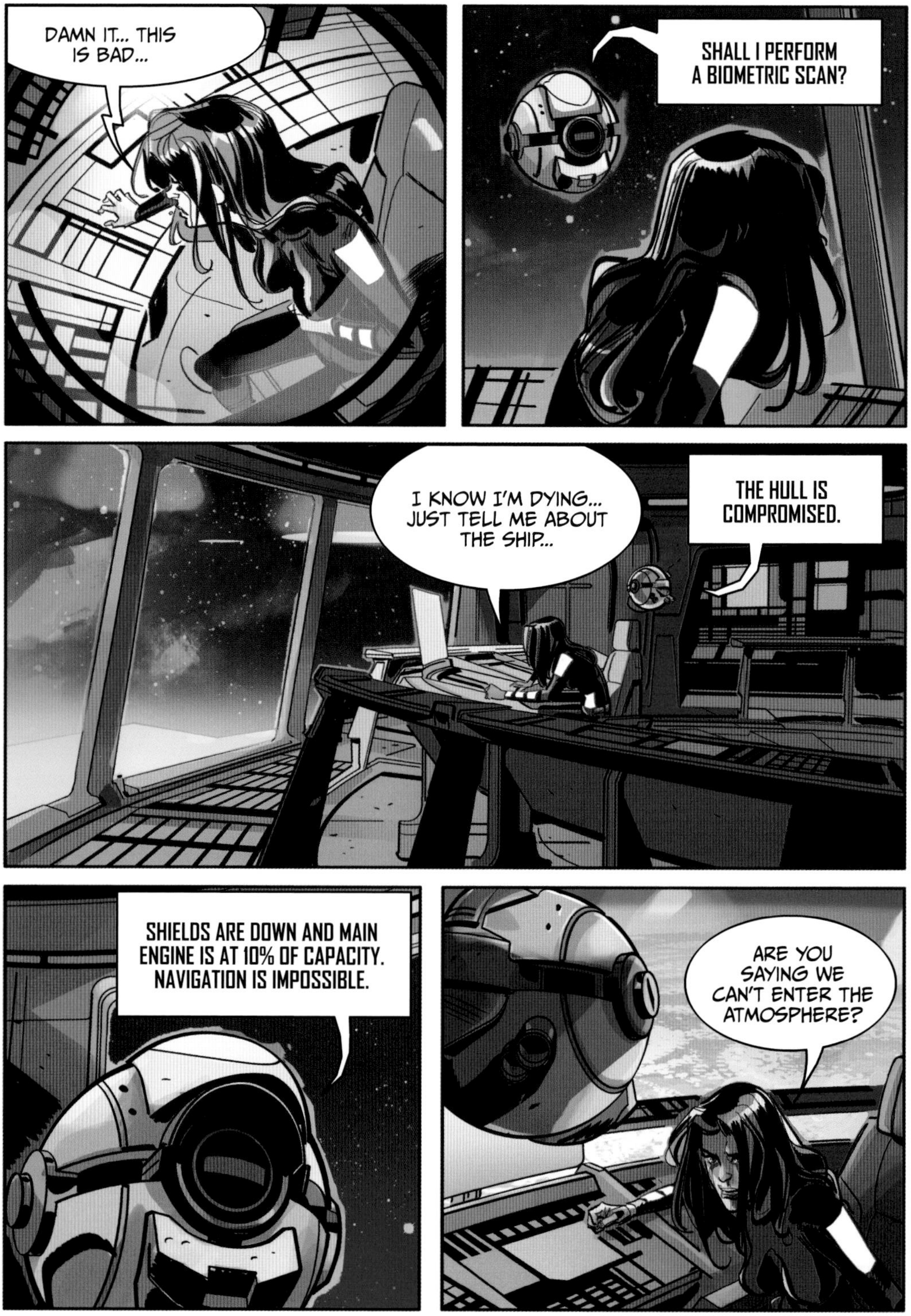
DAMN IT... THIS IS BAD...
SHALL I PERFORM A BIOMETRIC SCAN?
I KNOW I'M DYING... JUST TELL ME ABOUT THE SHIP...
THE HULL IS COMPROMISED.
SHIELDS ARE DOWN AND MAIN ENGINE IS AT 10% OF CAPACITY. NAVIGATION IS IMPOSSIBLE.
ARE YOU SAYING WE CAN'T ENTER THE ATMOSPHERE?

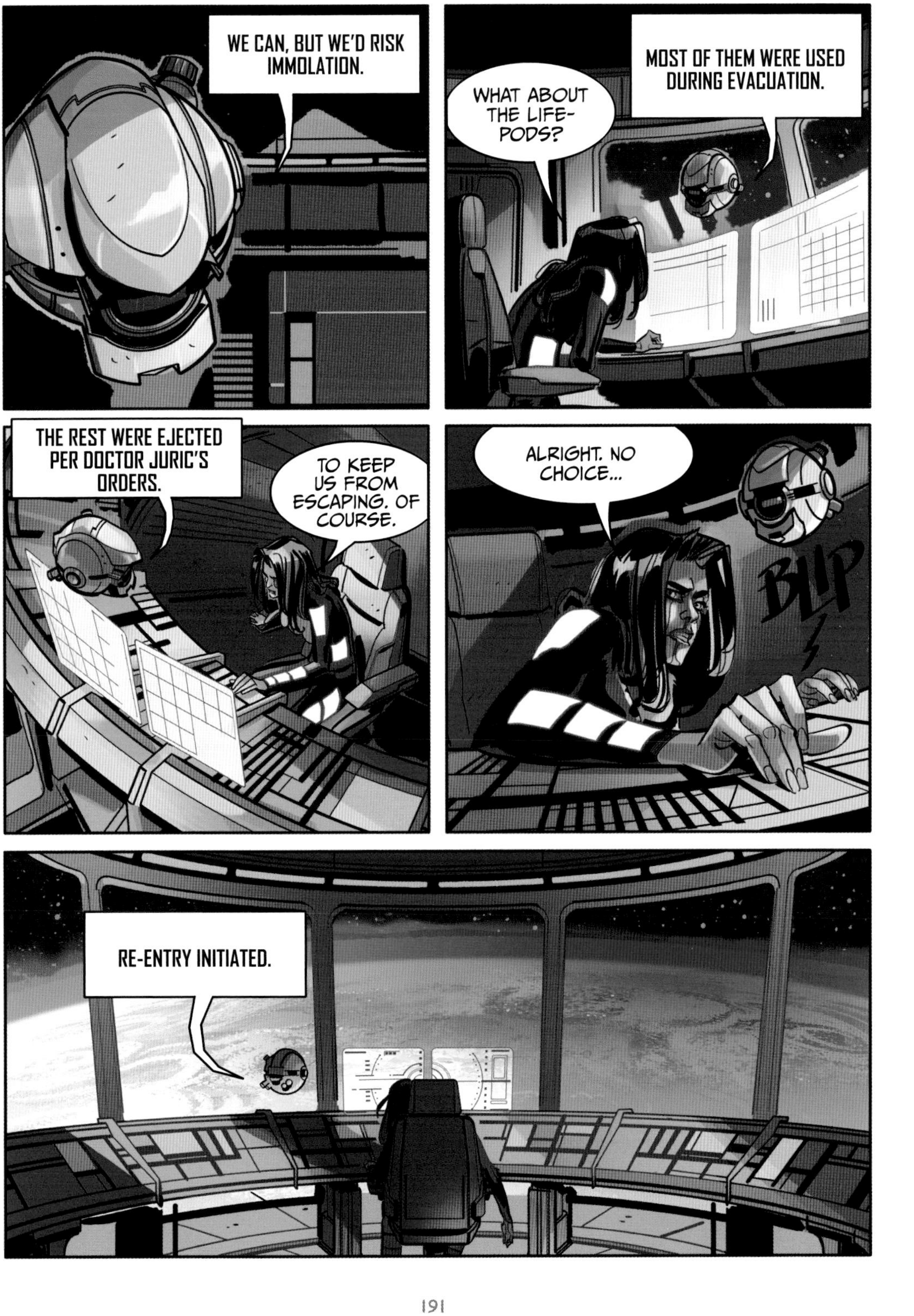
WE CAN, BUT WE'D RISK IMMOLATION.
WHAT ABOUT THE LIFE-PODS?
MOST OF THEM WERE USED DURING EVACUATION.
THE REST WERE EJECTED PER DOCTOR JURIC'S ORDERS.
TO KEEP US FROM ESCAPING. OF COURSE.
ALRIGHT. NO CHOICE...
BLIP
RE-ENTRY INITIATED.

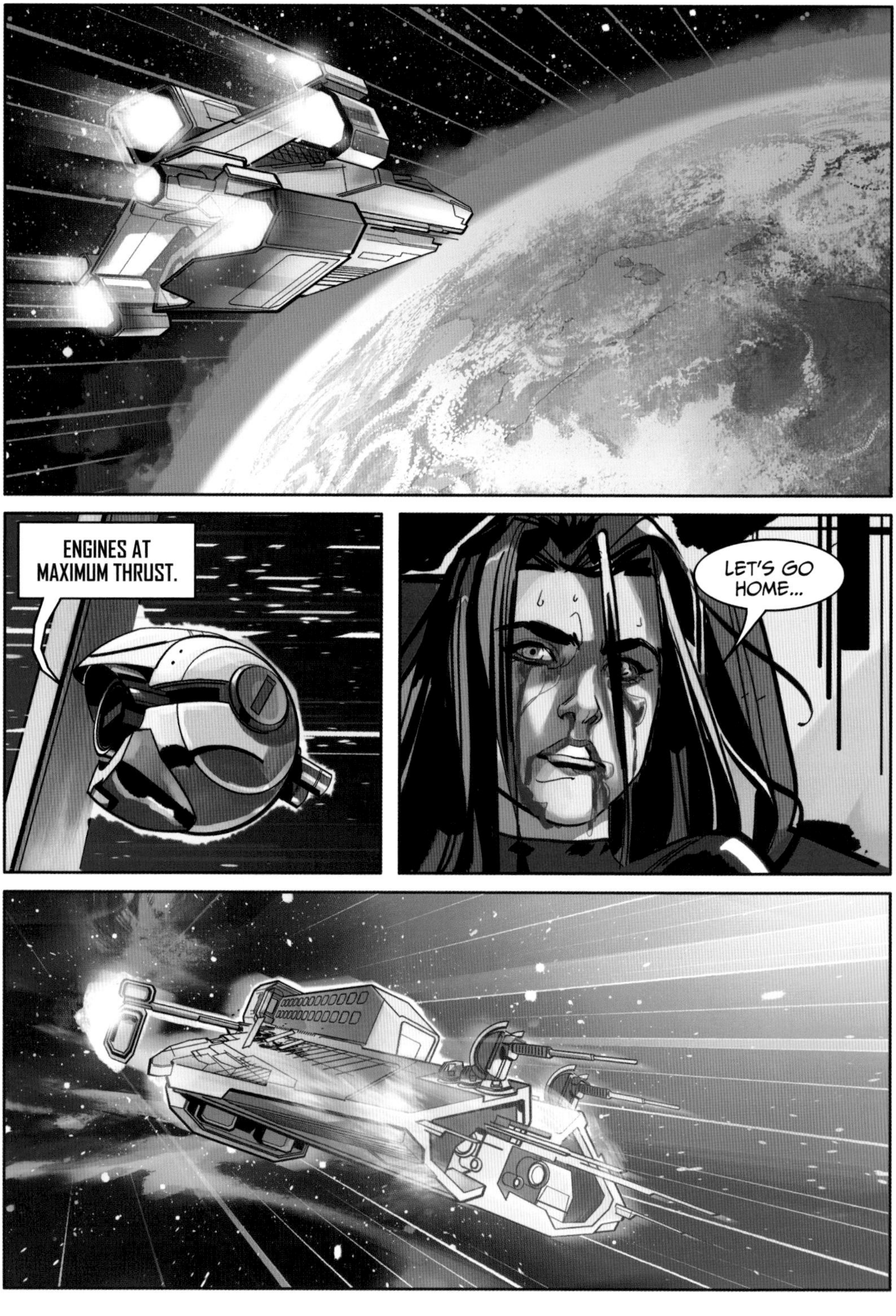
ENGINES AT MAXIMUM THRUST.
LET'S GO HOME...

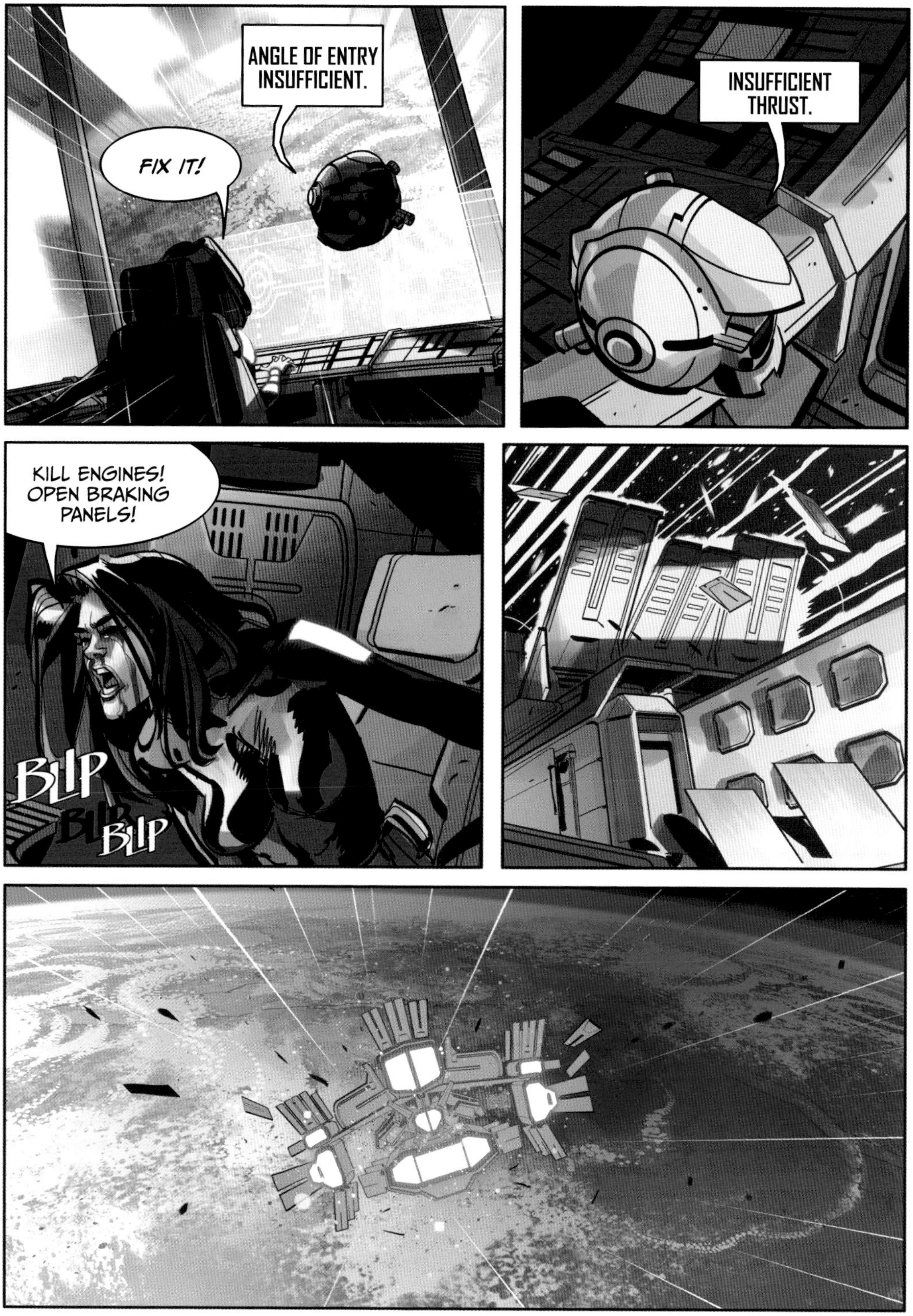
ANGLE OF ENTRY INSUFFICIENT.
FIX IT!
INSUFFICIENT THRUST.
KILL ENGINES! OPEN BRAKING PANELS!
BLIP
BLIP
BLIP

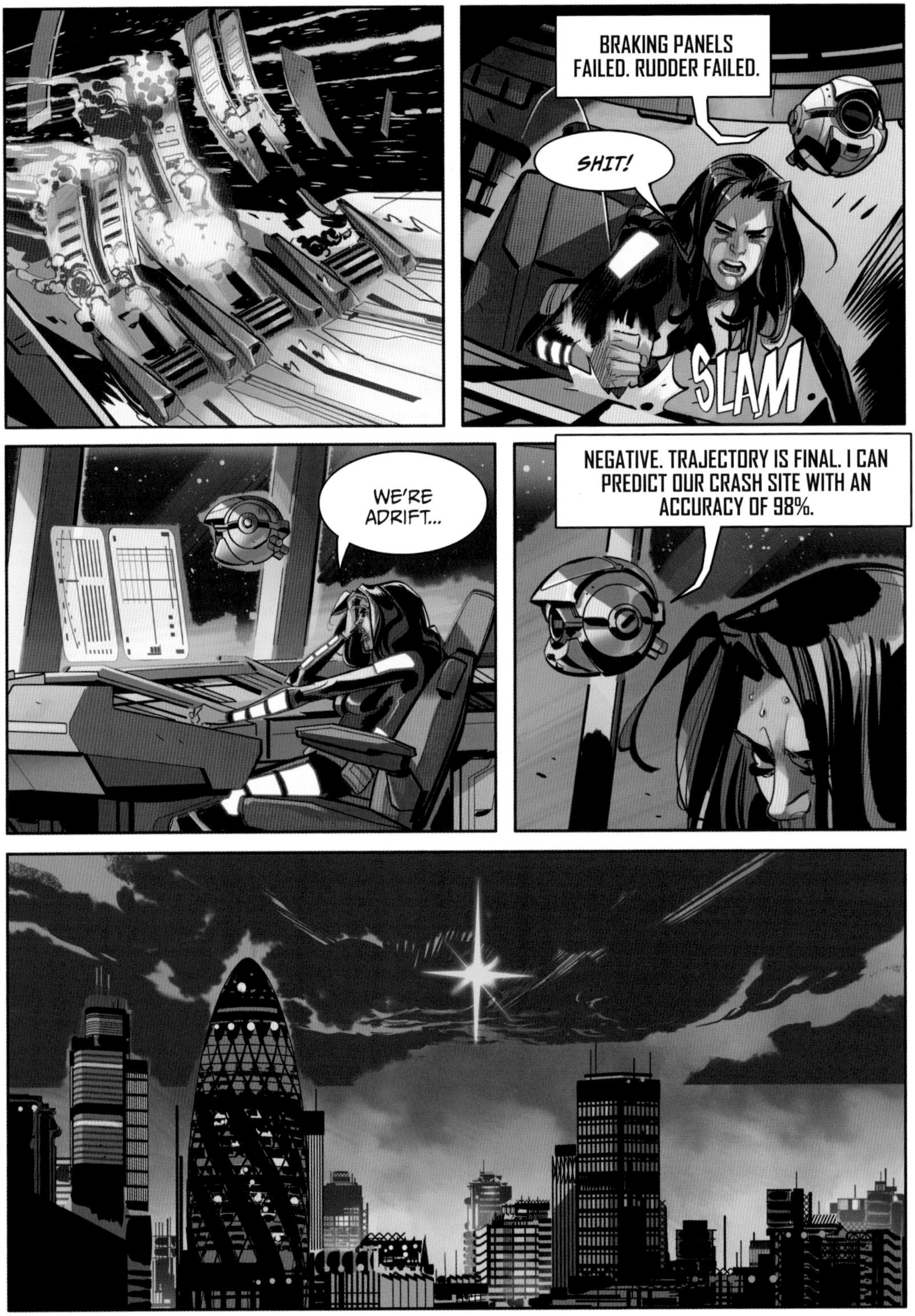
BRAKING PANELS FAILED. RUDDER FAILED.
SHIT!
SLAM
WE'RE ADRIFT...
NEGATIVE. TRAJECTORY IS FINAL. I CAN PREDICT OUR CRASH SITE WITH AN ACCURACY OF 98%.

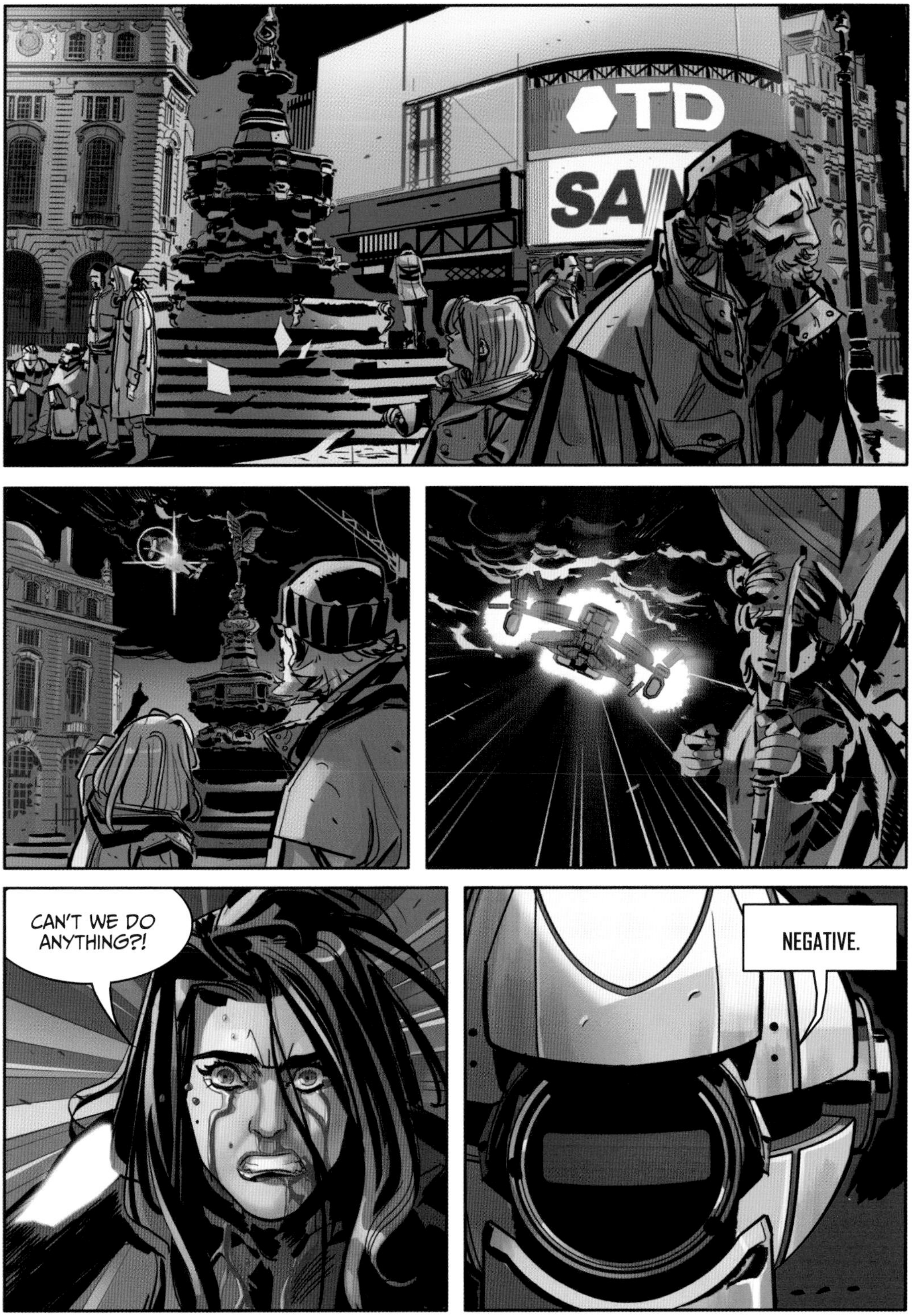
CAN'T WE DO ANYTHING?!
NEGATIVE.

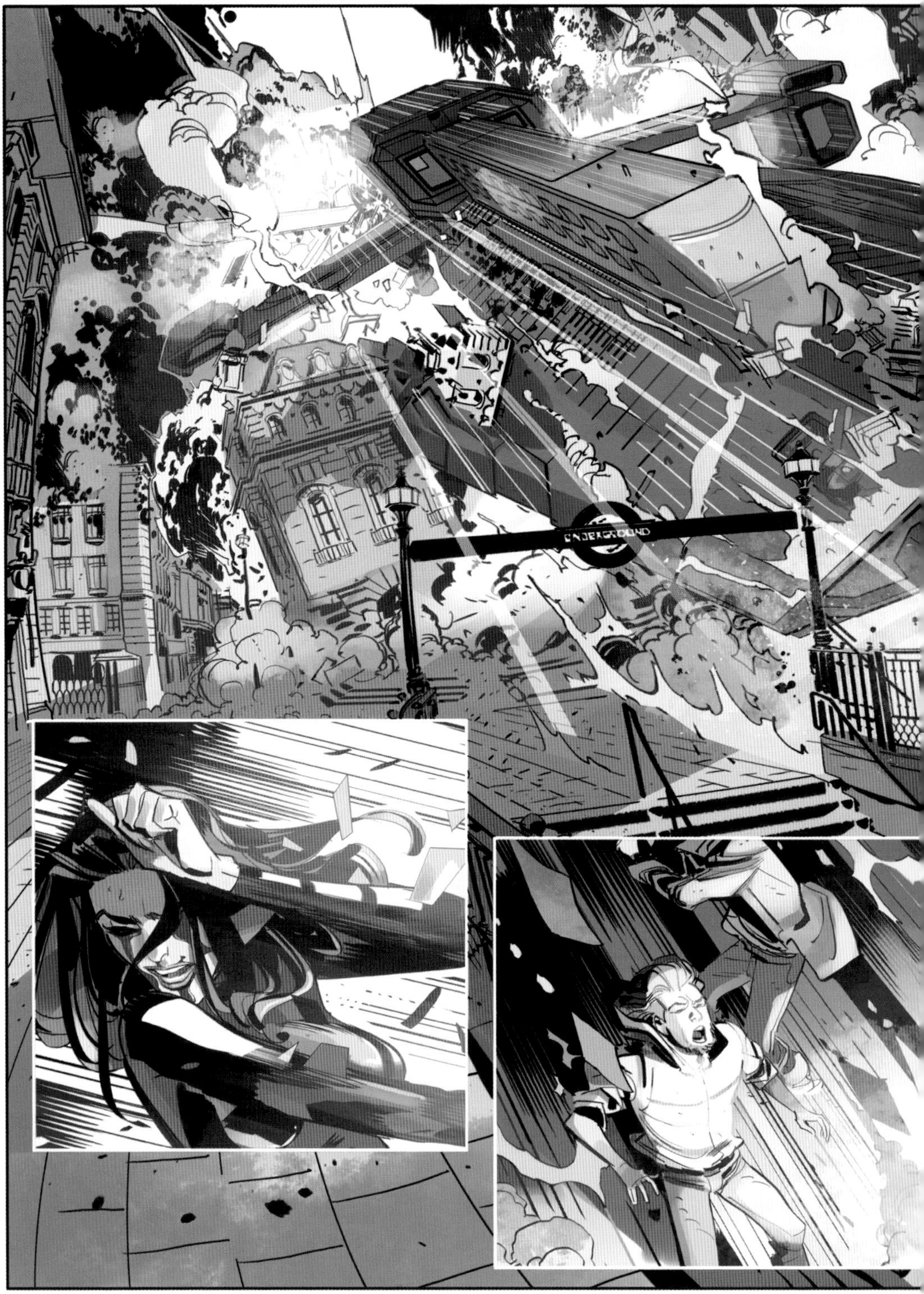
UNDERGROUND

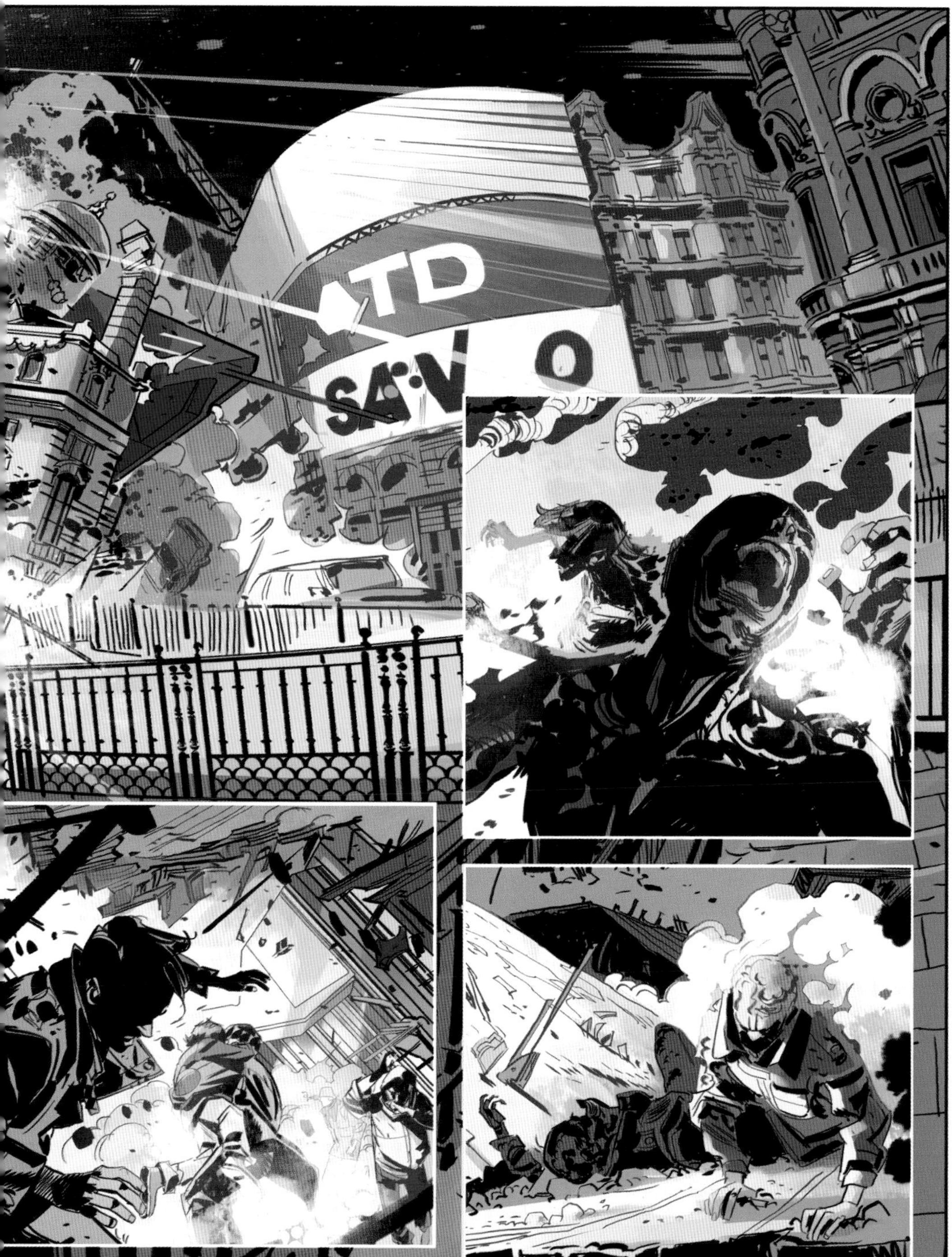
TD
SAV O

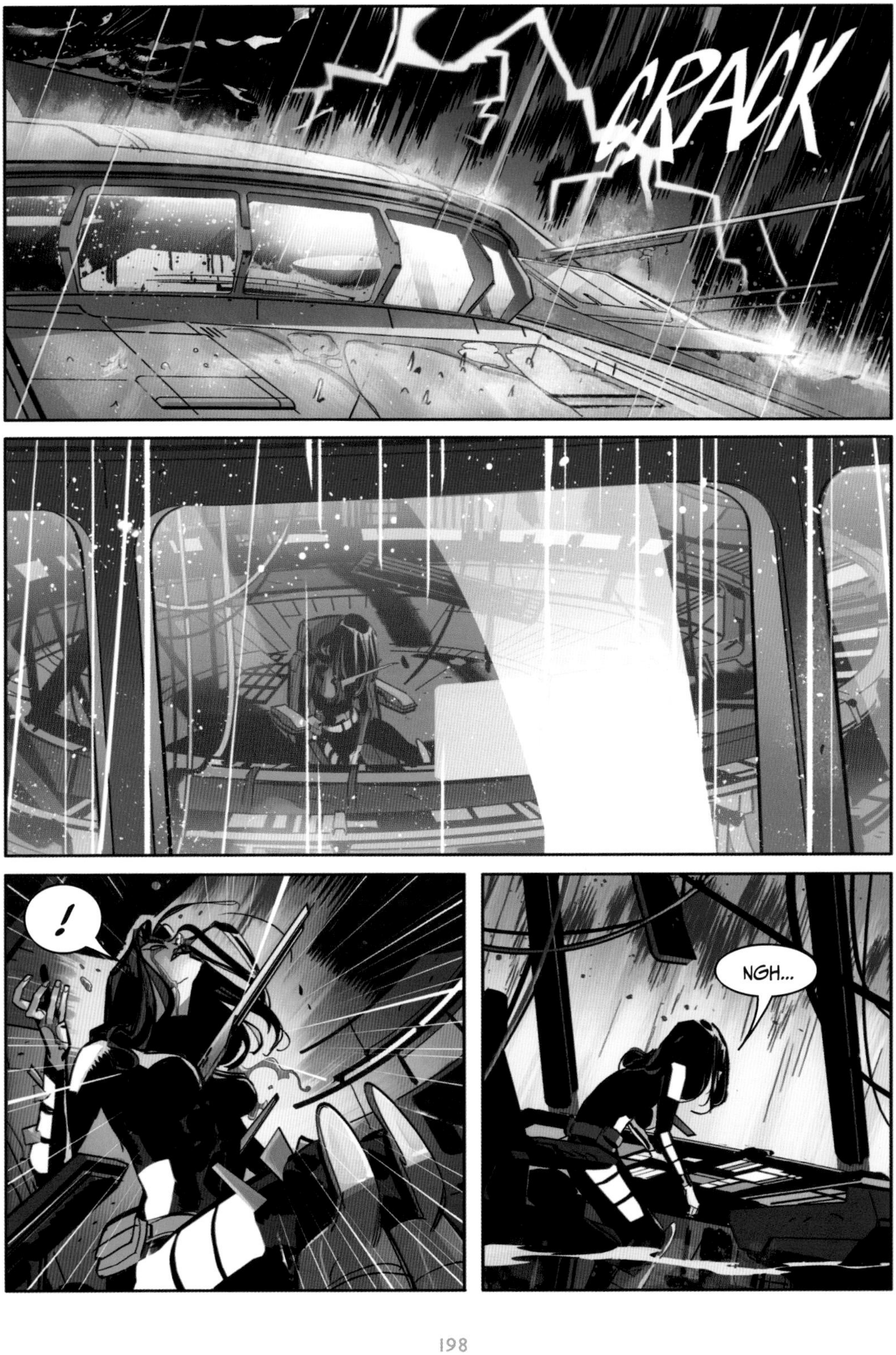
CRACK
!
NGH...

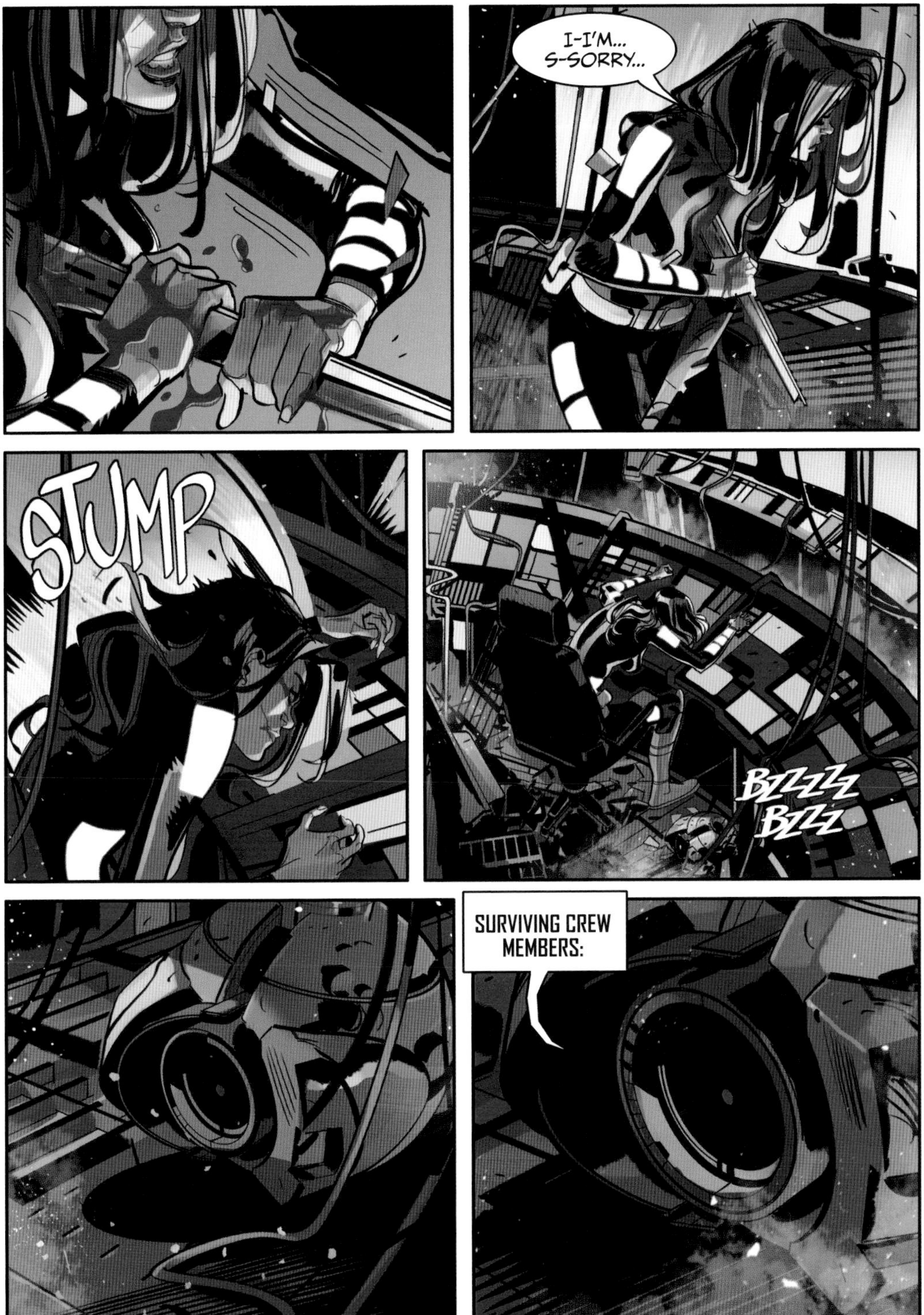
I-I'M... S-SORRY...
STUMP
BZZZZ BZZZ
SURVIVING CREW MEMBERS:

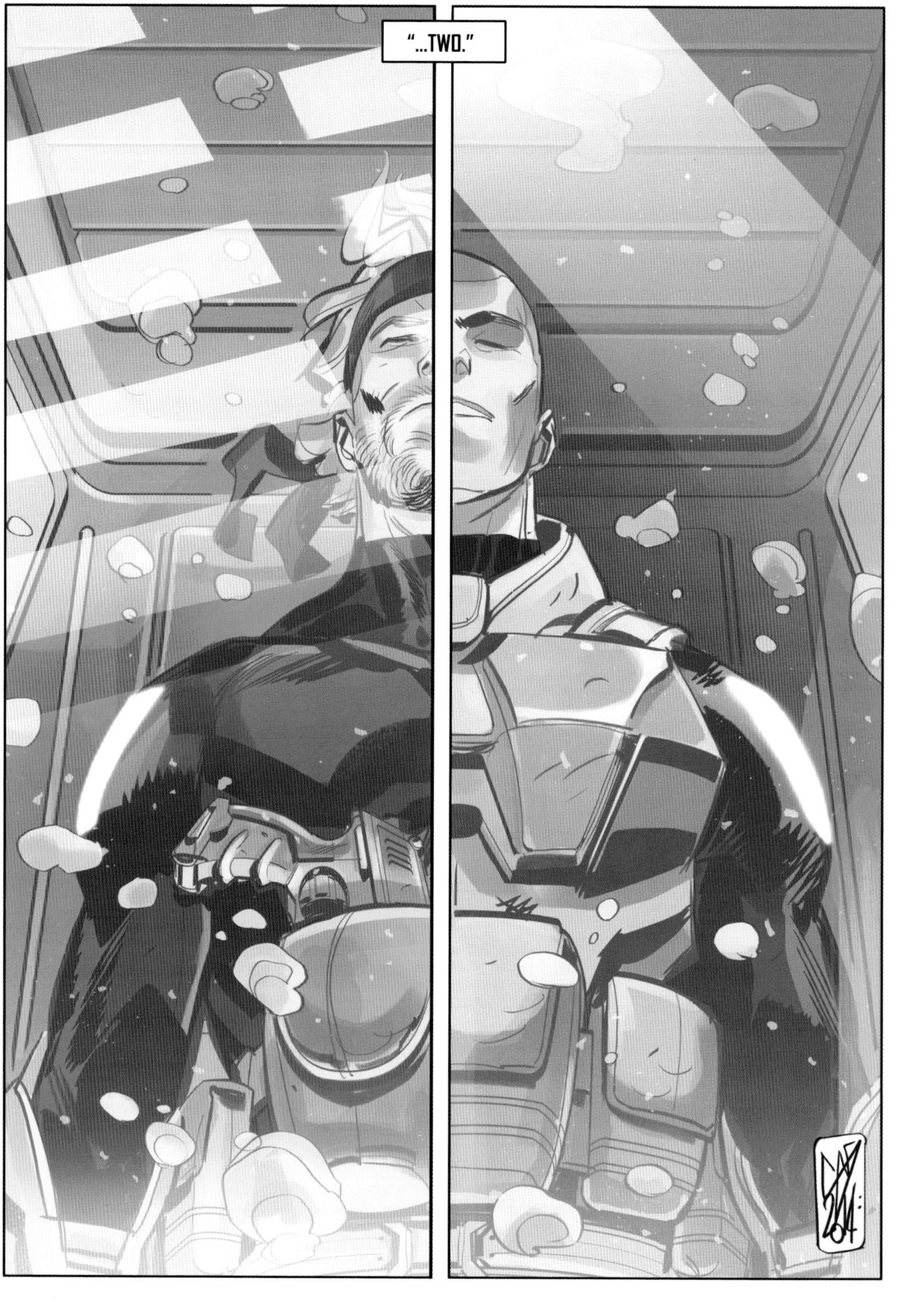
"...TWO."

GIGI CAVENAGO ARTIST

When and where were you born? Where do you live now?
I was born in Milan on October 12, 1982. I now live in Senago, Italy.

What sort of artistic education did you have?
I attended a class at the Comics School in Milan, but I also studied graphic design at the Rizzoli Institute for Graphic Arts.

Tell us about your previous works, before *Orphans*.
Jonathan Steele, by Memola and Marzia, published by Star Comics; the miniseries *Dr. Voodoo* with Giovanni Gualdoni for Free Books and, last but not least, *Cassidy*, a miniseries by Pasquale Rujo for Sergio Bonelli Editore.

When did you start working on *Orphans*, and when did you finish drawing this chapter?
I started in early November 2013. I remember it took a huge effort to get started: the first twenty pages went very slowly, while the last ones were finished in one breath.

What tools did you use?
Apart from one panel on the first page, I drew this episode digitally, both due to the complexity of some scenes and the fact that drawing digitally allowed me to work faster without losing quality. For example: to realize the "tree of sorrow" scene traditionally, I would have spent three times as much time if I hadn't done it digitally.

What was the most difficult scene and which one did you have to redraw more times?
Finishing my pages was a race against the clock, and during the entire process I felt on the same wavelength as Angel, as we were both chained to our desks trying to pilot something huge toward a grand finale. If at some point her eyes had bled, I'm pretty sure mine would have, too! I have to admit Alessia Pastorello (the colorist) didn't have it any easier, and we ended up consoling each other quite often.

If you could go back in time, what would you change about this chapter?
This chapter included a great number of splash pages and double page spreads which sometimes made our work faster and other times stalled us for days. The page where Ringo is at the weapon control console and the one where the spaceship crashes on Piccadilly Circus were some of the hardest ones for me: I spent the night awake trying to understand how to work out that last one.

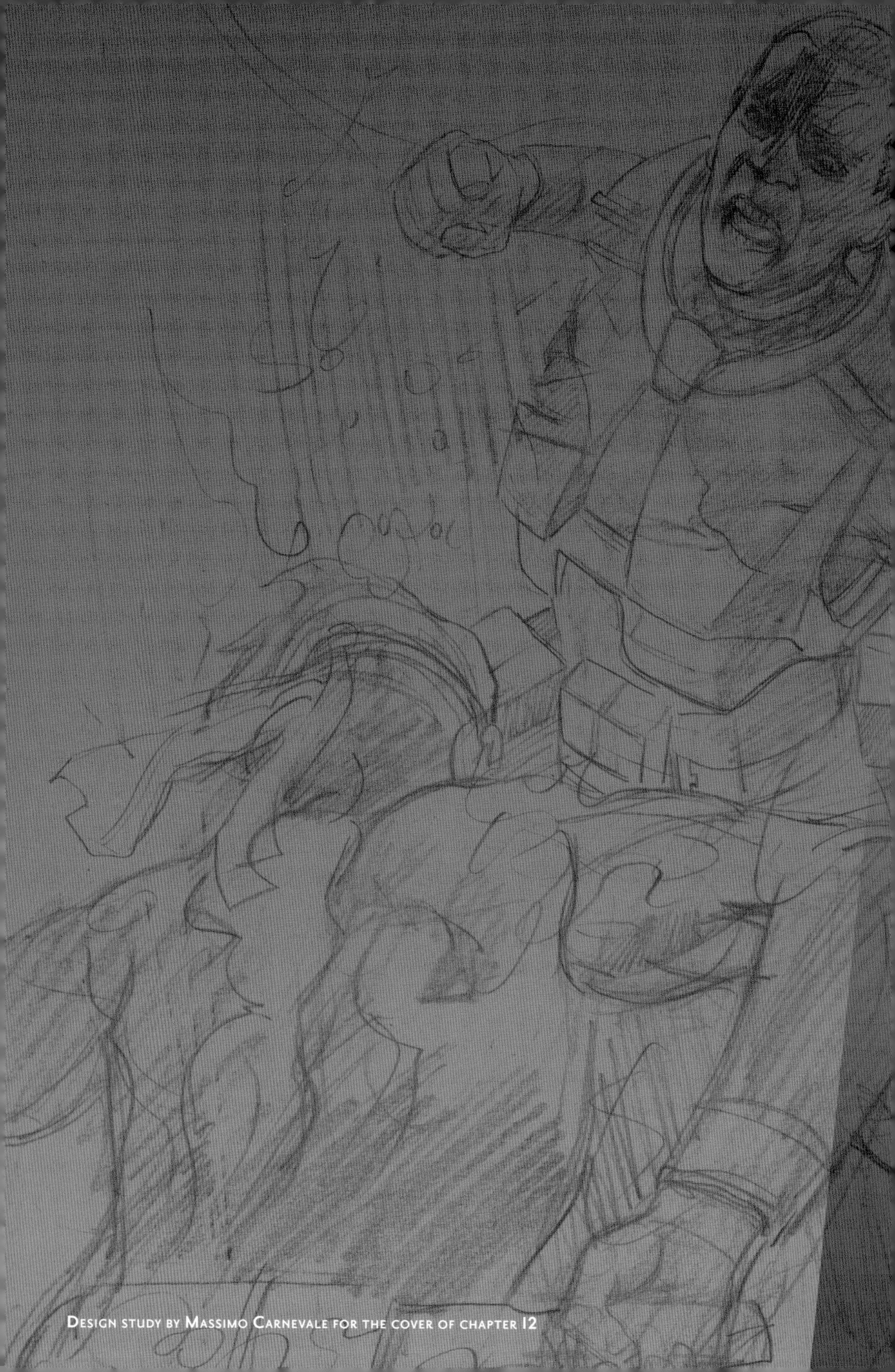

Design study by Massimo Carnevale for the cover of chapter 12

ROCK 'N' ROLL

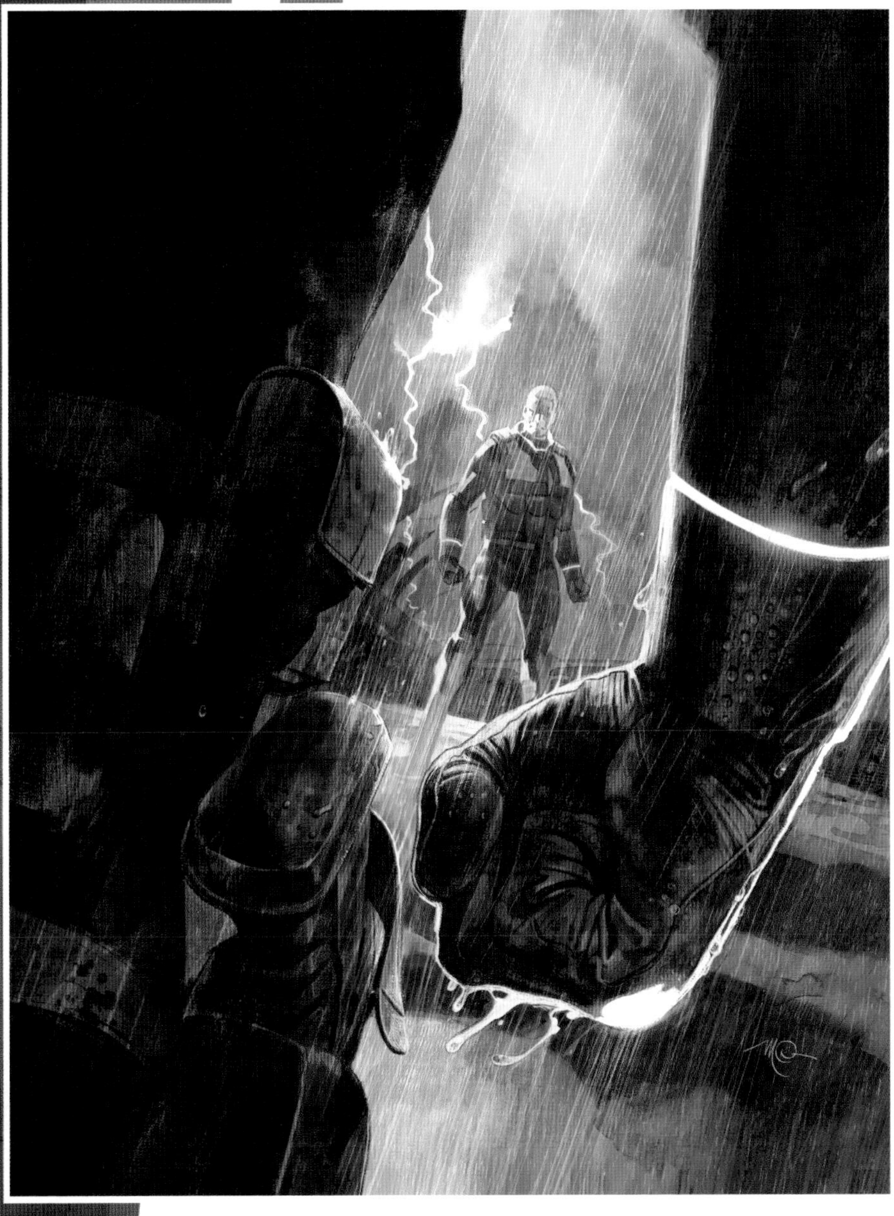

ORPHANS: CHAPTER 12

story: ROBERTO RECCHIONI
art: EMILIANO MAMMUCARI
colors: ANNALISA LEONI
cover: MASSIMO CARNEVALE

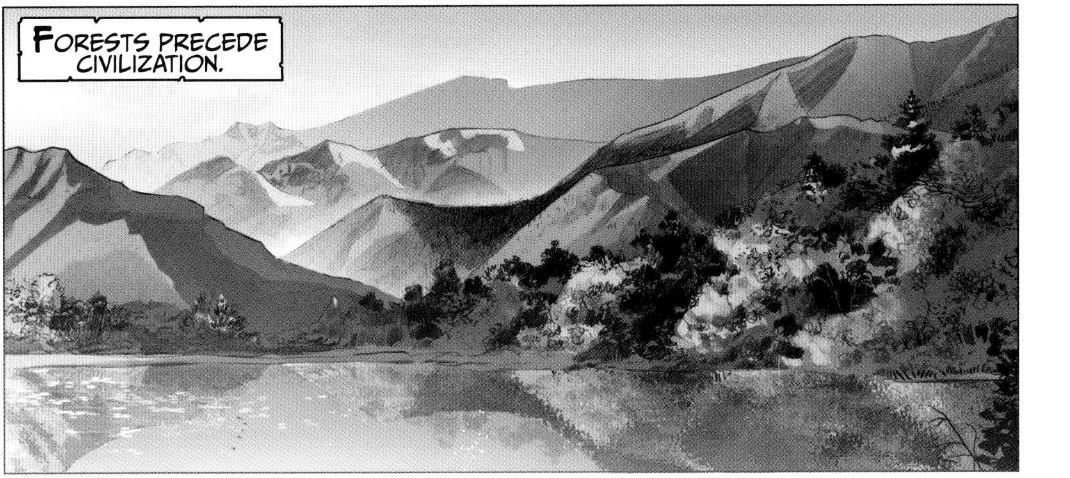
FORESTS PRECEDE CIVILIZATION.

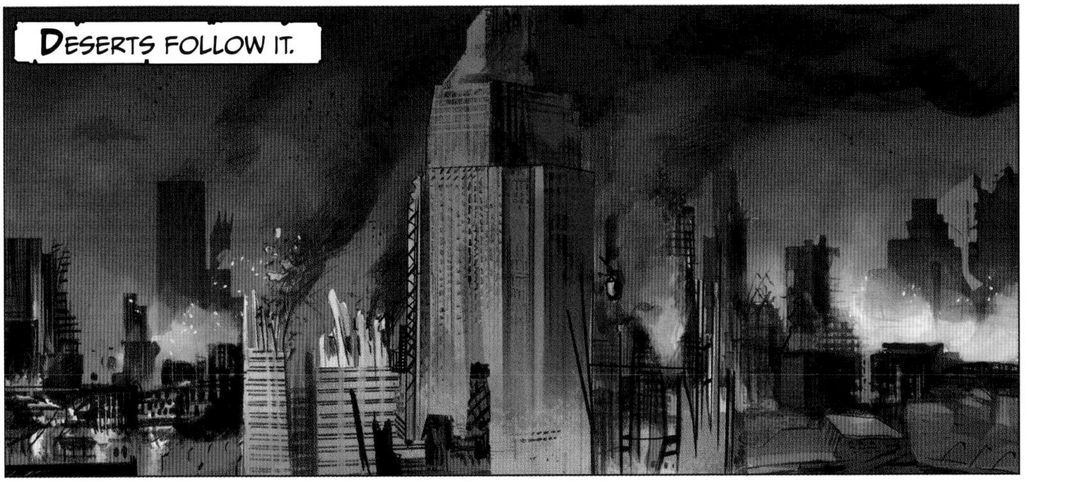
DESERTS FOLLOW IT.

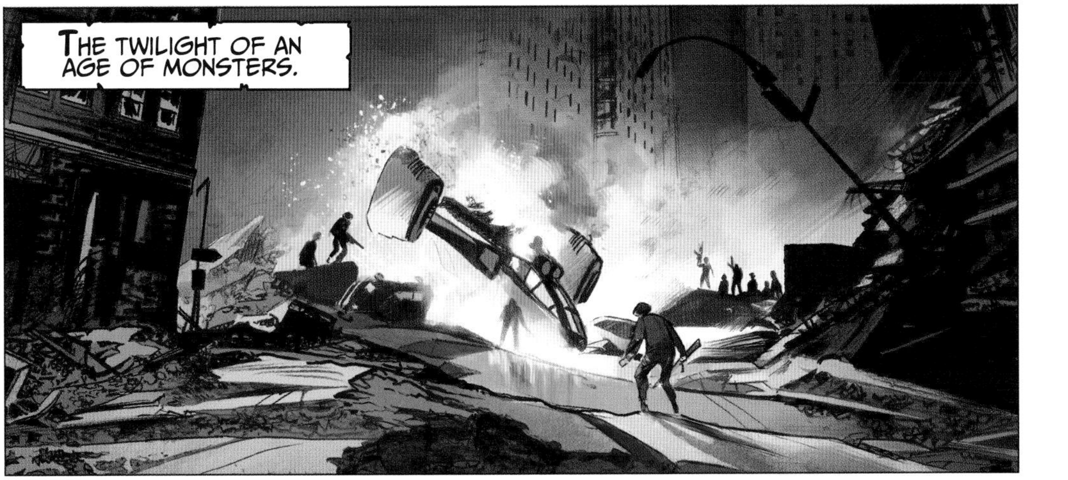
THE TWILIGHT OF AN AGE OF MONSTERS.

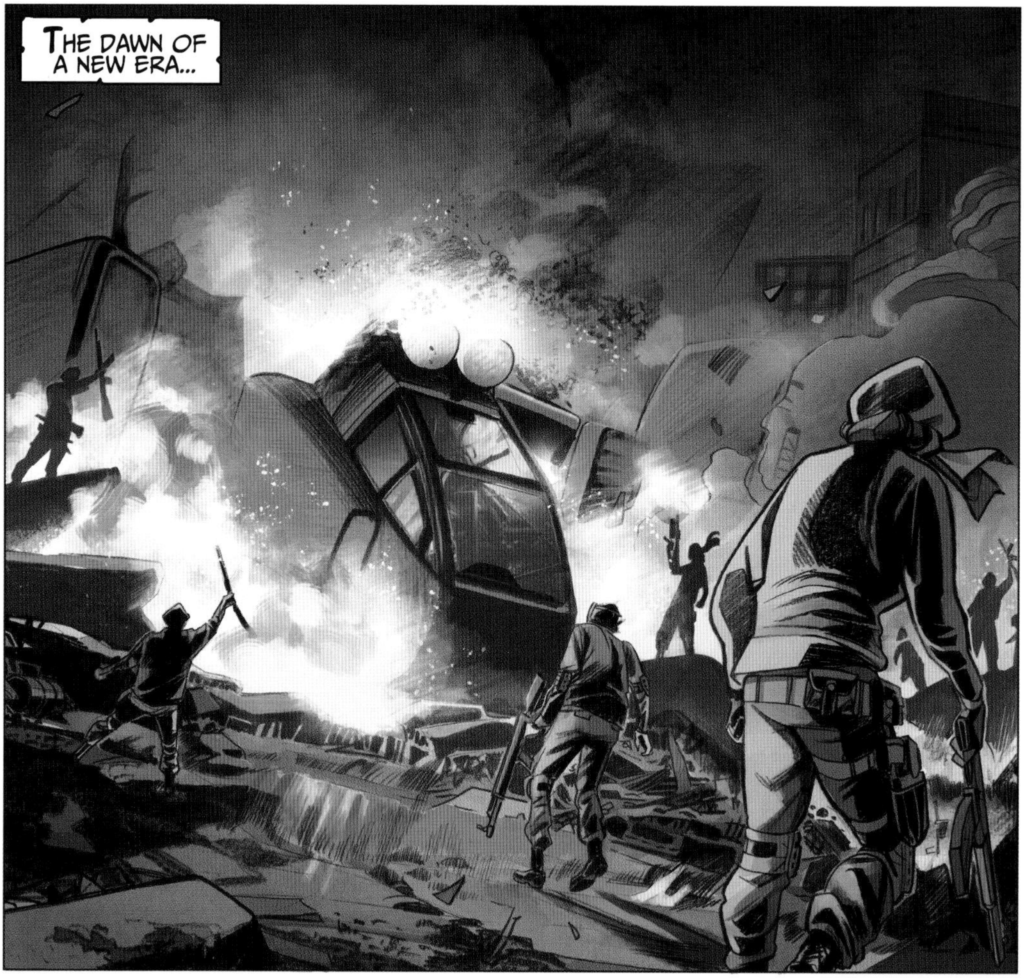
The dawn of a new era...

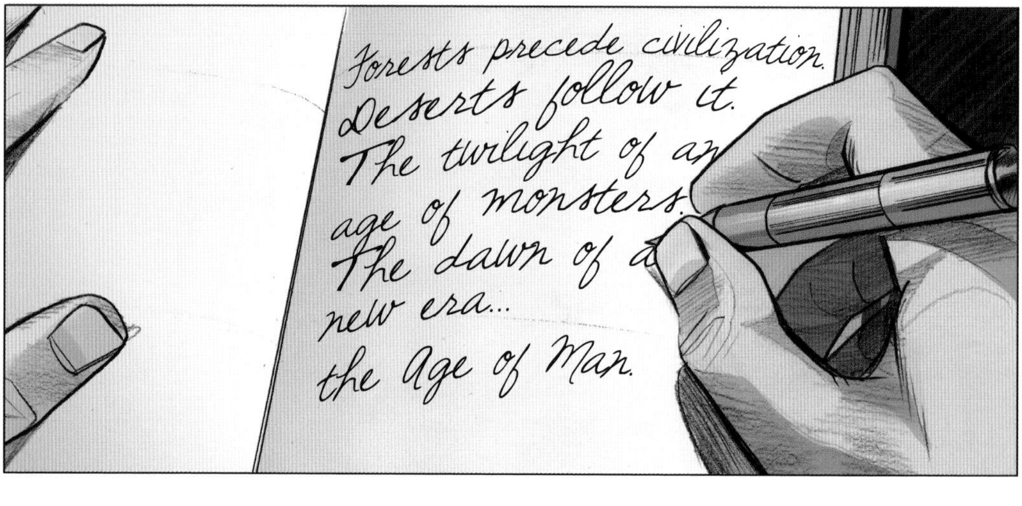
Forests precede civilization.
Deserts follow it.
The twilight of an
age of monsters.
The dawn of a
new era...
the age of Man.

NOW THIS IS NEW... BAD BOY RINGO DOING SOMETHING BESIDES SHOOTING EVERYTHING THAT MOVES OR GOOFING ON HIS TEAMMATES!

I'M A SENSITIVE SOUL. YOU GUYS JUST DON'T SEE IT.

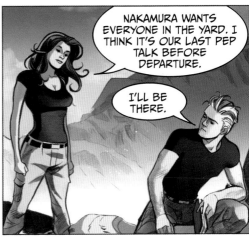

NAKAMURA WANTS EVERYONE IN THE YARD. I THINK IT'S OUR LAST PEP TALK BEFORE DEPARTURE.

I'LL BE THERE.

CAN I SEE YOUR DRAWINGS? YOU USED TO BE PRETTY GOOD...

I'VE KINDA LOST IT. MOSTLY SCRIBBLES NOW.

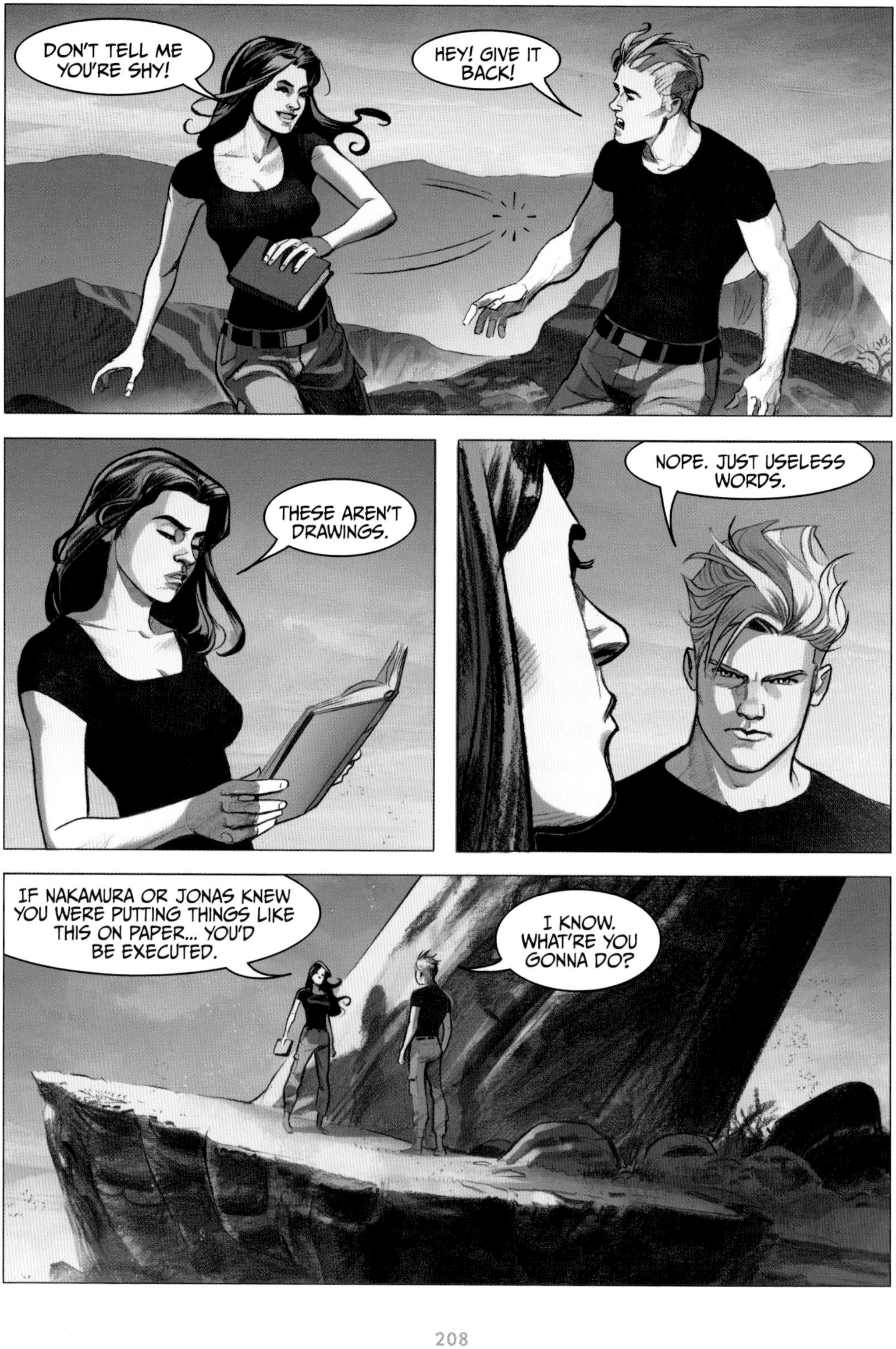
DON'T TELL ME YOU'RE SHY!
HEY! GIVE IT BACK!
THESE AREN'T DRAWINGS.
NOPE. JUST USELESS WORDS.
IF NAKAMURA OR JONAS KNEW YOU WERE PUTTING THINGS LIKE THIS ON PAPER... YOU'D BE EXECUTED.
I KNOW. WHAT'RE YOU GONNA DO?

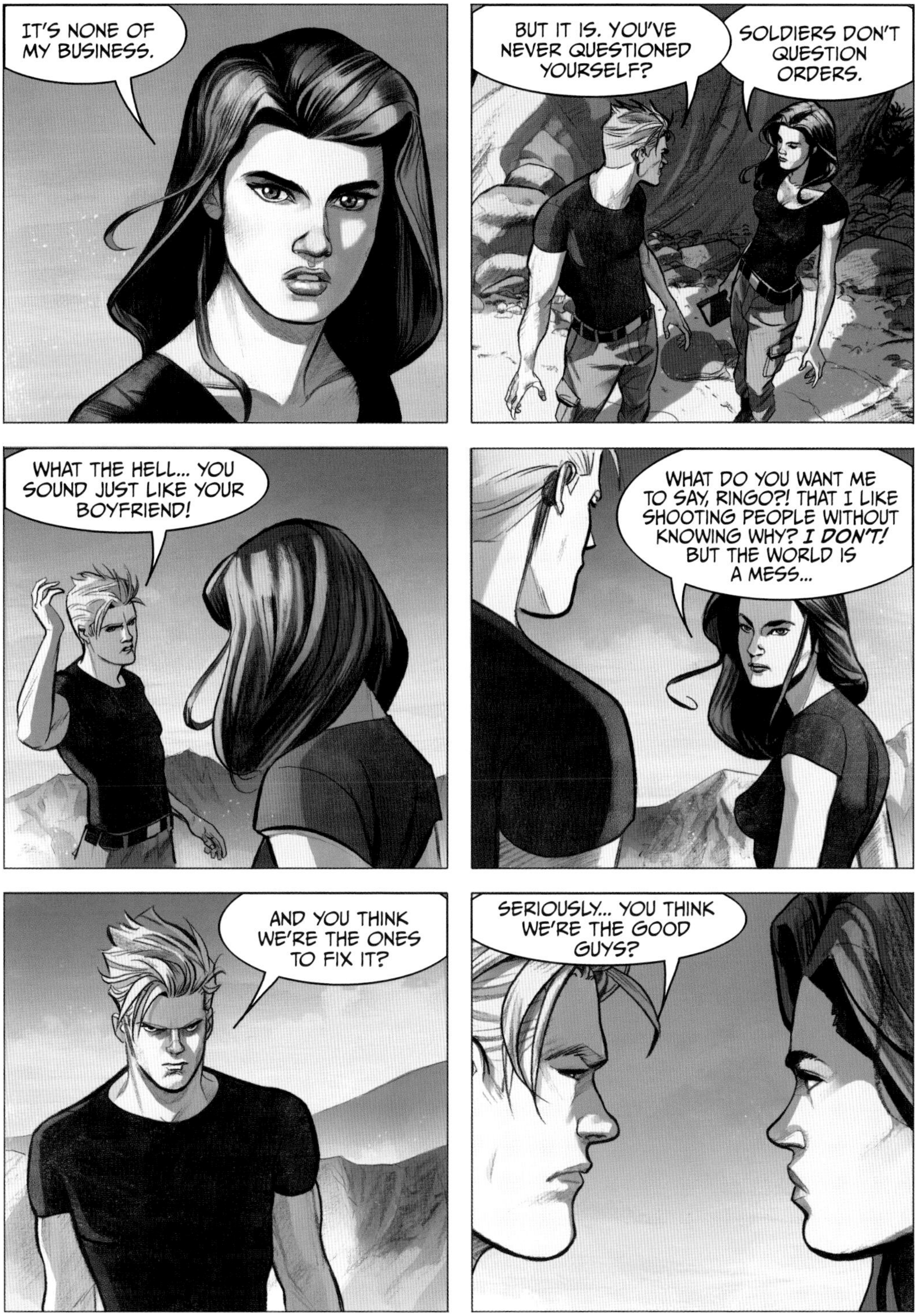
IT'S NONE OF MY BUSINESS.
BUT IT IS. YOU'VE NEVER QUESTIONED YOURSELF?
SOLDIERS DON'T QUESTION ORDERS.
WHAT THE HELL... YOU SOUND JUST LIKE YOUR BOYFRIEND!
WHAT DO YOU WANT ME TO SAY, RINGO?! THAT I LIKE SHOOTING PEOPLE WITHOUT KNOWING WHY? ***I DON'T!*** BUT THE WORLD IS A MESS...
AND YOU THINK WE'RE THE ONES TO FIX IT?
SERIOUSLY... YOU THINK WE'RE THE GOOD GUYS?

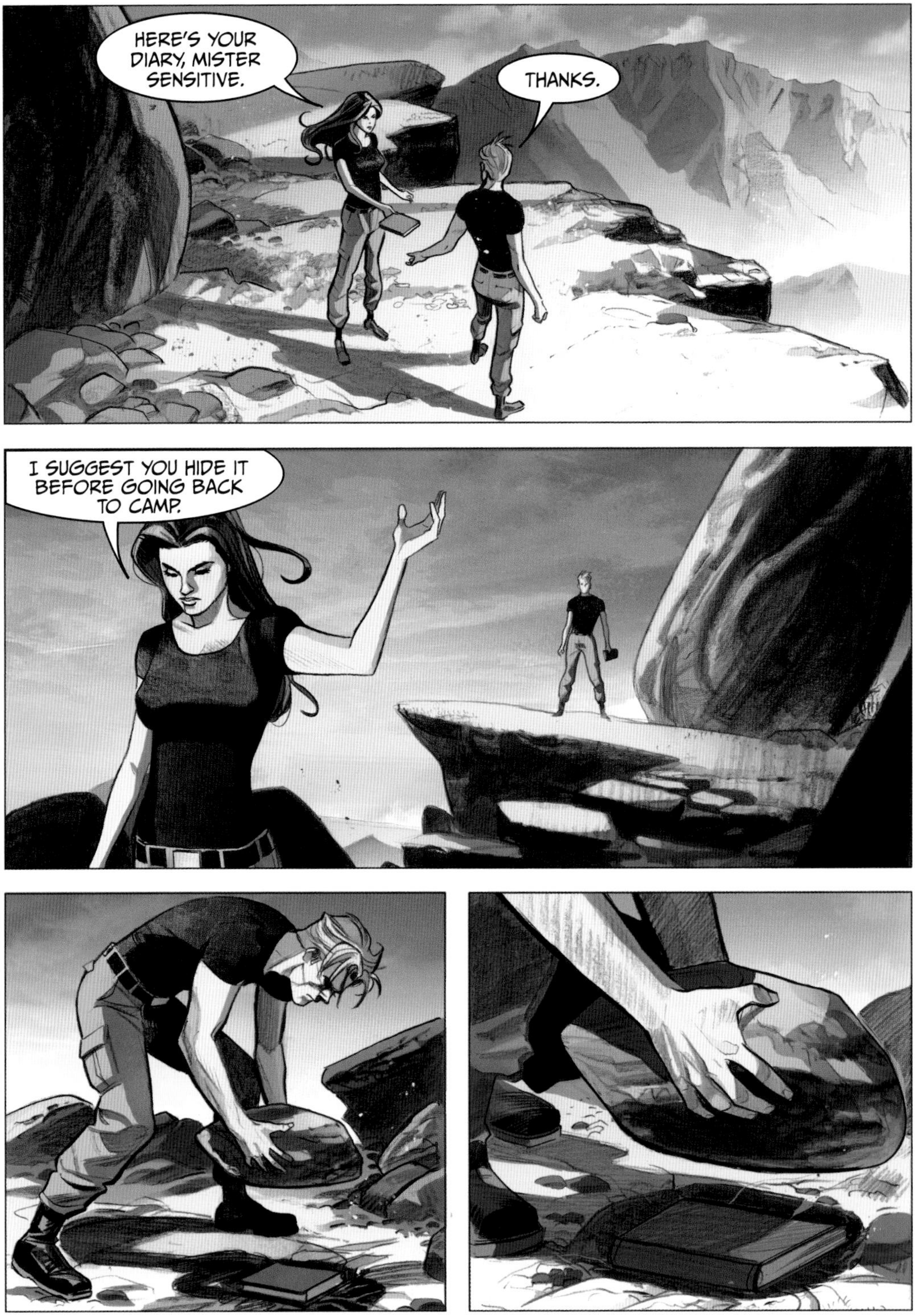
HERE'S YOUR DIARY, MISTER SENSITIVE.
THANKS.
I SUGGEST YOU HIDE IT BEFORE GOING BACK TO CAMP.

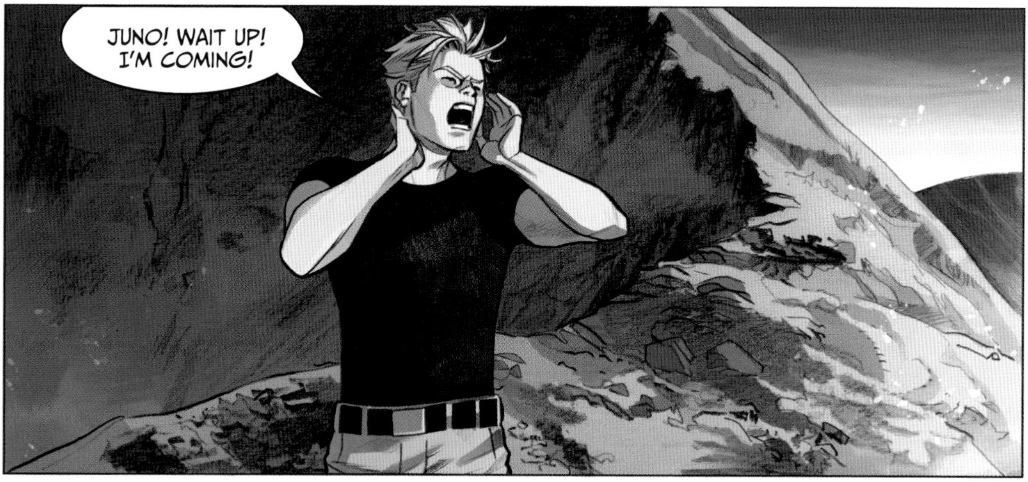
JUNO! WAIT UP! I'M COMING!

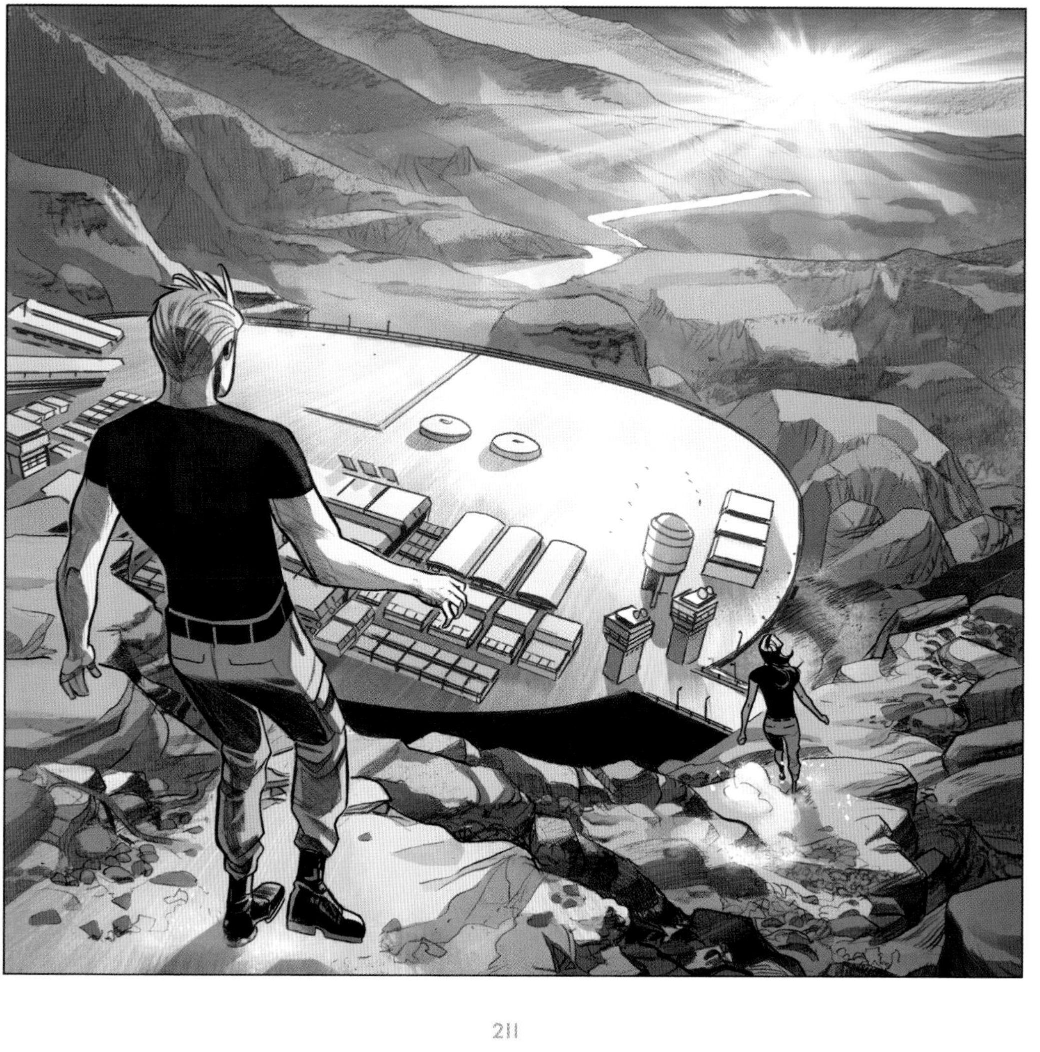

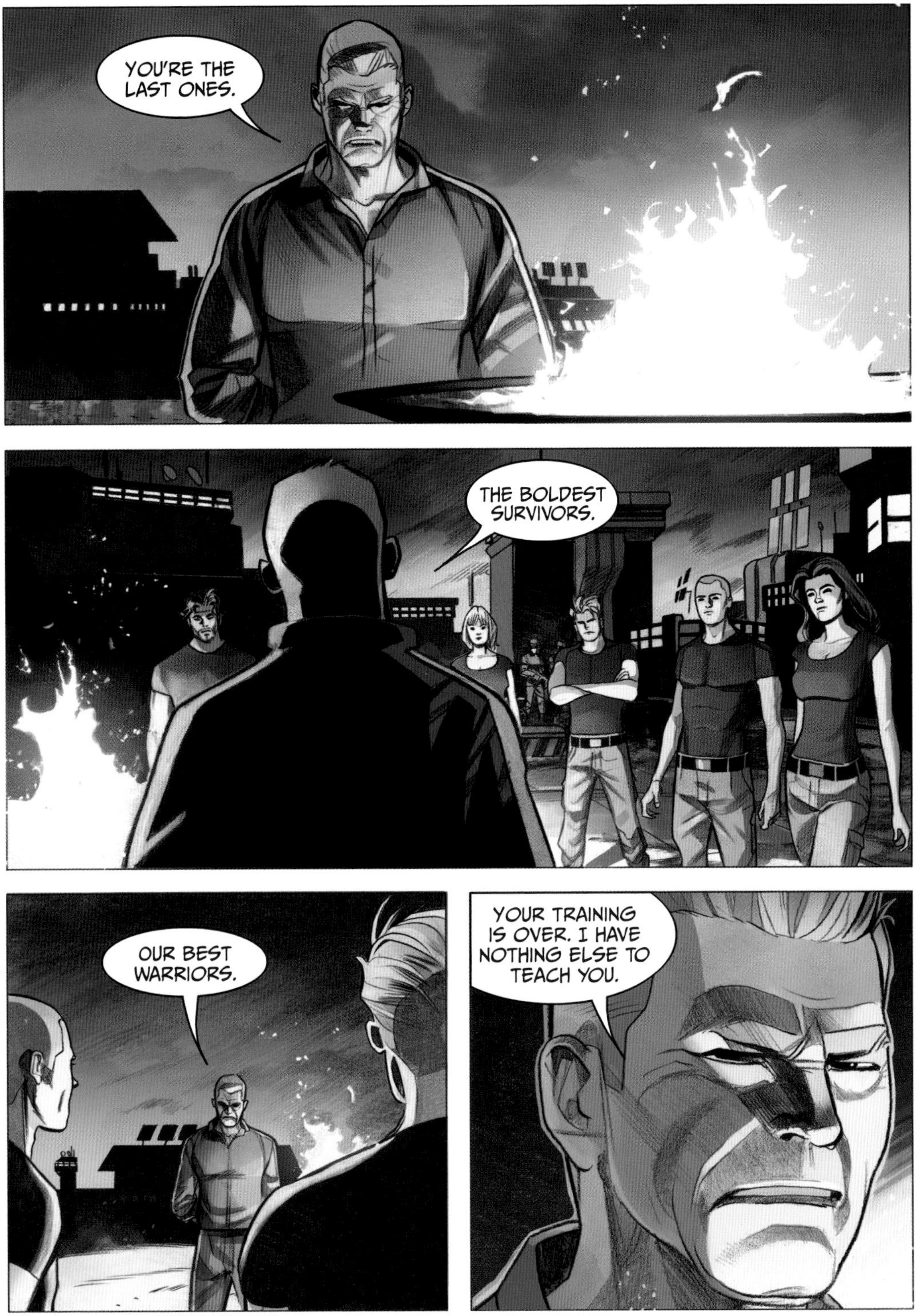
YOU'RE THE LAST ONES.
THE BOLDEST SURVIVORS.
OUR BEST WARRIORS.
YOUR TRAINING IS OVER. I HAVE NOTHING ELSE TO TEACH YOU.

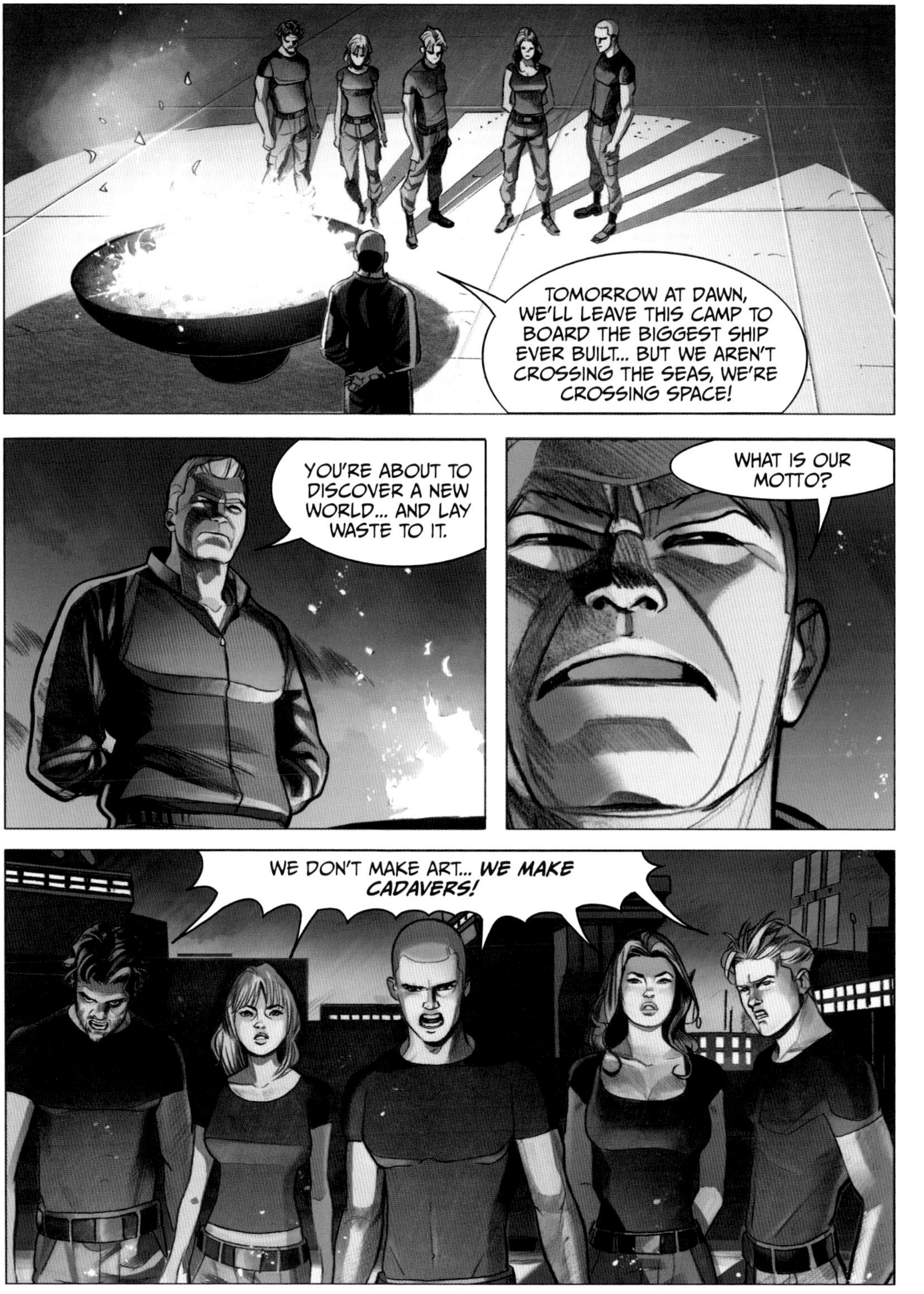
TOMORROW AT DAWN, WE'LL LEAVE THIS CAMP TO BOARD THE BIGGEST SHIP EVER BUILT... BUT WE AREN'T CROSSING THE SEAS, WE'RE CROSSING SPACE!
YOU'RE ABOUT TO DISCOVER A NEW WORLD... AND LAY WASTE TO IT.
WHAT IS OUR MOTTO?
WE DON'T MAKE ART... ***WE MAKE CADAVERS!***

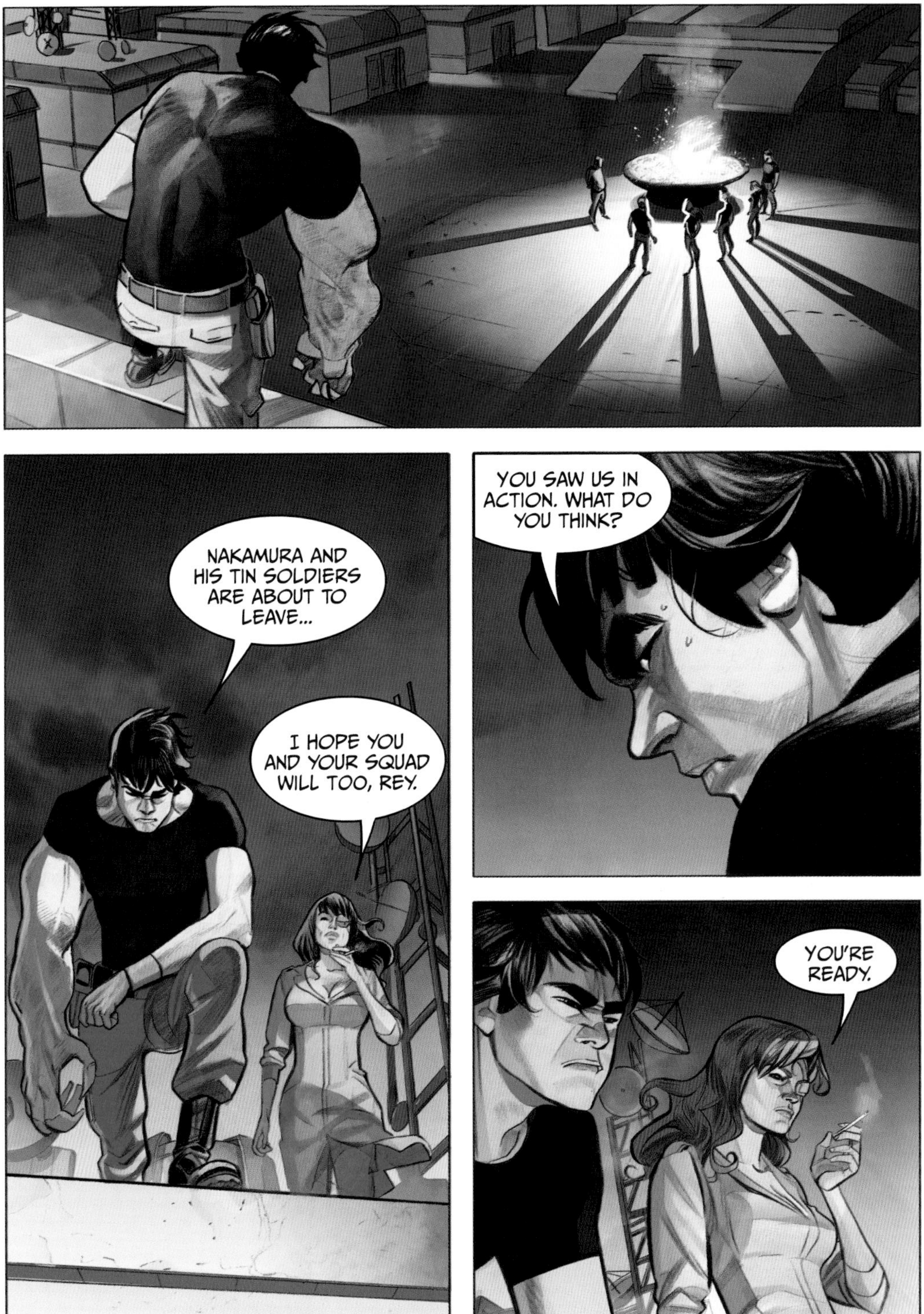
NAKAMURA AND HIS TIN SOLDIERS ARE ABOUT TO LEAVE...
I HOPE YOU AND YOUR SQUAD WILL TOO, REY.
YOU SAW US IN ACTION. WHAT DO YOU THINK?
YOU'RE READY.

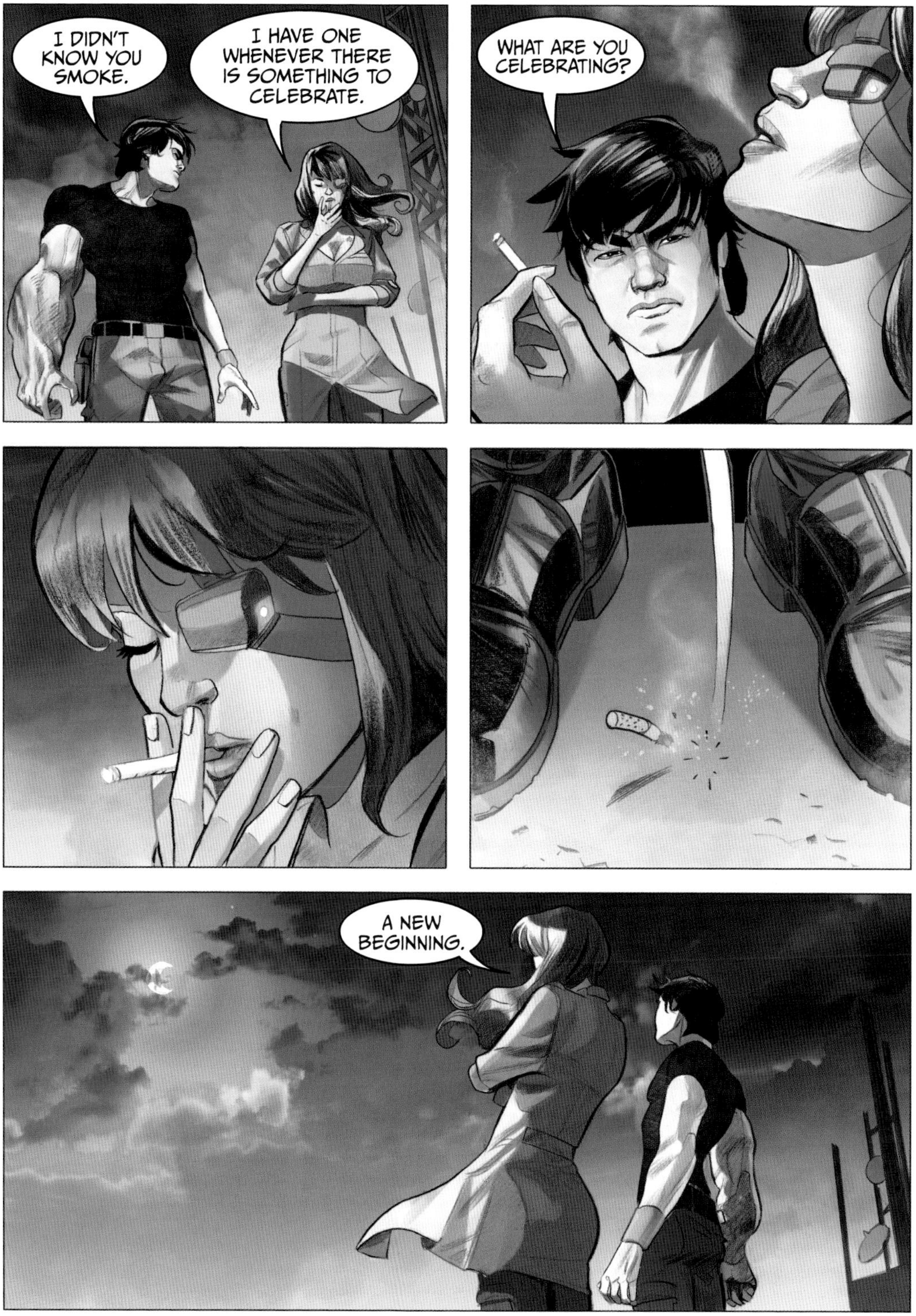
I DIDN'T KNOW YOU SMOKE.
I HAVE ONE WHENEVER THERE IS SOMETHING TO CELEBRATE.
WHAT ARE YOU CELEBRATING?
A NEW BEGINNING.

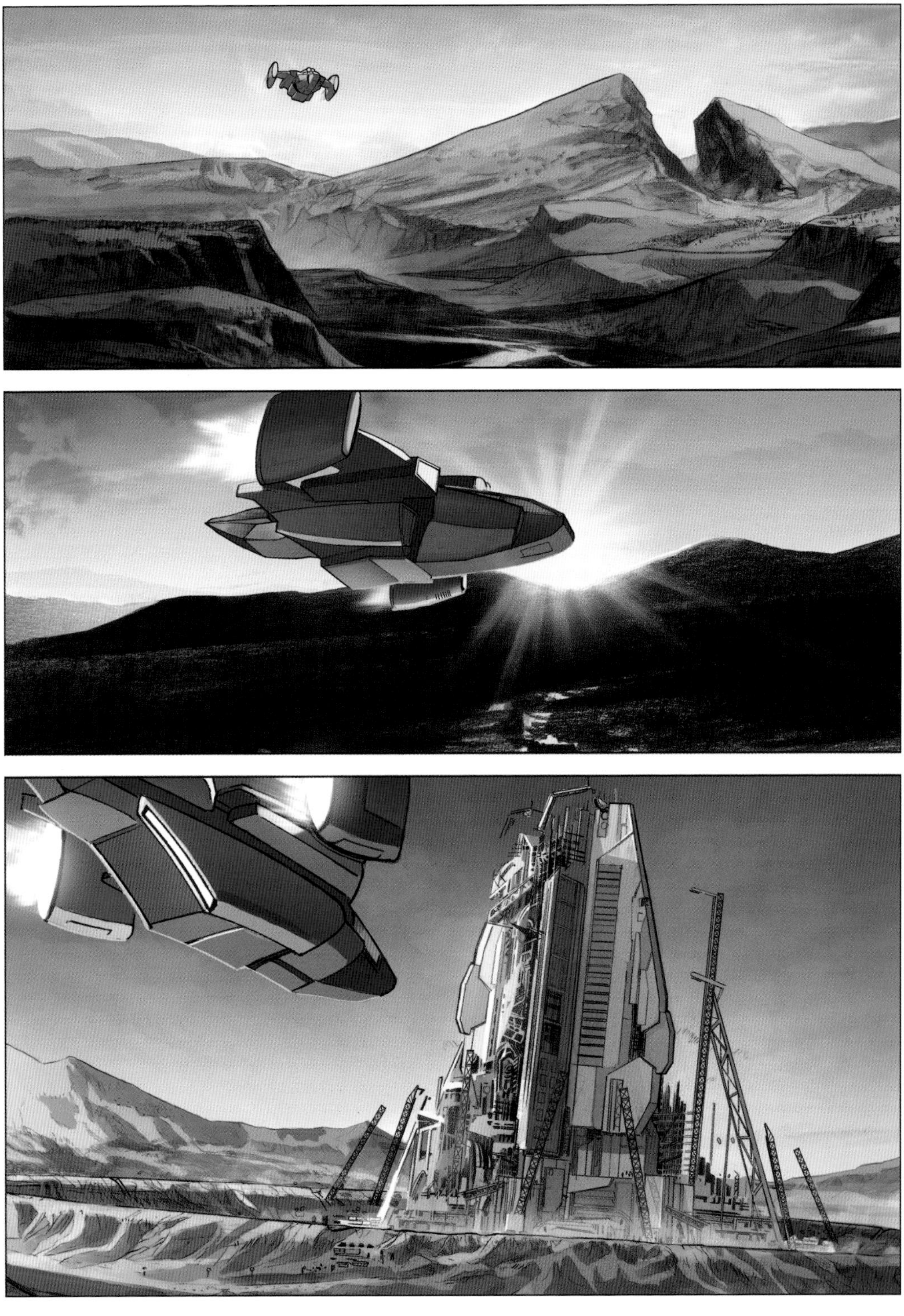

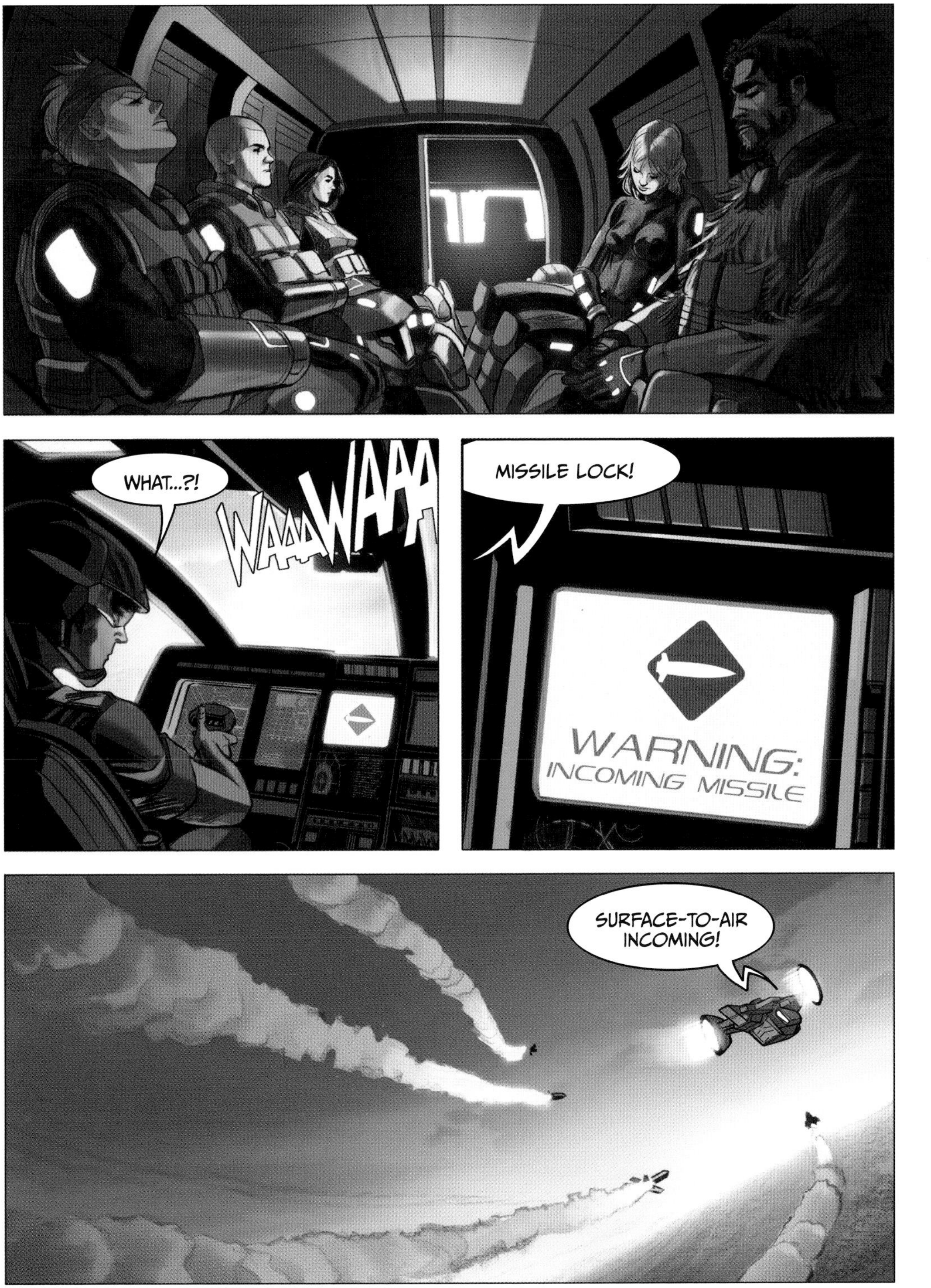
WHAT...?!
WAAAWAAA
MISSILE LOCK!
WARNING:
INCOMING MISSILE
SURFACE-TO-AIR INCOMING!

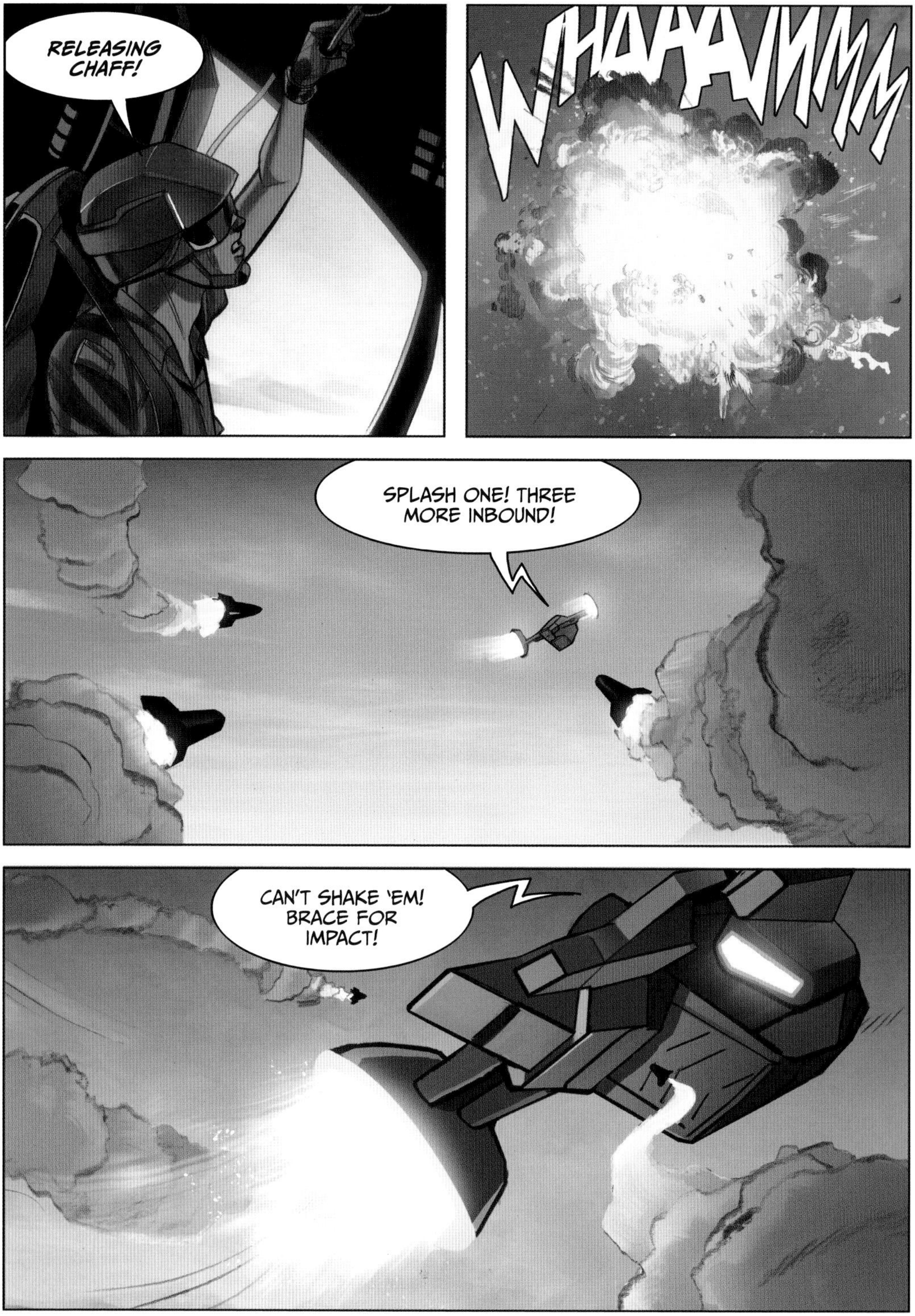
RELEASING CHAFF!
WHAAAMMM
SPLASH ONE! THREE MORE INBOUND!
CAN'T SHAKE 'EM! BRACE FOR IMPACT!

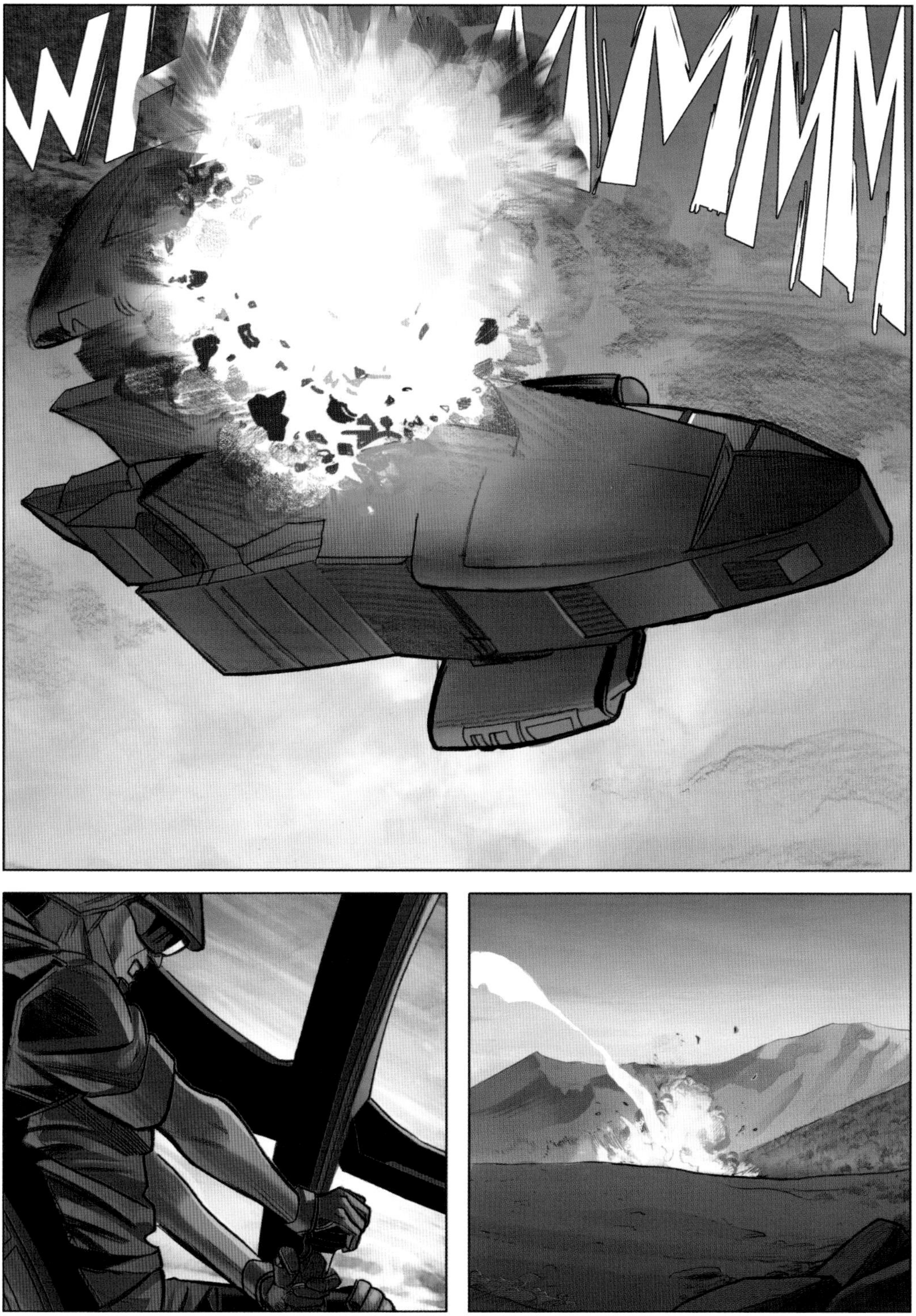
WH MMMMM

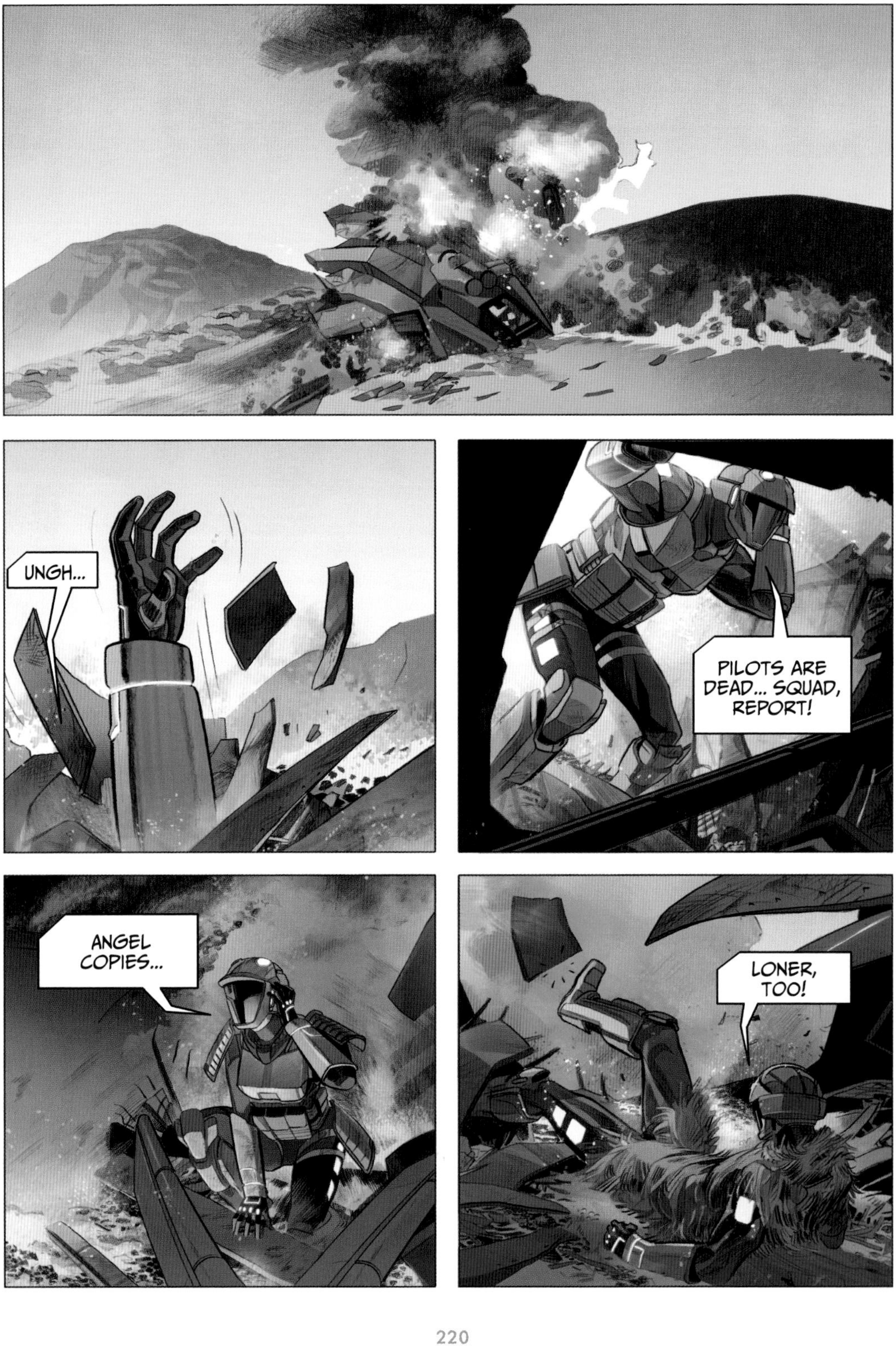
UNGH...
PILOTS ARE DEAD... SQUAD, REPORT!
ANGEL COPIES...
LONER, TOO!

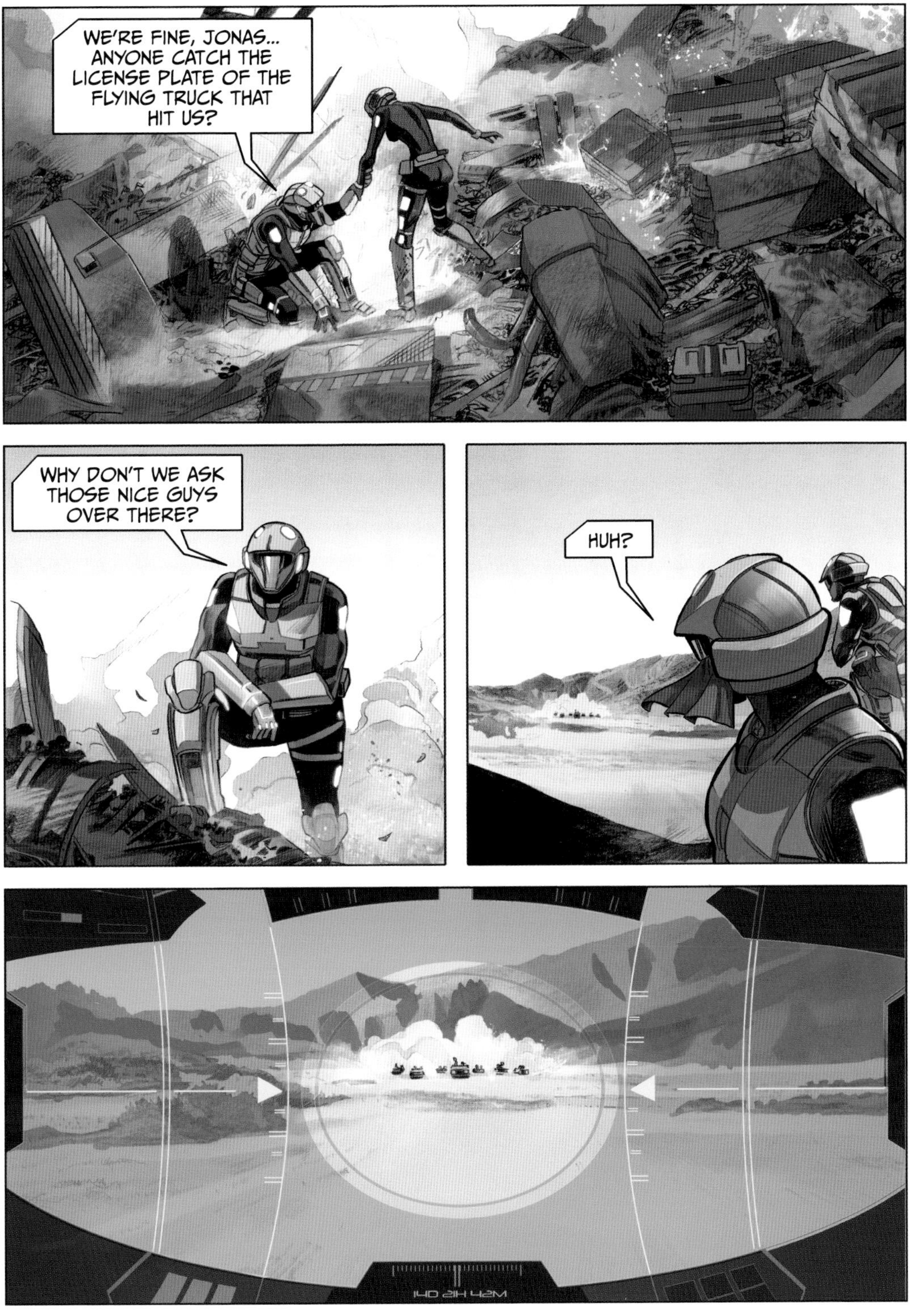
WE'RE FINE, JONAS... ANYONE CATCH THE LICENSE PLATE OF THE FLYING TRUCK THAT HIT US?
WHY DON'T WE ASK THOSE NICE GUYS OVER THERE?
HUH?
14D 21H 42M

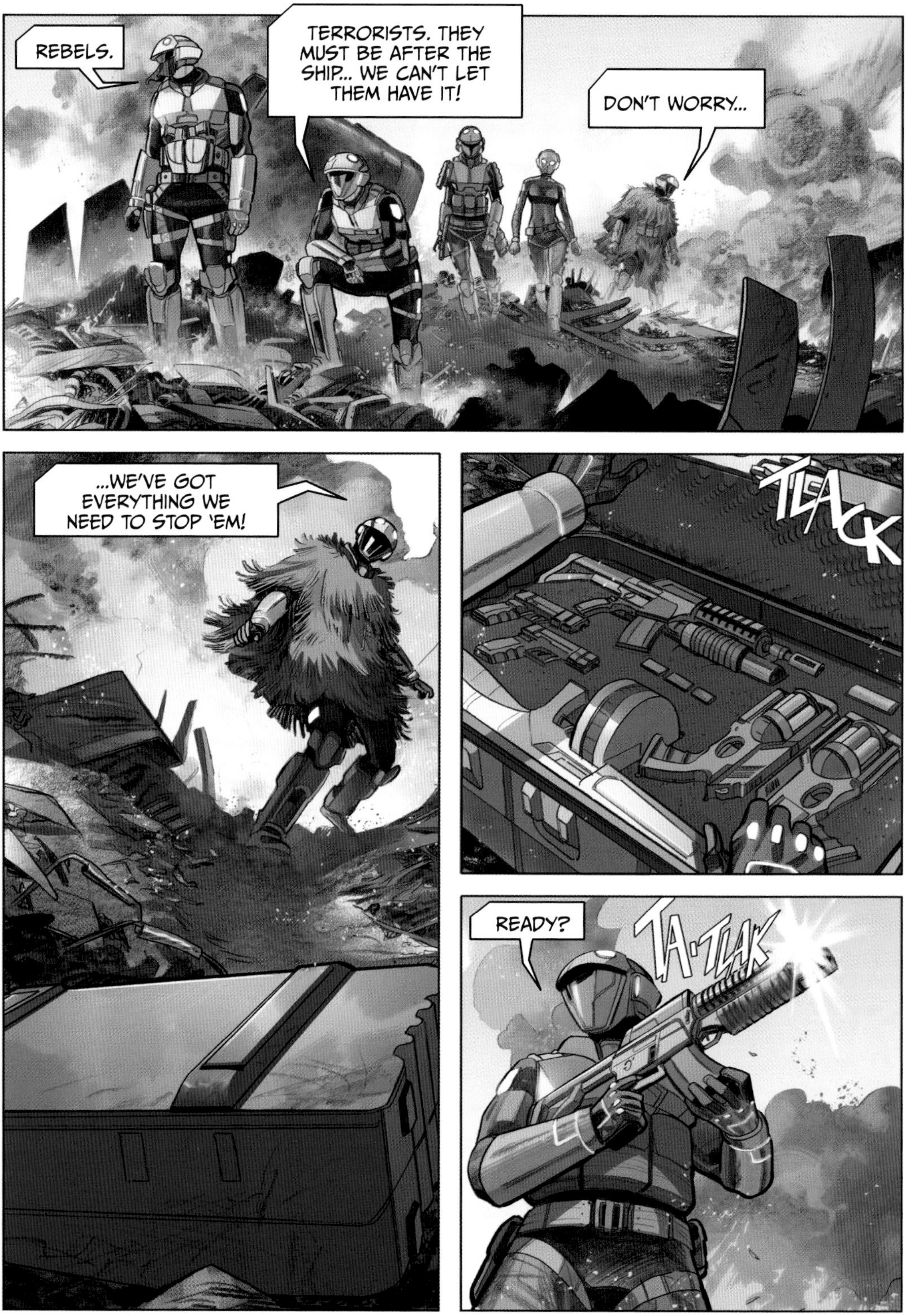
REBELS.
TERRORISTS. THEY MUST BE AFTER THE SHIP... WE CAN'T LET THEM HAVE IT!
DON'T WORRY...
...WE'VE GOT EVERYTHING WE NEED TO STOP 'EM!
TLACK
READY?
TA-TLAK

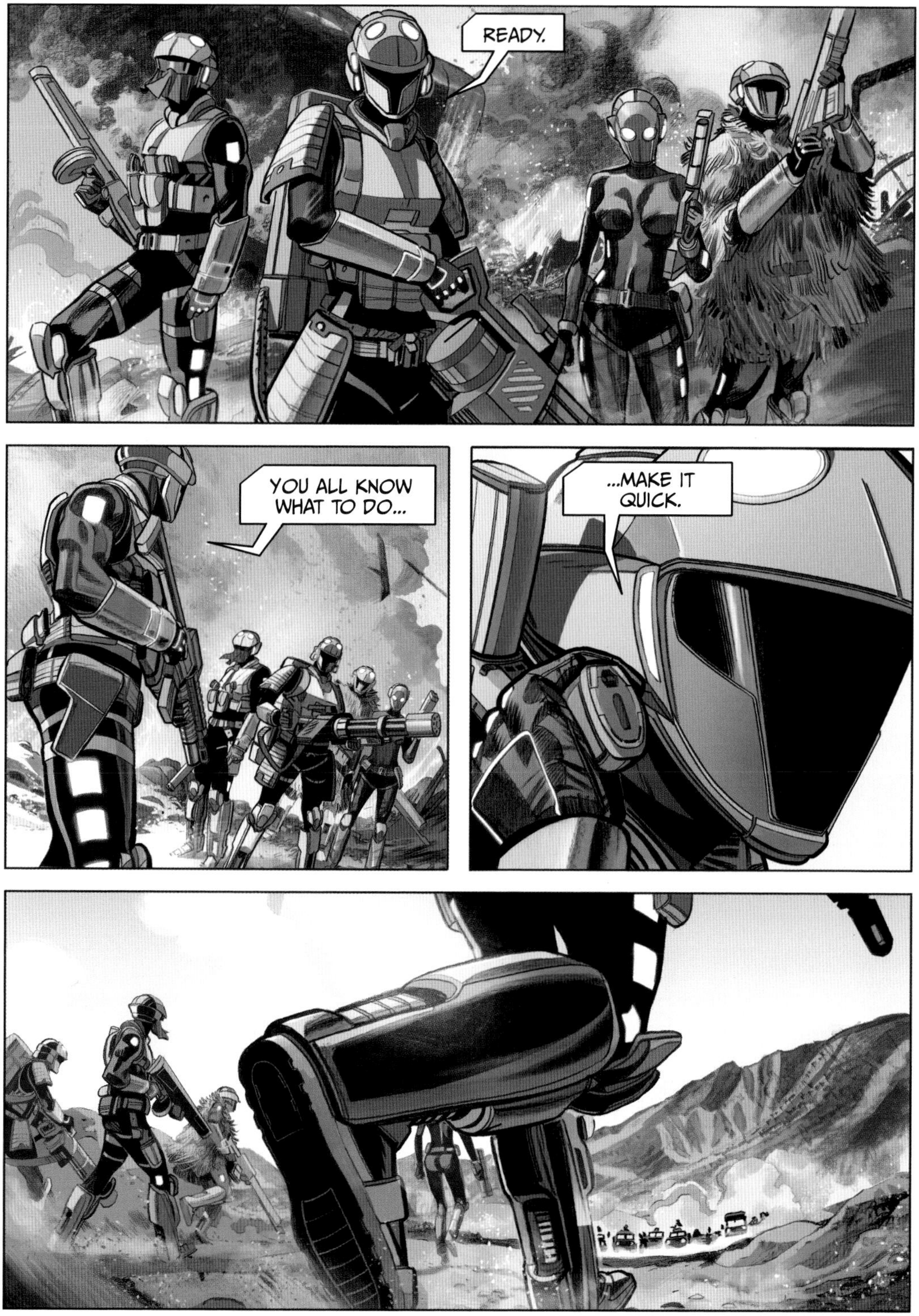
READY.
YOU ALL KNOW WHAT TO DO...
...MAKE IT QUICK.

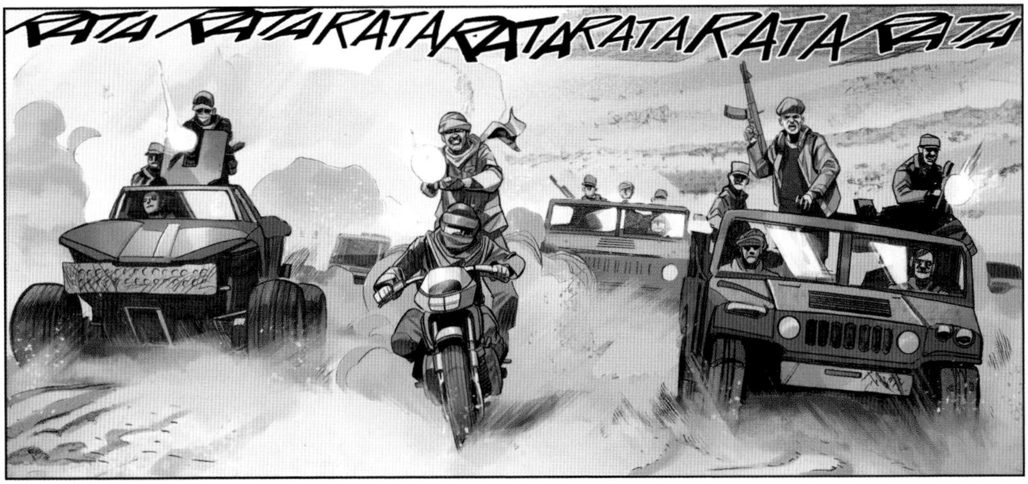
RATA RATA RATA RATA RATA RATA RATA

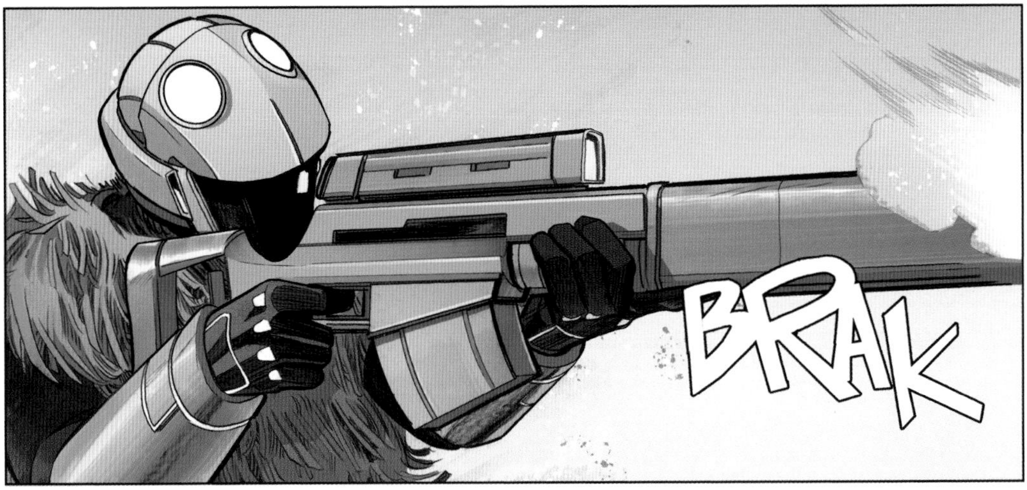
BRAK

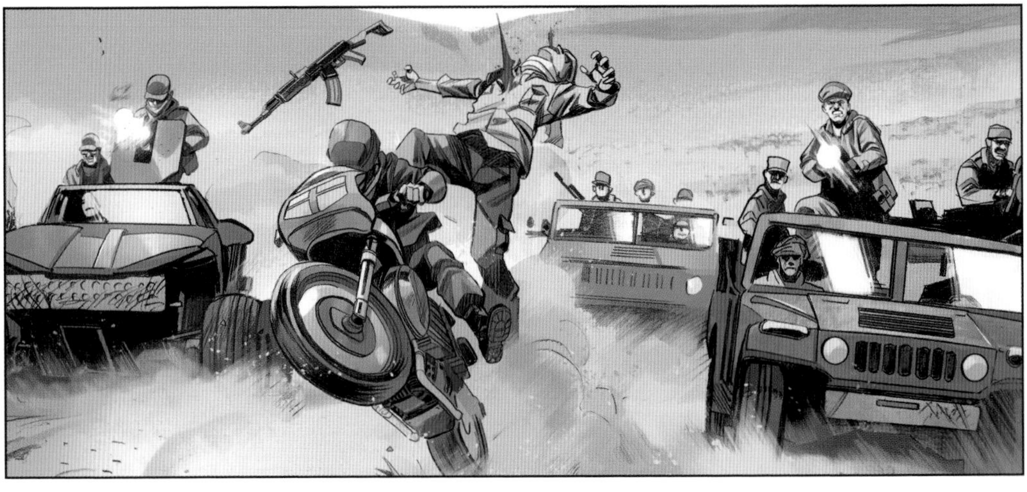

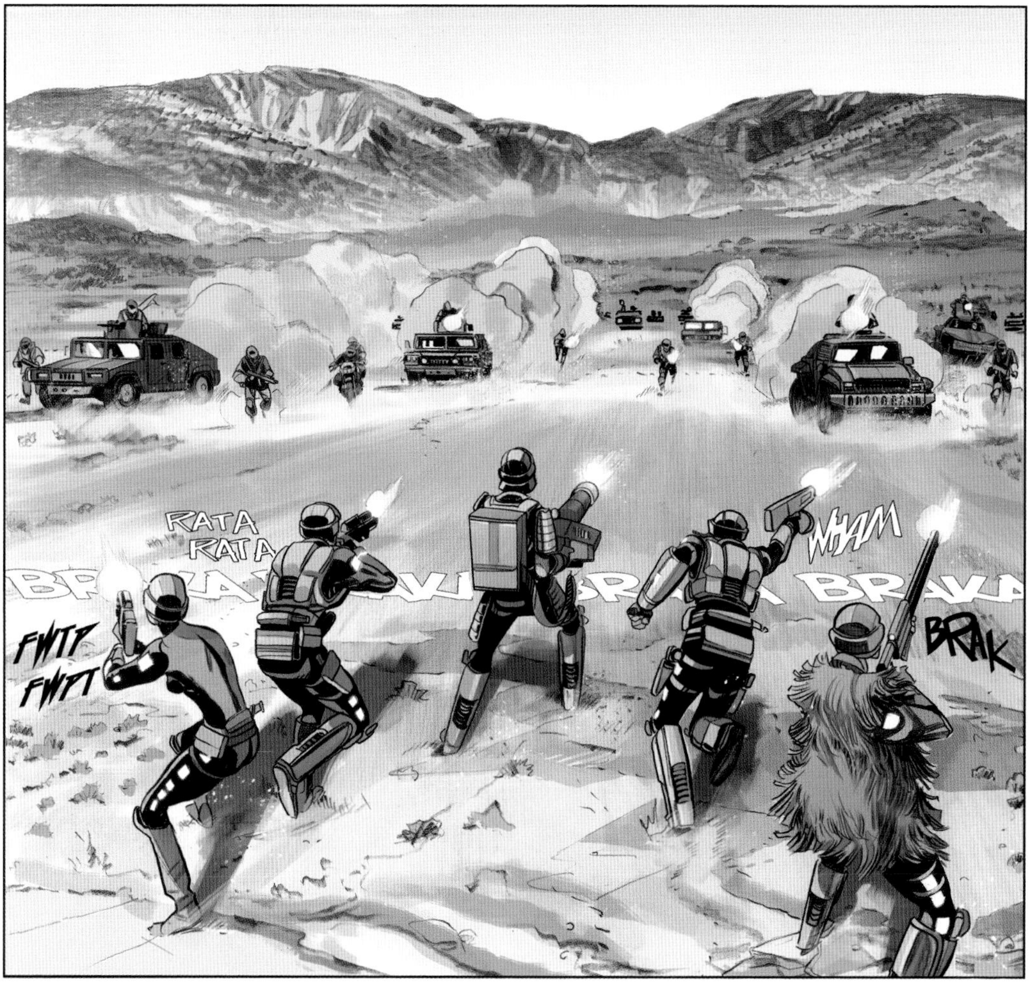
RATA
RATA
BRAKA BRAKA BRAKA BRAKA
WHAM
FWTP
FWPT
BRAK

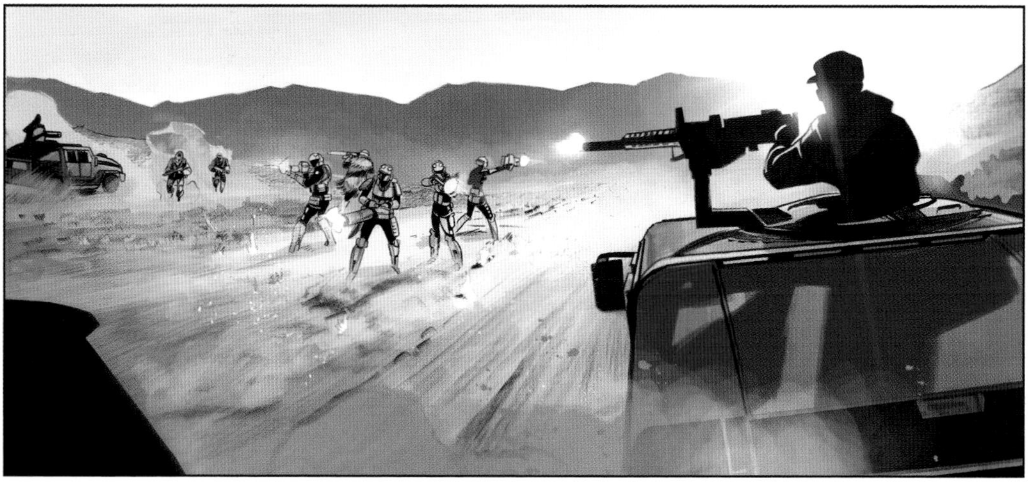

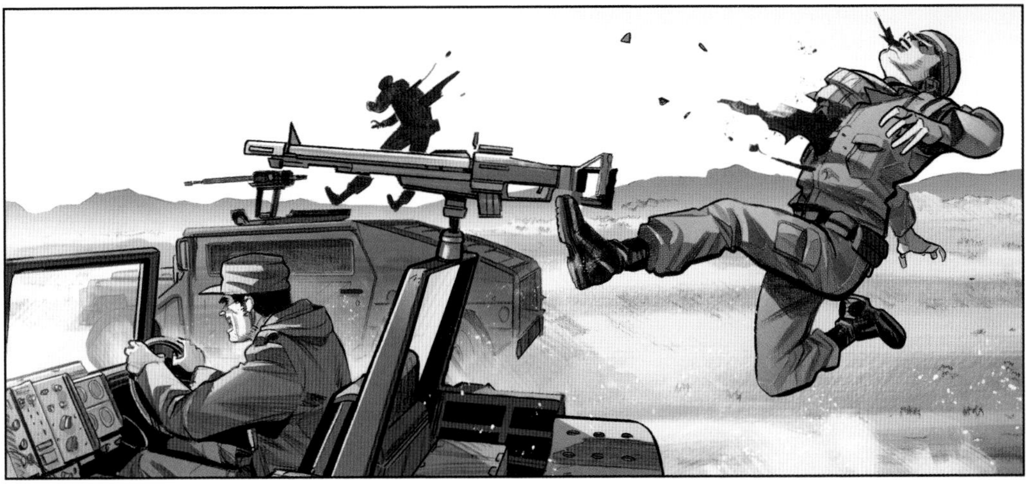

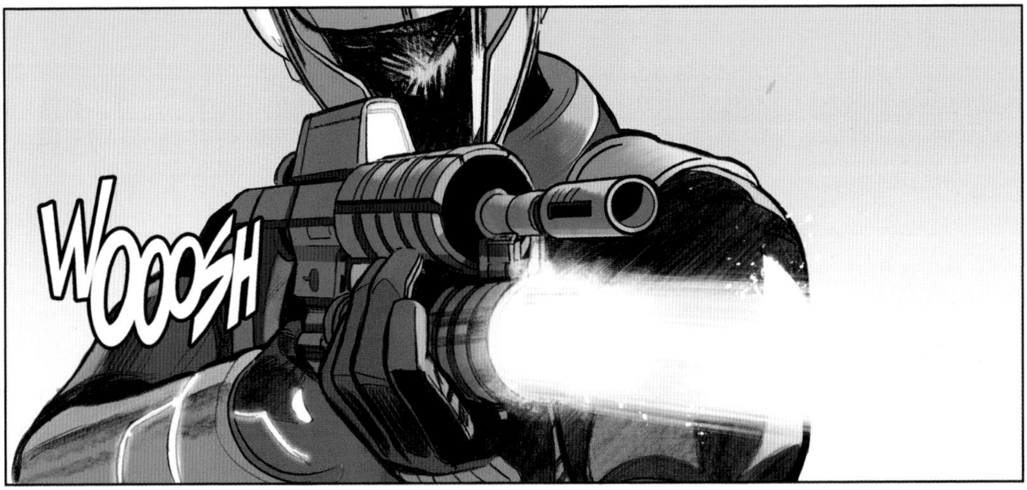
WOOOSH

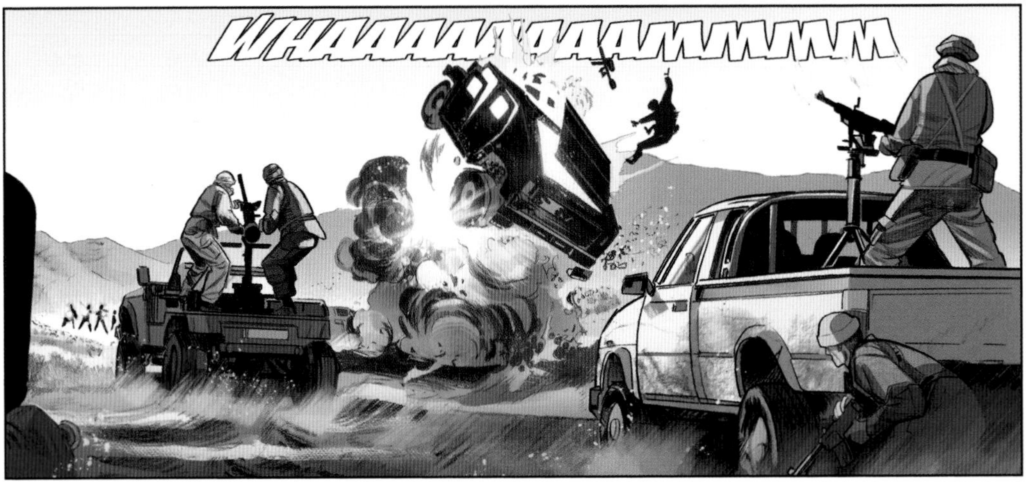
WHAAAAAAAAMMMMM

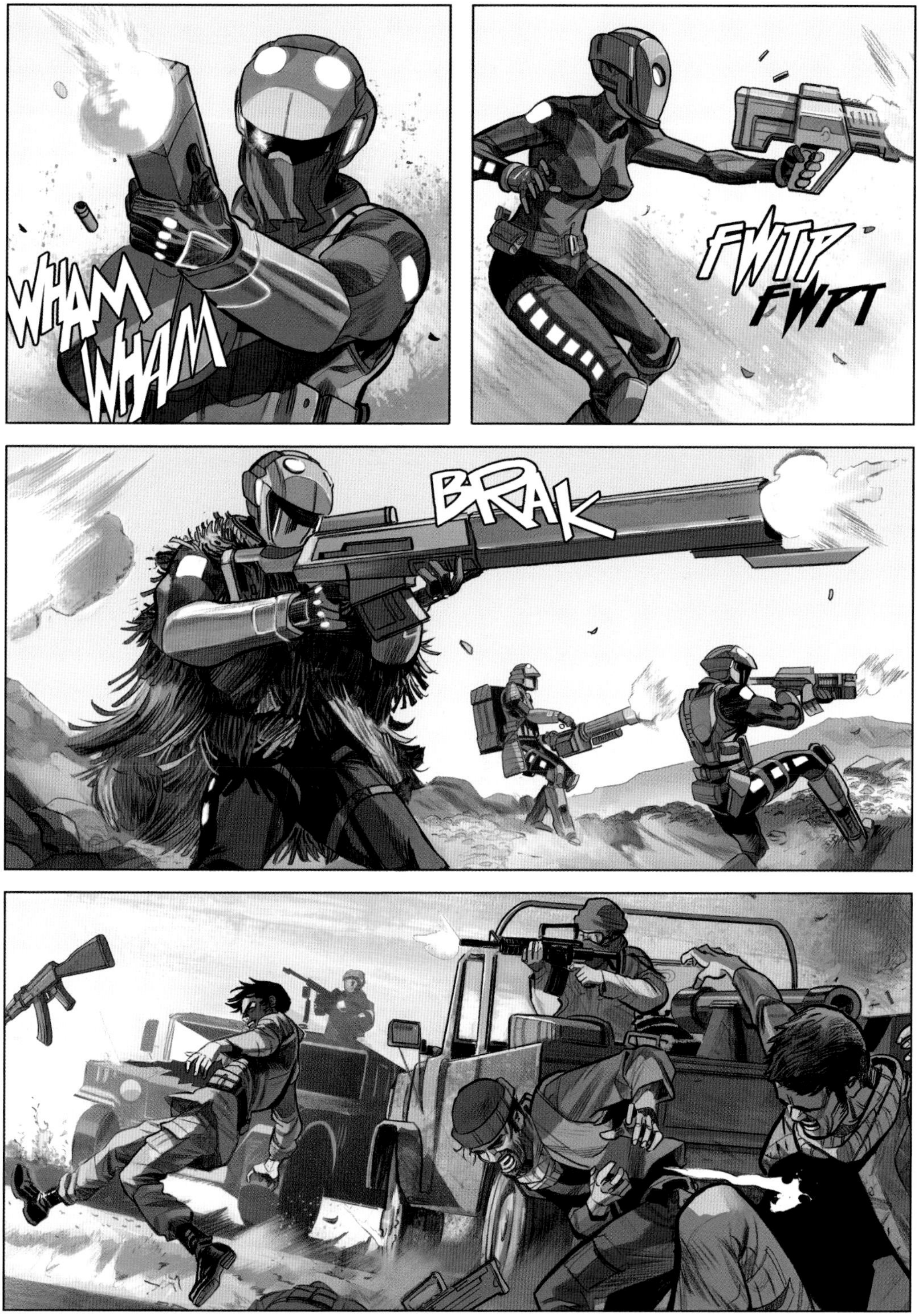
WHAM
WHAM
FWTP
FWPT
BRAK

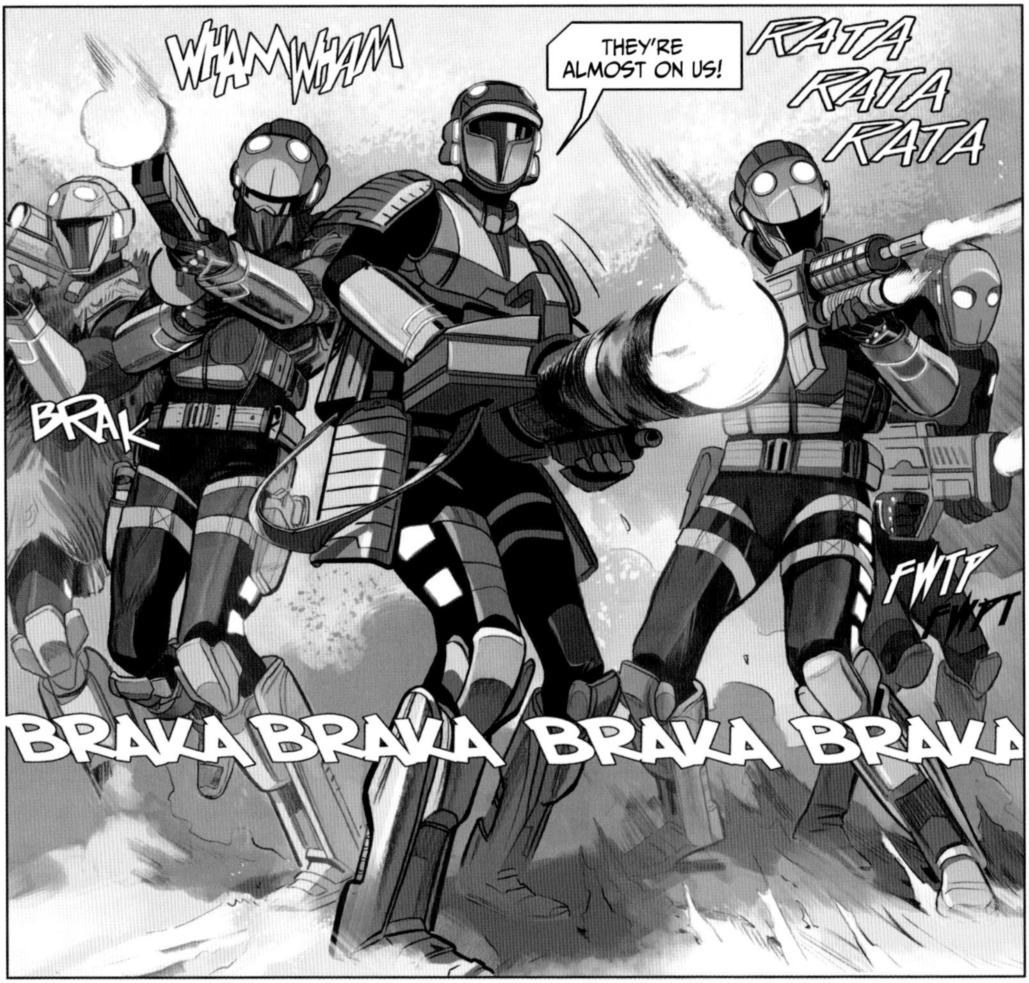
WHAMWHAM
THEY'RE ALMOST ON US!
RATA RATA RATA
BRAK
FWTP
BRAKA BRAKA BRAKA BRAKA

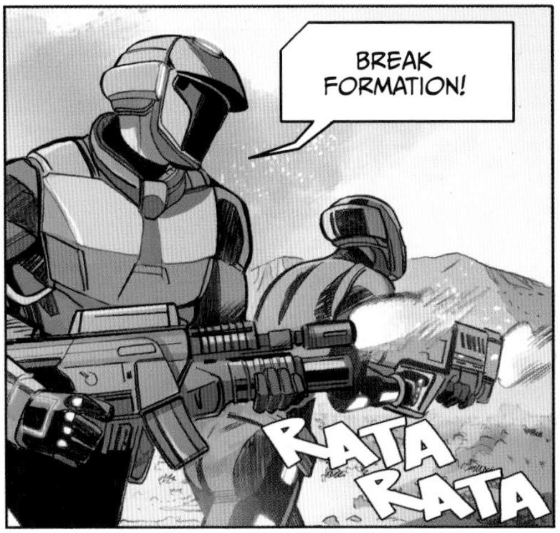
BREAK FORMATION!
RATA RATA

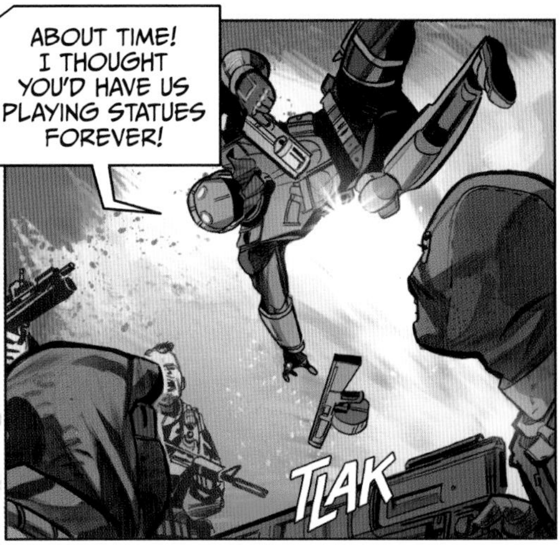
ABOUT TIME! I THOUGHT YOU'D HAVE US PLAYING STATUES FOREVER!
TLAK

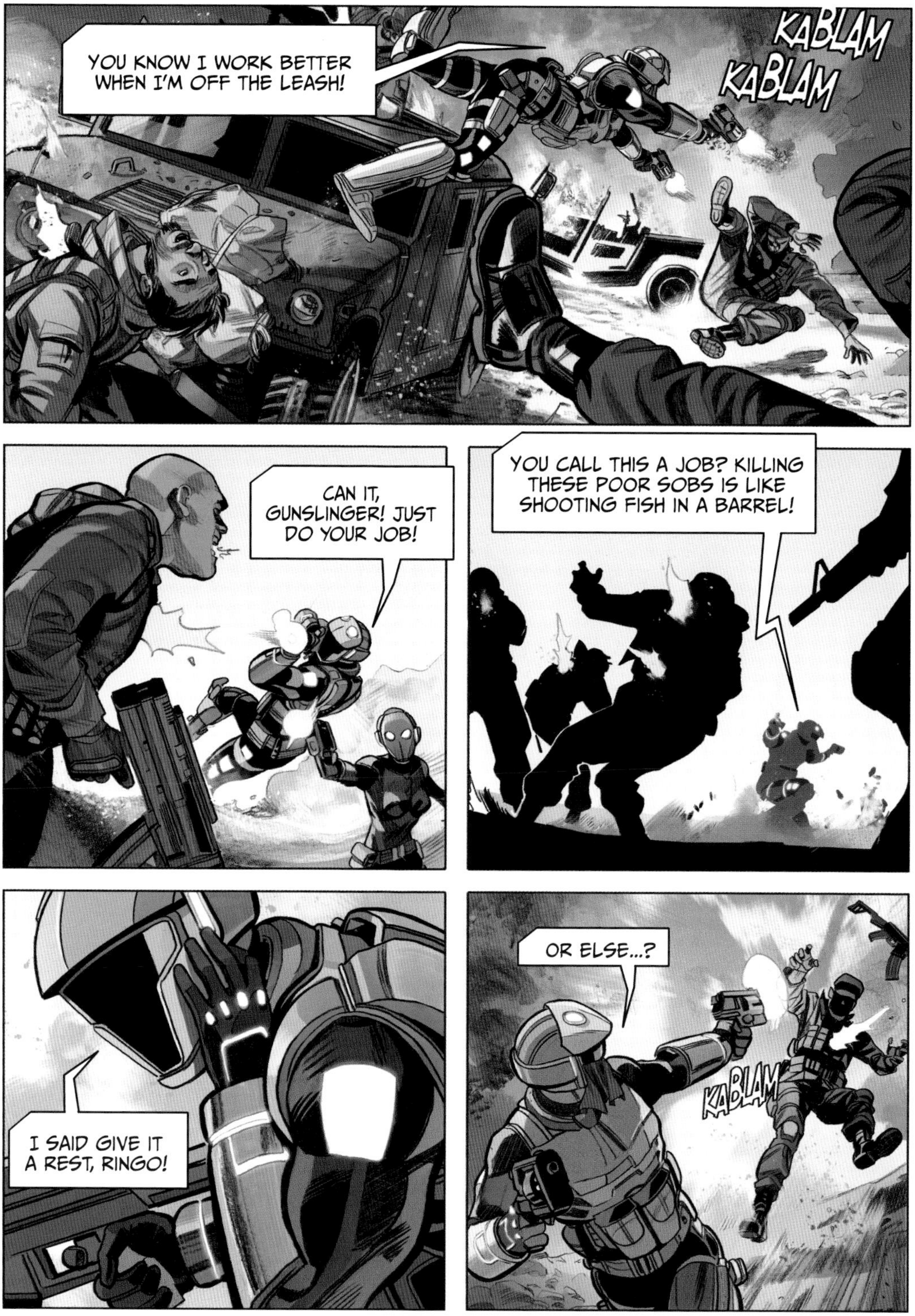
YOU KNOW I WORK BETTER WHEN I'M OFF THE LEASH!
KABLAM
KABLAM
CAN IT, GUNSLINGER! JUST DO YOUR JOB!
YOU CALL THIS A JOB? KILLING THESE POOR SOBS IS LIKE SHOOTING FISH IN A BARREL!
I SAID GIVE IT A REST, RINGO!
OR ELSE...?
KABLAM

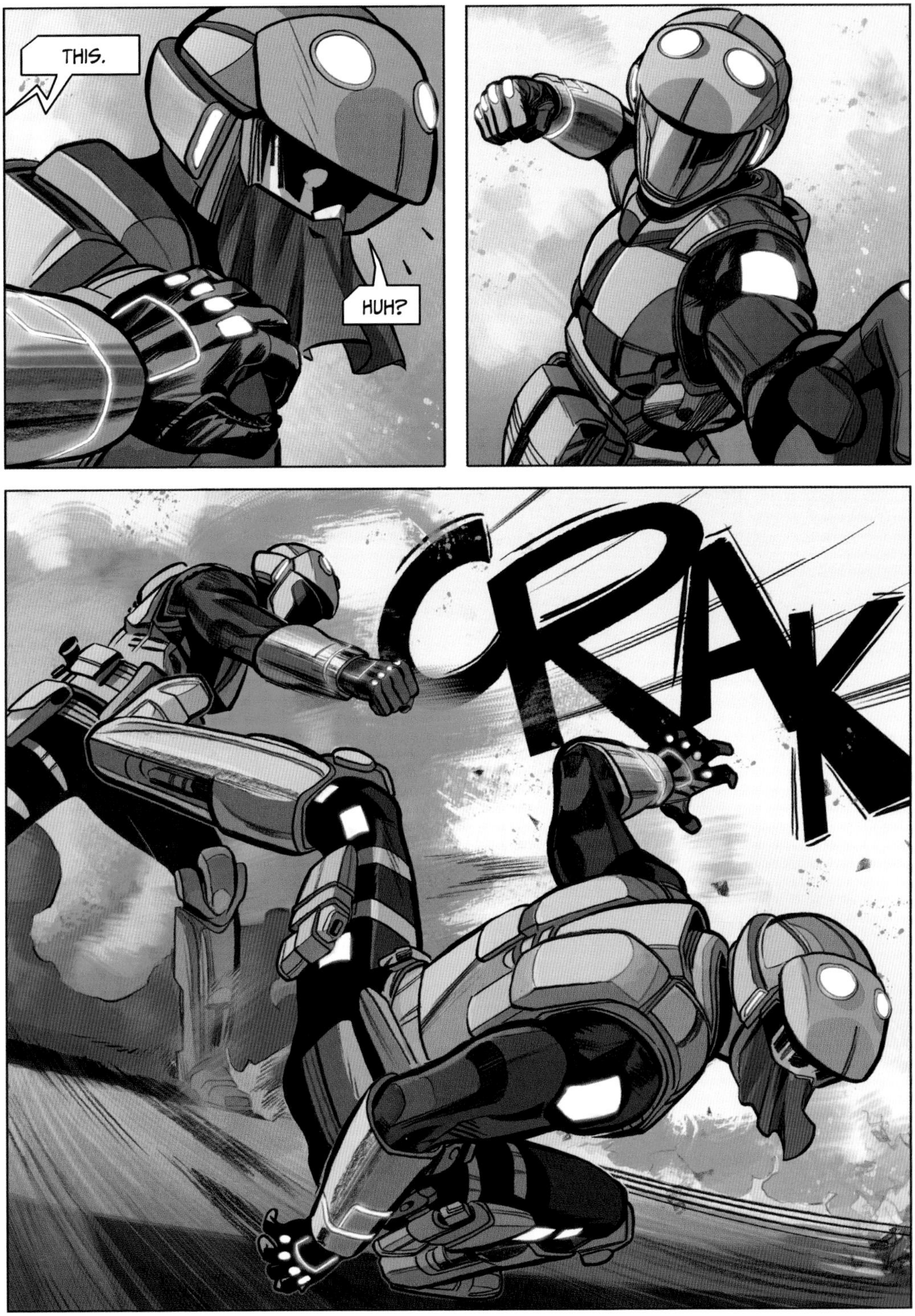
THIS.
HUH?
CRAK

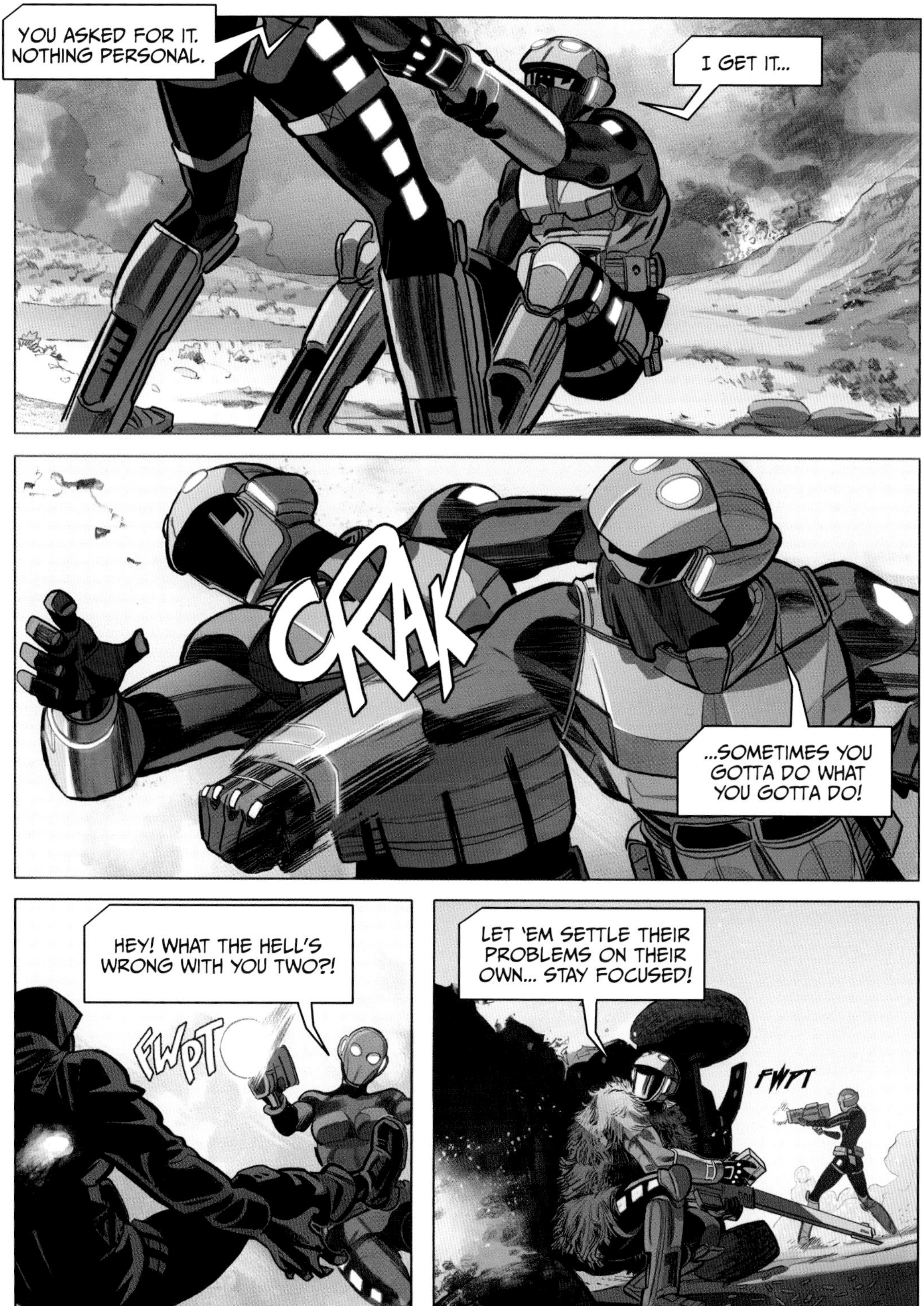
YOU ASKED FOR IT. NOTHING PERSONAL.
I GET IT...
CRAK
...SOMETIMES YOU GOTTA DO WHAT YOU GOTTA DO!
HEY! WHAT THE HELL'S WRONG WITH YOU TWO?!
FWPT
LET 'EM SETTLE THEIR PROBLEMS ON THEIR OWN... STAY FOCUSED!
FWPT

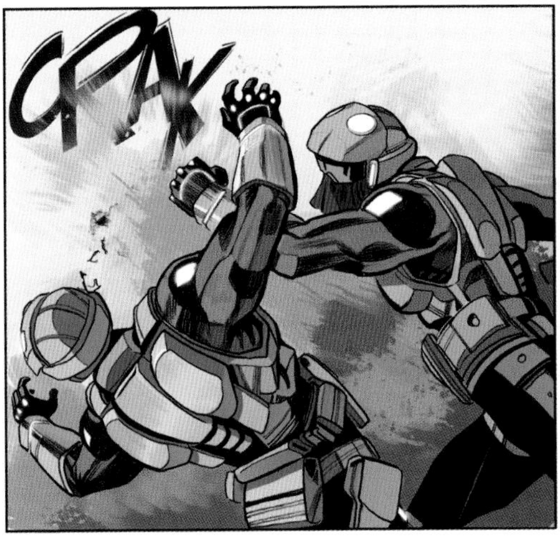
CRAK

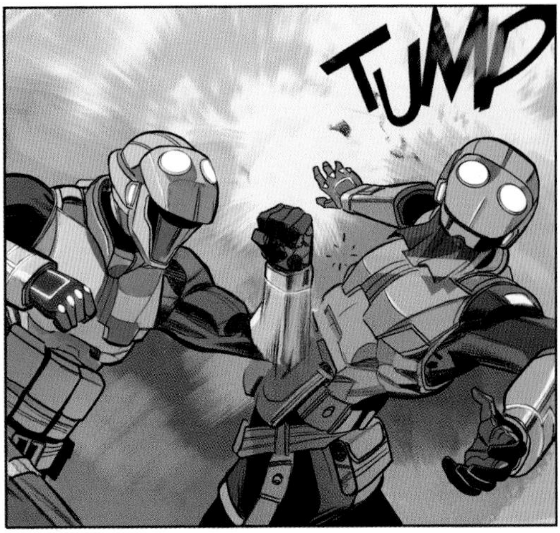
TUMP

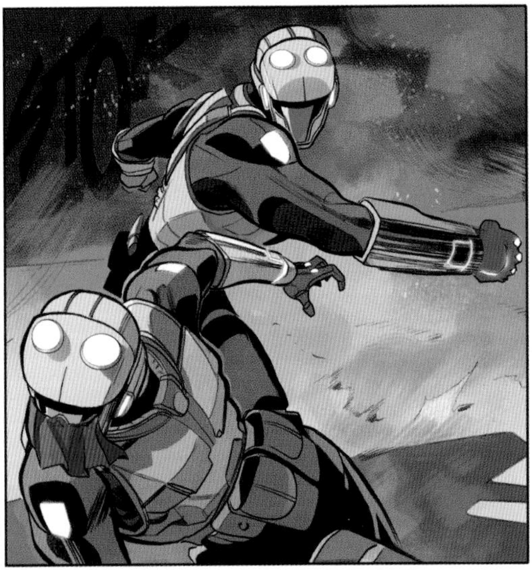

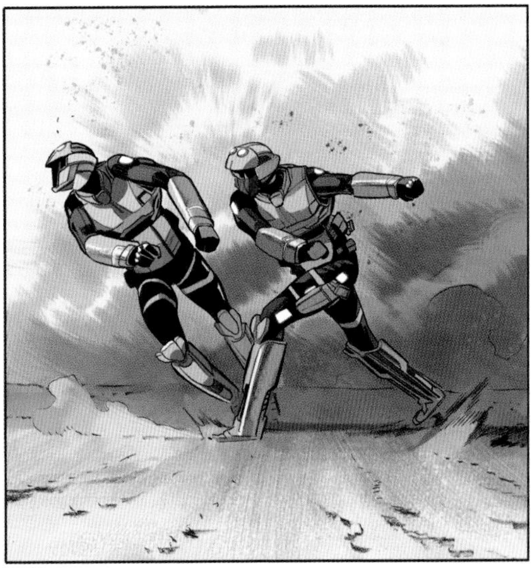

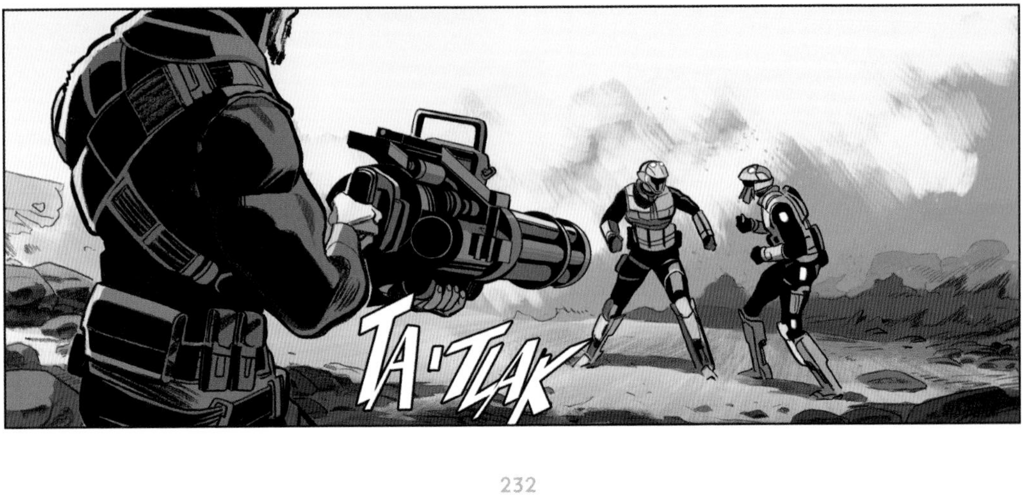
TA·TLAK

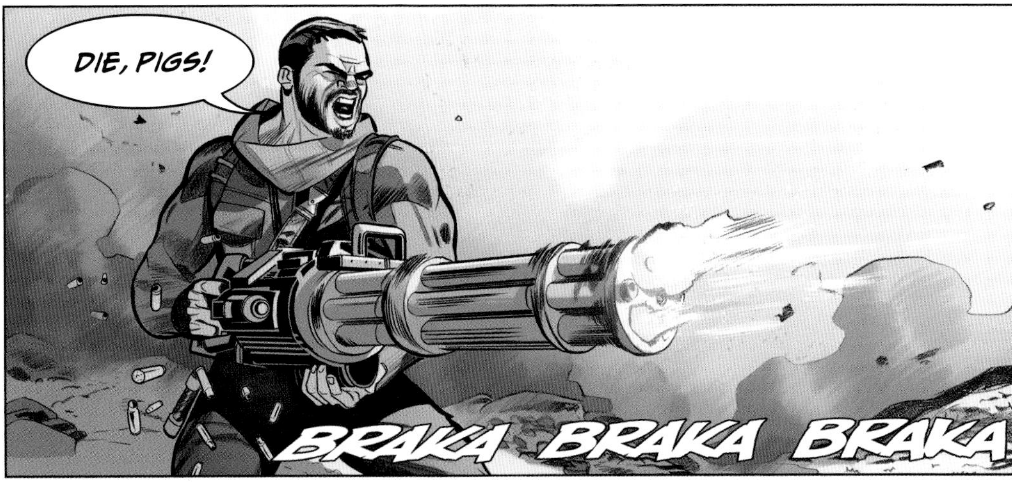
DIE, PIGS!
BRAKA BRAKA BRAKA

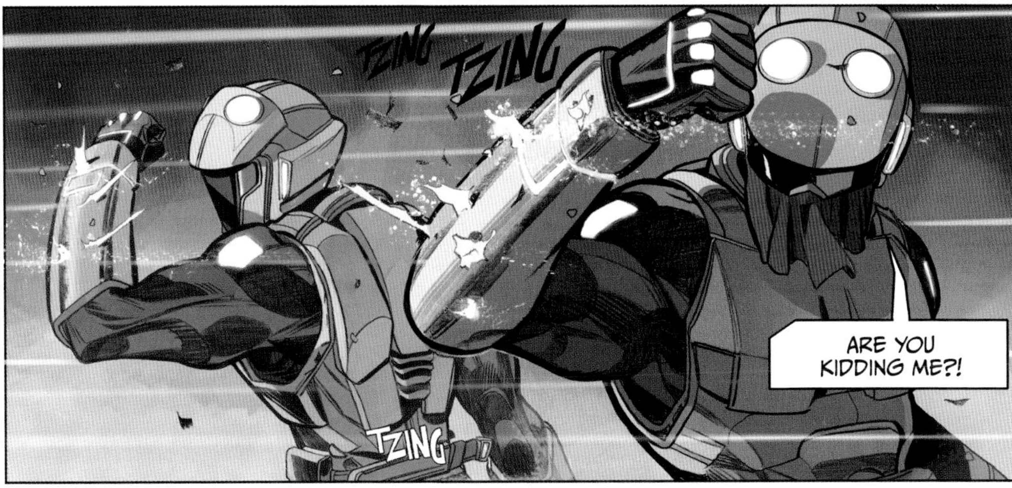
TZING
TZING
ARE YOU KIDDING ME?!
TZING

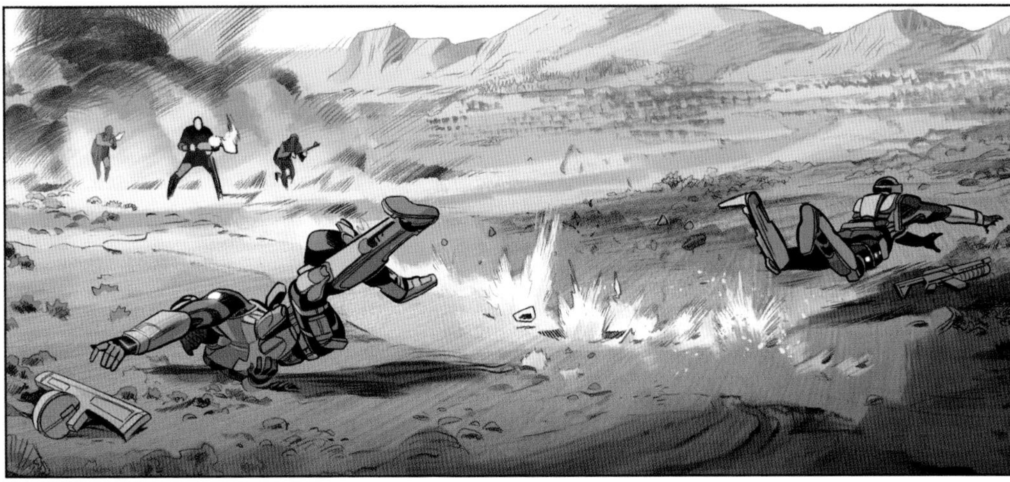

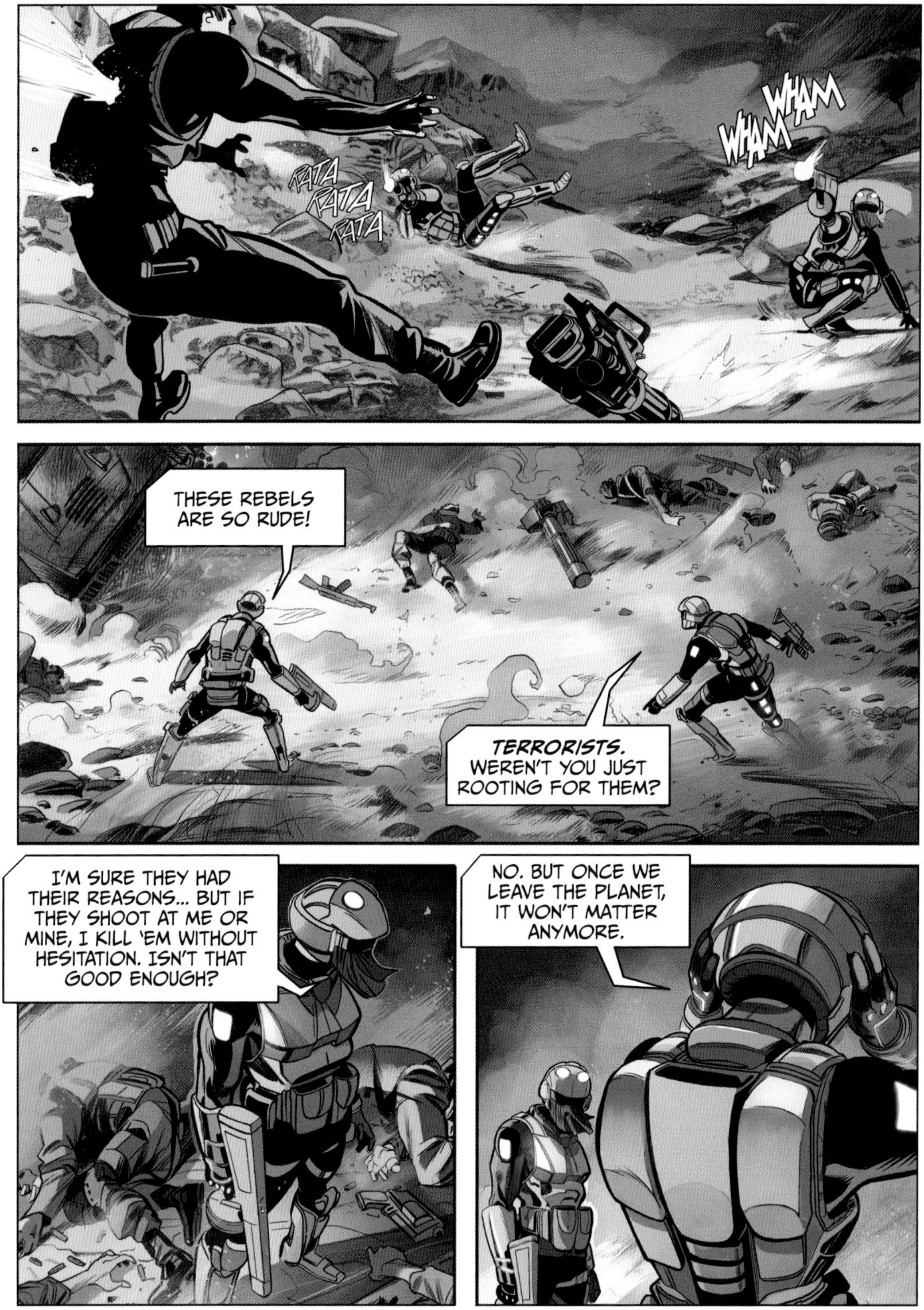
RATA RATA RATA
WHAM WHAM
THESE REBELS ARE SO RUDE!
TERRORISTS. WEREN'T YOU JUST ROOTING FOR THEM?
I'M SURE THEY HAD THEIR REASONS... BUT IF THEY SHOOT AT ME OR MINE, I KILL 'EM WITHOUT HESITATION. ISN'T THAT GOOD ENOUGH?
NO. BUT ONCE WE LEAVE THE PLANET, IT WON'T MATTER ANYMORE.

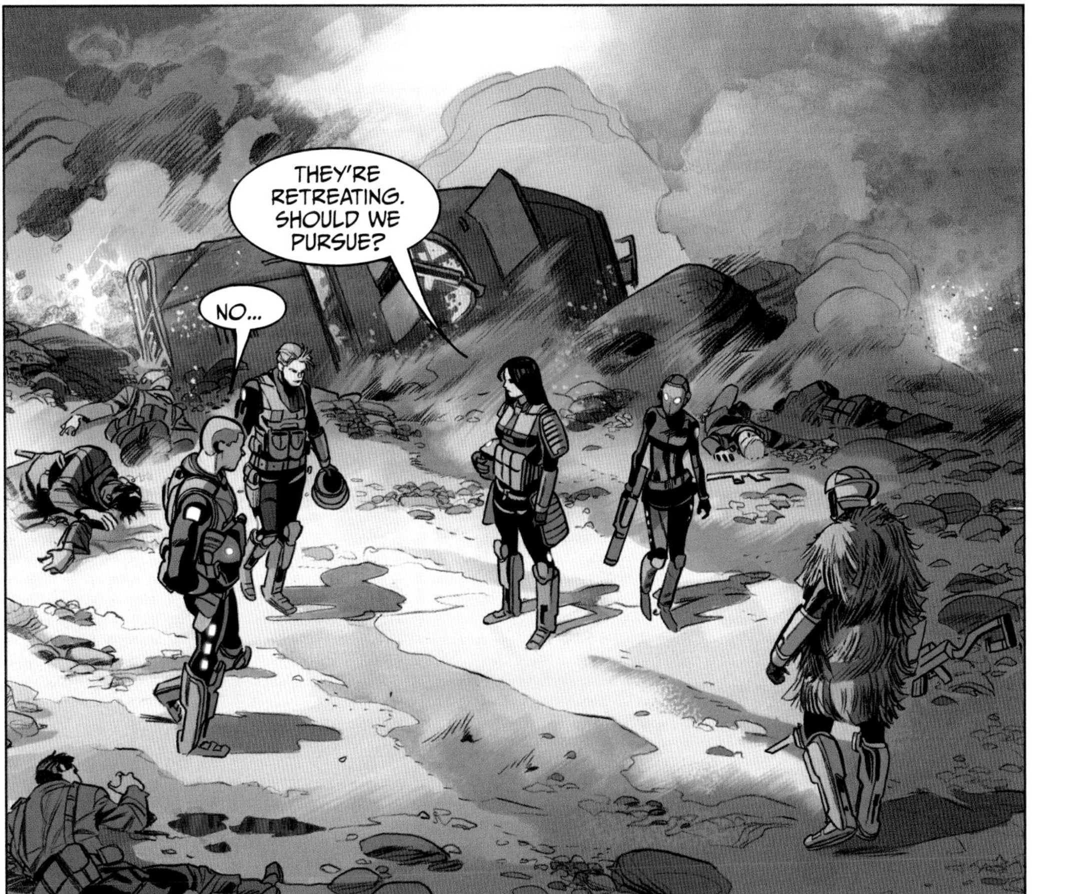
THEY'RE RETREATING. SHOULD WE PURSUE?
NO...

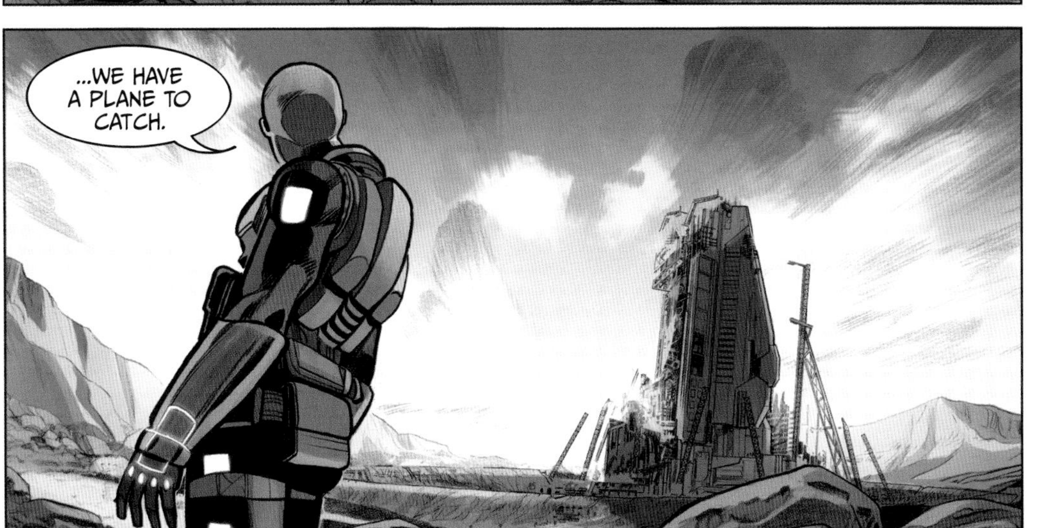
...WE HAVE A PLANE TO CATCH.

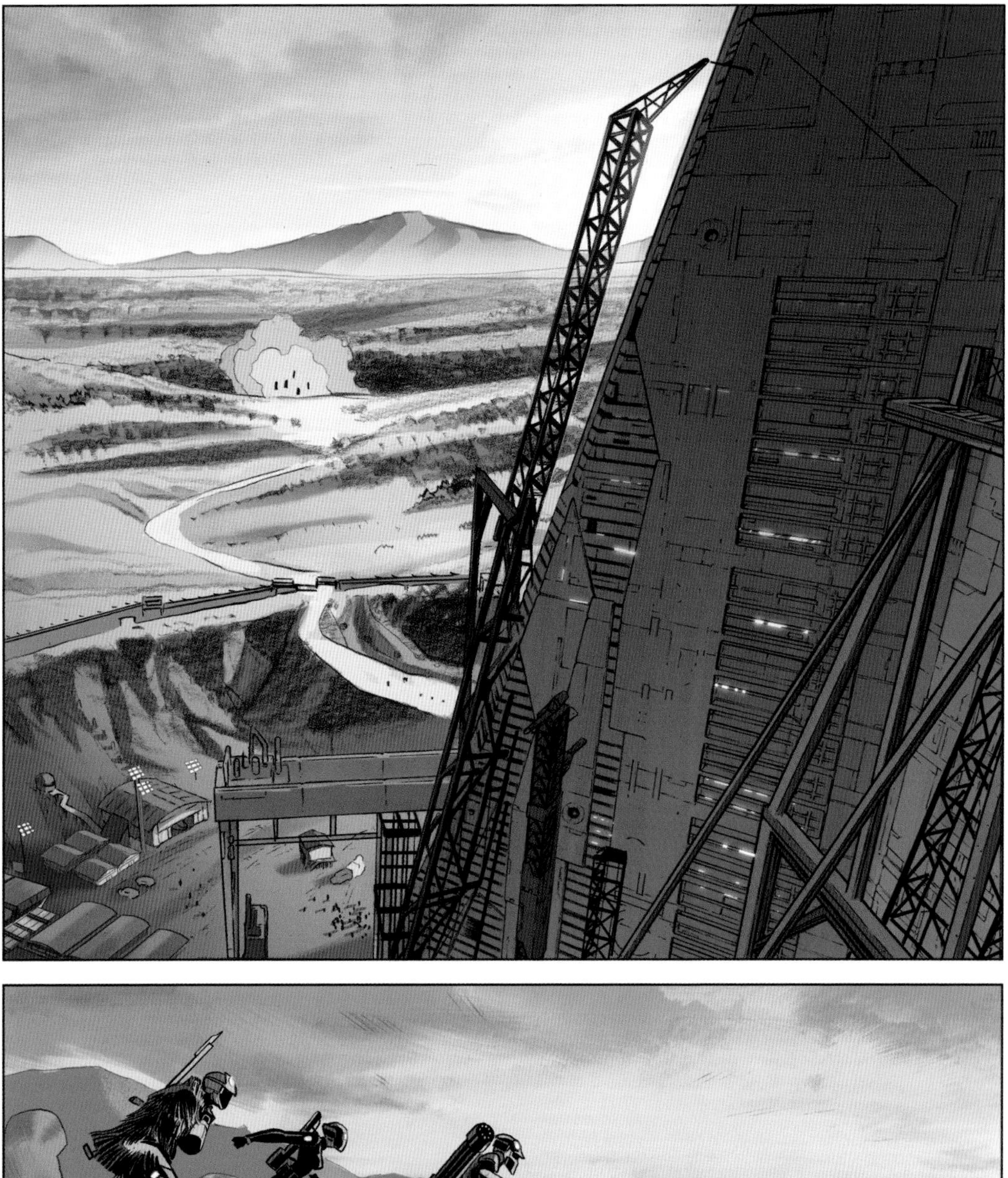

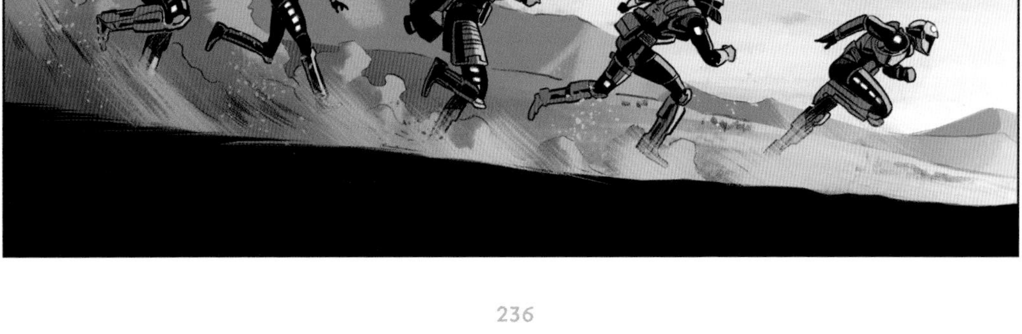

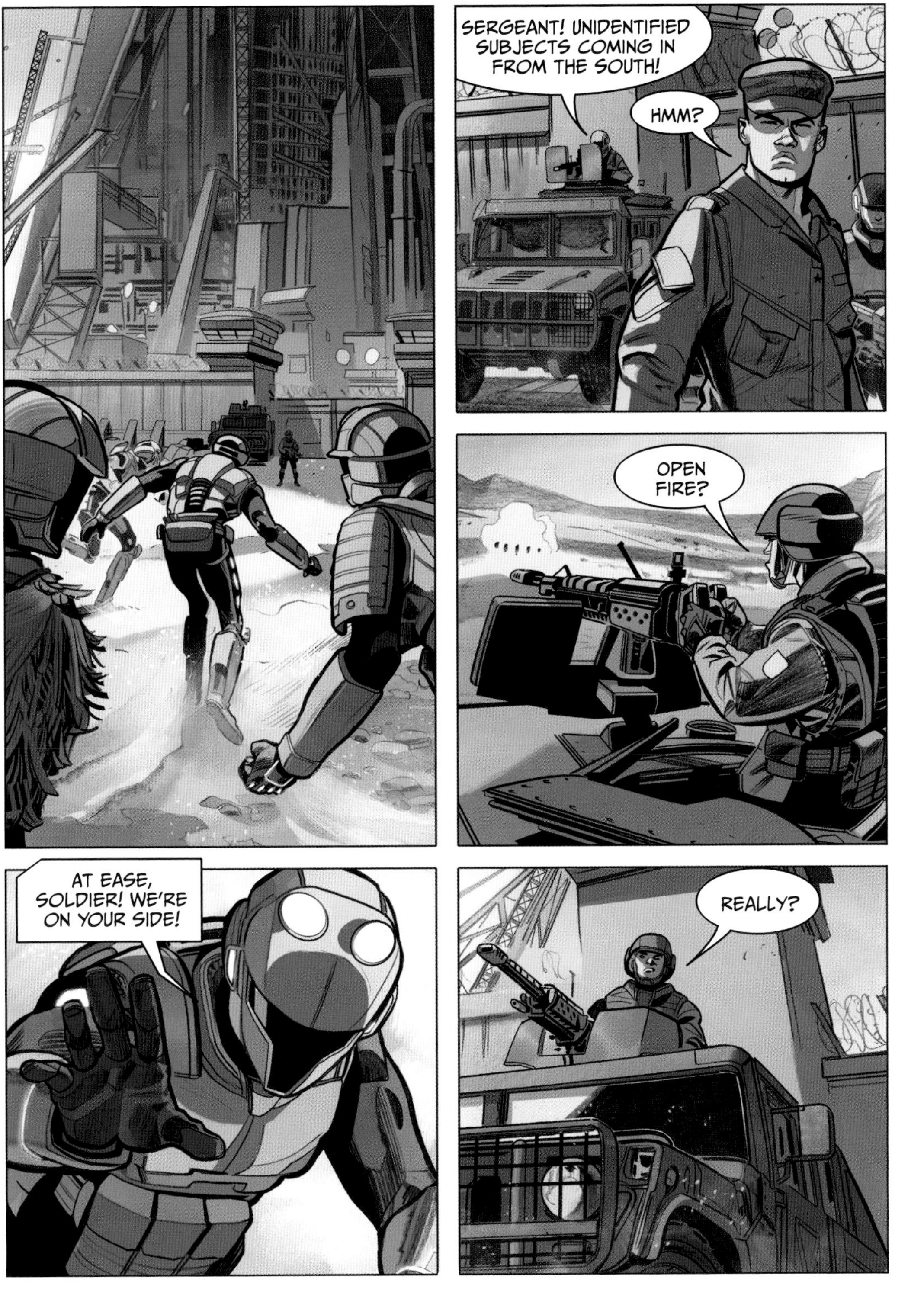
SERGEANT! UNIDENTIFIED SUBJECTS COMING IN FROM THE SOUTH!
HMM?
OPEN FIRE?
AT EASE, SOLDIER! WE'RE ON YOUR SIDE!
REALLY?

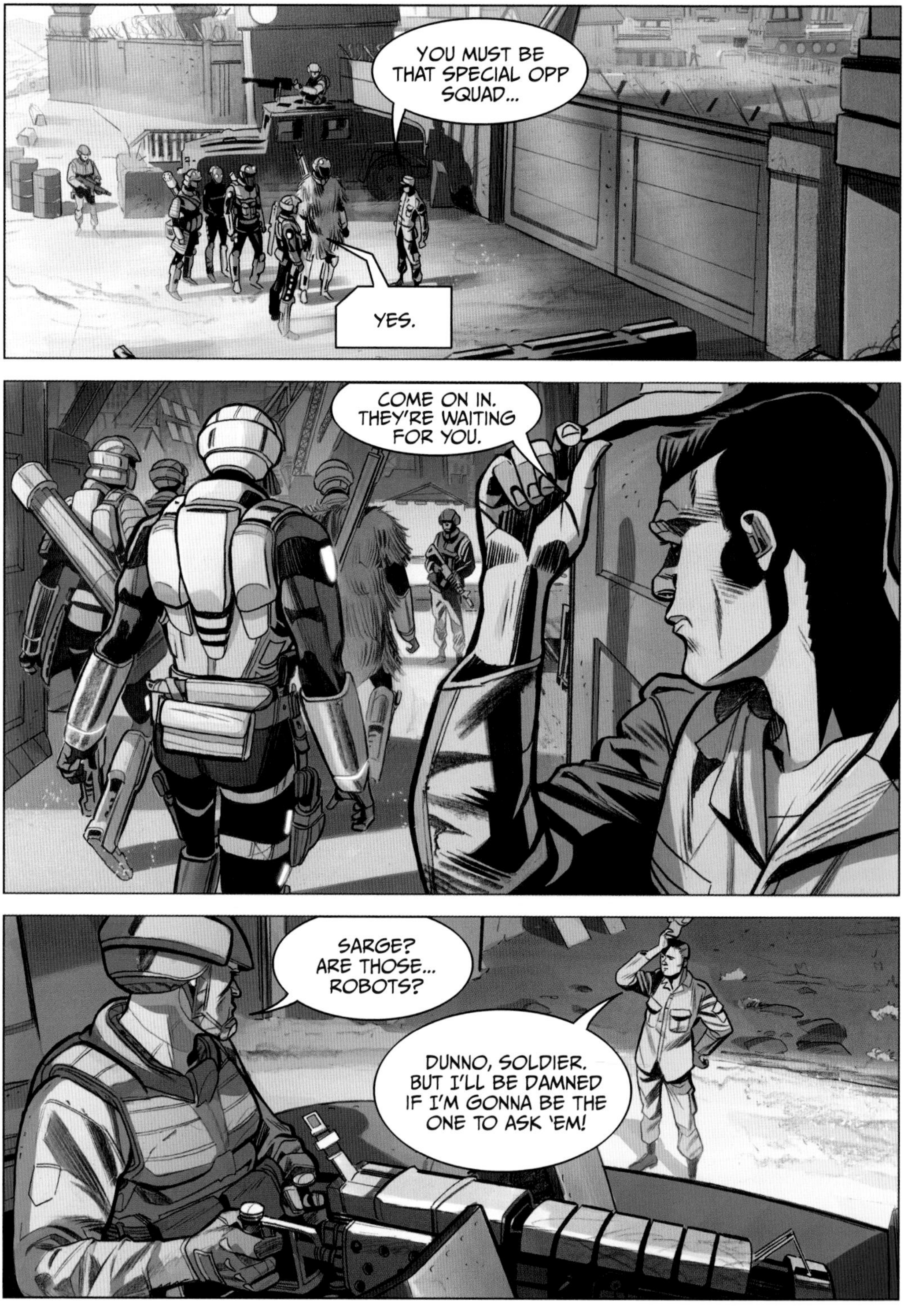
YOU MUST BE THAT SPECIAL OPP SQUAD...
YES.
COME ON IN. THEY'RE WAITING FOR YOU.
SARGE? ARE THOSE... ROBOTS?
DUNNO, SOLDIER. BUT I'LL BE DAMNED IF I'M GONNA BE THE ONE TO ASK 'EM!

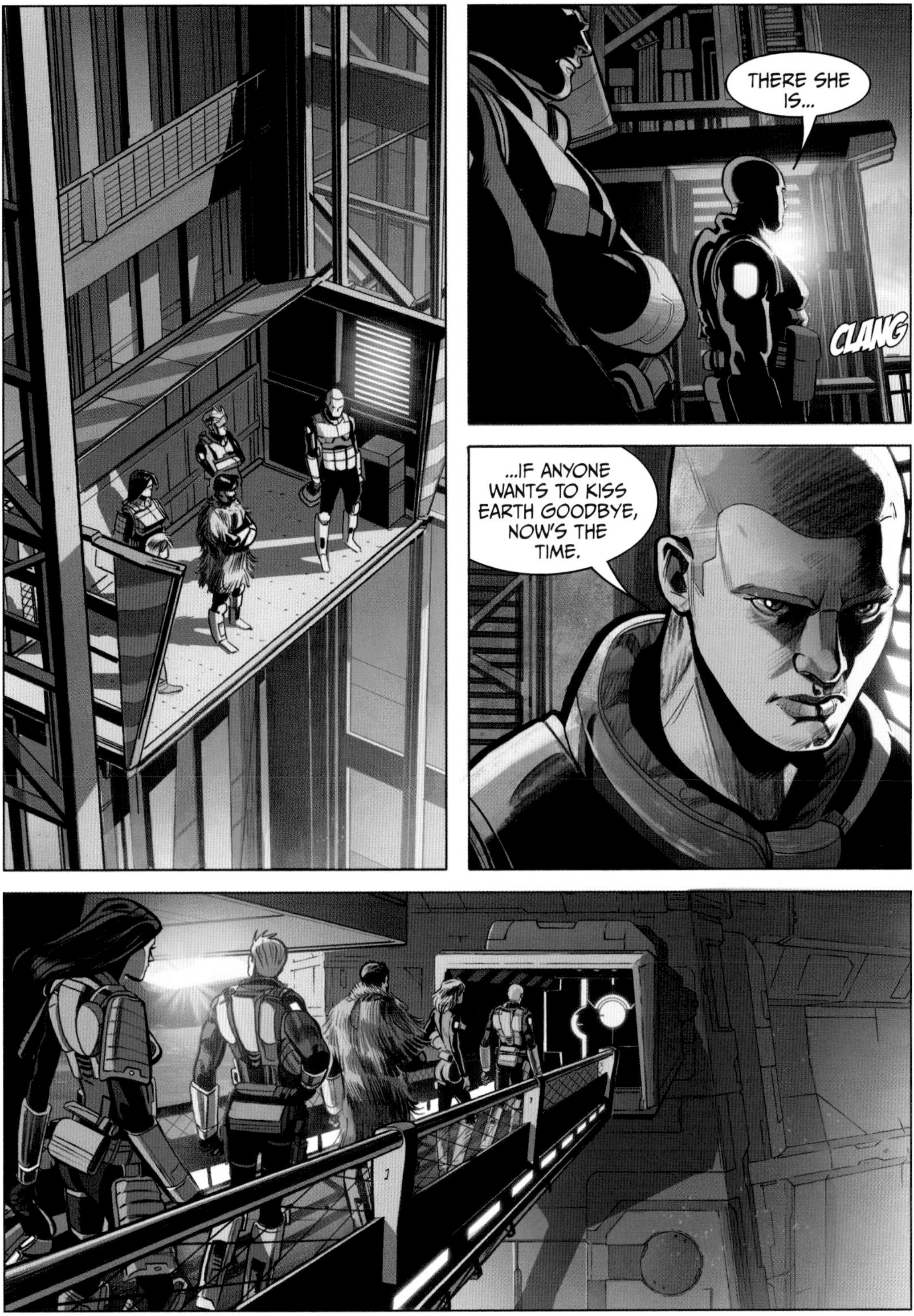
THERE SHE IS...
CLANG
...IF ANYONE WANTS TO KISS EARTH GOODBYE, NOW'S THE TIME.

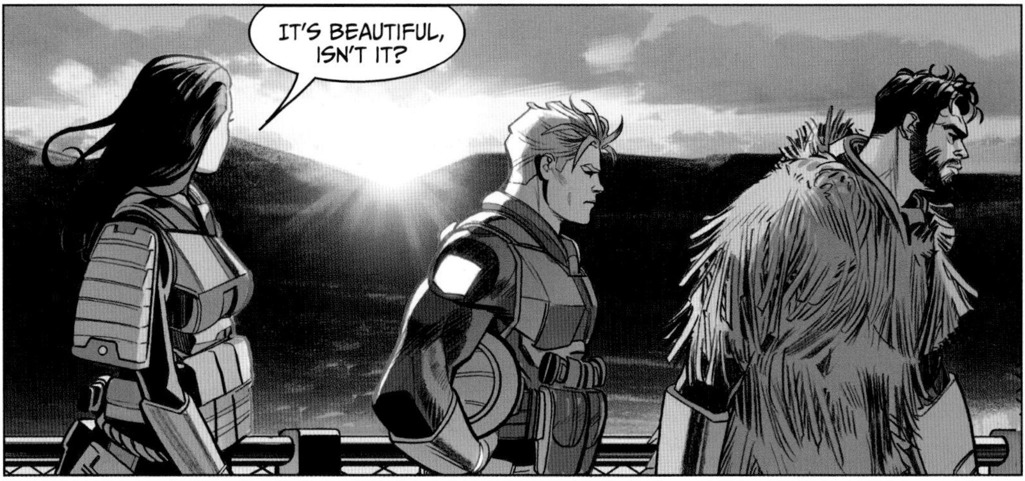
IT'S BEAUTIFUL, ISN'T IT?

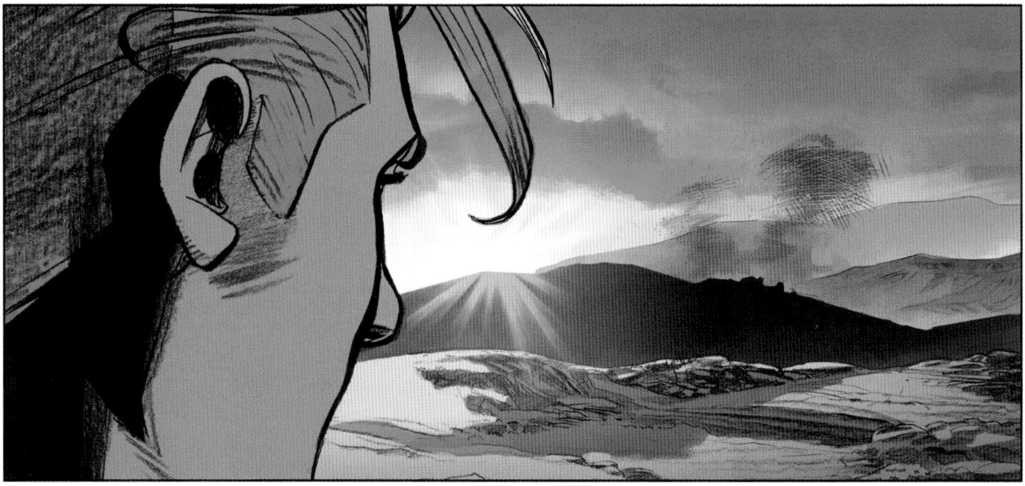

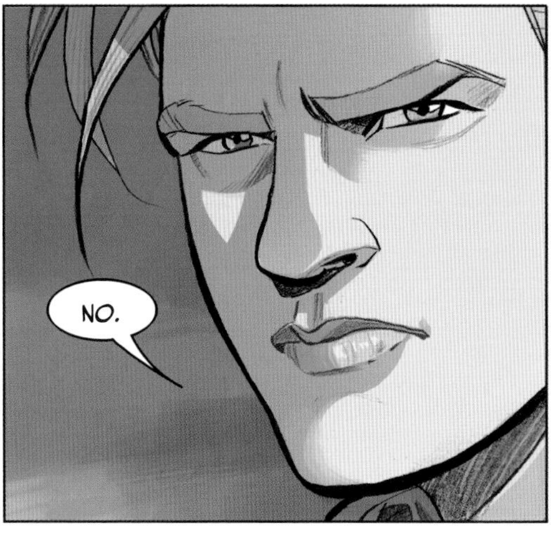
NO.

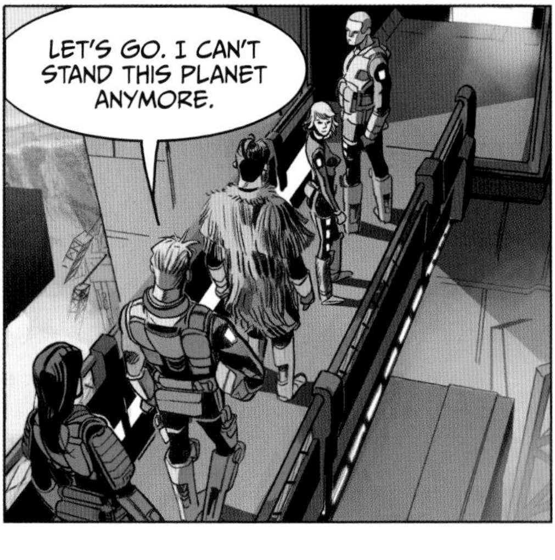
LET'S GO. I CAN'T STAND THIS PLANET ANYMORE.

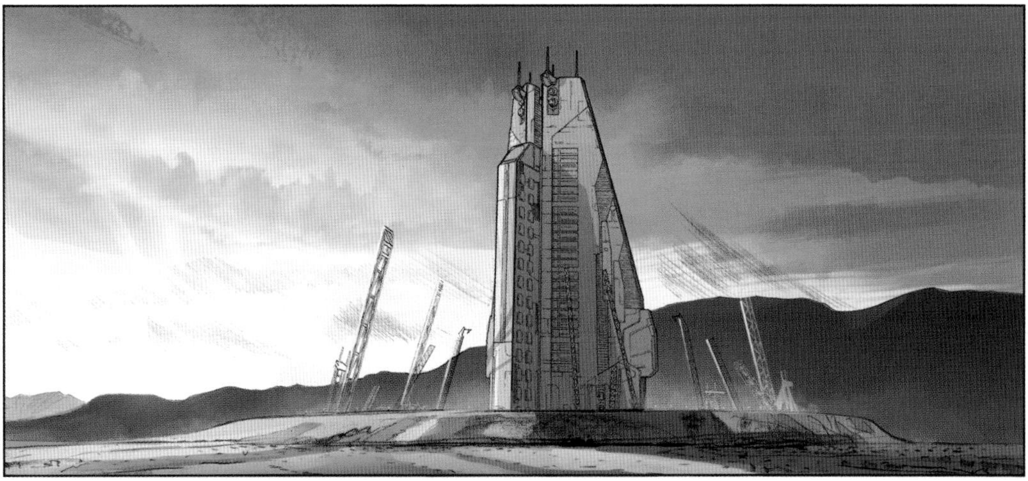

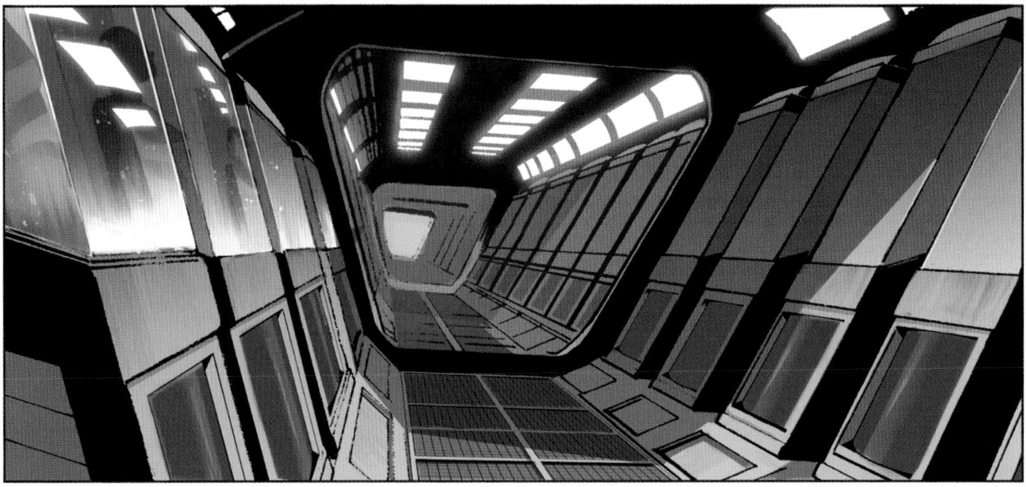

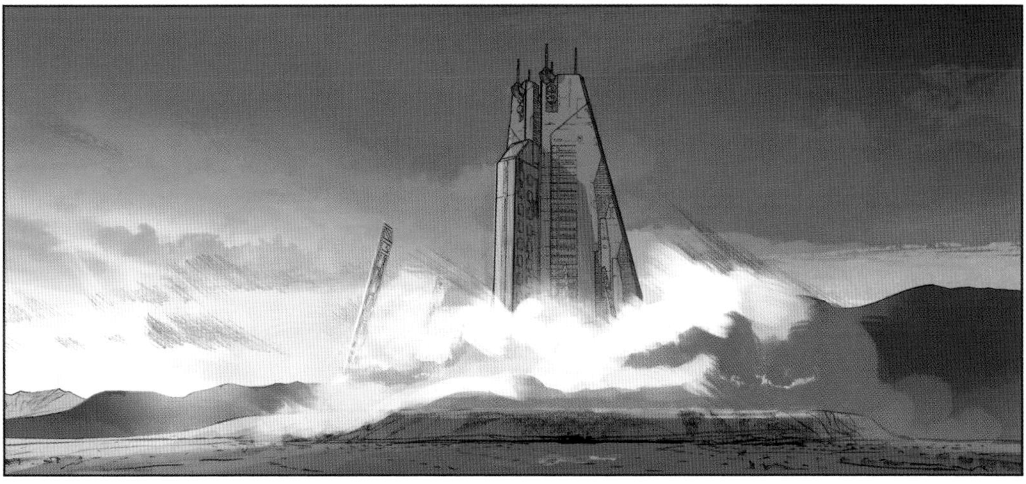

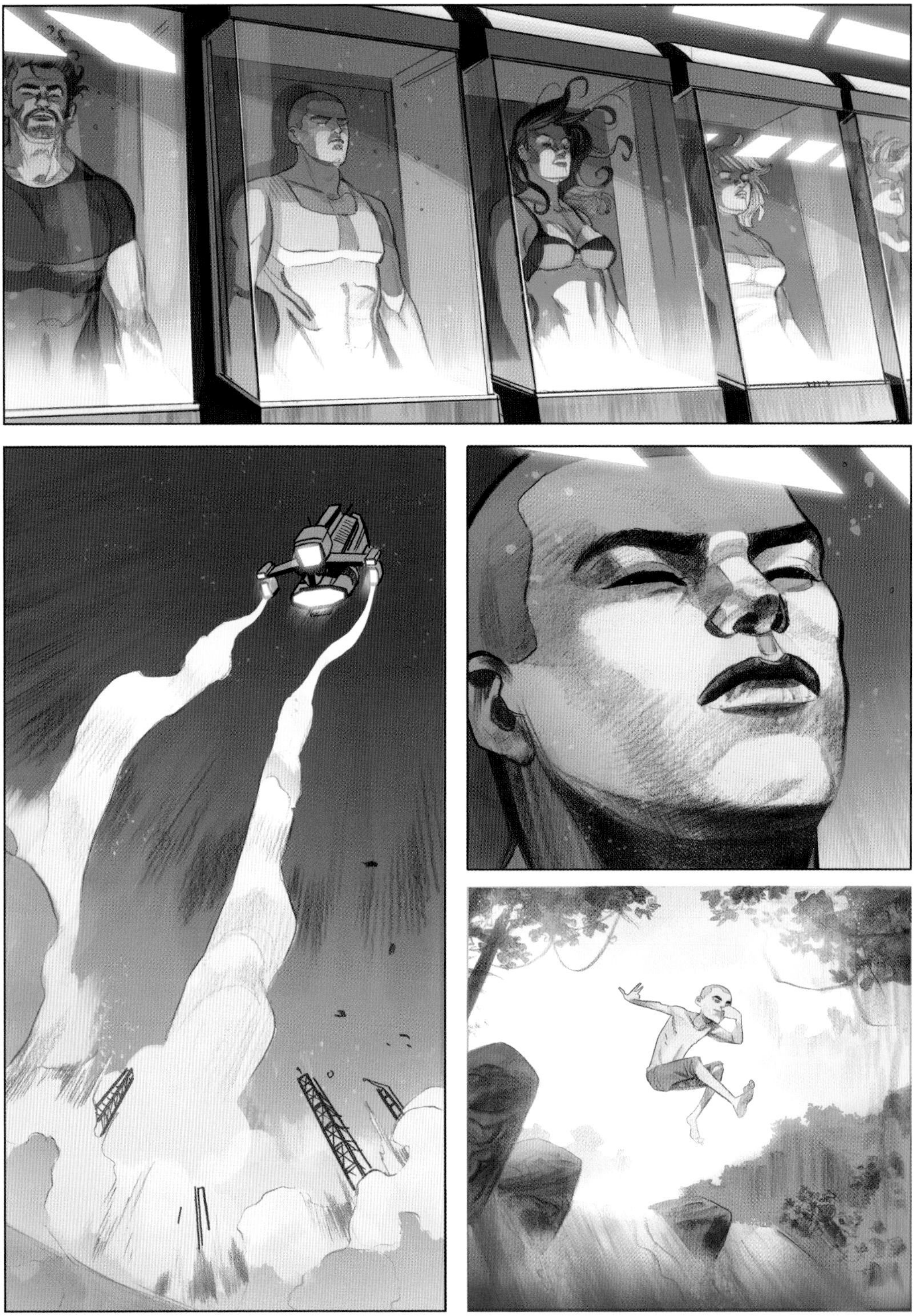

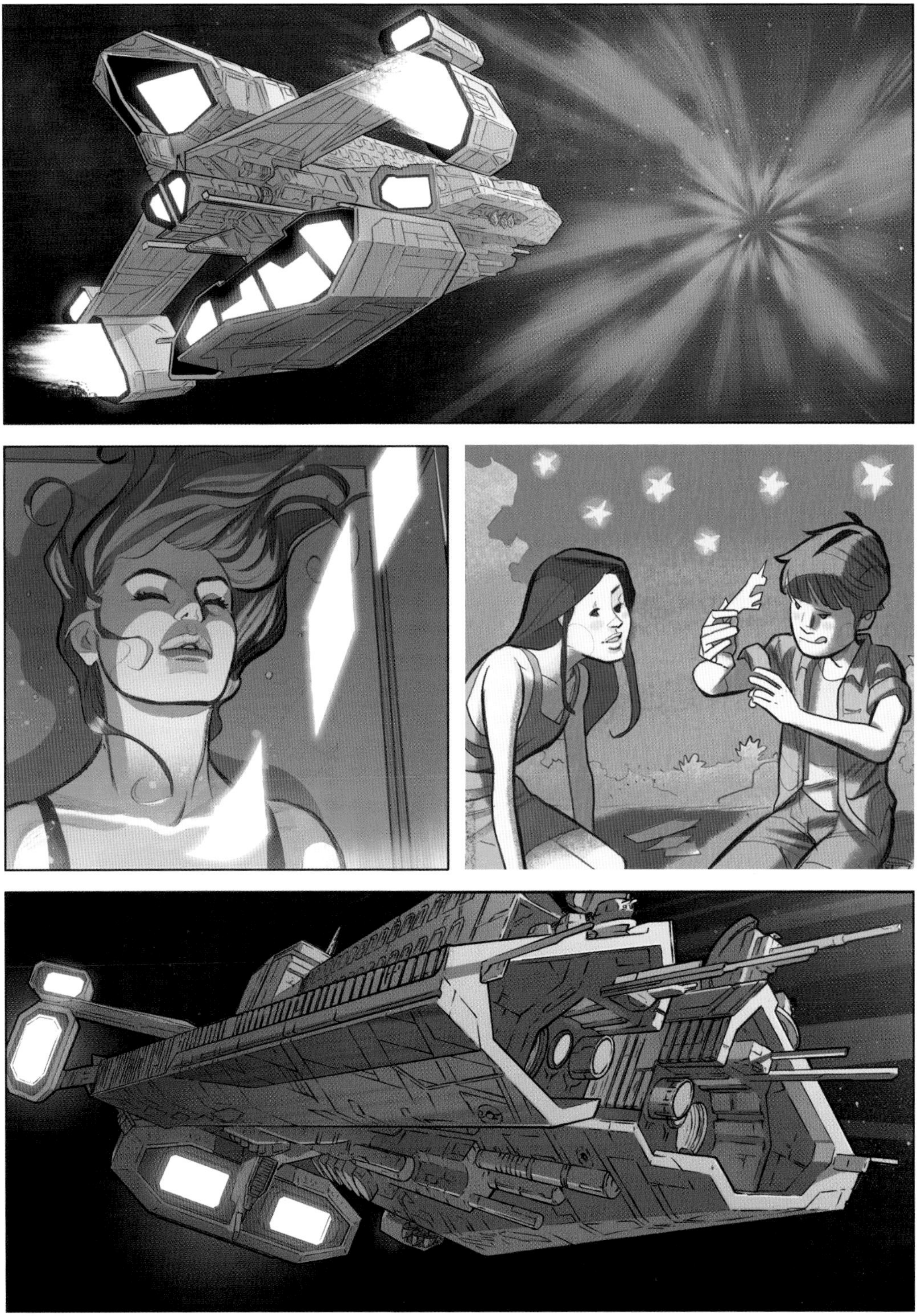

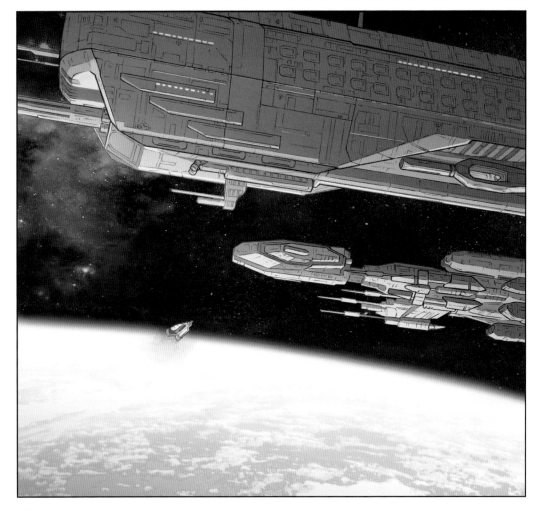

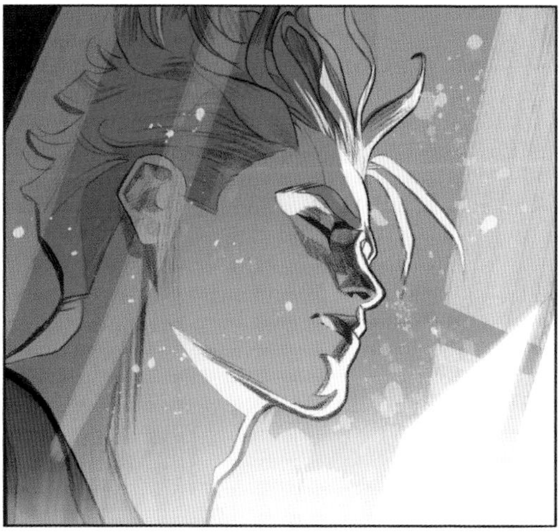

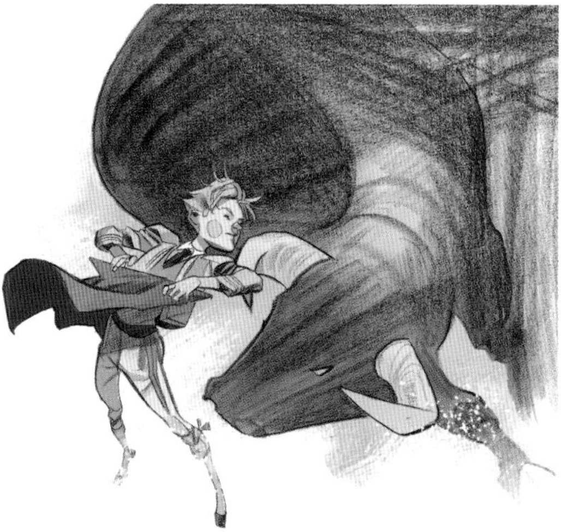

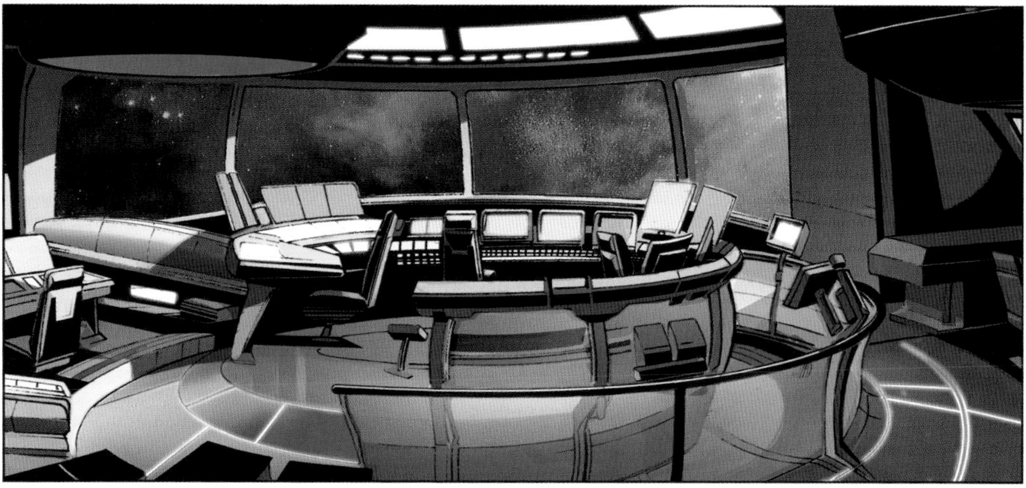

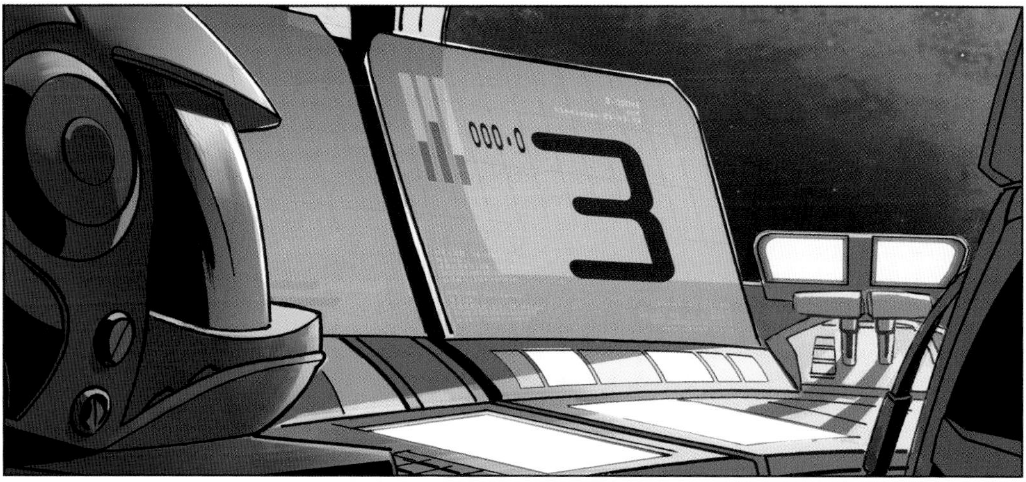
000.0
3

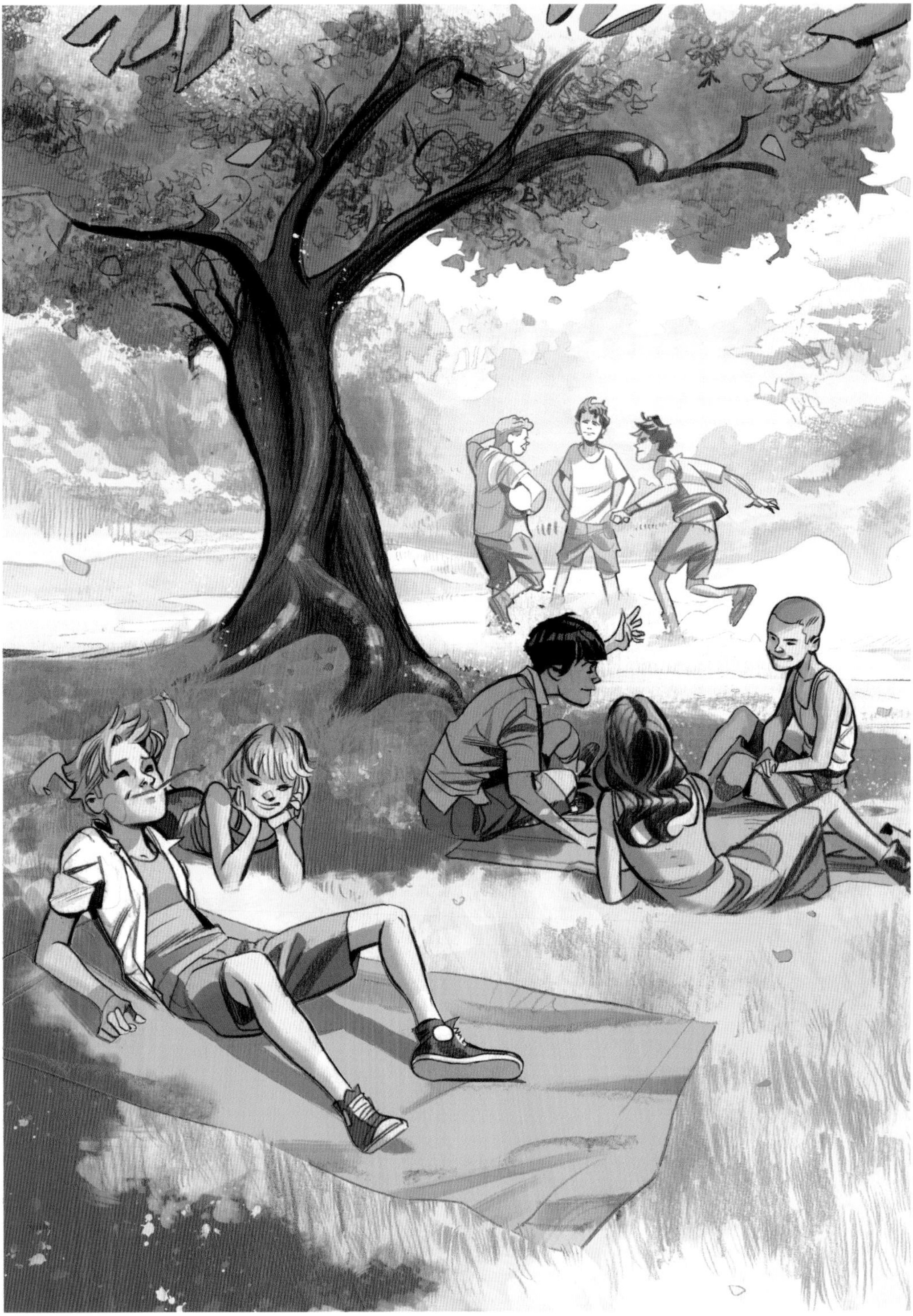

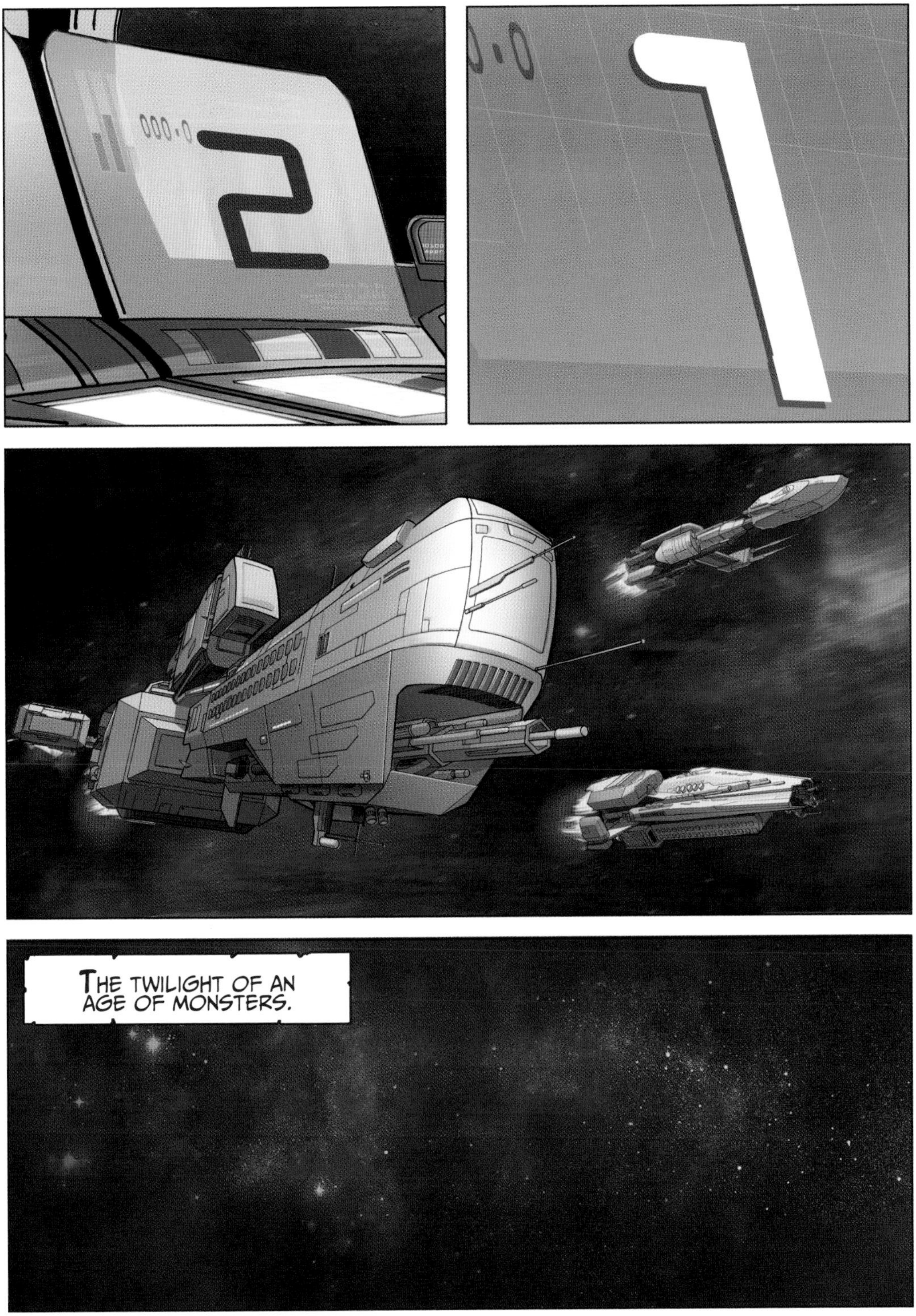
000.0
2
1
THE TWILIGHT OF AN
AGE OF MONSTERS.

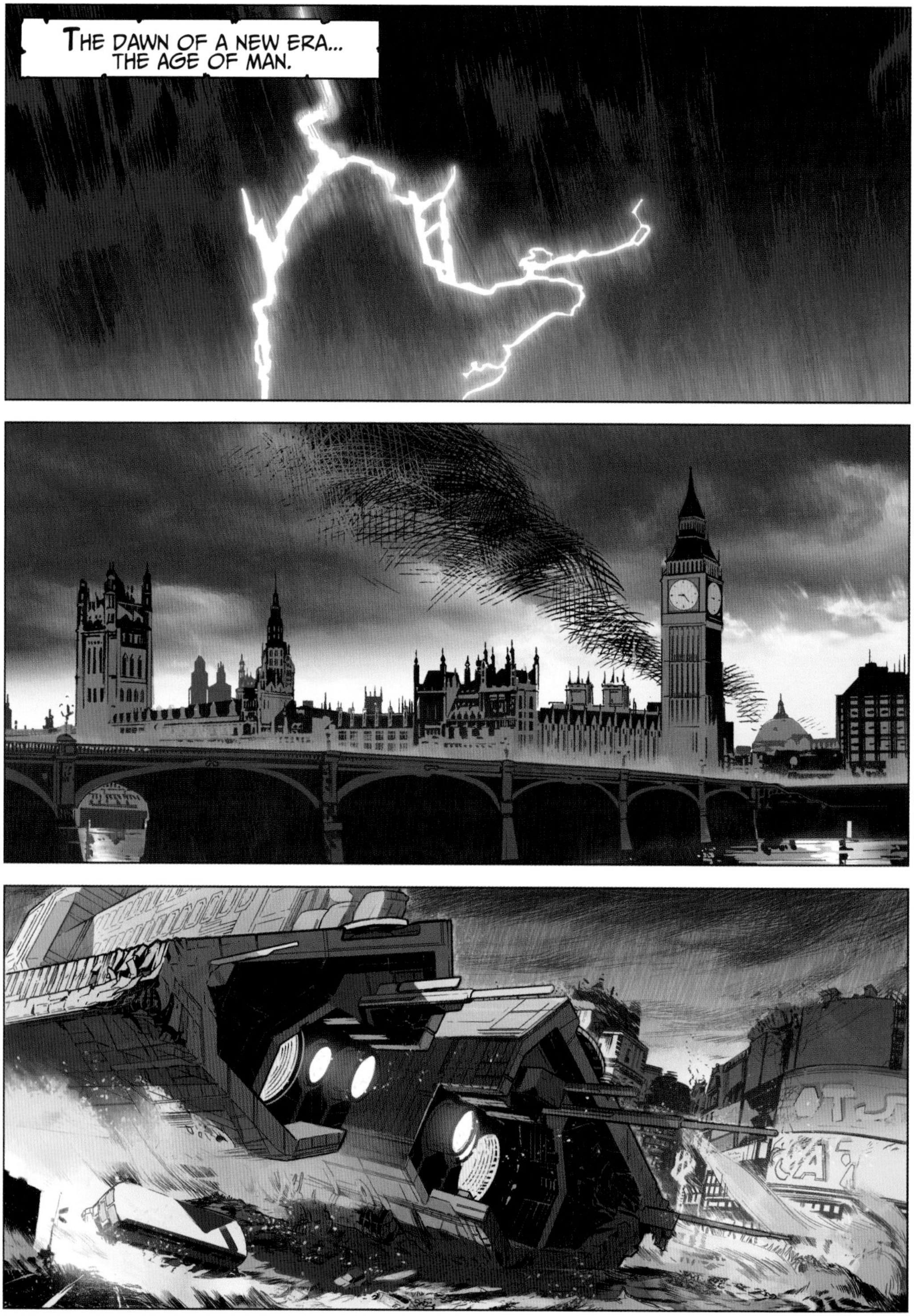
THE DAWN OF A NEW ERA... THE AGE OF MAN.

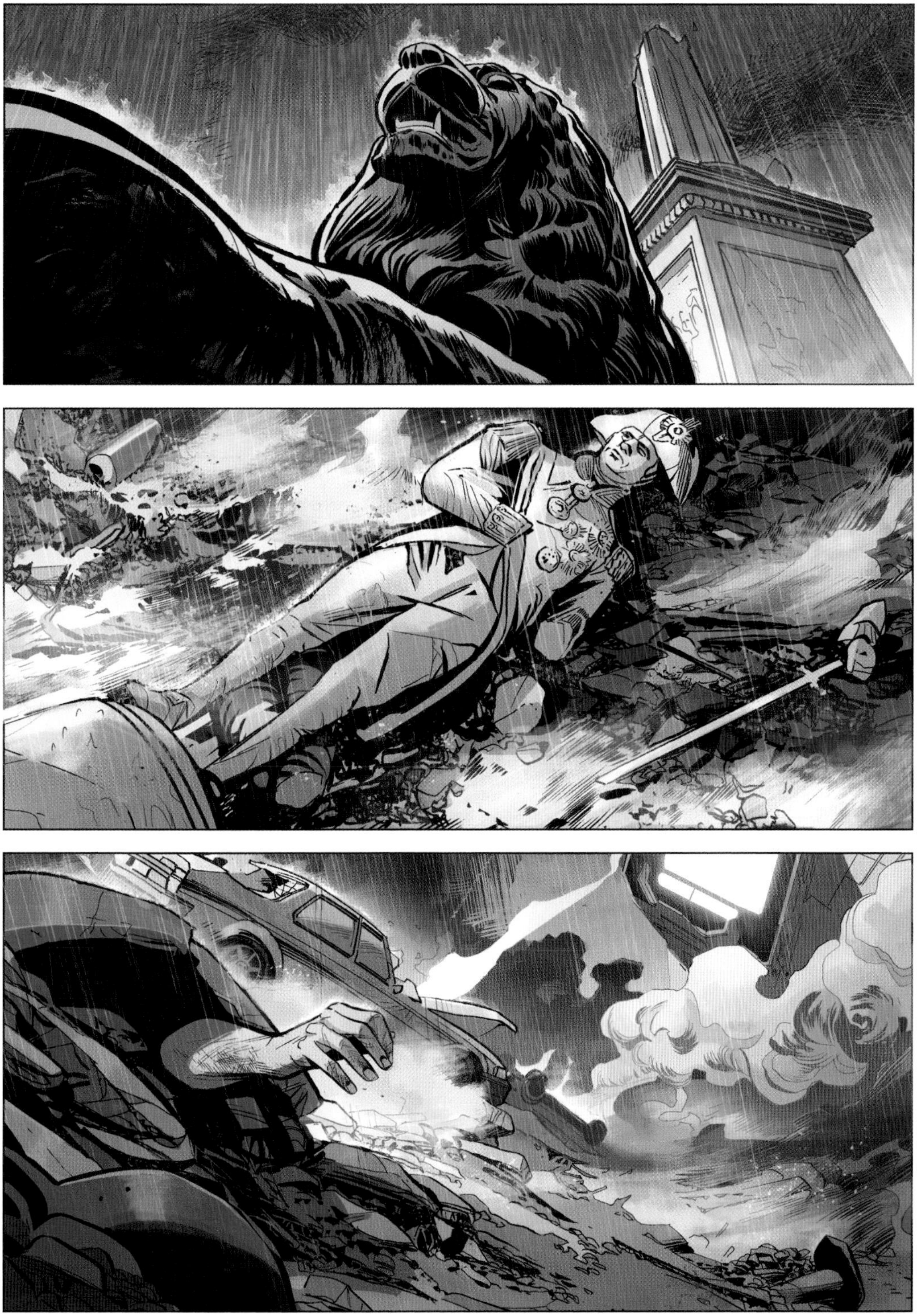

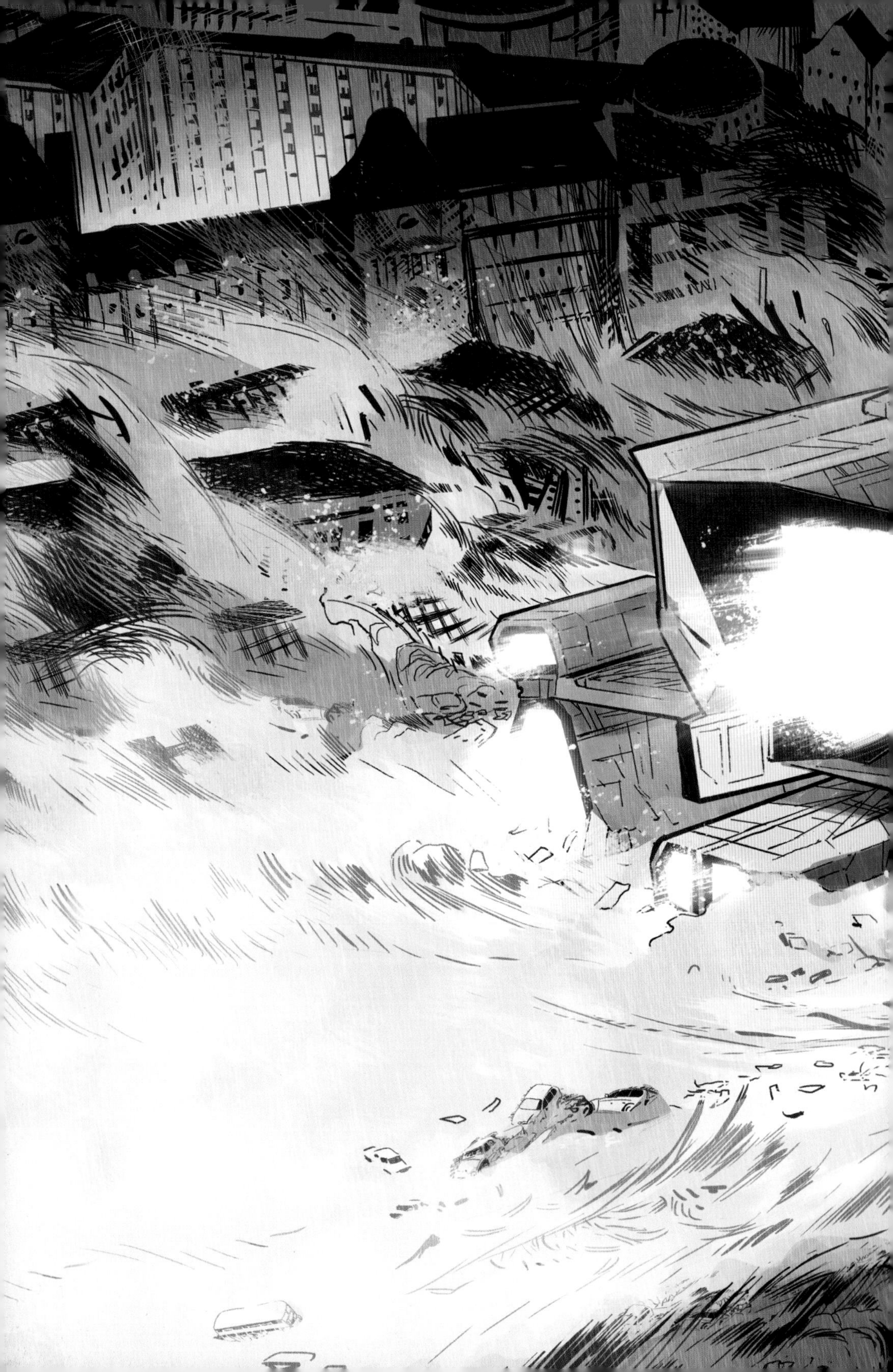

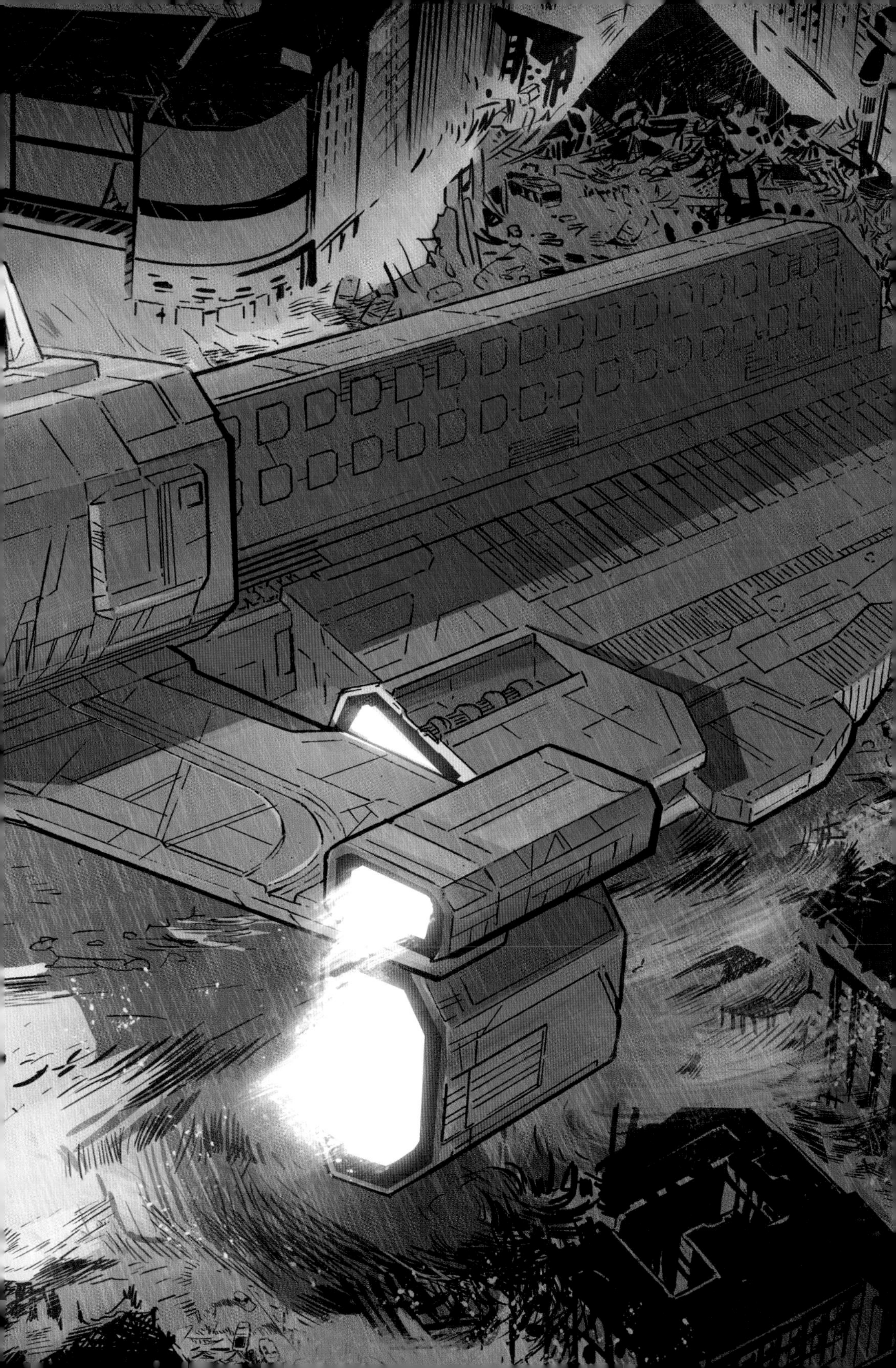

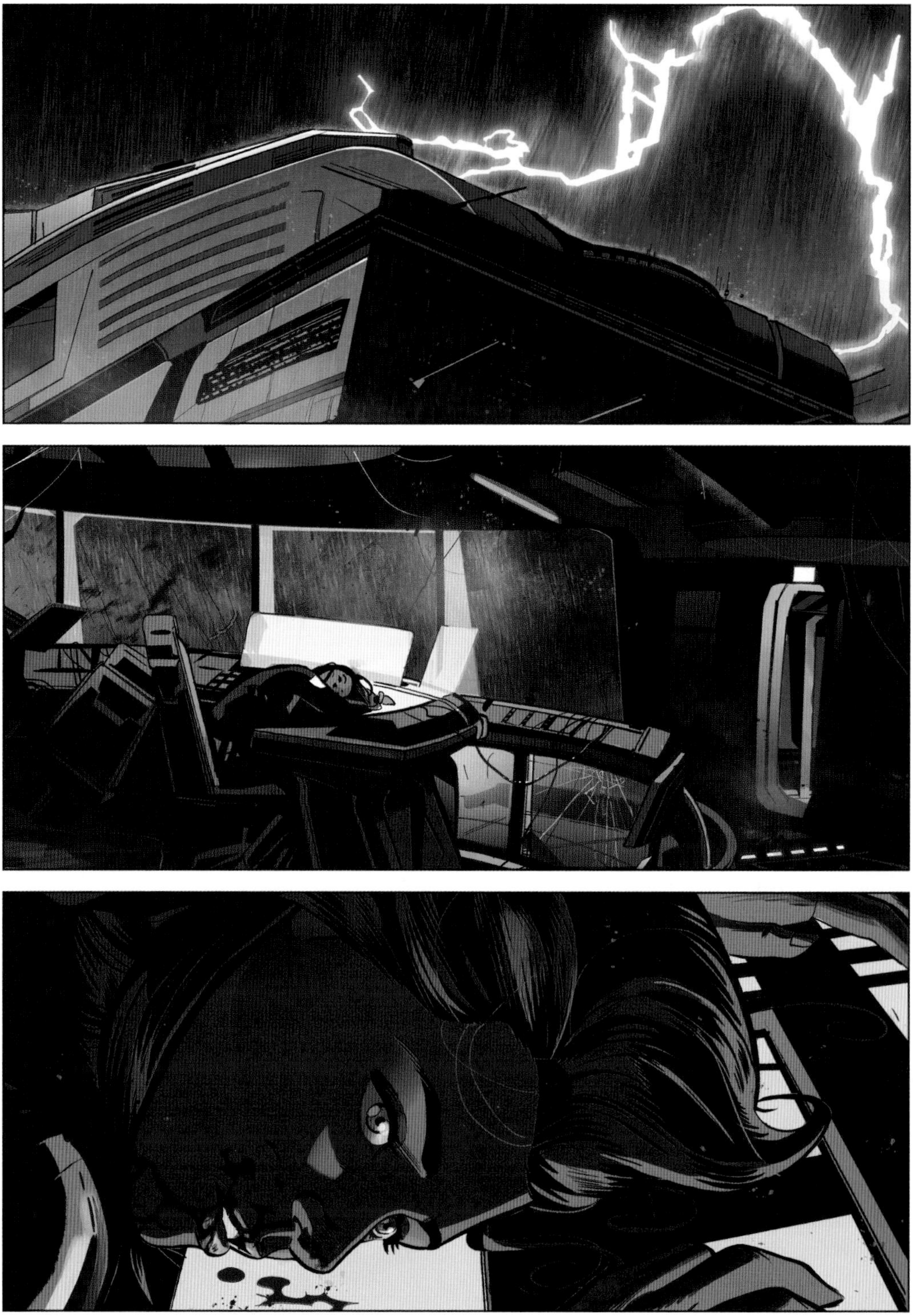

TING

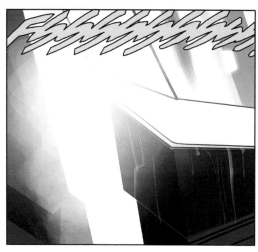

GUH!

WOOOOSHHHH

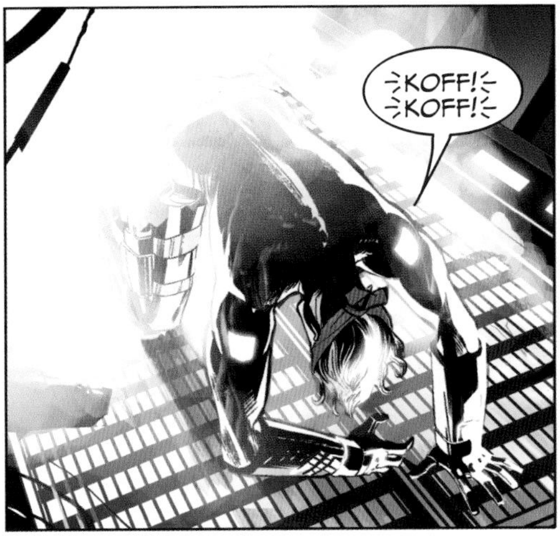
KOFF!
KOFF!

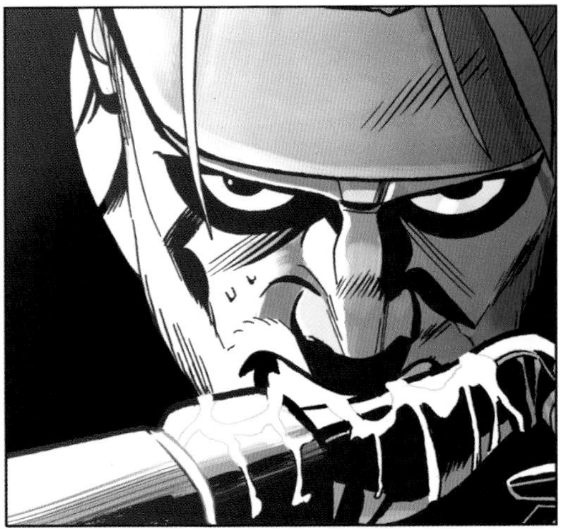

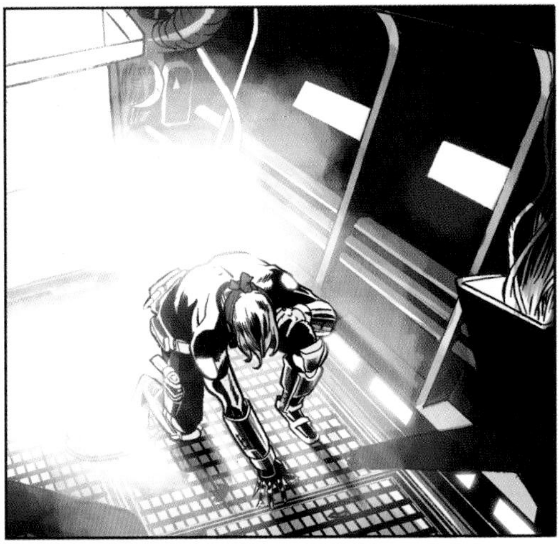

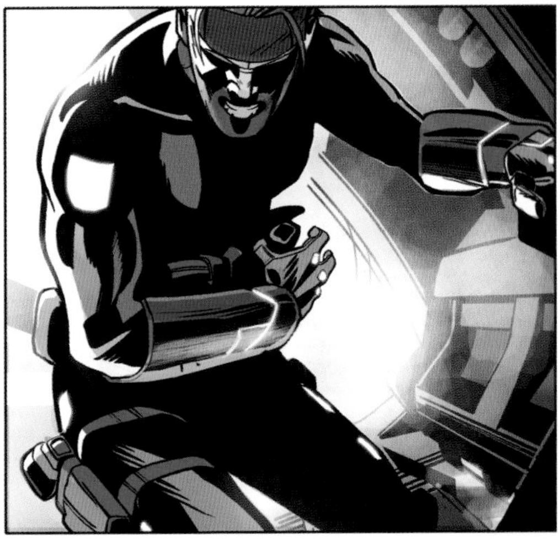

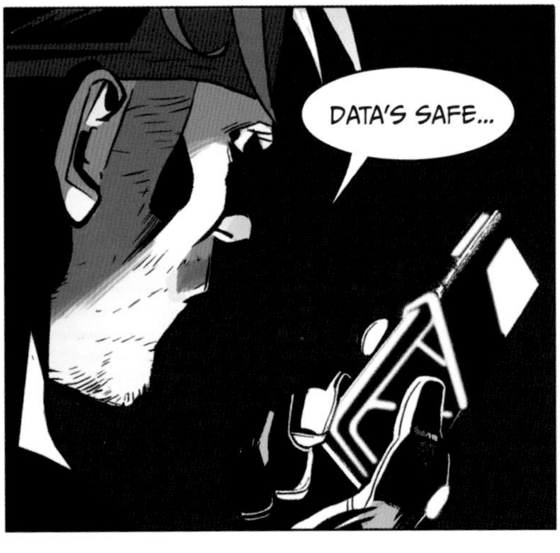
DATA'S SAFE...

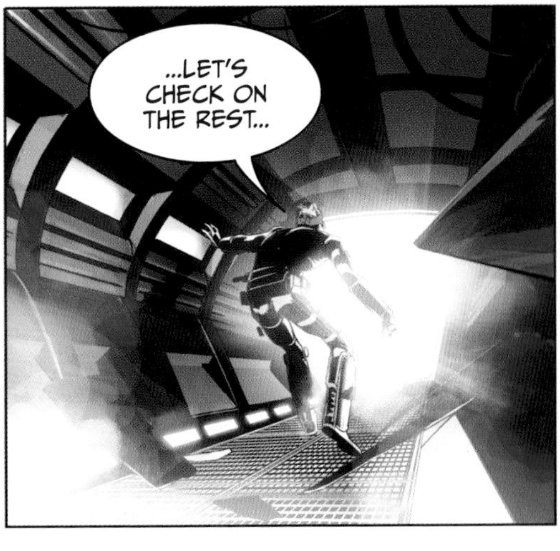
...LET'S CHECK ON THE REST...

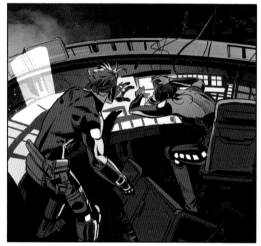

ANGEL... I'M SORRY...

...REST NOW.

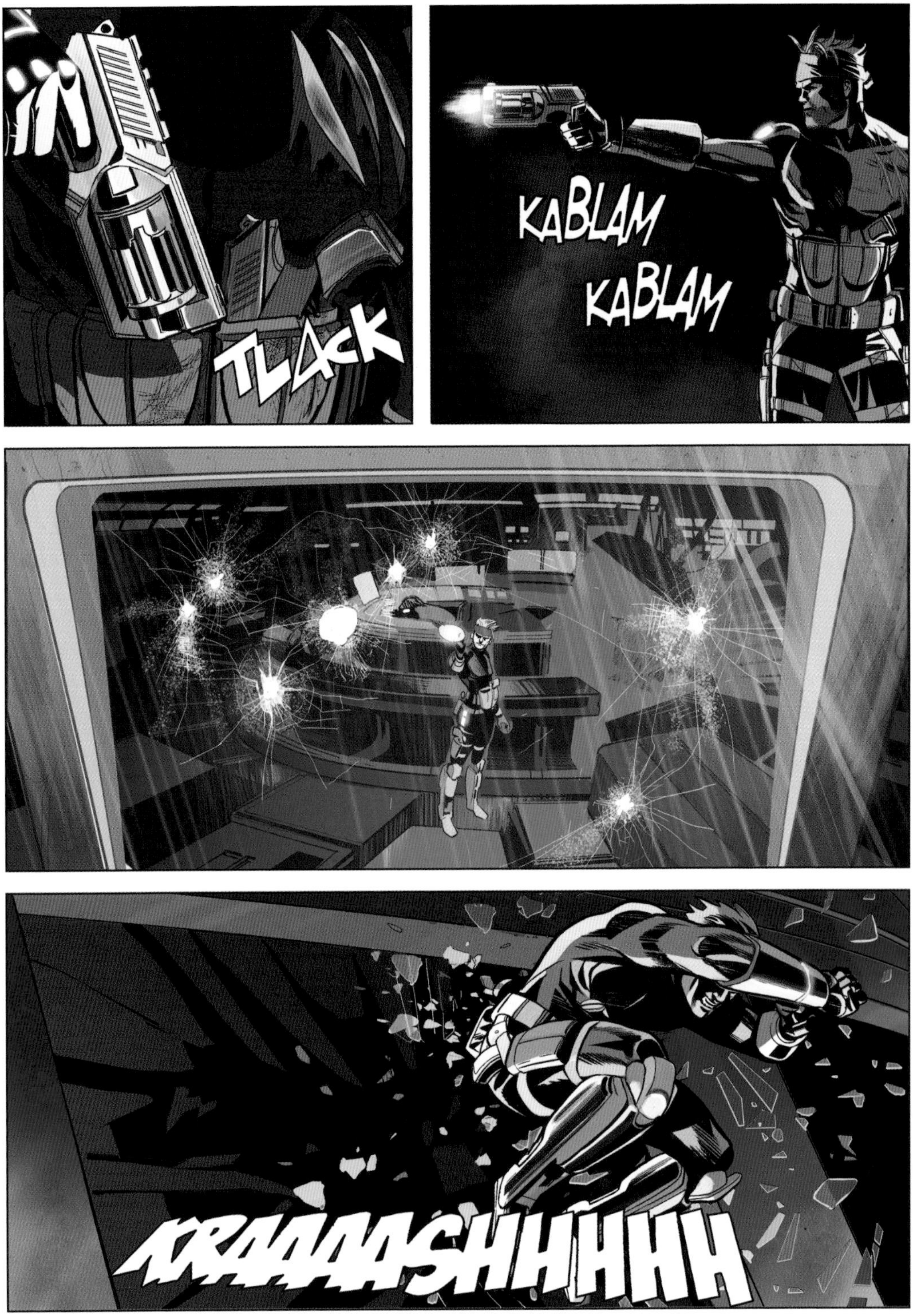
TLACK
KABLAM
KABLAM
KRAAAASHHHHHH

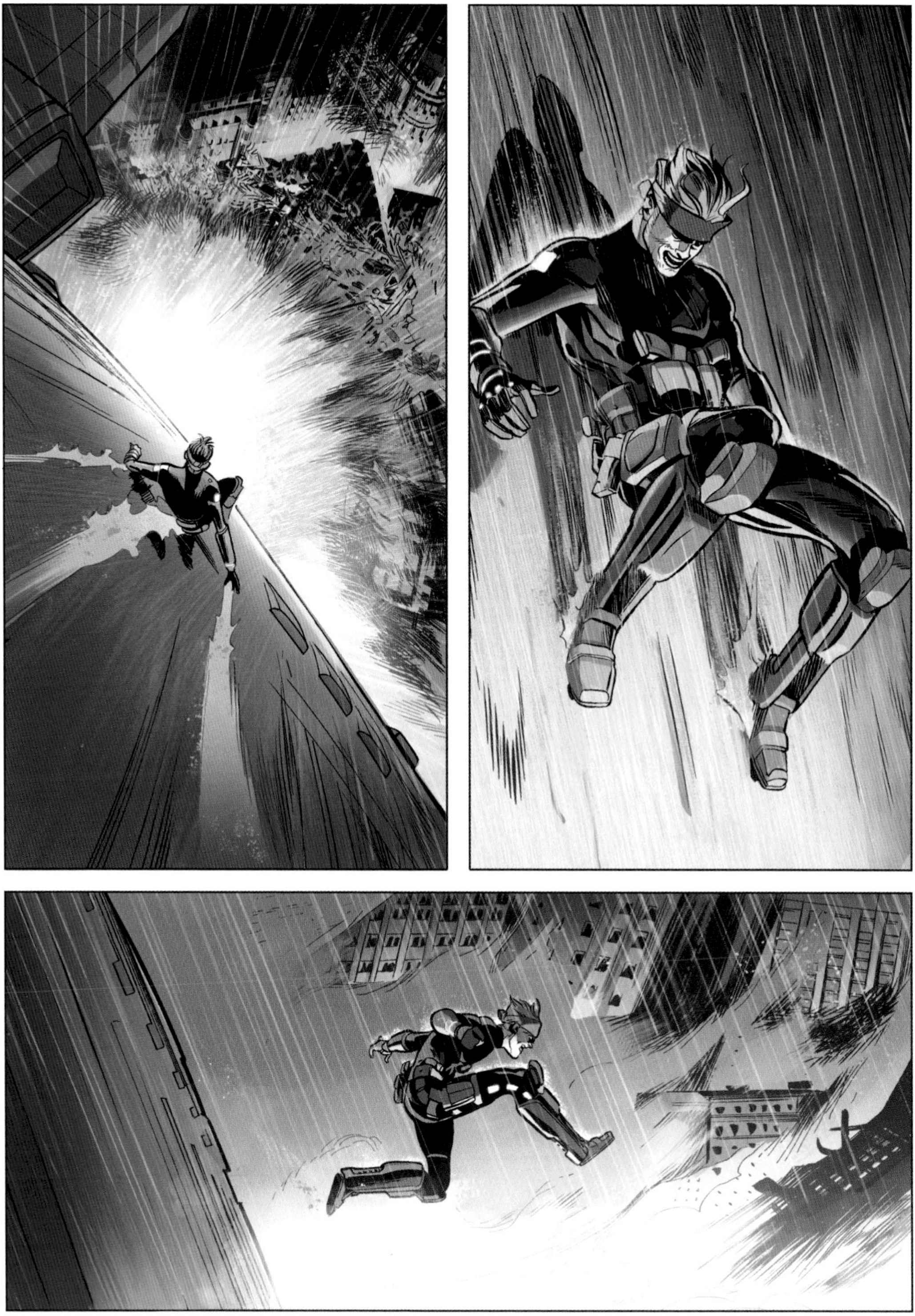

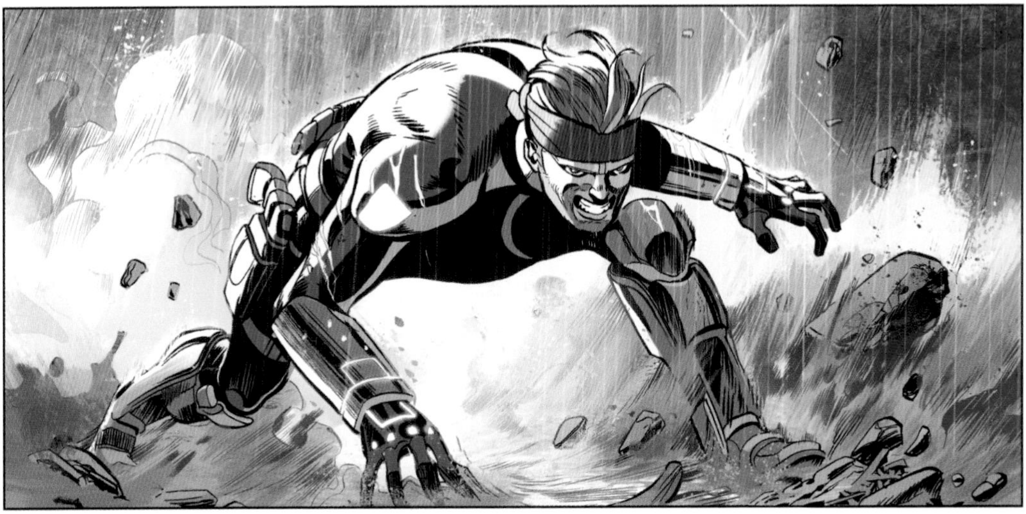

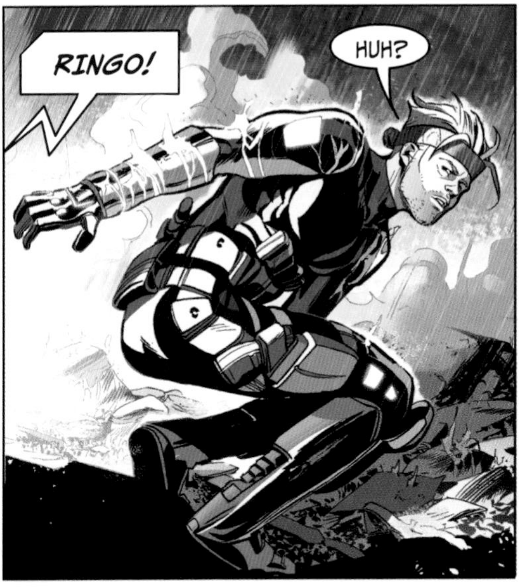
RINGO!
HUH?

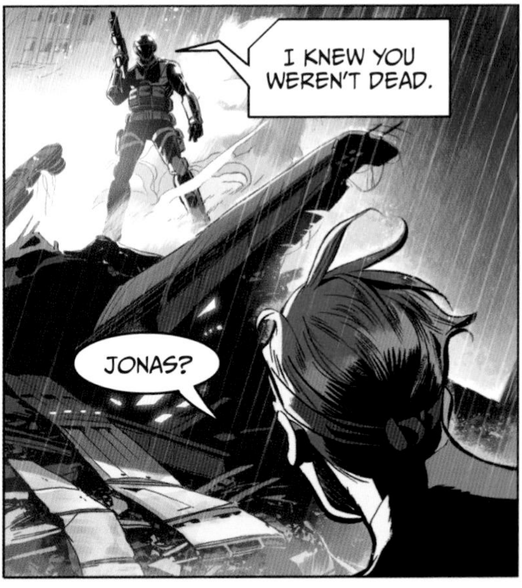
I KNEW YOU WEREN'T DEAD.
JONAS?

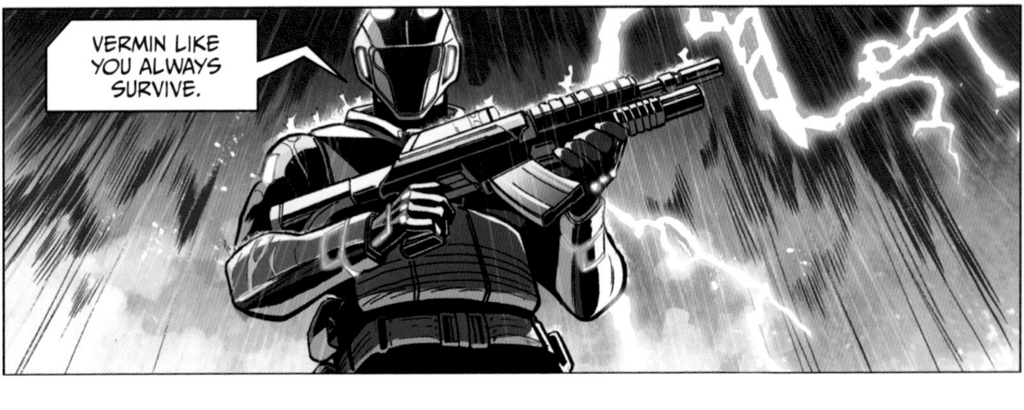
VERMIN LIKE YOU ALWAYS SURVIVE.

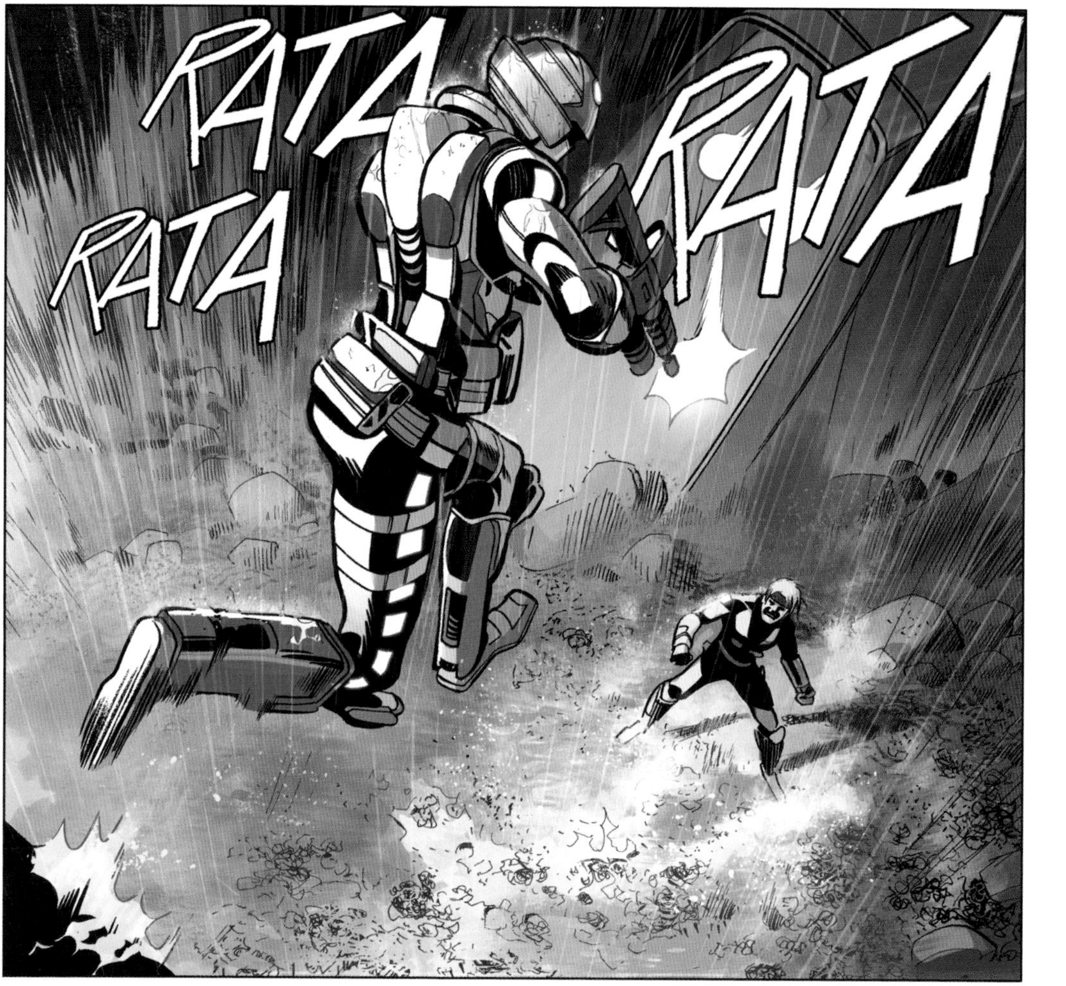
RATA
RATA
RATA

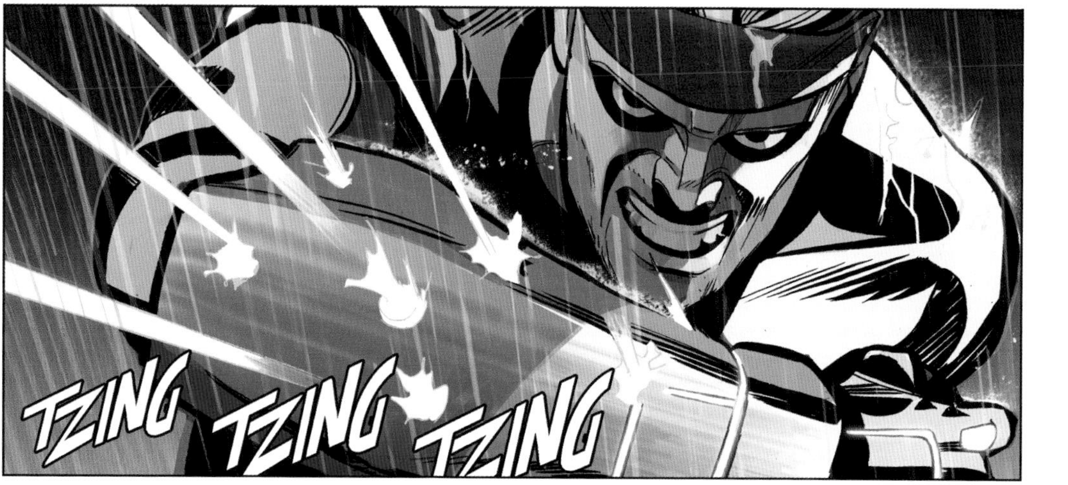
TZING TZING TZING

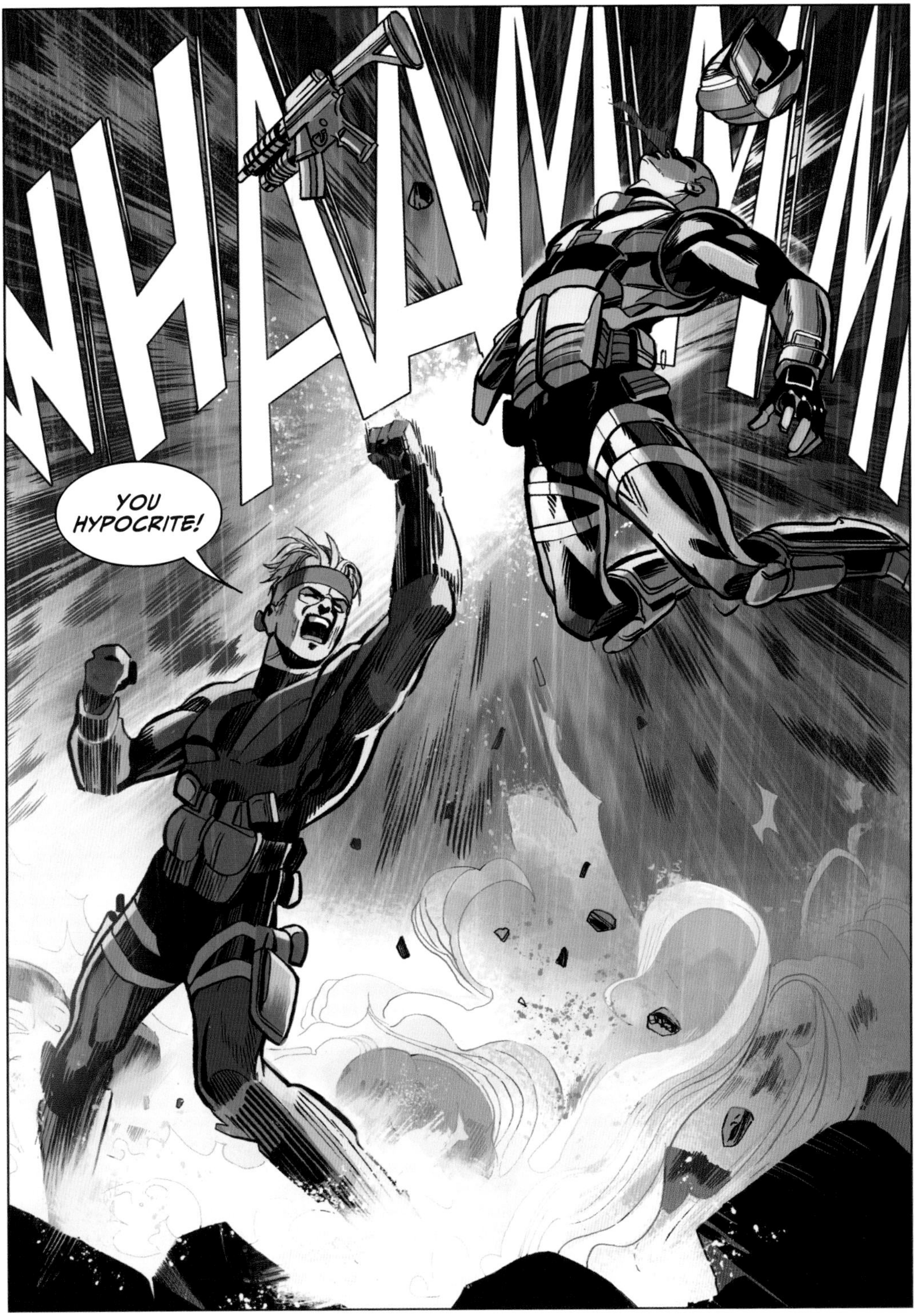
WHAM
YOU HYPOCRITE!

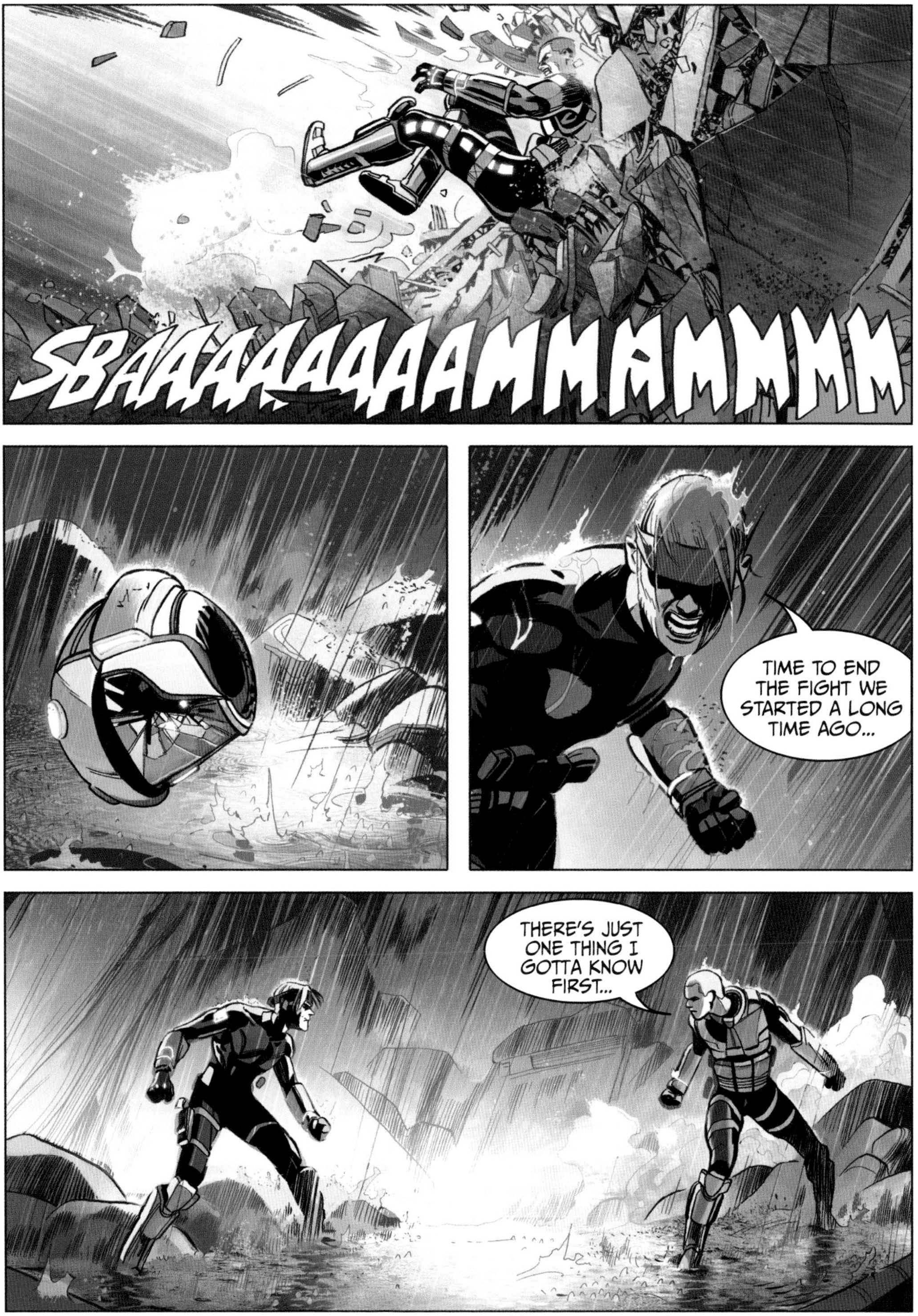
SBAAAAAAAAMMMMMMMM
TIME TO END THE FIGHT WE STARTED A LONG TIME AGO...
THERE'S JUST ONE THING I GOTTA KNOW FIRST...

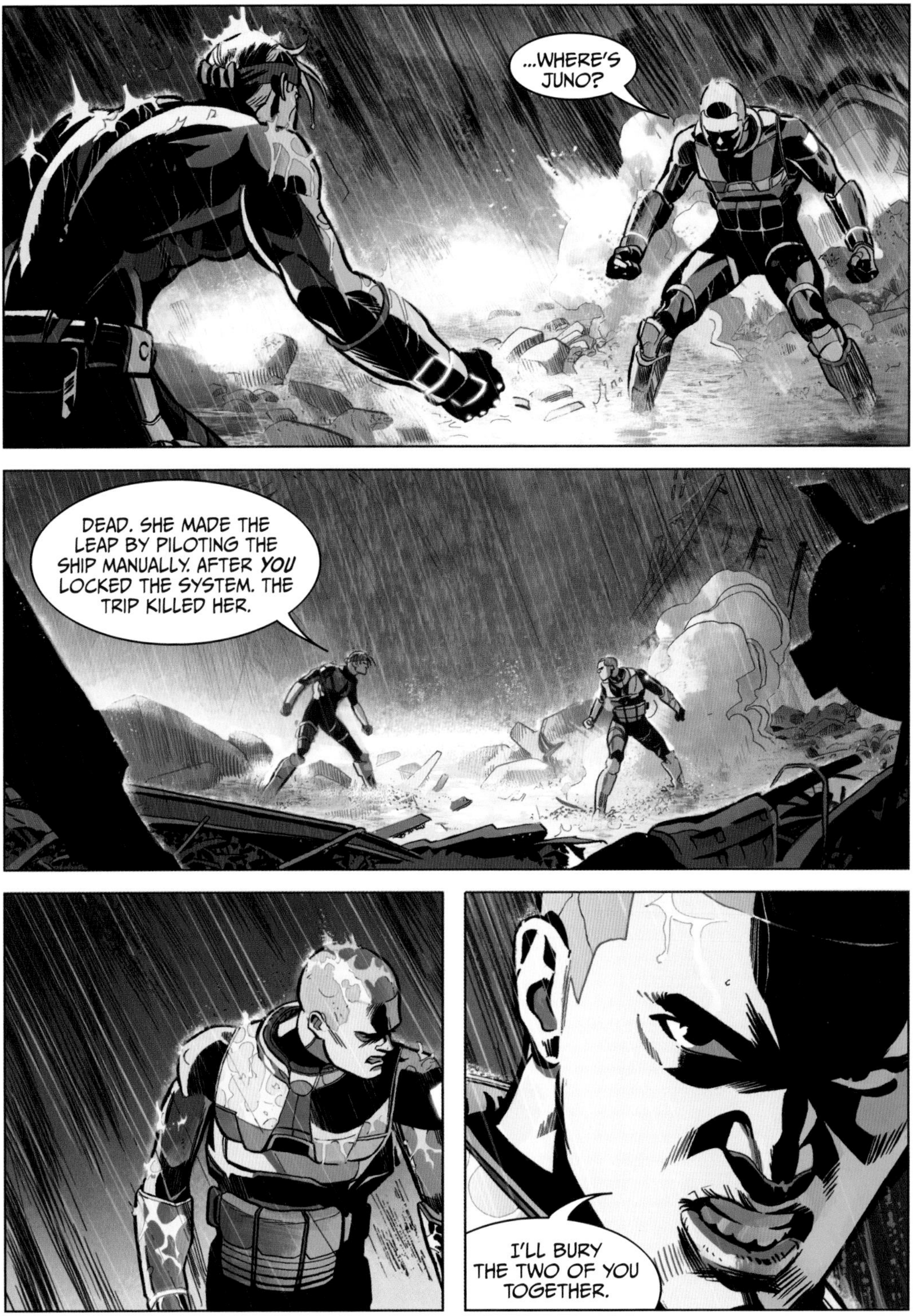
...WHERE'S JUNO?
DEAD. SHE MADE THE LEAP BY PILOTING THE SHIP MANUALLY. AFTER *YOU* LOCKED THE SYSTEM. THE TRIP KILLED HER.
I'LL BURY THE TWO OF YOU TOGETHER.

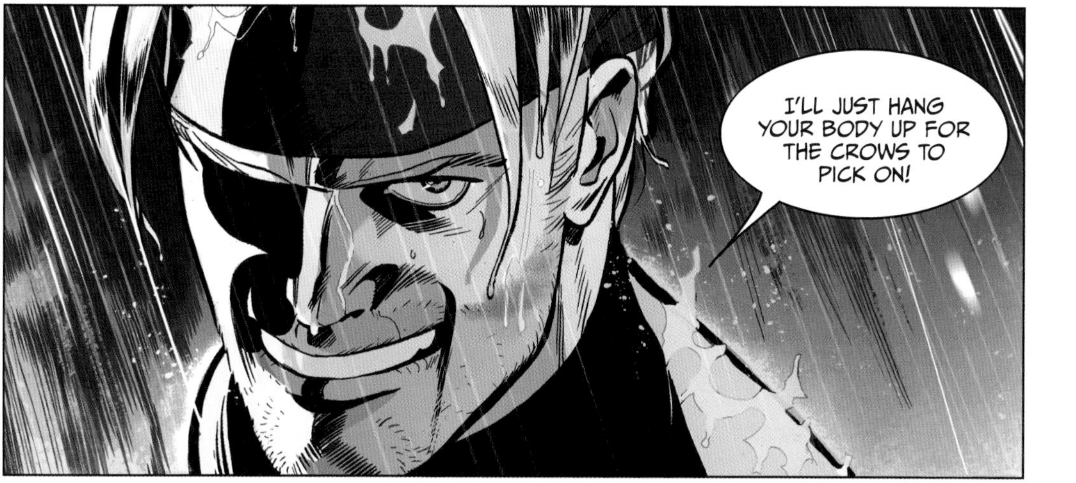
I'LL JUST HANG YOUR BODY UP FOR THE CROWS TO PICK ON!

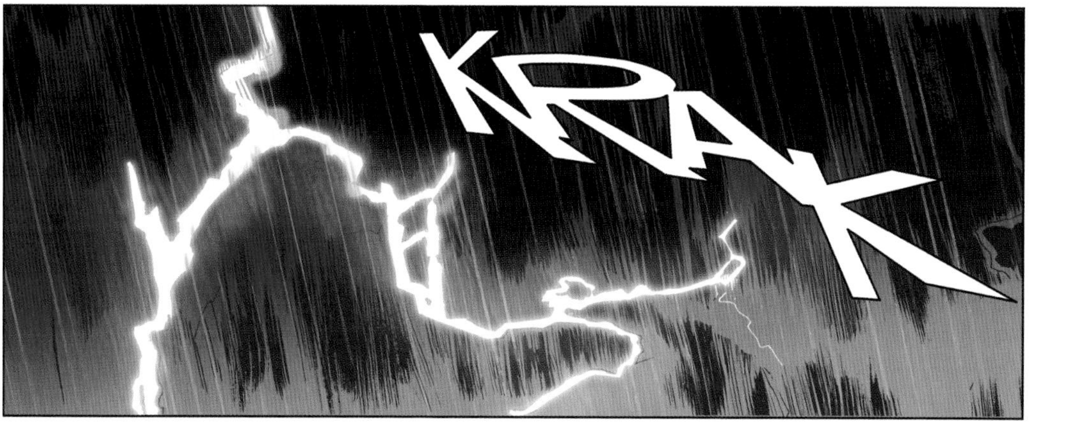
KRAK

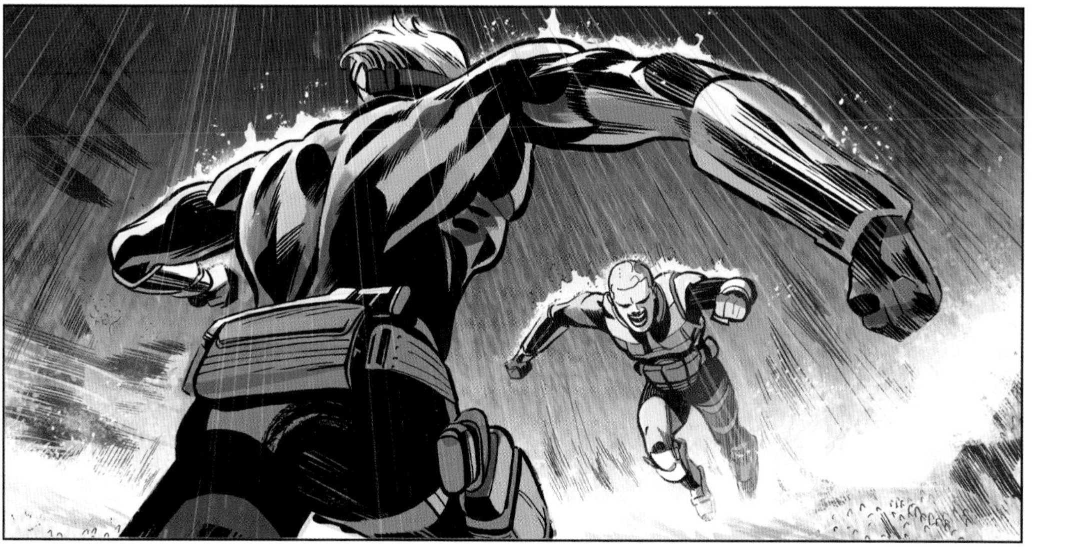

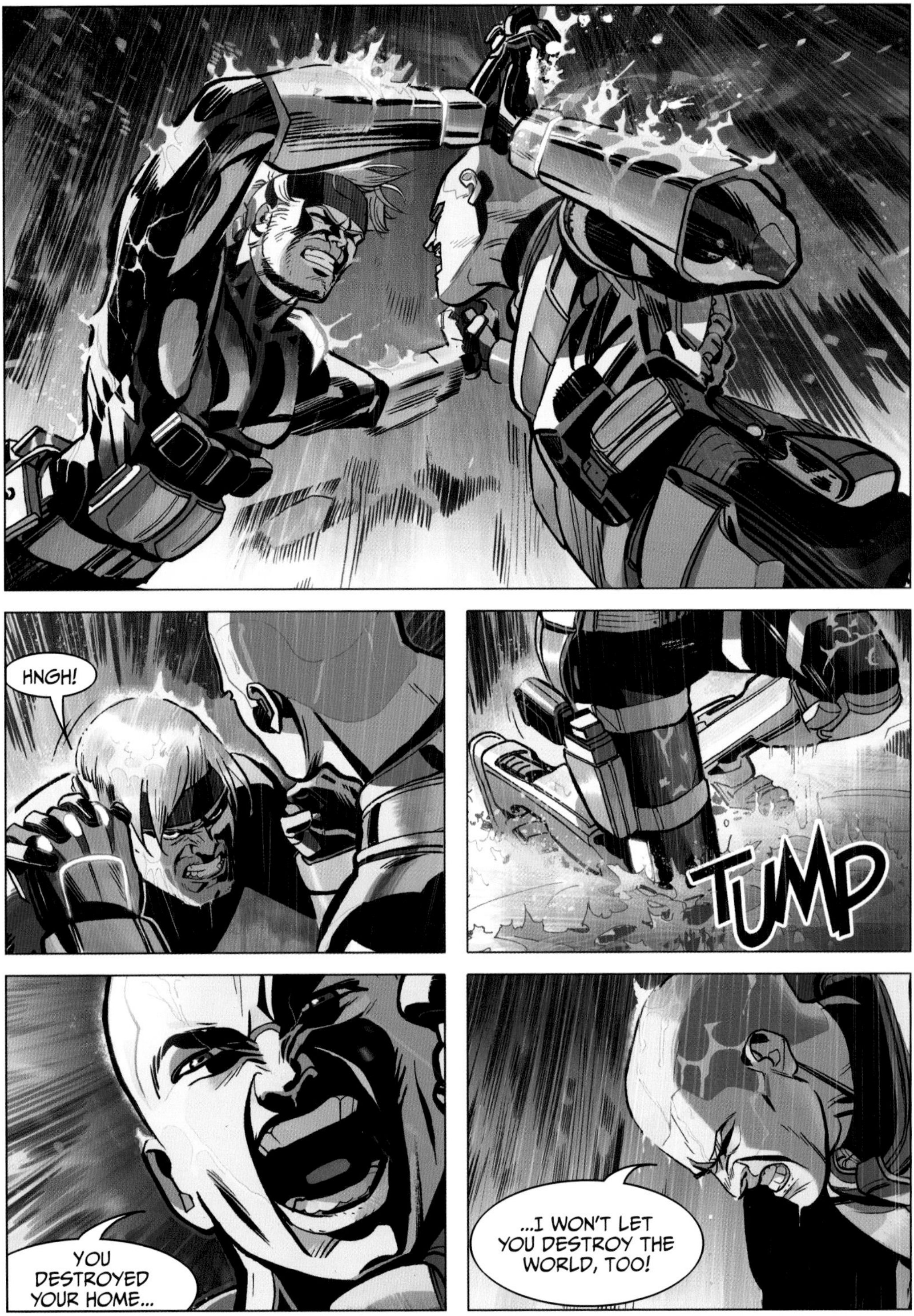
HNGH!
TUMP
YOU DESTROYED YOUR HOME...
...I WON'T LET YOU DESTROY THE WORLD, TOO!

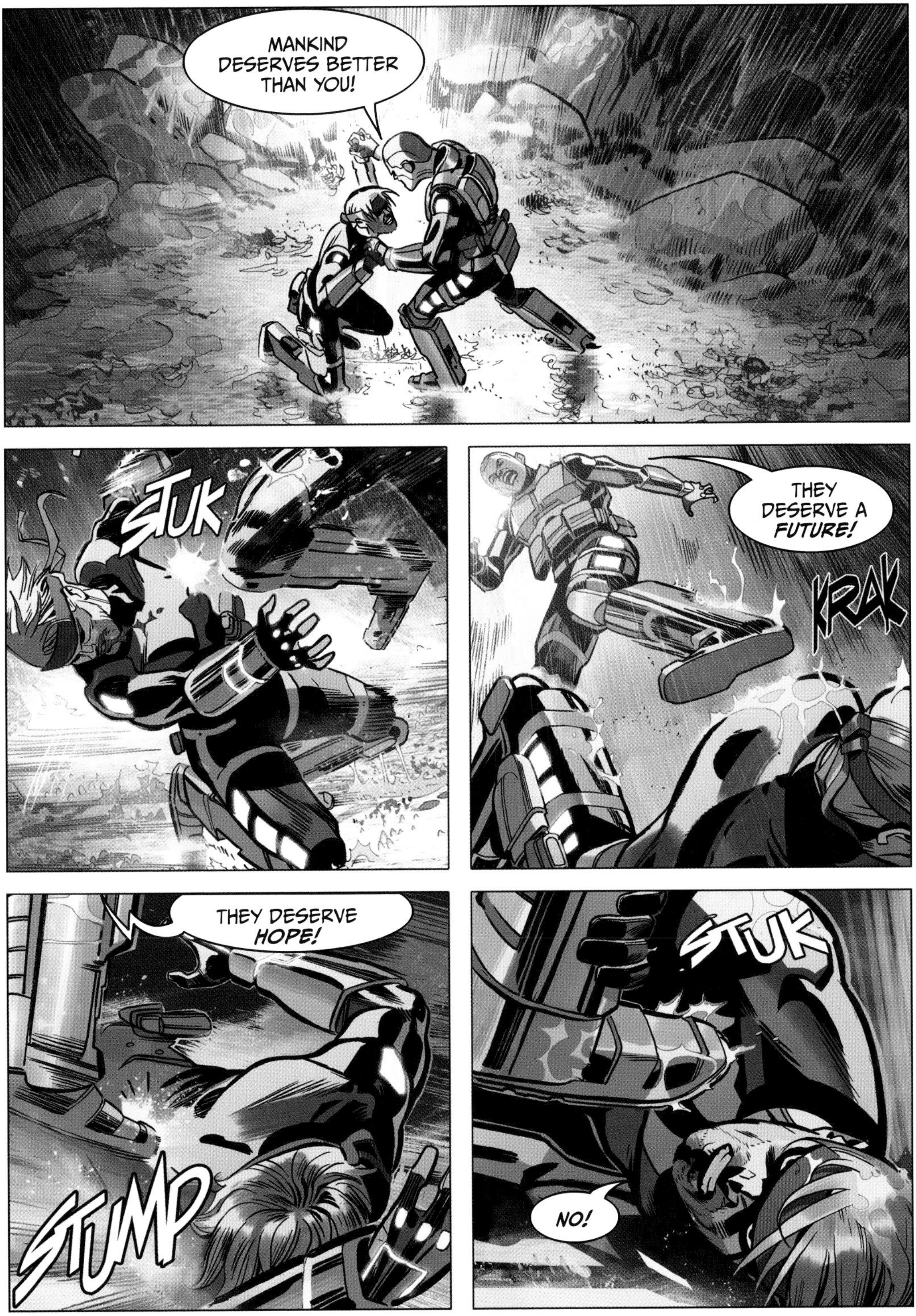
MANKIND DESERVES BETTER THAN YOU!
STUK
THEY DESERVE A FUTURE!
KRAK
THEY DESERVE HOPE!
STUMP
STUK
NO!

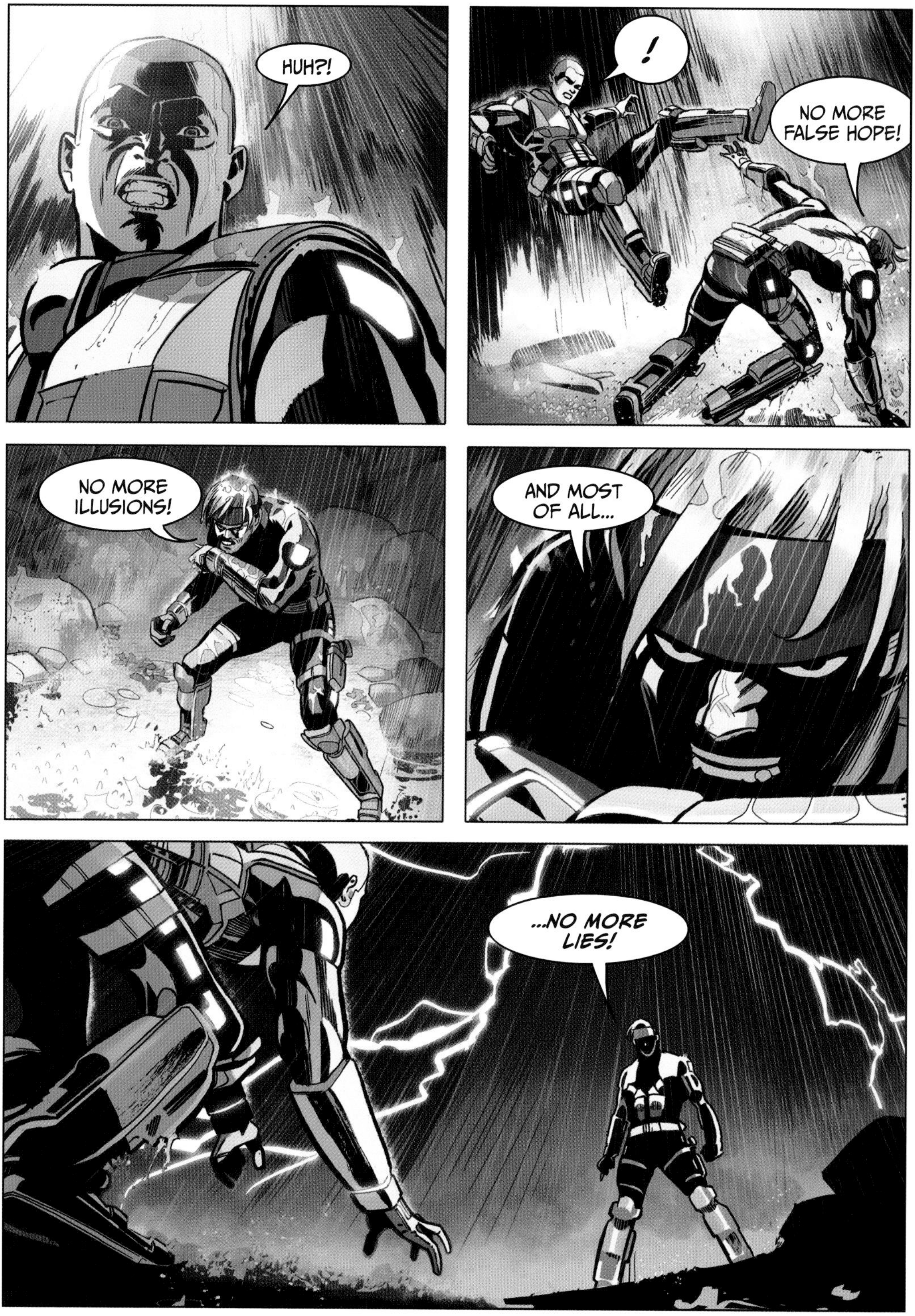
HUH?!
!
NO MORE FALSE HOPE!
NO MORE ILLUSIONS!
AND MOST OF ALL...
...NO MORE LIES!

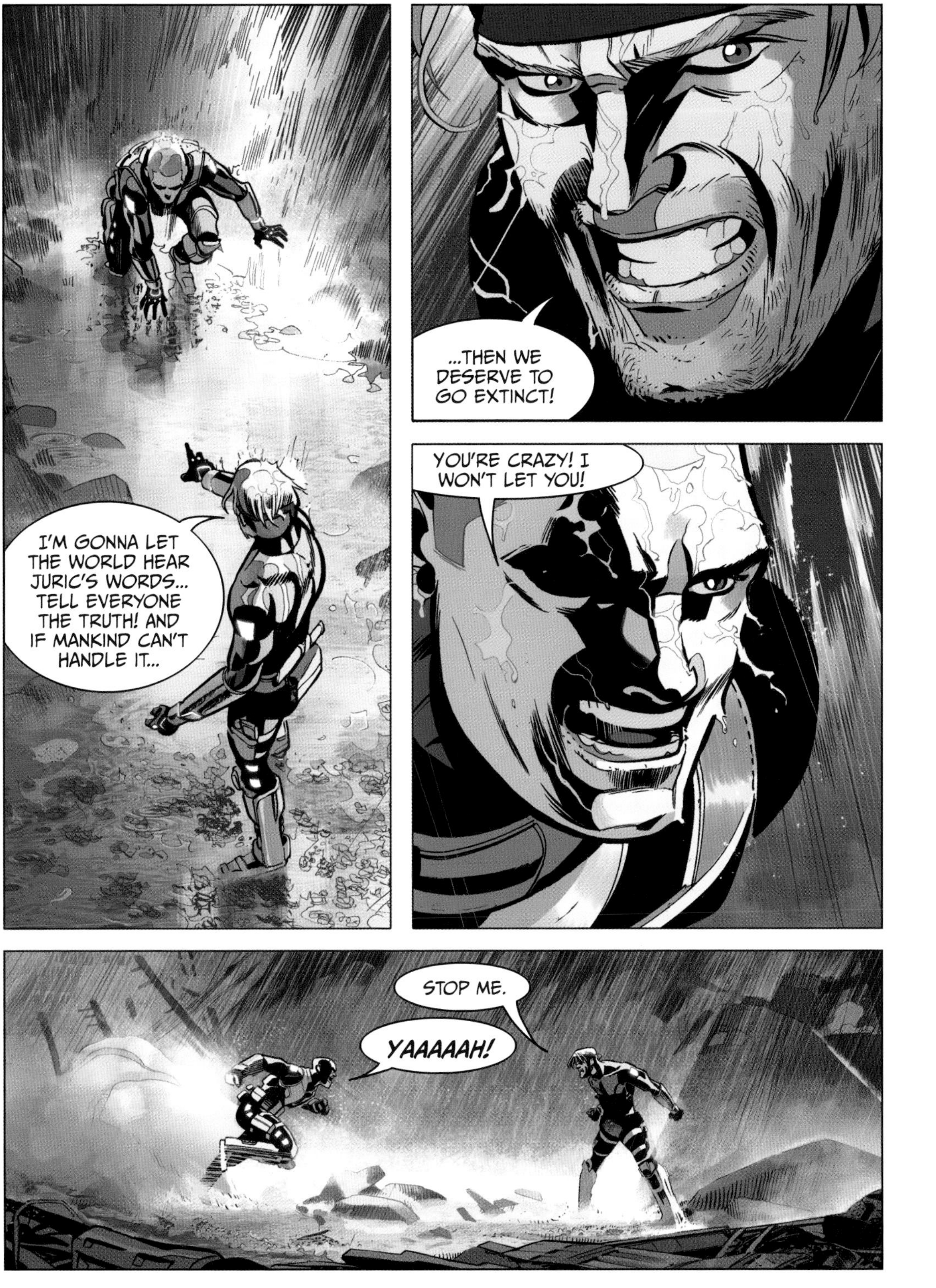
I'M GONNA LET THE WORLD HEAR JURIC'S WORDS... TELL EVERYONE THE TRUTH! AND IF MANKIND CAN'T HANDLE IT...
...THEN WE DESERVE TO GO EXTINCT!
YOU'RE CRAZY! I WON'T LET YOU!
STOP ME.
YAAAAAH!

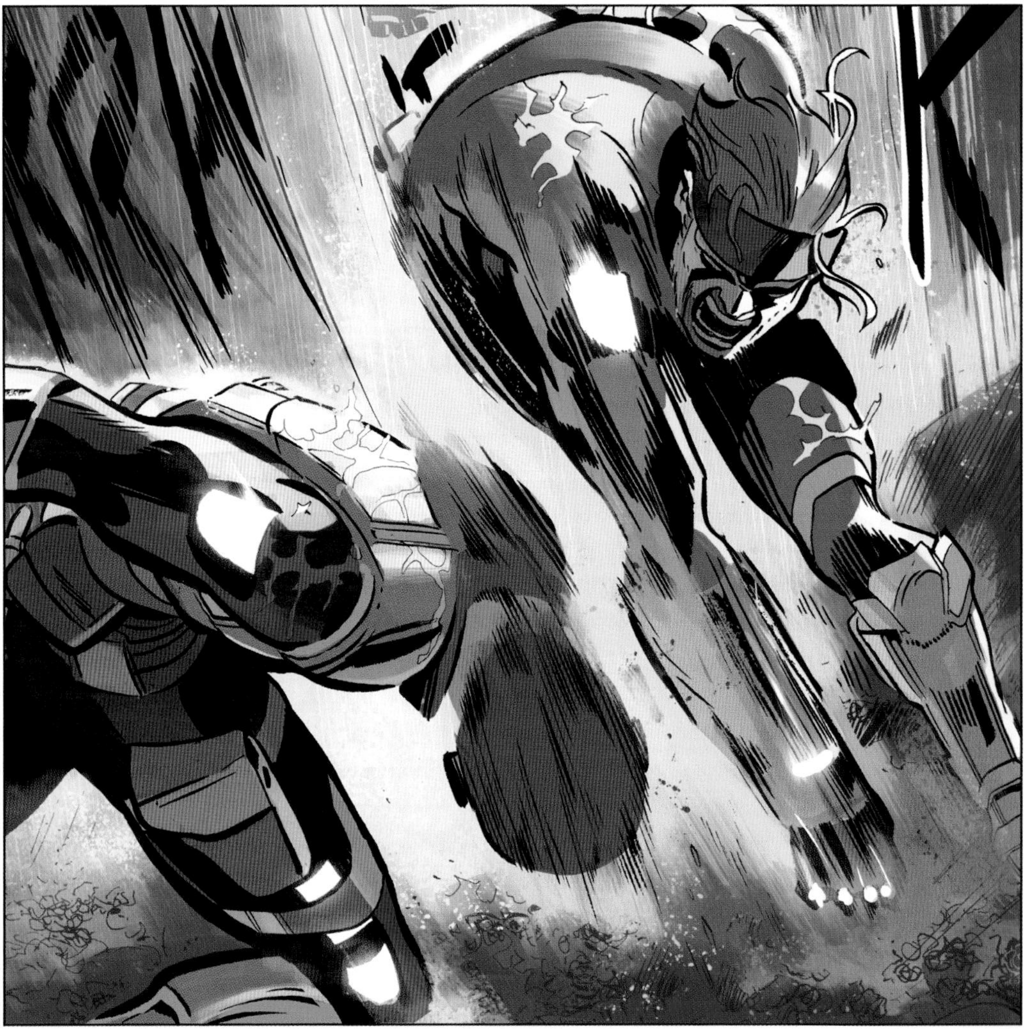

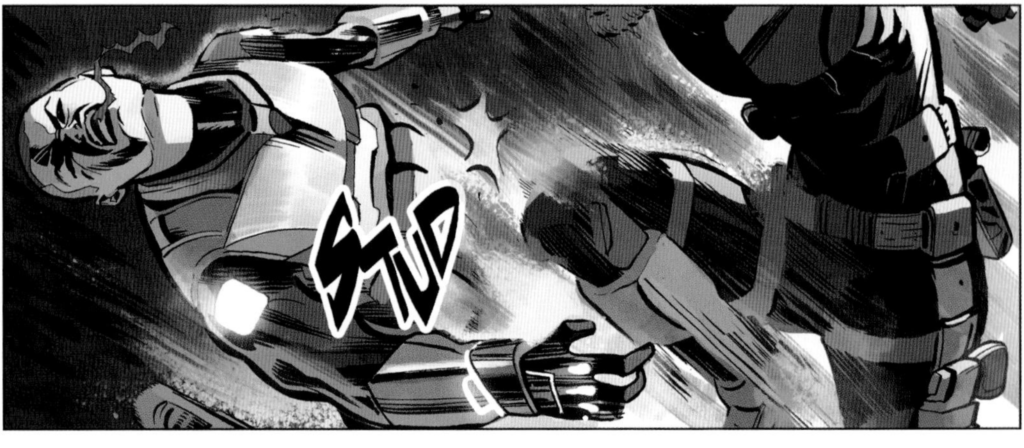
STUD

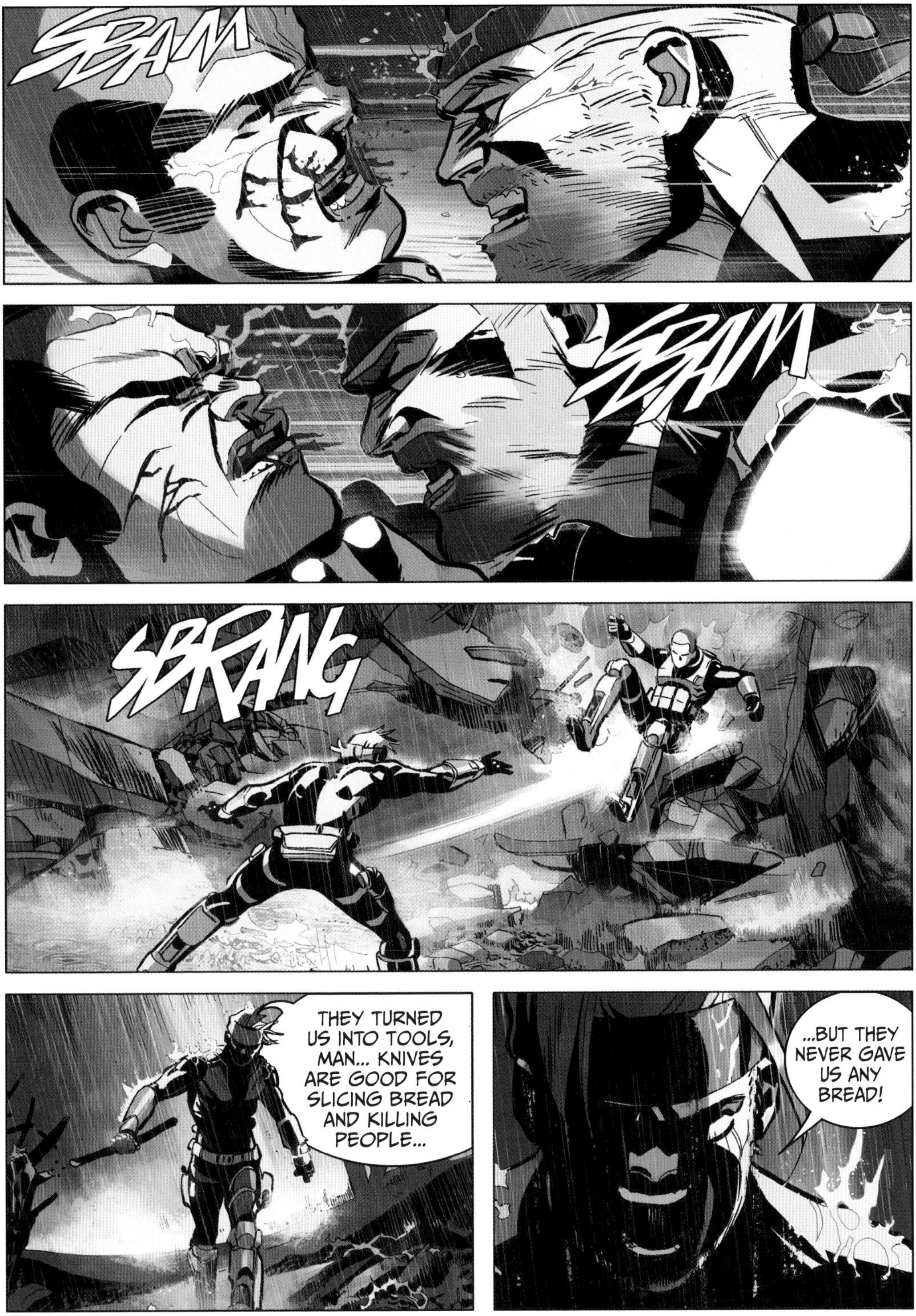
SBAM
SBAM
SBRANG
THEY TURNED US INTO TOOLS, MAN... KNIVES ARE GOOD FOR SLICING BREAD AND KILLING PEOPLE...
...BUT THEY NEVER GAVE US ANY BREAD!

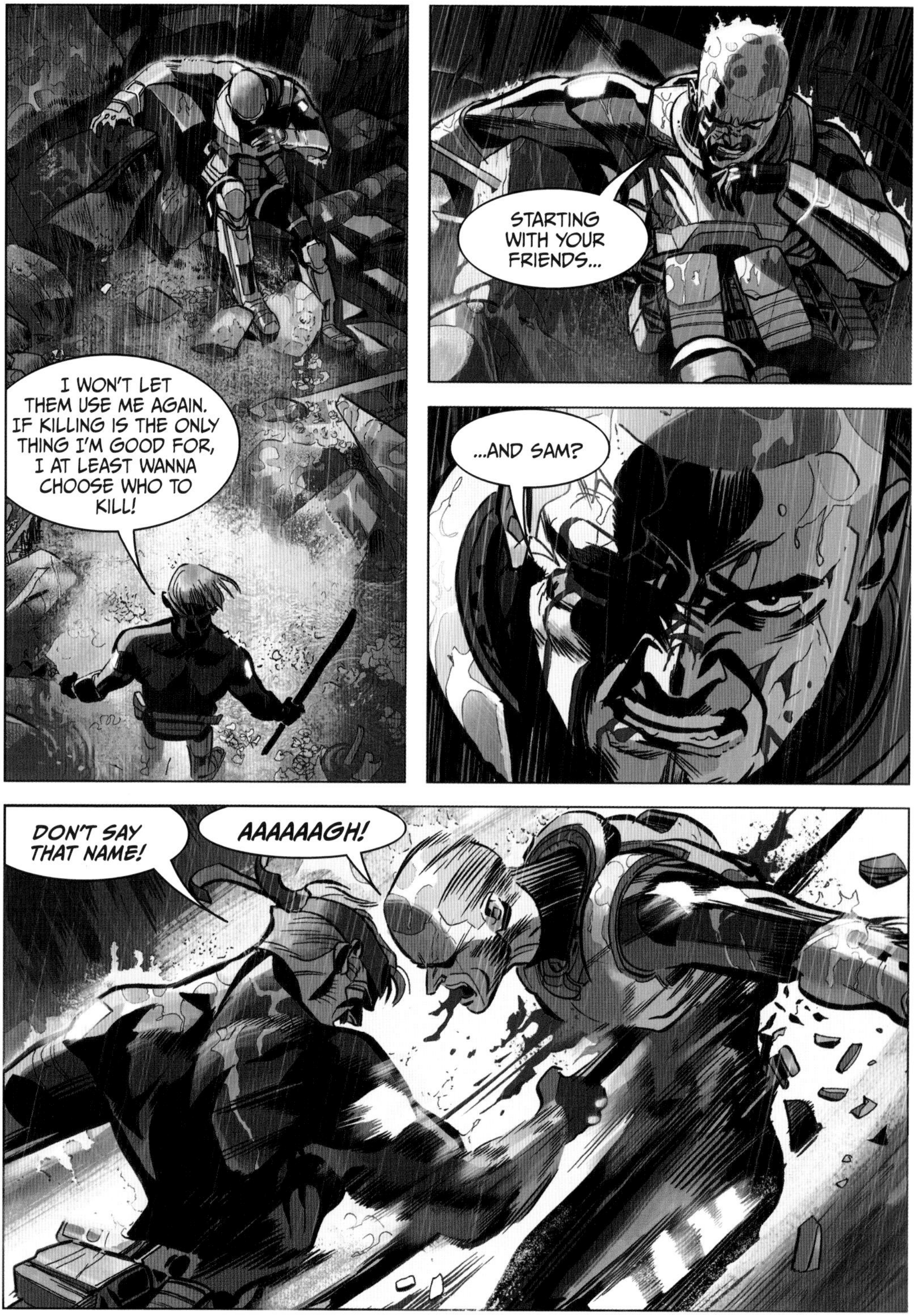
I WON'T LET THEM USE ME AGAIN. IF KILLING IS THE ONLY THING I'M GOOD FOR, I AT LEAST WANNA CHOOSE WHO TO KILL!
STARTING WITH YOUR FRIENDS...
...AND SAM?
DON'T SAY THAT NAME!
AAAAAAGH!

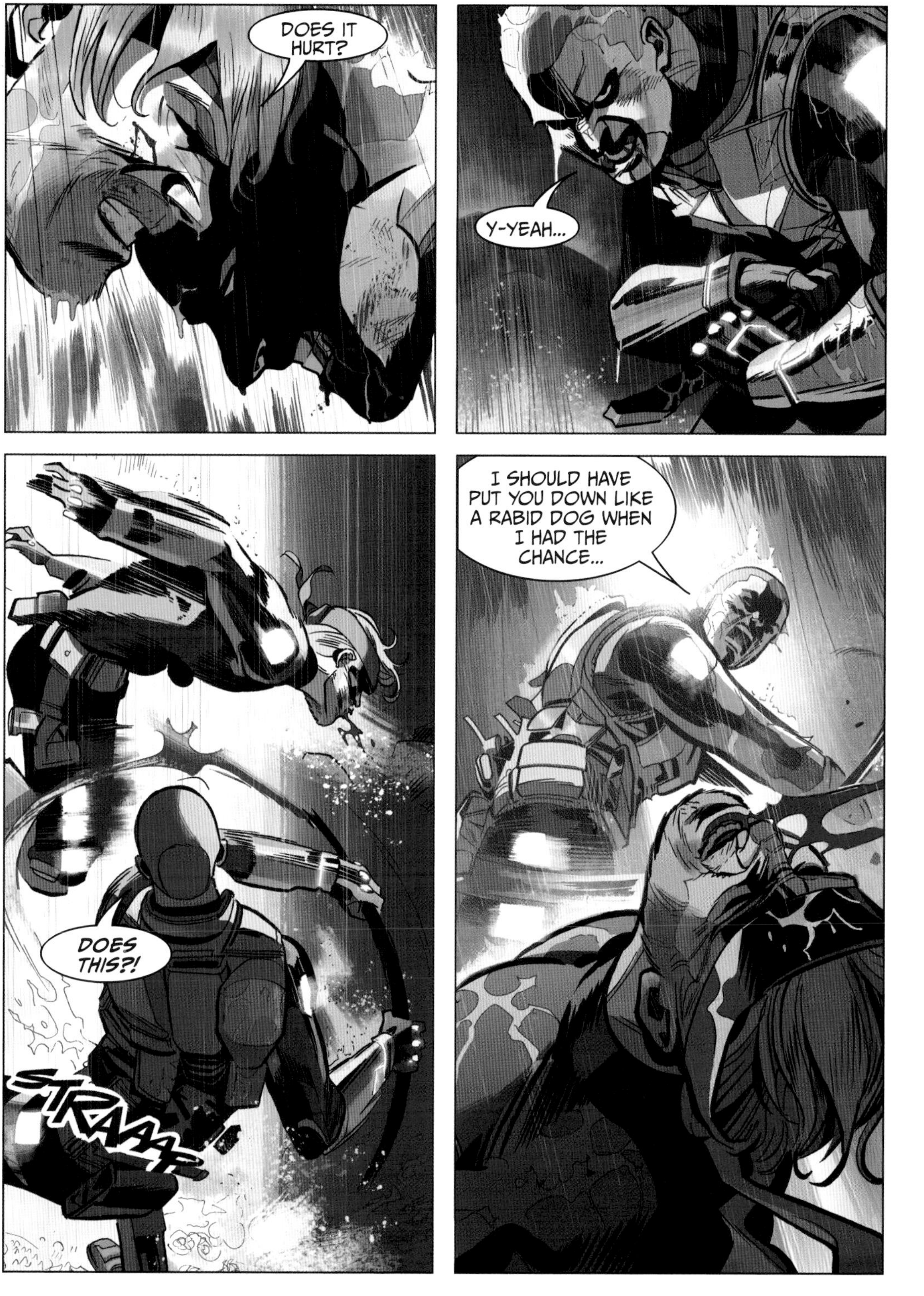
DOES IT HURT?
Y-YEAH...
DOES THIS?!
STRAAAP
I SHOULD HAVE PUT YOU DOWN LIKE A RABID DOG WHEN I HAD THE CHANCE...

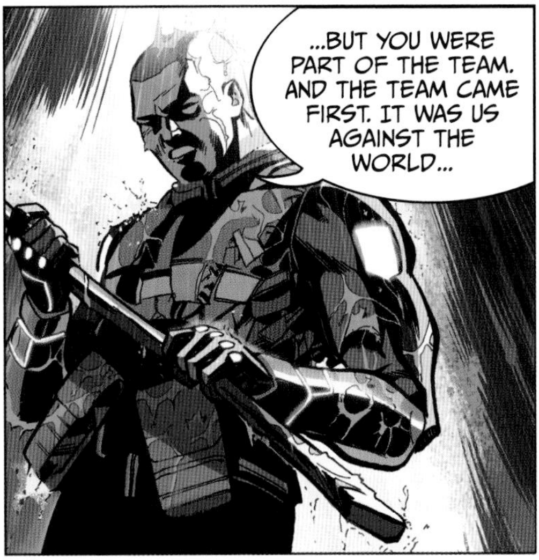
...BUT YOU WERE PART OF THE TEAM. AND THE TEAM CAME FIRST. IT WAS US AGAINST THE WORLD...

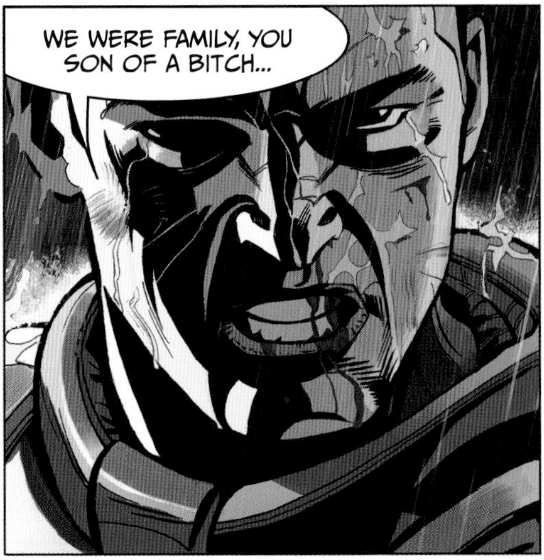
WE WERE FAMILY, YOU SON OF A BITCH...

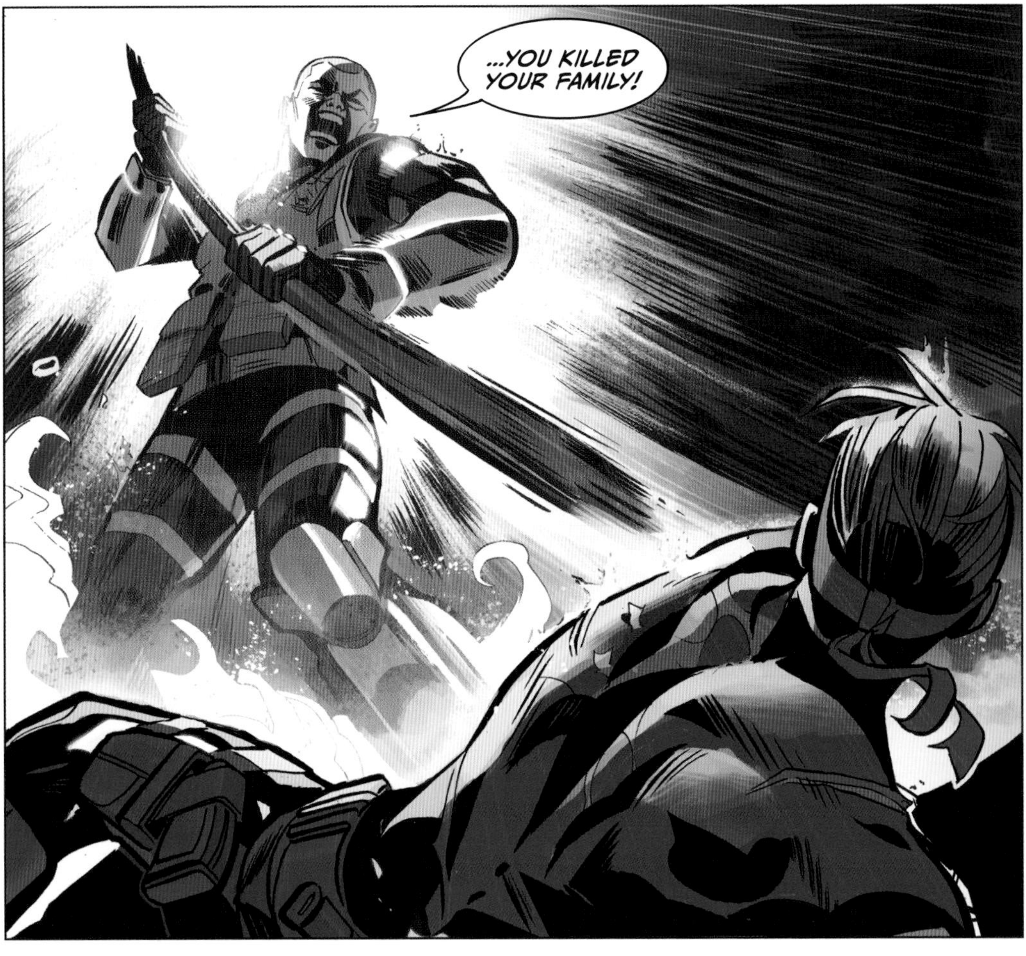
...YOU KILLED YOUR FAMILY!

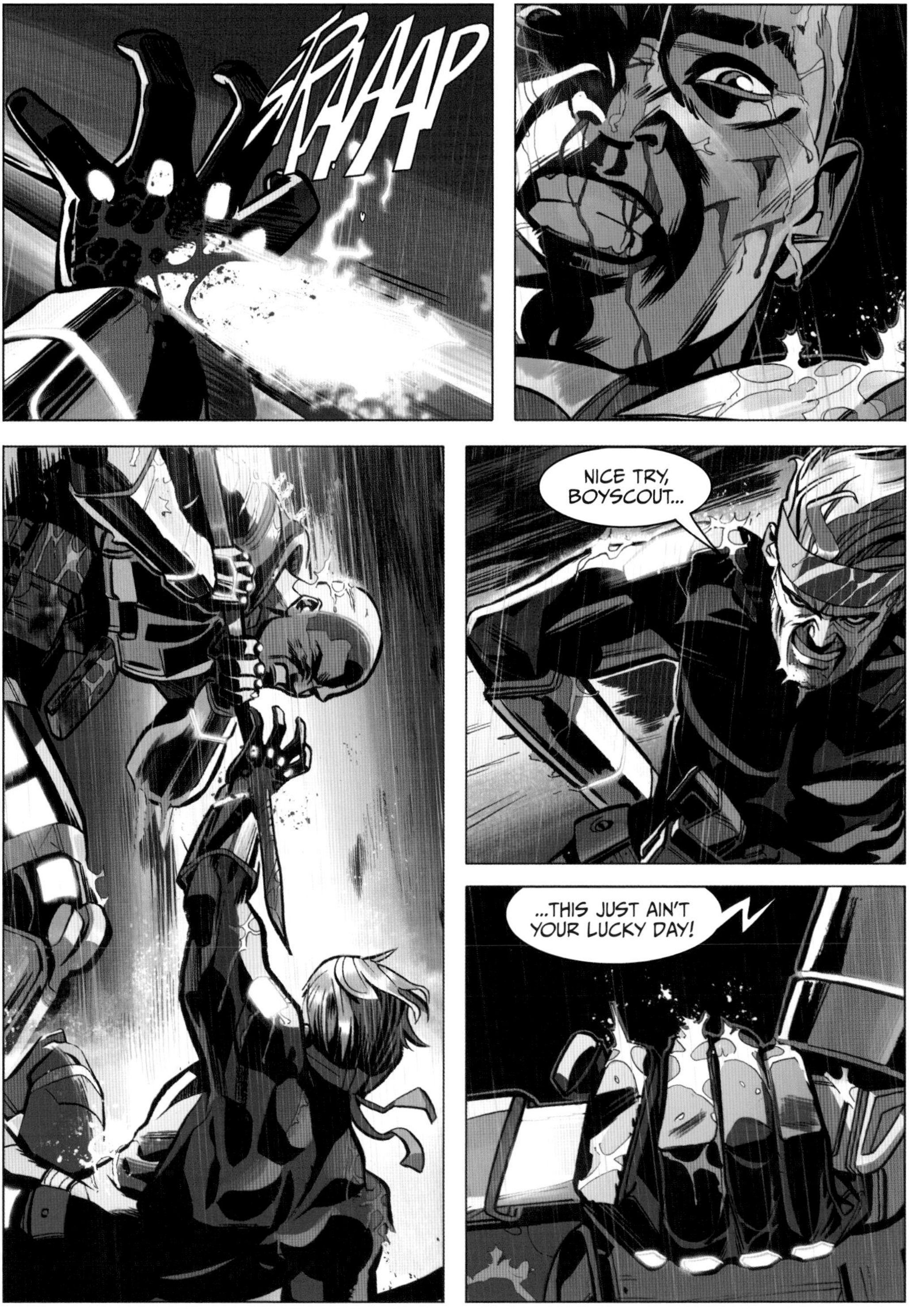
NICE TRY, BOYSCOUT...
...THIS JUST AIN'T YOUR LUCKY DAY!

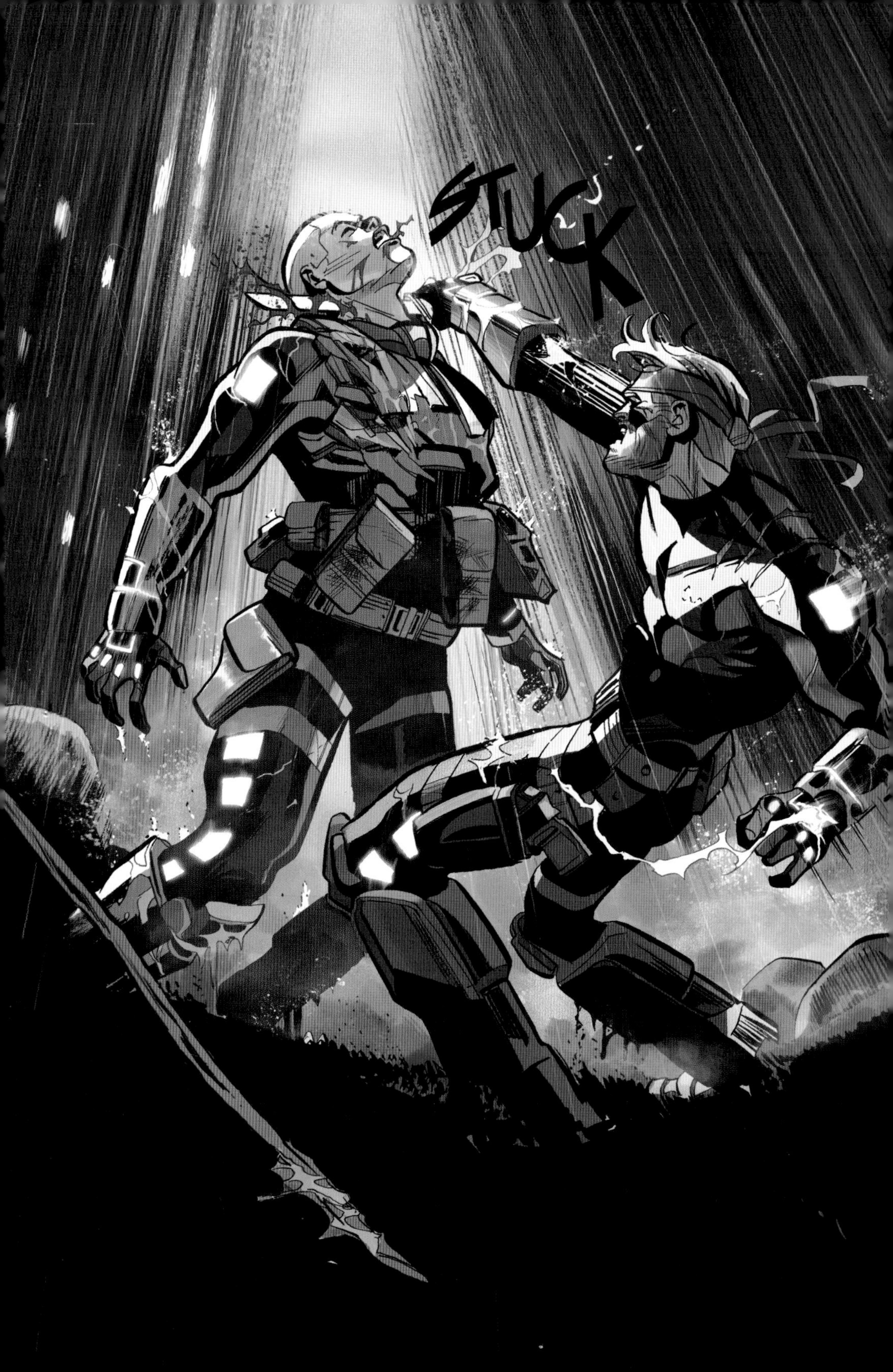
STUCK

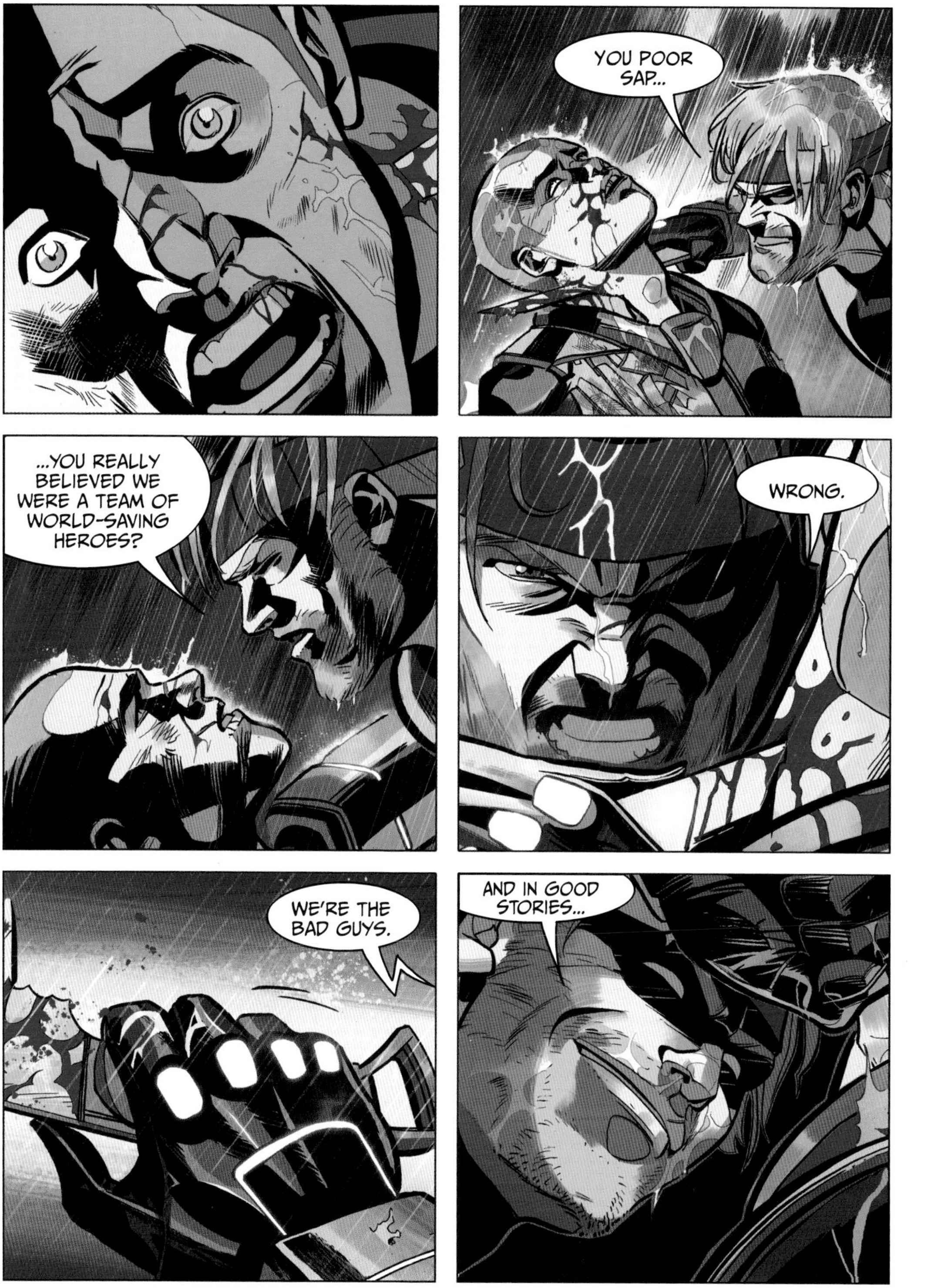
YOU POOR SAP...
...YOU REALLY BELIEVED WE WERE A TEAM OF WORLD-SAVING HEROES?
WRONG.
WE'RE THE BAD GUYS.
AND IN GOOD STORIES...

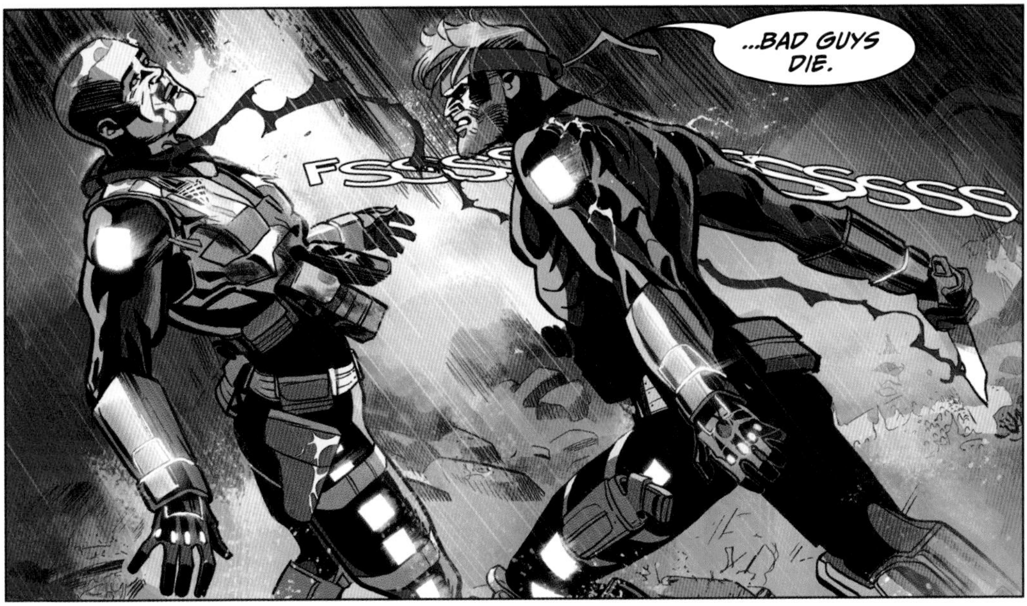
...BAD GUYS DIE.
FSSSSSSSSSSSSSS

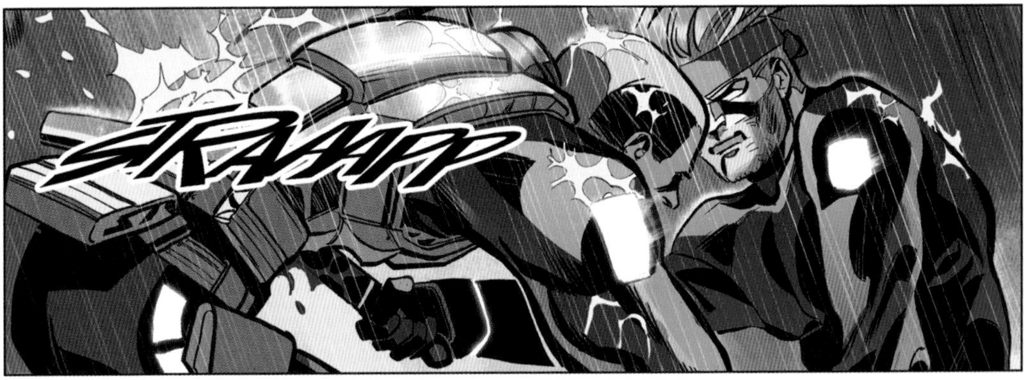
STRAAAPP

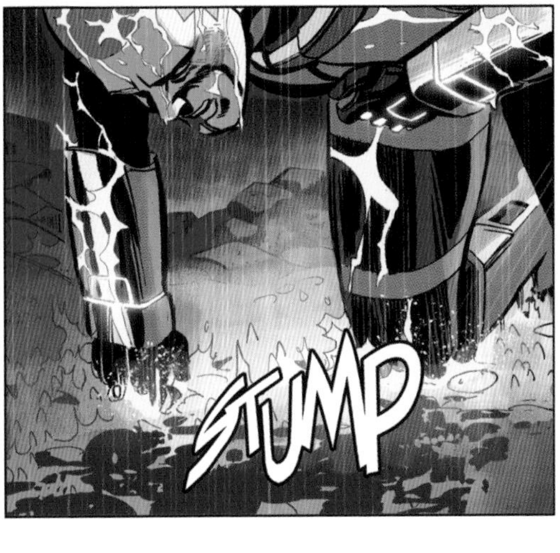
STUMP

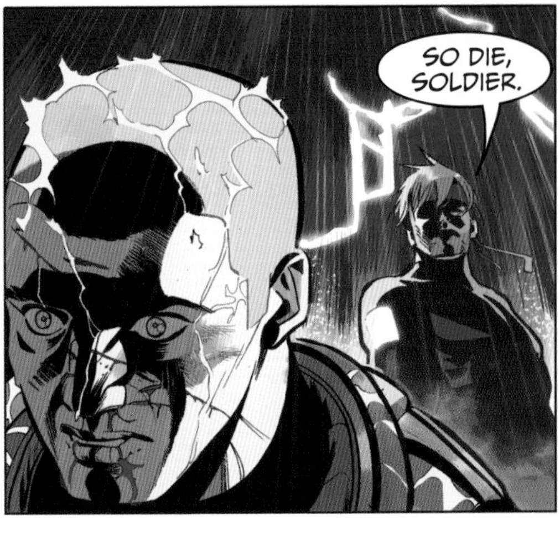
SO DIE, SOLDIER.

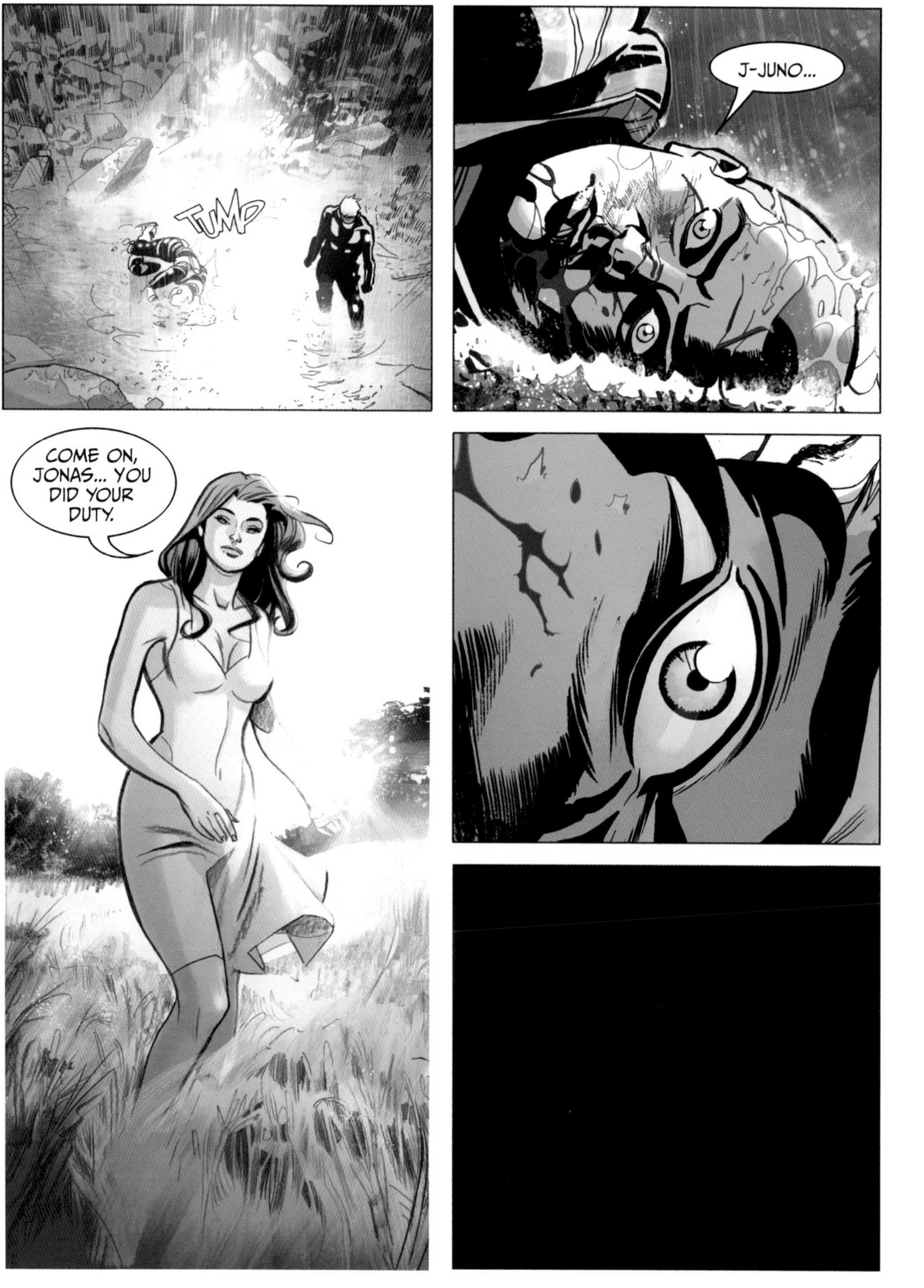
TUMP
J-JUNO...
COME ON, JONAS... YOU DID YOUR DUTY.

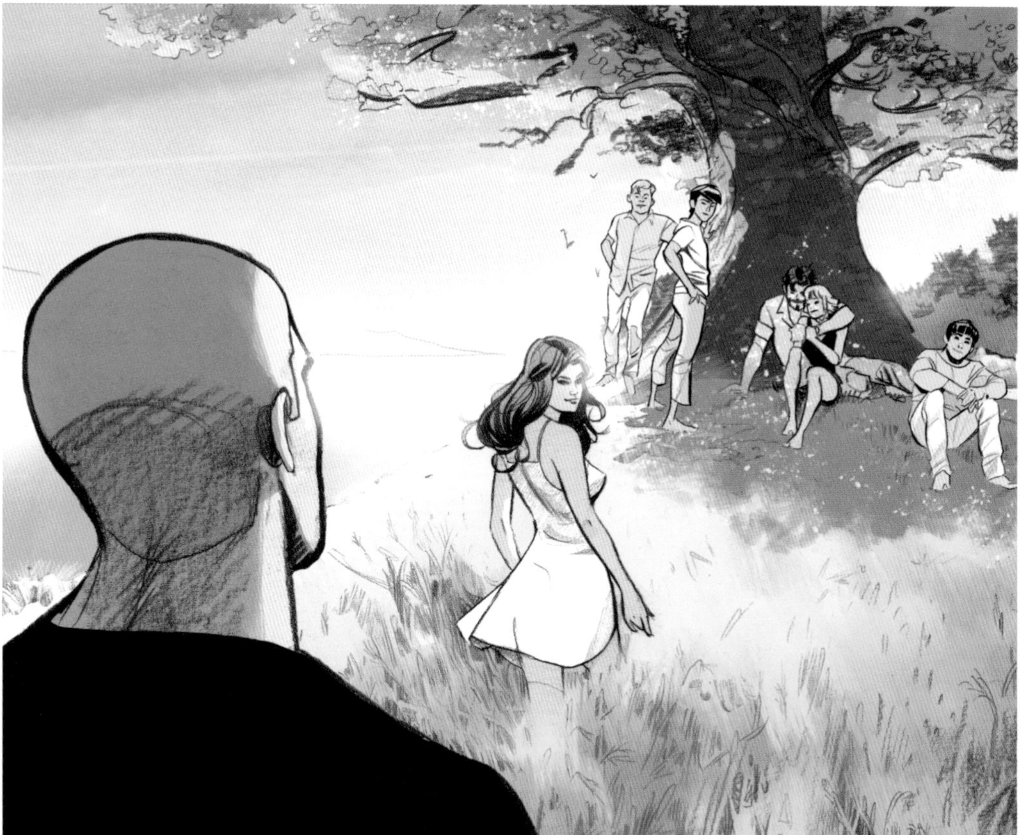

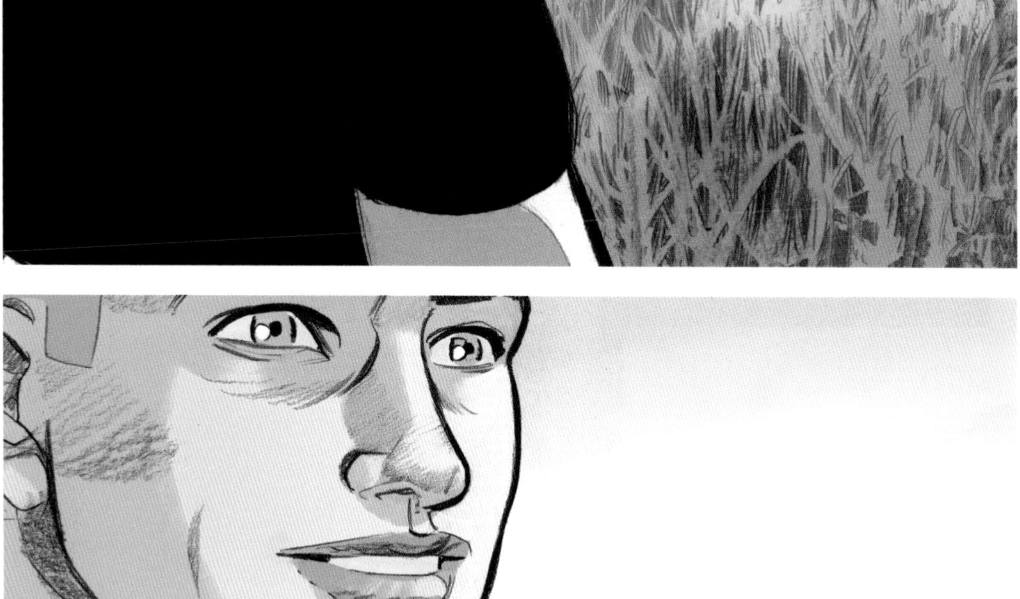

A PROMISE IS A PROMISE, OLD FRIEND...

FOR WHAT IT'S WORTH, I'M SORRY.

I HOPE YOU'RE IN A BETTER PLACE.

AS FOR ME... HOW DOES THAT SAYING GO?

* "I am not looking for peace. I cannot stand war…" translated from the poem "Pace non cerco" by Dino Campana.

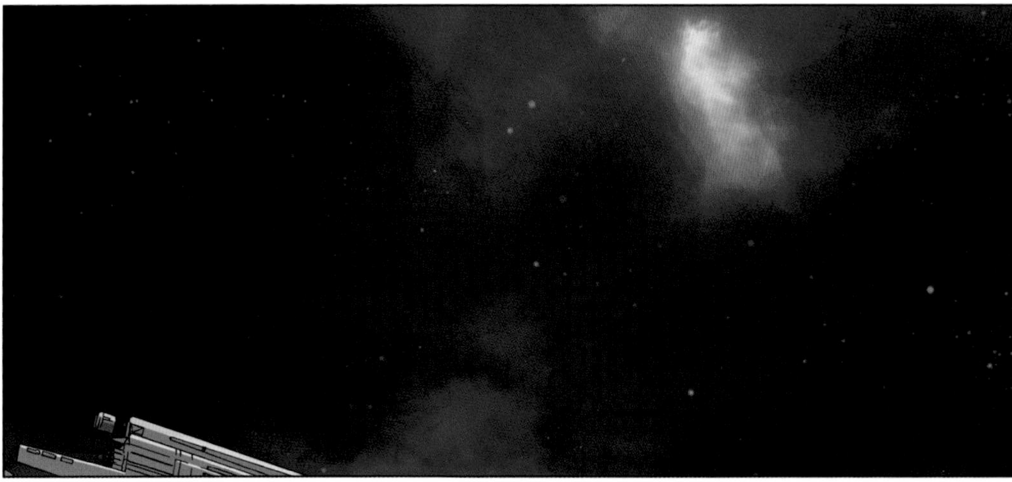

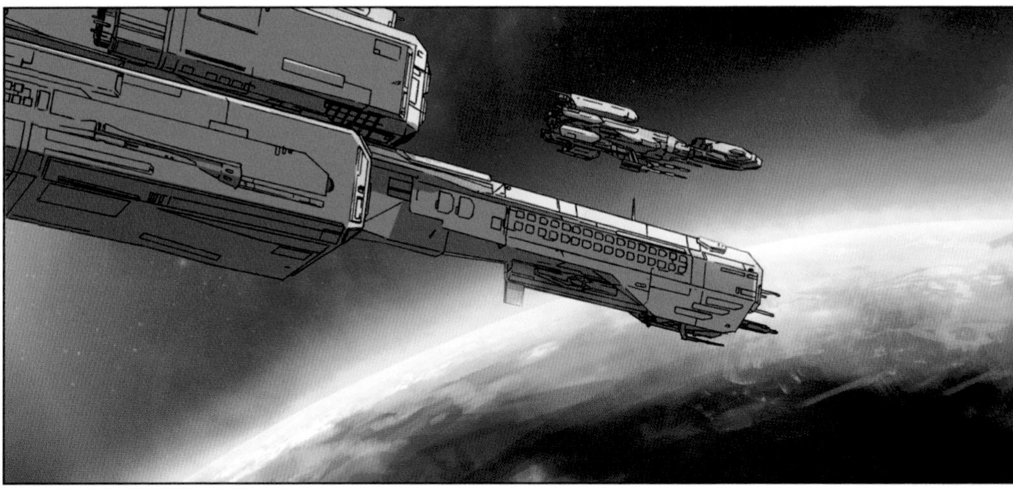

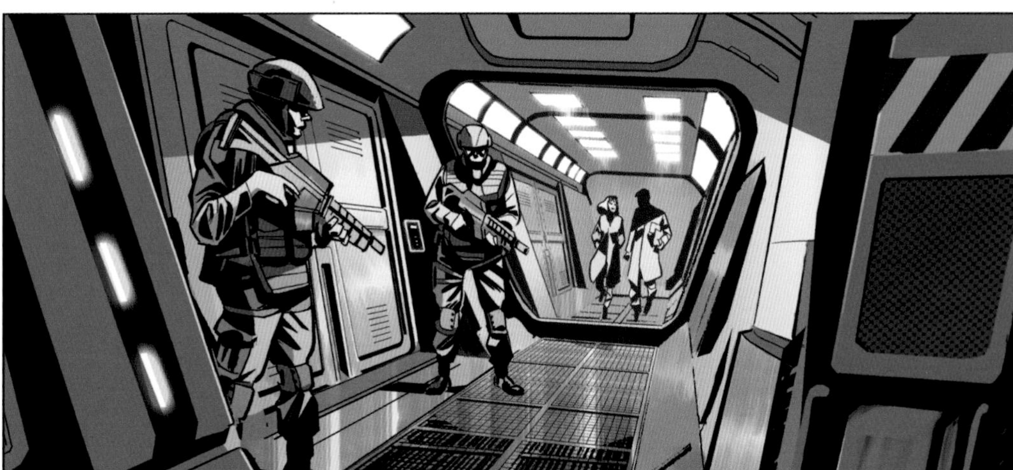

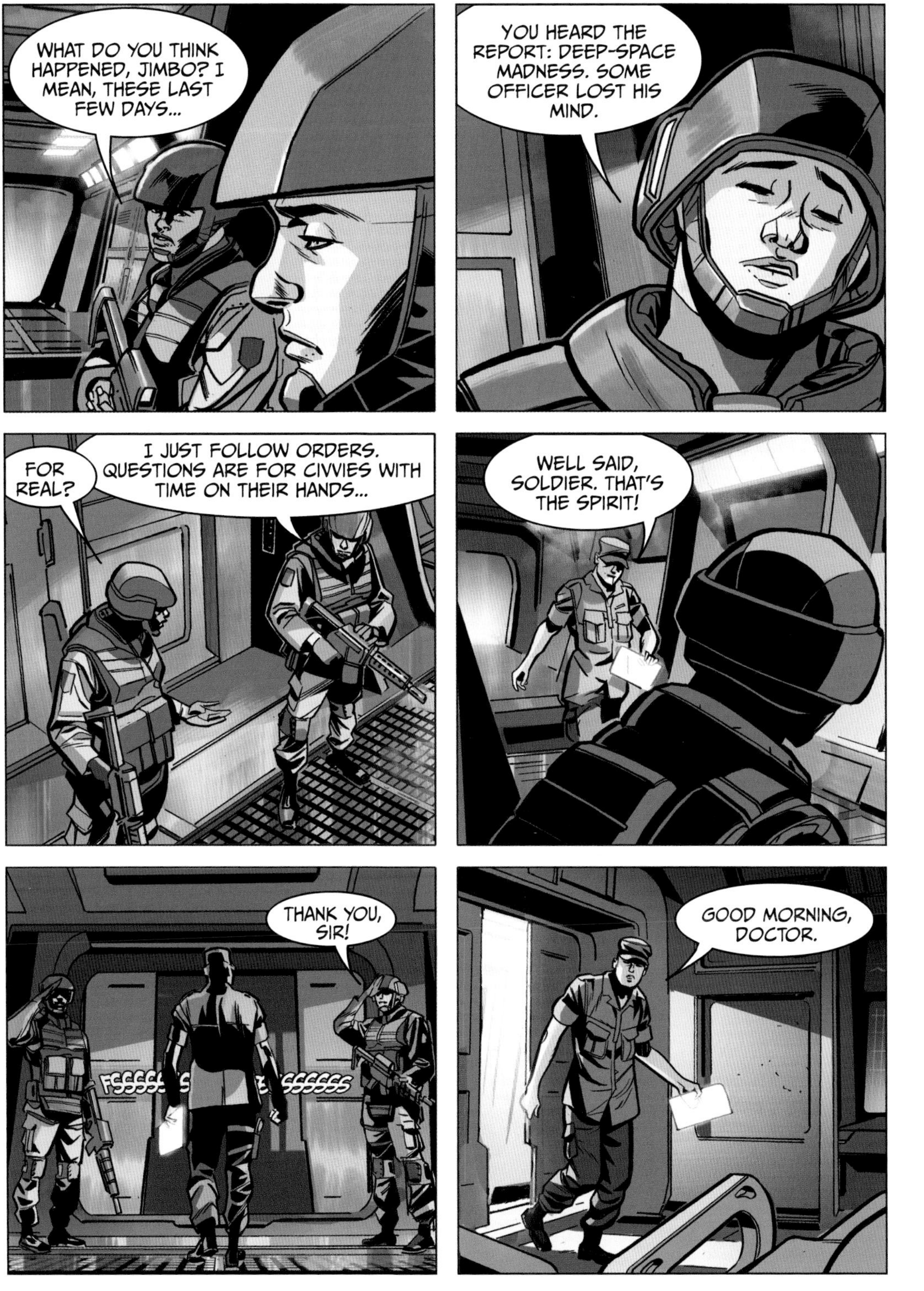
WHAT DO YOU THINK HAPPENED, JIMBO? I MEAN, THESE LAST FEW DAYS...
YOU HEARD THE REPORT: DEEP-SPACE MADNESS. SOME OFFICER LOST HIS MIND.
FOR REAL?
I JUST FOLLOW ORDERS. QUESTIONS ARE FOR CIVVIES WITH TIME ON THEIR HANDS...
WELL SAID, SOLDIER. THAT'S THE SPIRIT!
FSSSSSS SSSSSSS
THANK YOU, SIR!
GOOD MORNING, DOCTOR.

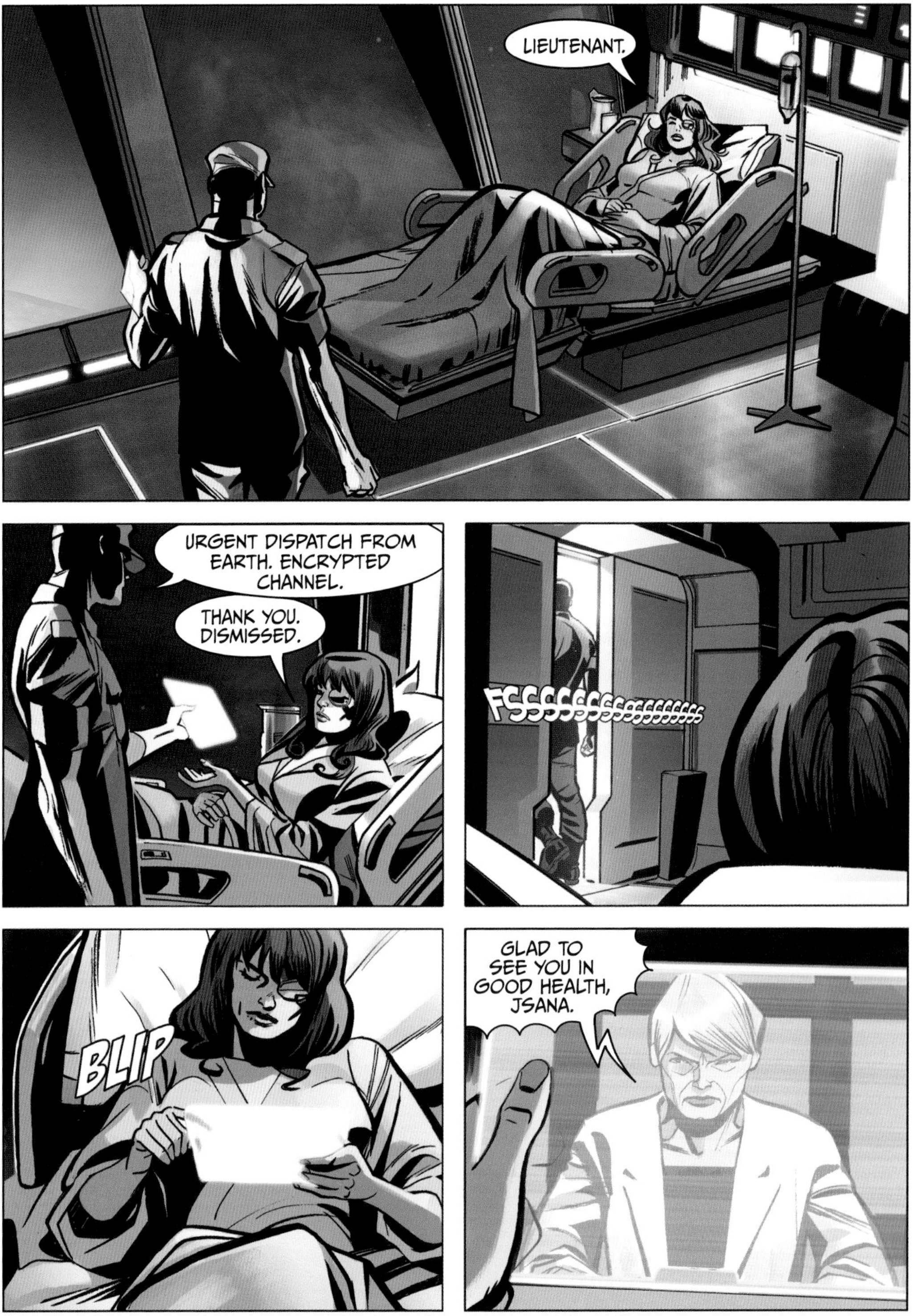
LIEUTENANT.
URGENT DISPATCH FROM EARTH. ENCRYPTED CHANNEL.
THANK YOU. DISMISSED.
FSSSSSSSSSSSSSSSSS
BLIP
GLAD TO SEE YOU IN GOOD HEALTH, JSANA.

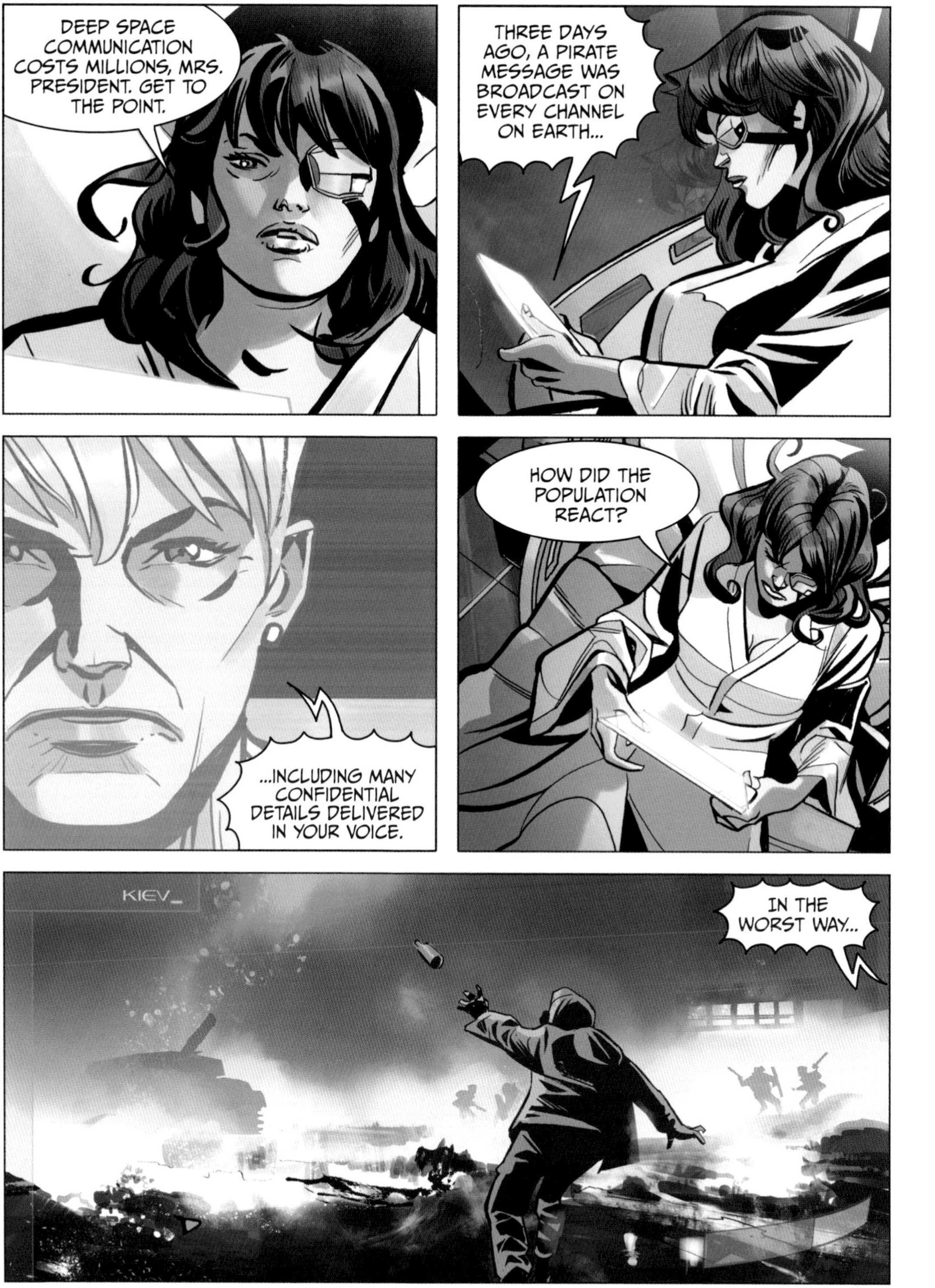
DEEP SPACE COMMUNICATION COSTS MILLIONS, MRS. PRESIDENT. GET TO THE POINT.
THREE DAYS AGO, A PIRATE MESSAGE WAS BROADCAST ON EVERY CHANNEL ON EARTH...
...INCLUDING MANY CONFIDENTIAL DETAILS DELIVERED IN YOUR VOICE.
HOW DID THE POPULATION REACT?
KIEV_
IN THE WORST WAY...

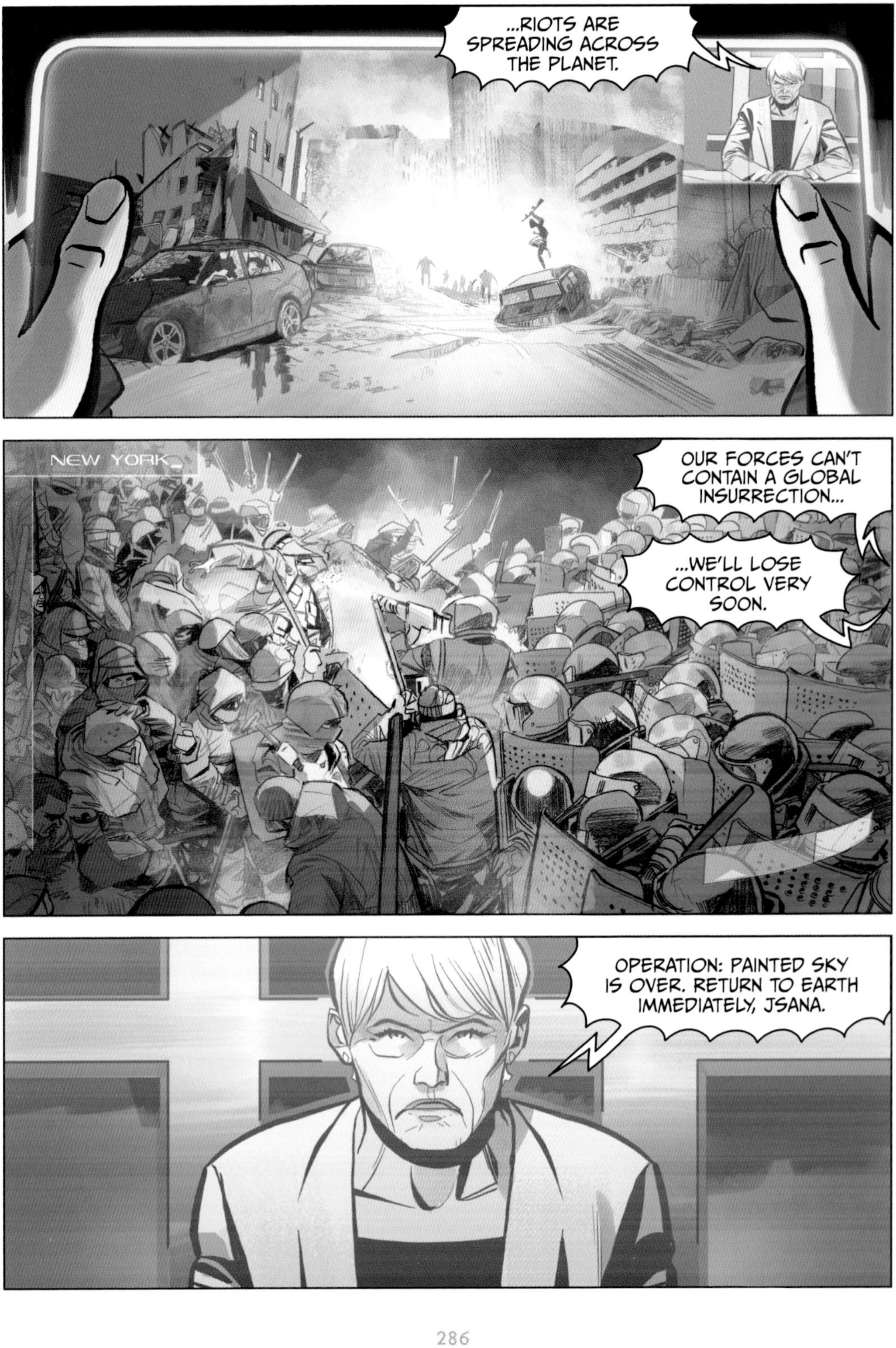
...RIOTS ARE SPREADING ACROSS THE PLANET.
NEW YORK_
OUR FORCES CAN'T CONTAIN A GLOBAL INSURRECTION...
...WE'LL LOSE CONTROL VERY SOON.
OPERATION: PAINTED SKY IS OVER. RETURN TO EARTH IMMEDIATELY, JSANA.

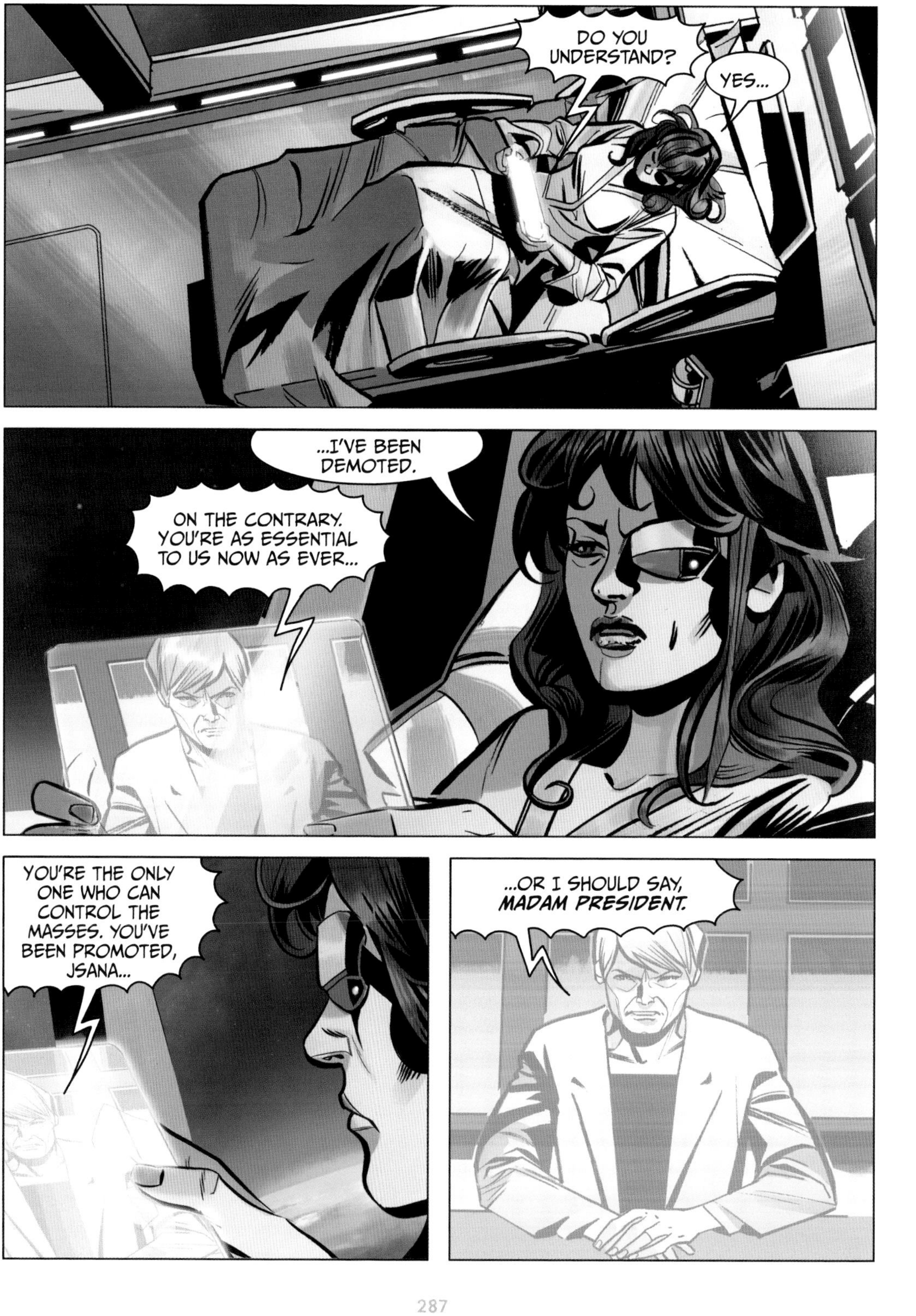
DO YOU UNDERSTAND?
YES...
...I'VE BEEN DEMOTED.
ON THE CONTRARY. YOU'RE AS ESSENTIAL TO US NOW AS EVER...
YOU'RE THE ONLY ONE WHO CAN CONTROL THE MASSES. YOU'VE BEEN PROMOTED, JSANA...
...OR I SHOULD SAY, *MADAM PRESIDENT.*

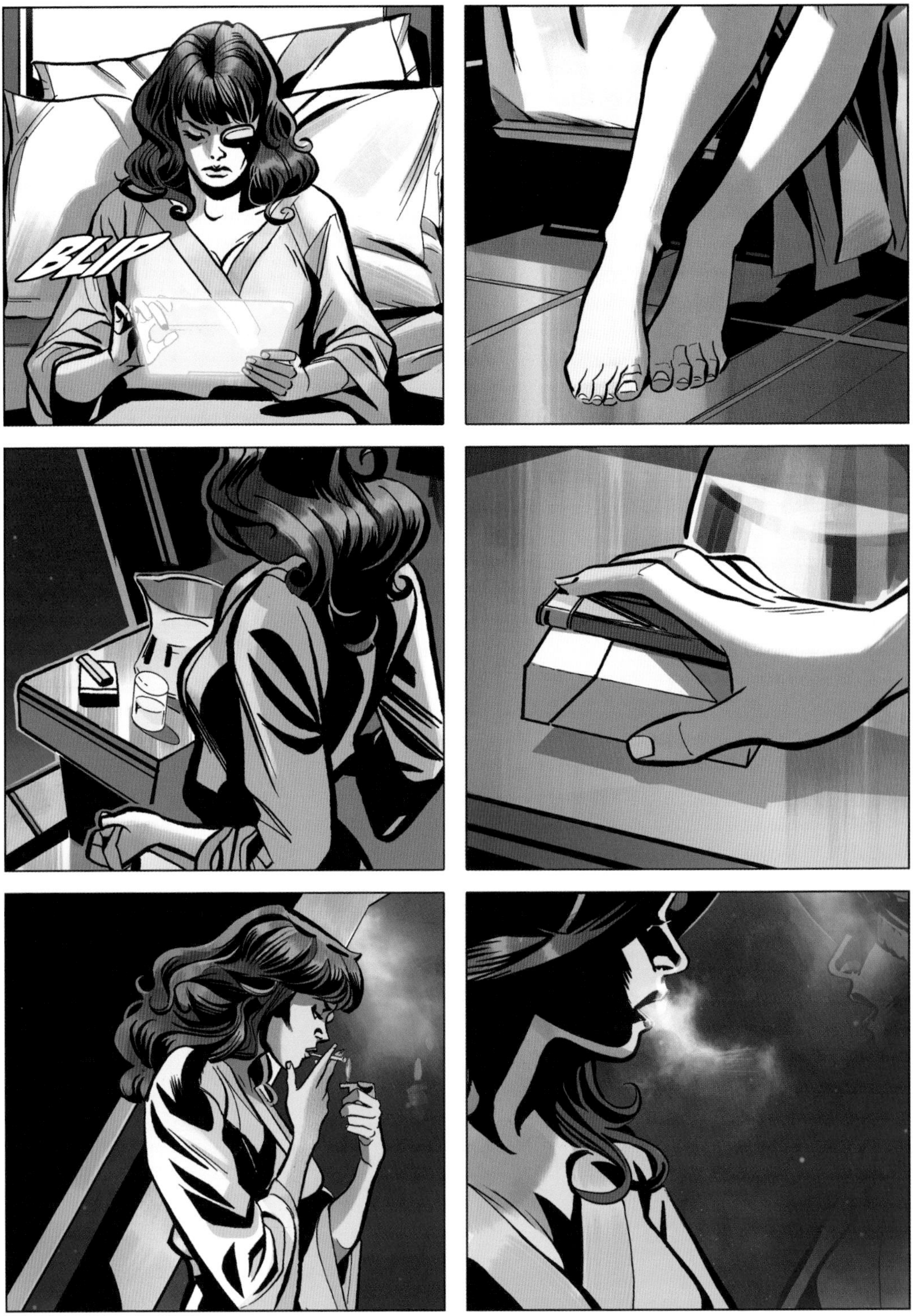
BLIP

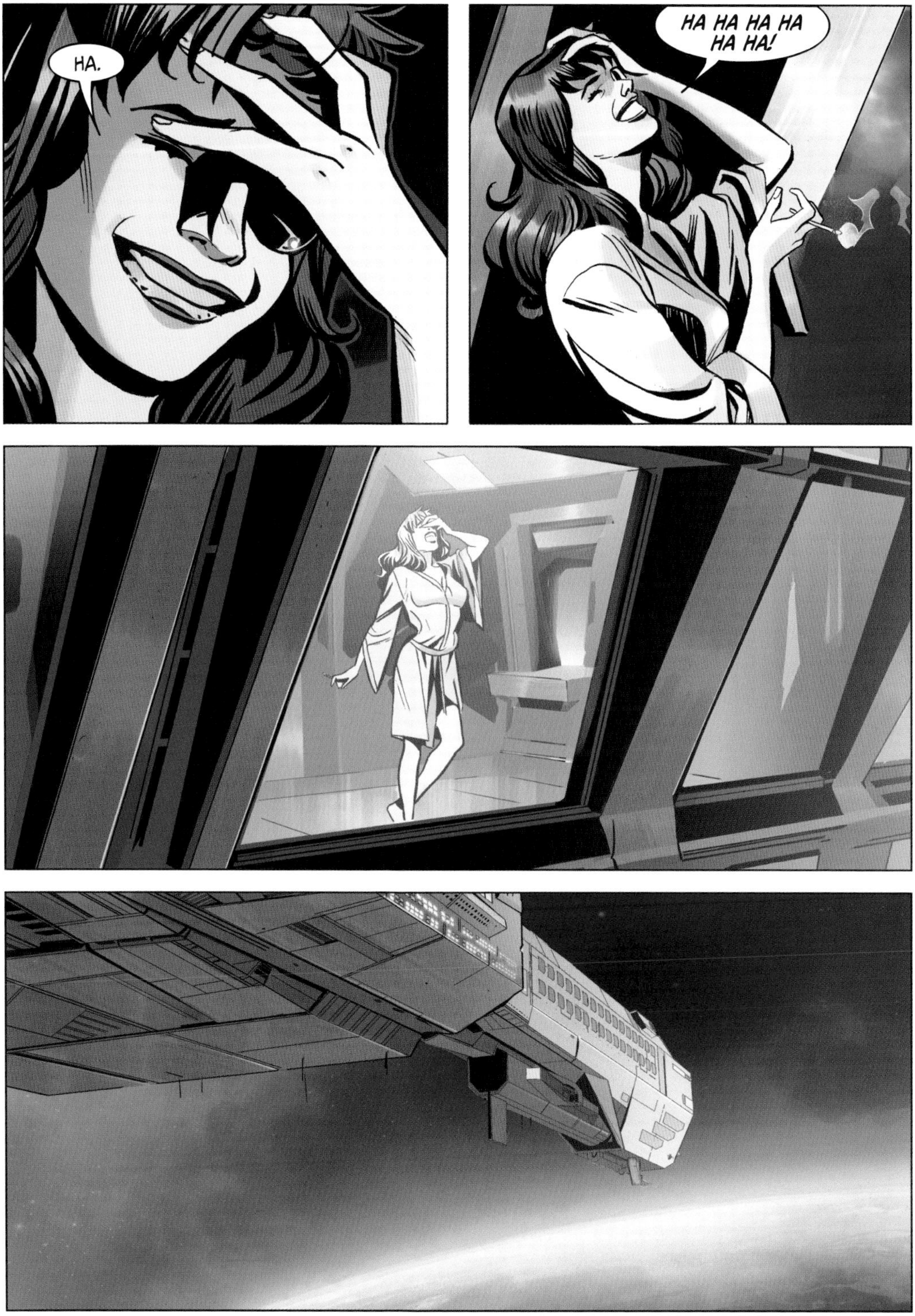
HA.
HA HA HA HA
HA HA!

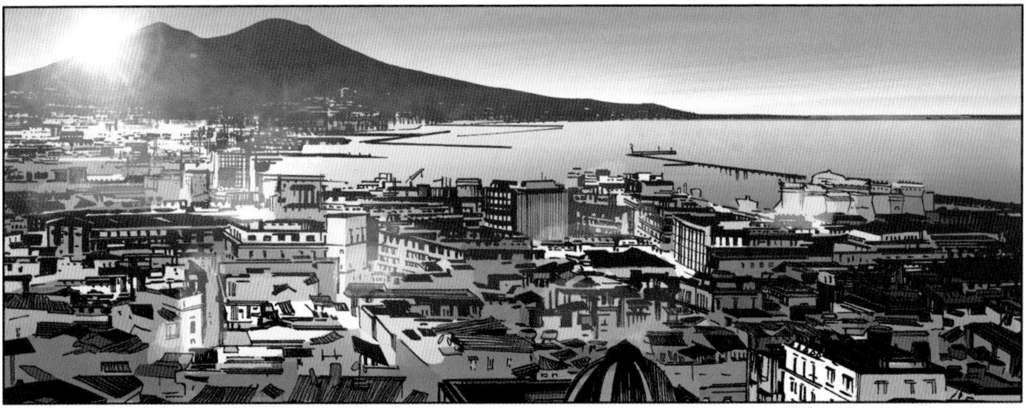

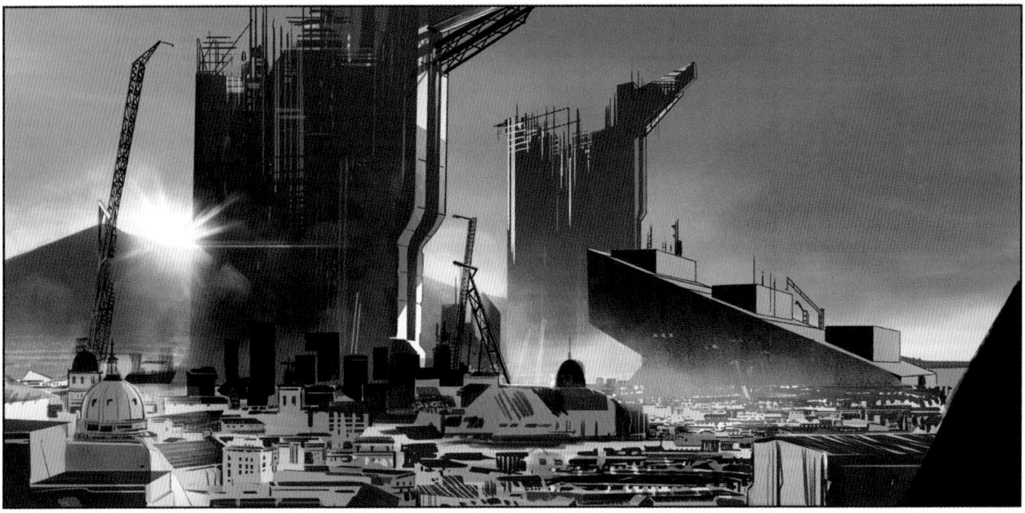

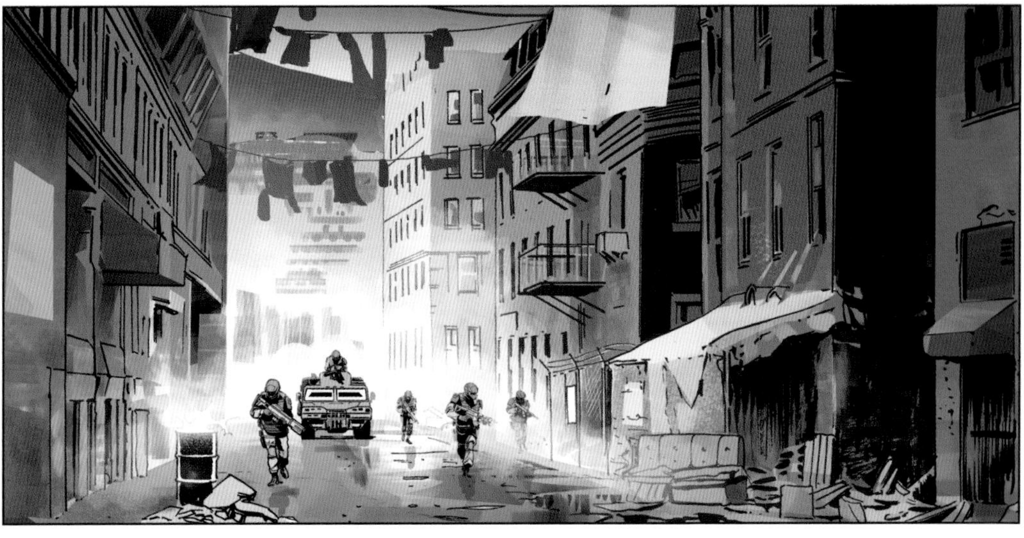

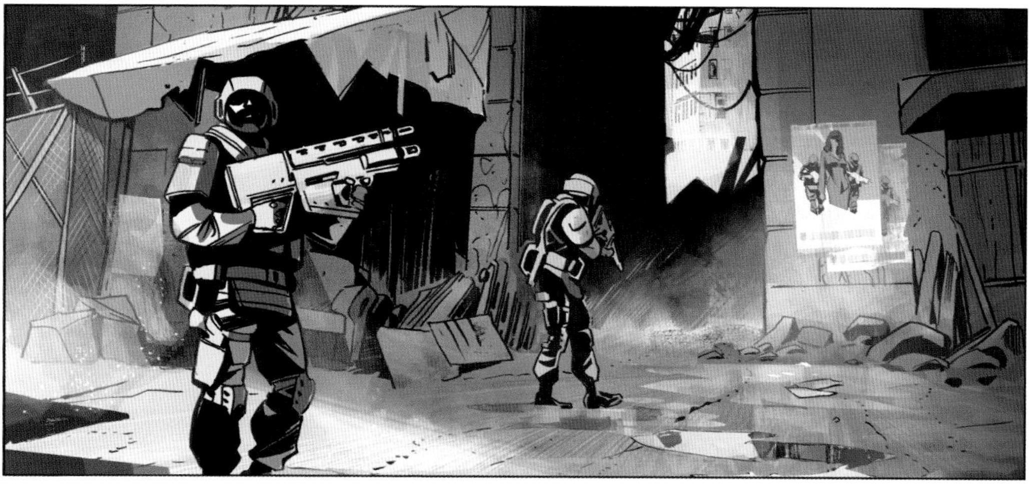

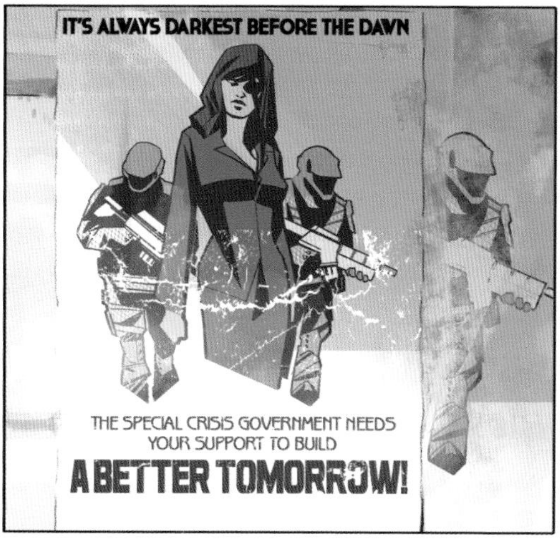
IT'S ALWAYS DARKEST BEFORE THE DAWN
THE SPECIAL CRISIS GOVERNMENT NEEDS YOUR SUPPORT TO BUILD
A BETTER TOMORROW!

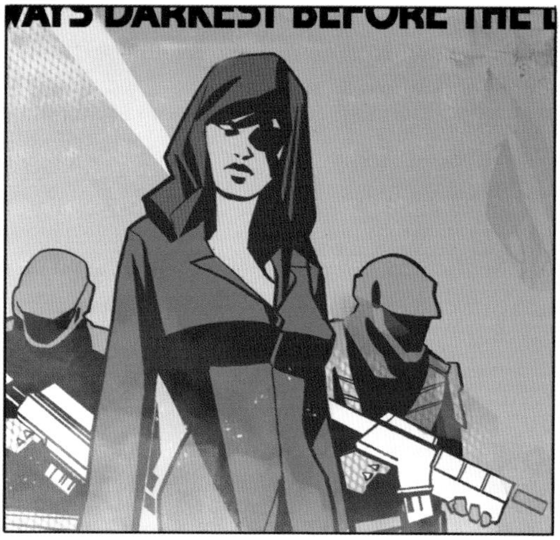

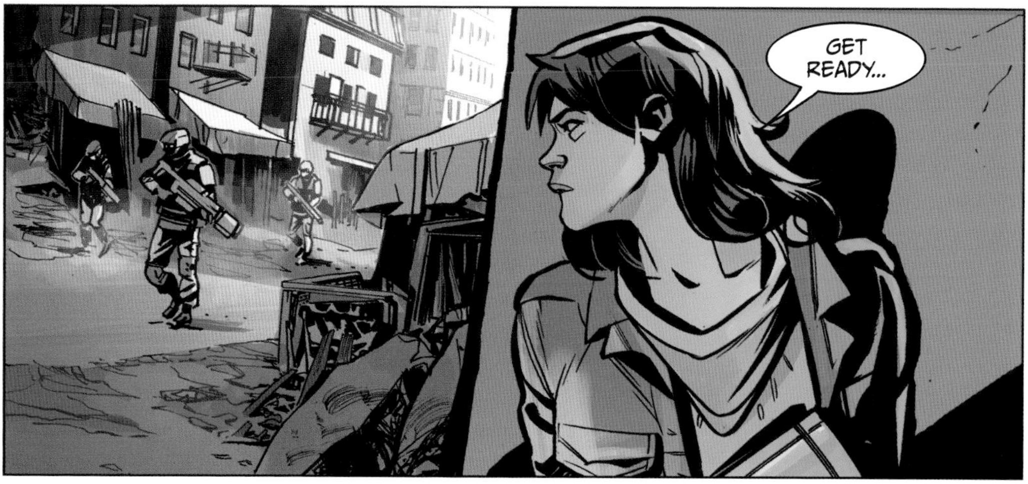
GET READY...

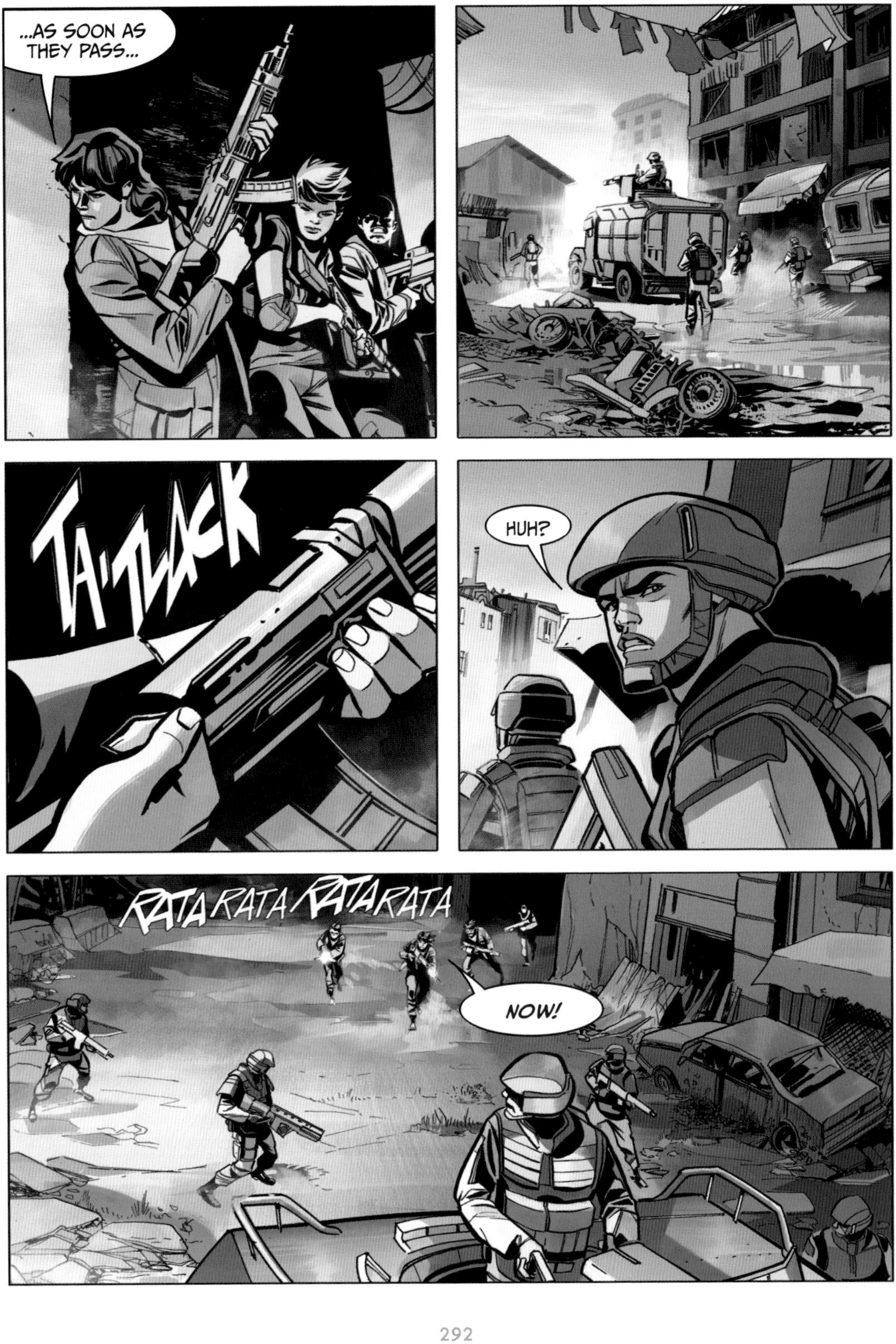
...AS SOON AS THEY PASS...
TA-TLACK
HUH?
RATA RATA RATA RATA
NOW!

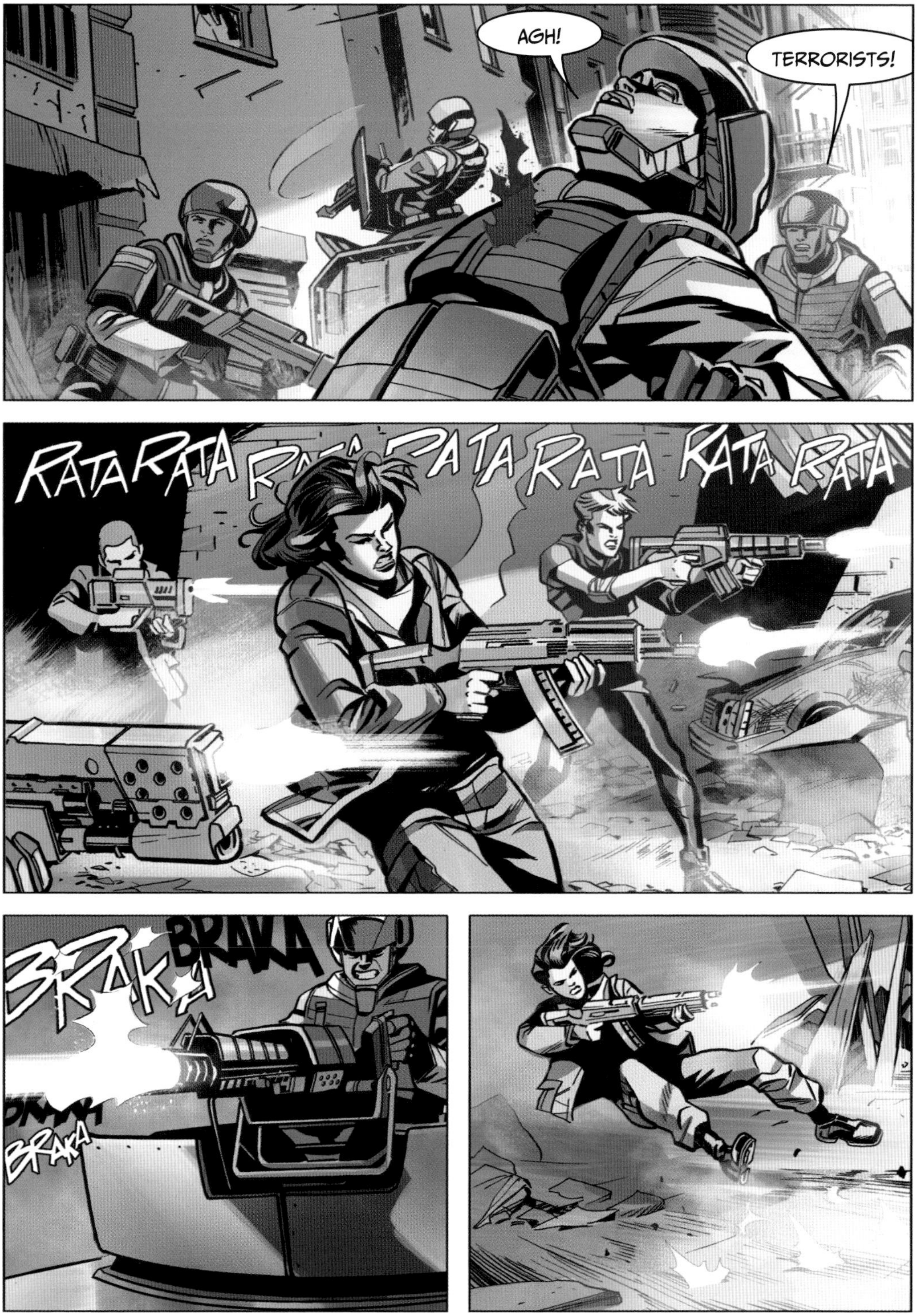
AGH!
TERRORISTS!
RATA RATA
RATA
RATA
RATA
RATA
BRAKA
BRAKA

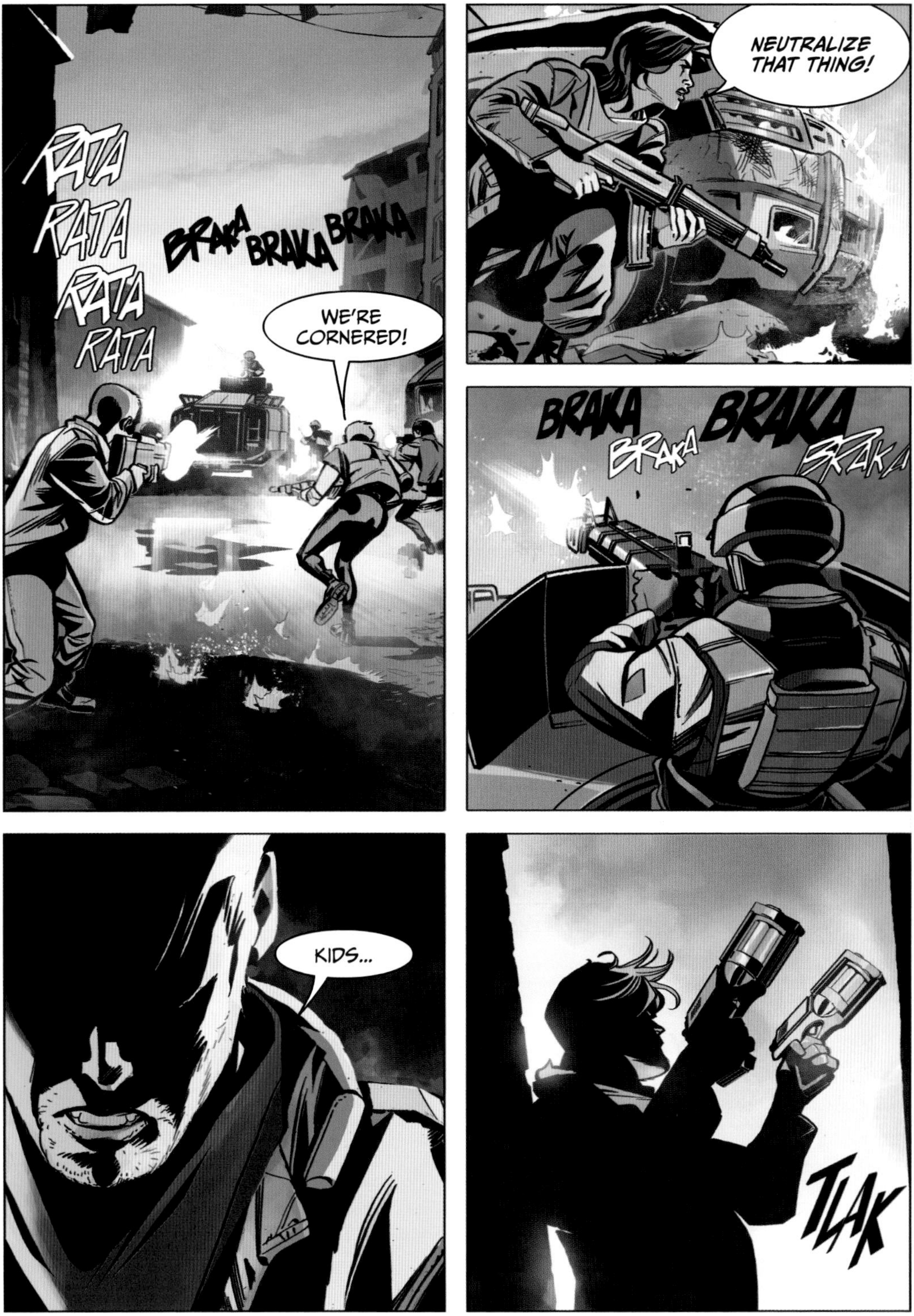
RATA
RATA
RATA
RATA
BRAKA
BRAKA
BRAKA
WE'RE CORNERED!
NEUTRALIZE THAT THING!
BRAKA
BRAKA
BRAKA
BRAKA
KIDS...
TLAK

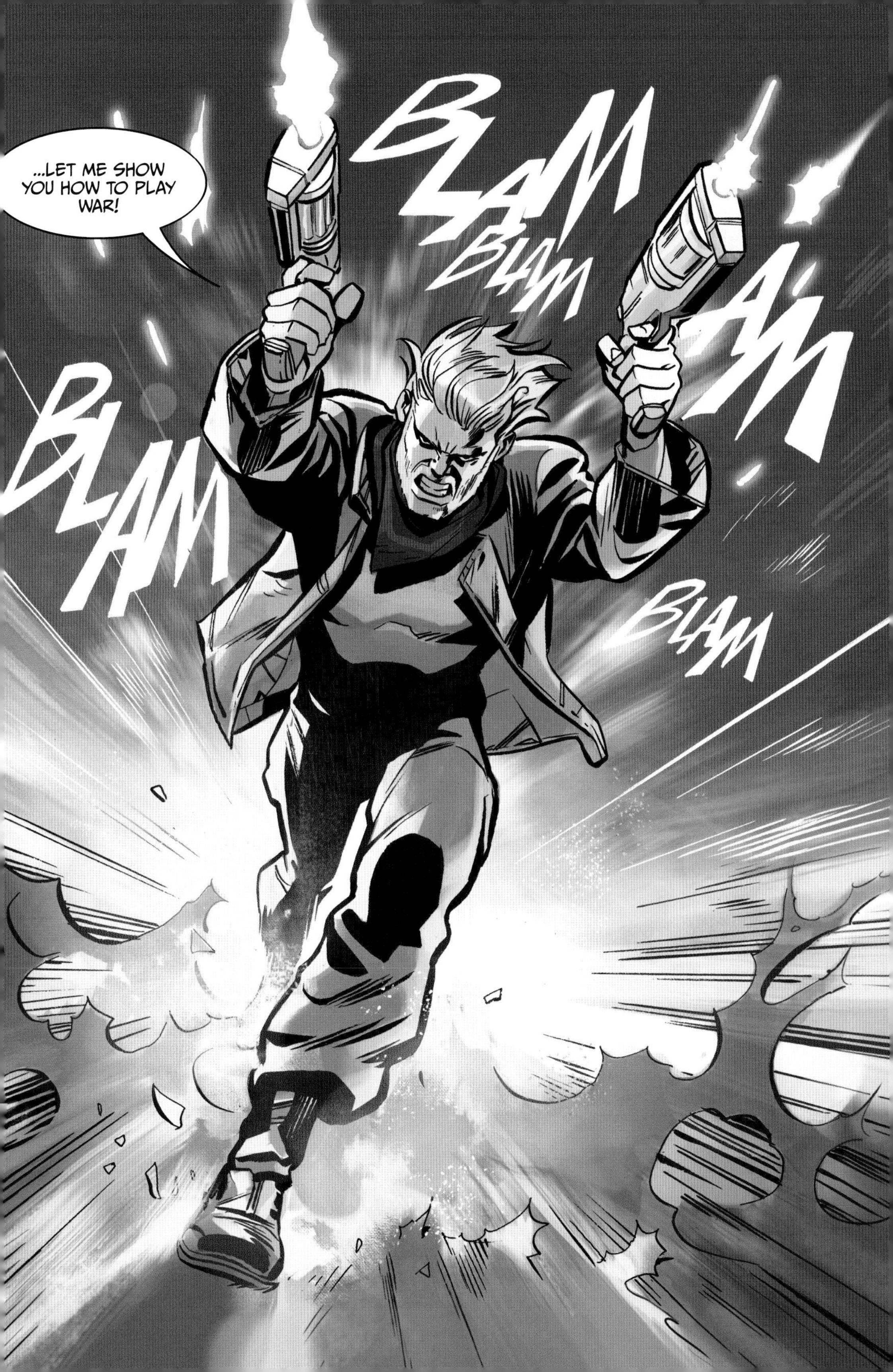
...LET ME SHOW YOU HOW TO PLAY WAR!
BLAM
BLAM
BLAM
BLAM
BLAM
BLAM

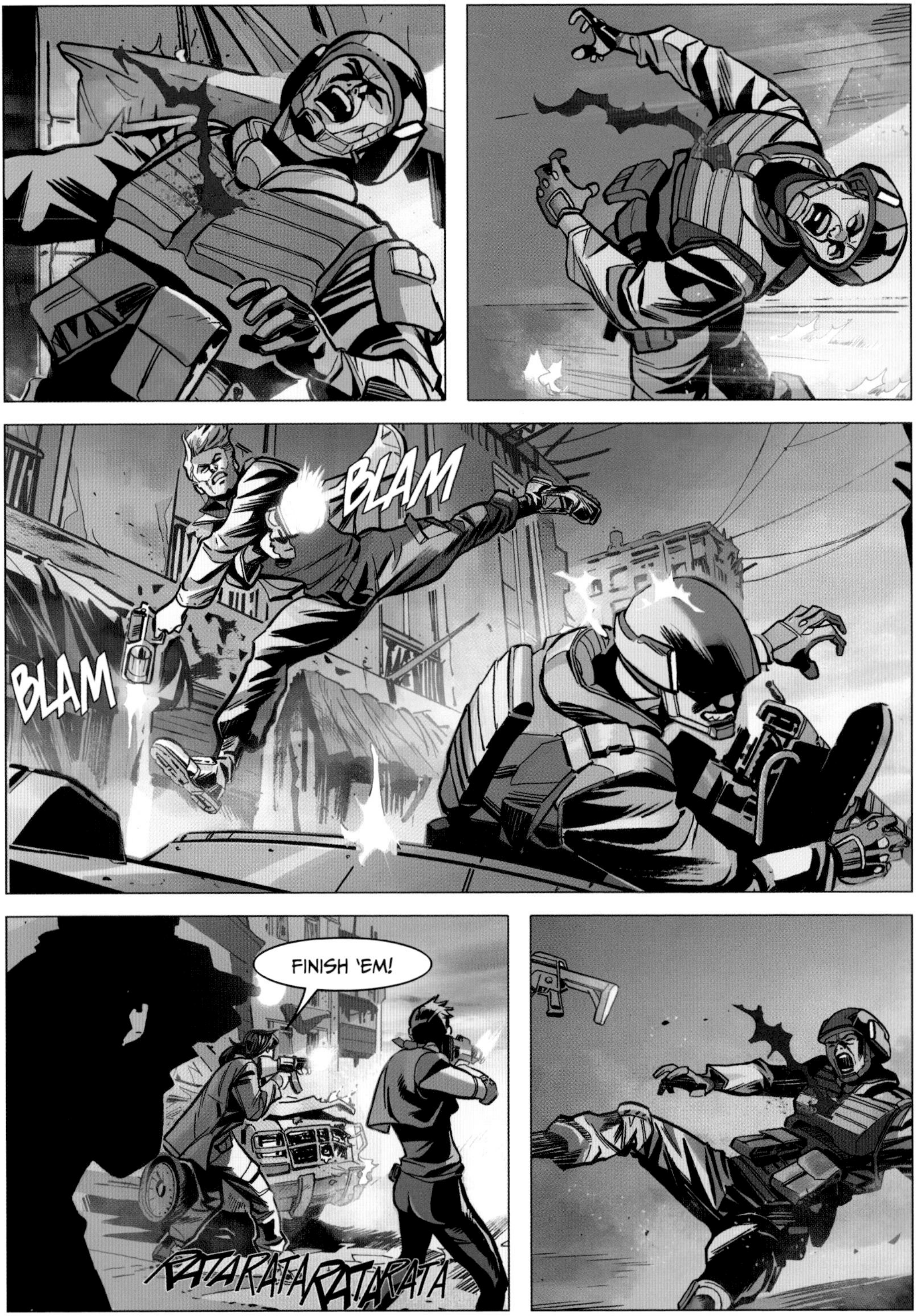
BLAM
BLAM
FINISH 'EM!
RATATARATATARATATARATA

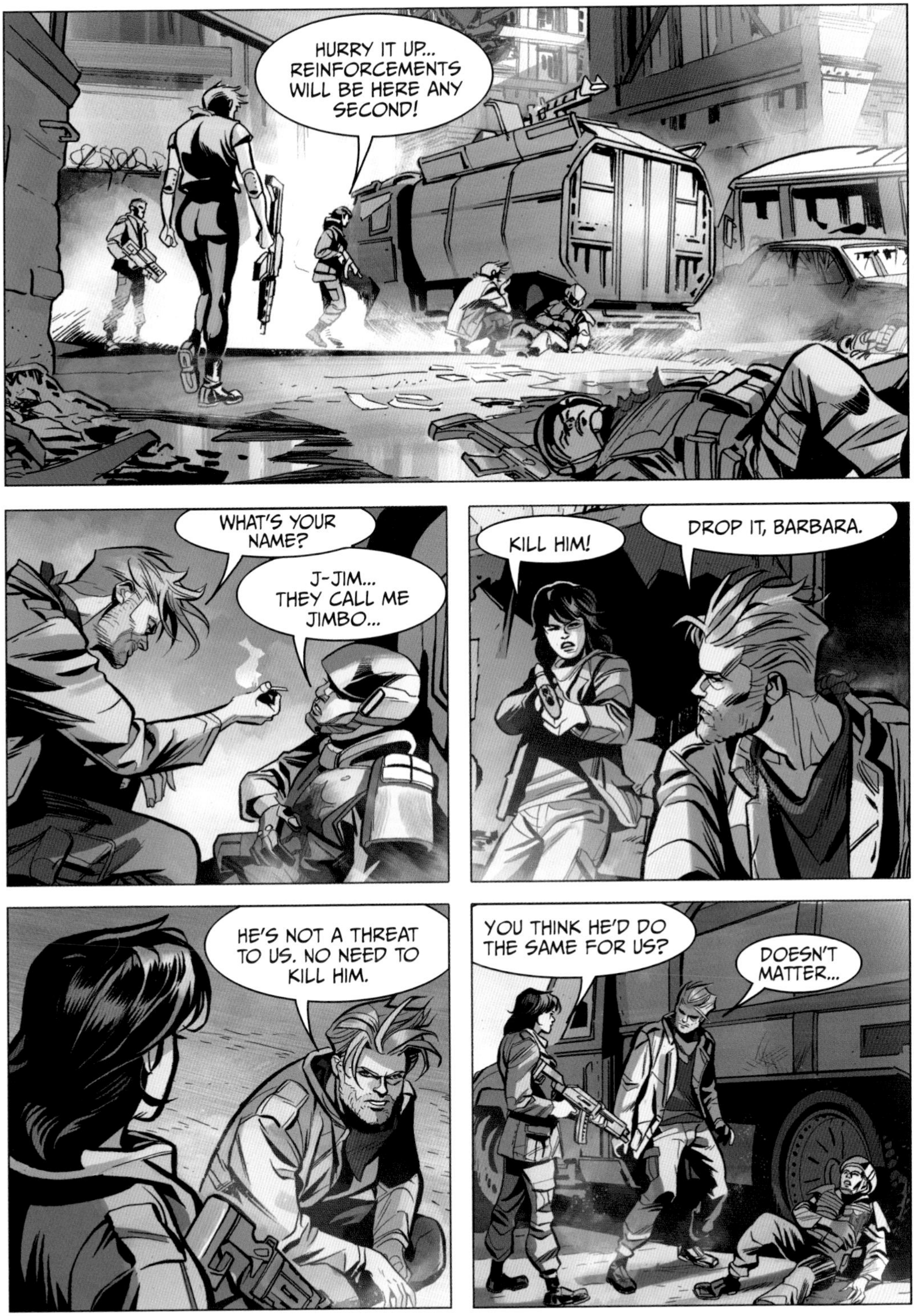
HURRY IT UP... REINFORCEMENTS WILL BE HERE ANY SECOND!
WHAT'S YOUR NAME?
J-JIM... THEY CALL ME JIMBO...
KILL HIM!
DROP IT, BARBARA.
HE'S NOT A THREAT TO US. NO NEED TO KILL HIM.
YOU THINK HE'D DO THE SAME FOR US?
DOESN'T MATTER...

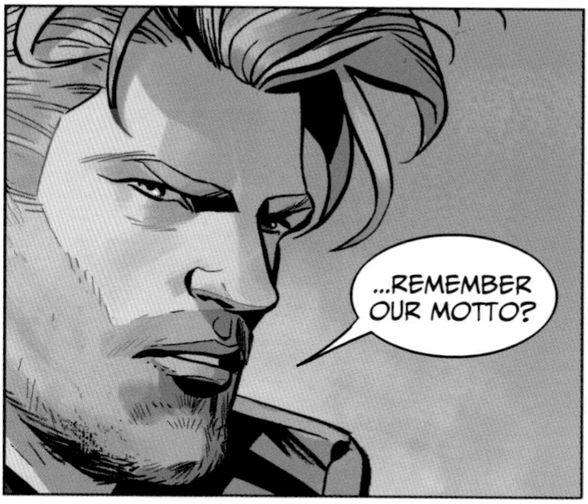
...REMEMBER OUR MOTTO?

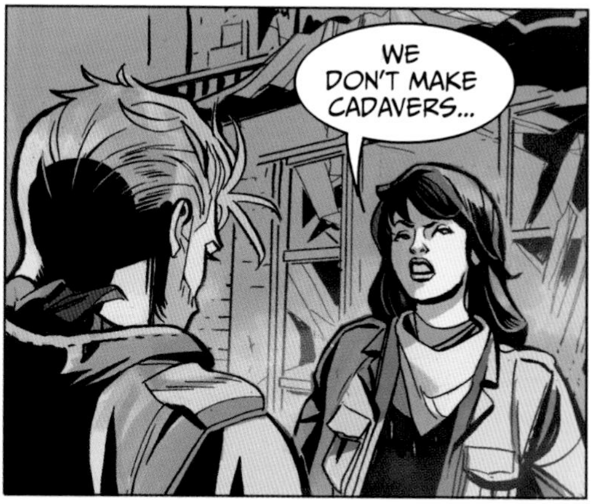
WE DON'T MAKE CADAVERS...

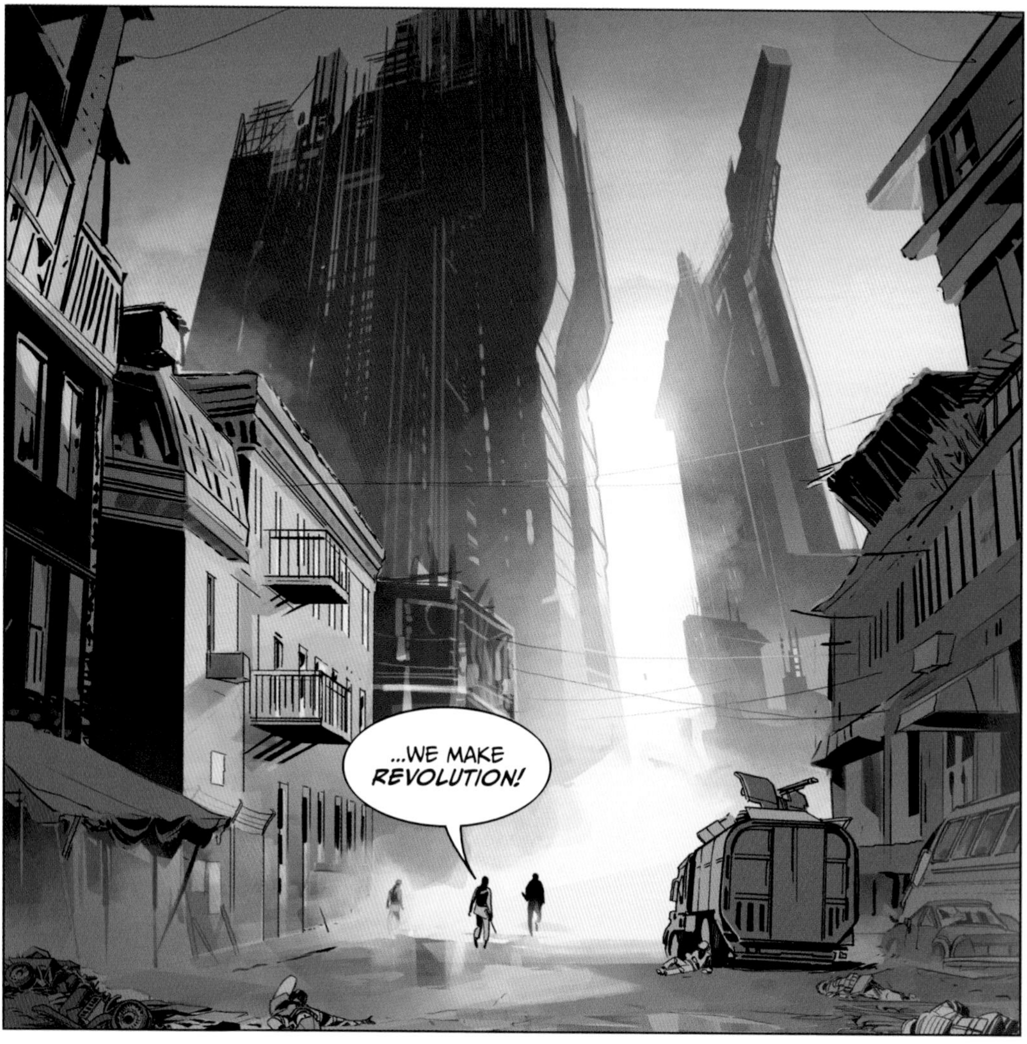
...WE MAKE *REVOLUTION!*

EMILIANO MAMMUCARI — ARTIST

When and where were you born? And where do you live now?

I was born in Velletri, Castelli Romani, on April 21st, 1975. I still live here in the country.

What is your artistic education?

I attended a classical high school, so I had no artistic education whatsoever. After graduating, I enrolled in a comics school and then immediately started working.

Let's talk about your previous works, before *Orphans*.

I started with *Povero Pinocchio*, a graphic novel (though at the time they weren't called that) published by Montego. After that, I drew the first episode of the successful series *John Doe* for Eura Editoriale and then started working for Bonelli, specifically on *Napoleone, Jan Dix, Caravan* and finally *Orphans*.

When did you start working on *Orphans*, and when did you finish drawing this chapter?

It was a complicated process. I started in April, 2012. When I was halfway through, I stopped to start designing the second season of *Orphans* before coming back to this episode about a year later. At a certain point, Roberto and I realized we lacked something in terms of rhythm, and what was initially a panel portraying London's destruction became a double page spread. We also disassembled and reassembled the dream sequence to create some balance with Jonas's dying hallucinations.

What tools did you use?

For the parts set in the past, I only used pencils. For the ones set in the present, I used ink. The final part, set in Naples, is digitally painted.

What was the most difficult scene and which one did you have to redraw more times?

The scene with Juno's corpse. It hurt. I lived with these characters for almost five years.

If you could go back in time, what would you change about this chapter?

This story is a nice snapshot of the period we lived through. There's chaos, confusion, and the intensity and pathos of those days. I find it asymmetric and unbalanced: it's perfect as it is.

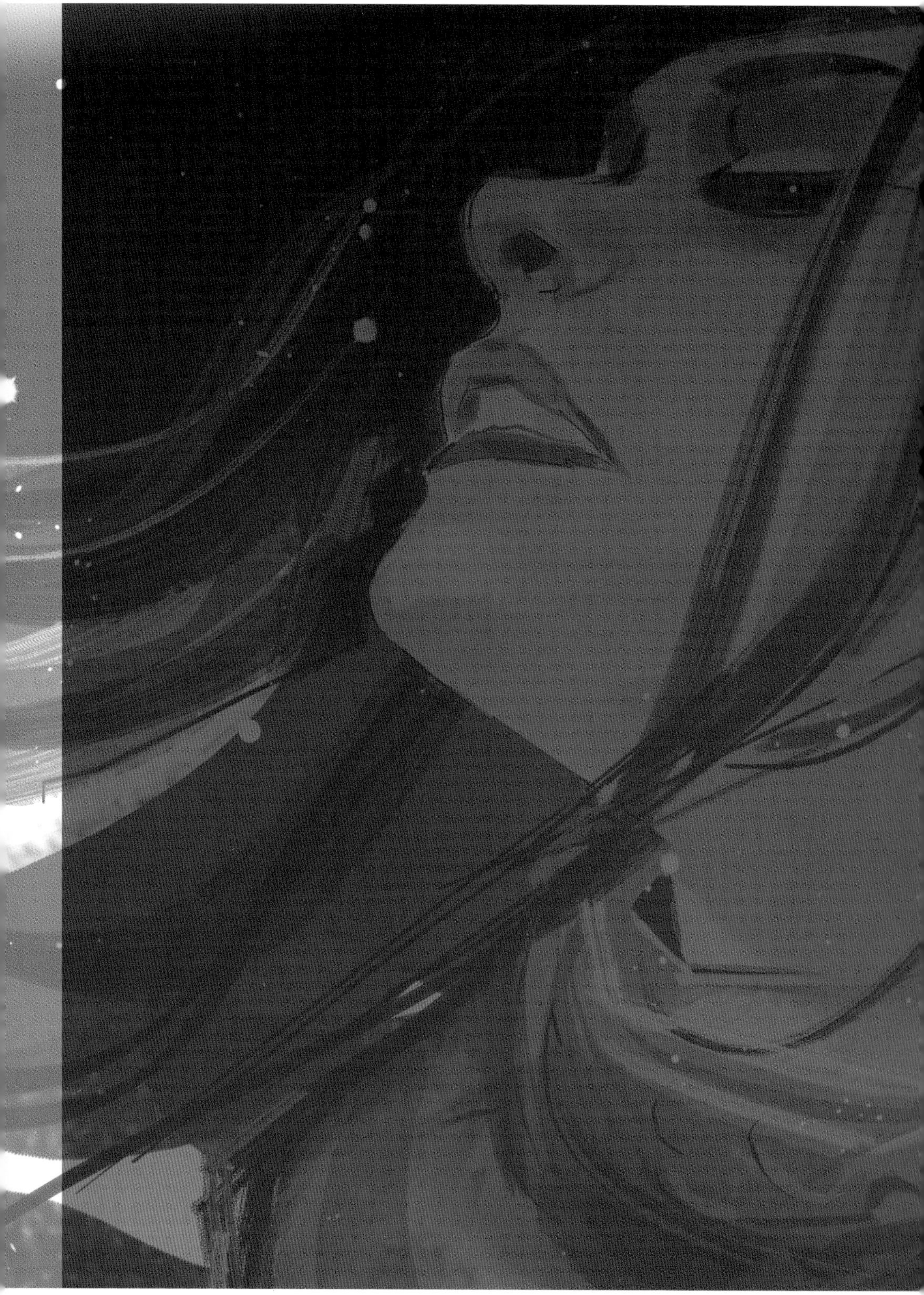

ORPHANS

EXTRA

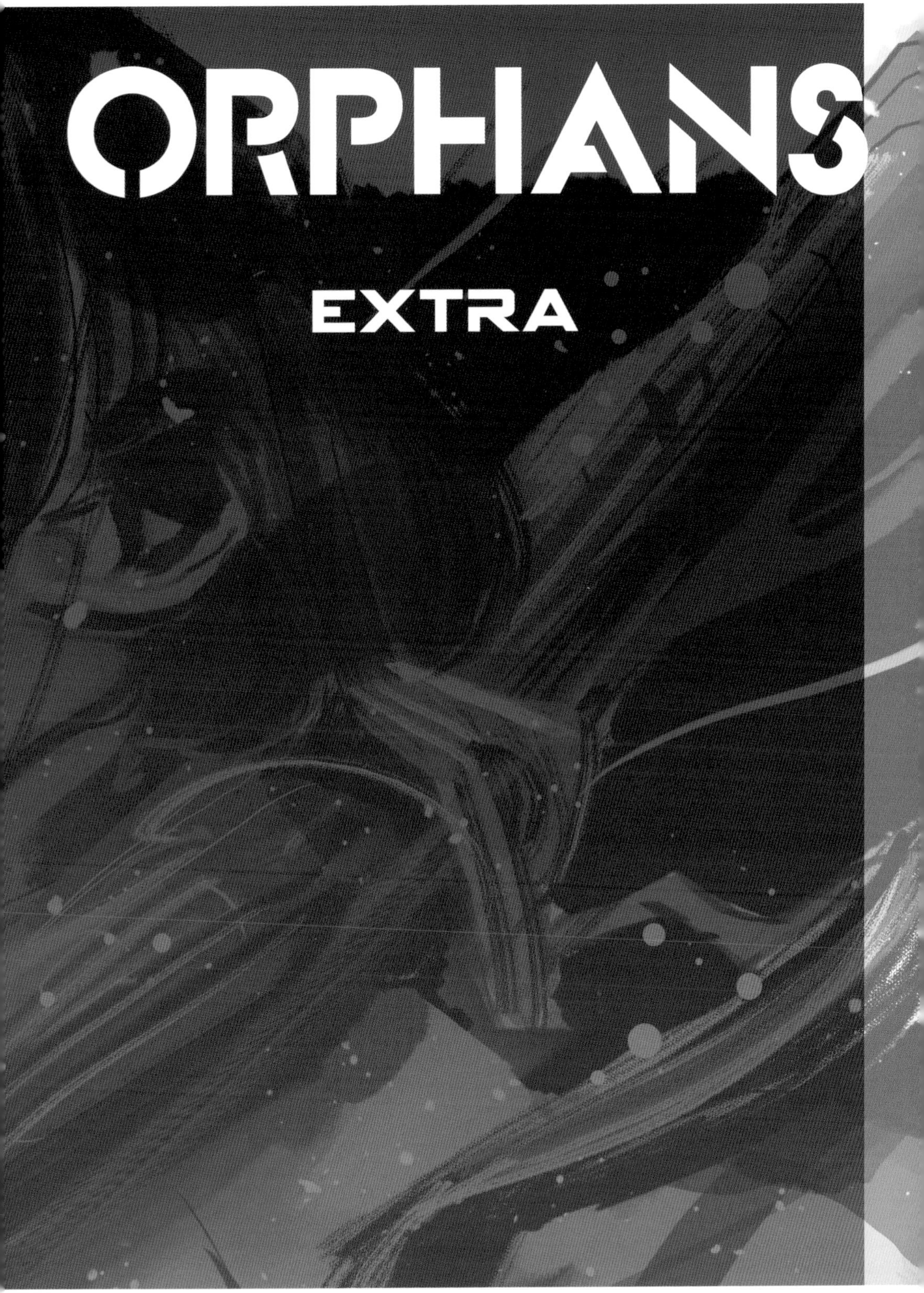

TO ME, WRITING A STORY IS ONE OF THE MOST POLITICAL ACTS ONE CAN DO. EVEN WHEN IT'S FULL OF EXPLOSIONS, FIGHTS, SPECIAL EFFECTS, AND DRAMATIC TURNS OF EVENTS.

– ROBERTO RECCHIONI

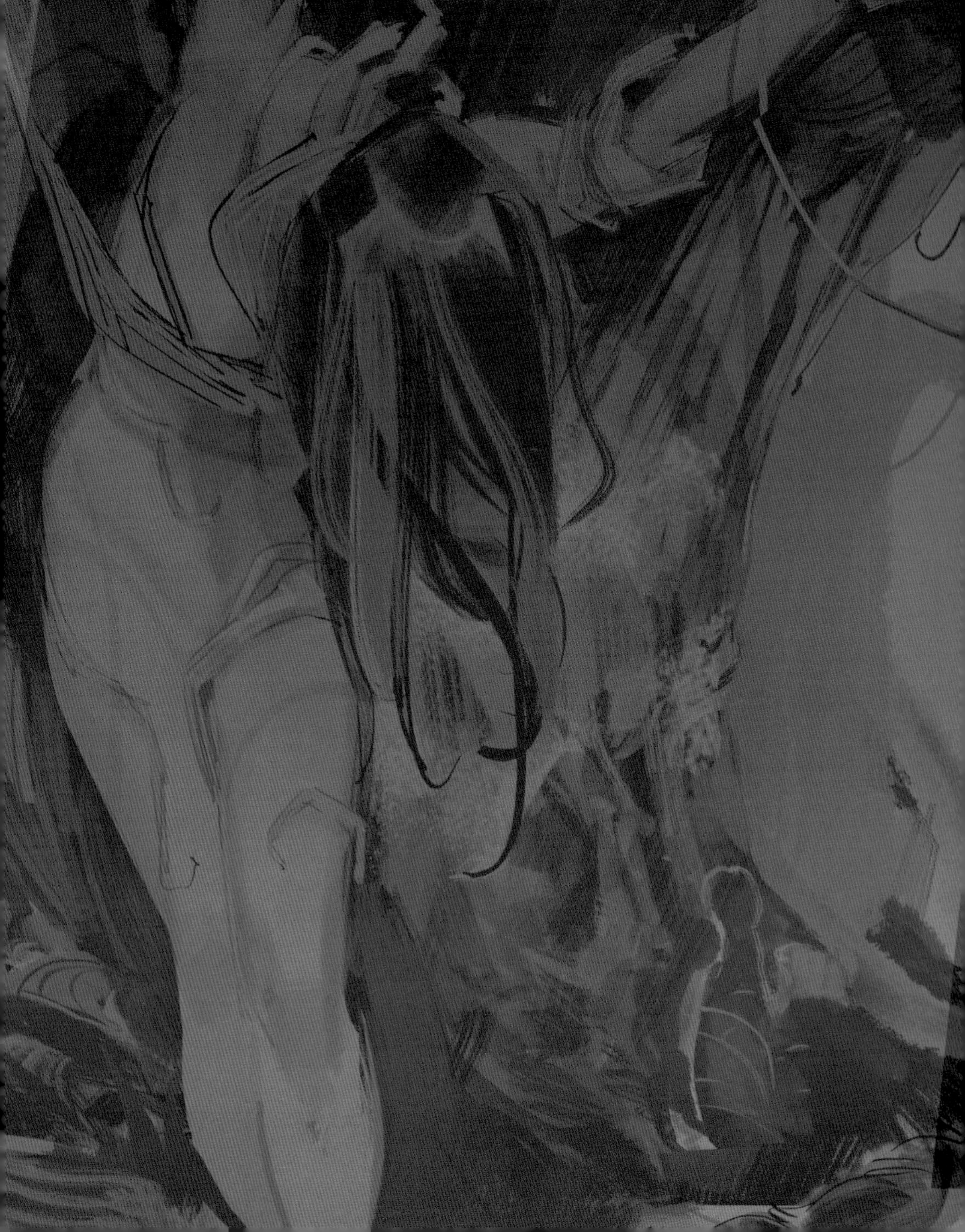

CHOOSE OR DIE

by *ROBERTO RECCHIONI*

I spent a great part of my life convinced that many of our choices
are political, even if we don't realize it: our actions, the causes we
choose to embrace or to fight, the jobs we accept to do and who
we accept to work for, as well as the jobs we refuse to do. Even the
people we choose to love. They're all political choices, that define
us within our universe.

Previous page: sketches by Gigi Cavenago

Below: sketch by Emiliano Mammucari

Needless to say, to me, writing a story is one of the most political acts one can do. Even when it's full of explosions, fights, special effects, and dramatic turns of events. In this regard, *Orphans* is one of the most political stories I've ever told. From the initial cue (a very simple metaphor of 9/11), continuing through the story (the war, an invasion of a strange land in search of non-existent weapons of mass destruction). In *Orphans*, Emiliano and I tried to talk about some of the tensions affecting our world today.

THESE TWO PAGES: DRAWINGS AND STUDIES BY EMILIANO MAMMUCARI

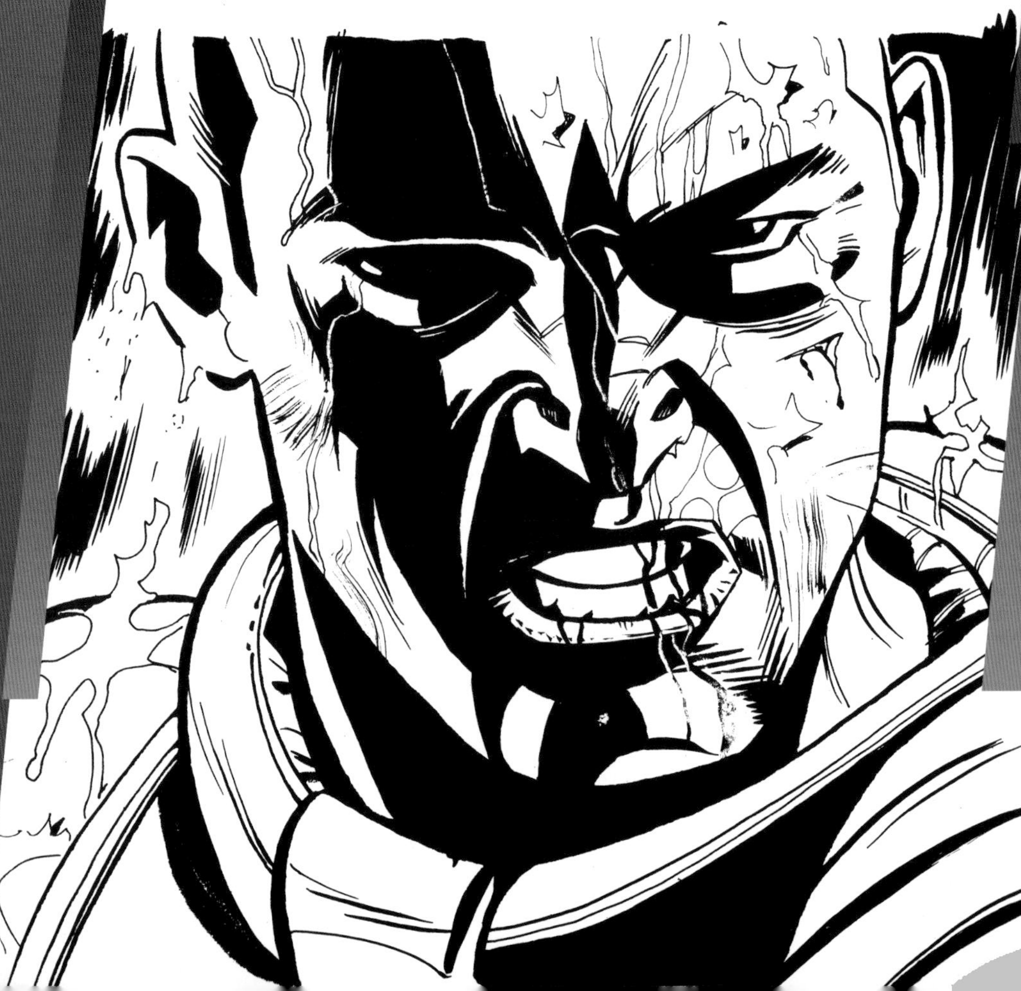

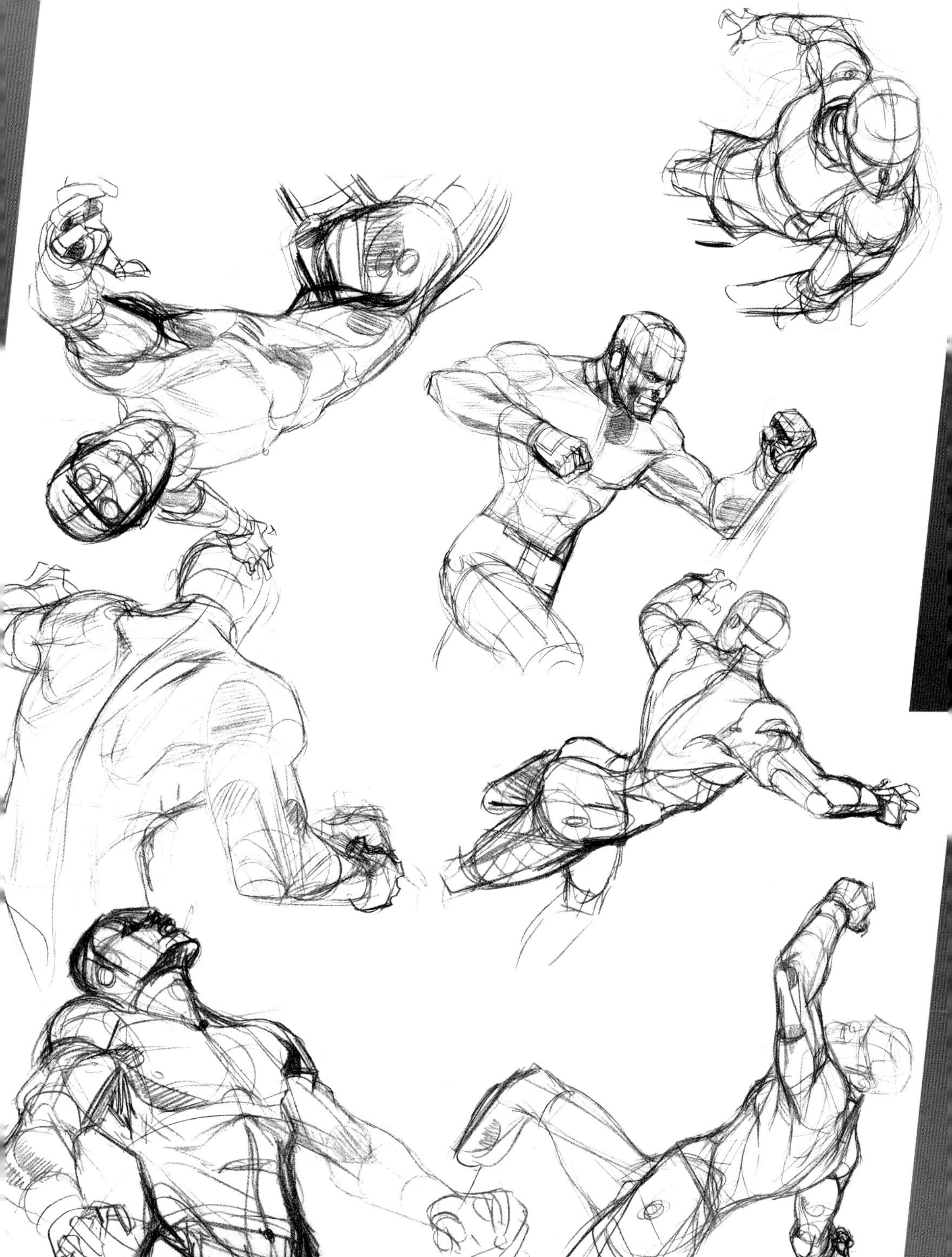

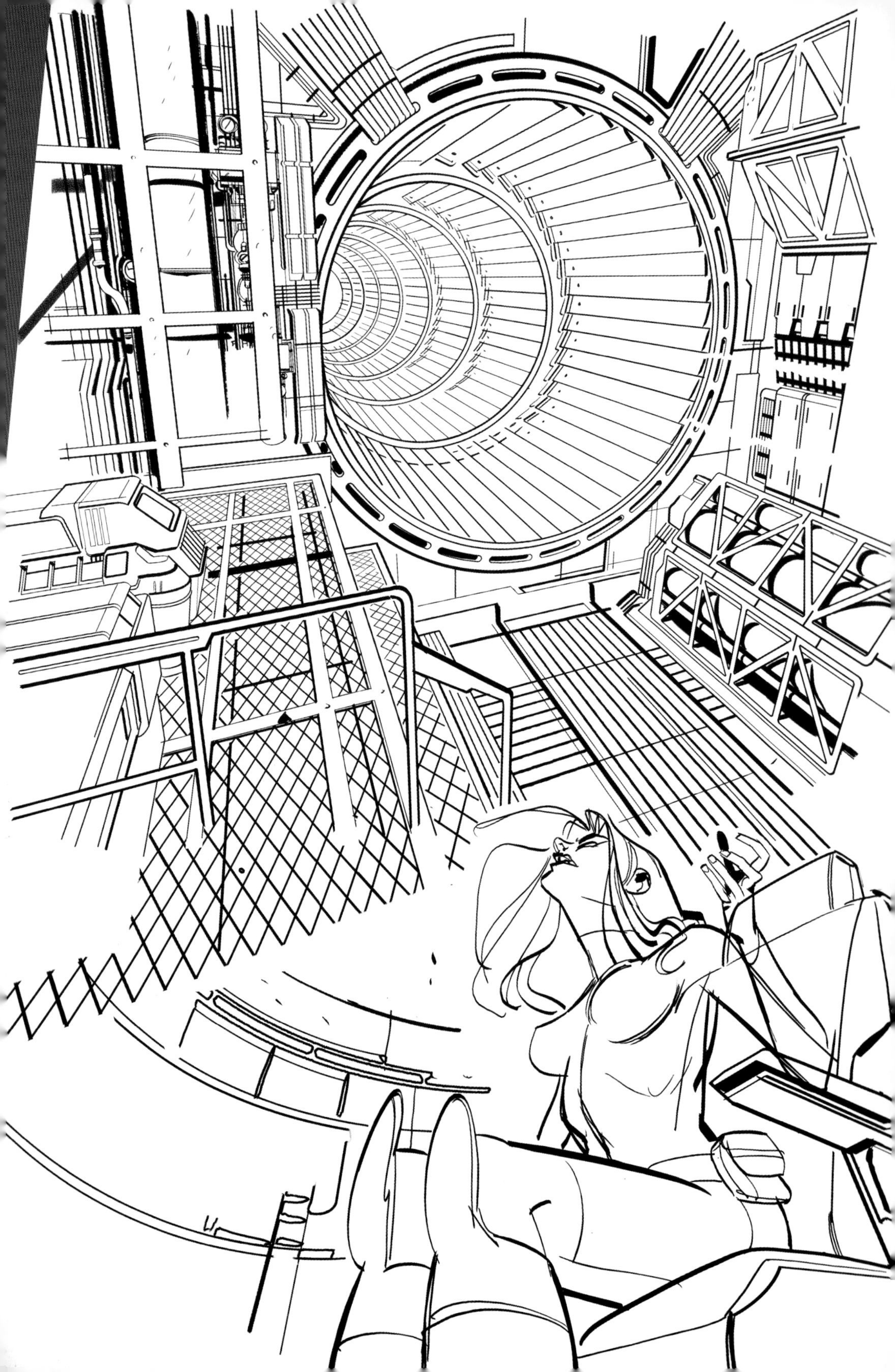

What is the political machine doing to new generations? How can the necessity of common safety and individual liberty coexist? Who's right and who's wrong between the ones who do their duty without asking questions and those who instead ask questions and rebel when the answers they find aren't what they expected?

BELOW: STUDY BY EMILIANO MAMMUCARI

PREVIOUS PAGE: DRAWING BY GIGI CAVENAGO

So, here's Jonas, trying to do his best by supporting the government, even though he clearly doesn't approve of its conduct. And Ringo, who believes the point is not whether people have the right to know, but that awareness is a duty and taking sides is a moral obligation. We have Juno and Rey, who can't get over their need for justice and revenge, Raul and Sam, who put their personal needs before the rest. And, at last, Jsana Juric, who takes the opposite direction, choosing the good of the many over the needs of the few.

These two pages: studies by Emiliano Mammucari

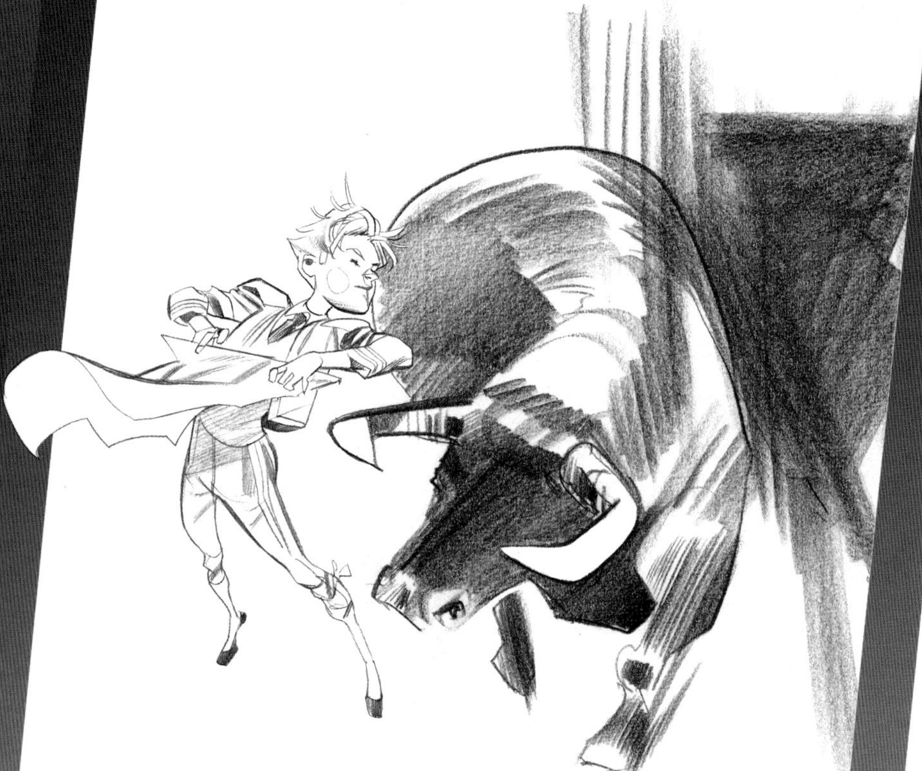

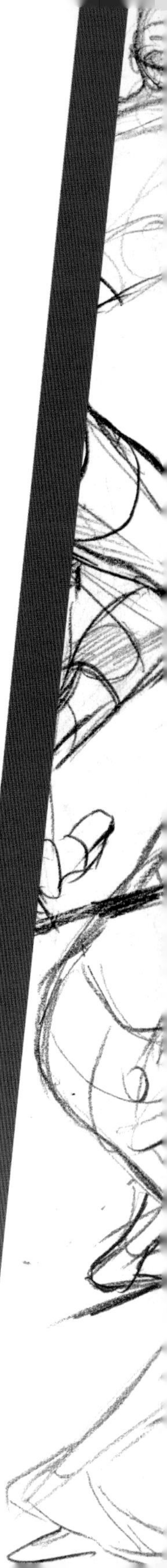

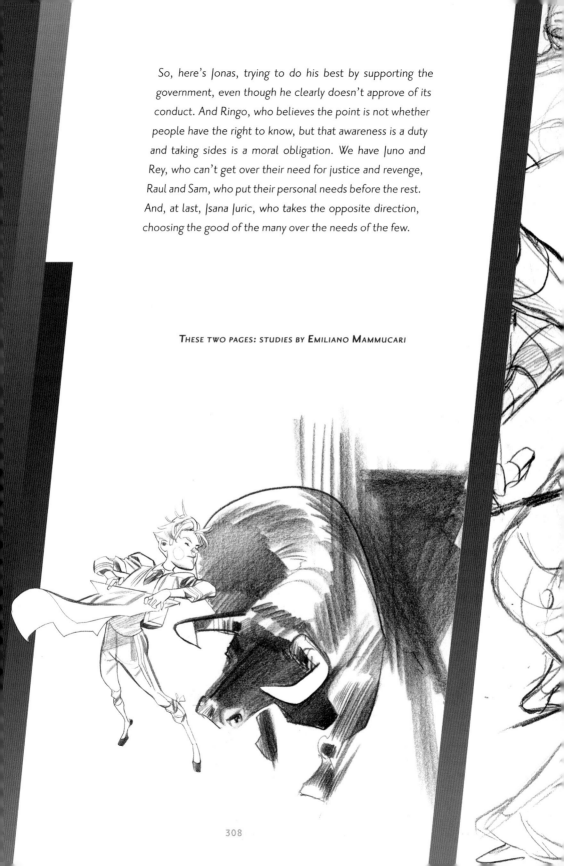

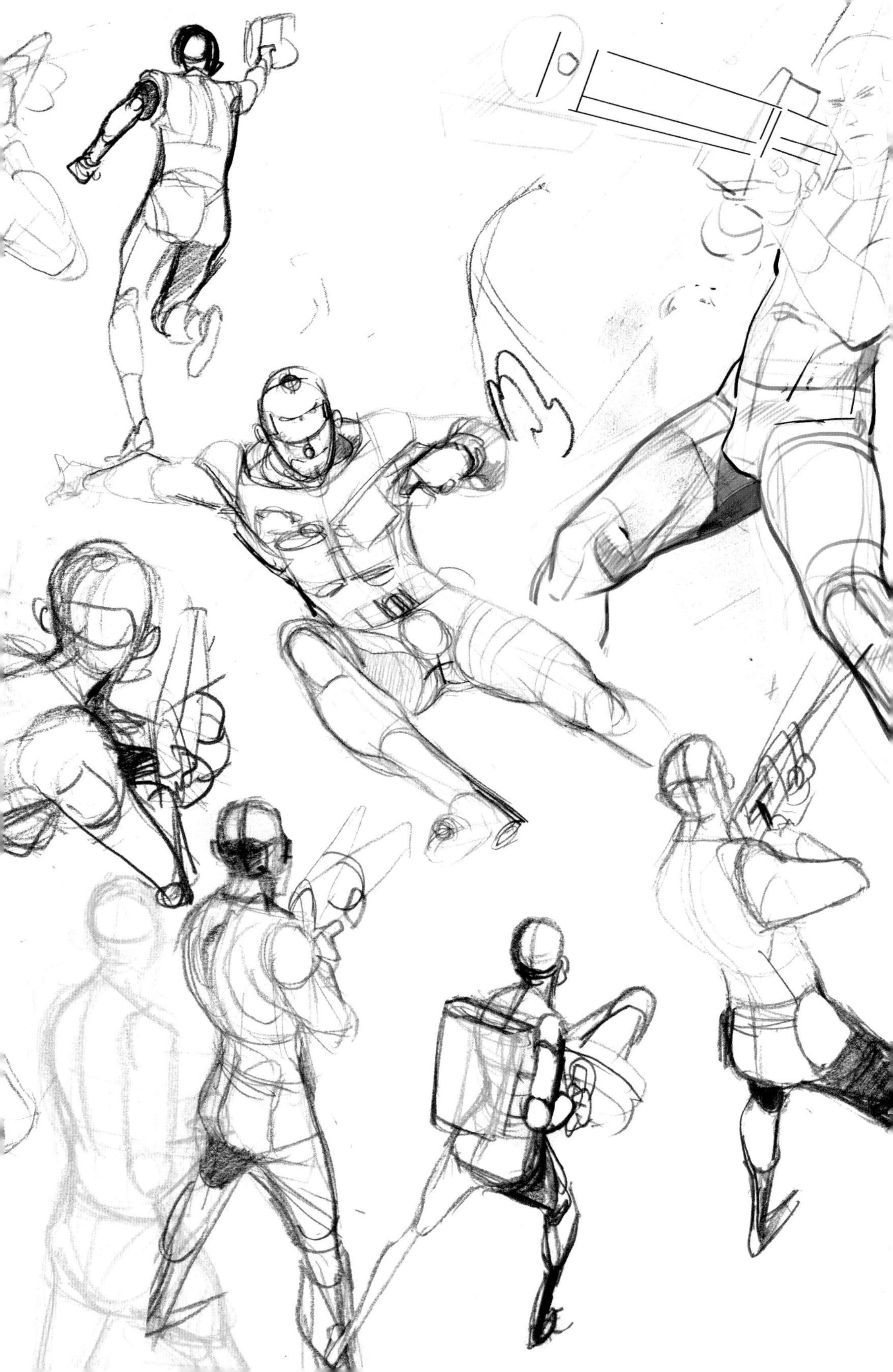

ORPHANS IS A SERIES WITH DIFFERENT READING LEVELS. IT DOESN'T MATTER IF YOU SEE THEM OR NOT -- THEY'RE THERE AND THEY PULL EACH TRIGGER, LIGHT EACH FUSE, SPARK EACH EXPLOSION.

– ROBERTO RECCHIONI

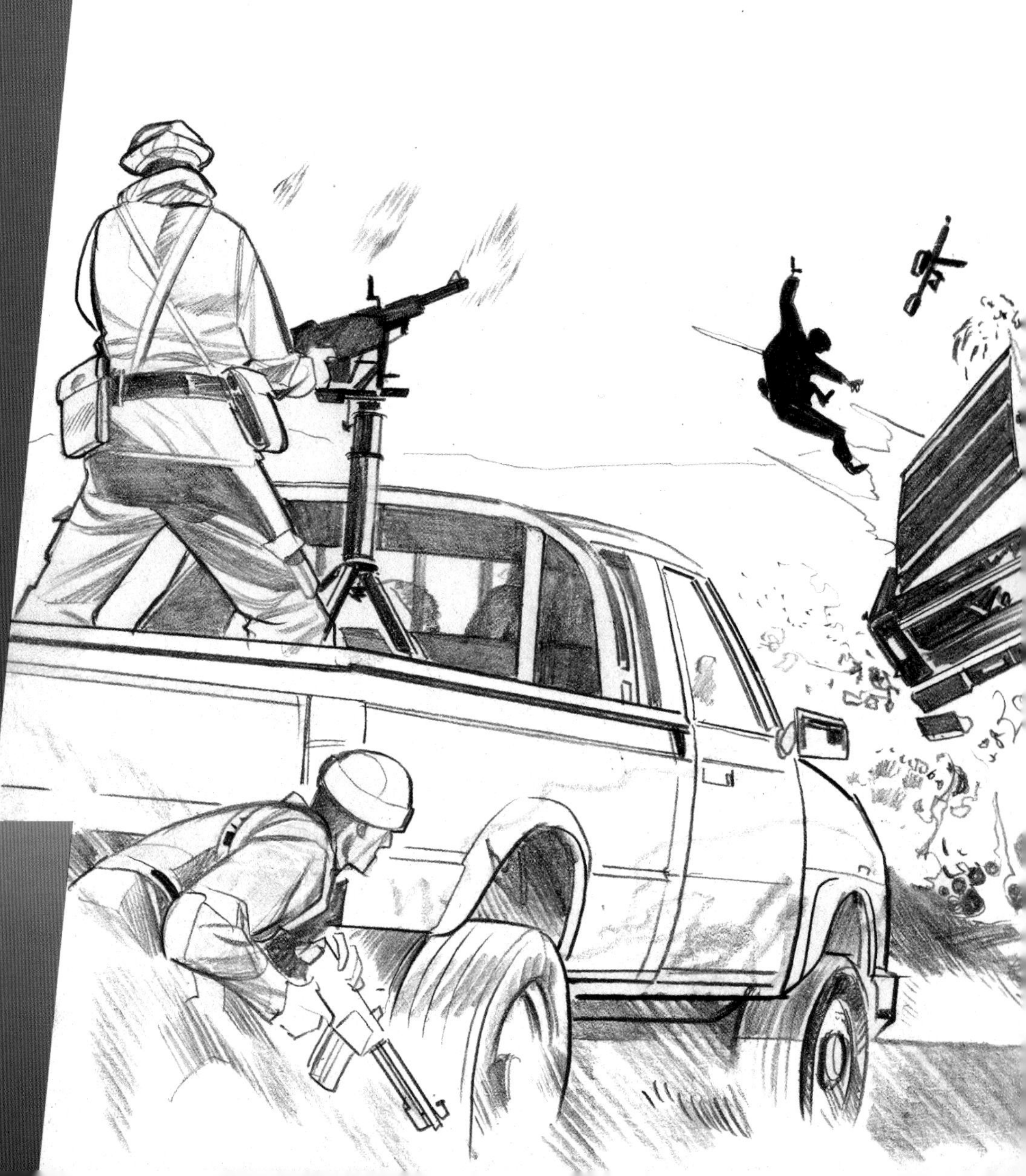

Moral choices. Ethical decisions. Political writing, masked as science fiction and dressed with frenetic action. Because without a doubt, *Orphans* is a series of pure entertainment, and it can be enjoyed as such. But it also has different reading levels. It doesn't matter if you see them or not -- they're there and they pull each trigger, light each fuse, spark each explosion. And they force the reader to take sides, be it with the rebels against the dictatorial and oppressive system or with the legitimate government defending against terrorists. To take the humans' side or the instruments' side. To support Hector or Achilles. To take Cain's side or Abel's. And my decision to force the passive reader to actively choose which side to take is the basis for my writing of this series. Because I have my favorites too, but I'll be damned if I tell you!

ILLUSTRATION BY EMILIANO MAMMUCARI

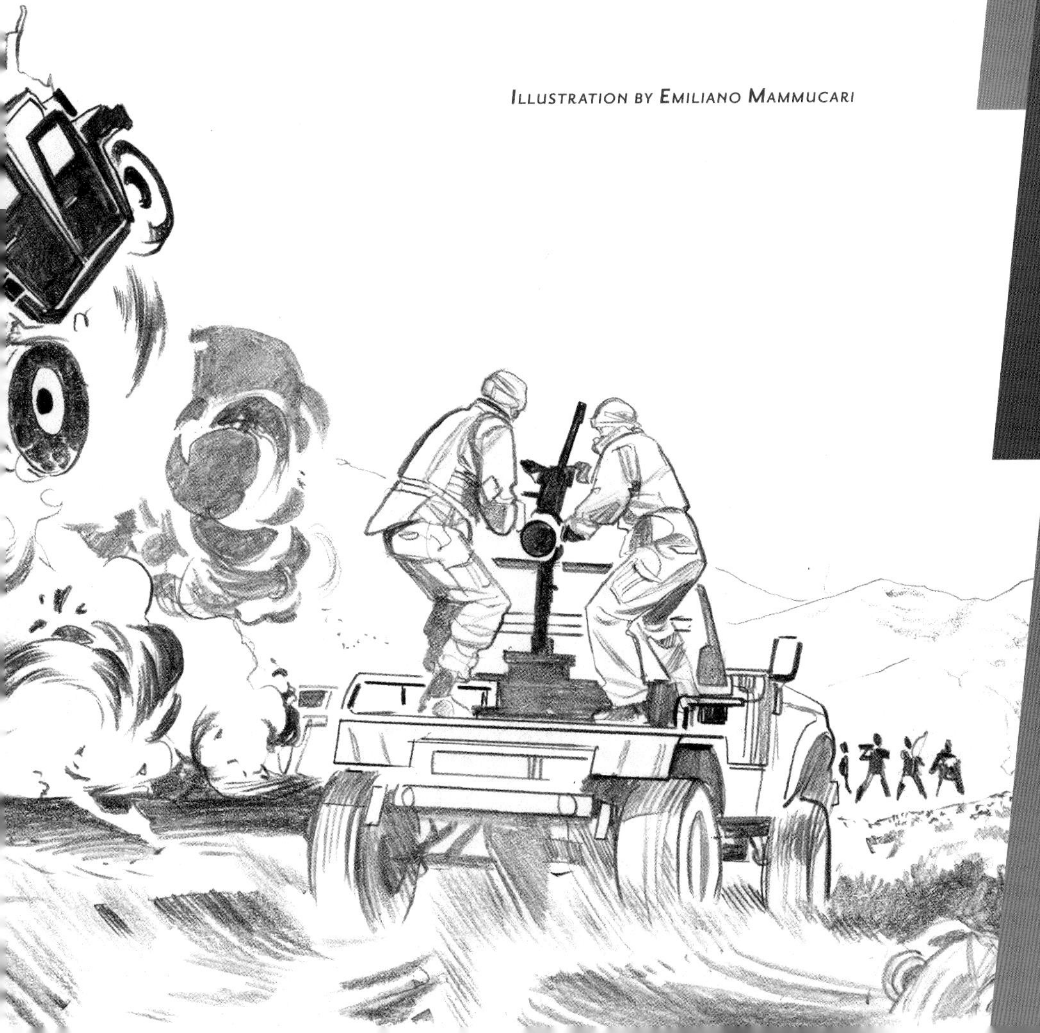

INITIALLY, I FEARED THAT CHANGING MY STYLE ALL OF A SUDDEN WOULD BE TRAUMATIC, BUT IT TURNED OUT TO BE AN INSPIRATION.

– Gigi Cavenago

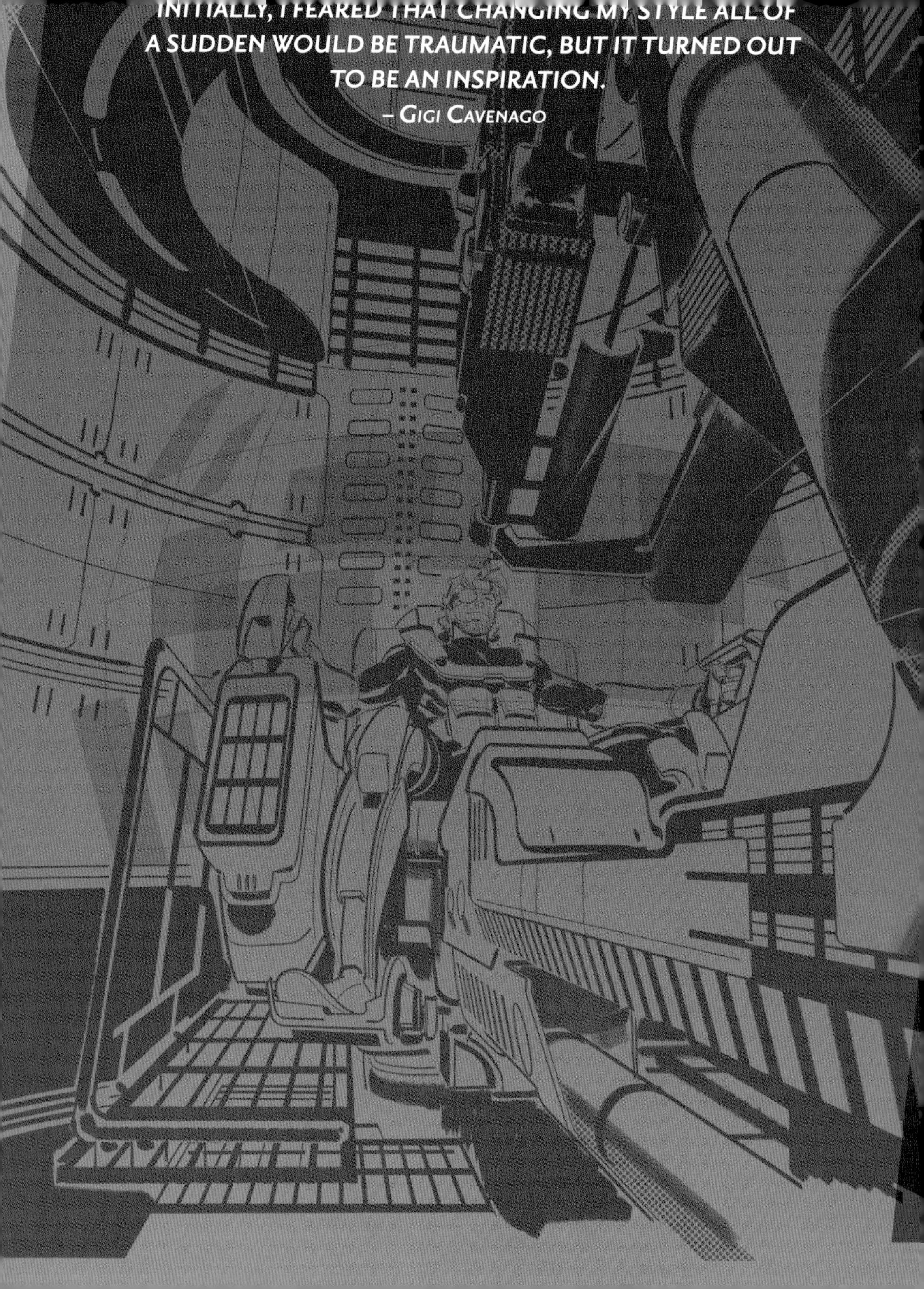

END OF THE GAME

GIGI CAVENAGO: *Chapter II is called "We All Fall Down" (like the nursery rhyme), but I remember suggesting to Roberto to give it a title that suggested martyrdom. Officially, it would have been Juno's martyrdom, but (and let's keep this between us) I thought I was the one sacrificing for the cause…!*

BELOW: ILLUSTRATION BY EMILIANO MAMMUCARI

PREVIOUS PAGE: ILLUSTRATION BY GIGI CAVENAGO

GIGI CAVENAGO: I'm really happy how the last page of the episode turned out: initially, Ringo and Jonas were framed full-body and from different angles inside their separate Schrödinger containment cells. I suggested we show them frontally and symmetrically, to form a single figure split in half, as if they were two sides of the same coin. It's a picture that closes the chapter nicely and prepares the reader for the upcoming clash between the last surviving Orphans.

THESE TWO PAGES: ART BY GIGI CAVENAGO

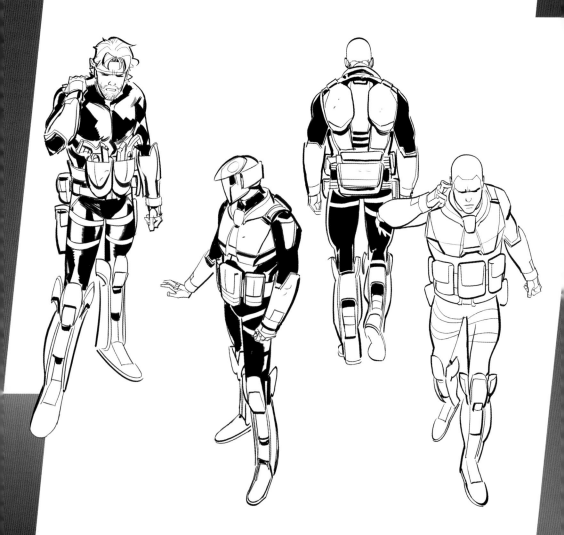

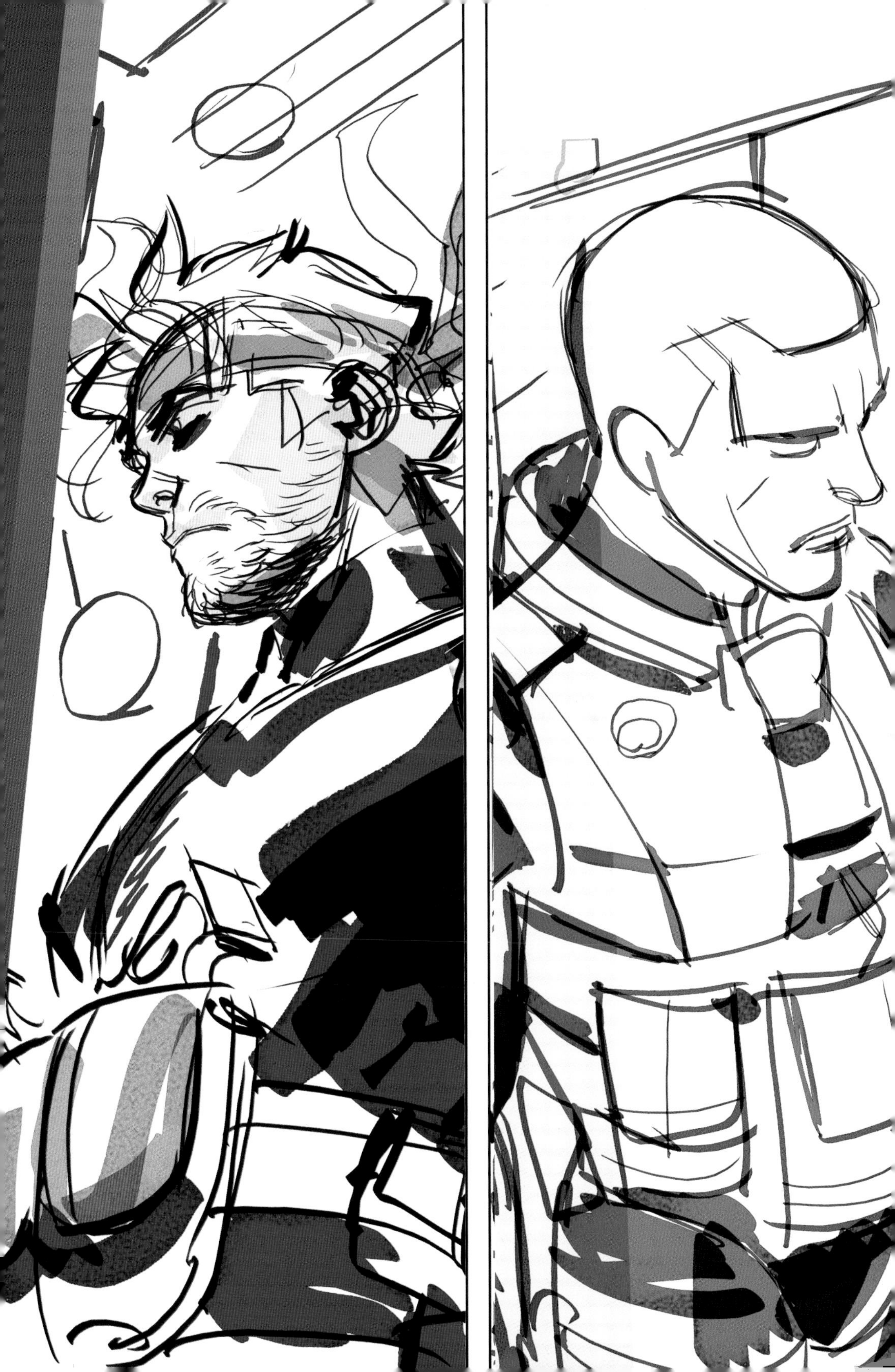

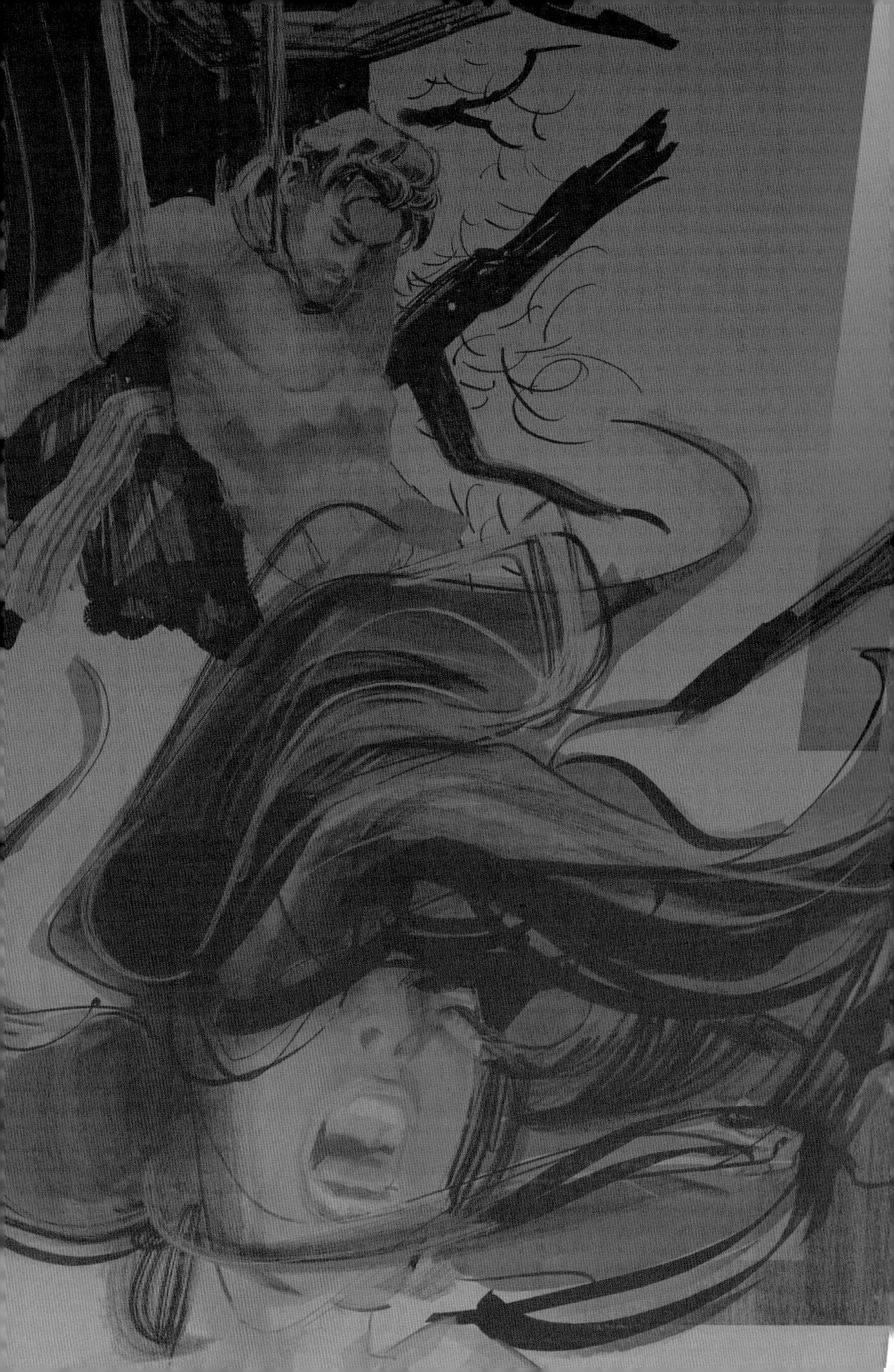

WERTHER DELL'EDERA: *In the sequence with Don Quixote and Sancho Panza, I managed to never draw their faces. I don't know why, I just remember I felt more uneasy drawing their faces than a horse and a donkey at a gallop.*

BELOW: ART BY WERTHER DELL'EDERA

PREVIOUS PAGE: ART BY GIGI CAVENAGO

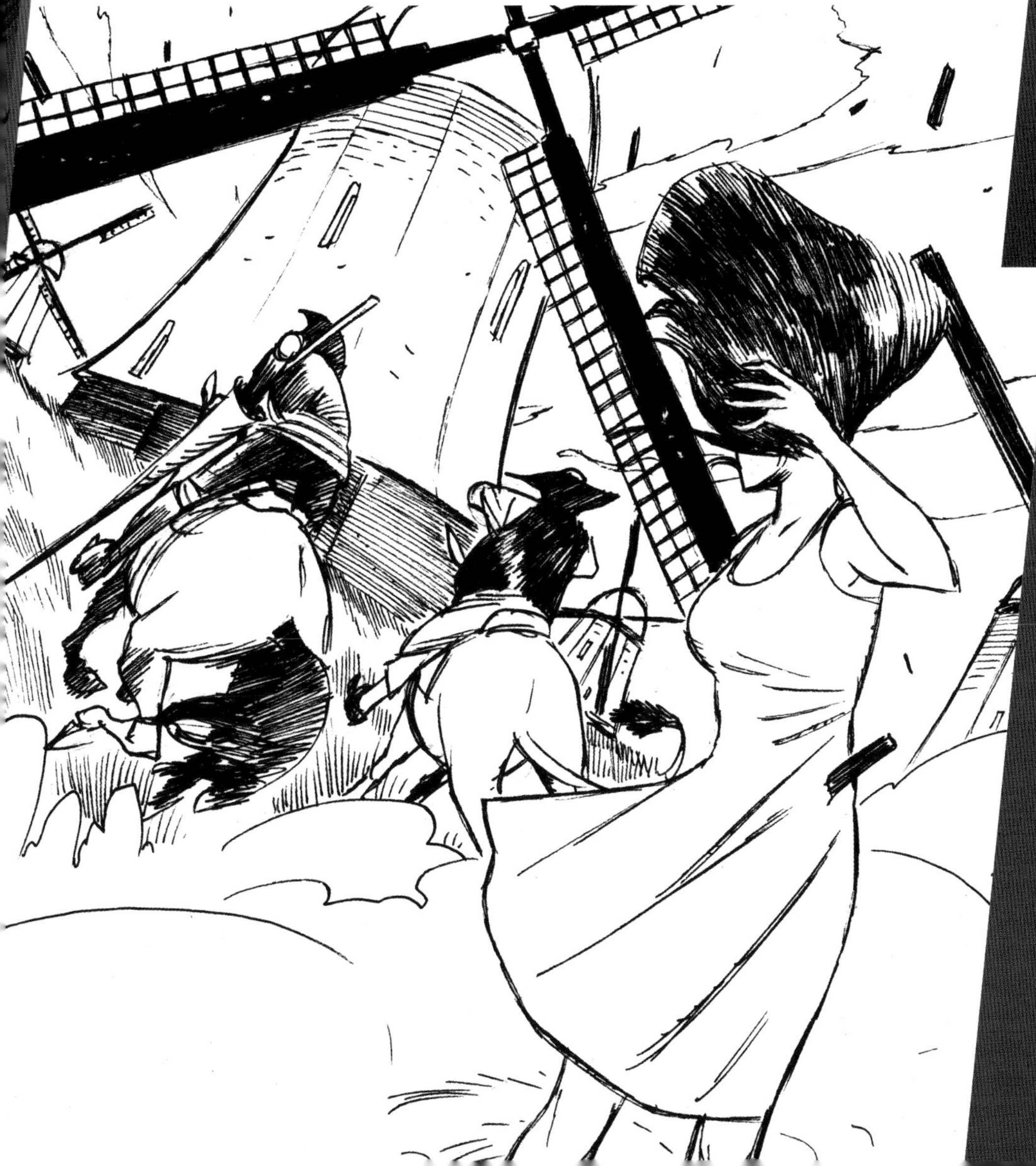

GIGI CAVENAGO: *One of the main sequences in this chapter was the one with the "Tree of Sorrow." Roberto suggested we make something unusual, and he wanted me to color those pages in a pictorial style. Just when I was on the verge of exhaustion from drawing the preceding traditional pages, moving to a new approach put some of my mental muscles to rest and let others wake up. Once I finished those pages, I could go back to the traditional pages feeling a bit refreshed.*

Below: study by **Emiliano Mammucari**
Next page: art by **Gigi Cavenago**

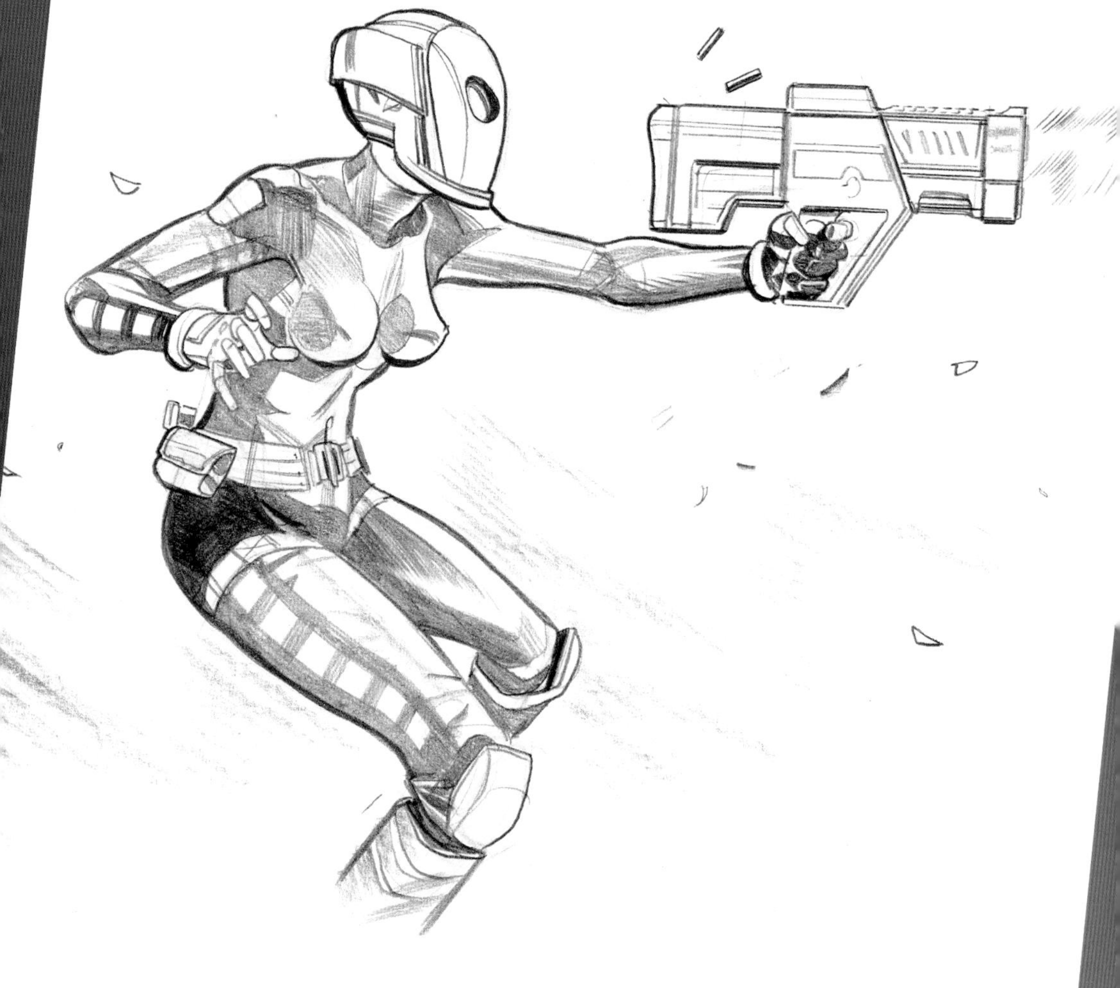

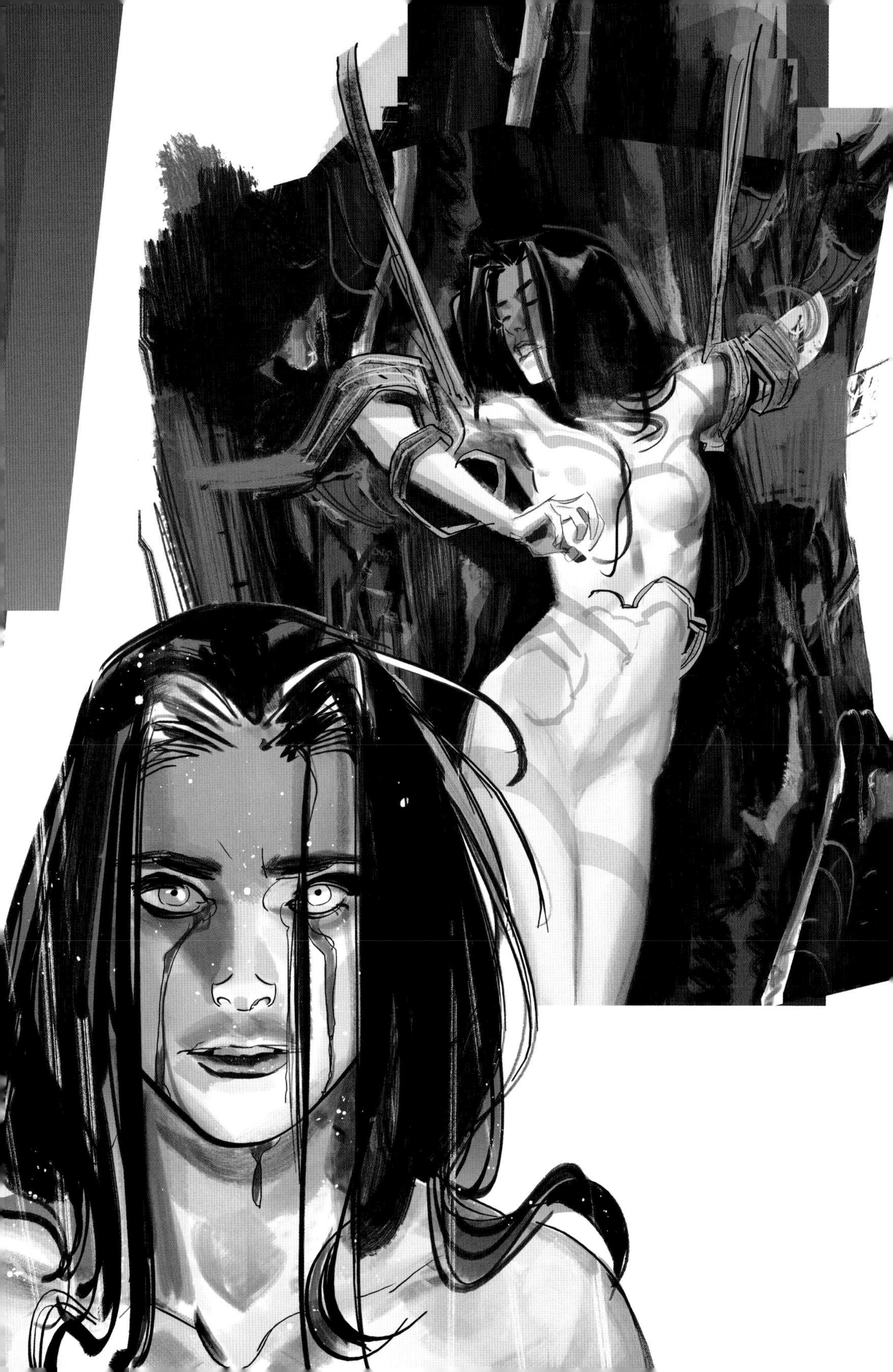

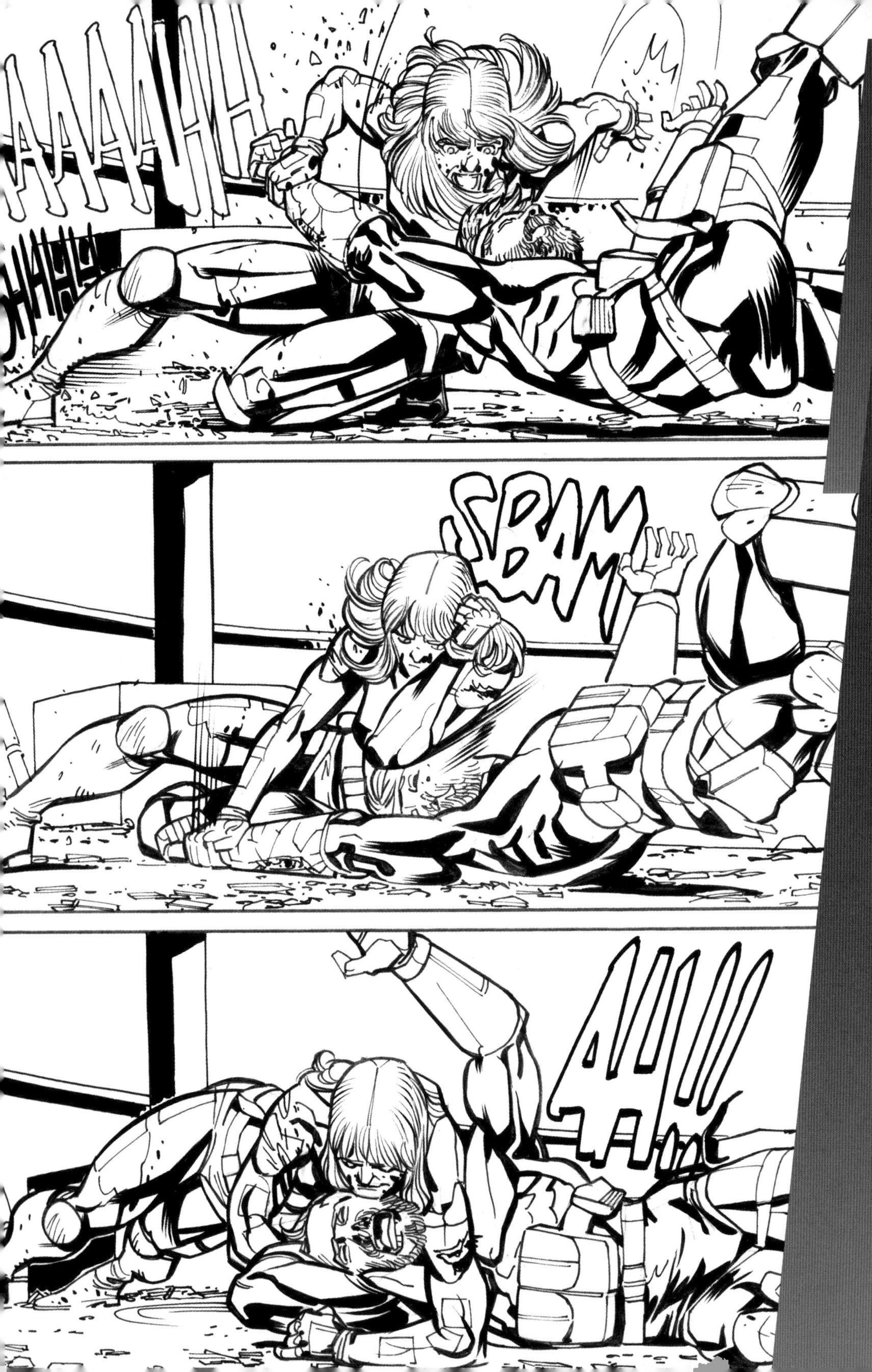
SBAM
SBAM

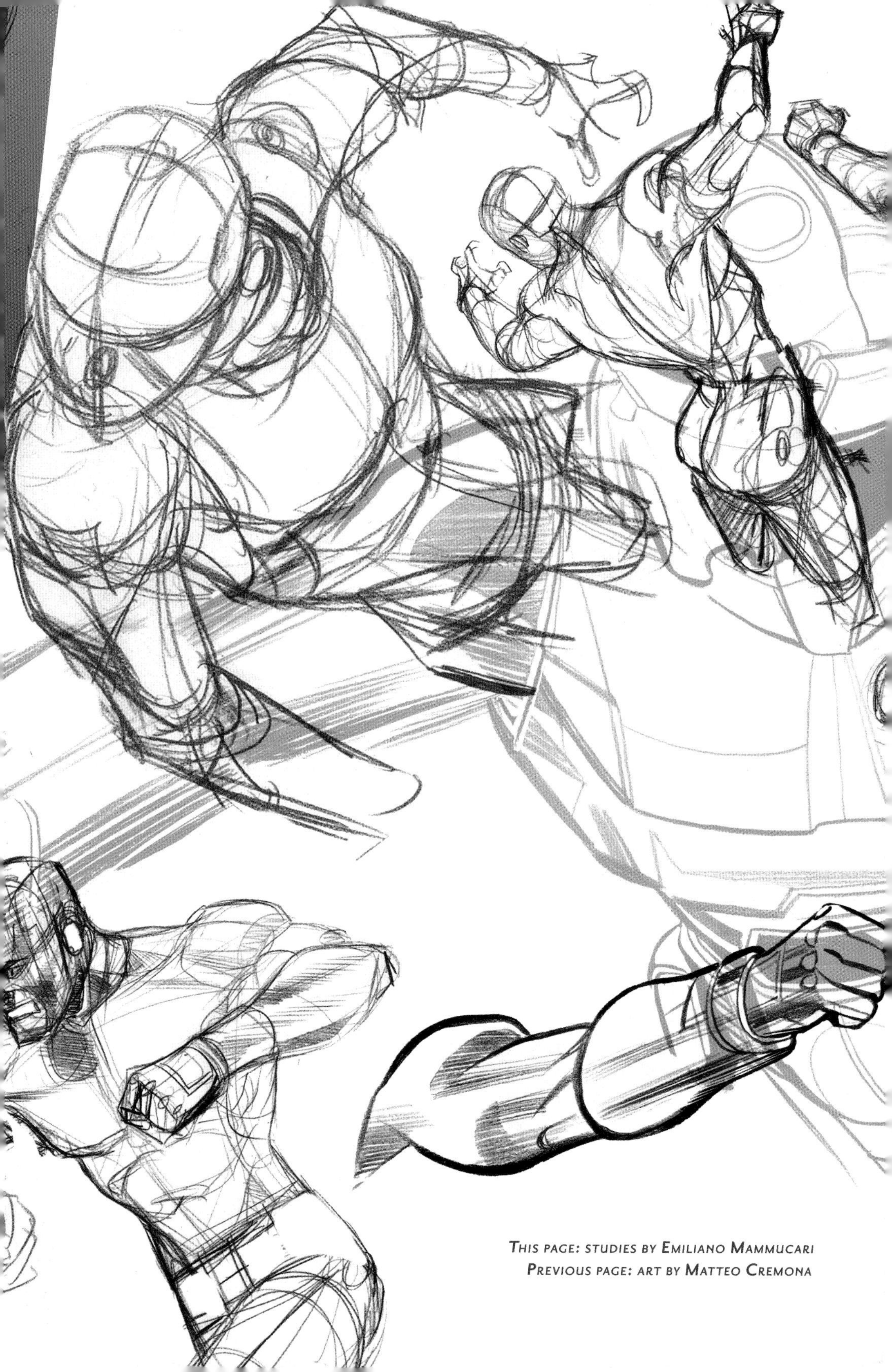

This page: studies by Emiliano Mammucari
Previous page: art by Matteo Cremona

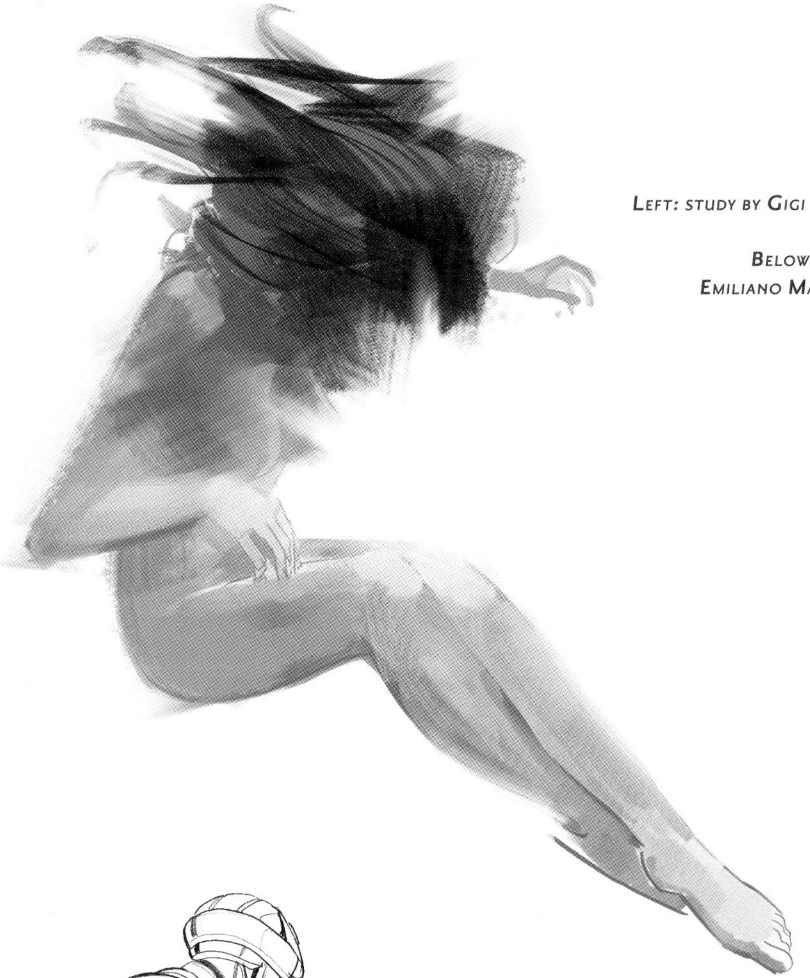

LEFT: STUDY BY GIGI CAVENAGO

BELOW: STUDY BY EMILIANO MAMMUCARI

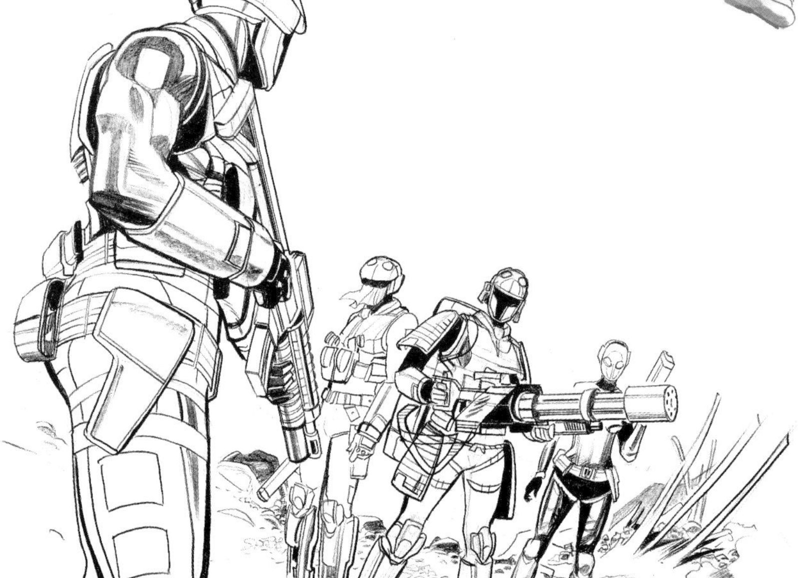

WERTHER DELL'EDERA: *Ringo is the protagonist of the first panel of this page, even though Raul tries to steal the show by getting up like a cool guy. It almost seems like after the director yells "cut," Ringo would have told him to quit with the silly faces or he'd start jumping around, guns in his hands!*

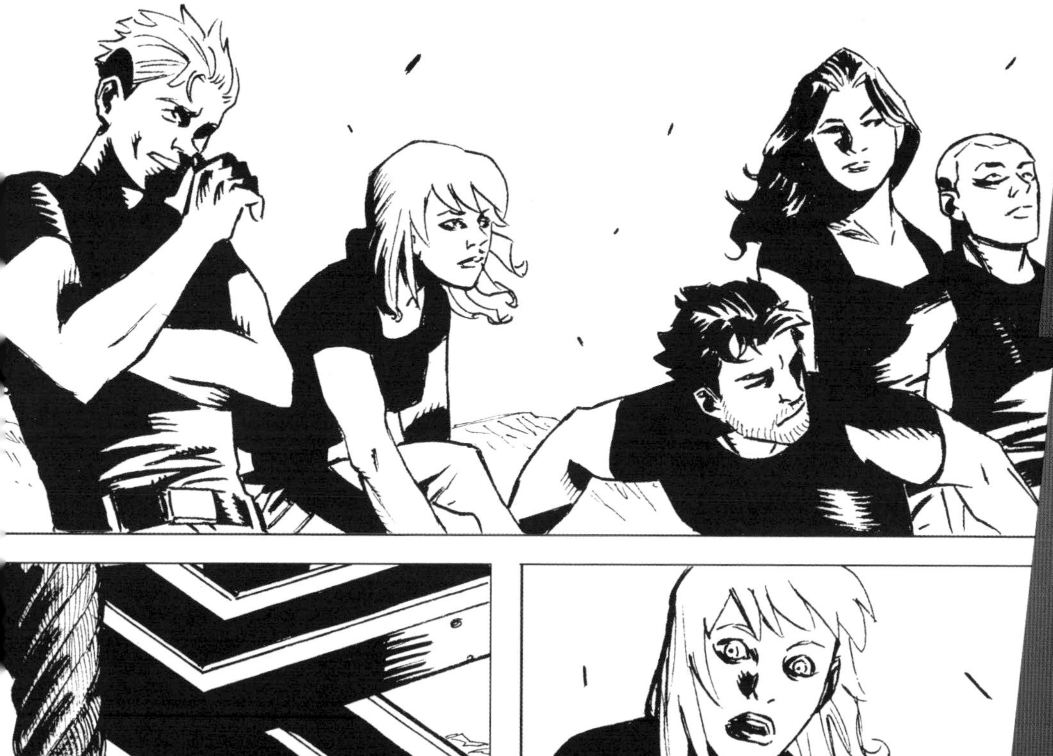

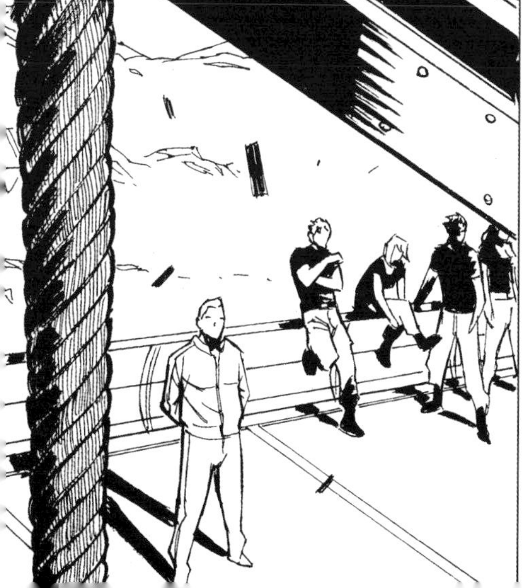

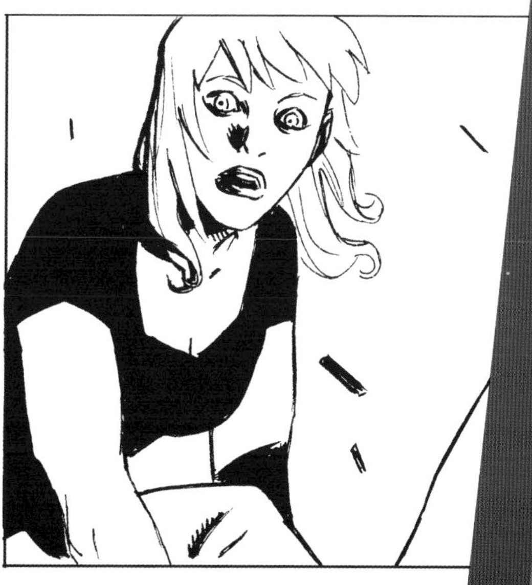

ART BY WERTHER DELL'EDERA

IN THE CONSTRUCTION SITE PANEL, I WANTED TO CONVEY A SENSE OF QUIET IN THE MIDDLE OF WHAT HAD BEEN A PIT OF RESTLESSNESS ACTIVITY UP TO THAT POINT.

– WERTHER DELL'EDERA

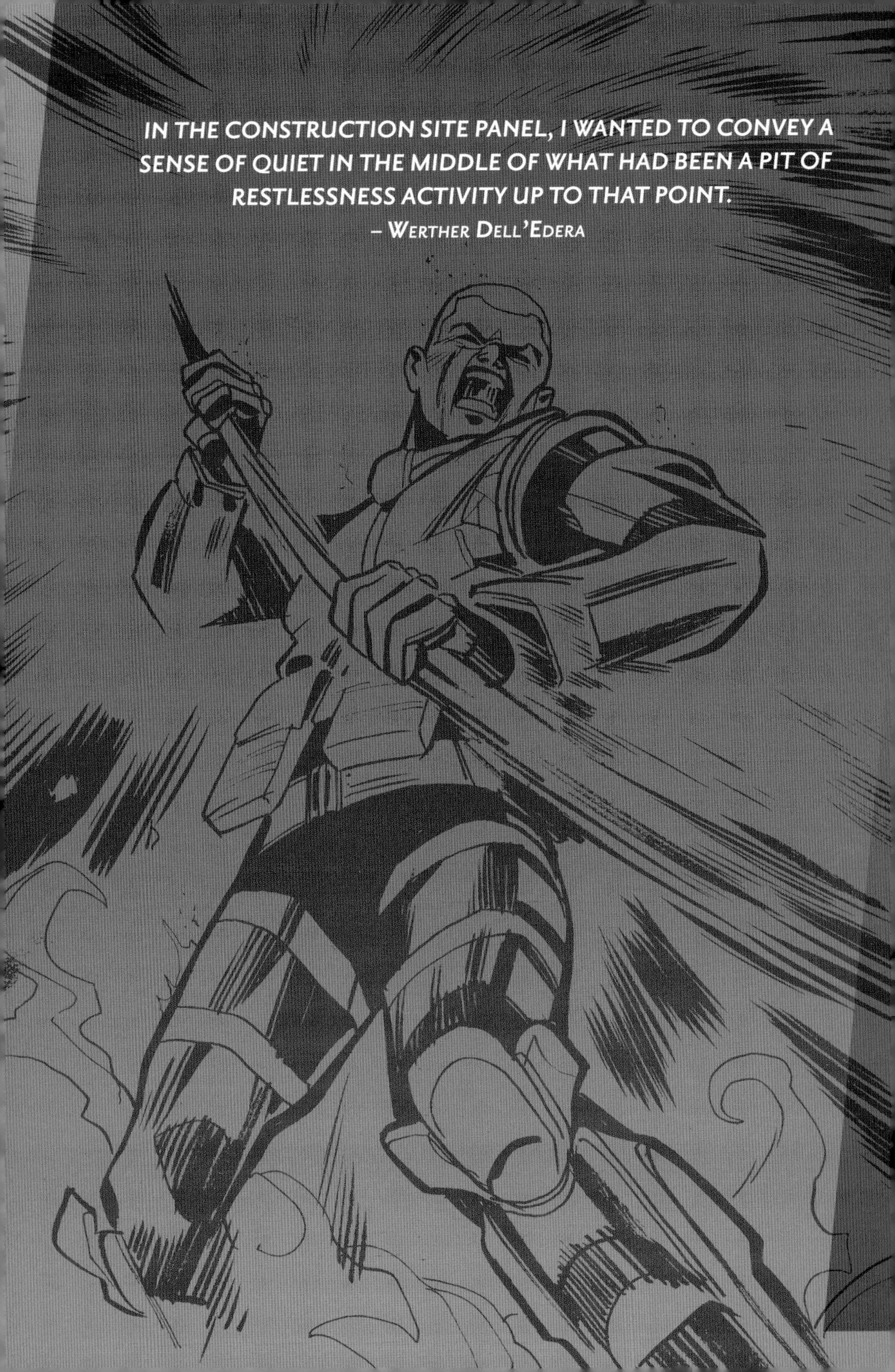

Below: art by Werther Dell'Edera

Previous page: art by Emiliano Mammucari

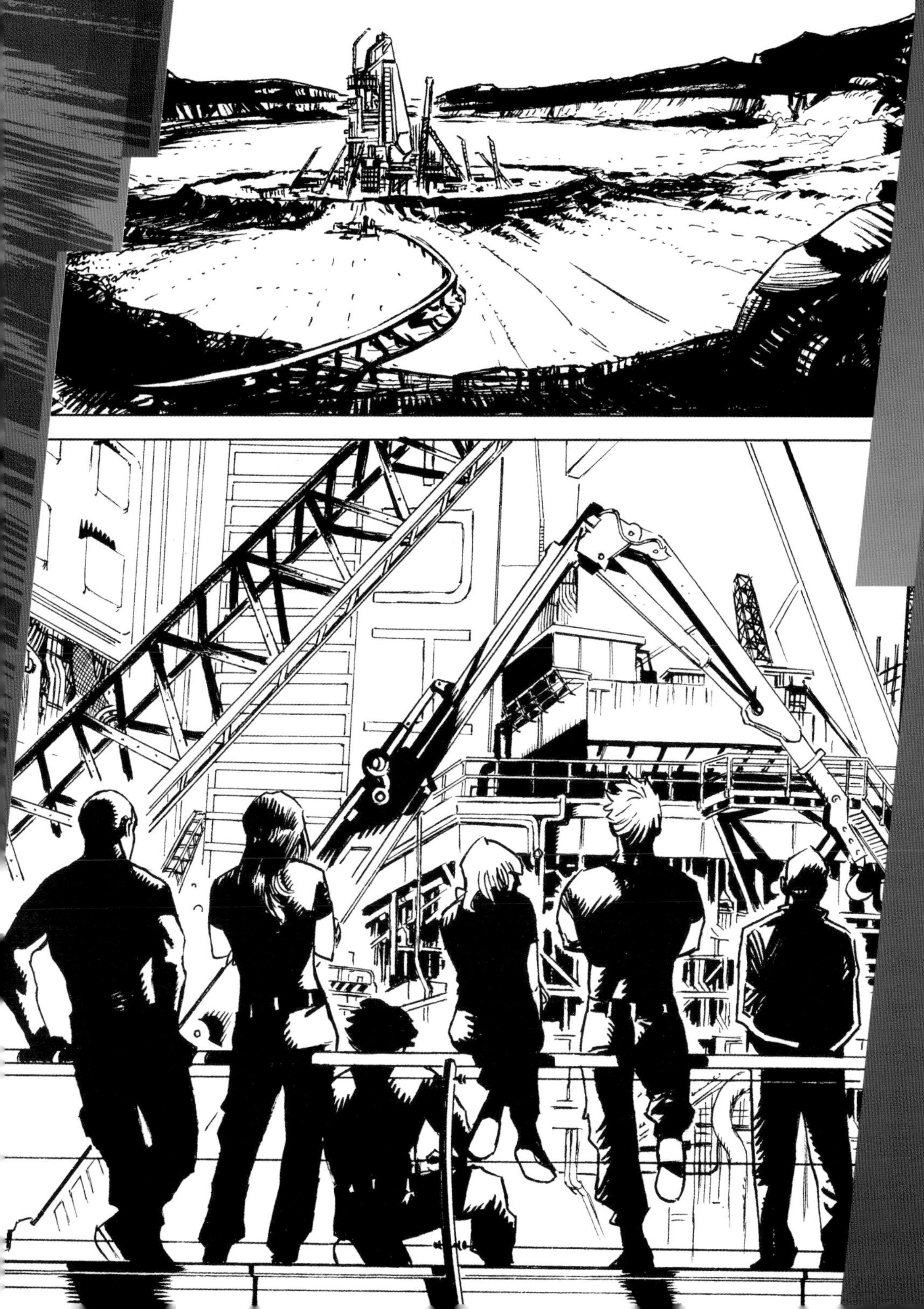

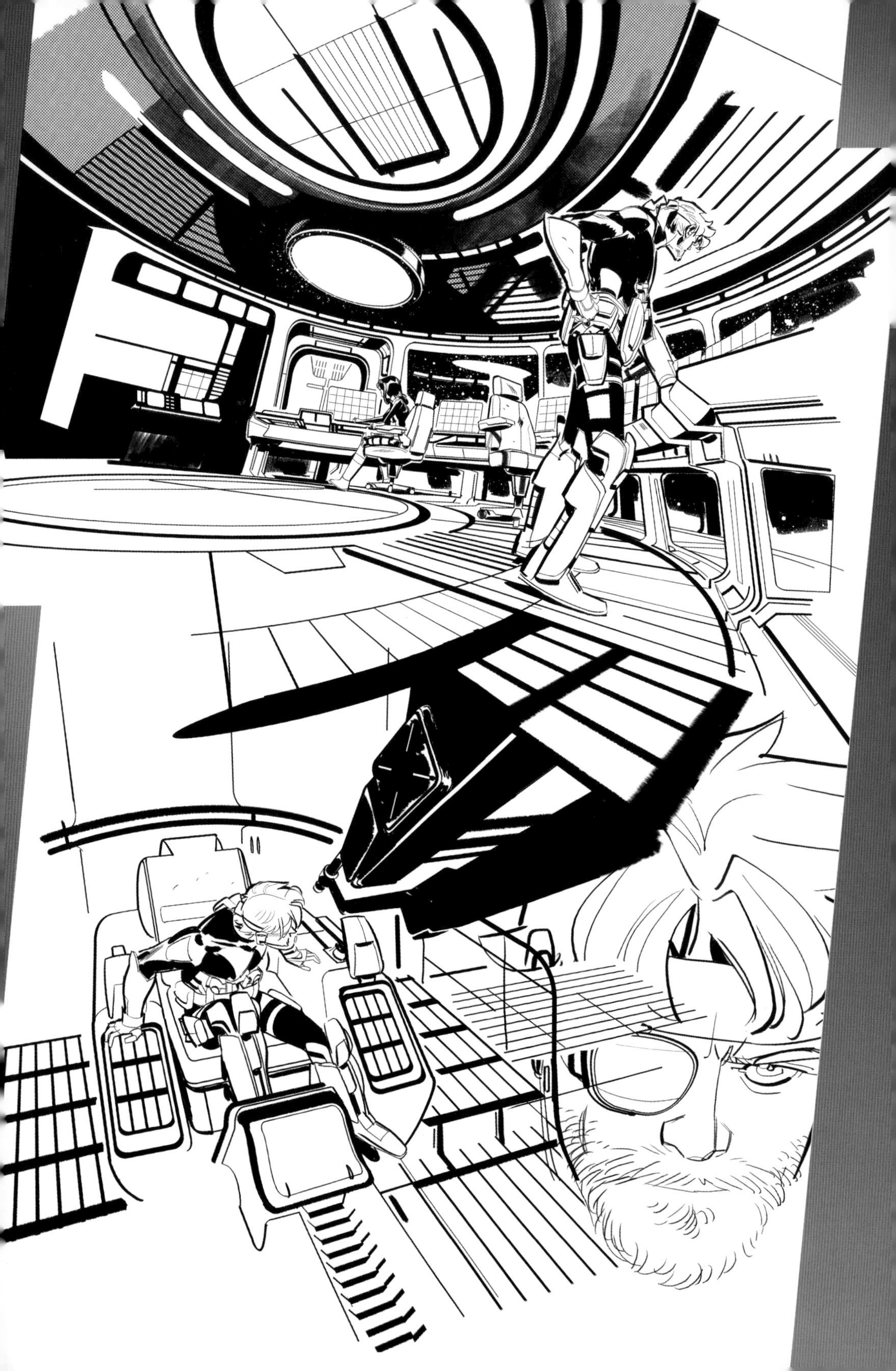

This page: studies by Matteo Cremona

Previous page: art by Gigi Cavenago

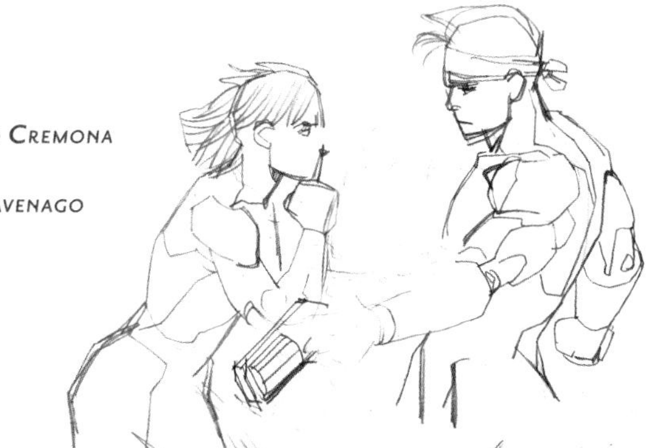

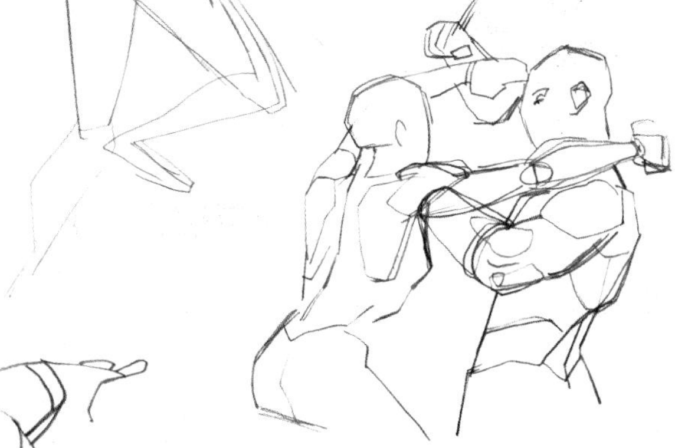

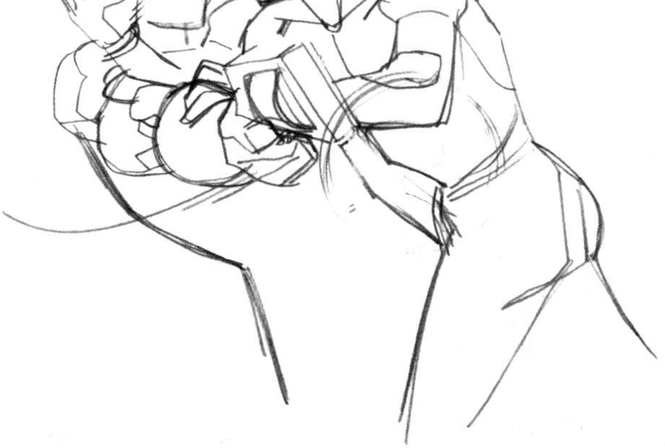

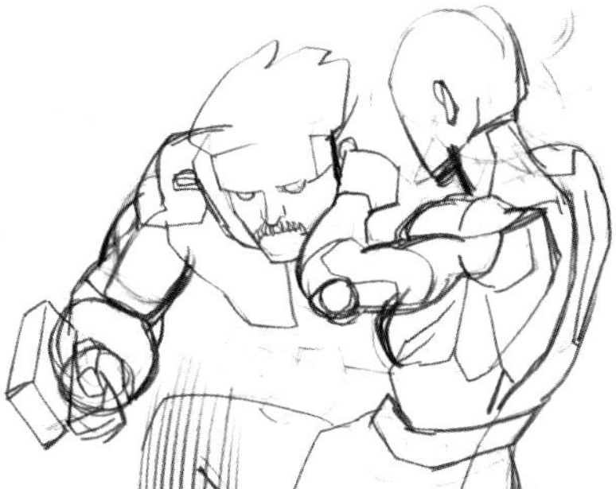

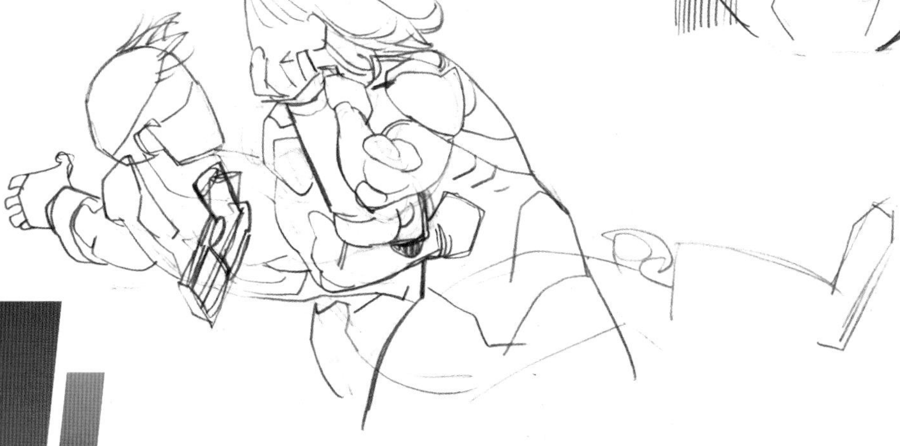

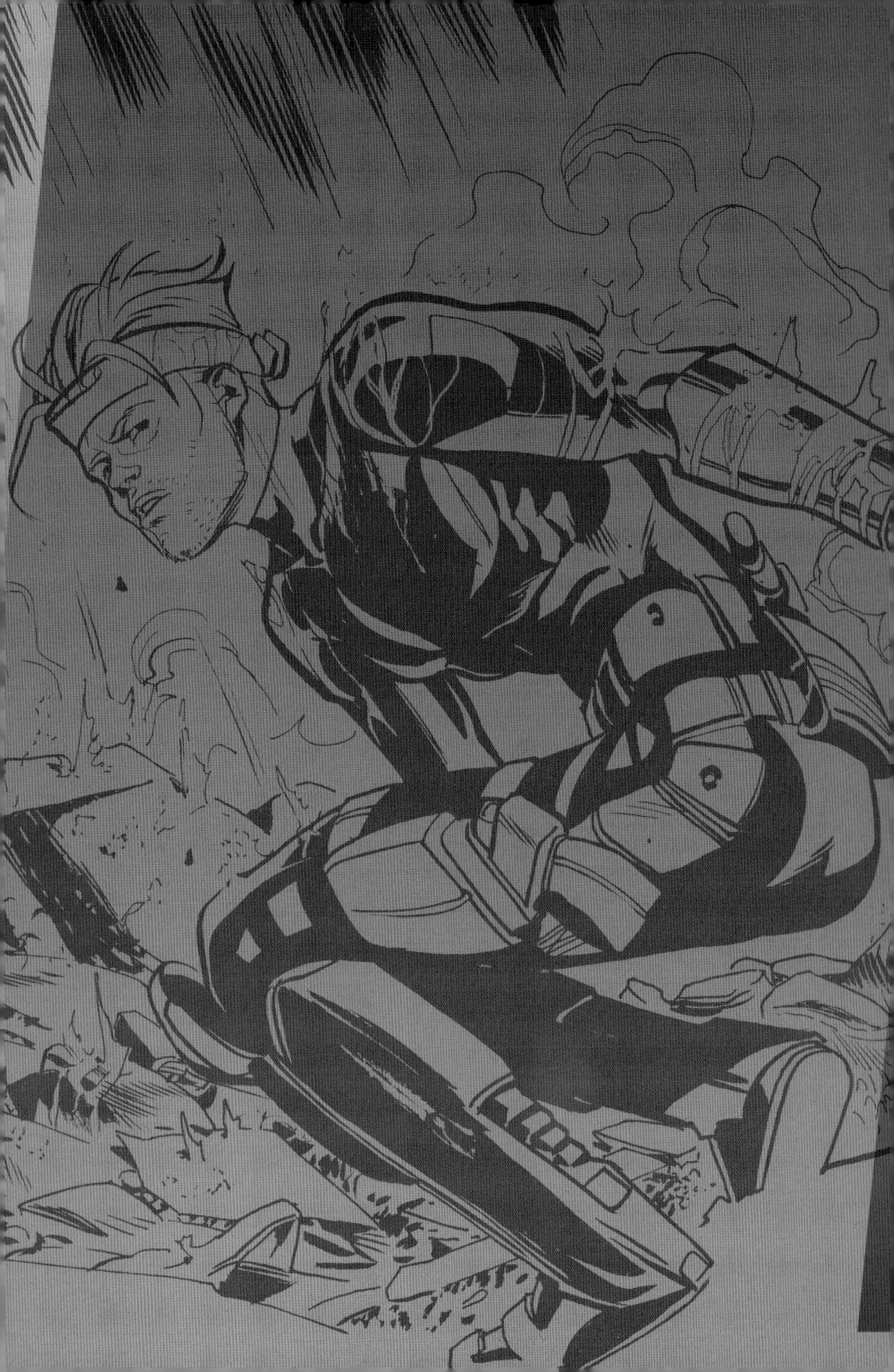

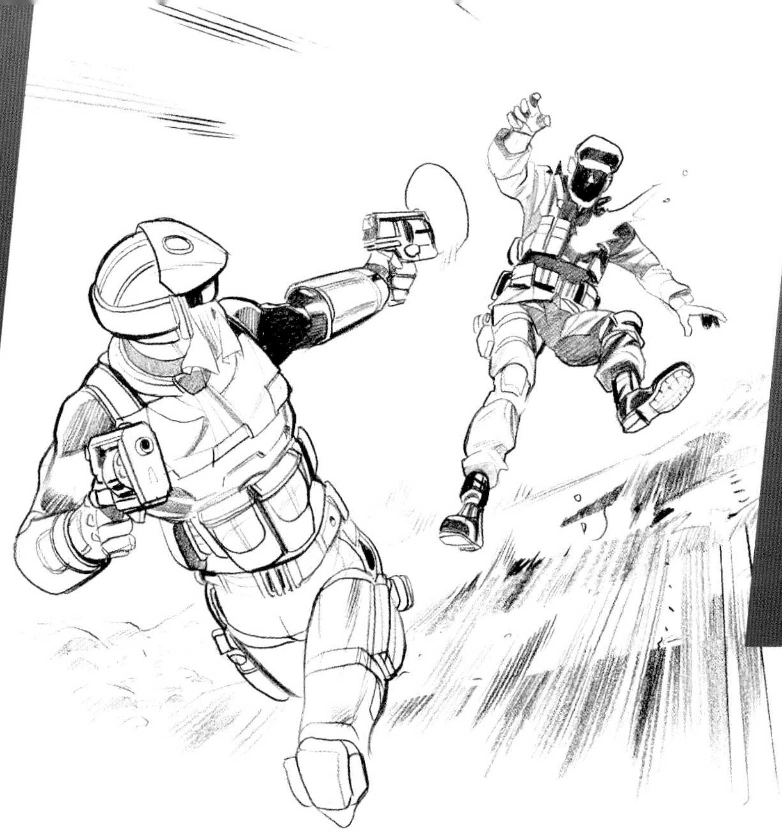

These two pages: illustrations and studies by Emiliano Mammucari

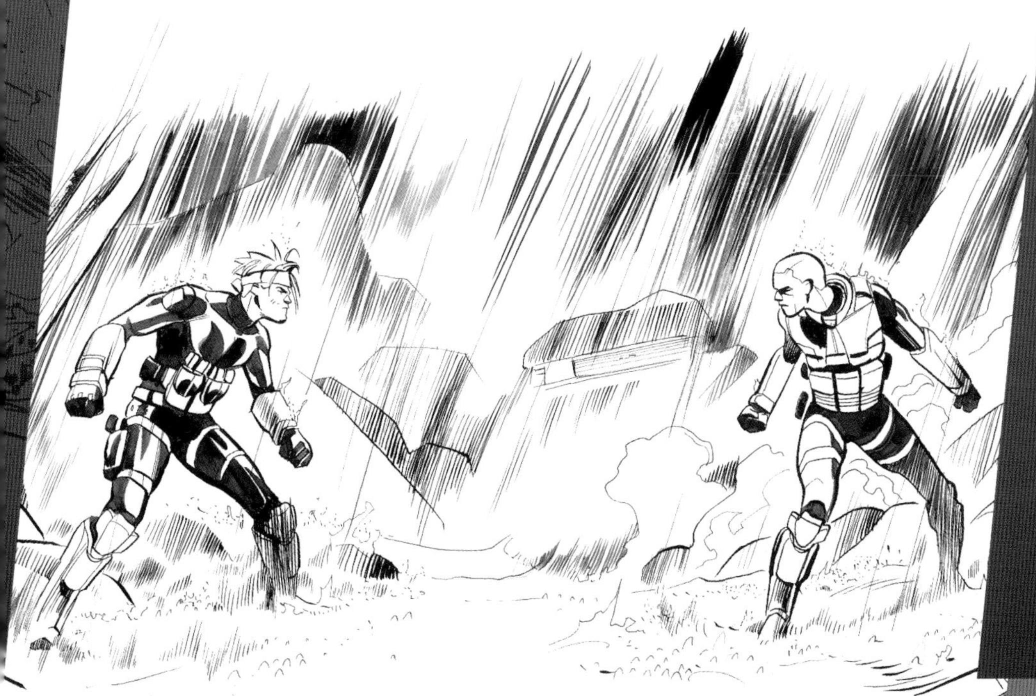

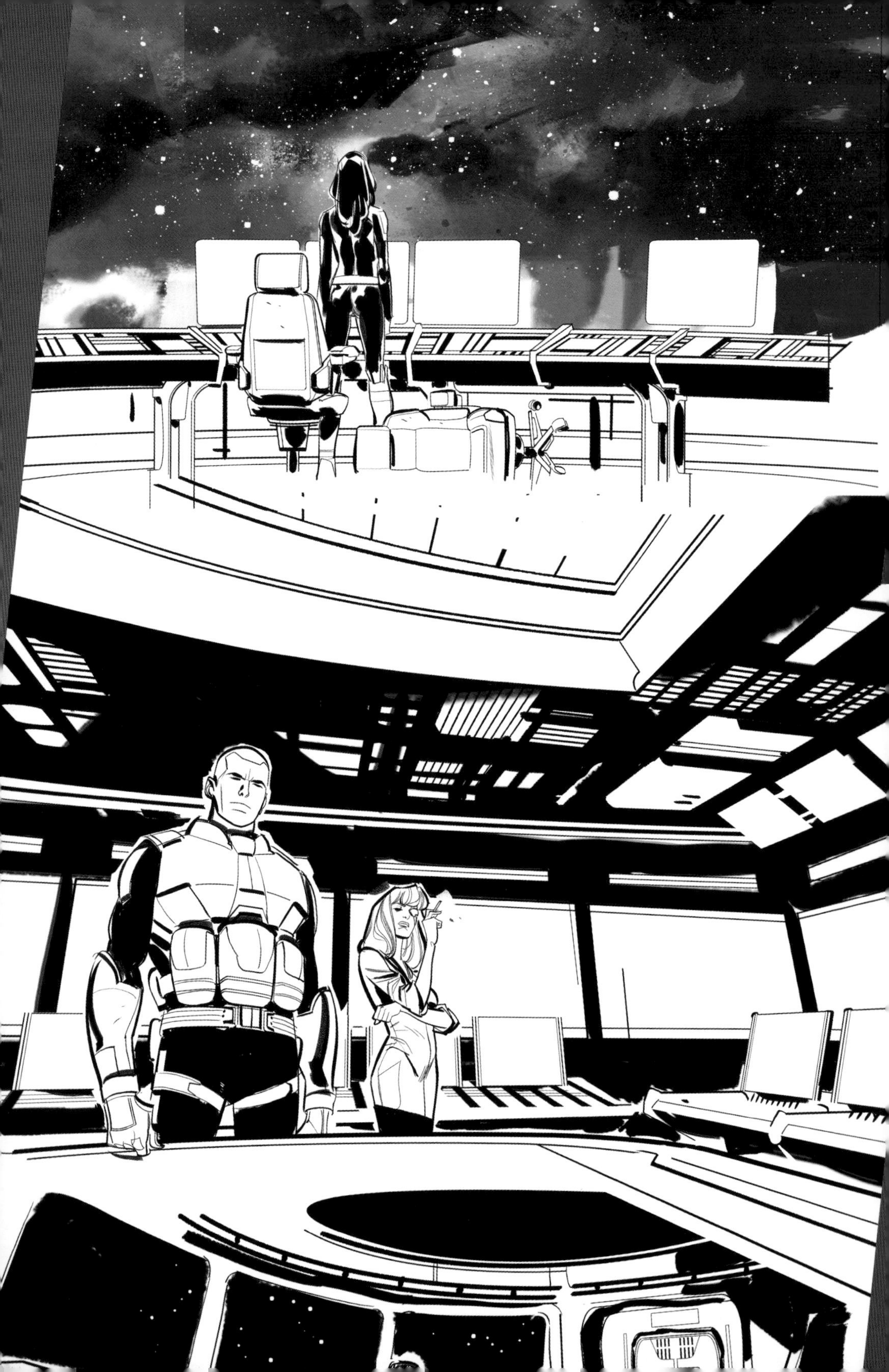

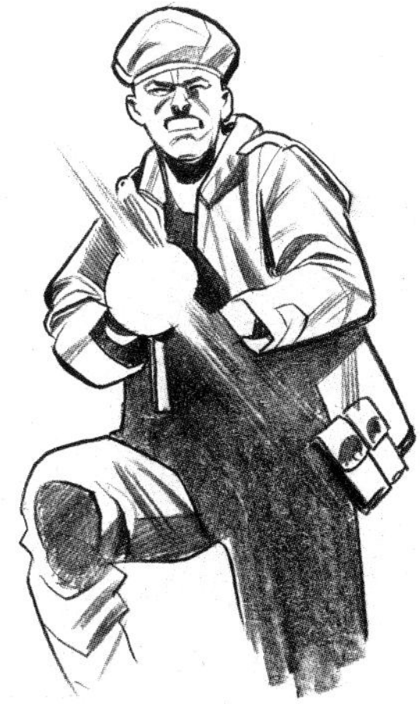

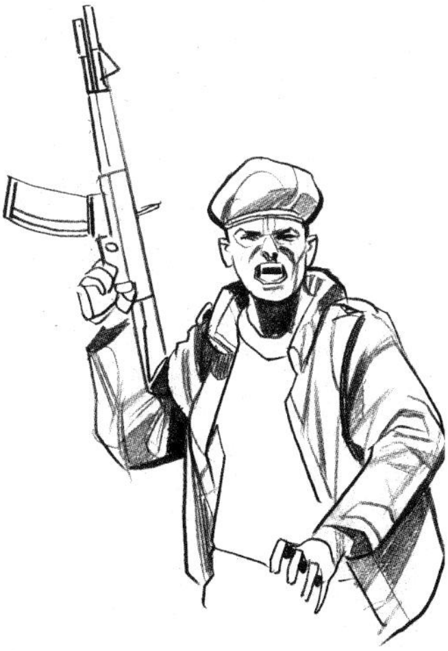

This page: studies by Emiliano Mammucari

Previous page: illustrations by Gigi Cavenago

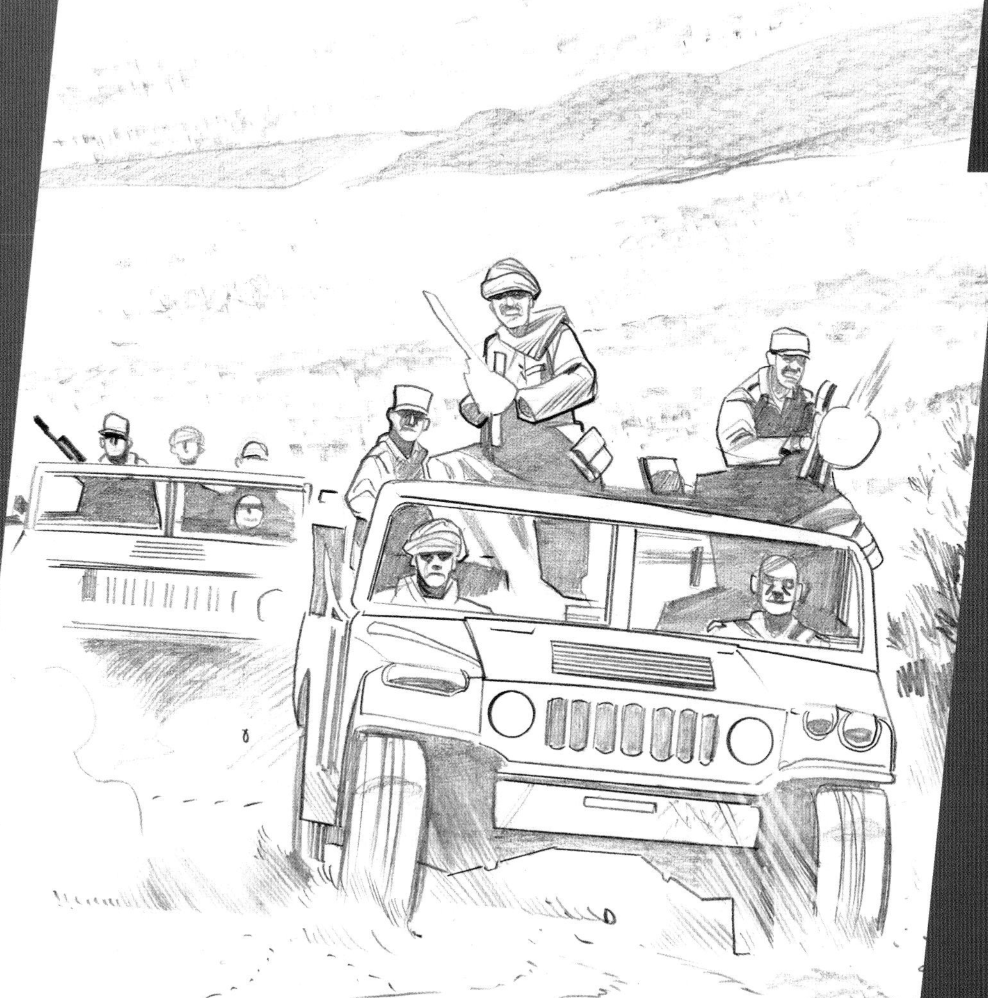

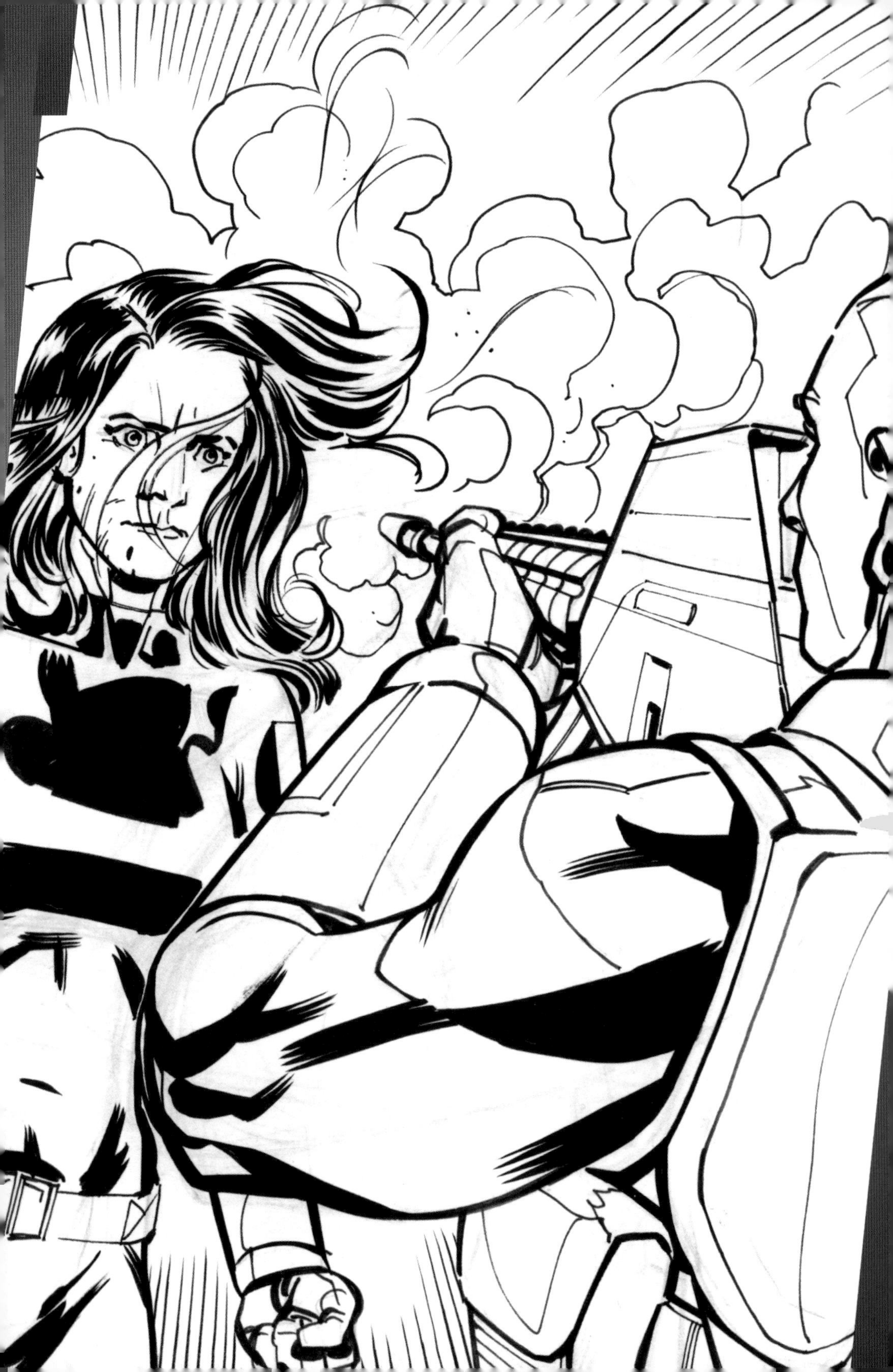

MATTEO CREMONA: *I "argued" a lot with faces, particularly with Juno's (which I don't think I rendered as well as she deserved) and also with environments. At first, I had problems with this kind of science fiction, maybe because it didn't match my personal taste. But in the course of working on it, I can say that I caught up and felt more connected to the world of* Orphans.

THESE TWO PAGES: STUDY AND DRAWING BY MATTEO CREMONA

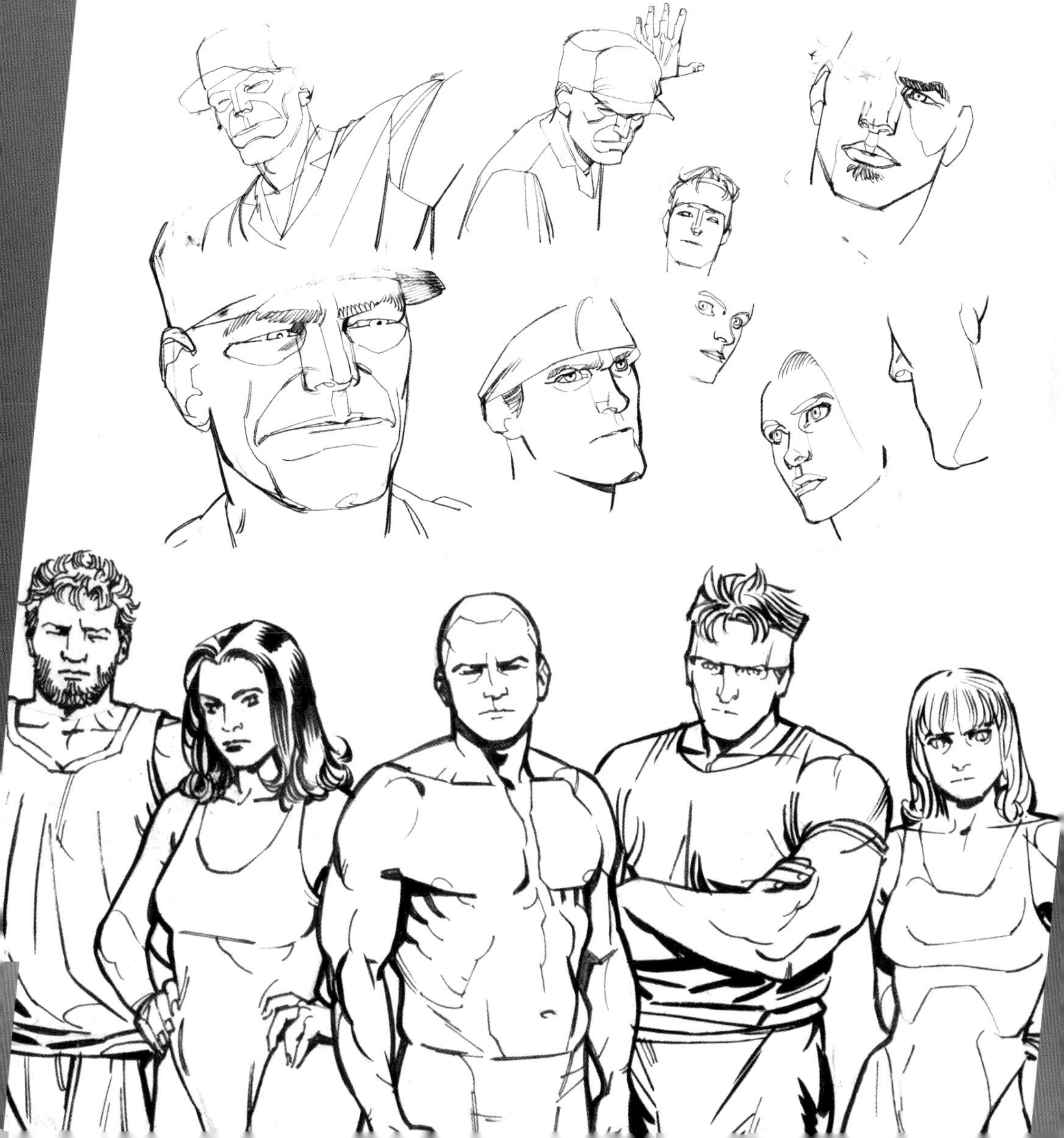

WERTHER DELL'EDERA: *It was really fun to work on the nightmare sequence, trying to sketch out the most disturbing details and exaggerating them with blacks, using rough brush strokes to make the scene as vibrant as possible.*

These two pages: study and drawings by Werther Dell'Edera

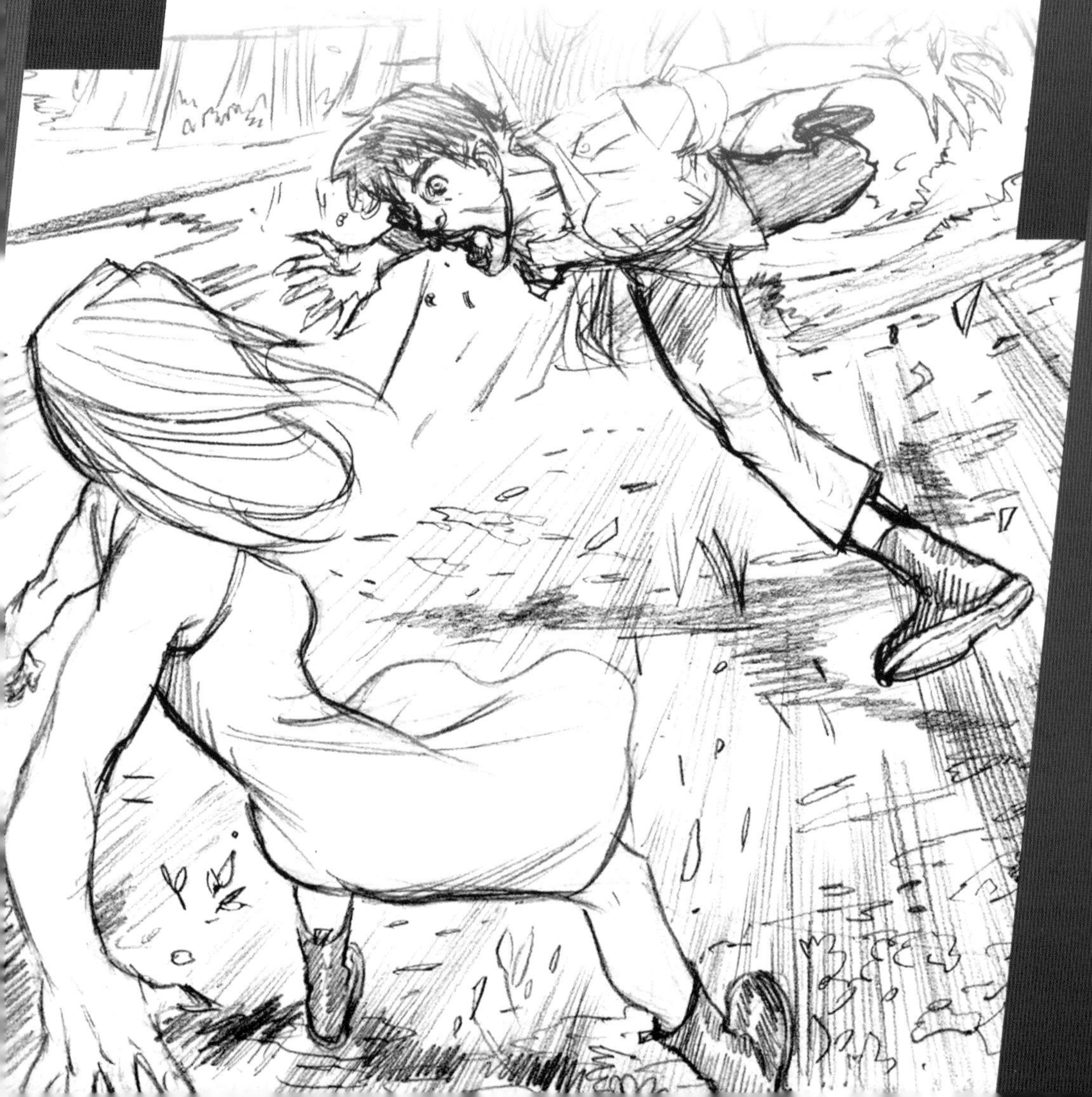

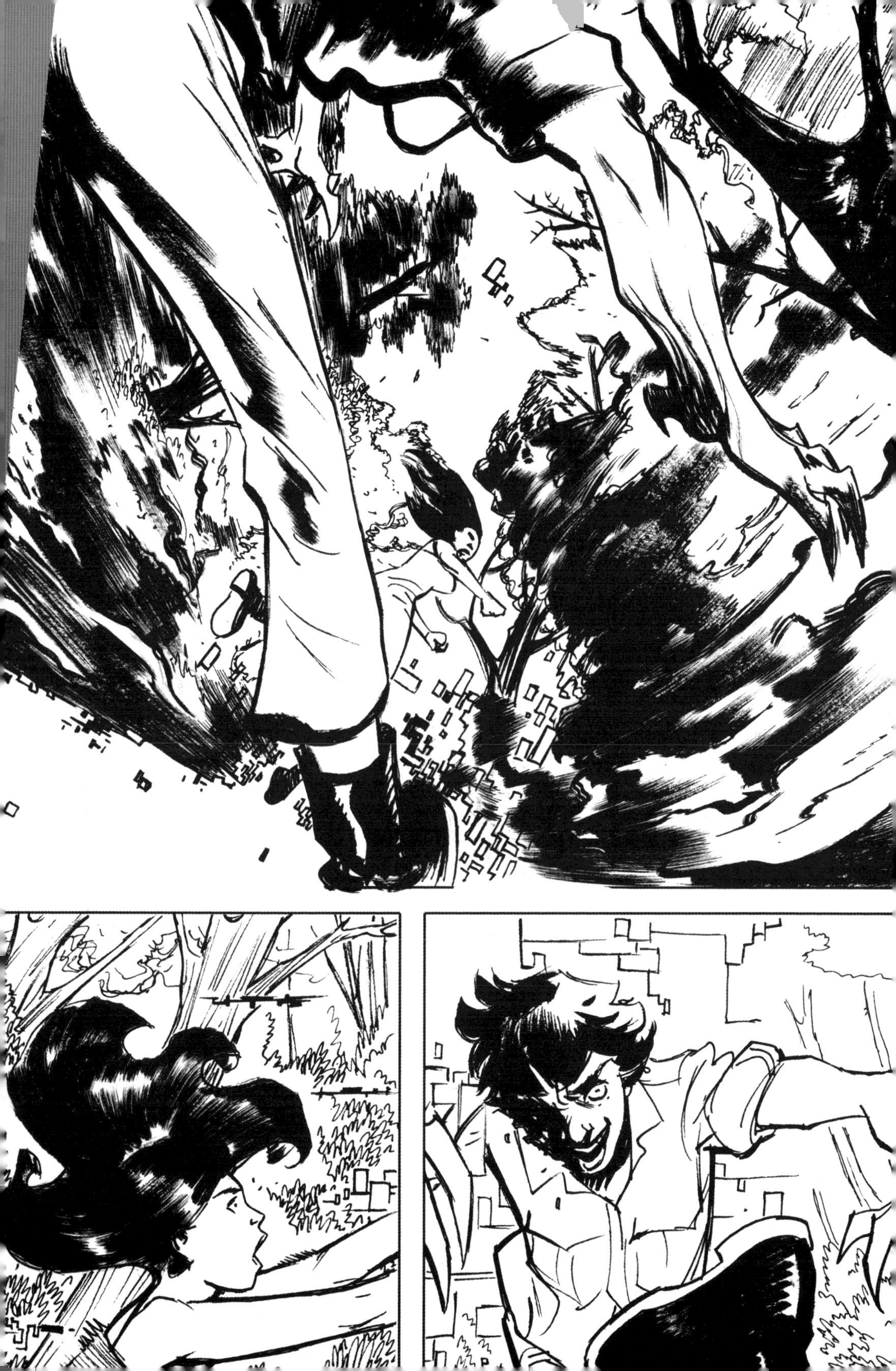

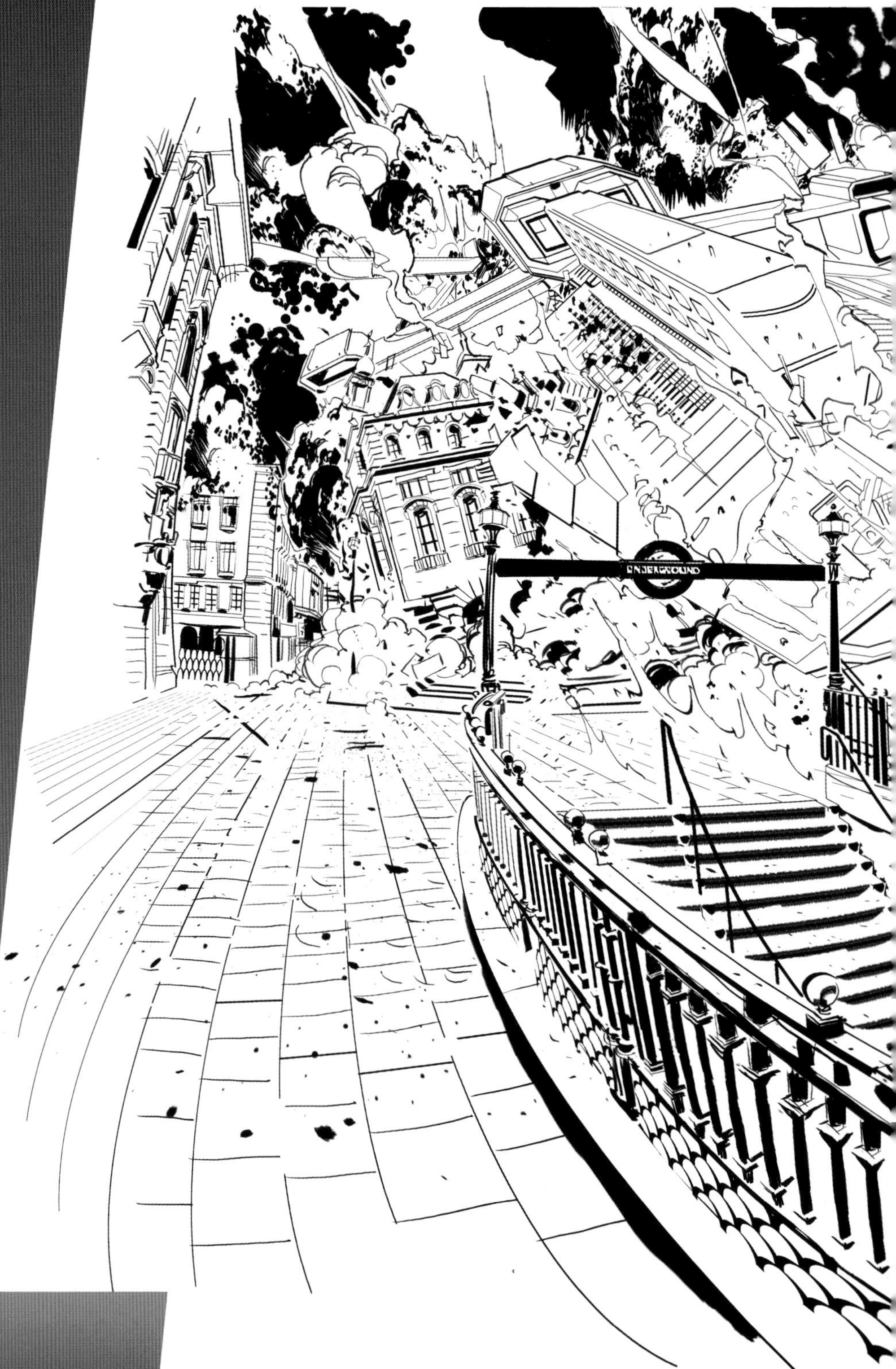
UNDERGROUND

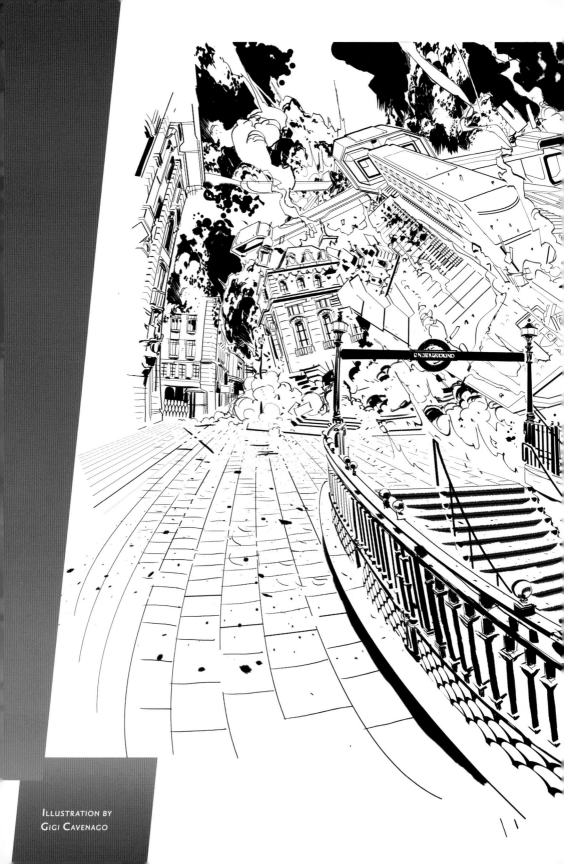

Illustration by
Gigi Cavenago

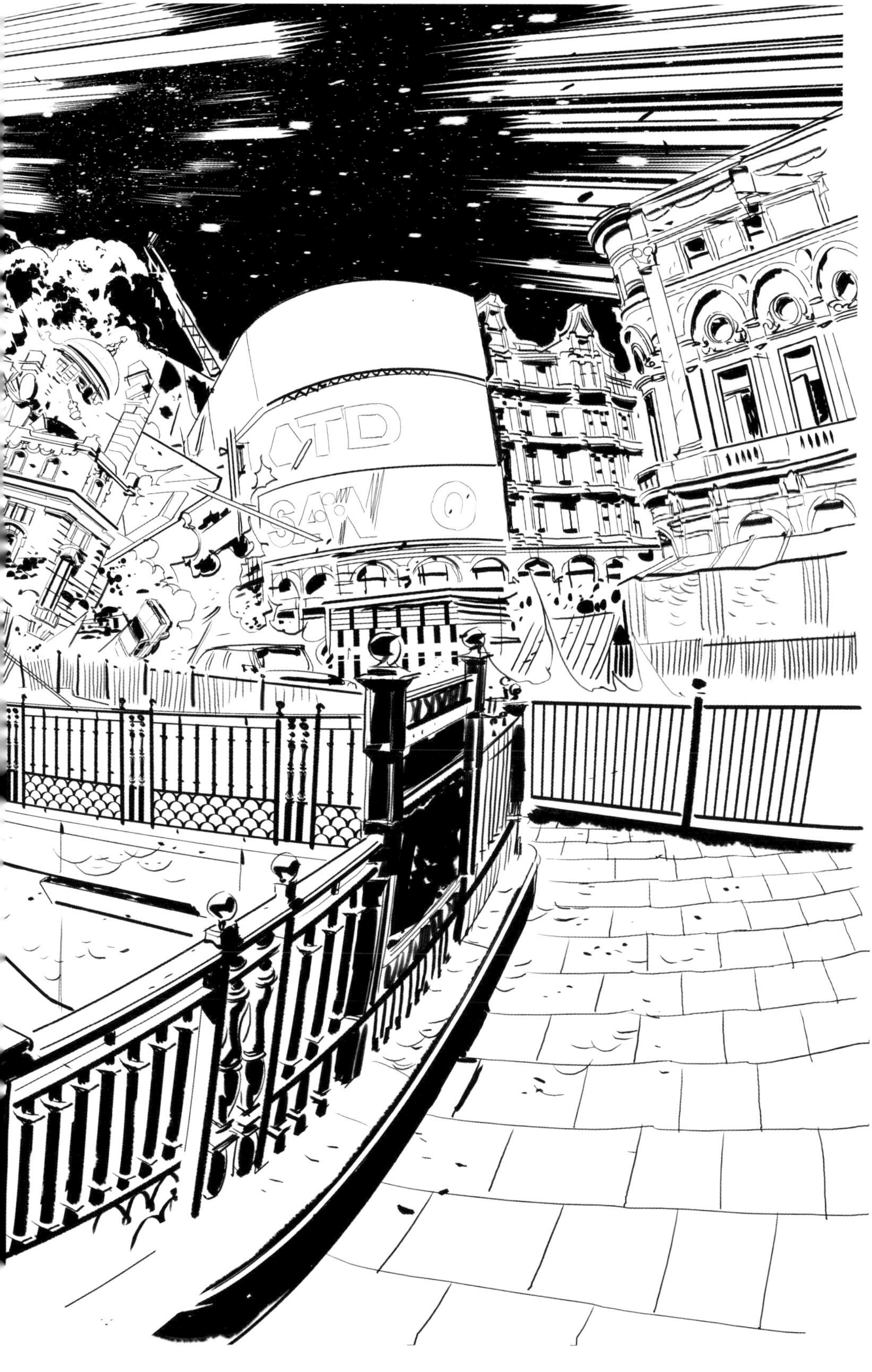

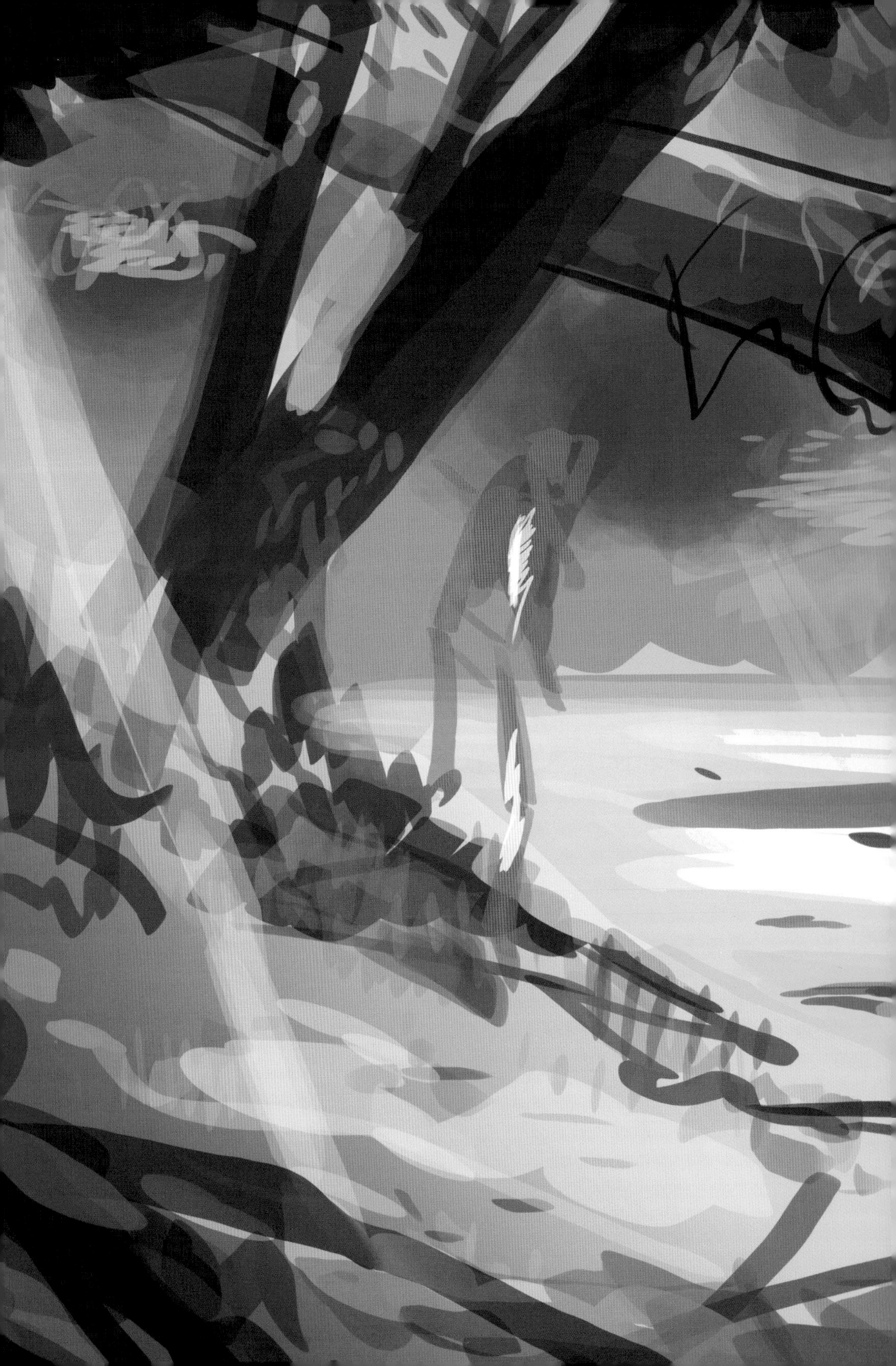

COVERS

When this first season of *Orphans* was initially collected into these four volumes, Emiliano Mammucari was asked to produce "variant covers" for each. His strikingly direct style was used to stand out among the vast array of other covers in bookstores. These four covers, which you can find in the next pages, introduced the world of *Orphans* to a public who hadn't yet been familiar with the series.

THESE TWO PAGES: STUDIES BY EMILIANO MAMMUCARI

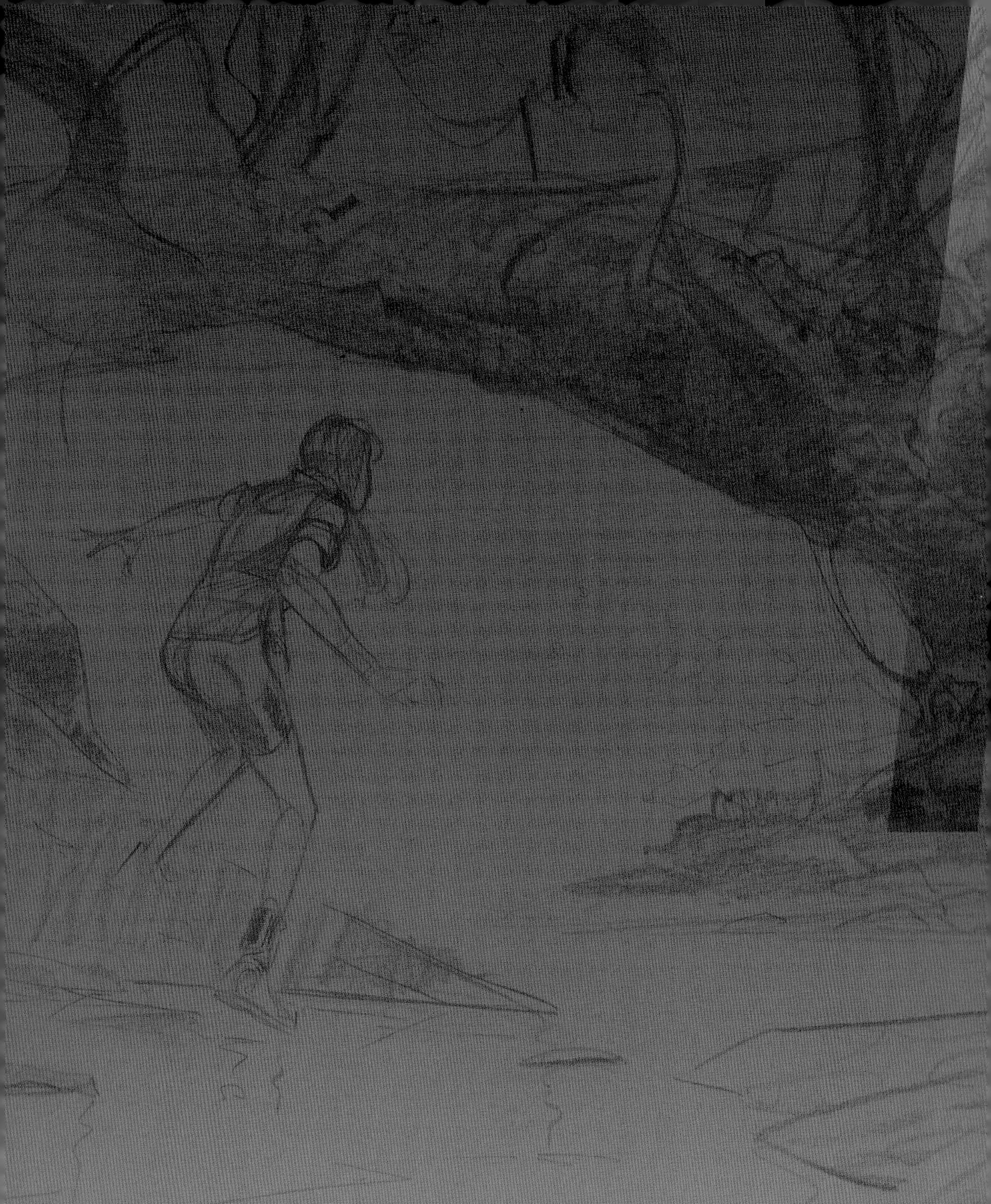

ONE BEAUTIFUL THING ABOUT COMICS IN BOOKSTORES IS THAT THEY CAN HAVE SOPHISTICATED COVERS. WHEN YOU APPROACH A SHELF AND SEE WHAT IS DRAWN ON THE COVER, YOU SIMPLY GET CURIOUS.

– EMILIANO MAMMUCARI

EMILIANO MAMMUCARI: With these covers, I wanted to tell people about the main protagonists of the story, one for each cover, taking a photo of them in a moment that represents them most. The instant in which they became characters.

Jonas, of course, starts the show. He's the leader. We intentionally decided not to tell the readers about his past precisely because he's a character who feels fulfilled by being a soldier. The first illustration goes without saying: Jonas becomes Jonas when he arrives at Ridgeback Camp.

On the second cover, we have Sam, the fragile little girl. The most ferocious of them all. I decided to draw the moment when she discovers the twisted pleasure of weaponry.

THESE TWO PAGES: STUDIES BY EMILIANO MAMMUCARI

THE NEXT PAGES: THE FOUR COVERS MADE BY EMILIANO MAMMUCARI
FOR THIS COLLECTED SERIES.

Orphans 1

CHAPTERS 1-3

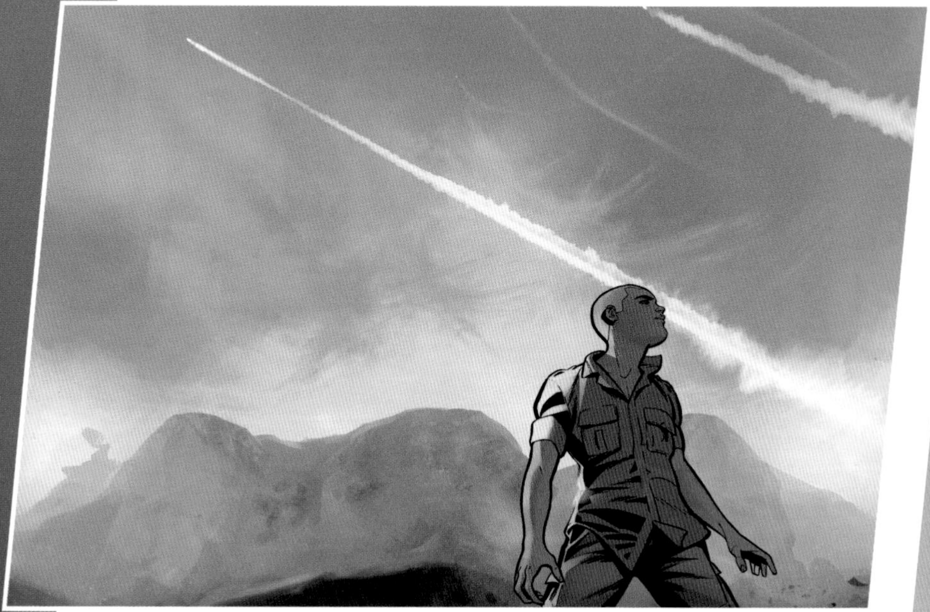

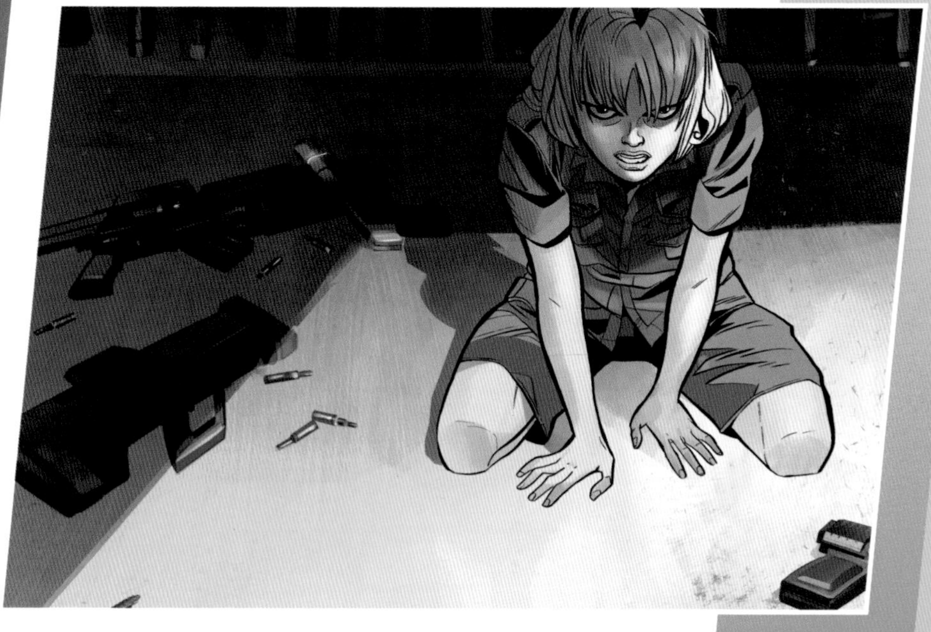

Orphans 2

CHAPTERS 4-6

Orphans 3

CHAPTERS 7-9

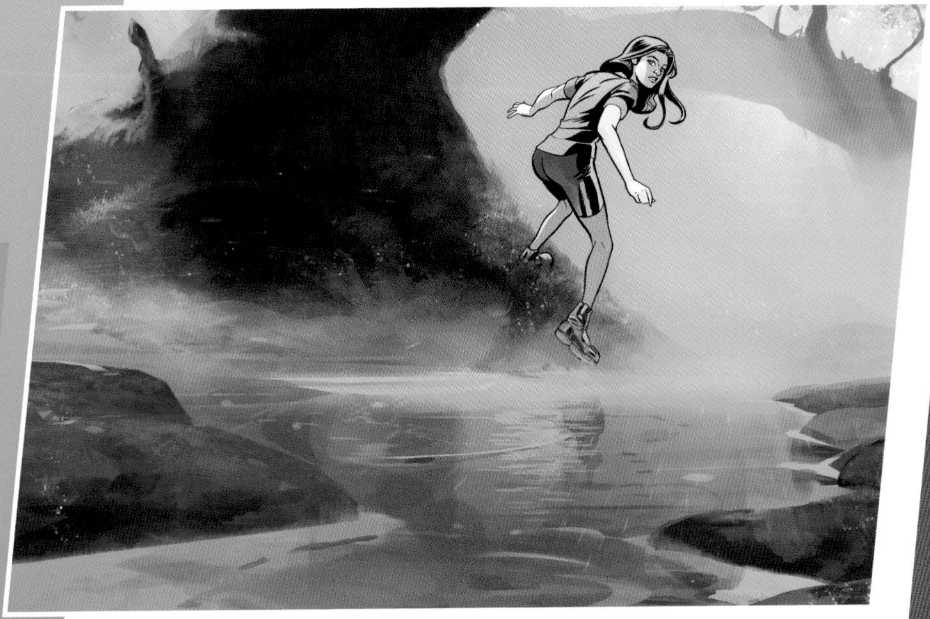

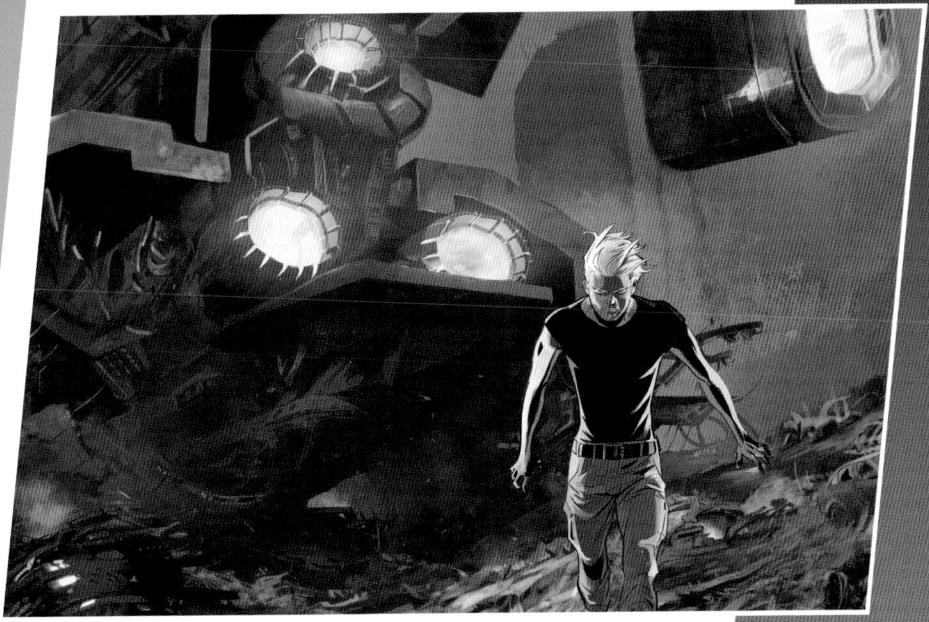

Orphans 4

CHAPTERS 10-12

EMILIANO MAMMUCARI: *The protagonist on the third cover is Juno. It took some time to decide on the subject of this illustration. Of the four of them, Juno is the only one that still clings to one specific event. She grows up and becomes stronger, but her development is always overshadowed by her brother's death. So I thought I could imprison her forever in the marshes where she saw Hector for the last time.*

The last in the line up is Ringo. He has to choose whether it's right to commit a massacre to prove he's right, and ultimately his answer is that yes, it is. It's the logic of a person that gives simple answers to complex questions. I drew him while he's coming back to Earth to start the uprising. This is the most unnatural illustration, because the Ringo that sets foot on Earth again is no longer a young boy.

THESE TWO PAGES: STUDIES BY EMILIANO MAMMUCARI

BOTTOM RIGHT: PREPARATORY STUDY FOR THE BACK COVER THIS EDITION

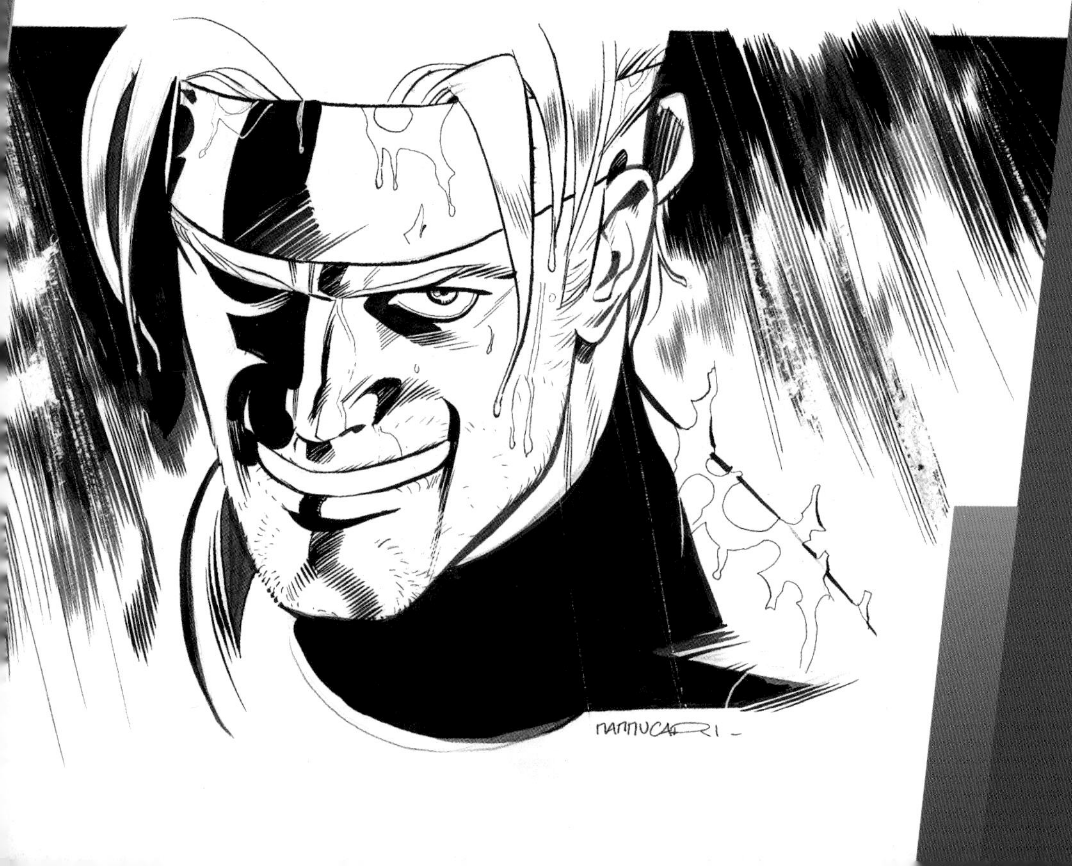
MAMMUCARI -

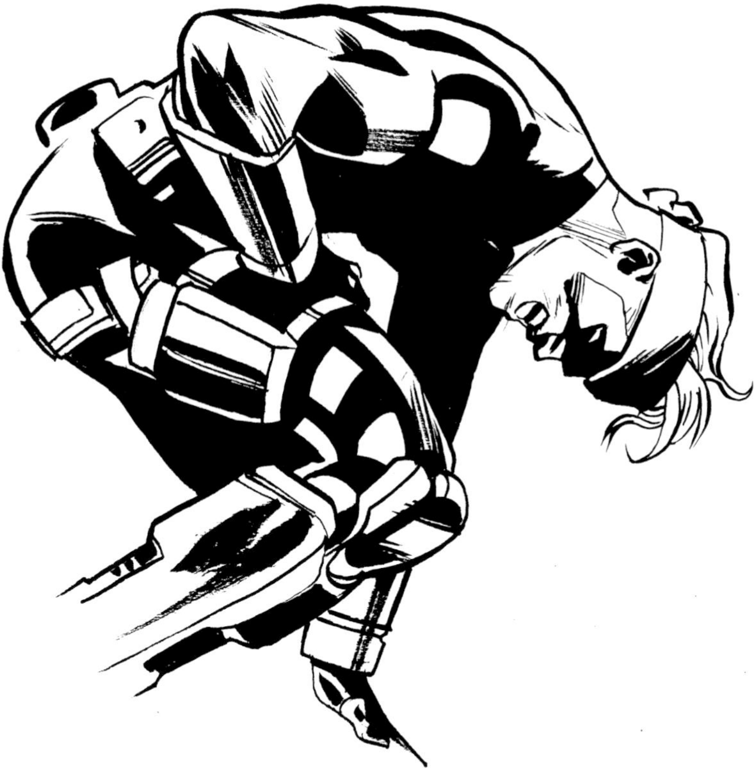

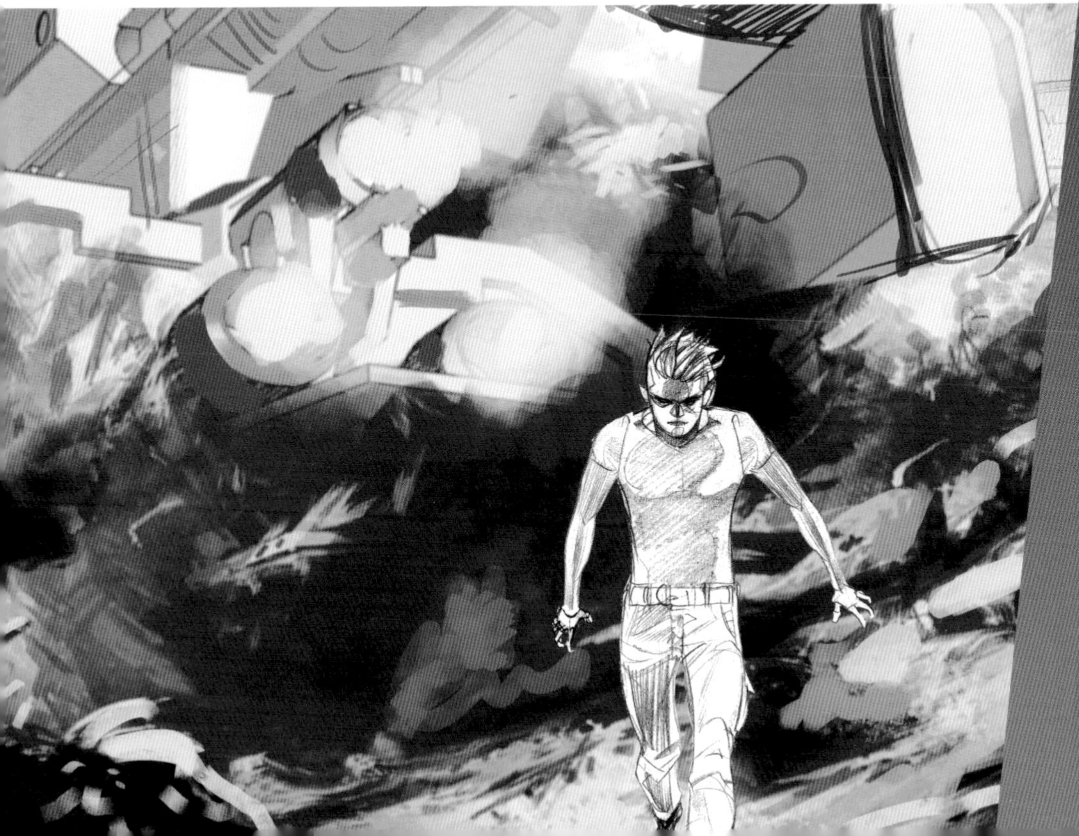

1

"The first step in coloring defines volumes and planes. I usually start with darker shades."

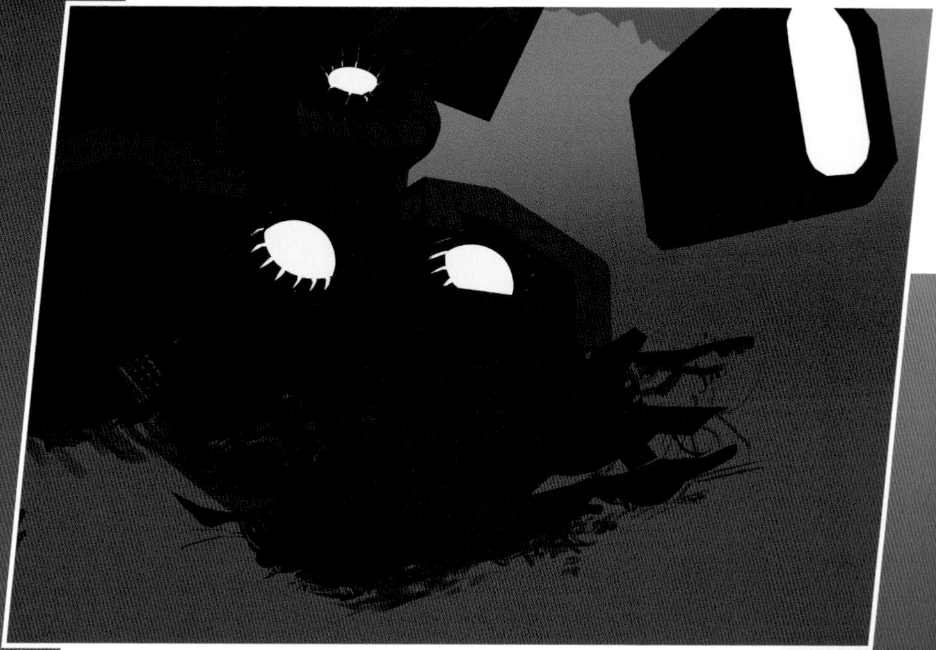

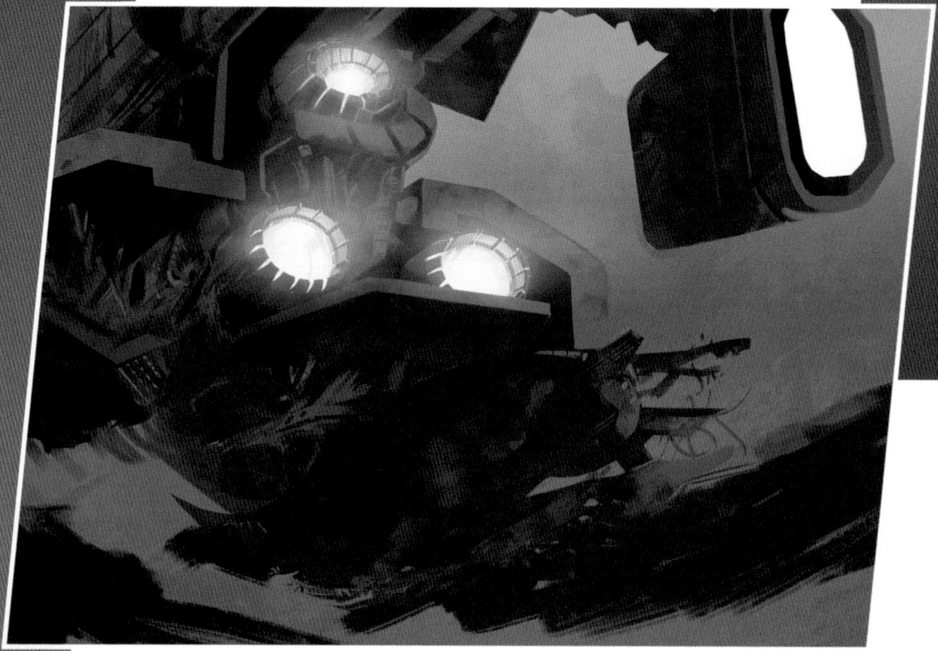

"The second step defines shapes. I polish objects with some initial lights."

2

3

"Then comes the atmosphere.
In this case, fire red and warm grays."

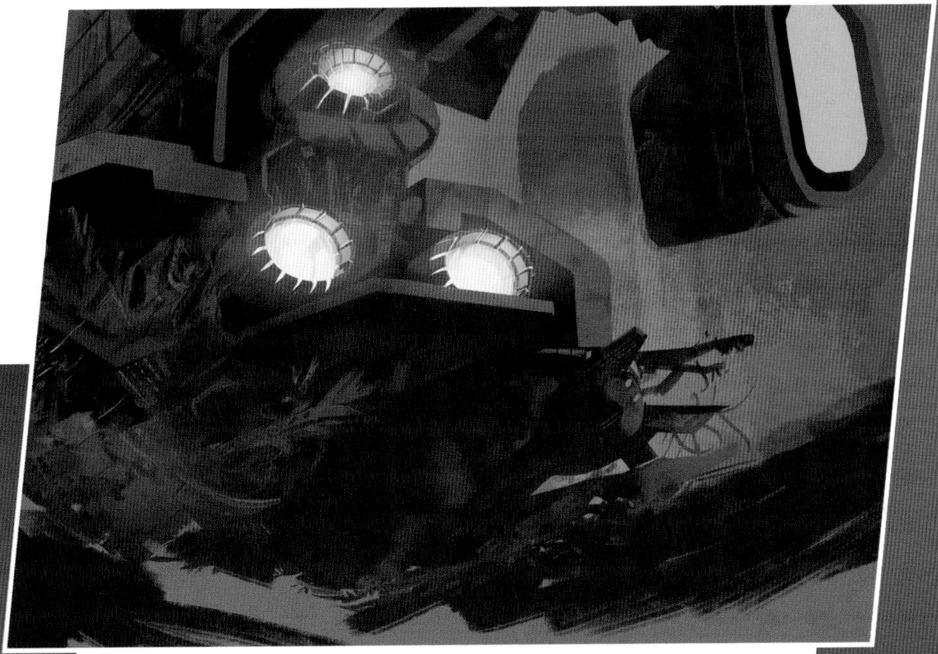

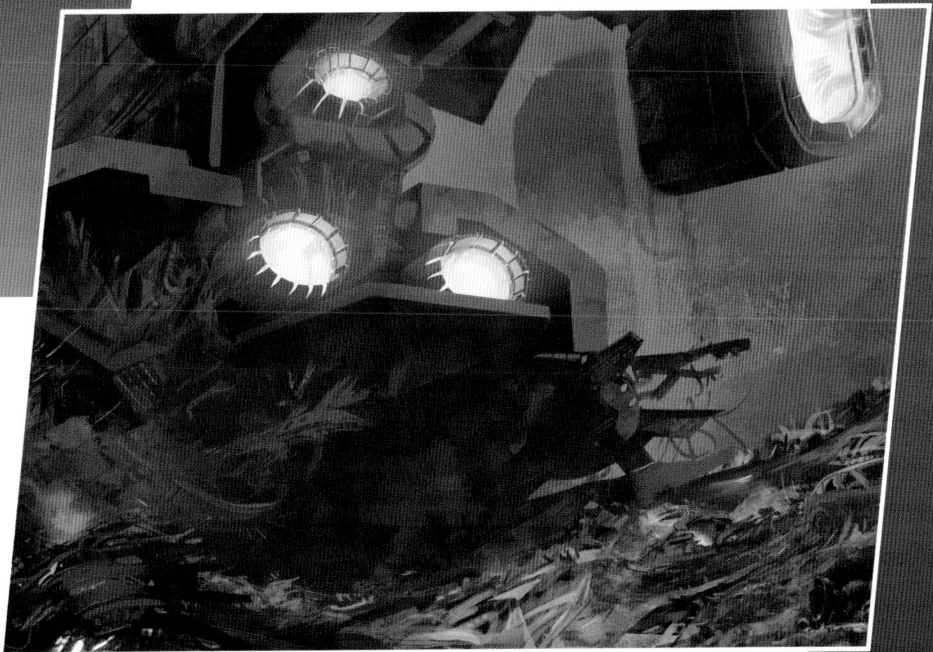

"Finally, I define the details step by step.
I always start from far away and come closer to the reader."

4

WHEN POPULAR COMICS ARE CONCERNED, YOU NEED TO USE HEAVY ARTILLERY ON THE COVER.

– Emiliano Mammucari

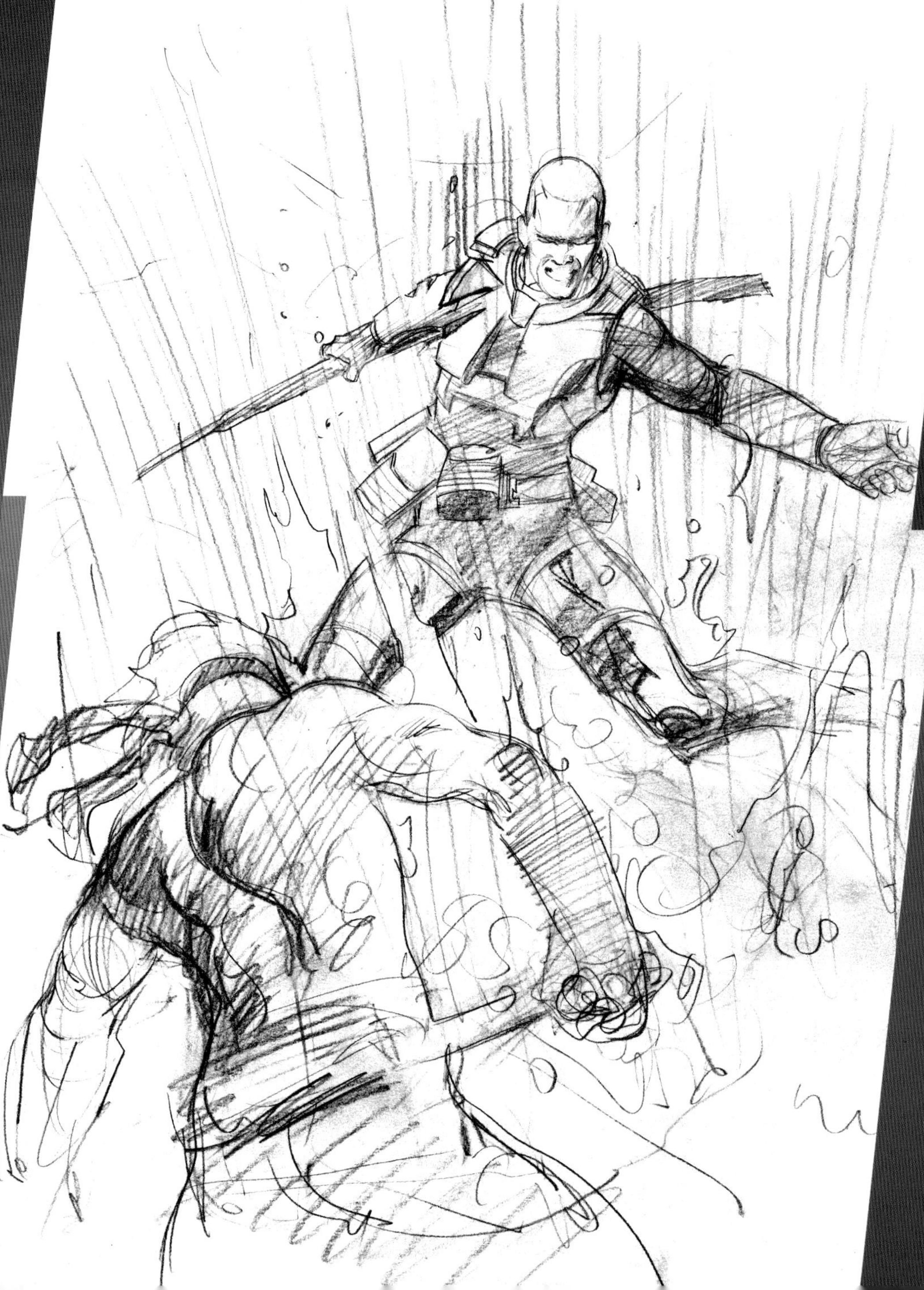

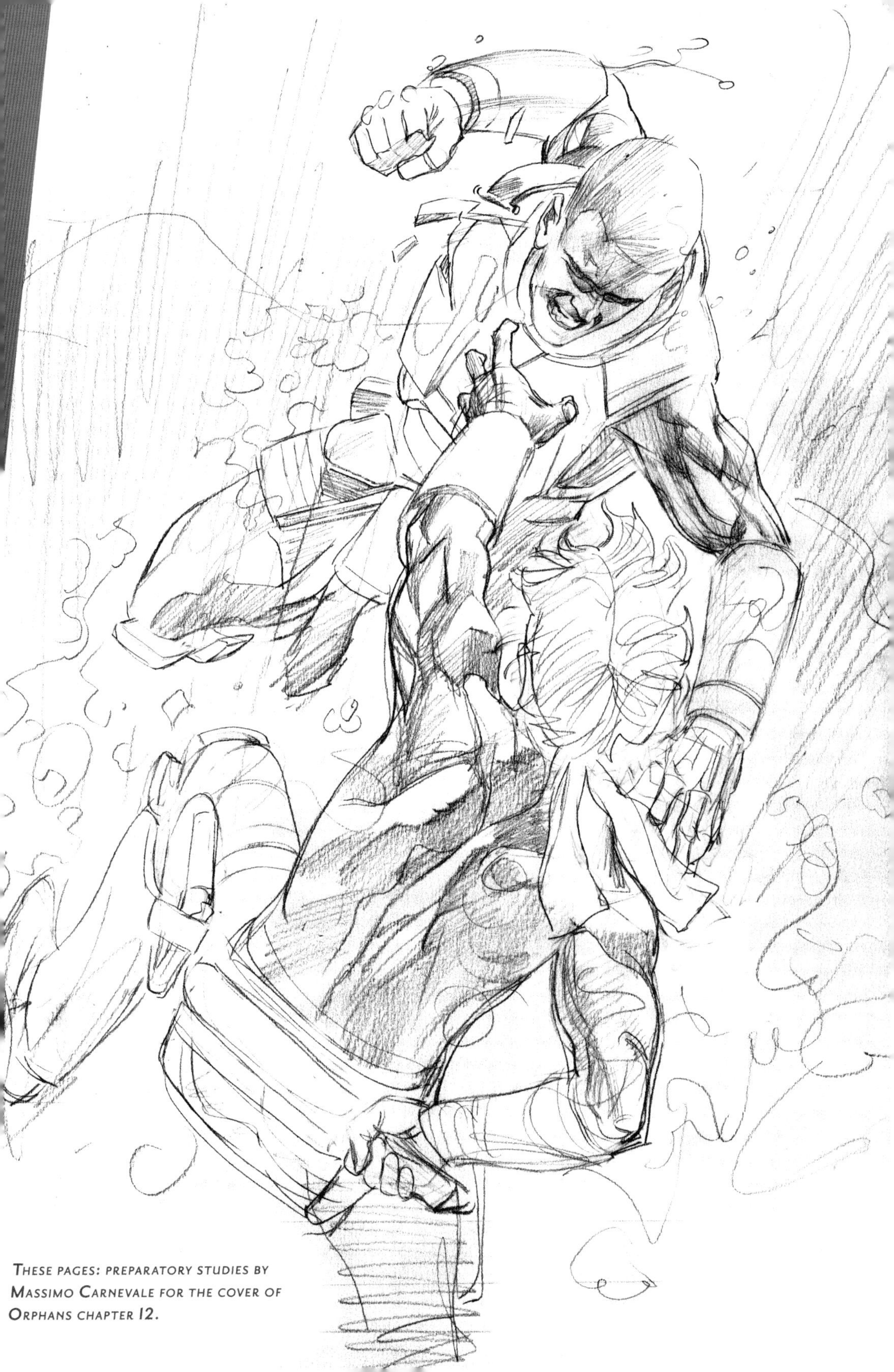

THESE PAGES: PREPARATORY STUDIES BY MASSIMO CARNEVALE FOR THE COVER OF ORPHANS CHAPTER 12.

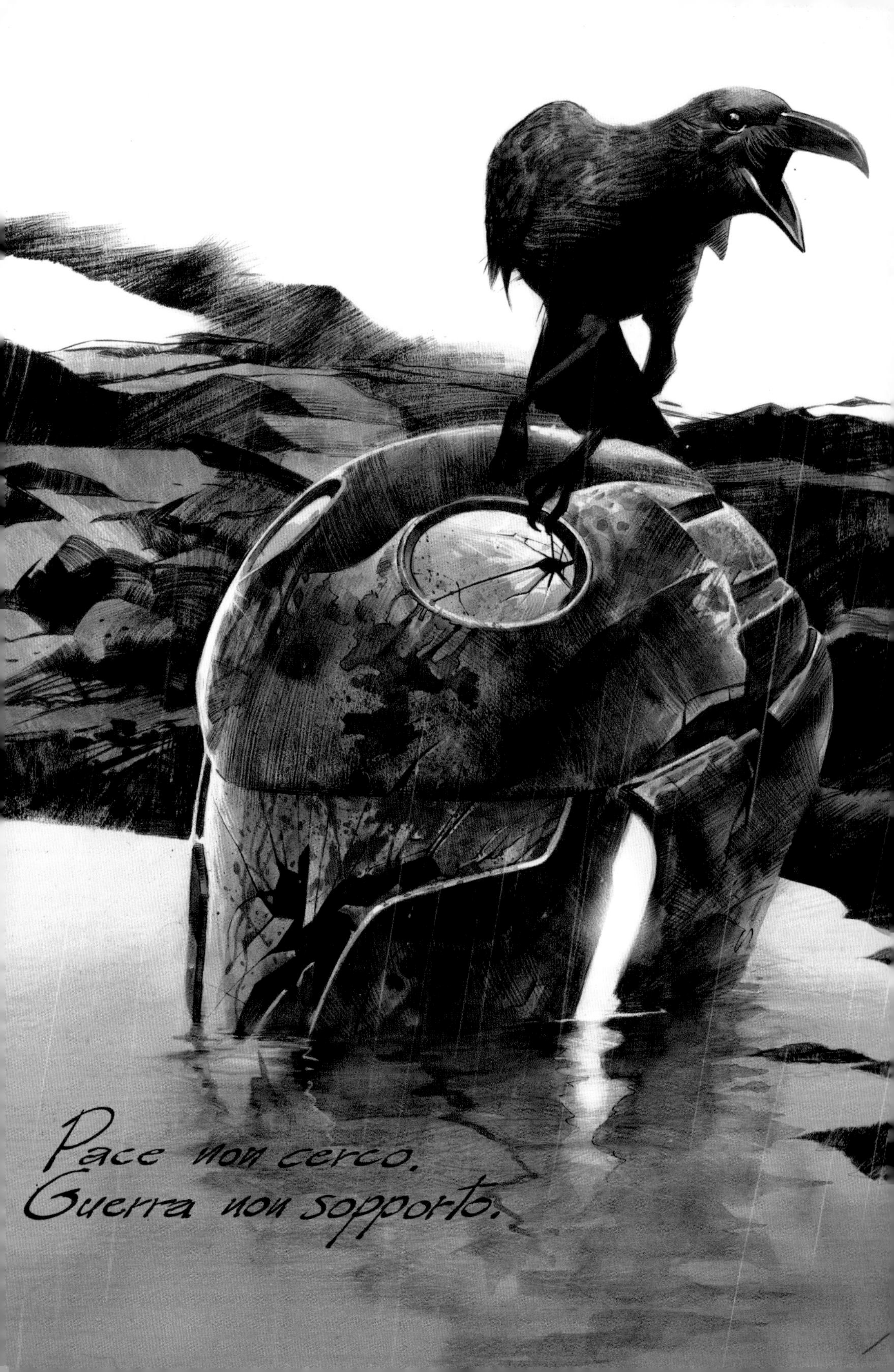
Pace non cerco.
Guerra non sopporto.

ILLUSTRATION BY MASSIMO CARNEVALE